Concepts in Programming Languages

This textbook for undergraduate and beginning graduate students explains and examines the central concepts used in modern programming languages, such as functions, types, memory management, and control. The book is unique in its comprehensive presentation and comparison of major object-oriented programming languages. Separate chapters examine the history of objects, Simula and Smalltalk, and the prominent languages C++ and Java.

The author presents foundational topics, such as lambda calculus and denotational semantics, in an easy-to-read, informal style, focusing on the main insights provided by these theories. Advanced topics include concurrency and concurrent object-oriented programming. A chapter on logic programming illustrates the importance of specialized programming methods for certain kinds of problems.

This book will give the reader a better understanding of the issues and trade-offs that arise in programming language design and a better appreciation of the advantages and pitfalls of the programming languages they use.

John C. Mitchell is Professor of Computer Science at Stanford University, where he has been a popular teacher for more than a decade. Many of his former students are successful in research and private industry. He received his Ph.D. from MIT in 1984 and was a Member of Technical Staff at AT&T Bell Laboratories before joining the faculty at Stanford. Over the past twenty years, Mitchell has been a featured speaker at international conferences; has led research projects on a variety of topics, including programming language design and analysis, computer security, and applications of mathematical logic to computer science; and has written more than 100 research articles. His previous textbook, *Foundations for Programming Languages* (MIT Press, 1996), covers lambda calculus, type systems, logic for program verification, and mathematical semantics of programming languages. Professor Mitchell was a member of the programming language subcommittee of the ACM/IEEE Curriculum 2001 standardization effort and the 2002 Program Chair of the ACM Principles of Programming Languages conference.

CONCEPTS IN PROGRAMMING LANGUAGES

John C. Mitchell
Stanford University

PUBLISHED BY THE PRESS SYNDICATE OF THE UNIVERSITY OF CAMBRIDGE
The Pitt Building, Trumpington Street, Cambridge, United Kingdom

CAMBRIDGE UNIVERSITY PRESS
The Edinburgh Building, Cambridge CB2 2RU, UK
40 West 20th Street, New York, NY 10011-4211, USA
477 Williamstown Road, Port Melbourne, VIC 3207, Australia
Ruiz de Alarcón 13, 28014 Madrid, Spain
Dock House, The Waterfront, Cape Town 8001, South Africa

http://www.cambridge.org

First published 2003

Printed in the United States of America

Typefaces Times Ten 10/12.5 pt., ITC Franklin Gothic, and Officina Serif
System LaTeX 2_ε [TB]

A catalog record for this book is available from the British Library.

Library of Congress Cataloging in Publication data available.

ISBN 0 521 78098 5 hardback

Contents

Preface

A good programming language is a conceptual universe for
thinking about programming.

Alan Perlis, NATO Conference on Software
Engineering Techniques, Rome, 1969

Programming languages provide the abstractions, organizing principles, and control
structures that programmers use to write good programs. This book is about the
concepts that appear in programming languages, issues that arise in their implementation, and the way that language design affects program development. The text is
divided into four parts:

- *Part 1:* Functions and Foundations
- *Part 2:* Procedures, Types, Memory Management, and Control
- *Part 3:* Modularity, Abstraction, and Object-Oriented Programming
- *Part 4:* Concurrency and Logic Programming

Part 1 contains a short study of Lisp as a worked example of programming language
analysis and covers compiler structure, parsing, lambda calculus, and denotational
semantics. A short Computability chapter provides information about the limits of
compile-time program analysis and optimization.

Part 2 uses procedural Algol family languages and ML to study types, memory
management, and control structures.

In Part 3 we look at program organization using abstract data types, modules, and
objects. Because object-oriented programming is the most prominent paradigm in
current practice, several different object-oriented languages are compared. Separate
chapters explore and compare Simula, Smalltalk, C++, and Java.

Part 4 contains chapters on language mechanisms for concurrency and on logic
programming.

The book is intended for upper-level undergraduate students and beginning
graduate students with some knowledge of basic programming. Students are expected to have some knowledge of C or some other procedural language and some

acquaintance with C++ or some form of object-oriented language. Some experience with Lisp, Scheme, or ML is helpful in Parts 1 and 2, although many students have successfully completed the course based on this book without this background. It is also helpful if students have some experience with simple analysis of algorithms and data structures. For example, in comparing implementations of certain constructs, it will be useful to distinguish between algorithms of constant-, polynomial-, and exponential-time complexity.

After reading this book, students will have a better understanding of the range of programming languages that have been used over the past 40 years, a better understanding of the issues and trade-offs that arise in programming language design, and a better appreciation of the advantages and pitfalls of the programming languages they use. Because different languages present different programming concepts, students will be able to improve their programming by importing ideas from other languages into the programs they write.

Acknowledgments

This book developed as a set of notes for Stanford CS 242, a course in programming languages that I have taught since 1993. Each year, energetic teaching assistants have helped debug example programs for lectures, formulate homework problems, and prepare model solutions. The organization and content of the course have been improved greatly by their suggestions. Special thanks go to Kathleen Fisher, who was a teaching assistant in 1993 and 1994 and taught the course in my absence in 1995. Kathleen helped me organize the material in the early years and, in 1995, transcribed my handwritten notes into online form. Thanks to Amit Patel for his initiative in organizing homework assignments and solutions and to Vitaly Shmatikov for persevering with the glossary of programming language terms. Anne Bracy, Dan Bentley, and Stephen Freund thoughtfully proofread many chapters.

Lauren Cowles, Alan Harvey, and David Tranah of Cambridge University Press were encouraging and helpful. I particularly appreciate Lauren's careful reading and detailed comments of twelve full chapters in draft form. Thanks also are due to the reviewers they enlisted, who made a number of helpful suggestions on early versions of the book. Zena Ariola taught from book drafts at the University of Oregon several years in a row and sent many helpful suggestions; other test instructors also provided helpful feedback.

Finally, special thanks to Krzystof Apt for contributing a chapter on logic programming.

John Mitchell

PART 1

Functions and Foundations

1

Introduction

"The Medium Is the Message"
Marshall McLuhan

1.1 PROGRAMMING LANGUAGES

Programming languages are the medium of expression in the art of computer programming. An ideal programming language will make it easy for programmers to write programs succinctly and clearly. Because programs are meant to be understood, modified, and maintained over their lifetime, a good programming language will help others read programs and understand how they work. Software design and construction are complex tasks. Many software systems consist of interacting parts. These parts, or software components, may interact in complicated ways. To manage complexity, the interfaces and communication between components must be designed carefully. A good language for large-scale programming will help programmers manage the interaction among software components effectively. In evaluating programming languages, we must consider the tasks of designing, implementing, testing, and maintaining software, asking how well each language supports each part of the software life cycle.

There are many difficult trade-offs in programming language design. Some language features make it easy for us to write programs quickly, but may make it harder for us to design testing tools or methods. Some language constructs make it easier for a compiler to optimize programs, but may make programming cumbersome. Because different computing environments and applications require different program characteristics, different programming language designers have chosen different trade-offs. In fact, virtually all successful programming languages were originally designed for one specific use. This is not to say that each language is good for only one purpose. However, focusing on a single application helps language designers make consistent, purposeful decisions. A single application also helps with one of the most difficult parts of language design: leaving good ideas out.

THE AUTHOR

I hope you enjoy using this book. At the beginning of each chapter, I have included pictures of people involved in the development or analysis of programming languages. Some of these people are famous, with major awards and published biographies. Others are less widely recognized. When possible, I have tried to include some personal information based on my encounters with these people. This is to emphasize that programming languages are developed by real human beings. Like most human artifacts, a programming language inevitably reflects some of the personality of its designers.

As a disclaimer, let me point out that I have not made an attempt to be comprehensive in my brief biographical comments. I have tried to liven up the text with a bit of humor when possible, leaving serious biography to more serious biographers. There simply is not space to mention all of the people who have played important roles in the history of programming languages.

Historical and biographical texts on computer science and computer scientists have become increasingly available in recent years. If you like reading about computer pioneers, you might enjoy paging through *Out of Their Minds: The Lives and Discoveries of 15 Great Computer Scientists* by Dennis Shasha and Cathy Lazere or other books on the history of computer science.

John Mitchell

Even if you do not use many of the programming languages in this book, you may still be able to put the conceptual framework presented in these languages to good use. When I was a student in the mid-1970s, all "serious" programmers (at my university, anyway) used Fortran. Fortran did not allow recursion, and recursion was generally regarded as too inefficient to be practical for "real programming." However, the instructor of one course I took argued that recursion was still an important idea and explained how recursive techniques could be used in Fortran by managing data in an array. I am glad I took that course and not one that dismissed recursion as an impractical idea. In the 1980s, many people considered object-oriented programming too inefficient and clumsy for real programming. However, students who learned about object-oriented programming in the 1980s were certainly happy to know about these "futuristic" languages in the 1990s, as object-oriented programming became more widely accepted and used.

Although this is not a book about the history of programming languages, there is some attention to history throughout the book. One reason for discussing historical languages is that this gives us a realistic way to understand programming language trade-offs. For example, programs were different when machines were slow and memory was scarce. The concerns of programming language designers were therefore different in the 1960s from the current concerns. By imaging the state of the art in some bygone era, we can give more serious thought to why language designers made certain decisions. This way of thinking about languages and computing may help us in the future, when computing conditions may change to resemble some past situation. For example, the recent rise in popularity of handheld computing devices and embedded processors has led to renewed interest in programming for devices with limited memory and limited computing power.

When we discuss specific languages in this book, we generally refer to the original or historically important form of a language. For example, "Fortran" means the Fortran of the 1960s and early 1970s. These early languages were called Fortran I, Fortran II, Fortran III, and so on. In recent years, Fortran has evolved to include more modern features, and the distinction between Fortran and other languages has blurred to some extent. Similarly, Lisp generally refers to the Lisps of the 1960s, Smalltalk to the language of the late 1970s and 1980s, and so on.

1.2 GOALS

In this book we are concerned with the basic concepts that appear in modern programming languages, their interaction, and the relationship between programming languages and methods for program development. A recurring theme is the trade-off between language expressiveness and simplicity of implementation. For each programming language feature we consider, we examine the ways that it can be used in programming and the kinds of implementation techniques that may be used to compile and execute it efficiently.

1.2.1 General Goals

In this book we have the following general goals:

- To understand the *design space* of programming languages. This includes concepts and constructs from past programming languages as well as those that may be used more widely in the future. We also try to understand some of the major conflicts and trade-offs between language features, including implementation costs.
- To develop a better understanding of the languages we currently use by comparing them with other languages.
- To understand the programming techniques associated with various language features. The study of programming languages is, in part, the study of conceptual frameworks for problem solving, software construction, and development.

Many of the ideas in this book are common knowledge among professional programmers. The material and ways of thinking presented in this book should be useful to you in future programming and in talking to experienced programmers if you work for a software company or have an interview for a job. By the end of the course, you will be able to evaluate language features, their costs, and how they fit together.

1.2.2 Specific Themes

Here are some specific themes that are addressed repeatedly in the text:

- *Computability:* Some problems cannot be solved by computer. The undecidability of the halting problem implies that programming language compilers and interpreters cannot do everything that we might wish they could do.
- *Static analysis:* There is a difference between compile time and run time. At compile time, the program is known but the input is not. At run time, the program and the input are both available to the run-time system. Although a program designer or implementer would like to find errors at compile time, many will not surface until run time. Methods that detect program errors at compile time are usually conservative, which means that when they say a program does not have a certain kind of error this statement is correct. However, compile-time error-detection methods will usually say that some programs contain errors even if errors may not actually occur when the program is run.
- *Expressiveness versus efficiency:* There are many situations in which it would be convenient to have a programming language implementation do something automatically. An example discussed in Chapter 3 is memory management: The Lisp run-time system uses garbage collection to detect memory locations no longer needed by the program. When something is done automatically, there is a cost. Although an automatic method may save the programmer from thinking about something, the implementation of the language may run more slowly. In some cases, the automatic method may make it easier to write programs and make programming less prone to error. In other cases, the resulting slowdown in program execution may make the automatic method infeasible.

1.3 PROGRAMMING LANGUAGE HISTORY

Hundreds of programming languages have been designed and implemented over the last 50 years. As many as 50 of these programming languages contained new concepts, useful refinements, or innovations worthy of mention. Because there are far too many programming languages to survey, however, we concentrate on six programming languages: Lisp, ML, C, C++, Smalltalk, and Java. Together, these languages contain most of the important language features that have been invented since higher-level programming languages emerged from the primordial swamp of assembly language programming around 1960.

The history of modern programming languages begins around 1958–1960 with the development of Algol, Cobol, Fortran, and Lisp. The main body of this book covers Lisp, with a shorter discussion of Algol and subsequent related languages. A brief account of some earlier languages is given here for those who may be curious about programming language prehistory.

In the 1950s, a number of languages were developed to simplify the process of writing sequences of computer instructions. In this decade, computers were very primitive by modern standards. Most programming was done with the native machine language of the underlying hardware. This was acceptable because programs were small and efficiency was extremely important. The two most important programming language developments of the 1950s were Fortan and Cobol.

Fortran was developed at IBM around 1954–1956 by a team led by John Backus. The main innovation of Fortran (a contraction of formula translator) was that it became possible to use ordinary mathematical notation in expressions. For example, the Fortran expression for adding the value of i to twice the value of j is i + 2*j. Before the development of Fortran, it might have been necessary to place i in a register, place j in a register, multiply j times 2 and then add the result to i. Fortran allowed programmers to think more naturally about numerical calculation by using symbolic names for variables and leaving some details of evaluation order to the compiler. Fortran also had subroutines (a form of procedure or function), arrays, formatted input and output, and declarations that gave programmers explicit control over the placement of variables and arrays in memory. However, that was about it. To give you some idea of the limitations of Fortran, many early Fortran compilers stored numbers $1, 2, 3 \ldots$ in memory locations, and programmers could change the values of numbers if they were not careful! In addition, it was not possible for a Fortran subroutine to call itself, as this required memory management techniques that had not been invented yet (see Chapter 7).

Cobol is a programming language designed for business applications. Like Fortran programs, many Cobol programs are still in use today, although current versions of Fortran and Cobol differ substantially from forms of these languages of the 1950s. The primary designer of Cobol was Grace Murray Hopper, an important computer pioneer. The syntax of Cobol was intended to resemble that of common English. It has been suggested in jest that if object-oriented Cobol were a standard today, we would use "add 1 to Cobol giving Cobol" instead of "C++".

The earliest languages covered in any detail in this book are Lisp and Algol, which both came out around 1960. These languages have stack memory management and recursive functions or procedures. Lisp provides higher-order functions (still not available in many current languages) and garbage collection, whereas the Algol family of languages provides better type systems and data structuring. The main innovations of the 1970s were methods for organizing data, such as records (or structs), abstract data types, and early forms of objects. Objects became mainstream in the 1980s, and the 1990s brought increasing interest in network-centric computing, interoperability, and security and correctness issues associated with active content on the Internet. The 21st century promises greater diversity of computing devices, cheaper and more powerful hardware, and increasing interest in correctness, security, and interoperability.

1.4 ORGANIZATION: CONCEPTS AND LANGUAGES

There are many important language concepts and many programming languages. The most natural way to summarize the field is to use a two-dimensional matrix, with languages along one axis and concepts along the other. Here is a partial sketch of such a matrix:

Language	Expressions	Functions	Heap storage	Exceptions	Modules	Objects	Threads
Lisp	x	x	x				
C	x	x	x				
Algol 60	x	x					
Algol 68	x	x	x				x
Pascal	x	x	x				
Modula-2	x	x	x		x		
Modula-3	x	x	x	x	x	x	
ML	x	x	x	x	x		
Simula	x	x	x			x	x
Smalltalk	x	x	x	x		x	x
C++	x	x	x	x	x	x	
Objective C	x	x	x			x	
Java	x	x	x	x	x	x	x

Although this matrix lists only a fraction of the languages and concepts that might be covered in a basic text or course on the programming languages, one general characteristic should be clear. There are some basic language concepts, such as expressions, functions, local variables, and stack storage allocation that are present in many languages. For these concepts, it makes more sense to discuss the concept in general than to go through a long list of similar languages. On the other hand, for concepts such as objects and threads, there are relatively few languages that exhibit these concepts in interesting ways. Therefore, we can study most of the interesting aspects of objects by comparing a few languages. Another factor that is not clear from the matrix is that, for some concepts, there is considerable variation from language to language. For example, it is more interesting to compare the way objects have been integrated into languages than it is to compare integer expressions. This is another reason why competing object-oriented languages are compared, but basic concepts related to expressions, statements, functions, and so on, are covered only once, in a concept-oriented way.

Most courses and texts on programming languages use some combination of language-based and concept-based presentation. In this book a concept-oriented organization is followed for most concepts, with a language-based organization used to compare object-oriented features.

The text is divided into four parts:

Part 1: Functions and Foundations   (Chapters 1–4)
Part 2: Procedures, Types, Memory Management, and Control   (5–8)
Part 3: Modularity, Abstraction and Object-Oriented Programming   (9–13)

Part 4: Concurrency and Logic Programming   (14 and 15)

In Part 1 a short study of Lisp is presented, followed by a discussion of compiler structure, parsing, lambda calculus, and denotational semantics. A short chapter provides a brief discussion of computability and the limits of compile-time program analysis and optimization. For C programmers, the discussion of Lisp should provide a good chance to think differently about programming and programming languages.

In Part 2, we progress through the main concepts associated with the conventional languages that are descended in some way from the Algol family. These concepts include type systems and type checking, functions and stack storage allocation, and control mechanisms such as exceptions and continuations. After some of the history of the Algol family of languages is summarized, the ML programming language is used as the main example, with some discussion and comparisons using C syntax.

Part 3 is an investigation of program-structuring mechanisms. The important language advances of the 1970s were abstract data types and program modules. In the late 1980s, object-oriented concepts attained widespread acceptance. Because object-oriented programming is currently the most prominent programming paradigm, in most of Part 3 we focus on object-oriented concepts and languages, comparing Smalltalk, C++, and Java.

Part 4 contains chapters on language mechanisms for concurrent and distributed programs and on logic programming.

Because of space limitations, a number of interesting topics are not covered. Although scripting languages and other "special-purpose" languages are not covered explicitly in detail, an attempt has been made to integrate some relevant language concepts into the exercises.

2

Computability

Some mathematical functions are computable and some are not. In all general-purpose programming languages, it is possible to write a program for each function that is computable in principle. However, the limits of computability also limit the kinds of things that programming language implementations can do. This chapter contains a brief overview of computability so that we can discuss limitations that involve computability in other chapters of the book.

2.1 PARTIAL FUNCTIONS AND COMPUTABILITY

From a mathematical point of view, a program defines a function. The output of a program is computed as a function of the program inputs and the state of the machine before the program starts. In practice, there is a lot more to a program than the function it computes. However, as a starting point in the study of programming languages, it is useful to understand some basic facts about computable functions.

The fact that not all functions are computable has important ramifications for programming language tools and implementations. Some kinds of programming constructs, however useful they might be, cannot be added to real programming languages because they cannot be implemented on real computers.

2.1.1 Expressions, Errors, and Nontermination

In mathematics, an expression may have a defined value or it may not. For example, the expression $3 + 2$ has a defined value, but the expression $3/0$ does not. The reason that $3/0$ does not have a value is that division by zero is not defined: division is defined to be the inverse of multiplication, but multiplication by zero cannot be inverted. There is nothing to try to do when we see the expression $3/0$; a mathematician would just say that this operation is undefined, and that would be the end of the discussion.

In computation, there are two different reasons why an expression might not have a value:

ALAN TURING

Alan Turing was a British mathematician. He is known for his early work on computability and his work for British Intelligence on code breaking during the Second World War. Among computer scientists, he is best known for the invention of the Turing machine. This is not a piece of hardware, but an idealized computing device. A Turing machine consists of an infinite tape, a tape read–write head, and a finite-state controller. In each computation step, the machine reads a tape symbol and the finite-state controller decides whether to write a different symbol on the current tape square and then whether to move the read–write head one square left or right. The importance of this idealized computer is that it is both very simple and very powerful.

Turing was a broad-minded individual with interests ranging from relativity theory and mathematical logic to number theory and the engineering design of mechanical computers. There are numerous published biographies of Alan Turing, some emphasizing his wartime work and others calling attention to his sexuality and its impact on his professional career.

The ACM Turing Award is the highest scientific honor in computer science, equivalent to a Nobel Prize in other fields.

- *Error termination:* Evaluation of the expression cannot proceed because of a conflict between operator and operand.
- *Nontermination:* Evaluation of the expression proceeds indefinitely.

An example of the first kind is division by zero. There is nothing to compute in this case, except possibly to stop the computation in a way that indicates that it could not proceed any further. This may halt execution of the entire program, abort one thread of a concurrent program, or raise an exception if the programming language provides exceptions.

The second case is different: There is a specific computation to perform, but the computation may not terminate and therefore may not yield a value. For example, consider the recursive function defined by

```
f(x:int) = if x = 0 then 0 else x + f(x-2)
```

This is a perfectly meaningful definition of a *partial* function, a function that has a value on some arguments but not on all arguments. The expression f(4) calling the function f above has value $4 + 2 + 0 = 6$, but the expression f(5) does not have a value because the computation specified by this expression does not terminate.

2.1.2 Partial Functions

A partial function is a function that is defined on some arguments and undefined on others. This is ordinarily what is meant by function in programming, as a function declared in a program may return a result or may not if some loop or sequence of recursive calls does not terminate. However, this is not what a mathematician ordinarily means by the word function.

The distinction can be made clearer by a look at the mathematical definitions. A reasonable definition of the word function is this: A function $f: A \to B$ from set A to set B is a rule associating a unique value $y = f(x)$ in B with every x in A. This is almost a mathematical definition, except that the word rule does not have a precise mathematical meaning. The notation $f: A \to B$ means that, given arguments in the set A, the function f produces values from set B. The set A is called the *domain* of f, and the set B is called the *range* or the *codomain* of f.

The usual mathematical definition of function replaces the idea of rule with a set of argument–result pairs called the graph of a function. This is the mathematical definition:

A *function* $f: A \to B$ is a set of ordered pairs $f \subseteq A \times B$ that satisfies the following conditions:

1. If $\langle x, y \rangle \in f$ and $\langle x, z \rangle \in f$, then $y = z$.
2. For every $x \in A$, there exists $y \in B$ with $\langle x, y \rangle \in f$.

When we associate a set of ordered pairs with a function, the ordered pair $\langle x, y \rangle$ is used to indicate that y is the value of the function on argument x. In words, the preceding two conditions can be stated as (1) a function has at most one value for every argument in its domain, and (2) a function has at least one value for every argument in its domain.

A partial function is similar, except that a partial function may not have a value for every argument in its domain. This is the mathematical definition:

A *partial function* $f: A \to B$ is a set of ordered pairs $f \subseteq A \times B$ satisfying the preceding condition

1. If $\langle x, y \rangle \in f$ and $\langle x, z \rangle \in f$, then $y = z$.

In words, a partial function is single valued, but need not be defined on all elements of its domain.

Programs Define Partial Functions

In most programming languages, it is possible to define functions recursively. For example, here is a function f defined in terms of itself:

```
f(x:int) = if x = 0 then 0 else x + f(x-2);
```

If this were written as a program in some programming language, the declaration would associate the function name f with an algorithm that terminates on every even $x \geq 0$, but diverges (does not halt and return a value) if x is odd or negative. The algorithm for f defines the following mathematical function f, expressed here as a set of ordered pairs:

$$f = \{\langle x, y \rangle \mid x \text{ is positive and even}, y = 0 + 2 + 4 + \cdots + x\}.$$

This is a partial function on the integers. For every integer x, there is at most one y with $f(x) = y$. However, if x is an odd number, then there is no y with $f(x) = y$. Where the algorithm does not terminate, the value of the function is undefined. Because a function call may not terminate, this program defines a partial function.

2.1.3 Computability

Computability theory gives us a precise characterization of the functions that are computable in principle. The class of functions on the natural numbers that are computable in principle is often called the class of *partial recursive functions*, as recursion is an essential part of computation and computable functions are, in general, partial rather than total. The reason why we say "computable in principle" instead of "computable in practice" is that some computable functions might take an extremely long time to compute. If a function call will not return for an amount of time equal to the length of the entire history of the universe, then in practice we will not be able to wait for the computation to finish. Nonetheless, computability in principle is an important benchmark for programming languages.

Computable Functions

Intuitively, a function is *computable* if there is some program that computes it. More specifically, a function $f: A \rightarrow B$ is computable if there is an algorithm that, given any $x \in A$ as input, halts with $y = f(x)$ as output.

One problem with this intuitive definition of computable is that a program has to be written out in some programming language, and we need to have some implementation to execute the program. It might very well be that, in one programming language, there is a program to compute some mathematical function and in another language there is not.

In the 1930s, Alonzo Church of Princeton University proposed an important principle, called Church's thesis. Church's thesis, which is a widely held belief about the relation between mathematical definitions and the real world of computing, states that the same class of functions on the integers can be computed by any general computing device. This is the class of partial recursive functions, sometimes called the class of *computable functions*. There is a mathematical definition of this class of functions that does not refer to programming languages, a second definition that uses a kind of idealized computing device called a *Turing machine*, and a third (equivalent) definition that uses lambda calculus (see Section 4.2). As mentioned in the biographical sketch on Alan Turing, a Turing machine consists of an infinite tape, a tape read–write head, and a finite-state controller. The tape is divided into contiguous cells, each containing a single symbol. In each computation step, the machine reads a tape symbol and the finite-state controller decides whether to write a different symbol on the current tape square and then whether to move the read–write head one square left or right. Part of the evidence that Church cited in formulating this thesis was the proof that Turing machines and lambda calculus are equivalent. The fact that all standard programming languages express precisely the class of partial recursive functions is often summarized by the statement that *all programming languages are Turing complete*. Although it is comforting to know that all programming languages are universal in a mathematical sense, the fact that all programming languages are Turing complete also means that computability theory does not help us distinguish among the expressive powers of different programming languages.

Noncomputable Functions

It is useful to know that some specific functions are not computable. An important example is commonly referred to as the *halting problem*. To simplify the discussion and focus on the central ideas, the halting problem is stated for programs that require one string input. If P is such a program and x is a string input, then we write $P(x)$ for the output of program P on input x.

> *Halting Problem:* Given a program P that requires exactly one string input and a string x, determine whether P halts on input x.

We can associate the halting problem with a function f_{halt} by letting $f_{halt}(P, x) =$ "halts" if P halts on input and $f_{halt}(P, x) =$ "does not halt" otherwise. This function f_{halt} can be considered a function on strings if we write each program out as a sequence of symbols.

The *undecidability of the halting problem* is the fact that the function f_{halt} is not computable. The undecidability of the halting problem is an important fact to keep in mind in designing programming language implementations and optimizations. It implies that many useful operations on programs cannot be implemented, even in principle.

Proof of the Undecidability of the Halting Problem. Although you will not need to know this proof to understand any other topic in the book, some of you may be interested in proof that the halting function is not computable. The proof is surprisingly short, but can be difficult to understand. If you are going to be a serious computer scientist, then you will want to look at this proof several times, over the course of several days, until you understand the idea behind it.

> Step 1: Assume that there is a program Q that solves the halting problem. Specifically, assume that program Q reads two inputs, both strings, and has the

following output:

$$Q(P, x) = \begin{cases} \text{halts} & \text{if } P(x) \text{ halts} \\ \text{does not halt} & \text{if } P(x) \text{ does not} \end{cases}.$$

An important part of this specification for Q is that $Q(P, x)$ always halts for every P and x.

Step 2: Using program Q, we can build a program D that reads one string input and sometimes does not halt. Specifically, let D be a program that works as follows:

$$D(P) = \text{if } Q(P, P) = \text{halts then } \textit{run forever} \text{ else } \textit{halt}.$$

Note that D has only one input, which it gives twice to Q. The program D can be written in any reasonable language, as any reasonable language should have some way of programming if-then-else and some way of writing a loop or recursive function call that runs forever. If you think about it a little bit, you can see that D has the following behavior:

$$D(P) = \begin{cases} \text{halt} & \text{if } P(P) \text{ runs forever} \\ \text{run forever} & \text{if } P(P) \text{ halts} \end{cases}.$$

In this description, the word halt means that $D(P)$ comes to a halt, and runs forever means that $D(P)$ continues to execute steps indefinitely. The program $D(P)$ halts or does not halt, but does not produce a string output in any case.

Step 3: Derive a contradiction by considering the behavior $D(D)$ of program D on input D. (If you are starting to get confused about what it means to run a program with the program itself as input, assume that we have written the program D and stored it in a file. Then we can compile D and run D with the file containing a copy of D as input.) Without thinking about how D works or what D is supposed to do, it is clear that either $D(D)$ halts or $D(D)$ does not halt. If $D(D)$ halts, though, then by the property of D given in step 2, this must be because $D(D)$ runs forever. This does not make any sense, so it must be that $D(D)$ runs forever. However, by similar reasoning, if $D(D)$ runs forever, then this must be because $D(D)$ halts. This is also contradictory. Therefore, we have reached a contradiction.

Step 4: Because the assumption in step 1 that there is a program Q solving the halting problem leads to a contradiction in step 3, it must be that the assumption is false. Therefore, there is no program that solves the halting problem.

Applications

Programming language compilers can often detect errors in programs. However, the undecidability of the halting problem implies that some properties of programs cannot be determined in advance. The simplest example is halting itself. Suppose someone writes a program like this:

```
i = 0;
while (i != f(i)) i = g(i);
printf(... i ...);
```

It seems very likely that the programmer wants the while loop to halt. Otherwise, why would the programmer have written a statement to print the value of i after the loop halts? Therefore, it would be helpful for the compiler to print a warning message if the loop will not halt. However useful this might be, though, it is not possible for a compiler to determine whether the loop will halt, as this would involve solving the halting problem.

2.2 CHAPTER SUMMARY

Computability theory establishes some important ground rules for programming language design and implementation. The following main concepts from this short overview should be remembered:

■ *Partiality:* Recursively defined functions may be partial functions. They are not always total functions. A function may be partial because a basic operation is not defined on some argument or because a computation does not terminate.

■ *Computability:* Some functions are computable and others are not. Programming languages can be used to define computable functions; we cannot write programs for functions that are not computable in principle.

■ *Turing completeness:* All standard general-purpose programming languages give us the same class of computable functions.

■ *Undecidability:* Many important properties of programs cannot be determined by any computable function. In particular, the halting problem is undecidable.

When the value of a function or the value of an expression is undefined because a basic operation such as division by zero does not make sense, a compiler or interpreter can cause the program to halt and report the error. However, the undecidability of the halting problem implies that there is no way to detect and report an error whenever a program is not going to halt.

There is a lot more to computability and complexity theory than is summarized in the few pages here. For more information, see one of the many books on computability and complexity theory such as *Introduction to Automata Theory, Languages, and Computation* by Hopcroft, Motwani, and Ullman (Addison Wesley, 2001) or *Introduction to the Theory of Computation* by Sipser (PWS, 1997).

EXERCISES

2.1 Partial and Total Functions

For each of the following function definitions, give the graph of the function. Say whether this is a partial function or a total function on the integers. If the function is partial, say where the function is defined and undefined.

For example, the graph of f(x) = if x > 0 then x + 2 else x/0 is the set of ordered pairs $\{\langle x, x + 2 \rangle \mid x > 0\}$. This is a partial function. It is defined on all integers greater than 0 and undefined on integers less than or equal to 0.

Functions:

(a) f(x) = if x + 2 > 3 then x * 5 else x/0
(b) f(x) = if x < 0 then 1 else f(x - 2)
(c) f(x) = if x = 0 then 1 else f(x - 2)

2.2 Halting Problem on No Input

Suppose you are given a function $Halt_\emptyset$ that can be used to determine whether a program that requires no input halts. To make this concrete, assume that you are writing a C or Pascal program that reads in another program as a string. Your program is allowed to call $Halt_\emptyset$ with a string input. Assume that the call to $Halt_\emptyset$ returns true if the argument is a program that halts and does not read any input and returns false if the argument is a program that runs forever and does not read any input. You should not make any assumptions about the behavior of $Halt_\emptyset$ on an argument that is not a syntactically correct program.

Can you solve the halting problem by using $Halt_\emptyset$? More specifically, can you write a program that reads a program text P as input, reads an integer n as input, and then decides whether P halts when it reads n as input? You may assume that any program P you are given begins with a read statement that reads a single integer from standard input. This problem does not ask you to write the program to solve the halting problem. It just asks whether it is possible to do so.

If you believe that the halting problem can be solved if you are given $Halt_\emptyset$, then explain your answer by describing how a program solving the halting problem would work. If you believe that the halting problem cannot be solved by using $Halt_\emptyset$, then explain briefly why you think not.

2.3 Halting Problem on All Input

Suppose you are given a function $Halt_\forall$ that can be used to determine whether a program halts on all input. Under the same conditions as those of problem 2.2, can you solve the halting problem by using $Halt_\forall$?

3

Lisp: Functions, Recursion, and Lists

Lisp is the medium of choice for people who enjoy free
style and flexibility.
Gerald J. Sussman

A Lisp programmer knows the value of everything, but the
cost of nothing.
Alan Perlis

Lisp is a historically important language that is good for illustrating a number of
general points about programming languages. Because Lisp is very different from
procedure-oriented and object-oriented languages you may use more frequently, this
chapter may help you think about programming in a different way. Lisp shows that
many goals of programming language design can be met in a simple, elegant way.

3.1 LISP HISTORY

The Lisp programming language was developed at MIT in the late 1950s for research
in artificial intelligence (AI) and symbolic computation. The name Lisp is an acronym
for the *LIS*t *P*rocessor. Lists comprise the main data structure of Lisp.

The strength of Lisp is its simplicity and flexibility. It has been widely used for
exploratory programming, a style of software development in which systems are built
incrementally and may be changed radically as the result of experimental evaluation.
Exploratory programming is often used in the development of AI programs, as a
researcher may not know how the program should accomplish a task until several
unsuccessful programs have been tested. The popular text editor emacs is written in
Lisp, as is the linux graphical toolkit gtk and many other programs in current use in
a variety of computing environments.

Many different Lisp implementations have been built over the years, leading
to many different dialects of the language. One influential dialect was Maclisp,

JOHN MCCARTHY

A programming language designer and a central figure in the field of artificial intelligence, John McCarthy led the original Lisp effort at MIT in the late 1950s and early 1960s. Among other seminal contributions to the field, McCarthy participated in the design of Algol 60 and formulated the concept of time sharing in a 1959 memo to the director of the MIT Computation Center. McCarthy moved to Stanford in 1962, where he has been on the faculty ever since.

Throughout his career, John McCarthy has advocated using formal logic and mathematics to understand programming languages and systems, as well as common-sense reasoning and other topics in artificial intelligence. In the early 1960s, he wrote a series of papers on what he called a *Mathematical Theory of Computation*. These identified a number of important problems in understanding and reasoning about computer programs and systems. He supported political freedom for scientists abroad during the Cold War and has been an advocate of free speech in electronic media.

Now a lively person with graying hair and beard, McCarthy is an independent thinker who suggests creative solutions to bureaucratic as well as technical problems. He has won a number of important prizes and honors, including the ACM Turing Award in 1971.

developed in the 1960s at MIT's Project MAC. Another was Scheme, developed at MIT in the 1970s by Guy Steele and Gerald Sussman. Common Lisp is a modern Lisp with complex forms of object-oriented primitives.

McCarthy's 1960 paper on Lisp, called "Recursive functions of symbolic expressions and their computation by machine" [*Communications of the Association for Computing Machinery*, **3**(4), 184–195 (1960)] is an important historical document with many good ideas. In addition to the value of the programming language ideas it contains, the paper gives us some idea of the state of the art in 1960 and provides some useful insight into the language design process. You might enjoy reading the first few sections of the paper and skim the other parts briefly to see what they contain. The journal containing the article will be easy to find in many computer science libraries or you can find a retypeset version of the paper in electronic form on the Web.

3.2 GOOD LANGUAGE DESIGN

Most successful language design efforts share three important characteristics with the Lisp project:

- *Motivating Application:* The language was designed so that a specific kind of program could be written more easily.
- *Abstract Machine:* There is a simple and unambiguous program execution model.
- *Theoretical Foundations:* Theoretical understanding was the basis for including certain capabilities and omitting others.

These points are elaborated in the subsequent subsections.

Motivating Application

An important programming problem for McCarthy's group was a system called *Advice Taker*. This was a common-sense reasoning system based on logic. As the name implies, the program was supposed to read statements written in a specific input language, perform logical reasoning, and answer simple questions. Another important problem used in the design of Lisp was symbolic calculation. For example, McCarthy's group wanted to be able to write a program that could find a symbolic expression for the indefinite integral (as in calculus) for a function, given a symbolic description of the function as input.

Most good language designs start from some specific need. For comparison, here are some motivating problems that were influential in the design of other programming languages:

Lisp	Symbolic computation, logic, experimental programming
C	Unix operating system
Simula	Simulation
PL/1	Tried to solve all programming problems; not successful or influential

A specific purpose provides focus for language designers. It helps us to set criteria for making design decisions. A specific, motivating application also helps us to solve one of the hardest problems in programming language design: deciding which features to leave out.

Program Execution Model

A language design must be specific about how all basic operations are done. The language design may either be very concrete, prescribing exactly how the parts of the language must be implemented, or more abstract, specifying only certain properties that must be satisfied in any implementation. It is possible to err in either direction. A language that is too closely tied to one machine will lead to programs that are not portable. When new technology leads to faster machine architectures, programs written in the language may become obsolete. At the other extreme, it is possible to be too abstract. If a language design specifies only what the eventual value of an expression must be, without any information about how it is to be evaluated, it may be difficult for programmers to write efficient code. Most programmers find it important to have a good understanding of how programs will be executed, with enough detail to predict program running time. Lisp was designed for a specific machine, the IBM 704. However, if the designers had built the language around a lot of special features of a particular computer, the language would not have survived as well as it has. Instead, by luck or by design, they identified a useful set of simple concepts that map easily onto the IBM 704 architecture, and also onto other computers. The Lisp execution model is discussed in more detail in Subsection 3.4.3.

A systematic, predictable machine model is critical to the success of a programming language. For comparison, here are some execution models associated with the design of other programming languages:

Fortran	Flat register machine
	No stacks, no recursion
	Memory arranged as linear array
Algol family	Stack of activation records
	Heap storage
Smalltalk	Objects, communicating by messages

Theoretical Foundations

McCarthy described Lisp as a "scheme for representing the *partial recursive functions* of a certain class of symbolic expressions." We discussed computability and partial recursive functions in Chapter 2. Here are the main points about computability theory that are relevant to the design of Lisp:

- Lisp was designed to be Turing complete, meaning that all partial recursive functions may be written in Lisp. The phrase "Turing complete" refers to a characterization of computability proposed by the mathematician A.M. Turing; see Chapter 2.
- The use of function expressions and recursion in Lisp take direct advantage of a mathematical characterization of computable functions based on lambda calculus.

Today it is unlikely that a team of programming language designers would advertise that their language is sufficient to define all partial recursive functions. Most computer scientists nowadays know about computability theory and assume that most languages intended for general programming are Turing complete. However, computability theory and other theoretical frameworks such as type theory continue to have important consequences for programming language design.

The connection between Lisp and lambda calculus is important, and lambda calculus remains an important tool in the study of programming languages. A summary of lambda calculus appears in Section 4.2.

3.3 BRIEF LANGUAGE OVERVIEW

The topic of this chapter is a language that might be called *Historical Lisp*. This is essentially Lisp 1.5, from the early 1960s, with one or two minor changes. Because there are several different versions of Lisp in common use, it is likely that some function names used in this book will differ from those you may have used in previous Lisp programming.

An engaging book that captures some of the spirit of contemporary Lisp is the Scheme-based paperback by D.P. Friedman and M. Felleisen, titled *The Little Schemer* (MIT Press, Cambridge, MA, 1995). This is similar to an earlier book by the same authors entitled *The Little LISPer*. Lisp syntax is extremely simple. To make parsing (see Section 4.1) easy, all operations are written in prefix form, with the operator in front of all the operands. Here are some examples of Lisp expressions, with corresponding infix form for comparison.

Lisp prefix notation	Infix notation
(+ 1 2 3 4 5)	(1 + 2 + 3 + 4 + 5)
(* (+ 2 3) (+ 4 5))	((2 + 3) * (4 + 5))
(f x y)	f(x, y)

Atoms

Lisp programs compute with atoms and cells. Atoms include integers, floating-point numbers, and symbolic atoms. Symbolic atoms may have more than one letter. For example, the atom duck is printed with four letters, but it is *atomic* in the sense that there is no Lisp operation for taking the atom apart into four separate atoms.

In our discussion of *Historical Lisp*, we use only integers and symbolic atoms. Symbolic atoms are written with a sequence of characters and digits, beginning with a character. The atoms, symbols, and numbers are given by the following Backus normal form (BNF) grammar (see Section 4.1 if you are not familiar with grammars):

```
<atom> ::= <smbl> | <num>
<smbl> ::= <char> | <smbl><char> | <smbl><digit>
<num> ::= <digit> | <num><digit>
```

An atom that is used for some special purposes is the atom nil.

S-Expressions and Lists

The basic data structures of Lisp are *dotted pairs*, which are pairs written with a dot between the two parts of the pair. Putting atoms or pairs together, we can write symbolic expressions in a form traditionally called S-expressions. The syntax of Lisp S-expressions is given by the following grammar:

```
<sexp> ::= <atom> | (<sexp> . <sexp>)
```

Although S-expressions are the basic data of Historical Lisp, most Lisp programs actually use lists. Lisp lists are built out of pairs in a particular way, as described in Subsection 3.4.3.

Functions and Special Forms

The basic functions of Historical Lisp are the operations

cons   car   cdr   eq   atom

on pairs and atoms, together with the general programming functions

cond   lambda   define   quote   eval

We also use numeric functions such as +, –, and ∗, writing these in the usual Lisp prefix notation. The function cons is used to combine two atoms or lists, and car and cdr take lists apart. The function eq is an equality test and atom tests whether its argument is an atom. These are discussed in more detail in Subsection 3.4.3 in connection with the machine representation of lists and pairs.

The general programming functions include cond for a conditional test (if... then...else...), lambda for defining functions, define for declarations, quote to delay or prevent evaluation, and eval to force evaluation of an expression.

The functions cond, lambda, define, and quote are technically called *special forms* since an expression beginning with one of these special functions is evaluated without evaluating all of the parts of the expression. More about this below.

The language summarized up to this point is called *pure Lisp*. A feature of pure Lisp is that expressions do not have *side effects*. This means that evaluating an expression only produces the value of that expression; it does not change the observable state of the machine. Some basic functions that *do* have side effects are

rplaca   rplacd   set   setq

We discuss these in Subsection 3.4.9. Lisp with one or more of these functions is sometimes called *impure Lisp*.

Evaluation of Expressions

The basic structure of the Lisp interpreter or compiler is the *read-eval-print* loop. This means that the basic action of the interpreter is to read an expression, evaluate it, and print the value. If the expression defines the meaning of some symbol, then the association between the symbol and its value is saved so that the symbol can be used in expressions that are typed in later.

In general, we evaluate a Lisp expression

(function arg_1 ... arg_n)

by evaluating each of the arguments in turn, then passing the list of argument values to the function. The exceptions to this rule are called special forms. For example, we evaluate a conditional expression

$$(\text{cond } (p_1 \ e_1) \dots (p_n \ e_n))$$

by proceeding from left to right, finding the first p_i with a value different from nil. This involves evaluating $p_1 \dots p_n$ and one e_i if p_i is nonnil. We return to this below.

Lisp uses the atoms T and nil for true and false, respectively. In this book, true and false are often written in Lisp code, as these are more intuitive and more understandable if you are have not done a lot of Lisp programming. You may read Lisp examples that contain true and false as if they appear inside a program for which we have already defined true and false as synonyms for T and nil, respectively.

A slightly tricky point is that the Lisp evaluator needs to distinguish between a string that is used to name an atom and a string that is used for something else, such as the name of a function. The form quote is used to write atoms and lists directly:

(quote cons)	expression whose value is the atom "cons"
(cons a b)	expression whose value is the pair containing the values of a and b
(cons (quote A) (quote B))	expression whose value is the pair containing the atoms "A" and "B"

In most dialects of Lisp, it is common to write 'bozo instead of (quote bozo). You can see from the preceding brief description that quote must be a special form. Here are some additional examples of Lisp expressions and their values:

(+ 4 5)	expression with value 9
(+ (+ 1 2) (+ 4 5))	first evaluate 1+2, then 4+5, then 3+9 to get value 12
(quote (+ 1 2))	evaluates to a list (+ 1 2)
'(+ 1 2)	same as (quote (+ 1 2))

Example. Here is a slightly longer Lisp program example, the definition of a function that searches a list. The find function takes two arguments, x and y, and searches the list y for an occurrence of x. The declaration begins with define, which indicates that this is a declaration. Then follows the name find that is being defined, and the expression for the find function:

```
(define find (lambda (x y)
      (cond ((equal y nil) nil)
             ((equal x (car y)) x)
             (true (find x (cdr y)))
)))
```

Lisp function expressions begin with lambda. The function has two arguments, x and y, which appear in a list immediately following lambda. The return value of the function is given by the expression that follows the parameters. The function body is a conditional expression, which returns nil, the empty list, if y is the empty list. Otherwise, if x is the first element (car) of the list y, then the function returns the element x. Otherwise the function makes a recursive call to see if x is in the cdr of the list y. The cdr of a list is the list of all elements that occur after the first element. We can use this function to find 'apple in the list '(pear peach apple fig banana) by writing the Lisp expression

```
(find 'apple '(pear peach apple fig banana))
```

Static and Dynamic Scope

Historically, Lisp was a dynamically scoped language. This means that a variable inside an expression could refer to a different value if it is passed to a function that declared this variable differently. When Scheme was introduced in 1978, it was a statically scoped variant of Lisp. As discussed in Chapter 7, static scoping is common in most modern programming languages. Following the widespread acceptance of Scheme, most modern Lisps have become statically scoped. The difference between static and dynamic scope is not covered in this chapter.

Lisp and Scheme

If you want to try writing Lisp programs by using a Scheme compiler, you will want to know that the names of some functions and special forms differ in Scheme and Lisp. Here is a summary of some of the notational differences:

Lisp	Scheme	Lisp	Scheme
defun	define	rplacaset	car!
defvar	define	rplacdset	cdr!
car, cdr	car, cdr	mapcar	map
cons	cons	t	#t
null	null?	nil	#f
atom	atom?	nil	nil
eq, equal	eq?, equal?	nil	'()
Setq	set!	progn	begin
cond...t	cond...else		

3.4 INNOVATIONS IN THE DESIGN OF LISP

3.4.1 Statements and Expressions

Just as virtually all natural languages have certain basic parts of speech, such as *nouns*, *verbs*, and *adjectives*, there are programming language parts of speech that occur in most languages. The most basic programming language parts of speech are *expressions*, *statements*, and *declarations*. These may be summarized as follows:

Expression: a syntactic entity that may be evaluated to determine its value. In some cases, evaluation may not terminate, in which case the expression has no value. Evaluation of some expressions may change the state of the machine, causing a side effect in addition to producing a value for the expression.

Statement : a command that alters the state of the machine in some explicit way. For example, the machine language statement load 4094 r1 alters the state of the machine by placing the contents of location 4094 into register r1. The programming language statement x := y + 3 alters the state of the machine by adding 3 to the value of variable y and storing the result in the location associated with variable x.

Declaration: a syntactic entity that introduces a new identifier, often specifying one or more attributes. For example, a declaration may introduce a variable i and specify that it is intended to have only integer values.

Errors and termination may depend on the order in which parts of expressions are evaluated. For example, consider the expression

```
if f(2)=2 or f(3)=3 then 4 else 4
```

where f is a function that halts on even arguments but runs forever on odd arguments. In many programming languages, a Boolean expression A or B would be evaluated from left to right, with B evaluated only if A is false. In this case, the value of the preceding expression would be 4. However, if we evaluate the test A or B from right to left or evaluate both A and B regardless of the value of A, then the value of the expression is undefined.

Traditional machine languages and assembly languages are based on statements. Lisp is an expression-based language, meaning that the basic constructs of the language are expressions, not statements. In fact, pure Lisp has no statements and no expressions with side effects. Although it was known from computability theory that it was possible to define all computable functions without using statements or side effects, Lisp was the first programming language to try to put this theoretical possibility into practice.

3.4.2 Conditional Expressions

Fortran and assembly languages used before Lisp had conditional statements. A typical statement might have the form

```
if (condition) go to 112
```

If the condition is true when this command is executed, then the program jumps to the statement with the label 112. However, conditional expressions that produce a value instead of causing a jump were new in Lisp. They also appeared in Algol 60, but this seems to have been the result of a proposal by McCarthy, modified by a syntactic suggestion of Backus.

The Lisp conditional expression

$(\text{cond } (p_1 \ e_1) \dots (p_n \ e_n))$

---

could be written as

---

if p_1 then e_1
   else if p_2 then e_2
     ...
       else if p_n then e_n
        else *no_value*

---

in an Algol-like notation, except that most programming languages do not have a direct way of specifying the absence of a value. In brief, the value of $(\text{cond } (p_1 \ e_1) \dots (p_n \ e_n))$ is the first e_i, proceeding from left to right, with p_i nonnil and p_j nil (representing false) for all $j < i$. If there is no such e_i then the conditional expression has no value. If any of the expressions $p_1 \dots p_n$ have side effects, then these will occur from left to right as the conditional expression is evaluated.

The Lisp conditional expression would now be called a *sequential conditional expression*. The reason it is called sequential is that the parts of this expression are evaluated in sequence from left to right, with evaluation terminating as soon as a value for the expression can be determined.

It is worth noting that $(\text{cond } (p_1 \ e_1) \dots (p_n \ e_n))$ is undefined if

$p_1, \dots, p_n$ are all nil
$p_1, \dots, p_i$ false and p_{i+1} undefined
$p_1, \dots, p_i$ false, p_{i+1} true, and e_{i+1} undefined

Here are some example conditional expressions and their values:

$(\text{cond } ((< 2 \ 1) \ 2) \ ((< 1 \ 2) \ 1))$	has value 1
$(\text{cond } ((< 2 \ 1) \ 2) \ ((< 3 \ 2) \ 3))$	is undefined
$(\text{cond } (\text{diverge } 1) \ (\text{true } 0))$	is undefined, if diverge does not terminate
$(\text{cond } (\text{true } 0) \ (\text{diverge } 1))$	has value 0

Strictness. An important part of the Lisp cond expression is that a conditional expression may have a value even if one or more subexpressions do not. For example, $(\text{cond } (\text{true } e_1) \ (\text{false } e_2))$ may be defined even if e_2 is undefined. In contrast, $e_1 + e_2$ is undefined if either e_1 or e_2 is undefined. In standard programming language terminology, an operator or expression form is *strict* if all operands or subexpressions are evaluated. Lisp cond is not strict, but addition is. (Some operators from C that are not strict are && and ||.)

3.4.3 The Lisp Abstract Machine

What is an Abstract Machine?

The phrase *abstract machine* is generally used to refer to an idealized computing device that can execute a specific programming language directly. Typically an abstract machine may not be fully implementable: An abstract machine may provide infinitely many memory locations or infinite-precision arithmetic. However, as we use the phrase in this book, an abstract machine should be sufficiently realistic to provide useful information about the real execution of real programs on real hardware. Our goal in discussing abstract machines is to identify the mental model of the computer that a programmer uses to write and debug programs. For this reason, there is a tendency to refer to *the* abstract machine associated with a specific programming language.

The Abstract Machine for Lisp

The abstract machine for Pure Lisp has four parts:

- A *Lisp expression* to be evaluated.
- A *continuation*, which is a function representing the remaining program to evaluate when done with the current expression.
- An *association list*, commonly called the *A-list* in much of the literature on Lisp and called the *run-time stack* in the literature on Algol-based languages. The purpose of the A-list is to store the values of variables that may occur either in the current expression to be evaluated or in the remaining expressions in the program.
- A *heap*, which is a set of cons cells (pairs stored in memory) that might be pointed to by pointers in the A-list.

The structure of this machine is not investigated in detail. The main idea is that when a Lisp expression is evaluated some bindings between identifiers and values may be created. These are stored on the A-list. Some of these values may involve cons cells that are placed in the heap. When the evaluation of an expression is completed, the value of that expression is passed to the continuation, which represents the work to be done by the program after that expression is evaluated.

This abstract machine is similar to a standard register machine with a stack, if we think of the current expression as representing the program counter and the continuation as representing the remainder of the program.

There are four main equality functions in Lisp: eq, eql, equal, and =. The function eq tests whether its arguments are represented by the same sequence of memory locations, and = is numeric equality. The function eql tests whether its arguments are the same symbol or number, and equal is a recursive equality test on lists or atoms that is implemented by use of eq and =. For simplicity, we generally use equal in sample code.

Cons Cells

Cons cells (or dotted pairs) are the basic data structure of the Lisp abstract machine. Cons cells have two parts, historically called the *address* part and the *decrement* part. The words address and decrement come from the IBM 704 computer and are hardly ever used today. Only the letters a and d remain in the acronyms car (for "contents of the address register") and cdr (for "contents of the decrement register"). We draw cons cells as follows:

Cons cells

- provide a simple model of memory in the machine,
- are efficiently implementable, and
- are not tightly linked to particular computer architecture.

We may represent an atom may be represented with a cons cell by putting a "tag" that tells what kind of atom it is in the address part and the actual atom value in the decrement part. For example, the letter "a" could be represented as a Lisp atom as

where atm indicates that the cell represents an atom and a indicates that the atom is the letter a.

Because putting a pointer in one or both parts of a cons cell represents lists, the bit pattern used to indicate an atom must be different from every pointer value. There are five basic functions on cons cells, which are evaluated as follows:

atom, a function with one argument: If a value is an atom, then the word storing the value has a special bit pattern in its address part that flags the value as being an atom. The atom function returns true if this pattern indicates that the function argument is an atom. (In Scheme, the function atom is written atom?, which reminds us that the function value will be true or false.)

eq, a function with two arguments: compares two arguments for equality by checking to see if they are stored in the same location. This is meaningful for atoms as well as for cons cells because conceptually the Lisp compiler behaves as if each atom (including every number) is stored once in a unique location.

cons, a function with two arguments: The expression (cons x y) is evaluated as follows:

1. Allocate new cell c.
2. Set the address part of c to point to the value of x.
3. Set the decrement part of c to point to the value of y.
4. Return a pointer to c.

car, a function with one argument: If the argument is a cons cell c, then return the *c*ontents of the *a*ddress *r*egister of c. Otherwise the application of car results in an error.

cdr, a function with one argument: If the argument is a cons cell c, then return the *c*ontents of the *d*ecrement *r*egister of c. Otherwise the application of cdr results in an error.

In drawing cons cells, we draw the contents of a cell as either a pointer to another cell or as an atom. For our purposes, it is not important how an atom is represented inside a cons cell. (It could be represented as either a specific bit pattern inside a cell or as a pointer to a location that contains the representation of an atom.)

Example 3.1

We evaluate the expression (cons 'A 'B) by creating a new cons cell and then setting the car of this cell to the atom 'A and the cdr of the cell to 'B. The expression '(A . B) would have the same effect, as this is the syntax for a dotted pair of atom A and atom B. Although this dotted-pair notation was a common part of early Lisp, Scheme and later Lisps emphasize lists over pairs.

Example 3.2

When the expression (cons (cons 'A 'B) (cons 'A 'B)) is evaluated, a new structure of the following form is created:

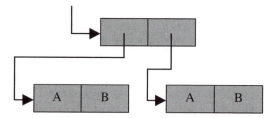

The reason that there are two cons cells with the same parts is that each evaluation of (cons 'A 'B) creates a new cell. This structure is printed as ((A . B) . (A . B)).

Example 3.3

It is also possible to write a Lisp expression that creates the following structure, which is also printed ((A . B) . (A . B)):

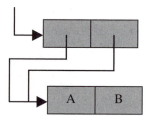

One expression whose evaluation produces this structure is ((lambda (x) (cons x x)) (cons 'A 'B)). We proceed with the evaluation of this expression by first evaluating the function argument (cons 'A 'B) to produce the cons cell drawn here, then passing the cell to the function (lambda (x) (cons x x)) that creates the upper cell with two pointers to the (A.B) cell. Lisp lambda expressions are described in this chapter in Subsection 3.4.5.

Representation of Lists by Cons Cells

Because a cons cell may contain two pointers, cons cells may be used to construct trees. Because Lisp programs often use lists, there are conventions for representing lists as a certain form of trees. Specifically, the list $a_1, a_2, \ldots a_n$ is represented by a cons cell whose car is a_1 and whose cdr points to the cells representing list $a_2, \ldots a_n$. For the empty list, we use a pointer set to NIL.

For example, here is representation for the list (A B C), also written as (A . (B . (C . NIL))):

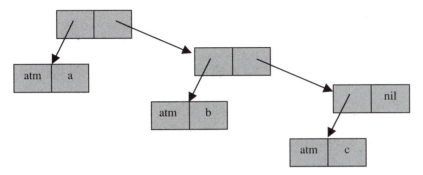

In this illustration, atoms are shown as cons cells, with a bit pattern indicating atom in the first part of the cell and the actual atom value in the second. For simplicity, we often draw lists by placing an atom inside half a cons cells. For example, we could write A in the address part of the top-left cell instead of drawing a pointer to the cell representing atom A, and similarly for list cells pointing to atoms B and C. In the rest of the book, we use the simpler form of drawing; the illustration here is just to remind us that atoms as well as lists must be represented inside the machine in some way.

3.4.4 Programs as Data

Lisp data and Lisp programs have the same syntax and internal representation. This makes it easy to manipulate Lisp programs as data. One feature that sets Lisp apart from many other languages is that it is possible for a program to build a data structure that represents an expression and then evaluates the expression as if it were written as part of the program. This is done with the function eval.

Example. We can write a Lisp function to substitute expression x for all occurrences of y in expression z and then evaluate the resulting expression. To make the logical structure of the substitute-and-eval function clear, we define substitute first and then use it in substitute-and-eval. The substitute function has three arguments, exp1, var, and exp2. The result of (substitute exp1 var exp2) is the expression obtained from exp2 when all occurrences of var are replaced with exp1:

```
(define substitute (lambda (exp1 var exp2)
     (cond  ((atom exp2) (cond ((eq exp2 var) exp1) (true exp2)))
            (true (cons (substitute exp1 var (car exp2))
                    (substitute exp1 var (cdr exp2)))))))
(define substitute-and-eval (lambda (x y z) (eval (substitute x y z))))
```

The ability to use list operations to build programs at run time and then execute them is a distinctive feature of Lisp. You can appreciate the value of this feature if you think about how you would write a C program to read in a few C expressions and execute them. To do this, you would have to write some kind of C interpreter or compiler. In Lisp, you can just read in an expression and apply the built-in function eval to it.

3.4.5 Function Expressions

Lisp computation is based on functions and recursive calls instead of on assignment and iterative loops. This was radically different from other languages in 1960, and is fundamentally different from many languages in common use now.

A Lisp function expression has the form

(lambda (⟨parameters⟩) ⟨function_body⟩)

---

where ⟨parameters⟩ is a list of identifiers and ⟨function_body⟩ is an expression. For example, a function that places its argument in a list followed by atoms A and B may be written as

---

(lambda (x) (cons x '(A B)))

Another example is this function that, with a primitive function used for addition, adds its two arguments:

(lambda (x y) (+ x y))

The idea of writing expressions for functions may be traced to lambda calculus, which was developed by Alonzo Church and others, beginning in the 1930s. One fact about lambda calculus that was known in the 1930s was that every function computable by a Turing machine could also be written in the lambda calculus and conversely.

In lambda calculus, function expressions are written with the Greek lowercase letter lambda (λ), rather than with the word lambda, as in Lisp. Lambda calculus also uses different conventions about parenthesization. For example, the function that squares its argument and adds the result to y is written as

$$\lambda x.(x^2 + y)$$

in lambda calculus, but as

(lambda (x) (+ (square x) y))

---

in Lisp. In this function, x is called the *formal parameter*; this means that x is a placeholder in the function definition that will refer to the actual parameter when the function is applied. More specifically, consider the expression

((lambda (x) (+ (square x) y)) 4)

that applies a function to the integer 4. This expression can be evaluated only in a context in which y already has a value. The value of this expression will be 16 plus the value of y. This will be computed by the evaluation of (plus (square x) y) with x set to 4. The identifier y is a said to be a *global variable* in this function expression because its value must be given a value by some definition outside the function expression. More information about variables, binding, and lambda calculus may be found in Section 4.2.

3.4.6 Recursion

Recursive functions were new at the time Lisp appeared. McCarthy, in addition to including them in Lisp, was the main advocate for allowing recursive functions in Algol 60. Fortran, by comparison, did not allow a function to call itself.

Members of the Algol 60 committee later wrote that they had no idea what they were in for when they agreed to include recursive functions in Algol 60. (They might have been unhappy for a few years, but they would probably agree now that it was a visionary decision.)

Lisp lambda makes it possible to write *anonymous functions*, which are functions that do not have a declared name. However, it is difficult to write recursive functions with this notation. For example, suppose we want to write an expression for the function f such that

(f x) = (cond   ((eq x 0) 0)
                  (true (+ x (f (- x 1))))
)

A first attempt might be

(lambda (x) (cond ((eq x 0) 0) (true (+ x (f (- x 1))))))

However, this does not make any sense because the f inside the function expression is not defined anywhere. McCarthy's solution in 1960 was to add an operator called label so that

(label f (lambda (x) (cond ((eq x 0) 0) (true (+ x (f (- x 1)))))))

defines the recursive f suggested previously. In later Lisps, it became accepted style just to declare a function by use of the define declaration form. In particular, a recursive function f can be declared by

```
(define f (lambda (x) (cond ((eq x 0) 0) (true (+ x (f (- x 1)))))))
```

Another notation in some versions of Lisps is defun for "define function," which eliminates the need for lambda:

```
(defun f (x) (cond ((eq x 0) 0) (true (+ x (f (- x 1))))))
```

McCarthy's 1960 paper comments that the lambda notation is inadequate for expression recursive functions. This statement is false. Lambda calculus, and therefore Lisp, is capable of expressing recursive functions without any additional operator such as label. This was known to experts in lambda calculus in the 1930s, but apparently not known to McCarthy and his group in the 1950s. (See Subsection 4.2.3 for an explanation of how to do it.)

3.4.7 Higher-Order Functions

The phrase *higher-order function* means a function that either takes a function as an argument or returns a function as a result (or both). This use of higher-order comes from a convention that calls a function whose arguments and results are not functions a *first-order function*. A function that takes a first-order function as an argument is called a *second-order function*, functions on second-order functions are called *third-order functions*, and so on.

Example 3.4

If f and g are mathematical functions, say functions on the integers, then their composition $f \circ g$ is the function such that for every integer x, we have

$$(f \circ g)(x) = f(g(x)).$$

We can write composition as a Lisp function compose that takes two functions as arguments and returns their composition:

```
(define compose (lambda (f g) (lambda (x) (f (g x)))))
```

The first lambda is used to identify the arguments to compose. The second lambda is used to define the return value of the function, which is a function. You might enjoy calculating the value of the expression

```
(compose (lambda (x) (+ x x)) (lambda (x) (* x x)))
```

Example 3.5

A maplist is a function that takes a function and list and applies the function to every element in the list. The result is a list that contains all the results of function application. Using define to define a recursive function, we can write the maplist as follows:

```
(define maplist (lambda (f x)
    (cond ((eq x nil) nil) (true (cons (f (car x)) (maplist f (cdr x)))))))
```

We cannot say whether the maplist is a second-order or third-order function, as the elements of the list might be atoms, functions, or higher-order functions. As an example of the use of this function, we have

```
(maplist square '(1 2 3 4 5)) ⇒ (1 4 9 16 25),
```

where the symbol ⇒ means "evaluates to."

Higher-order functions require more run-time support than first-order functions, as discussed in some detail in Chapter 7.

3.4.8 Garbage Collection

In computing, *garbage* refers to memory locations that are not accessible to a program. More specifically, we define garbage as follows:

> At a given point in the execution of a program P, a memory location m is *garbage* if no completed execution of P from this point can access location m. In other words, replacing the contents of m or making this location inaccessible to P cannot affect any further execution of the program.

Note that this definition does not give an algorithm for finding garbage. However, if we could find all locations that are garbage (by this definition), at some point in the suspended execution of a program, it would be safe to deallocate these locations or use them for some other purpose.

In Lisp, the memory locations that are accessible to a program are cons cells. Therefore the garbage associated with a running Lisp program will be a set of cons cells that are not needed to complete the execution of the program. Garbage collection is the process of detecting garbage during the execution of a program and making it available for other uses. In garbage-collected languages, the run-time system receives requests for memory (as when Lisp cons cells are created) and allocates memory from some list of available space. The list of available memory locations is called the free list. When the run-time system detects that the available space is below some threshold, the program may be suspended and the garbage collector invoked. In Lisp and other garbage-collected languages, it is generally not necessary for the program to invoke the garbage collector explicitly. (In some modern implementations, the garbage collector may run in parallel with the program. However, because concurrent garbage collection raises some additional considerations, we will assume that the program is suspended when the garbage collector is running.)

The idea and implementation of automatic garbage collection appear to have originated with Lisp.

Here is an example of garbage. After the expression

```
(car (cons e₁ e₂ ))
```

is evaluated, any cons cells created by evaluation of e_2 will typically be garbage. However, it is not always correct to deallocate the locations used in a list after applying car to the list. For example, consider the expression

```
((lambda (x) (car (cons x x))) '(A B))
```

When this expression is evaluated, the function car will be applied to a cons cell whose "a" and "d" parts both point to the same list.

Many algorithms for garbage collection have been developed over the years. Here is a simple example called mark-and-sweep. The name comes from the fact that the algorithm first marks all of the locations reachable from the program, then "sweeps" up all the unmarked locations as garbage. This algorithm assumes that we can tell which bit sequences in memory are pointers and which are atoms, and it also assumes that there is a tag bit in each location that can be switched to 0 or 1 without destroying the data in that location.

Mark-and-Sweep Garbage Collection
1. Set all tag bits to 0.
2. Start from each location used directly in the program. Follow all links, changing the tag bit of each cell visited to 1.
3. Place all cells with tags still equal to 0 on the free list.

Garbage collection is a *very* useful feature, at least as far as programmer convenience goes. There is some debate about the efficiency of garbage-collected languages, however. Some researchers have experimental evidence showing that garbage collection adds of the order of 5% overhead to program execution time. However, this sort of measurement depends heavily on program design. Some simple programs could be written in C without the use of any user-allocated memory, but when translated into Lisp could create many cons cells during expression evaluation and therefore involve a lot of garbage-collection overhead. On the other hand, explicit memory management in C and C++ (in place of garbage collection) can be cumbersome and error prone, so that for certain programs it is highly advantageous to have automatic garbage collection. One phenomenon that indicates the importance and difficulty of memory management in C programs is the success of program analysis tools that are aimed specifically at detecting memory management errors.

Example. In Lisp, we can write a function that takes a list lst and an entry x, returning the part of the list that follows x, if any. This function, which we call select, can be written as follows:

```
(define select (lambda (x lst)
    (cond ((equal lst nil) nil)
          ((equal x (car lst)) (cdr lst))
          (true (select x (cdr lst)))
)))
```

Here are two analogous C programs that have different effects on the list they are passed. The first one leaves the list alone, returning a pointer to the cdr of the first cell that has its car equal to x:

```
typedef struct cell cell;
struct cell {
      cell * car, * cdr;
};
cell * select (cell *x, cell *lst) {
    cell *ptr;
    for (ptr=lst; ptr != 0; ) {
          if (ptr->car == x) return(ptr->cdr);
          else ptr = ptr->cdr;
    };
};
```

A second C program might be more appropriate if only the part of the list that follows x will be used in the rest of the program. In this case, it makes sense to free the cells that will no longer be used. Here is a C function that does just this:

```
cell * select1 (cell *x; cell *lst) {
    cell *ptr, *previous;
    for (ptr=lst; ptr != 0; ) {
          if (ptr->car == x) return(ptr->cdr);
          else previous = ptr;
          ptr = ptr->cdr;
          free(previous);
    }
}
```

An advantage of Lisp garbage collection is that the programmer does not have to decide which of these two functions to call. In Lisp, it is possible to just return a pointer to the part of the list that you want and let the garbage collector figure out whether you may need the rest of the list ever again. In C, on the other hand, the programmer must decide, while traversing the list, whether this is the last time that these cells will be referenced by the program.

Question to Ponder. It is interesting to observe that programming languages such as Lisp, in which most computation is expressed by recursive functions and linked data structures, provide automatic garbage collection. In contrast, simple imperative languages such as C require the programmer to free locations that are no longer needed. Is it just a coincidence that function-oriented languages have garbage collection and assignment-oriented languages do not? Or is there something intrinsic to function-oriented programming that makes garbage collection more appropriate for these languages? Part of the answer lies in the preceding example. Another part of the answer seems to lie in the problems associated with storage management for higher-order functions, studied in Section 7.4.

3.4.9 Pure Lisp and Side Effects

Pure Lisp expressions do not have side effects, which are visible changes in the state of the machine as the result of evaluating an expression. However, for efficiency, even early Lisp had expressions with side effects. Two historical functions with side effects are rplaca and rplacd:

(rplaca x y) — replace the address field of cons cell x with y,

(rplacd x y) — replace the decrement field of cons cell x with y.

In both cases, the value of the expression is the cell that has been modified. For example, the value of

```
(rplaca (cons 'A 'B) 'C)
```

is the cons cell with car 'C and cdr 'B produced when a new cons cell is allocated in the evaluation of (cons 'A 'B) and then the car 'A is replaced with 'C.

With these constructs, two occurrences of the same expression may have different values. (This is really what side effect means.) For example, consider the following code:

```
(lambda (x) (cons (car x) (cons (rplaca x c) (car x)))) (cons a b)
```

The expression (car x) occurs twice within the function expression, but there will be two different values in the two places this expression is evaluated. When rplaca and rplacd are used, it is possible to create circular list structures, something that is not possible in pure Lisp.

One situation in which rplaca and rplacd may increase efficiency is when a program modifies a cell in the middle of a list. For example, consider the following list of four elements:

Suppose we call this list x and we want to change the third element of list x to '. In pure Lisp, we cannot change any of the cells of this list, but we can define a new list with elements A, B, y, D. The new list can be defined with the following expression, where cadr x means "car of the cdr of x" and cdddr x means "cdr of cdr of cdr of x":

```
(cons (car x) (cons (cadr x) (cons y (cdddr x))))
```

Note that evaluating this expression will involve creating new cons cells for the first three elements of the list and, if there is no further use for them, eventually garbage collecting the old cells used for the first three elements of x. In contrast, in impure Lisp we can change the third cell directly by using the expression

```
(rplaca (cddr x) y)
```

If all we need is the list we obtained by replacing the third element of x with y, then this expression gets the result we want far more efficiently. In particular, there is no need to allocate new memory or free memory used for the original list.

Although this example may suggest that side effects lead to efficiency, the larger picture is more complicated. In general, it is difficult to compare the efficiency of different languages if the same problem would be best solved in very different ways. For example, if we write a program by using pure Lisp, we might be inclined to use different algorithms than those for impure Lisp. Once we begin to compare the efficiency of different solutions for the same problem, we should also take into account the amount of effort a programmer must spend writing the program, the ease of debugging, and so on. These are complex properties of programming languages that are difficult to quantify.

3.5 CHAPTER SUMMARY: CONTRIBUTIONS OF LISP

Lisp is an elegant programming language designed around a few simple ideas. The language was intended for symbolic computation, as opposed to the kind of numeric computation that was dominant in most programming outside of artificial intelligence research in 1960. This innovative orientation can be seen in the basic data structure, lists, and in the basic control structures, recursion and conditionals. Lists can be used to store sequences of symbols or represent trees or other structures. Recursion is a natural way to proceed through lists that may contain atomic data or other lists.

Three important aspects of programming language design contributed to the success of Lisp: a specific motivation application, an unambiguous program execution model, and attention to theoretical considerations. Among the main theoretical considerations, Lisp was designed with concern for the mathematical class of partial recursive functions. Lisp syntax for function expressions is based on lambda calculus.

The following contributions are some that are important to the field of programming languages:

- *Recursive functions.* Lisp programming is based on functions and recursion instead of assignment and while loops. Lisp introduces recursive functions and supports functions with function arguments and functions that return functions as results.

■ *Lists.* The basic data structure in early Lisp was the cons cell. The main use of cons cells in modern forms of Lisp is for building lists, and lists are used for everything. The list data structure is extremely useful. In addition, the Lisp presentation of memory as an unlimited supply of cons cells provides a more useful abstract machine for nonnumerical programming than do arrays, which were primary data structures in other languages of the early days of computing.

■ *Programs as data.* This is still a revolutionary concept 40 years after its introduction in Lisp. In Lisp, a program can build the list representation of a function or other forms of expression and then use the eval function to evaluate the expression.

■ *Garbage collection.* Lisp was the first language to manage memory for the programmer automatically. Garbage collection is a useful feature that eliminates the program error of using a memory location after freeing it.

In the years since 1960, Lisp has continued to be successful for symbolic mathematics and exploratory programming, as in AI research projects and other applications of symbolic computation or logical reasoning. It has also been widely used for teaching because of the simplicity of the language.

EXERCISES

3.1 Cons Cell Representations

(a) Draw the list structure created by evaluating (cons 'A (cons 'B 'C)).

(b) Write a pure Lisp expression that will result in this representation, with no sharing of the (B . C) cell. Explain why your expression produces this structure.

(c) Write a pure Lisp expression that will result in this representation, with sharing of the (B . C) cell. Explain why your expression produces this structure.

While writing your expressions, use only these Lisp constructs: lambda abstraction, function application, the atoms 'A 'B 'C, and the basic list functions (cons, car, cdr, atom, eq). Assume a simple-minded Lisp implementation that does not try to do any clever detection of common subexpressions or advanced memory allocation optimizations.

3.2 Conditional Expressions in Lisp

The semantics of the Lisp conditional expression

$$(\text{cond } (p_1\ e_1) \ldots (p_n\ e_n))$$

is explained in the text. This expression does not have a value if $p_1, \ldots, p_k$ are false and p_{k+1} does not have a value, regardless of the values of $p_{k+2}, \ldots, p_n$.

Imagine you are an MIT student in 1958 and you and McCarthy are considering alternative interpretations for conditionals in Lisp:

(a) Suppose McCarthy suggests that the value of (cond $(p_1\ e_1) \ldots (p_n\ e_n)$) should be the value of e_k if p_k is true and if, for every $i<k$, the value of expression p_i is either false or undefined. Is it possible to implement this interpretation? Why or why not? (*Hint:* Remember the halting problem.)

(b) Another design for conditional might allow any of several values if more than one of the guards $(p_1, \ldots, p_n)$ is true. More specifically (and be sure to read carefully), suppose someone suggests the following meaning for conditional:

i. The conditional's value is undefined if none of the p_k is true.

ii. If some p_k are true, then the implementation *must* return the value of e_j for *some* j with p_j true. However, it need not be the first such e_j.

Note that in (cond (a b) (c d) (e f)), for example, if a runs forever, c evaluates to true, and e halts in error, the value of this expression should be the value of d, if it has one. Briefly describe a way to implement conditional so that properties i and ii are true. You need to write only two or three sentences to explain the main idea.

(c) Under the original interpretation, the function

```
(defun odd (x) (cond ((eq x 0) nil)
                     ((eq x 1) t)
                     ((> x 0) (odd (- x 2)))
                     (t (odd (+ x 2)))))
```

would give us t for odd numbers and nil for even numbers. Modify this expression so that it would always give us t for odd numbers and nil for even numbers under the alternative interpretation described in part (b).

(d) The normal implementation of Boolean OR is designed not to evaluate a subexpression unless it is necesary. This is called the *short-circuiting* OR, and it may be defined as follows:

$$\text{SCOR}(e_1, e_2) = \begin{cases} true & \text{if } e_1 = true \\ true & \text{if } e_1 = false \text{ and } e_2 = true \\ false & \text{if } e_1 = e_2 = false \\ undefined & \text{otherwise} \end{cases}.$$

It allows e_2 to be undefined if e_1 is true.

The *parallel* OR is a related construct that gives an answer whenever possible (possibly doing some unnecessary subexpression evaluation). It is defined similarly:

$$\text{POR}(e_1, e_2) = \begin{cases} true & \text{if } e_1 = true \\ true & \text{if } e_2 = true \\ false & \text{if } e_1 = e_2 = false \\ undefined & \text{otherwise} \end{cases}$$

It allows e_2 to be undefined if e_1 is true and also allows e_1 to be undefined if e_2 is true. You may assume that e_1 and e_2 do not have side effects.

Of the original interpretation, the interpretation in part (a), and the interpretation in part (b), which ones would allow us to implement SCOR most easily? What about POR? Which interpretation would make implementations of short-circuiting OR difficult? Which interpretation would make implementation of parallel OR difficult? Why?

3.3 Detecting Errors

Evaluation of a Lisp expression can either terminate normally (and return a value), terminate abnormally with an error, or run forever. Some examples of expressions that terminate with an error are (/ 3 0), division by 0; (car 'a), taking the car of an atom; and (+ 3 "a"), adding a string to a number. The Lisp system detects these errors, terminates evaluation, and prints a message to the screen. Your boss wants to handle errors in Lisp programs without terminating the computation, but doesn't know how, so your boss asks you to...

(a) ...implement a Lisp construct (error? E) that detects whether an expression E will cause an error. More specifically, your boss wants the evaluation of (error? E) to halt with the value *true* if the evaluation of E terminates in error and to halt with the value *false* otherwise. Explain why it is not possible to implement the error? construct as part of the Lisp environment.

(b) ...implement a Lisp construct (guarded E) that either executes E and returns its value, or, if E halts with an error, returns 0 without performing any side effects. This could be used to try to evaluate E and, if an error occurs, just use 0 instead. For example,

    (+ (guarded E) E')   ; just E' if E halts with an error; E+E' otherwise

will have the value of E' if the evaluation of E halts in error and the value of E + E' otherwise. How might you implement the guarded construct? What difficulties might you encounter? Note that, unlike that of (error? E), evaluation of (guarded E) does not need to halt if evaluation of E does not halt.

3.4 Lisp and Higher-Order Functions

Lisp functions compose, mapcar, and maplist are defined as follows, with #t written for *true* and () for the empty list. Text beginning with ;; and continuing to the end of a line is a comment.

```
(define compose
    (lambda (f g)   (lambda (x) (f (g x)))))

(define mapcar
  (lambda (f xs)
    (cond
      ((eq? xs ()) ())   ;; If the list is empty, return the empty list
      (#t              ;; Otherwise, apply f to the first element...
          (cons (f (car xs))
                        ;; and map f on the rest of the list
              (mapcar f (cdr xs))
)))))

(define maplist
  (lambda (f xs)
    (cond
      ((eq? xs ()) ())   ;; If the list is empty, return the empty list
      (#t              ;; Otherwise, apply f to the list...
          (cons (f xs)
                        ;; and map f on the rest of the list
```

(maplist f (cdr xs))
)))))

The difference between maplist and mapcar is that maplist applies f to every sublist, whereas mapcar applies f to every element. (The two function expressions differ in only the sixth line.) For example, if inc is a function that adds one to any number, then

(mapcar inc '(1 2 3 4)) = (2 3 4 5)

whereas

(maplist (lambda (xs) (mapcar inc xs)) '(1 2 3 4))
= ((2 3 4 5) (3 4 5) (4 5) (5))

However, you can almost get mapcar from maplist by composing with the car function. In particular, note that

(mapcar f '(1 2 3 4))
= ((f (car (1 2 3 4))) (f (car (2 3 4))) (f (car (3 4))) (f (car (4))))

Write a version of compose that lets us define mapcar from maplist. More specifically, write a definition of compose2 so that

((compose2 maplist car) f xs) = (mapcar f xs)

for any function f and list xs.

(a) Fill in the missing code in the following definition. The correct answer is short and fits here easily. You may also want to answer parts (b) and (c) first.

```
(define compose2
    (lambda (g h)
        (lambda (f xs)
            (g (lambda (xs) (_____ )) xs )
```

)))

(b) When (compose2 maplist car) is evaluated, the result is a function defined by (lambda (f xs) (g ...)) above, with
   i. which function replacing g?
   ii. and which function replacing h?

(c) We could also write the subexpression (lambda (xs) (...)) as (compose (...) (...)) for two functions. Which two functions are these? (Write them in the correct order.)

3.5 Definition of Garbage

This question asks you to think about garbage collection in Lisp and compare our definition of garbage in the text to the one given in McCarthy's 1960 paper on Lisp. McCarthy's definition is written for Lisp specifically, whereas our definition is stated generally for any programming language. Answer the question by comparing the definitions as they apply to Lisp only. Here are the two definitions.

Garbage, our definition: At a given point in the execution of a program P, a memory location m is garbage if no continued execution of P from this point can access location m.

Garbage, McCarthy's definition: "Each register that is accessible to the program is accessible because it can be reached from one or more of the base registers by a chain of car and cdr operations. When the contents of a base register are changed, it may happen that the register to which the base register formerly pointed cannot be reached by a car–cdr chain from any base register. Such a register may be considered abandoned by the program because its contents can no longer be found by any possible program."

(a) If a memory location is garbage according to our definition, is it necessarily garbage according to McCarthy's definition? Explain why or why not.

(b) If a location is garbage according to McCarthy's definition, is it garbage by our definition? Explain why or why not.

(c) There are garbage collectors that collect everything that is garbage according to McCarthy's definition. Would it be possible to write a garbage collector to collect everything that is garbage according to our definition? Explain why or why not.

3.6 Reference Counting

This question is about a possible implementation of garbage collection for Lisp. Both impure and pure Lisp have lambda abstraction, function application, and elementary functions atom, eq, car, cdr, and cons. Impure Lisp also has rplaca, rplacd, and other functions that have side effects on memory cells.

Reference counting is a simple garbage-collection scheme that associates a reference count with each datum in memory. When memory is allocated, the associated reference count is set to 0. When a pointer is set to point to a location, the count for that location is incremented. If a pointer to a location is reset or destroyed, the count for the location is decremented. Consequently, the reference count always tells how many pointers there are to a given datum. When a count reaches 0, the datum is considered garbage and is returned to the free-storage list. For example, after evaluation of (cdr (cons (cons 'A 'B) (cons 'C 'D))), the cell created for (cons 'A 'B) is garbage, but the cell for (cons 'C 'D) is not.

(a) Describe how reference counting could be used for garbage collection in evaluating the following expression:

    (car (cdr (cons (cons a b) (cons c d))))

where a, b, c, and d are previously defined names for cells. Assume that the reference counts for a, b, c, and d are initially set to some numbers greater than 0, so that these do not become garbage. Assume that the result of the entire expression is not garbage. How many of the three cons cells generated by the evaluation of this expression can be returned to the free-storage list?

(b) The "impure" Lisp function rplaca takes as arguments a cons cell *c* and a value *v* and modifies *c*'s address field to point to *v*. Note that this operation does *not* produce a new cons cell; it modifies the one it receives as an argument. The function rplacd performs the same function with respect the decrement portion of its argument cons cell.

Lisp programs that use rplaca or rplacd may create memory structures that cannot be garbage collected properly by reference counting. Describe a configuration of cons cells that can be created by use of operations of pure Lisp and rplaca and rplacd. Explain why the reference-counting algorithm deos not work properly on this structure.

3.7 Regions and Memory Management

There are a wide variety of algorithms to chose from when implementing garbage collection for a specific language. In this problem, we examine one algorithm for finding garbage in pure Lisp (Lisp without side effects) based on the concept of *regions*. Generally speaking, a region is a section of the program text. To make things simple, we consider each function as a separate region. Region-based collection reclaims garbage each time program execution leaves a region. Because we are treating functions as regions in this problems, our version of region-based collection will try to find garbage each time a program returns from a function call.

(a) Here is a simple idea for region-based garbage collection:

> When a function exits, free all the memory that was allocated during execution of the function.

However, this is not correct as some memory locations that are freed may still be accessible to the program. Explain the flaw by describing a program that could possibly access a previously freed piece of memory. You do not need to write more than four or five sentences; just explain the aspects of an example program that are relevant to the question.

(b) Fix the method in part (a) to work correctly. It is not necessary for your method to find all garbage, but the locations that are freed should really be garbage. Your answer should be in the following form:

> When a function exits, free all memory allocated by the function except....

Justify your answer. (*Hint:* Your statement should not be more than a sentence or two. Your justification should be a short paragraph.)

(c) Now assume that you have an correctly functioning region-based garbage collector. Does your region-based collector have any advantages or disadvantages over a simple mark-and-sweep collector?

(d) Could a region-based collector like the one described in this problem work for impure Lisp? If you think the problem is more complicated for impure Lisp, briefly explain why. You may consider the problem for C instead of for impure Lisp if you like, but do not give an answer that depends on specific properties of C such as pointer arithmetic. The point of this question is to explore the relationship between side effects and a simple form of region-based collection.

3.8 Concurrency in Lisp

The concept of *future* was popularized by R. Halstead's work on the language Multilisp for concurrent Lisp programming. Operationally, a future consists of a location in memory (part of a cons cell) and a process that is intended to place a value in this location at some time "in the future." More specifically, the evaluation of (future e) proceeds as follows:

(i) The location ℓ that will contain the value of (future e) is identified (if the value is going to go into an existing cons cell) or created if needed.

(ii) A process is created to evaluate e.

(iii) When the process evaluating e completes, the value of e is placed in the location ℓ.

(iv) The process that invoked (future e) continues in parallel with the new process. If the originating process tries to read the contents of location ℓ while it is still empty, then the process blocks until the location has been filled with the value of e.

Other than this construct, all other operations in this problem are defined as in pure Lisp. For example, if expression e evaluates to the list (1 2 3), then the expression

> (cons 'a (future e))

produces a list whose first element is the atom 'a and whose tail becomes (1 2 3) when the process evaluating e terminates. The value of the future construct is that the program can operate on the car of this list while the value of the cdr is being computed in parallel. However, if the program tries to examine the cdr of the list before the value has been placed in the empty location, then the computation will block (wait) until the data is available.

(a) Assuming an unbounded number of processors, how much time would you expect the evaluation of the following fib function to take on positive-integer argument n?

> ```
> (defun fib (n)
>         (cond ( (eq n 0) 1)
>               ((eq n 1) 1)
>               (T (plus (future (fib (minus n 1)))
>                        (future (fib (minus n 2)))))))
> ```

We are interested only in time up to a multiplicative constant; you may use "big Oh" notation if you wish. If two instructions are done at the same time by two processors, count that as one unit of time.

(b) At first glance, we might expect that two expressions

> (... e ...)
> (... (future e) ...)

which differ only because an occurrence of a subexpression e is replaced with (future e), would be equivalent. However, there are some circumstances in which the result of evaluating one might differ from the other. More specifically, side effects may cause problems. To demonstrate this, write an expression of the form (... e ...) so that when the e is changed to (future e), the expression's value or behavior might be different because of side effects, and explain why. Do not be concerned with the efficiency of either computation or the degree of parallelism.

(c) Side effects are not the only cause for different evaluation results. Write a pure Lisp expression of the form (... e' ...) so that when the e' is changed to (future e'), the expression's value or behavior might be different, and explain why.

(d) Suppose you are part of a language design team that has adopted futures as an approach to concurrency. The head of your team suggests an error-handling feature called a *try block*. The syntactic form of a try block is

```
(try e
    (error-1 handler-1)
    (error-2 handler-2)
    ...
    (error-n handler-n))
```

This construct would have the following characteristics:

i. Errors are programmer defined and occur when an expression of the form (raise error-i) is evaluated inside e, the main expression of the try block.

ii. If no errors occur, then (try e (error-1 handler-1)...) is equivalent to e.

iii. If the error named error-i occurs during the evaluation of e, the rest of the computation of e is aborted, the expression handler-i is evaluated, and this becomes the value of the try block.

The other members of the team think this is a great idea and, claiming that it is a completely straightforward construct, ask you to go ahead and implement it. You think the construct might raise some tricky issues. Name two problems or important interactions between error handling and concurrency that you think need to be considered. Give short code examples or sketches to illustrate your point(s). (*Note:* You are not being asked to solve any problems associated with futures and try blocks; just identify the issues.) Assume for this part that you are using pure Lisp (no side effects).

4

Fundamentals

In this chapter some background is provided on programming language implementation through brief discussions of syntax, parsing, and the steps used in conventional compilers. We also look at two foundational frameworks that are useful in programming language analysis and design: lambda calculus and denotational semantics. Lambda calculus is a good framework for defining syntactic concepts common to many programming languages and for studying symbolic evaluation. Denotational semantics shows that, in principle, programs can be reduced to functions.

A number of other theoretical frameworks are useful in the design and analysis of programming languages. These range from computability theory, which provides some insight into the power and limitations of programs, to type theory, which includes aspects of both syntax and semantics of programming languages. In spite of many years of theoretical research, the current programming language theory still does not provide answers to some important foundational questions. For example, we do not have a good mathematical theory that includes higher-order functions, state transformations, and concurrency. Nonetheless, theoretical frameworks have had an impact on the design of programming languages and can be used to identify problem areas in programming languages. To compare one aspect of theory and practice, we compare functional and imperative languages in Section 4.4.

4.1 COMPILERS AND SYNTAX

A program is a description of a dynamic process. The text of a program itself is called its syntax; the things a program does comprise its semantics. The function of a programming language implementation is to transform program syntax into machine instructions that can be executed to cause the correct sequence of actions to occur.

4.1.1 Structure of a Simple Compiler

Programming languages that are convenient for people to use are built around concepts and abstractions that may not correspond directly to features of the underlying machine. For this reason, a program must be translated into the basic instruction

JOHN BACKUS

An early pioneer, John Backus became a computer programmer at IBM in 1950. In the 1950s, Backus developed Fortran, the first high-level computer language, which became commercially available in 1957. The language is still widely used for numerical and scientific programming. In 1959, John Backus invented Backus naur form (BNF), the standard notation for defining the syntax of a programming language. In later years, he became an advocate of pure functional programming, devoting his 1977 ACM Turing Award lecture to this topic.

I met John Backus through IFIP WG 2.8, a working group of the International Federation of Information Processing on functional programming. Backus continued to work on functional programming at IBM Almaden through the 1980s, although his group was disbanded after his retirement. A mild-mannered and unpretentious individual, here is a quote that gives some sense of his independent, pioneering spirit:

"I really didn't know what the hell I wanted to do with my life. I decided that what I wanted was a good hi fi set because I liked music. In those days, they didn't really exist so I went to a radio technicians' school. I had a very nice teacher – the first good teacher I ever had – and he asked me to cooperate with him and compute the characteristics of some circuits for a magazine."

"I remember doing relatively simple calculations to get a few points on a curve for an amplifier. It was laborious and tedious and horrible, but it got me interested in math. The fact that it had an application – that interested me."

set of the machine before it can be executed. This can be done by a *compiler*, which translates the entire program into machine code before the program is run, or an *interpreter*, which combines translation and program execution. We discuss programming language implementation by using compilers, as this makes it easier to separate the main issues and to discuss them in order.

The main function of a compiler is illustrated in this simple diagram:

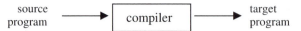

Given a program in some *source language*, the compiler produces a program in a *target language*, which is usually the instruction set, or machine language, of some machine.

Most compilers are structured as a series of phases, with each phase performing one step in the translation of source program to target program. A typical compiler might consist of the phases shown in the following diagram:

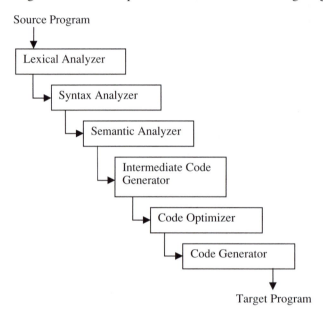

Each of these phases is discussed briefly. Our goal with this book is only to understand the parts of a compiler so that we can discuss how different programming language features might be implemented. We do not discuss how to build a compiler. That is the subject of many books on compiler construction, such as *Compilers: Principles, Techniques and Tools* by Aho, Sethi, and Ullman (Addison-Wesley, 1986), and *Modern Compiler Implementation in Java/ML/C* by Appel (Cambridge Univ. Press, 1998).

Lexical Analysis

The input symbols are scanned and grouped into meaningful units called *tokens*. For example, lexical analysis of the expression temp := x+1, which uses Algol-style notation := for assignment, would divide this sequence of symbols into five tokens: the identifier temp, the assignment "symbol" :=, the variable x, the addition symbol +, and the number 1. Lexical analysis can distinguish numbers from identifiers. However, because lexical analysis is based on a single left-to-right (and top-to-bottom) scan, lexical analysis does not distinguish between identifiers that are names of variables and identifiers that are names of constants. Because variables and constants are declared differently, variables and constants are distinguished in the semantic analysis phase.

Syntax Analysis

In this phase, tokens are grouped into syntactic units such as expressions, statements, and declarations that must conform to the grammatical rules of the programming language. The action performed during this phase, called *parsing*, is described in Subsection 4.1.2. The purpose of parsing is to produce a data structure called a parse tree, which represents the syntactic structure of the program in a way that is convenient for subsequent phases of the compiler. If a program does not meet the syntactic requirements to be a well-formed program, then the parsing phase will produce an error message and terminate the compiler.

Semantic Analysis

In this phase of a compiler, rules and procedures that depend on the context surrounding an expression are applied. For example, returning to our sample expression temp := x+1, we find that it is necessary to make sure that the types match. If this assignment occurs in a language in which integers are automatically converted to floats as needed, then there are several ways that types could be associated with parts of this expression. In standard semantic analysis, the types of temp and x would be determined from the declarations of these identifiers. If these are both integers, then the number 1 could be marked as an integer and + marked as integer addition, and the expression would be considered correct. If one of the identifiers, say x, is a float, then the number 1 would be marked as a float and + marked as a floating-point addition. Depending on whether temp is a float or an integer, it might also be necessary to insert a conversion around the subexpression x+1. The output of this phase is an augmented parse tree that represents the syntactic structure of the program and includes additional information such as the types of identifiers and the place in the program where each identifier is declared.

Although the phase following parsing is commonly called *semantic analysis*, this use of the word *semantic* is different from the standard use of the term for *meaning*. Some compiler writers use the word semantic because this phase relies on context information, and the kind of grammar used for syntactic analysis does not capture context information. However, in the rest of this book, the word semantics is used to refer to how a program executes, not the essentially syntactic properties that arise in the third phase of a compiler.

Intermediate Code Generation

Although it might be possible to generate a target program from the results of syntactic and semantic analysis, it is difficult to generate efficient code in one phase. Therefore, many compilers first produce an intermediate form of code and then optimize this code to produce a more efficient target program.

Because the last phase of the compiler can translate one set of instructions to another, the intermediate code does not need to be written with the actual instruction set of the target machine. It is important to use an intermediate representation that is easy to produce and easy to translate into the target language. The intermediate representation can be some form of generic low-level code that has properties common to several computers. When a single generic intermediate representation is used, it is possible to use essentially the same compiler to generate target programs for several different machines.

Code Optimization

There are a variety of techniques that may be used to improve the efficiency of a program. These techniques are usually applied to the intermediate representation. If several optimization techniques are written as transformations of the intermediate representation, then these techniques can be applied over and over until some termination condition is reached.

The following list describes some standard optimizations:

- *Common Subexpression Elimination:* If a program calculates the same value more than once and the compiler can detect this, then it may be possible to transform the program so that the value is calculated only once and stored for subsequent use.
- *Copy Propagation:* If a program contains an assignment such as x=y, then it may be possible to change subsequent statements to refer to y instead of to x and to eliminate the assignment.
- *Dead-Code Elimination:* If some sequence of instructions can never be reached, then it can be eliminated from the program.
- *Loop Optimizations:* There are several techniques that can be applied to remove instructions from loops. For example, if some expression appears inside a loop but has the same value on each pass through the loop, then the expression can be moved outside the loop.
- *In-Lining Function Calls:* If a program calls function f, it is possible to substitute the code for f into the place where f is called. This makes the target program more efficient, as the instructions associated with calling a function can be eliminated, but it also increases the size of the program. The most important consequence of in-lining function calls is usually that they allow other optimizations to be performed by removing jumps from the code.

Code Generation

The final phase of a standard compiler is to convert the intermediate code into a target machine code. This involves choosing a memory location, a register, or both, for each variable that appears in the program. There are a variety of register allocation algorithms that try to reuse registers efficiently. This is important because many machines have a fixed number of registers, and operations on registers are more efficient than transferring data into and out of memory.

4.1.2 Grammars and Parse Trees

We use grammars to describe various languages in this book. Although we usually are not too concerned about the pragmatics of parsing, we take a brief look in this subsection at the problem of producing a parse tree from a sequence of tokens.

Grammars

Grammars provide a convenient method for defining infinite sets of expressions. In addition, the structure imposed by a grammar gives us a systematic way of processing expressions.

A *grammar* consists of a start symbol, a set of nonterminals, a set of terminals, and a set of productions. The nonterminals are symbols that are used to write out the grammar, and the terminals are symbols that appear in the language generated by the grammar. In books on automata theory and related subjects, the productions of a grammar are written in the form $s \rightarrow tu$, with an arrow, meaning that in a string containing the symbol s, we can replace s with the symbols tu. However, here we use a more compact notation, commonly referred to as BNF.

The main ideas are illustrated by example. A simple language of numeric expressions is defined by the following grammar:

```
e ::= n | e+e | e-e
n ::= d | nd
d ::= 0 | 1 | 2 | 3 | 4 | 5 | 6 | 7 | 8 | 9
```

where e is the *start symbol*, symbols e, n, and d are nonterminals, and 0, 1, 2, 3, 4, 5, 6, 7, 8, 9, +, and - are the terminals. The language defined by this grammar consists of all the sequences of terminals that we can produce by starting with the start symbol e and by replacing nonterminals according to the preceding productions. For example, the first preceding production means that we can replace an occurrence of e with the symbol n, the three symbols e+e, or the three symbols e-e. The process can be repeated with any of the preceding three lines.

Some expressions in the language given by this grammar are

```
0, 1 + 3 + 5, 2 + 4 - 6 - 8
```

Sequences of symbols that contain nonterminals, such as

```
e, e + e, e + 6 - e
```

are not expressions in the language given by the grammar. The purpose of nonterminals is to keep track of the form of an expression as it is being formed. All nonterminals must be replaced with terminals to produce a well-formed expression of the language.

Derivations

A sequence of replacement steps resulting in a string of terminals is called a *derivation*.

Here are two derivations in this grammar, the first given in full and the second with a few missing steps that can be filled in by the reader (be sure you understand how!):

$$e \rightarrow n \rightarrow nd \rightarrow dd \rightarrow 2d \rightarrow 25$$
$$e \rightarrow e \text{ - } e \rightarrow e \text{ - } e+e \rightarrow \cdots \rightarrow n\text{-}n+n \rightarrow \cdots \rightarrow 10\text{-}15+12$$

Parse Trees and Ambiguity

It is often convenient to represent a derivation by a tree. This tree, called the *parse tree* of a derivation, or *derivation tree*, is constructed with the start symbol as the root of the tree. If a step in the derivation is to replace s with $x_1, \ldots, x_n$, then the children of s in the tree will be nodes labeled $x_1, \ldots, x_n$.

The parse tree for the derivation of 10-15+12 in the preceding subsection has some useful structure. Specifically, because the first step yields e-e, the parse tree has the form

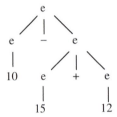

where we have contracted the subtrees for each two-digit number to a single node. This tree is different from

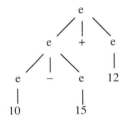

which is another parse tree for the same expression. An important fact about parse trees is that each corresponds to a unique parenthesization of the expression. Specifically, the first tree corresponds to 10-(15+12) whereas the second corresponds to (10-15)+12. As this example illustrates, the value of an expression may depend on how it is parsed or parenthesized.

A grammar is *ambiguous* if some expression has more than one parse tree. If every expression has at most one parse tree, the grammar is *unambiguous*.

Example 4.1

There is an interesting ambiguity involving if-then-else. This can be illustrated by the following simple grammar:

```
s ::= v := e | s;s | if b then s | if b then s else s
v ::= x | y | z
e ::= v | 0 | 1 | 2 | 3 | 4
b ::= e=e
```

where s is the start symbol, s, v, e, and b are nonterminals, and the other symbols are terminals. The letters s, v, e, and b stand for statement, variable, expression, and Boolean test, respectively. We call the expressions of the language generated by this grammar *statements*. Here is an example of a well-formed statement and one of its parse trees:

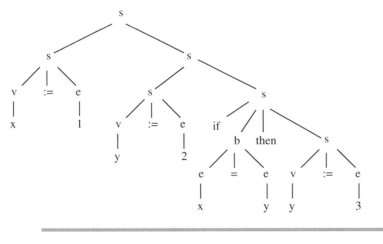

---

x := 1; y := 2; if x=y then y := 3

This statement also has another parse tree, which we obtain by putting two assignments to the left of the root and the if-then statement to the right. However, the difference between these two parse trees will not affect the behavior of code generated by an ordinary compiler. The reason is that $s_1;s_2$ is normally compiled to the code for s_1 followed by the code for s_2. As a result, the same code would be generated whether we consider $s_1;s_2;s_3$ as $(s_1;s_2);s_3$ or $s_1;(s_2;s_3)$.

A more complicated situation arises when if-then is combined with if-then-else in the following way:

---

if b_1 then if b_2 then s_1 else s_2

What should happen if b_1 is true and b_2 is false? Should s_2 be executed or not? As you can see, this depends on how the statement is parsed. A grammar that allows this combination of conditionals is ambiguous, with two possible meanings for statements of this form.

4.1.3 Parsing and Precedence

Parsing is the process of constructing parse trees for sequences of symbols. Suppose we define a language L by writing out a grammar G. Then, given a sequence of symbols s, we would like to determine if s is in the language L. If so, then we would like to compile or interpret s, and for this purpose we would like to find a parse tree for s. An algorithm that decides whether s is in L, and constructs a parse tree if it is, is called a *parsing algorithm* for G.

There are many methods for building parsing algorithms from grammars. Many of these work for only particular forms of grammars. Because parsing is an important part of compiling programming languages, parsing is usually covered in courses and textbooks on compilers. For most programming languages you might consider, it is either straightforward to parse the language or there are some changes in syntax that do not change the structure of the language very much but make it possible to parse the language efficiently.

Two issues we consider briefly are the syntactic conventions of precedence and right or left associativity. These are illustrated briefly in the following example.

Example 4.2

A programming language designer might decide that expressions should include addition, subtraction, and multiplication and write the following grammar:

```
e ::= 0 | 1 | e+e | e-e | e*e
```

This grammar is ambiguous, as many expressions have more than one parse tree. For expressions such as 1-1+1, the value of the expression will depend on the way it is parsed. One solution to this problem is to require complete parenthesization. In other words, we could change the grammar to

```
e ::= 0 | 1 | (e+e) | (e-e) | (e*e)
```

so that it is no longer ambiguous. However, as you know, it can be awkward to write a lot of parentheses. In addition, for many expressions, such as 1+2+3+4, the value of the expression does not depend on the way it is parsed. Therefore, it is unnecessarily cumbersome to require parentheses for every operation.

The standard solution to this problem is to adopt parsing conventions that specify a single parse tree for every expression. These are called *precedence* and *associativity*. For this specific grammar, a natural precedence convention is that multiplication ($*$) has a higher precedence than addition ($+$) and subtraction ($-$). We incorporate precedence into parsing by treating an unparenthesized expression e op_1 e op_2 e as if parentheses are inserted around the operator of higher precedence. With this rule in effect, the expression 5*4-3 will be parsed as if it were written as (5*4)-3. This coincides with the way that most of us would ordinarily think about the expression 5*4-3. Because there is no standard way that most readers would parse 1+1-1, we might give addition and subtraction equal precedence. In this case, a compiler could issue an error message requiring the programmer to parenthesize 1+1-1. Alternatively, an expression like this could be disambiguated by use of an additional convention.

Associativity comes into play when two operators of equal precedence appear next to each other. Under left associativity, an expression e op_1 e op_2 e would be parsed as (e op_1 e) op_2 e, if the two operators have equal precedence. If we adopted a right-associativity convention instead, e op_1 e op_2 e would be parsed as e op_1 (e op_2 e).

Expression	Precedence	Left Associativity	Right Associativity
5*4-3	(5*4)-3	(no change)	(no change)
1+1-1	(no change)	(1+1)-1	1+(1-1)
2+3-4*5+2	2+3-(4*5)+2	((2+3)-(4*5))+2	2+(3-((4*5)+2))

4.2 LAMBDA CALCULUS

Lambda calculus is a mathematical system that illustrates some important programming language concepts in a simple, pure form. Traditional lambda calculus has three main parts: a notation for defining functions, a proof system for proving equations between expressions, and a set of calculation rules called reduction. The first word in the name lambda calculus comes from the use of the Greek letter lambda (λ) in function expressions. (There is no significance to the letter λ.) The second word comes from the way that reduction may be used to *calculate* the result of applying a function to one or more arguments. This calculation is a form of symbolic evaluation of expressions. Lambda calculus provides a convenient notation for describing programming languages and may be regarded as the basis for many language constructs. In particular, lambda calculus provides fundamental forms of parameterization (by means of function expressions) and binding (by means of declarations). These are basic concepts that are common to almost all modern programming languages. It is therefore useful to become familiar enough with lambda calculus to regard expressions in your favorite programming language as essentially a form of lambda expression. For simplicity, the untyped lambda calculus is discussed; there are also typed versions of lambda calculus. In typed lambda calculus, there are additional type-checking constraints that rule out certain forms of expressions. However, the basic concepts and calculation rules remain essentially the same.

4.2.1 Functions and Function Expressions

Intuitively, a function is a rule for determining a value from an argument. This view of functions is used informally in most mathematics. (See Subsection 2.1.2 for a discussion of functions in mathematics.) Some examples of functions studied in mathematics are

$$f(x) = x^2 + 3,$$
$$g(x + y) = \sqrt{x^2 + y^2}.$$

In the simplest, pure form of lambda calculus, there are no domain-specific operators such as addition and exponentiation, only function definition and application. This allows us to write functions such as

$$h(x) = f(g(x))$$

because h is defined solely in terms of function application and other functions that we assume are already defined. It is possible to add operations such as addition and exponentiation to pure lambda calculus. Although purists stick to pure lambda calculus without addition and multiplication, we will use these operations in examples as this makes the functions we define more familiar.

The main constructs of lambda calculus are *lambda abstraction* and *application*. We use lambda abstraction to write functions: If M is some expression, then $\lambda x.M$ is the function we get by treating M as a function of the variable x. For example,

$$\lambda x.x$$

is a lambda abstraction defining the identity function, the function whose value at x is x. A more familiar way of defining the identity function is by writing

$$I(x) = x.$$

However, this way of defining a function forces us to make up a name for every function we want. Lambda calculus lets us write anonymous functions and use them inside larger expressions.

In lambda notation, it is traditional to write function application just by putting a function expression in front of one or more arguments; parentheses are optional. For example, we can apply the identity function to the expression M by writing

$$(\lambda x.x)M.$$

The value of this application is the identity function, applied to M, that just ends up being M. Thus, we have

$$(\lambda x.x)M = M.$$

Part of lambda calculus is a set of rules for deducing equations such as this. Another example of a lambda expression is

$$\lambda f.\lambda g.\lambda x.f(g\,x).$$

Given functions f and g, this function produces the composition $\lambda x.f(g\,x)$ of f and g.

We can extend pure lambda calculus by adding a variety of other constructs. We call an extension of pure lambda calculus with extra operations an *applied lambda calculus*. A basic idea underlying the relation between lambda calculus and computer science is the slogan

$$\text{Programming language} = \text{applied } \lambda\text{-calculus}$$
$$= \text{pure } \lambda\text{-calculus} + \text{additional data types.}$$

This works even for programming languages with side effects, as the way a program depends on the state of the machine can be represented by explicit data structures for the machine state. This is one of the basic ideas behind Scott–Strachey denotational semantics, as discussed in Section 4.3.

4.2.2 Lambda Expressions

Syntax of Expressions

The syntax of untyped lambda expressions may be defined with a BNF grammar. We assume we have some infinite set V of *variables* and use x, y, z, ..., to stand for arbitrary variables. The grammar for lambda expressions is

$$M ::= x \mid MM \mid \lambda x.M$$

where x may be any variable (element of V). An expression of the form $M_1 M_2$ is called an *application*, and an expression of the form $\lambda x.M$ is called a *lambda abstraction*. Intuitively, a variable x refers to some function, the particular function being determined by context; $M_1 M_2$ is the application of function M_1 to argument M_2; and $\lambda x.M$ is the function that, given argument x, returns the value M. In the lambda calculus literature, it is common to refer to the expressions of lambda calculus as *lambda terms*.

Here are some example lambda terms:

$\lambda x.x$ a lambda abstraction called the *identity function*
$\lambda x.(f(gx))$ another lambda abstraction
$(\lambda x.x)5$ an application

There are a number of syntactic conventions that are generally convenient for lambda calculus experts, but they are confusing to learn. We can generally avoid these by writing enough parentheses. One convention that we will use, however, is that in an expression containing a λ, the scope of λ extends as far to the right as possible. For example, $\lambda x.xy$ should be read as $\lambda x.(xy)$, not $(\lambda x.x)y$.

Variable Binding

An occurrence of a variable in an expression may be either free or bound. If a variable is *free* in some expression, this means that the variable is not declared in the expression. For example, the variable x is free in the expression $x + 3$. We cannot evaluate the expression $x + 3$ as it stands, without putting it inside some larger expression that will associate some value with x. If a variable is not free, then that must be because it is *bound*.

The symbol λ is called a *binding operator*, as it binds a variable within a specific scope (part of an expression). The variable x is bound in $\lambda x.M$. This means that x is just a place holder, like x in the integral $\int f(x)\, dx$ or the logical formula $\forall x.P(x)$, and the meaning of $\lambda x.M$ does not depend on x. Therefore, just as $\int f(x)\, dx$ and $\int f(y)\, dy$ describe the same integral, we can rename a λ-bound x to y without changing the meaning of the expression. In particular,

$\lambda x.x$ defines the same function as $\lambda y.y$.

Expressions that differ in only the names of bound variables are called α equivalent. When we want to emphasize that two expressions are α equivalent, we write $\lambda x.x =_\alpha \lambda y.y$, for example.

In $\lambda x.M$, the expression M is called the *scope* of the binding λx. A variable x appearing in an expression M is bound if it appears in the scope of some λx and is free otherwise. To be more precise about this, we may define the set $\mathrm{FV}(M)$ of *free variables of M* by induction on the structure of expressions, as follows:

$$FV(x) = \{x\},$$
$$FV(MN) = FV(M) \cup FV(N),$$
$$FV(\lambda x.M) = FV(M) - x,$$

where $-$ means set difference, that is, $S - x = \{y \in S \mid y \neq x\}$. For example, $FV(\lambda x.x) = \emptyset$ because there are no free variables in $\lambda x.x$, whereas FV $(\lambda f.\lambda x.$ $(f(g(x)))) = \{g\}$.

It is sometimes necessary to talk about different occurrences of a variable in an expression and to distinguish free and bound occurrences. In the expression

$$\lambda x.(\lambda y.xy)y,$$

the first occurrence of x is called a *binding occurrence*, as this is where x becomes bound. The other occurrence of x is a bound occurrence. Reading from left to right, we see that the first occurrence of y is a binding occurrence, the second is a bound occurrence, and the third is free as it is outside the scope of the λy in parentheses.

It can be confusing to work with expressions that use the same variable in more than one way. A useful convention is to rename bound variables so that all bound variables are different from each other and different from all of the free variables. Following this convention, we will write $(\lambda y.(\lambda z.z)y)x$ instead of $(\lambda x.(\lambda x.x)x)x$. The variable convention will be particularly useful when we come to equational reasoning and reduction.

Lambda Abstraction in Lisp and Algol

Lambda calculus has an obvious syntactic similarity to Lisp: the Lisp lambda expression

```
(lambda (x) function_body)
```

looks like the lambda calculus expression

$$\lambda x. function\_body,$$

and both expressions define functions. However, there are some differences between Lisp and lambda calculus. For example, lists are the basic data type of Lisp, whereas functions are the only data type in pure lambda calculus. Another difference is evaluation order, but that topic will not be discussed in detail.

Although the syntax of block-structured languages is farther from lambda calculus than from Lisp, the basic concepts of declarations and function parameterizations in Algol-like languages are fundamentally the same as in lambda calculus. For example, the C program fragment

```
int f (int x) {return x};
block_body;
```

with a function declaration at the beginning of a block is easily translated into lambda calculus. The translation is easier to understand if we first add declarations to lambda calculus.

The simple let declaration,

let $x = M$ in N,

which declares that x has value M in the body N, may be regarded as syntactic sugar for a combination of lambda abstraction and application:

let $x = M$ in N is sugar for $(\lambda x.N)M$.

For those not familiar with the concept of *syntactic sugar*, this means that let $x = M$ in N is "sweeter" to write in some cases, but we can just think of the syntax let $x = M$ in N as standing for $(\lambda x.N)M$.

Using let declarations, we can write the C program from above as

---

let $f = (\lambda x.x)$ in *block_body*

Note that the C form expression and the lambda expression have the same free and bound variables and a similar structure. One difference between C and lambda calculus is that C has assignment statements and side effects, whereas lambda calculus is purely functional. However, by introducing *stores*, mappings from variable locations to values, we can translate C programs with side effects into lambda terms as well. The translation preserves the overall structure of programs, but makes programs look a little more complicated as the dependencies on the state of the machine are explicit.

Equivalence and Substitution

We have already discussed α equivalence of terms. This is one of the basic axioms of lambda calculus, meaning that it is one of the properties of lambda terms that defines the system and that is used in proving other properties of lambda terms. Stated more carefully than before, the equational proof system of lambda calculus has the equational axiom

$$\lambda x.M = \lambda y.[y/x]M, \tag{α}$$

where $[y/x]M$ is the result of substituting y for free occurrences of x in M and y cannot already appear in M. There are three other equational axioms and four inference rules for proving equations between terms. However, we look at only one other equational axiom.

The central equational axiom of lambda calculus is used to calculate the value of a function application $(\lambda x.M)N$ by substitution. Because $\lambda x.M$ is the function we get by treating M as a function of x, we can write the value of this function at N by substituting N for x. Again writing $[N/x]M$ for the result of substituting N for free occurrences of x in M, we have

$$(\lambda x.M)N = [N/x]M, \tag{β}$$

which is called the axiom of β-equivalence. Some important warnings about substitution are discussed in the next subsection. The value of $\lambda f. fx$ applied to $\lambda y. y$ may be calculated if the argument $\lambda y. y$ is substituted in for the bound variable f:

$$(\lambda f. fx)(\lambda y. y) = (\lambda y. y)x$$

Of course, $(\lambda y. y)x$ may be simplified by an additional substitution, and so we have

$$(\lambda f. fx)(\lambda y. y) = (\lambda y. y)x = x$$

Any readers old enough to be familiar with the original documentation of Algol 60 will recognize β-equivalence as the *copy rule* for evaluating function calls. There are also parallels between (β) and macroexpansion and in-line substitution of functions.

Renaming Bound Variables

Because λ bindings in M can conflict with free variables in N, substitution $[N/x]M$ is a little more complicated than we might think at first. However, we can avoid all of the complications by following the variable convention: renaming bound variables in $(\lambda x. M)N$ so that all of the bound variables are different from each other and different from all of the free variables. For example, let us reduce the term $(\lambda f. \lambda x. f(fx))(\lambda y. y + x)$. If we first rename bound variables and then perform β-reduction, we get

$$(\lambda f. \lambda z. f(fz))(\lambda y. y + x) = \lambda z.((\lambda y. y + x)((\lambda y. y + x)z)) = \lambda z. z + x + x$$

If we were to forget to rename bound variables and substitute blindly, we might simplify as follows:

$$(\lambda f. \lambda x. f(fx))(\lambda y. y + x) = \lambda x.((\lambda y. y + x)((\lambda y. y + x)x)) = \lambda x. x + x + x$$

However, we should be suspicious of the second reduction because the variable x is free in $(\lambda y. y + x)$ but becomes bound in $\lambda x. x + x + x$. *Remember:* In working out $[N/x]M$, we must rename any bound variables in M that might be the same as free variables in N. To be precise about renaming bound variables in substitution, we define the result $[N/x]M$ of substituting N for x in M by induction on the structure of M:

$[N/x]x = N$,

$[N/x]y = y$, where y is any variable different from x,

$[N/x](M_1 M_2) = ([N/x]M_1)([N/x]M_2)$,

$[N/x](\lambda x. M) = \lambda x. M$,

$[N/x](\lambda y. M) = \lambda y.([N/x]M)$, where y is not free in N.

Because we are free to rename the bound variable y in $\lambda y. M$, the final clause $\lambda y.([N/x]M)$ always makes sense. With this precise definition of substitution, we now have a precise definition of β-equivalence.

4.2.3 Programming in Lambda Calculus

Lambda calculus may be viewed as a simple functional programming language. We will see that, even though the language is very simple, we can program fairly naturally if we adopt a few abbreviations. Before declarations and recursion are discussed, it is worth mentioning the problem of multiargument functions.

Functions of Several Arguments

Lambda abstraction lets us treat any expression M as a function of any variable x by writing $\lambda x.M$. However, what if we want to treat M as function of two variables, x and y? Do we need a second kind of lambda abstraction $\lambda_2 x, y.M$ to treat M as function of the pair of arguments x, y? Although we could add lambda operators for sequences of formal parameters, we do not need to because ordinary lambda abstraction will suffice for most purposes.

We may represent a function f of two arguments by a function $\lambda x.(\lambda y.M)$ of a single argument that, when applied, returns a second function that accepts a second argument and then computes a result in the same way as f. For example, the function

$$f(g, x) = g(x)$$

has two arguments, but can be represented in lambda calculus by ordinary lambda abstraction. We define f_{curry} by

$$f_{\mathrm{curry}} = \lambda g.\lambda x.gx$$

The difference between f and f_{curry} is that f takes a pair (g, x) as an argument, whereas f_{curry} takes a single argument g. However, f_{curry} can be used in place of f because

$$f_{\mathrm{curry}} g\, x = gx = f(g, x)$$

Thus, in the end, f_{curry} does the same thing as f. This simple idea was discovered by Schönfinkel, who investigated functionality in the 1920s. However, this technique for representing multiargument functions in lambda calculus is usually called *Currying*, after the lambda calculus pioneer Haskell Curry.

Declarations

We saw in Subsection 4.2.2 that we can regard simple let declarations,

$$\mathtt{let}\, x = M\, \mathtt{in}\, N$$

as lambda terms by adopting the abbreviation

$$\mathtt{let}\, x = M\, \mathtt{in}\, N = (\lambda x.N)M$$

The let construct may be used to define a composition function, as in the expression

$$\mathtt{let}\, compose = \lambda f.\lambda g.\lambda x.\, f(gx)\, \mathtt{in}\, compose\, h\, h$$

Using β-equivalence, we can simplify this let expression to $\lambda x.\, h(hx)$, the composition of h with itself. In programming language parlance, the let construct provides local declarations.

Recursion and Fixed Points

An amazing fact about pure lambda calculus is that it is possible to write recursive functions by use of a self-application "trick." This does not have a lot to do with comparisons between modern programming languages, but it may interest readers with a technical bent. (Some readers and some instructors may wish to skip this subsection.)

Many programming languages allow recursive function definitions. The characteristic property of a recursive definition of a function f is that the body of the function contains one or more calls to f. To choose a specific example, let us suppose we define the factorial function in some programming language by writing a declaration like

```
function f(n) {if n=0 then 1 else n*f(n-1)};
```

where the body of the function is the expression inside the braces. This definition has a straightforward computational interpretation: when f is called with argument a, the function parameter n is set to a and the function body is evaluated. If evaluation of the body reaches the recursive call, then this process is repeated. As definitions of a computational procedure, recursive definitions are clearly meaningful and useful.

One way to understand the lambda calculus approach to recursion is to associate an equation with a recursive definition. For example, we can associate the equation

$$f(n) = \text{if } n=0 \text{ then } 1 \text{ else } n*f(n-1)$$

with the preceding recursive declaration. This equation states a property of factorial.

Specifically, the value of the expression f(n) is equal to the value of the expression if n=0 then 1 else n*f(n-1) when f is the factorial function. The lambda calculus approach may be viewed as a method of finding solutions to equations in which an identifier (the name of the recursive function) appears on both sides of the equation.

We can simplify the preceding equation by using lambda abstraction to eliminate n from the left-hand side. This gives us

$$f = \lambda n. \text{ if } n=0 \text{ then } 1 \text{ else } n*f(n-1)$$

Now consider the function G that we obtain by moving f to the right-hand-side of the equation:

$$G = \lambda f. \lambda n. \text{ if } n=0 \text{ then } 1 \text{ else } n*f(n-1)$$

Although it might not be clear what sort of "algebra" is involved in this manipulation of equations, we can check, by using lambda calculus reasoning and basic understanding of function equality, that the factorial function f satisfies the equation

$$f = G(f)$$

This shows that recursive declarations involve finding fixed points.

A *fixed point* of a function G is a value f such that $f = G(f)$. In lambda calculus, fixed points may be defined with the *fixed-point operator*:

$$Y = \lambda f.(\lambda x. f(xx))(\lambda x. f(xx)).$$

The surprising fact about this perplexing lambda expression is that, for any f, the application Yf is a fixed point of f. We can see this by calculation. By β-equivalence, we have

$$Yf = (\lambda x. f(xx))(\lambda x. f(xx)).$$

Using β-equivalence again on the right-hand term, we get

$$Yf = (\lambda x. f(xx))(\lambda x. f(xx)) = f(\lambda x. f(xx))(\lambda x. f(xx)) = f(Yf).$$

Thus Yf is a fixed point of f.

Example 4.3

We can define factorial by $fact = YG$, where lambda terms Y and G are as given above, and calculate $fact\ 2 = 2!$ by using the calculation rules of lambda calculus. Here are the calculation steps representing the first "call" to factorial:

$$
\begin{aligned}
fact\ 2 &= (YG)\,2 \\
&= G(YG)\,2 \\
&= (\lambda f.\lambda n.\,\text{if } n = 0 \text{ then } 1 \text{ else } n* f(n-1))(YG)\,2 \\
&= (\lambda n.\,\text{if } n = 0 \text{ then } 1 \text{ else } n*((YG)(n-1))\,2 \\
&= \text{if } 2 = 0 \text{ then } 1 \text{ else } 2*((YG)(2-1)) \\
&= \text{if } 2 = 0 \text{ then } 1 \text{ else } 2*((YG)\,1) \\
&= 2*((YG)\,1).
\end{aligned}
$$

Using similar steps, we can calculate $(YG)\,1 = 1! = 1$ to complete the calculation.

It is worth mentioning that Y is not the only lambda term that finds fixed points of functions. There are other expressions that would work as well. However, this particular fixed-point operator played an important role in the history of lambda calculus.

4.2.4 Reduction, Confluence, and Normal Forms

The computational properties of lambda calculus are usually described with a form of symbolic evaluation called reduction. In simple terms, reduction is equational reasoning, but in a certain direction. Specifically, although β-equivalence was written as an equation, we have generally used it in one direction to "evaluate" function calls. If we write $\rightarrow$ instead of $=$ to indicate the direction in which we intend to use the equation, then we obtain the basic computation step called β-reduction:

$$(\lambda x. M)N \rightarrow [N/x]M, \qquad\qquad (\beta)$$

We say that M β-reduces to N, and write $M \rightarrow N$, if N is the result of applying one β-reduction step somewhere inside M. Most of the examples of calculation in this section use β-reduction, i.e., β-equivalence is used from left to right rather than from right to left. For example,

$$(\lambda f.\lambda z.\ f(fz))(\lambda y.y + x) \to \lambda z.((\lambda y.y + x)((\lambda y.y + x)z)) \to \lambda z.z + x + x.$$

Normal Forms

Intuitively, we think of $M \to N$ as meaning that, in one computation step, the expression M can be evaluated to the expression N. Generally, this process can be repeated, as illustrated in the preceding subsection. However, for many expressions, the process eventually reaches a stopping point. A stopping point, or expression that cannot be further evaluated, is called a *normal form*. Here is an example of a reduction sequence that leads to a normal form:

$$(\lambda f.\lambda x.\ f(fx))(\lambda y.y + 1)\,2$$
$$\to (\lambda x.(\lambda y.y + 1)((\lambda y.y + 1)x))\,2$$
$$\to (\lambda x.(\lambda y.y + 1)(x + 1))\,2$$
$$\to (\lambda x.(x + 1 + 1))\,2$$
$$\to (2 + 1 + 1).$$

This last expression is a normal form if our only computation rule is β-reduction, but not a normal form if we have a computation rule for addition. Assuming the usual evaluation rule for expressions with addition, we can continue with

$$2 + 1 + 1$$
$$\to 3 + 1$$
$$\to 4.$$

This example should give a good idea of how reduction in lambda calculus corresponds to computation. Since the 1930s, lambda calculus has been a simple mathematical model of expression evaluation.

Confluence

In our example starting with $(\lambda f.\lambda x.\ f(fx))(\lambda y.y + 1)\,2$, there were some steps in which we had to chose from several possible subexpressions to evaluate. For example, in the second expression,

$$(\lambda x.(\lambda y.y + 1)((\lambda y.y + 1)x))\,2,$$

we could have evaluated either of the two function calls beginning with λy. This is not an artifact of lambda calculus itself, as we also have two choices in evaluating the purely arithmetic expression

$$2 + 1 + 1.$$

An important property of lambda calculus is called *confluence*. In lambda calculus, as a result of confluence, evaluation order does not affect the final value of an expression. Put another way, if an expression M can be reduced to a normal form, then there is exactly one normal form of M, independent of the order in which we choose to evaluate subexpressions. Although the full mathematical statement of confluence is a bit more complicated than this, the important thing to remember is that, in lambda calculus, expressions can be evaluated in any order.

4.2.5 Important Properties of Lambda Calculus

In summary, lambda calculus is a mathematical system with some syntactic and computational properties of a programming language. There is a general notation for functions that includes a way of treating an expression as a function of some variable that it contains. There is an equational proof system that leads to calculation rules, and these calculation rules are a simple form of symbolic evaluation. In programming language terminology, these calculation rules are a form of macro expansion (with renaming of bound variables!) or function in-lining. Because of the relation to in-lining, some common compiler optimizations may be defined and proved correct by use of lambda calculus.

Lambda calculus has the following imortant properties:

- Every computable function can be represented in pure lambda calculus. In the terminology of Chapter 2, lambda calculus is Turing complete. (Numbers can be represented by functions and recursion can be expressed by Y.)
- Evaluation in lambda calculus is order independent. Because of confluence, we can evaluate an expression by choosing any subexpression. Evaluation in pure functional programming languages (see Section 4.4) is also confluent, but evaluation in languages whose expressions may have side effects is not confluent.

Macro expansion is another setting in which a form of evaluation is confluent. If we start with a program containing macros and expand all macro calls with the macro bodies, then the final fully expanded program we obtain will not depend on the order in which macros are expanded.

4.3 DENOTATIONAL SEMANTICS

In computer science, the phrase denotational semantics refers to a specific style of mathematical semantics for imperative programs. This approach was developed in the late 1960s and early 1970s, following the pioneering work of Christopher Strachey and Dana Scott at Oxford University. The term denotational semantics suggests that a meaning or *denotation* is associated with each program or program phrase (expression, statement, declaration, etc.). The denotation of a program is a mathematical object, typically a function, as opposed to an algorithm or a sequence of instructions to execute.

In denotational semantics, the meaning of a simple program like

```
x := 0; y:=0; while x ≤ z do y := y+x; x := x+1
```

is a mathematical function from *states* to *states*, in which a state is a mathematical function representing the values in memory at some point in the execution of a program. Specifically, the meaning of this program will be a function that maps any state in which the value of z is some nonnegative integer n to the state in which $x=n$, y is the sum of all numbers up to n, and all other locations in memory are left unchanged. The function would not be defined on machine states in which the value of z is not a nonnegative integer.

Associating mathematical functions with programs is good for some purposes and not so good for others. In many situations, we consider a program correct if we get the correct output for any possible input. This form of correctness depends on only the denotational semantics of a program, the mathematical function from input to output associated with the program. For example, the preceding program was designed to compute the sum of all the nonnegative integers up to n. If we verify that the actual denotational semantics of this program is this mathematical function, then we have proved that the program is correct. Some disadvantages of denotational semantics are that standard denotational semantics do not tell us anything about the running time or storage requirements of a program. This is sometimes an advantage in disguise because, by ignoring these issues, we can sometimes reason more effectively about the correctness of programs.

Forms of denotational semantics are commonly used for reasoning about program optimization and static analysis methods. If we are interested in analyzing running time, then operational semantics might be more useful, or we could use more detailed denotational semantics that also involves functions representing time bounds. An alternative to denotational semantics is called operational semantics, which involves modeling machine states and (generally) the step-by-step state transitions associated with a program. Lambda calculus reduction is an example of operational semantics.

Compositionality

An important principle of denotational semantics is that the meaning of a program is determined from its text *compositionally*. This means that the meaning of a program must be defined from the meanings of its parts, not something else, such as the text of its parts or the meanings of related programs obtained by syntactic operations. For example, the denotation of a program such as *if B then P else Q* must be explained with only the denotations of B, P, and Q; it should not be defined with programs constructed from B, P, and Q by syntactic operations such as substitution.

The importance of compositionality, which may seem rather subtle at first, is that if two program pieces have the same denotation, then either may safely be substituted for the other in any program. More specifically, if B, P, and Q have the same denotations as B', P', and Q', respectively, then *if B then P else Q* must have the same denotation as *if B' then P' else Q'*. Compositionality means that the denotation of an expression or program statement must be detailed enough to capture everything that is relevant to its behavior in larger programs. This makes denotational semantics useful for understanding and reasoning about such pragmatic issues as program transformation and optimization, as these operations on programs involve replacing parts of programs without changing the overall meaning of the whole program.

4.3.1 Object Language and Metalanguage

One source of confusion in talking (or writing) about the interpretation of syntactic expressions is that everything we write is actually syntactic. When we study a programming language, we need to distinguish the programming language we study from the language we use to describe this language and its meaning. The language we study is traditionally called the object language, as this is the object of our attention, whereas the second language is called the metalanguage, because it transcends the object language in some way.

To pick an example, let us consider the mathematical interpretation of a simple algebraic expression such as $3 + 6 - 4$ that might appear in a program written in C, Java, or ML. The ordinary "mathematical" meaning of this expression is the number obtained by doing the addition and subtraction, namely 5. Here, the symbols in the expression $3 + 6 - 4$ are in our object language, whereas the number 5 is meant to be in our metalanguage. One way of making this clearer is to use an outlined number, such as $\mathbb{1}$, to mean "the mathematical entity called the natural number 1." Then we can say that the meaning of the object language expression $3 + 6 - 4$ is the natural number $\mathbb{5}$. In this sentence, the symbol $\mathbb{5}$ is a symbol of the metalanguage, whereas the expression $3 + 6 - 4$ is written with symbols of the object language.

4.3.2 Denotational Semantics of Binary Numbers

The following grammar for binary expressions is similar to the grammar for decimal expressions discussed in Subsection 4.1.2:

```
e ::= n | e+e | e-e
n ::= b | nb
b ::= 0 | 1
```

We can give a mathematical interpretation of these expressions in the style of denotational semantics. In denotational semantics and other studies of programming languages, it is common to forget about how expressions are converted into parse trees and just give the meaning of an expression as a function of its parse tree.

We may interpret the expressions previously defined as natural numbers by using induction on the structure of parse trees. More specifically, we define a function from parse trees to natural numbers, defining the function on a compound expression by referring to its value on simpler expressions. A historical convention is to write [[e]] for any parse tree of the expression e. When we write [[e₁+e₂]], for example, we mean a parse tree of the form

$$
\begin{array}{ccc}
 & e & \\
\diagup & | & \diagdown \\
[[e_1]] & + & [[e_2]]
\end{array}
$$

with [[e₁]] and [[e₂]] as immediate subtrees.

Using this notation, we may define the meaning $E[[e]]$ of an expression e, according to its parse tree $[[e]]$, as follows:

$$E[[0]] = 0$$
$$E[[1]] = 1$$
$$E[[nb]] = E[[n]] * 2 + E[[b]]$$
$$E[[e_1+e_2]] = E[[e_1]] + E[[e_2]]$$
$$E[[e_1-e_2]] = E[[e_1]] - E[[e_2]]$$

In words, the value associated with a parse tree of the form $[[e_1+e_2]]$, for example, is the sum of the values given to the subtrees $[[e_1]]$ and $[[e_2]]$. This is not a circular definition because the parse trees $[[e_1]]$ and $[[e_2]]$ are smaller than the parse tree $[[e_1+e_2]]$.

On the right-hand side of the equal signs, numbers and arithmetic operations $*$, $+$, and $-$ are meant to indicate the actual natural numbers and the standard integer operations of multiplication, addition, and subtraction. In contrast, the symbols $+$ and $-$ in expressions surrounded by double square brackets on the left-hand side of the equal signs are symbols of the object language, the language of binary expressions.

4.3.3 Denotational Semantics of While Programs

Without going into detail about the kinds of mathematical functions that are used, let us take a quick look at the form of semantics used for a simplified programming language with assignment and loops.

Expressions with Variables

Program statements contain expressions with variables. Here is a grammar for arithmetic expressions with variables. This is the same as the grammar in Subsection 4.1.2, except that expressions can contain variables in addition to numbers:

```
e ::= v | n | e+e | e-e
n ::= d | nd
d ::= 0 | 1 | 2 | 3 | 4 | 5 | 6 | 7 | 8 | 9
v ::= x | y | z | ...
```

In the simplified programming language we consider, the value of a variable depends on the state of the machine. We model the state of the machine by a function from variables to numbers and write $E[[e]](s)$ for the value of expression e in state s. The value of an expression in a state is defined as follows.

$$E[[x]](s) = s(x)$$
$$E[[0]](s) = 0$$
$$E[[1]](s) = 1$$
$$\ldots = \ldots$$

$$E[[9]](s) = 9$$
$$E[[nd]](s) = E[[n]](s) * 10 + E[[d]](s)$$
$$E[[e_1+e_2]](s) = E[[e_1]](s) + E[[e_2]](s)$$
$$E[[e_1- e_2]](s) = E[[e_1]](s) - E[[e_2]](s)$$

Note that the state matters in the definition in the base case, the value of a variable. Otherwise, this is essentially the same definition as that in the semantics of variable-free expressions in the preceding subsection.

The syntax and semantics of Boolean expressions can be defined similarly.

While Programs

The language of *while* programs may be defined over any class of value expressions and Boolean expressions. Without specifying any particular basic expressions, we may summarize the structure of while programs by the grammar

$$P ::= x := e \mid P; P \mid \text{if } e \text{ then } P \text{ else } P \mid \text{while } e \text{ do } P$$

where we assume that x has the appropriate type to be assigned the value of e in the assignment x :=e and that the test e has type *bool* in if-then-else and while statements. Because this language does not have explicit input or output, the effect of a program will be to change the values of variables. Here is a simple example:

$$x := 0; \; y:=0; \; \text{while } x \le z \text{ do } (y := y+x; \; x := x+1)$$

We may think of this program as having input z and output y. This program uses an additional variable x to set y to the sum of all natural numbers up to z.

States and Commands

The meaning of a program is a function from states to states. In a more realistic programming language, with procedures or pointers, it is necessary to model the fact that two variable names may refer to the same location. However, in the simple language of while programs, we assume that each variable is given a different location. With this simplification in mind, we let the set *State* of mathematical representations of machine states be

$$State = Variables \rightarrow Values$$

In words, a state is a function from variables to values. This is an idealized view of machine states in two ways: We do not explicitly model the locations associated with variables, and we use infinite states that give a value to every possible variable.

The meaning of a program is an element of the mathematical set *Command* of commands, defined by

$$Command = State \rightarrow State$$

In words, a command is a function from states to states. Unlike states themselves, which are total functions, a command may be a *partial* function. The reason we need partial functions is that a program might not terminate on an initial state.

A basic function on states that is used in the semantics of assignment is *modify*, which is defined as follows:

$$modify(s,x,a) = \lambda v \in Variables. \text{ if } v=x \text{ then } a \text{ else } s(v)$$

In words, $modify(s,x,a)$ is the state (function from variables to values) that is just like state s, except that the value of x is a.

Denotational Semantics

The denotational semantics of while programs is given by the definition of a function C from parsed programs to commands. As with expressions, we write [[P]] for a parse tree of the program P. The semantics of programs are defined by the following clauses, one for each syntactic form of program:

C[[x := e]](s) = modify(s,x, E[[e]](s))
C[[P₁;P₂]](s) = C[[P₂]](C[[P₁]](s))
C[[if e then P₁ else P₂]](s) = if E[[e]](s) then C[[P₁]](s) else C[[P₂]](s)
C[[while e do P]](s) = if not E[[e]](s) then s
                                        else C[[while e do P]](C[[P]](s))

Because e is an expression, not a statement, we apply the semantic function E to obtain the value of e in a given state.

In words, we can describe the semantics of programs as follows:

C[[x := e]](s) is the state similar to s, but with x having the value of e.
C[[P₁;P₂]](s) is the state we obtain by applying the semantics of P₂ the to the state we obtain by applying the semantics of P₁ to state s.
C[[if e then P₁ else P₂]](s) is the state we obtain by applying the semantics of P₁ to s if e is true in s and P₂ to s otherwise.
C[[while e do P]](s) is a recursively defined function f, from states to states. In words, $f(s)$ is either s if e is false or the state we obtain by applying f to the state resulting from executing P once in s.

The recursive function definition in the while clause is relatively subtle. It also raises some interesting mathematical problems, as it is not always mathematically reasonable to define functions by arbitrary recursive conditions. However, in the interest of keeping our discussion simple and straightforward, we just assume that a definition of this form can be made mathematically rigorous.

Example 4.4

We can calculate the semantics of various programs by using this definition. To begin with, let us consider a simple loop-free program,

```
if x>y then x :=y else y :=x
```

which sets both x and y to the minimum of their initial values. For concreteness, let us calculate the semantics of this program in the state s_0, where $s_0(x) = 1$ and $s_0(y)=2$.

Because $E[[x>y]](s_0) =$ false, we have

$$
\begin{aligned}
C[[\text{if } x>y \text{ then } x :=y \text{ else } y := x]](s_0) \\
= \text{if } E[[x>y]](s_0) \text{ then } C[[x := y]](s_0) \text{ else } C[[y := x]](s_0) \\
= C[[y := x]](s_0) \\
= \text{modify}(s_0, y, E[[x]](s_0))
\end{aligned}
$$

In words, if the program if x>y then x :=y else y := x is executed in the state s_0, then the result will be the state that is the same as s_0, but with variable y given the value that x has in state s_0.

Example 4.5

Although it takes a few more steps than the previous example, it is not too difficult to work out the semantics of the program

---

$x := 0; y:=0; \text{while } x \leq z \text{ do } (y := y+x; x := x+1)$

---

in the state s_0, where $s_0(z)=2$. A few preliminary definitions will make the calculation easier. Let s_1 and s_2 be the states

$$
\begin{aligned}
s_1 &= C[[x:= 0]](s_0) \\
s_2 &= C[[y := 0]](s_1)
\end{aligned}
$$

Using the semantics of assignment, as above, we have

$$
\begin{aligned}
s_1 &= \text{modify}(s_0 , x, 0) \\
s_2 &= \text{modify}(s_1 , y, 0)
\end{aligned}
$$

Returning to the preceding program, we have

$$
\begin{aligned}
&C[[x := 0; y:=0; \text{while } x \leq z \text{ do } (y := y+x; x := x+1)]](s_0) \\
&= C[[y:=0; \text{while } x \leq z \text{ do } (y := y+x; x := x+1)]](C [[x := 0]](s_0)) \\
&= C[[y:=0; \text{while } x \leq z \text{ do } (y := y+x; x := x+1)]](s_1) \\
&= C[[\text{while } x \leq z \text{ do } (y := y+x; x := x+1)]](C [[y := 0]](s_1)) \\
&= C[[\text{while } x \leq z \text{ do } (y := y+x; x := x+1)]](s_2) \\
&= \text{if not } E[[x \leq z]](s_2) \text{ then } s_2 \\
&\quad \text{else } C[[\text{while } x \leq z \text{ do } (y := y+x; x := x+1)]](C[[y := y+x; x := x+1]](s_2)) \\
&= C[[\text{while } x \leq z \text{ do } (y := y+x; x := x+1)]](s_3)
\end{aligned}
$$

where s_3 has y set to 0 and x set to 1. Continuing in the same manner, we have

$$
\begin{aligned}
&C[[\text{while } x \leq z \text{ do } (y := y+x; x := x+1)]](s_3) \\
&= \text{if not } E[[x \leq z]](s_3) \text{ then } s_3 \\
&\quad \text{else } C[[\text{while } x \leq z \text{ do } (y := y+x; x := x+1)]](C[[y := y+x; x := x+1]](s_3)) \\
&= C[[\text{while } x \leq z \text{ do } (y := y+x; x := x+1)]](s_4) \\
&= \text{if not } E[[x \leq z]](s_4) \text{ then } s_4 \\
&\quad \text{else } C[[\text{while } x \leq z \text{ do } (y := y+x; x := x+1)]](C[[y := y+x; x := x+1]](s_4)) \\
&= C[[\text{while } x \leq z \text{ do } (y := y+x; x := x+1)]](s_5) \\
&= s_5
\end{aligned}
$$

where s_4 has y set to 1 and x to 2 and s_5 has y set to 3 and x to 3. The steps are tedious to write out, but you can probably see without doing so that if $s_0(z) = 5$, for example, then this program will yield a state in which the value of x is 0+1+2+3+4+5.

As these examples illustrate, the denotational semantics of while programs unambiguously associates a partial function from states to states with each program. One important issue we have not discussed in detail is what happens when a loop does not terminate. The meaning C[[while x=x do x := x]] of a loop that does not terminate in any state is a partial function that is not defined on any state. In other words, for any state s, C[[while x=x do x := x]](s) is not defined. Similarly, C[[while x=y do x := y]](s) is s if $s(x) \neq s(y)$ and undefined otherwise. If you are interested in more information, there are many books that cover denotational semantics in detail.

4.3.4 Perspective and Nonstandard Semantics

There are several ways of viewing the standard methods of denotational semantics. Typically, denotational semantics is given by the association of a function with each program. As many researchers in denotational semantics have observed, a mapping from programs to functions must be written in some metalanguage. Because lambda calculus is a useful notation for functions, it is common to use some form of lambda calculus as a metalanguage. Thus, most denotational semantics actually have two parts: a translation of programs into a lambda calculus (with some extra operations corresponding to basic operations in programs) and a semantic interpretation of the lambda calculus expressions as mathematical objects. For this reason, denotational semantics actually provides a general technique for translating imperative programs into functional programs.

Although the original goal of denotational semantics was to define the meanings of programs in a mathematical way, the techniques of denotational semantics can also be used to define useful "nonstandard" semantics of programs.

One useful kind of nonstandard semantics is called *abstract interpretation*. In abstract interpretation, programs are assigned meaning in some simplified domain. For example, instead of interpreting integer expressions as integers, integer expressions could be interpreted elements of the finite set {0, 1, 2, 3, 4, 5, . . . , 100, >100}, where >100 is a value used for expressions whose value might be greater than 100. This might be useful if we want to see if two array expressions $A[e_1]$ and $A[e_2]$ refer to the same array location. More specifically, if we assign values to e_1 from the preceding set, and similarly for e_2, we might be able to determine that $e_1=e_2$. If both are assigned the value >100, then we would not know that they are the same, but if they are assigned the same ordinary integer between 0 and 100, then we would know that these expressions have the same value. The importance of using a finite set of values is that an algorithm could iterate over all possible states. This is important for calculating properties of programs that hold in all states and also for calculating the semantics of loops.

Example. Suppose we want to build a program analysis tool that checks programs to make sure that every variable is initialized before it is used. The basis for this kind of program analysis can be described by denotational semantics, in which the meaning of an expression is an element of a finite set.

Because the halting problem is unsolvable, program analysis algorithms are usually designed to be *conservative*. Conservative means that there are no false positivies: An algorithm will output *correct* only if the program is correct, but may sometimes output *error* even if there is no error in the program. We cannot expect a computable analysis to decide correctly whether a program will ever access a variable before it is initialized. For example, we cannot decide whether

---

(complictated error-free program); x := y

---

executes the assignment x := y without deciding whether complictated error-free program halts. However, it is often possible to develop efficient algorithms for conservative analysis. If you think about it, you will realize that most compiler warnings are conservative: Some warnings could be a problem in general, but are not a problem in a specific program because of program properties that the compiler is not "smart" enough to understand.

We describe initialize-before-use analysis by using an abstract representation of machine states that keep track only of whether a variable has been initialized or not. More precisely, a state will either be a special error state called *error* or a function from variable names to the set {*init, uninit*} with two values, one representing any value of initialized variable and the other an uninitialized one. The set *State* of mathematical abstractions of machine states is therefore

$$State = \{\text{error}\} \cup (Variables \rightarrow \{init, uninit\})$$

As usual, the meaning of a program will be a function from states to states. Let us assume that $E[[e]](s) = error$ if e contains any variable y with $s(y) = uninit$ and $E[[e]](s) = Ok$ otherwise.

The semantics of programs is given by a set of clauses, one for each program form, as usual. For any program P, we let $C[[P]](error) = error$. The semantic clause for assignment in state $s \neq error$ can be written as

$$C[[x := e]](s) = \text{if } E[[e]](s) = Ok \text{ then modify}(s, x, init) \text{ else } error$$

In words, if we execute an assignment x:= e in a state s different from *error*, then the result is either a state that has x initialized or *error* if there is some variable in e that was not initialized in s. For example, let

$$s_0 = \lambda v \in Variables. \ uninit$$

be the state with every variable uninitialized. Then

$$C[[x := 0]](s_0) = \text{modify}(s_0, x, init)$$

is the state with variable x initialized and all other variables uninitialized.

The clauses for sequences P1; P2 are essentially straightforward. For $s \neq error$,

$$C[[P_1;P_2]](s) = \text{if } C[[P_1]](s) = error \text{ then } error \text{ else } C[[P_2]](\ C[[P_1]](s)\ )$$

The clause for conditional is more complicated because our analysis tool is not going to try to evaluate a Boolean expression. Instead, we treat conditional as if it were possible to execute either branch. (This is the conservative part of the analysis.) Therefore, we change a variable to initialized only if it is initialized in both branches. If s_1 and s_2 are states different from *error*, then let $s_1 \dotplus s_2$ be the state

$$s_1 \dotplus s_2 = \lambda v \in \textit{Variables}. \text{ If } s_1(v) = s_2(v) = \textit{init} \text{ then } \textit{init} \text{ else } \textit{uninit}$$

We define the meaning of a conditional statement by

$$C[[\text{if e then } P_1 \text{ else } P_2]](s)$$
$$= \text{if } E[[e]](s) = \textit{error} \text{ or } C[[P_1]](s) = \textit{error} \text{ or } C[[P_2]](s) = \textit{error}$$
$$\text{then } \textit{error}$$
$$\text{else } C[[P_1]](s) \dotplus C[[P_2]](s)$$

For example, using s_0 as above, we have

$$C[[\text{ if 0=1 then x := 0 else x := 1; y := 2 }]](s_0) = \text{modify}(s_0, x, \textit{init})$$

as only x is initialized in both branches of the conditional.

For simplicity, we do not consider the clause for while e do P.

4.4 FUNCTIONAL AND IMPERATIVE LANGUAGES

4.4.1 Imperative and Declarative Sentences

The languages that humans speak and write are called *natural languages* as they developed naturally, without concern for machine readability. In natural languages, there are four main kinds of sentences: imperative, declarative, interrogative, and exclamatory.

In an imperative sentence, the subject of the sentence is implicit. For example, the subject of the sentence

Pick up that fish

is (implicitly) the person to whom the command is addressed. A declarative sentence expresses a fact and may consist of a subject and a verb or subject, verb, and object. For example,

Claude likes bananas

is a declarative sentence.

Interrogatives are questions. An exclamatory sentence may consist of only an interjection, such as *Ugh!* or *Wow!*

In many programming languages, the basic constructs are imperative statements. For example, an assignment statement such as

```
x:=5
```

is a command to the computer (the implied subject of the utterance) to store the value 5 in a certain location. Programming languages also contain declarative constructs such as the function declaration

```
function f(int x) { return x+1;}
```

that states a fact. One reading of this as a declarative sentence is that the subject is the name f and the sentence about f is "f is a function whose return value is 1 greater than its argument."

In programming, the distinction between imperative and declarative constructs rests on the distinction between changing an existing value and declaring a new value. The first is imperative, the latter declarative. For example, consider the following program fragment:

```
{ int x = 1;              /* declares new x */
    x = x+1;              /* assignment to existing x */
    { int y = x+1;        /* declares new y */
        { int x = y+1;    /* declares new x */
}}}
```

Here, only the second line is an imperative statement. This is an imperative command that changes the state of the machine by storing the value 2 in the location associated with variable x. The other lines contain declarations of new variables.

A subtle point is that the last line in the preceding code declares a new variable with the same name as that of a previously declared variable. The simplest way to understand the distinction between declaring a new variable and changing the value of an old one is by variable renaming. As we saw in lambda calculus, a general principle of binding is that bound variables can be renamed without changing the meaning of an expression or program. In particular, we can rename bound variables in the preceding program fragment to get

```
{ int x = 1;              /* declares new x */
    x = x+1;              /* assignment to existing x */
    { int y = x+1;        /* declares new y */
        { int z = y+1;    /* declares new z */
}}}
```

(If there were additional occurrences of x inside the inner block, we would rename them to z also.) After rewriting the program to this equivalent form, we easily see that the declaration of a new variable z does not change the value of any previously existing variable.

4.4.2 Functional versus Imperative Programs

The phrase *functional language* is used to refer to programming languages in which most computation is done by evaluation of expressions that contain functions. Two examples are Lisp and ML. Both of these languages contain declarative and imperative constructs. However, it is possible to write a substantial program in either language without using any imperative constructs.

Some people use the phrase functional language to refer to languages that do not have expressions with side effects or any other form of imperative construct.

However, we will use the more emphatic phrase *pure functional language* for declarative languages that are designed around flexible constructs for defining and using functions. We learned in Subsection 3.4.9 that pure Lisp, based on atom, eq, car, cdr, cons, lambda, define, is a pure functional language. If rplaca, which changes the car of a cell, and rplacd, which changes the cdr of a cell, are added, then the resulting Lisp is not a pure functional language.

Pure functional languages pass the following test:

> *Declarative Language Test*: Within the scope of specific declarations of $x_1, \ldots,$ x_n, all occurrences of an expression e containing only variables $x_1, \ldots, x_n$ have the same value.

As a consequence, pure functional languages have a useful optimization property: If expression e occurs several places within a specific scope, this expression needs to be evaluated only once. For example, suppose a program written in pure Lisp contains two occurrences of (cons a b). An optimizing Lisp compiler could compute (cons a b) once and use the same value both places. This not only saves time, but also space, as evaluating cons would ordinarily involve a new cell.

Referential Transparency

In some of the academic literature on programming languages, including some textbooks on programming language semantics, the concept that is used to distinguish declarative from imperative languages is called *referential transparency*. Although it is easy to define this phrase, it is a bit tricky to use it correctly to distinguish one programming language from another.

In linguistics, a name or noun phrase is considered *referentially transparent* if it may be replaced with another noun phrase with the same referent (i.e., referring to the same thing) without changing the meaning of the sentence that contains it. For example, consider the sentence

I saw Walter get into *his car*.

If Walter owns a Maserati Biturbo, say, and no other car, then the sentence

I saw Walter get into *his Maserati Biturbo*

has the same meaning because the noun phrases (in italics) have the same meaning. A traditional counterexample to referential transparency, attributed to the language philosopher Willard van Orman Quine, occurs in the sentence

He was called *William Rufus* because of his red beard.

The sentence refers to William IV of England and rufus means reddish or orange in color. If we replace William Rufus with William IV, we get a sentence that makes no sense:

He was called *William IV* because of his red beard.

Obviously, the king was called William IV because he was the fourth William, not because of the color of his beard.

Returning to programming languages, it is traditional to say that a language is referentially transparent if we may replace one expression with another of equal value anywhere in a program without changing the meaning of the program. This is a property of pure functional languages.

The reason referential transparency is subtle is that it depends on the value we associate with expressions. In imperative programming languages, we can say that a variable x refers to its value or to its location. If we say that a variable refers to its location in memory, then imperative languages *are* referentially transparent, as replacing one variable with another that names the same memory location will not change the meaning of the program. On the other hand, if we say that a variable refers to the value stored in that location, then imperative languages are not referentially transparent, as the value of a variable may change as the result of assignment.

Historical Debate

John Backus received the 1977 ACM Turing Award for the development of Fortran. In his lecture associated with this award, Backus argued that pure functional programming languages are better than imperative ones. The lecture and the accompanying paper, published by the Association for Cumputing Machinery, helped inspire a number of research projects aimed at developing practical pure functional programming languages. The main premise of Backus' argument is that pure functional programs are easier to reason about because we can understand expressions independently of the context in which they occur.

Backus asserts that, in the long run, program correctness, readability, and reliability are more important than other factors such as efficiency. This was a controversial position in 1977, when programs were a lot smaller than they are today and computers were much slower. In the 1990s, computers finally reached the stage at which commercial organizations began to choose software development methods that value programmer development time over run-time efficiency. Because of his belief in the importance of correctness, readability, and reliability, Backus thought that pure functional languages would be appreciated as superior to languages with side effects.

To advance his argument, Backus proposed a pure functional programming language called FP, an acronym for functional programming. FP contains a number of basic functions and a rich set of combining forms with which to build new functions from old ones. An example from Backus' paper is a simple program to compute the inner product of two vectors. In C, the inner product of vectors stored in arrays a and b could be written as

```
int i, prod;
prod=0;
for (i=0; i < n; i++) prod = prod + a[i] * b[i];
```

In contrast, the inner product function would be defined in FP by combining functions + and × (multiplication) with vector operations. Specifically, the inner product would be expressed as

```
Inner_product = (Insert +) ° (ApplyToAll x) ° Transpose
```

where ° is function composition and Insert, ApplyToAll, and Transpose are vector operations. Specifically, the Transpose of a pair of lists produces a list of pairs and ApplyToAll applies the given operation to every element in a list, like the maplist function in Subsection 3.4.7. Given a binary operation and a list, Insert has the effect of inserting the operation between every pair of adjacent list elements and calculating the result. For example, (Insert +) <1, 2, 3, 4> = 1+2+3+4=10, where <1, 2, 3, 4> is the FP notation for the list with elements 1, 2, 3, 4.

Although the C syntax may seem clearer to most readers, it is worth trying to imagine how these would compare if you had not seen either before. One facet of the FP expression is that all of its parts are functions that we can understand without thinking about how vectors are represented in memory. In contrast, the C program has extra variables i and prod that are not part of the function we are trying to compute. In this sense, the FP program is higher level, or more abstract, than the C code.

A more general point about FP programs is that if one functional expression is equivalent to another, then we can replace one with the other in any program. This leads to a set of algebraic laws for FP programs. In addition to algebraic laws, an advantage of functional programming languages is the possibility of parallelism in implementations. This is subsequently discussed.

In retrospect, Backus' argument seems more plausible than his solution. The importance of program correctness, readability, and reliability has increased compared with that of run-time efficiency. The reason is that these affect the amount of time that people must spend in developing, debugging, and maintaining code. When computers become faster, it is acceptable to run less efficient programs – hardware improvements can compensate for software. However, increases in computer speed do not make humans more efficient. In this regard, Backus was absolutely right about the aspects of programming languages that would be important in the future.

Backus' language FP, on the other hand, was not a success. In the years since his lecture, there was an effort to develop a FP implementation at IBM, but the language was not widely used. One problem is that the language has a difficult syntax. Perhaps more importantly, there are severe limitations in the kind of data structures and control structures that can be defined. FP languages that allow variable names and binding (as in Lisp and lambda calculus) have been more successful, as have all programming languages that support modularity and reuse of library components. However, Backus raised an important issue that led to useful reflection and debate.

Functional Programming and Concurrency

An appealing aspect of pure functional languages and of programs written in the pure functional subset of larger languages is that programs can be executed concurrently. This is a consequence of the declarative language test mentioned at the beginning of this subsection. We can see how parallelism arises in pure functional languages by using the example of a function call $f(e_1,...,e_n)$, where function arguments $e_1,...,e_n$ are expressions that may need to be evaluated.

Functional Programming: We can evaluate $f(e_1,...,e_n)$ by evaluating $e_1,...,e_n$ in parallel because values of these expressions are independent.

Imperative Programming: For an expression such as $f(g(x), h(x))$, the function g might change the value of x. Hence the arguments of functions in imperative languages must be evaluated in a fixed, sequential order. This ordering restricts the use of concurrency.

Backus used the term *von Neumann bottleneck* for the fact that in executing an imperative program, computation must proceed one step at a time. Because each step in a program may depend on the previous one, we have to pass values one at a time from memory to the CPU and back. This sequential channel between the CPU and memory is what he called the von Neumann bottleneck.

Although functional programs provide the opportunity for parallelism, and parallelism is often an effective way of increasing the speed of computation, effectively taking advantage of inherent parallelism is difficult. One problem that is fairly easy to understand is that functional programs sometimes provide too much parallelism. If all possible computations are performed in parallel, many more computation steps will be executed than necessary. For example, full parallel evaluation of a conditional

---

if e_1 then e_2 else e_3

---

will involve evaluating all three expressions. Eventually, when the value of e_1 is found, one of the other computations will turn out to be irrelevant. In this case, the irrelevant computation can be terminated, but in the meantime, resources will have been devoted to calculation that does not matter in the end.

In a large program, it is easy to generate so many parallel tasks that the time setting up and switching between parallel processes will detract from the efficiency of the computation. In general, parallel programming languages need to provide some way for a programmer to specify where parallelism may be beneficial. Parallel implementations of functional languages often have the drawback that the programmer has little control over the amount of parallelism used in execution.

Practical Functional Programming

Backus' Turing Award lecture raises a fundamental question:

> Do pure functional programming languages have significant practical advantages over imperative languages?

Although we have considered many of the potential advantages of pure FP languages in this section, we do not have a definitive answer. From one theoretical point of view, FP languages are as good as imperative programming languages. This can be demonstrated when a translation is made of C programs into FP programs, lambda calculus expressions, or pure Lisp. Denotational semantics provides one method for doing this.

To answer the question in practice, however, we would need to carry out large projects in a functional language and see whether it is possible to produce usable software in a reasonable amount of time. Some work toward answering this question was done at IBM on the FP project (which was canceled soon after Backus retired). Additional efforts with other languages such as Haskell and Lazy ML are still being carried out at other research laboratories and universities. Although most programming is done in imperative languages, it is certainly possible that, at some future time, pure or mostly pure FP languages will become more popular. Whether or not that happens, FP projects have generated many interesting language design ideas and implementation techniques that have been influential beyond pure functional programming.

4.5 CHAPTER SUMMARY

In this chapter, we studied the following topics:

- the outline of a simple compiler and parsing issues,
- lambda calculus,
- denotational semantics,
- the difference between functional and imperative languages.

A standard compiler transforms an input program, written in a source language, into an output program, written in a target language. This process is organized into a series of six phases, each involving more complex properties of programs. The first three phases, lexical analysis, syntax analysis, and semantic analysis, organize the input symbols into meaningful tokens, construct a parse tree, and determine context-dependent properties of the program such as type agreement of operators and operands. (The name semantic analysis is commonly used in compiler books, but is somewhat misleading as it is still analysis of the parse tree for context-sensitive syntactic conditions.) The last three phases, intermediate code generation, optimization, and target code generation, are aimed at producing efficient target code through language transformations and optimizations.

Lambda calculus provides a notation and symbolic evaluation mechanism that is useful for studying some properties of programming languages. In the section on lambda calculus, we discussed binding and α conversion. Binding operators arise in many programming languages in the form of declarations and in parameter lists of functions, modules, and templates. Lambda expressions are symbolically evaluated by use of β-reduction, with the function argument substituted in place of the formal parameter. This process resembles macro expansion and function in-lining, two transformations that are commonly done by compilers. Although lambda calculus is a very simple system, it is theoretically possible to write every computable function in the lambda calculus. Untyped lambda calculus, which we discussed, can be extended with type systems to produce various forms of typed lambda calculus.

Denotational semantics is a way of defining the meanings of programs by specifying the mathematical value, function, or function on functions that each construct denotes. Denotational semantics is an abstract way of analyzing programs because it does not consider issues such as running time and memory requirements. However, denotational semantics is useful for reasoning about correctness and has been used to develop and study program analysis methods that are used in compilers and programming environments. Some of the exercises at the end of the chapter present applications for type checking, initialization-before-use analysis, and simplified security analysis. From a theoretical point of view, denotational semantics shows that every imperative program can be transformed into an equivalent functional program.

In pure functional programs, syntactically identical expressions within the same scope have identical values. This property allows certain optimizations and makes it possible to execute independent subprograms in parallel. Because functional languages are theoretically as powerful as imperative languages, we discussed some of the pragmatic differences between functional and imperative languages. Although functional languages may be simpler to reason about in certain ways, imperative languages often make it easier to write efficient programs. Although Backus argues that functional programs can eliminate the von Neumann bottleneck, practical parallel execution of functional programs has not proven as successful as he anticipated in his Turing Award lecture.

EXERCISES

4.1 Parse Tree

Draw the parse tree for the derivation of the expression 25 given in Subsection 4.1.2. Is there another derivation for 25? Is there another parse tree?

4.2 Parsing and Precedence

Draw parse tress for the following expressions, assuming the grammar and precedence described in Example 4.2:

(a) 1 - 1 $*$ 1.

(b) 1 - 1 + 1.

(c) 1 - 1 + 1 - 1 + 1, if we give + higher precedence than −.

4.3 Lambda Calculus Reduction

Use lambda calculus reduction to find a shorter expression for $(\lambda x.\lambda y.xy)(\lambda x.xy)$. Begin by renaming bound variables. You should do all possible reductions to get the shortest possible expression. What goes wrong if you do not rename bound variables?

4.4 Symbolic Evaluation

The Algol-like program fragment

```
function f(x)
    return x+4
end;
function g(y)
    return 3-y
end;
f(g(1));
```

can be written as the following lambda expression:

$$\left(\underbrace{(\lambda f.\lambda g. f(g\ 1))}_{\text{main}}\ \underbrace{(\lambda x.x + 4)}_{f} \right)\ \underbrace{(\lambda y.3 - y)}_{g}.$$

Reduce the expression to a normal form in two different ways, as described below.

(a) Reduce the expression by choosing, at each step, the reduction that eliminates a λ as far to the *left* as possible.

(b) Reduce the expression by choosing, at each step, the reduction that eliminates a λ as far to the *right* as possible.

4.5 Lambda Reduction with Sugar

Here is a "sugared" lambda expression that uses let declarations:

$$\text{let } compose = \lambda f. \lambda g. \lambda x.\ f(g\,x) \text{ in}$$
$$\text{let } h = \lambda x. x + x \text{ in}$$
$$compose\,h\,h\,3$$

The "desugared" lambda expression, obtained when each let $z = U$ in V is replaced with $(\lambda z.\ V)\,U$ is

$$(\lambda compose.$$
$$(\lambda h.\ compose\,h\,h\,3)\ \lambda x. x + x)$$
$$\lambda f. \lambda g. \lambda x. f(g\,x).$$

This is written with the same variable names as those of the let form to make it easier to read the expression.

Simplify the desugared lambda expression by using reduction. Write one or two sentences explaining why the simplified expression is the answer you expected.

4.6 Translation into Lambda Calculus

A programmer is having difficulty debugging the following C program. In theory, on an "ideal" machine with infinite memory, this program would run forever. (In practice, this program crashes because it runs out of memory, as extra space is required every time a function call is made.)

```
int f(int (*g)(...)){ /* g points to a function that returns an int */
   return g(g);
}
int main(){
  int x;
  x = f(f);
  printf("Value of x = %d\n", x);
  return 0;
}
```

Explain the behavior of the program by translating the definition of f into lambda calculus and then reducing the application f(f). This program assumes that the type checker does not check the types of arguments to functions.

4.7 Order of Evaluation

In pure lambda calculus, the order of evaluation of subexpressions does not effect the value of an expression. The same is true for pure Lisp: if a pure Lisp expression has a value under the ordinary Lisp interpreter, then changing the order of evaluation of subterms cannot produce a different value.

To give a concrete example, consider the following section of Lisp code:

```
(define a ( ... ))
(define b ( ... ))
...
(define f (lambda (x y z) (cons (car x) (cons (car y) (cdr z)))))
...
(f e1 e2 e3)
```

The ordinary evaluation order for the function call

> (f e1 e2 e3)

is to evaluate the arguments e1 e2 e3 from left to right and then pass this list of values to the function f.

Give an example of Lisp expressions e1 e2 e3, possibly by using functions rplaca or rplacd with side effects, so that evaluating expressions from left to right gives a different result from that obtained by evaluating them from right to left. You may fill in specific declarations for a or b if you like and refer to a or b in your expressions. Explain briefly, in one or two sentences, why one order of evaluation is different from the other.

4.8 Denotational Semantics

The text describes a denotational semantics for the simple imperative language given by the grammar

$$P ::= x := e \mid P_1; P_2 \mid \text{if } e \text{ then } P_1 \text{ else } P_2 \mid \text{while } e \text{ do } P.$$

Each program denotes a function from *states* to *states*, in which a *state* is a function from *variables* to *values*.

(a) Calculate the meaning $C[\![\, x := 1; x := x + 1; \,]\!](s_0)$ in approximately the same detail as that of the examples given in the text, where $s_0 = \lambda v \in variables.\, 0$, giving every variable the value 0.

(b) Denotational semantics is sometimes used to justify ways of reasoning about programs. Write a few sentences, referring to your calculation in part (a), explaining why

$$C[\![x := 1; x := x + 1;]\!](s) = C[\![x := 2;]\!](s)$$

for every state s.

4.9 Semantics of Initialize-Before-Use

A nonstandard denotational semantics describing initialize-before-use analysis is presented in the text.

(a) What is the meaning of

$$C[\![x := 0; y := 0; \text{if } x = y \text{ then } z := 0 \text{ else } w := 1]\!](s_0)$$

in the state $s_0 = \lambda y \in variables.uninit$? Show how to calculate your answer.

(b) Calculate the meaning

$$C[\![\text{if } x = y \text{ then } z := y \text{ else } z := w]\!](s)$$

in state s with $s(x) = init$, $s(y) = init$, and $s(v) = uninit$ or every other variable v.

4.10 Semantics of Type Checking

This problem asks about a nonstandard semantics that characterizes a form of type analysis for expressions given by the following grammar:

$$e ::= 0 \mid 1 \mid true \mid false \mid x \mid e + e \mid \text{if } e \text{ then } e \text{ else } e \mid \text{let } x{:}\tau{=}e \text{ in } e$$

In the let expresion, which is a form of local declaration, the type τ may be either *int* or *bool*. The meaning $V[\![e]\!](\eta)$ of an expression e depends on an environment.

An environment η is a mapping from variables to values. In type analysis, we use three values,

$$Values = \{integer, boolean, type\_error\}.$$

Intuitively, $\mathcal{V}[\![e]\!](\eta) = integer$ means that the value of expression e is an integer (in environment η) and $\mathcal{V}[\![e]\!](\eta) = type\_error$ means that evaluation of e *may* involve a type error.

Here are the semantic clauses for the first few expression forms.

$$
\begin{aligned}
\mathcal{V}[\![0]\!]\eta &= integer, \\
\mathcal{V}[\![1]\!]\eta &= integer, \\
\mathcal{V}[\![true]\!]\eta &= boolean, \\
\mathcal{V}[\![false]\!]\eta &= boolean.
\end{aligned}
$$

The value of a variable in some environment is simply the value the environment gives to that variable:

$$\mathcal{V}[\![x]\!]\eta = \eta(x)$$

For addition, the value will be *type_error* unless both operands are integers:

$$\mathcal{V}[\![e_1 + e_2]\!]\eta = \begin{cases} integer & \text{if } \mathcal{V}[\![e_1]\!]\eta = integer \text{ and } \mathcal{V}[\![e_2]\!]\eta = integer \\ type\_error & \text{otherwise} \end{cases}.$$

Because declarations involve setting the types of variables, and the types of variables are recorded in an environment, the semantics of declarations involves changing the environment. Before giving the clause for declarations, we define the notation $\eta[x \mapsto \sigma]$ for an environment that is similar to η, except that it must map the variable x to type σ. More precisely,

$$\eta[x \mapsto \sigma] = \lambda y \in Variables. \text{ if } y = x \text{ then } \sigma \text{ else } \eta(y).$$

Using this notation, we can define the semantics of declarations by

$$\mathcal{V}[\![let\ x{:}\tau = e_1\ in\ e_2]\!]\eta$$
$$= \begin{cases} \mathcal{V}[\![e_2]\!](\eta[x \mapsto integer]) & \text{if } \mathcal{V}[\![e_1]\!]\eta = integer \text{ and } \tau = int \\ \mathcal{V}[\![e_2]\!](\eta[x \mapsto boolean]) & \text{if } \mathcal{V}[\![e_1]\!]\eta = boolean \text{ and } \tau = bool. \\ type\_error & \text{otherwise} \end{cases}$$

The clause for conditional is

$$\mathcal{V}[\![if\ e_1\ then\ e_2\ else\ e_3]\!]\eta$$
$$= \begin{cases} boolean & \text{if } \mathcal{V}[\![e_1]\!]\eta = \mathcal{V}[\![e_2]\!]\eta = \mathcal{V}[\![e_3]\!]\eta = boolean \\ integer & \text{if } \mathcal{V}[\![e_1]\!]\eta = boolean \text{ and } \mathcal{V}[\![e_2]\!]\eta = \mathcal{V}[\![e_3]\!]\eta = integer. \\ type\_error & \text{otherwise} \end{cases}$$

For example, with $\eta_0 = \lambda y \in Var. type\_error$,

$$\mathcal{V}[\![if\ true\ then\ 0 + 1\ else\ x + 1]\!]\eta_0 = type\_error$$

as the expression $x + 1$ produces a type error if evaluating x produces a type error. On the other hand,

$$\mathcal{V}[\![let\ x{:}int = (1{+}1)\ in\ (if\ true\ then\ 0\ else\ x)]\!]\eta_0 = integer$$

as the let expression declares that x is an integer variable.

Questions:

(a) Show how to calculate the meaning of the expression if false then 0 else 1 in the environment $\eta_0 = \lambda y \in Var. type\_error$.

(b) Suppose e_1 and e_2 are expressions with $\mathcal{V}[\![e_1]\!]\eta = integer$ and $\mathcal{V}[\![e_2]\!]\eta = boolean$ in every environment. Show how to calculate the meaning of the expression let $x{:}int{=}e_1$ in (if e_2 then e_1 else x) in environment $\eta_0 = \lambda y \in Var. type\_error$.

(c) In declaration let $x{:}\tau{=}e$ in e, the type of x is given explicitly. It is also possible to leave the type out of the declaration and infer it from context. Write a semantic clause for the alternative form, let $x{=}e_1$ in e_2 by using the following partial solution (i.e., fill in the missing parts of this definition):

$$\mathcal{V}[\![let\ x{=}e_1\ in\ e_2]\!]\eta = \begin{cases} \mathcal{V}[\![e_2]\!](\eta[x \mapsto \sigma]) & \text{if} \\ type\_error & \text{otherwise} \end{cases}$$

4.11 Lazy Evaluation and Parallelism

In a "lazy" language, we evaluate a function call f(e) by passing the *unevaluated* argument to the function body. If the value of the argument is needed, then it is evaluated as part of the evaluation of the body of f. For example, consider the function g defined by

```
fun g(x,y) = if = x=0
                then 1
                else if x+y=0
                        then 2
                        else 3;
```

In a lazy language, we evaluate the call g(3,4+2) by passing some representation of the expressions 3 and 4+2 to g. We evaluate the test x=0 by using the argument 3. If it were true, the function would return 1 without ever computing 4+2. Because the test is false, the function must evaluate x+y, which now causes the actual parameter 4+2 to be evaluated. Some examples of lazy functional languages are Miranda, Haskell, and Lazy ML; these languages do not have assignment or other imperative features with side effects.

If we are working in a pure functional language without side effects, then for any function call f(e_1, e_2), we can evaluate e_1 before e_2 or e_2 before e_1. Because neither can have side effects, neither can affect the value of the other. However, if the language is lazy, we might not need to evaluate both of these expression. Therefore, something can go wrong if we evaluate both expressions and one of them does not terminate.

As Backus argues in his Turing Award lecture, an advantage of pure functional languages is the possibility of parallel evaluation. For example, in evaluating a function call f(e_1, e_2) we can evaluate both e_1 and e_2 in parallel. In fact, we could even start evaluating the body of f in parallel as well.

(a) Assume we evaluate g(e_1, e_2) by starting to evaluate g, e_1, and e_2 in parallel, where g is the function defined above. Is it possible that one process will have to wait for another to complete? How can this happen?

(b) Now, suppose the value of e_1 is zero and evaluation of e_2 terminates with an error. In the normal (i.e., eager) evaluation order that is used in C and other common languages, evaluation of the expression g(e_1, e_2) will terminate in error. What will happen with lazy evaluation? Parallel evaluation?

(c) Suppose you want the same value, for every expression, as lazy evaluation, but you want to evaluate expressions in parallel to take advantage of your new pocket-sized multiprocessor. What actions should happen, if you evaluate $g(e_1, e_2)$ by starting g, e_1, and e_2 in parallel, if the value of e_1 is zero and evaluation of e_2 terminates in an error?

(d) Suppose now that the language contains side effects. What if e_1 is z and e_2 contains an assignment to z; can you still evaluate the arguments of $g(e_1, e_2)$ in parallel? How? Or why not?

4.12 Single-Assignment Languages

A number of so-called *single-assignment languages* have been developed over the years, many designed for parallel scientific computing. Single-assignment conditions are also used in program optimization and in hardware description languages. Single-assignment conditions arise in hardware as only one assignment to each variable may occur per clock cycle.

One example of a single-assignment language is *SISAL,* which stands for streams and iteration in a single-assignment language. Another is *SAC,* or single-assignment C. Programs in single-assignment languages must satisfy the following condition:

> *Single-Assignment Condition:* During any run of the program, each variable may be assigned a value only once, within the scope of the variable.

The following program fragment satisfies this condition,

    if (y>3) then x = 42+29/3 else x = 13.39;

because only one branch of the if-then-else will be executed on any run of the program. The program x=2; loop_forever; x=3 also satisfies the condition because no execution will complete both assignments.

Single-assignment languages often have specialized loop constructs, as otherwise it would be impossible to execute an assignment inside a loop body that gets executed more than once. Here is one form, from SISAL:

    for ⟨range⟩
      ⟨body⟩
    returns ⟨returns clause⟩
    end for

An example illustrating this form is the following loop, which computes the dot (or inner) product of two vectors:

    for i in 1, size
      elt_prod := x[i]*y[i]
    returns value of sum elt_prod
    end for

This loop is parallelizable because different products x[i]*y[i] can be computed in parallel. A typical SISAL program has a sequential outer loop containing a set of parallel loops.

Suppose you have the job of building a parallelizing compiler for a single-assignment language. Assume that the programs you compile satisfy the single-assignment condition and do not contain any explicit process fork or other parallelizing instructions. Your implementation must find parts of programs that can be safely executed in parallel, producing the same output values as if the program were executed sequentially on a single processor.

Assume for simplicity that every variable is assigned a value before the value of the variable is used an in expression. Also assume that there is no potential source of side effects in the language other than assignment.

(a) Explain how you might execute parts of the sample program

```
x = 5;
y = f(g(x),h(x));
if y==5 then z=g(x) else z=h(x);
```

in parallel. More specifically, assume that your implementation will schedule the following processes in some way:

```
process 1 - set x to 5
process 2 - call g(x)
process 3 - call h(x)
process 4 - call f(g(x),h(x)) and set y to this value
process 5 - test y==5
process 6 - call g(x) and then set z=g(x)
process 7 - call h(x) and then set z=h(x)
```

For each process, list the processes that this process must wait for and list the processes that can be executed in parallel with it. For simplicity, assume that a call cannot be executed until the parameters have been evaluated and assume that processes 6 and 7 are *not* divided into smaller processes that execute the calls but do not assign to z. Assume that parameter passing in the example code is by value.

(b) If you further divide process 6 into two processes, one that calls g(x) and one that assigns to z, and similarly divide process 7 into two processes, can you execute the calls g(x) and h(x) in parallel? Could your compiler correctly eliminate these calls from processes 6 and 7? Explain briefly.

(c) Would the parallel execution of processes you describe in parts (a) and (b), if any, be correct if the program does not satisfy the single-assignment condition? Explain briefly.

(d) Is the single-assignment condition decidable? Specifically, given an program written in a subset of C, for concreteness, is it possible for a compiler to decide whether this program satisfies the single-assignment condition? Explain why or why not. If not, can you think of a decidable condition that implies the single-assignment condition and allows many useful single-assignment programs to be recognized?

(e) Suppose a single-assignment language has no side-effect operations other than assignment. Does this language pass the declarative language test? Explain why or why not.

4.13 Functional and Imperative Programs

Many more lines of code are written in imperative languages than in functional ones. This question asks you to speculate about reasons for this. First, however, an explanation of what the reasons *are not* is given:

- It is not because imperative languages can express programs that are not possible in functional languages. Both classes can be made Turing complete, and indeed a denotational sematics of an imperative language can be used to translate it into a functional language.

- It is not because of syntax. There is no reason why a functional language could not have a syntax similar to that of C, for example.

- It is not because imperative languages are always compiled whereas functional languages are always interpreted. Basic is imperative, but is usually interpreted, whereas Haskell is functional and usually compiled.

For this problem, consider general properties of imperative and functional languages. Assume that a functional language supports higher-order functions and garbage collection, but not assignment. For the purpose of this question, an imperative language is a language that supports assignment, but not higher-order functions or garbage collection. Use only these assumptions about imperative and functional languages in your answer.

(a) Are there inherent reasons why imperative languages are superior to functional ones for the majority of programming tasks? Why?

(b) Which variety (imperative or functional) is easier to implement on machines with limited disk and memory sizes? Why?

(c) Which variety (imperative or functional) would require bigger executables when compiled? Why?

(d) What consequence might these facts have had in the early days of computing?

(e) Are these concerns still valid today?

4.14 Functional Languages and Concurrency

It can be difficult to write programs that run on several processors concurrently because a task must be decomposed into independent subtasks and the results of subtasks often must be combined at certain points in the computation. Over the past 20 years, many researchers have tried to develop programming languages that would make it easier to write concurrent programs. In his Turing Lecture, Backus advocated functional programming because he believed functional programs would be easier to reason about and because he believed that functional programs could be executed efficiently in parallel.

Explain why functional programming languages do not provide a complete solution to the problem of writing programs that can be executed efficiently in parallel. Include two specific reasons in your answer.

PART 2

Procedures, Types, Memory Management, and Control

5

The Algol Family and ML

The Algol-like programming languages evolved in parallel with the Lisp family of languages, beginning with Algol 58 and Algol 60 in the late 1950s. The most prominent Algol-like programming languages are Pascal and C, although C differs from most of the Algol-like languages in some significant ways.

In this chapter, we look at some of the historically important languages from the Algol family, including Algol 60, Pascal, and C. Because many of the central features of the Algol family are used in ML, we then use the ML programming language to discuss some important concepts in more detail. The ML section of this chapter is also a useful reference for later chapters that use ML examples to illustrate concepts that are not found in C.

There are many Algol-related languages that we do not have time to cover, such as Algol 58, Algol W, Euclid, EL1, Mesa, Modula-2, Oberon, and Modula-3. We will discuss Modula and modules in Chapter 9.

5.1 THE ALGOL FAMILY OF PROGRAMMING LANGUAGES

A number of important language ideas were developed in the Algol family, which began with work on Algol 58 and Algol 60 in the late 1950s. The Algol family developed in parallel with Lisp languages and led to the late development of ML and Modula.

The main characteristics of the Algol family are the familiar colon-separated sequence of statements used in most languages today, block structure, functions and procedures, and static typing.

5.1.1 Algol 60

Algol 60 was designed between 1958 and 1963 by a committee that included many important computer pioneers, such as John Backus (designer of Fortran), John McCarthy (designer of Lisp), and Alan Perlis. Algol 60 was intended to be a general-purpose language, which at the time meant there was emphasis on scientific and numerical applications. Compared with Fortran, Algol 60 provided better ways to

ROBIN MILNER

A thoughtful, engaging, and optimistic person, Robin Milner has had a profound effect on several areas of computer science and on computing in the United Kingdom in general. Always looking for new insight and open to new ideas, Robin is an unassuming but forceful presence at any discussion over coffee after a conference talk or workshop presentation.

Milner was awarded the 1991 ACM Turing Award for "several distinct and complete achievements: LCF, probably the first theoretically based yet practical tool for machine-assisted proof construction; ML, the first language to include polymorphic type inference and a type-safe exception-handling mechanism; CCS, a general theory of concurrency; and full abstraction, the study of the relationship between operational and denotational semantics."

After approximately 20 years in Edinburgh, Robin returned to Cambridge University, where he held a Chair in Computer Science and was Head of the Computer Laboratory until his retirement in 1999.

represent data structures and, like LISP, allowed functions to be called recursively. Until the development of Pascal, Algol 60 was the academic standard for describing complex algorithms in scientific and engineering publications.

The following characteristics are some important features of Algol 60:

- simple statement-oriented syntax, involving colon-separated sequences of statements
- blocks indicated by begin ... end (corresponding to curly braces {...} in C)
- recursive functions and stack storage allocation

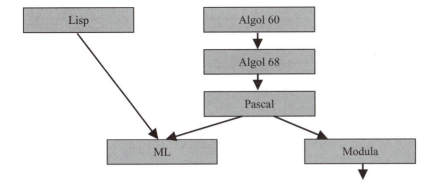

- fewer ad hoc restrictions than previous languages. For example,
  □ general expressions inside array indices
  □ procedures that could be called with procedure parameters
- a primitive static type system, later improved on in Algol 68 and Pascal.

Here is an example program (subsequently explained) that will give you some feel for Algol 60 syntax:

```
real procedure average(A,n);
    real array A; integer n;
    begin
        real sum; sum := 0;
        for i = 1 step 1 until n do
            sum := sum + A[i];
        average := sum/n
    end;
```

In Algol, the two-character sequence := is used for assignment, and the single character = for test for equality. In this program, note that the types of the parameters to the procedure (function) are declared in the line following the procedure name. Although A is declared to be a real array, no array bounds are given as part of the declaration. The return value of the procedure is given when a value is assigned to the name of the procedure. (This is the assignment to average in the last line.) An irritating syntactic peculiarity of Algol 60 is the way that semicolons must be (and must not be) used between statements. In particular, it would be a syntactic error to place a semicolon after the last assignment and before the keyword end. There is a systematic explanation for why semicolons are needed some places and not others in Algol 60, but the systematic reason is hard for programmers to learn, remember, and apply when programs are edited.

There were a number of trouble spots in Algol 60 that motivated computer scientists to develop better programming languages:

- The Algol 60 type discipline had some shortcomings. There are two examples that are illustrated in more detail in the exercises:

▫ The type of a procedure parameter to a procedure does not include the types of parameters.

▫ An array parameter to a procedure is given type array, without array bounds.

■ Algol 60 was designed around two parameter-passing mechanisms, pass-by-value and pass-by-name:

▫ Pass-by-name interacts badly with side effects.

▫ Pass-by-value is expensive for arrays.

■ There are some awkward issues related to control flow, such as memory management, when a program jumps out of a nested block.

Pass-by-Name. Perhaps the strangest feature of Algol 60, in retrospect, is the use of pass-by-name. In pass-by-name, the result of a procedure call is the same as if the formal parameter were substituted into the body of the procedure. This rule for defining the result of a procedure call by copying the procedure and substituting for the formal parameters is called the Algol 60 *copy rule*. Although the copy rule works well for pure functional programs, as illustrated by β reduction in lambda calculus, the interaction with side effects to the formal parameter are a bit strange. Here is an example program showing a technique referred to as *Jensen's device*: passing an expression and a variable it contains to a procedure so that the procedure can use one parameter to change the location referred to by the other:

```
begin integer i;
    integer procedure sum(i, j);
        integer i, j;
            comment parameters passed by name;
        begin integer sm; sm := 0;
            for i := 1 step 1 until 100 do sm := sm + j;
            sum := sm
        end;
    print(sum(i, i*10 ))
end
```

In this program, the procedure sum(i,j) adds up the values of j as i goes from 1 to 100. If you look at the code, you will realize that the procedure makes no sense unless changes to i cause some change in the value of j; otherwise, the procedure just computes 100∗j. In the call sum(i, i∗10) shown here, the for loop in the body of procedure sum adds up the value of i∗10 as i goes from 1 to 100.

BNF. An important by-product of the Algol 60 design effort was the invention of Backus Normal Form (or BNF), which was used in the Algol 60 report to define the well-formed programs of the language. BNF, summarized in Subsection 4.1.2, remains the standard notation for describing the syntax of programming languages. Although Algol 60 was very influential and commonly used in academic circles and in Europe, it was not a commercial success in the United States.

5.1.2 Algol 68

Algol 68 was intended to remove some of the difficulties found in Algol 60 and to improve the expressiveness of the language. However, in the end, the Algol 68 committee produced a design that was more problematic than that of Algol 60. One main problem is that, although programming in Algol 68 appears no more difficult than that of Algol 60, some features of Algol 68 made it difficult to compile efficiently. One source of difficulty was the combination of procedure parameters and procedure return values, which was not well understood at the time. (We will discuss the implementation consequences of higher-order functions in Section 7.4.) Another reason that Algol 68 was not entirely successful was that the authors chose to define entirely new terminology for the language and its documentation. This made it difficult for programmers to move from Algol 60 to Algol 68.

One contribution of Algol 68 was its regular, systematic type system. For some reason, the Algol 68 designers chose to call types *modes*. The modes of Algol 68 are either primitive or compound modes. The primitive modes included int, real, char, bool, string, complex, bits, bytes, semaphore, format (for input and output), and file.

The compound modes include modes formed with the forms array, structure, procedure, set, and pointer.

These type constructions can be combined without restriction, so that a programmer can build an array of pointers to procedures, for example. The decision to allow unrestricted combinations of the mode constructors made the type system seem more systematic than previous languages.

Some other advances in Algol 68 were in the areas of memory management and parameter passing. (The general concepts of memory management, parameter passing, and related issues are covered in Chapter 7.) Algol 68 memory management involves a stack for local variables and heap storage for data that are intended to live beyond the current function call. As in C, Algol 68 data on the heap are explicitly allocated, but unlike C, heap data are reclaimed by garbage collection. This combination of explicit allocation and garbage collection carried over into Pascal. Algol 68 parameter passing is pass-by-value, with pass-by-reference accomplished by pointer types. This is essentially the same design as that adopted in C some years later. The decision to allow independent constructs to be combined without restriction also led to some complex features, such as assignable procedure variables.

5.1.3 Pascal

Pascal was design in the 1970s by Niklaus Wirth, who used the data-structuring ideas advanced by C.A.R. (Tony) Hoare. Wirth first designed and implemented a language called Algol W and then refined the design of Algol W to produce Pascal. Wirth designed Pascal around a series of teaching exercises, enumerated in his book *Algorithms + Data Structures = Programs* (Prentice-Hall, 1975). He also designed the language so that it could have a simple one-pass compiler.

Pascal was significantly simpler than Algol 68 and achieved more widespread acceptance than either Algol 60 or Algol 68. Although the use of Pascal declined in the 1990s, Pascal was one of the most widely used programming languages over approximately a 20-year period. Pascal was very successful as a programming language for teaching, in part because it was designed explicitly for this purpose. Pascal was also used for a significant number of production programming projects, including operating systems and applications for the Apple Macintosh.

The Pascal type system is more expressive than the Algol 60 type system. The type system also repairs some of the Algol 60 type loopholes, such as Algol 60 procedure types that do not include the types of parameters. The Pascal type system is also simpler and more limited than the Algol 68 type system, eliminating some of the compilation difficulties of Algol 68.

An important contribution of the Pascal type system is the rich set of data-structuring concepts. These include records (similar to C structs), variant records (a form of union type), and subranges. For example, the subrange [1 .. 10] of integers between 1 and 10 became a type for the first time in Pascal. A restriction that made Pascal simpler than Algol 68 was that procedure parameters could not be procedures with procedure parameters. More specifically, in Pascal syntax, procedures of the form

```
procedure DoSomething( j, k : integer );
procedure DoSomething( procedure P(i:integer); j,k, : integer);
```

are allowed. The first is a procedure with integer parameters, and the second is a procedure whose parameter is a procedure with integer parameters. However, a procedure of the form

```
procedure NotAllowed( procedure MyProc( procedure P(i:integer)));
```

with a procedure parameter that has a procedure parameter, is *not* allowed.

One place where Wirth's focus on teaching and on systematic language design caused a small problem was in the typing of array parameters. In Pascal, the type of an array has the form

```
array ⟨indexType⟩ of ⟨entryType⟩
```

where ⟨indexType⟩ is often a subrange type. The important detail here is that the index type is part of the type of an array, and two array types are equal only if they have the same index type and entry type. This definition of array type allows a procedure declaration such as

```
procedure p(a : array [1..10] of integer)
```

where the argument to the procedure is an array of some array type, but does not allow

---

procedure p(n: integer, a : array [1..n] of integer)

---

as array [1..n] of integer is not considered a legal type in Pascal. A procedure of the form

---

procedure p(a : array [1..10] of integer)

---

may be called only with an array of length 10 as an actual parameter. This is an unfortunate limitation. If we want to write a sort procedure, for example, then we will have to write the procedure out for sorting arrays of some fixed length. If we want to sort arrays of several different lengths, then Pascal (as originally designed) would make it necessary to copy over the procedure several times, changing the array length in each copy.

Not only is this awkward, it is also unnecessary because the memory associated with an array is already allocated before it is passed to any procedure. Therefore there is no reason, other than type checking, for a procedure to allow array parameters of only a fixed length. Because this aspect of the Pascal design was awkward and unnecessary, later versions of Pascal have this limitation removed.

5.1.4 Modula

The Modula programming language is a descendent of Pascal, developed by Pascal designer Niklaus Wirth in Switzerland in the late 1970s. The main innovation of Modula over Pascal is a module system, used for grouping sets of related declarations into program units. Some examples of Modula-2, a successful version of the language, appear in Subsection 9.3.1 as part of the discussion of program modules.

5.2 THE DEVELOPMENT OF C

Although Pascal was a successful academic and teaching language, C eventually eclipsed Pascal as a production programming language. There are several reasons for the success of C. One reason, which is unrelated to the design of the language itself, is the popularity of the Unix operating system, which was written in C. When programs are written to run under Unix, all of the basic system calls are immediately available in C. Therefore, it is easier to write many Unix applications in C than in other programming languages. Another reason for the popularity of C is that it has a distinctive memory model that is close to the underlying hardware. Although C has many of the same concepts as Pascal, C is less rigid in its enforcement of basic principles and restrictions. Many C programmers like the resulting flexibility of C.

C was originally designed and implemented from 1969 to 1973, as part of the Unix operating system project at Bell Laboratories. C was designed by Dennis Ritchie, one of the original designers of Unix, so that he and Ken Thompson could build Unix in a language that they liked. The design evolved from Ritchie's and Thompson's B language (hence the name C, the next letter in the alphabet), which was in turn based on a language called BCPL. Significant changes in C occurred from 1977 to 1979, as part of a push to achieve portability of the Unix system, and in the mid-1980s when committee of the American National Standards Institute (ANSI) standardized the language. BCPL was a systems programming language designed in the 1960s and used by Bell Laboratories members of the Multics operating system project. B was a pared-down version of BCPL, designed to run on the small (PDP) computer used by the Unix project. The main difference between B and C is that B was untyped whereas the C language has types and type-checking rules.

One characteristic that distinguishes C from other popular languages is the treatment of memory locations, arrays, and pointers. This part of C is inherited from BCPL and B. The only data type in B is the "word," or "cell," a fixed-length bit pattern. Memory in BCPL and B is presented to the programmer as a linear array of words. Pointers are treated as integer indices into this array, and programmer-declared arrays are treated as contiguous words drawn from the larger array of all memory words. This view has several consequences. One is that arrays and pointers are largely equivalent, as described below. Another consequence is that, because pointers are integer indices in the memory array, pointer arithmetic is considered meaningful: If p is the address of a memory location, then p+1 is the address of the next location.

C Arrays and Pointers

In C, pointers and arrays are declared differently, as if pointers and arrays are different types of values. For example, the following code declares a pointer p to an integer location and an array A of integers:

```
int * p;
int A[5];
```

In most languages, there is some operation for dereferencing a pointer. Dereferencing is the operation that returns the location pointed to by the pointer. In most languages with arrays, there is an indexing operation that can be used to find one of the locations within the array. There are some similarities between these two operations, but most typed languages (including others in the Algol family) would consider dereferencing an array name or indexing a pointer illegal. In C, however, arrays are effectively treated as pointers. To quote Dennis Ritchie's 1975 C Reference Manual,

> Every time an identifier of array type appears in an expression, it is converted into a pointer to the first member of the array. . . . By definition, the subscript operator [ ] is interpreted in such a way that "E1[E2]" is identical to "*((E1)+(E2))." Because of the conversion rules which apply to +, if E1 is an array and E2 is an integer, then E1[E2] refers to the E2-th member of E1.

There is no other programming language in widespread use that allows pointer arithmetic in this way.

Critique

An important feature of C has been the tolerance of C compilers to type errors. This is partly because C evolved from typeless languages. Ritchie had to adapt existing programs as the language developed and to make an allowance for existing code in a typeless language. As C evolved further and was later standardized by an ANSI committee, backward compatibility with the then-existing C code also prevented strong typing restrictions. Although some C programmers have liked the ability to write and compile programs with type errors, most C programmers have eventually come to consider the weak type checking of many C compilers to be a disadvantage. In fact, one of the most commonly cited advantages of C++ over C is the fact that C++ provides better type checking.

As Dennis Ritchie says in The Development of the C Language (ACM Second History of Programming Languages conference, ACM 1993), "C is quirky, flawed, and an enormous success." Although accidents of history surely helped, C evidently satisfied a need for a system implementation language efficient enough to displace assembly language, yet sufficiently abstract and fluent to describe algorithms and interactions in a wide variety of environments.

An interesting discussion may be found in Kernighan's "Why Pascal is not my favorite programming language," Bell Labs CSTR 100, July 1981. If you are interested in doing extra reading, you can find this document on the web.

5.3 THE LCF SYSTEM AND ML

ML might be called a mostly functional language with imperative features or perhaps a *function-oriented imperative language*. ML has very flexible function features, similar to Lisp, allowing functions to be created in-line as parts of expressions, passed as arguments to functions, and returned as function results. At the same time, it is possible to write imperative Algol-like programs in a syntax that resembles that of the Algol family with approximately the same degree of ease as for modern descendants of Algol. ML also has concurrent extensions, making it suitable for developing concurrent systems, and an object-oriented extension. However, our main use of ML in this part of the book is to examine concepts common to Algol-like languages, Lisp-like languages, and concurrent and object-oriented extensions of these languages. Therefore, we focus primarily on the core fragment of ML.

The following list enumerates our main reasons for looking at ML in some detail:

- ML illustrates most of the important concepts of the Lisp/Algol families of languages.
- Type systems have been an important part of programming language design from 1960 to the present day, and the ML type system is often considered the cleanest and most expressive type system to date.
- Because most readers are familiar with C and many have not written a lot of programs in significantly different languages, it is useful to have a language other than C to use for examples in the following chapters.

■ ML allows higher-order functions and other constructions that are discussed in the following chapters.

One distinguishing feature of ML is its type system, which extends the successful Pascal type system in a number of ways. Unlike C, which has numerous loopholes, the ML type system is sound in a precise mathematical sense. Specifically, if the type checker determines that an expression has a certain type, then any terminating evaluation of that expression is guaranteed to produce a legitimate value of that type. For example, if an expression has a type such as "pointer to string," then the value of that expression is guaranteed to be a pointer to allocated memory that contains a string. It cannot be a dangling pointer to a location that has been deallocated or used to store some value other than a string.

Before ML, programming languages with sound type systems were generally considered unpleasantly restrictive. Many C programmers have considered it important to "break" the type system in various ways (confusing integers and pointers, for example), and Lisp fans have valued their freedom from static typing. However, the ML type system is unobtrusive, as many type declarations are automatically deduced by the compiler, and flexible, as the type system allows an expression to have many possible types. We will explore these aspects of the ML type system in more detail in Chapter 6.

Most successful programming languages were originally designed for a single application or a set of closely related programming tasks. The ML programming language was designed by Robin Milner and his associates as part of the LCF project. The LCF project, aimed at developing a *Logic for Computable Functions*, drew inspiration from a set of logical principles outlined by Dana Scott. Robin Milner's goal was to build a system that would make it practical to prove interesting properties of functional programs in an automated or semiautomated manner. His LCF project started at Stanford in 1970 and continued at Edinburgh through the 1980s, making substantial progress toward this goal and stimulating a number of related efforts in the process.

ML was designed as the *Meta-Language* (hence its name) of the LCF System. Its original purpose was for writing programs that would attempt to construct mathematical proofs. As any reader who has developed mathematical proofs will know, this can be a very difficult task. In many cases, it is necessary to try a number of methods for finding proofs. A fundamental concept in the LCF system is that of *proof tactic*. A proof tactic is a function that, given a formula making some assertion, tries to find a proof of the formula. Because a tactic may search indefinitely or reach some situation in which it is clear that no further search is likely to produce a proof, there are three possible results of applying a tactic to a formula:

$$
\text{tactic(formula)} = \begin{cases} \text{succeed and return proof} \\ \text{search forever} \\ \text{fail} \end{cases}
$$

We may use the concept of tactic to understand some basic properties of the ML programming language. Because the goal of LCF is to find correct proofs, a programming language mechanism that ensures correctness, in whole or in part, might improve the LCF system. An idea that was adopted in LCF was to try to use a type system to distinguish successful proofs from unsuccessful ones. In particular, there was a type proof, with the intent that values of type proof are correct proofs, not incorrect ones.

Once we have a type of correct proofs, a problem arises. If a tactic fails to find a proof, what should the function do? More specifically, because a tactic is a function from formulas to proofs, the type of a tactic would be a function type:

tactic : formula $\longrightarrow$ proof

However, this type seems to say that if a tactic is applied to a function, the result will be a proof. However, what if the formula is not a correct statement and therefore has no proof? The solution was to develop an exception mechanism and allow a tactic to raise an exception if the computation determines that no proof will be found. From this inspiration, Milner developed the first type-safe exception mechanism, one of the accomplishments that led to his Turing Award in 1991. Allowing for the possibility of exceptions, a function f that maps A to B, written as

f : A $\longrightarrow$ B

in ML, means that, for all x in A, if $f(x)$ terminates normally without raising an exception, then $f(x)$ is in B.

Thus type correctness and exceptions, two basic concepts in ML, arose naturally as the result of the intended application of ML.

Another emphasis of ML is the use of higher-order functions. This can also be attributed to the interest in defining complex proof-search tactics: Because a tactic is a function, a method for combining tactics into a proof-search strategy is a function from functions to functions. For example, here is the outline of a function that combines two tactics according to an if-then-else strategy:

f(tactic$_1$, tactic$_2$) =
$\qquad$ λformula. try tactic$_1$(formula)
$\qquad\qquad\qquad$ else tactic$_2$(formula)

Given two tactics tactic$_1$ and tactic$_2$, the function f returns a tactic that, given a formula, first tries to prove the formula by using tactic$_1$ and then uses tactic$_2$ if tactic$_1$ fails.

5.4 THE ML PROGRAMMING LANGUAGE

Because ML is used in the next few chapters of the book to illustrate properties of programming languages, we will study ML in a little more detail than we will study some other languages. The version of ML that we will use is called Standard ML 97 (SML97). Compilers for SML97 are available on the Internet without charge.

Several books and manuals covering the language are available. In addition to on-line sources easily located by web search, Ullman's *Elements of ML Programming* (Prentice-Hall, 1994) is a good reference.

5.4.1 Interactive Sessions and the Run-Time System

Most ML compilers are based on the same kind of read-eval-print loop as many Lisp implementations. The standard way of interacting with the ML system is to enter expressions and declarations one at a time. As each is entered, the source code is type checked, compiled, and executed. Once an identifier has been given a value by a declaration, that identifier can be used in subsequent expressions.

Expressions

For expressions, user interaction with the ML compiler has the form

```
— <expression>;
val it = <print_value> : <type>
```

where "—" is the prompt for user input and the line below is output from the ML compiler and run-time system. The preceding lines show that if you type in an expression, the compiler will compile the expression and evaluate it. The output is a bit cryptic: it is a special identifier bound to the value of the last expression entered, so it = <print_value> : <type> means that the value of the expression is <print_value> and this is a value of type <type>. It is probably easier to understand the idea from a few examples. Here are four lines of input and the resulting compiler output:

```
— (5+3) -2;
val it = 6 : int
— it + 3;
val it = 9 : int
— if true then 1 else 5;
val it = 1 : int
— (5 = 4);
val it = false : bool
```

In words, the value of the first expression is the integer 6. The second expression adds 3 to the value it of the previous expression, giving integer value 9. The third expression is an if-then-else, which evaluates to the integer 1, and the fourth expression is a Boolean-valued expression (comparison for equality) with value false.

Each expression is parsed, type checked, compiled, and executed before the next input is read. If an expression does not parse correctly or does not pass the type-checking phase of the compiler, no code is generated and no code is executed. The ill-typed expression

---

if true then 3 else false;

---

for example, parses correctly because this has the correct form for an if-then-else. However, the type checker rejects this expression because the ML type checker requires the then and else parts of an if-then-else expression to have the same types, as described in the next subsection. The compiler output for this expression includes the error message

---

stdIn:1.1-29.10 Error: types of rules don't agree [literal]

---

indicating a type mismatch. A full discussion of ML type checking appears in Chapter 6.

Declarations

User input can be an expression or a declaration. The standard form for ML declarations, followed by compiler output, is

---

— val <identifier> = <expression>;
val <identifier> = <print_value> : <type>

The keyword val stands for value. When a declaration is given to the compiler, the value associated with the identifier is computed and bound to that identifier. Because the value of the expression used in a declaration has a name, the compiler output uses this name instead of it for the value of the expression. Here are some examples:

— val x=7+2;
val x = 9 : int
— val y = x+3;
val y = 12 : int
— val z = x*y - (x div y);
val z = 108 : int

In words, the first declaration binds the integer value 9 to the identifier x. The second declaration refers to the value of x from the first declaration and binds the value 12 to the identifier y. The third declaration refers to both of the previous declarations and binds the integer value 108 to the identifier z.

You might note that integer division in ML is written as div instead of /. There are a few syntactic peculiarities of ML like this, especially when it comes to integer and real-number arithmetic. As you will see from the discussion of ML type inference in Chapter 6, it is useful for the compiler to distinguish operations of different types.

In ML, / is used for real-number (floating-point) division, and there is no automatic conversion from integer to real. Therefore x/y would not have been syntactically well formed if we had written this instead of x div y in the declaration of z.

Functions can be declared with the keyword fun (which stands for function) instead of val. The general form of user input and compiler output is

— fun <identifier> <arguments> = <expression>;
val <identifier> = fn <arg_type> $\longrightarrow$ <result_type>

This declares a function whose name is <identifier>. The argument type is determined by the form of <arguments> and the result type is determined by the form of <expression>.

Here is an example:

— fun f(x) = x + 5;
val f = fn : int $\longrightarrow$ int

This declaration binds a function value to the identifier f. The value of f is a function from integers to integers. The same function can be declared by a val declaration, written as

— val f = fn x => x+5;
val f = fn : int $\longrightarrow$ int

In this declaration, the identifier f is given the value of expression fn x => x+5, which is a function expression like (lambda (x) (+ x 5)) in Lisp or $\lambda x.\ x + 5$ in lambda calculus. We will discuss function declarations and function expressions further in Subsection 5.4.3.

The system prints fn for the value of f because the value of a function is not printable. One reason why function values are not printed is that most functions are infinite values in principle – an integer function has infinitely many possible results, one for each possible integer argument. After a function is declared, the compiler stores compiled code for the function. It would be possible to print the compiled code, but this is not in ML. It is in some other target low-level language, and printing it would not usually be useful to a programmer.

Identifiers vs. Variables. An important aspect of ML is that the value of an identifier cannot be changed by assignment. More specifically, if an identifier x is declared by val x = 3, for example, then the value of x will always be 3. It is not possible to change the value of x by assignment. In other words, ML declarations introduce constants, not variables. The way to declare an assignable variable in ML is to define a reference cell, which is similar to a cons cell in Lisp, except that reference cells do not come in pairs. References and assignment are explained in Subsection 5.4.5.

Although most readers will initially think otherwise, the ML treatment of identifiers and variables is more uniform than the treatment of identifiers and variables in languages such as Pascal and C. If an integer identifier is declared in C or Pascal, it is treated as an assignable variable. On the other hand, if a function is declared and given a name in either of these languages, the name of the function is a constant, not a variable. It is not possible to assign to the function name and change it to a different function. Thus, Pascal and C choose between variables and constants according to the type of the value given to the identifier. In ML, a val declaration works the same way for all types of values.

5.4.2 Basic Types and Type Constructors

The core expression, declaration, and statement parts of ML are best summarized by a list of the basic types along with the expression forms associated with each type.

Unit
The type unit has only one element, written as empty parentheses:

```
( ) : unit
```

Like void in C, unit is used as the result type for functions that are executed only for side effects. The type unit is also used as the type of argument for functions that have no arguments. C programmers may be confused by the fact that unit suggests one element, whereas void seems to mean no elements. From a mathematical point of view, "one element" is correct. In particular, if a function is supposed to return an element of an empty type, then that function cannot return because the empty set (or empty type) has no elements. On the other hand, a function that returns an element of a one-element type can return. However, we do not need to keep track of what value such a function returns, as there is only one thing that it could possibly return. The ML type system is based on years of theoretical study of types; most of the typing concepts in ML have been considered with great care.

Bool
There are two values of type bool, true and false:

```
true : bool
false : bool
```

The most common expression form associated with Booleans is conditional, with

```
if e1 then e2 else e3
```

having the same type as e2 and e3 if these have the same type and e1 has type bool. There is no if-then without else, as a conditional expression must have a value whether the test is true or false. For example, an expression

```
— val nonsense = if a then 3;
```

is not legal ML because there is no value for nonsense if the expression a is false. More specifically, the input if a then 3 does not even parse correctly; there is no parse tree for this string in the syntax of ML.

There are also ML Boolean operations for and, or, not, and so on. These are similar to AND, OR, and NOT in Pascal or &&, ||, and ! in C, with some minor differences. Negation is written as not, conjunction (and) is written as andalso and disjunction (or) is written as orelse.

For example, here is a function that determines whether its two arguments have the same Boolean value, followed by an expression that calls this function:

```
— fun equiv(x,y) = (x andalso y) orelse ((not x) andalso (not y));
val equiv = fn : bool * bool -> bool
— equiv(true,false);
val it = false : bool
```

In words, Boolean arguments x and y are the same Boolean value if they are either both true or both false. The first subexpression, (x andalso y), is true if x and y are both true and the second subexpression, ((not x) andalso (not y)), is true if they are both false.

The reason for the long names andalso and orelse is to emphasize evaluation order. In the expression (a andalso b), where a and b are both expressions, a is evaluated first. If a is true, then b is evaluated. Otherwise the value of the expression (a andalso b) is determined to be false without evaluating b. Similarly, b in (a orelse b) is evaluated only if the value of a is false.

Integers

Many ML integer expressions are written in the usual way, with number constants and standard arithmetic operations:

```
0,1,2, . . . ,-1,-2, . . . : int
+, -, *, div : int * int → int
```

The operator div is a binary infix operator on integers, used as follows:

```
— fun quotient(x,y) = x div y;
val quotient = fn : int * int → int
```

The identifier div by itself is not an expression, though. Similarly, +, -, and * are infix binary operators.

Strings

Strings are written as a sequence of symbols between double quotes:

"William Jefferson Clinton" : string
"Boris Yeltsin" : string

String concatenation is written as ^, so we have

— "Chelsey" ^ " " ^ "Clinton";
val it = "Chelsey Clinton" : string

Real

The ML type for floating-point numbers is real. For reasons that will be easier to understand when we come to type inference, ML requires a decimal point in real constants:

1.0, 2.0, 3.14159, 4.44444, . . . : real

The arithmetic operators +, -, and * may be applied to either integers or real numbers. Here are some example expressions and the resulting compiler output:

— 3+4;
val it = 7 : int
— 4.0 + 5.1;
val it = 9.1 : real

Note that when + has two integer arguments the result is an integer, and when + has two real arguments the result is a real number. However, it is a type error to combine integer and real arguments. Here is part of the compiler output for an expression that adds an integer to a real number:

— 4+5.1;
stdIn:1.1-1.6 Error: operator and operand don't agree [literal]
operator domain: int * int
operand: int * real

This error message is telling us that, because the first argument is an integer, the + symbol is considered to be integer addition. Therefore, the operator + has domain int * int, which is ML notation for the type of pairs of integers. However, the operand is applied to a pair of type int * real, which is ML notation for the type of pairs with one integer and one real number.

Conversion from integer to real is done by the explicit conversion function real. For example, the value of the expression real(3) is 3.0. Conversion from real to integer can be done with functions floor (round down), ceil (round up), round, and trunc.

Although arithmetic expressions in ML are a little more cumbersome than in some other languages, the language is generally usable for most purposes. In part, explicit typing of numeric constants and explicit conversion is the price to pay for automatic type inference, a useful feature of ML that is described in Chapter 6.

Tuples

A tuple may be a pair, triple, quadruple, and so on. In ML, tuples may be formed of any types of values. Tuple values are written with parentheses and tuple types are written with *. For example, here is the compiler output for a pair, a triple, and a quadruple:

```
— (3,4);
val it = (3,4) : int * int
— (4,5,true);
val it = (4,5,true) : int * int * bool
— ("Bob", "Carol", "Ted", "Alice");
val it = ("Bob","Carol","Ted","Alice") : string * string * string * string
```

For all types τ_1 and τ_2, the type $\tau_1 * \tau_2$ is the type of pairs whose first component has type τ_1 and whose second component has type τ_2. The type $\tau_1 * \tau_2 * \tau_3$ is a type of triples, the type $\tau_1 * \tau_2 * \tau_3 * \tau_4$ a type of quadruples, and so on.

Components of a tuple are accessed by functions that name the position of the desired component. For example, #1, selects the first component of any tuple, #2 selects the second component of any tuple with at least two components, and so on. Here are some examples:

```
— #2(3,4);
val it = 4 : int
— #3("John", "Paul", "George", "Ringo");
val it = "George" : string
```

Records

Like Pascal records and C structs, ML records are similar to tuples, but with named components. Record values and record types are written with curly braces, as follows:

```
— { First_name = "Donald", Last_name = "Knuth" };
val it = {First_name="Donald",Last_name="Knuth"}
  : {First_name:string, Last_name:string}
```

The expression here has two components, one called First_name and the other called Last_name. The type of this record tells us the type of each component. Record components can be accessed with # functions like tuples, but are named according to the component names instead of position. Here is one example:

— #First_name({First_name="Donald", Last_name="Knuth"});
val it = "Donald" : string

Another way of selecting components of tuples and records is by pattern matching, which is described in Subsection 5.4.3.

Lists
ML lists can have any length, but all elements of a list must have the same type. We can write lists by listing their elements, separated by commas, between brackets. Here are some example lists of different types:

— [1,2,3,4];
val it = [1,2,3,4] : int list
— [true, false];
val it = [true,false] : bool list
— ["red", "yellow", "blue"];
val it = ["red","yellow","blue"] : string list
— [fn x => x+1, fn x => x+2];
val it = [fn,fn] : (int -> int) list

For short lists, the compiler prints the elements of the list when showing that a list expression has been evaluated. For longer lists, the last elements are replaced with an ellipsis (three dots; . . .). As the last list example above shows, it is possible to write a list of functions.

In general, a τ list is the type of all lists whose elements have type τ.

As in Lisp, the empty list is written nil in ML. List cons is an infix operator written as a pair of colons:

— 3 :: nil;
val it = [3] : int list
— 4 :: 5 :: it;
val it = [4,5,3] : int list

In the first list expression, 3 is "consed" onto the front of the empty list. The result is a list containing the single element 3. In the second expression, 4 and 5 are consed onto this list. In both cases, the result is an int list.

5.4.3 Patterns, Declarations, and Function Expressions

The declarations we have seen so far bind a value to a single identifier. One very convenient syntactic feature of ML is that declarations can also bind values to a set of identifiers by using patterns.

Value Declarations

The general form of value declaration associates a value with a pattern. A pattern is an expression containing variables (such as x, y, z ...) and constants (such as true, false, 1, 2, 3 ...), combined by certain forms such as tupling, record expressions, and a form of operation called a constructor. The general form of value declaration is

---

val <pattern> = <exp> ;

---

where the common forms of patterns are summarized by the following grammar:

<pattern> ::= <id> | <tuple> | <cons> | <record> | <constr>
<tuple> ::= (<pattern>, ..., <pattern>)
<cons> ::= <pattern>::pattern
<record> ::= {<id>=<pattern>, ..., <id>=<pattern>}
<constr> ::= <id>(<pattern>, ..., <pattern>)

In words, a pattern can be an identifier, a tuple pattern, a list cons pattern, a record pattern, or a declared data-type constructor pattern. A tuple pattern is a sequence of patterns between parentheses, a list cons pattern is two patterns separated by double colons, a record pattern is a recordlike expression with each field in the form of a pattern, and a constructor pattern is an identifier (a declared constructor) applied to the right number of pattern arguments. This BNF does not define the set of patterns exactly, as some conditions on patterns are not context free and therefore cannot be expressed by BNF. For example, the conditions that in a constructor pattern the identifier must be a declared constructor and that the constructor must be applied to the right number of pattern arguments are not context free conditions. An additional condition on patterns, subsequently discussed in connection with function declarations, is that no variable can occur twice in any pattern.

Because a variable is a pattern, a value declaration can simply associate a value with a variable. For example, here is a declaration that binds a tuple to one identifier, followed by a declaration that uses a tuple pattern to bind components of the tuple:

```
— val t = (1,2,3);
val t = (1,2,3) : int * int * int
— val (x,y,z) = t;
val x = 1 : int
val y = 2 : int
val z = 3 : int
```

Note that there are two lines of input in this example and four lines of compiler output. In the first declaration, the identifier t is bound to a tuple. In the second declaration, the tuple pattern (x,y,z) is given the value of t. When the pattern (x,y,z) is matched against the triple t, identifier x gets value 1, identifier y gets value 2, and identifier z gets value 3.

Function Declarations

The general form of a function declaration uses patterns. A single-clause definition has the form

```
fun f( <pattern> ) = <exp>
```

and a multiple-clause definition has the form

```
fun f( <pattern1> ) = <exp1> | ... | f( <patternn> ) = <expn>
```

For example, a function adding its arguments can be written as

```
fun f(x,y) = x + y;
```

Technically, the formal parameter of this function is a pattern (x, y) that must match the actual parameter on a call to f. The formal parameter to f is a tuple, which is broken down by pattern matching into its first and second components. You may think you are calling a function of two arguments. In reality, you are calling a function of one argument. That argument happens to be a pair of values. Pattern matching takes the tuple apart, binding x to what you might think is the first parameter and y to the second.

An example in which more than one clause is used is the following function, which computes the length of a list:

```
— fun length(nil) = 0
|   length( x :: xs ) = 1 + length(xs);
val length = fn : 'a list → int
```

This code is subsequently explained. The first two lines here are input (the declaration of function length) and the last line is the compiler output giving the type of this function. Here is an example application of length and the resulting value:

```
— length ["a", "b", "c", "d"];
val it = 4 : int
```

When the function length is applied to an argument, the clauses are matched in the order they are written. If the argument matches the constant nil (i.e., the argument is the empty list), then the function returns the value 0, as specified by the first clause. Otherwise the argument is matched against the pattern given in the second clause (x::xs), and then the code for the second branch is executed. Because type checking guarantees that length will be applied only to a list, these two clauses cover all values that could possibly be passed to this function. The type of length, 'a list → int, will be explained in the next chapter.

In addition to declarations, ML has syntax for anonymous functions. We have already seen some simple examples. The general form allows the argument to be given by a pattern:

```
fn <pattern> => <exp>,
```

As mentioned briefly in passing in an earlier example, fn <pattern> => <exp> is like (lambda (<parameters>) (<exp>)) in Lisp. Here is an example, with compiler output:

```
— fn (x,y) => x+y;
val it = fn : int * int → int
```

The function expressed here takes a pair and adds its two components. The type of this function is int * int → int, meaning a function that maps a pair of integers to a single integer.

Here are some more examples illustrating other forms of patterns, each shown with an associated compiler output:

```
— fun f(x, (y,z)) = y;
val f = fn : 'a * ('b * 'c) -> 'b
— fun g(x::y::z) = x::z;
val g = fn : 'a list -> 'a list
— fun h {a=x, b=y, c=z} = {d=y, e=z};
val h = fn : {a:'a, b:'b, c:'c} -> {d:'b, e:'c}
```

The first is a function on nested tuples, the second a function on lists that have at least two elements, and the third a function on records. The second declaration produces a compiler warning, as the function g is not defined for lists that have fewer than two elements.

Pattern matching is applied in order. For example, when the function

```
fun f (x,0) = x
  |   f (0,y) = y
  |   f (x,y) = x+y;
```

is applied to an argument (a,b), the first clause is used if b=0, the second clause if b≠0 and a=0, and the third clause if b≠0 and a≠0. The ML type system will keep f from being applied to any argument that is not a pair (a,b).

An important condition on patterns is that no variable can occur twice in any pattern. For example, the following function declaration is not syntactically correct because the identifier x occurs twice in the pattern:

```
— fun eq(x,x) = true
   |   eq(x,y) = false;
stdIn:24.5-25.20 Error: duplicate variable in pattern(s):
```

This function is not allowed because multiple occurrences of variables express equality, and equality must be written explicitly into the body of a function.

5.4.4 ML Data-Type Declaration

The ML data-type declaration is a special form of type declaration that declares a type name and operations for building and making use of elements of the type. The ML data-type declaration has the syntactic form

```
datatype <type_name> = <constructor_clause> | ... | <constructor_clause>
```

where a constructor clause has the form

```
<constructor_clause> ::= <constructor> | <constructor> of <arg_types>
```

The idea is that each constructor clause tells one way to construct elements of the type. Elements of the type may be "deconstructed" into their constituent parts by pattern matching. This is illustrated by three examples that show some common ways of using data-type declarations in ML programs.

Example. An Enumerated Data Type: Types consisting of a finite set of tokens can be declared as ML data types. Here is a type consisting of three tokens, named to indicate three specific colors:

```
— datatype color = Red | Blue | Green;
datatype color = Blue | Green | Red
```

The compiler output, which looks just like the ML input code, indicates that the three elements of type color are Blue, Green, and Red. Technically, values Blue, Green, and Red are called *constructors*. They are called constructors because they are the ways of constructing values with type color.

Example. A Tagged Union Data Type: ML constructors can be declared so that they must be applied to arguments when constructing elements of the data type. Constructors do not actually do anything to their arguments, other than to "tag" their arguments so that values constructed in different ways can be distinguished by pattern matching.

Suppose we are keeping student records, with names of B.S. students, names and undergraduate institutions of M.S. students, and names and faculty supervisors of Ph.D. students. Then we could define a type student that allows these three forms of tuples as follows:

— datatype student = BS of name | MS of name*school | PhD of name*faculty;

In this data-type declaration, BS, MS, and PhD are each constructors. However, unlike in the color example, each student constructor must be applied to arguments to construct a value of type student. We must apply BS to a name, MS to a pair consisting of a name and a school, and PhD to a pair consisting of a name and a faculty name in order to produce a value of type student.

In effect, the type student is the union of three types,

student ≈ union {name, name*school, name*faculty }

except that in ML "unions" (which are defined by datatype), each value of the union is tagged by a constructor that tells which of the constituent types the value comes from. This is illustrated in the following function, which returns the name of a student:

```
— fun name(BS(n)) = n
   |   name(MS(n,s)) = n
   |   name(PhD(n,f)) = n;
val name = fn : student → name
```

The first three lines are the declaration of the function name, and the last line is the compiler output indicating that name is a function from students to names. The function has three clauses, one for each form of student.

Example. A Recursive Type: Data-type declaration may be recursive in that the type name may appear in one or more of the constructor argument types. Because of the way type recursion is implemented, ML data type provides a convenient, high-level language construct that hides a common form of routine pointer manipulation.

The set of trees with integer labels at the leaves may be defined mathematically as follows:

A *tree* is either

a leaf, with an associated integer label, or

a compound tree, consisting of a left subtree and a right subtree.

This definition can be expressed as an ML data-type declaration, with each part of the definition corresponding to a clause of the data-type declaration:

```
datatype tree = LEAF of int | NODE of (tree * tree);
```

The identifiers LEAF and NODE are constructors, and the elements of the data type are all values that can be produced by the application of constructors to legal (type-correct) arguments. In words, a tree is either the result of applying the constructor LEAF to an integer (signifying a leaf with that integer label) or the result of applying the constructor NODE to two trees. These two trees, of course, must be produced similarly with constructors LEAF and NODE.

The following function shows how the constructors may be used to define a function on trees:

```
— fun inTree(x, LEAF(y)) = x = y
    |    inTree(x, NODE(y,z)) = inTree(x, y) orelse inTree(x, z);
val inTree = fn : int * tree → bool
```

This function looks for a specific integer value x in a tree. If the tree has the form LEAF(y), then x is in the tree only if x=y. If the tree has the form NODE(y,z), with subtrees y and z, then x is in the tree only if x is in the subtree y or the subtree z. The type output by the compiler shows that inTree is a function that, given an integer and a tree, returns a Boolean value.

An example of a polymorphic data-type declaration appears in Subsection 6.5.3, after the discussion of polymorphism in Section 6.4.

5.4.5 ML Reference Cells and Assignment

None of the ML constructs discussed in earlier sections of this chapter have side effects. Each expression has a value, but evaluating an expression does not have the side effect of changing the value of any other expression. Although most large ML programs are written in a style that avoids side effects when possible, most large ML programs do use assignment occasionally to change the value of a variable.

The way that assignable variables are presented in ML is different from the way that assignable variables appear in other programming languages. The main reasons for this are to preserve the uniformity of ML as a programming language and to separate side effects from pure expressions as much as possible.

ML assignment is restricted to reference cells. In ML, a reference cell has a different type than immutable values such as integers, strings, lists, and so on. Because reference cells have specific reference types, restrictions on ML assignment are enforced as part of the type system. This is part of the elegance of ML: Almost all restrictions on the structure of programs are part of the type system, and the type system has a systematic, uniform definition.

L-values and R-values

Before looking at assignment in ML, let us think about the difference between memory locations and their contents. This distinction is part of machine architectures (memory locations contain data) and relevant to many programming languages. The following pseudocode fragment illustrates the idea:

```
x : int;
y : int;
x := y + 3;
```

In the assignment, the *value* stored in variable y is added to 3 and the result stored in the *location* for x. The central point is that the two variables are used differently. The command uses only the value stored in y and does not depend on the location of y. In contrast, the command uses the location of x, but does not depend on the value stored in x before the assignment occurs.

The location of a variable is called its *L-value*, and the value stored in this location is called the *R-value* of the variable. This is standard terminology that you will see in many books on programming languages. The two values are called L and R to stand for left and right, as typically we use L-values on the left-hand sides of an assignment statement and R-values on the right-hand side.

ML Reference Cells

In ML, L-values and R-values have different types. In other words, an assignable region of memory has a different type than a value that cannot be changed. In ML, an L-value, or assignable region of memory, is called a *reference cell*. The type of a reference cell indicates that it is a reference cell and specifies the type of value that it contains. For example, a reference cell that contains an integer has type int ref, meaning an integer reference cell.

When a reference cell is created, it must be initialized to a value of the correct type. Therefore ML does not have uninitialized variables or dangling pointers. When an assignment changes the value stored in a reference cell, the assignment must be consistent with the type of the reference cell: An integer reference cell will always contain an integer, a list reference cell will always contain (or refer to) a list, and so on.

Operations on Reference Cells

ML has operations to create reference cells, to access their contents, and to change their contents. These are ref, !, and :=, which behave as follows:

```
ref v   — creates a reference cell containing value v
! r     — returns the value contained in reference cell r
r := v  — places value v in reference cell r
```

Here are some examples:

```
— val x = ref 0;
val x = ref 0 : int ref
— x := 3*(!x) + 5;
val it = () : unit
— !x;
val it = 5 : int
```

The first input line binds identifier x to a new reference cell with contents 0. As the compiler output indicates, the value of x is this reference cell, which has type int ref. The next input line multiplies 3 times the contents of x, adds 5, and stores the resulting integer value in cell x. Because ML is expression oriented, this "statement" is an ML expression. The type of this expression is unit, which, as described earlier, is the type used for expressions that are evaluated for side effect. The last input line is an expression reading the contents of x, which is the integer 5.

Because ML does not have any operations for computing the address of a value, there is no way to observe whether assignment is by value or by pointer. As a result, it is a convenient and accurate abstraction to regard a reference cell as a box holding a value of any size and to regard assignment as an operation that places a value inside the box. For example, the preceding code that creates a reference cell named x and changes its contents can be visualized as follows, with the double arrow indicating changes as a result of assignment:

Because reference cells can be created for any type of value, we can define a string reference cell and change its contents by assignment:

```
— val y = ref "Apple";
val y = ref "Apple" : string ref
— y := "Fried green tomatoes";
val it = () : unit
— !y;
val it = "Fried green tomatoes" : string
```

As in the integer example, the associated reference cell can be visualized as a box that can contain any string:

As you know, different strings may require different amounts of memory. Therefore, it does not seem likely that the memory cell bound to y can hold any string of any length.

In fact, when the declaration val y = ref "Apple" is processed, storage is allocated to contain the string "Apple" and the reference cell y is initialized to a pointer to this location. When the assignment y := "Fried green tomatoes" is executed, the contents of the cell y are changed to a pointer to "Fried green tomatoes". Comparing the integer and string examples, ML assignment is implemented as ordinary value assignment for some types of cells and pointer assignment for others. However, because ML has no way of finding the address of an expression, this implementation difference is completely hidden from the programmer. If a compiler writer wanted to implement integer assignment as pointer assignment, all programs would behave in exactly the same way.

Here is one last simple code example to show how ML reference cells may be used in an iterative loop. This loop sums the numbers between 1 and 10:

```
val i = ref 0;
val j = ref 0;
while !i < 10 do (i := !i + 1;j := !j + !i);
!j;
```

In the first two lines, the identifiers i and j are bound to new reference cells initialized to value 0. The while loop increments i until !i, the contents of i, is not less than 10. The final expression reveals the final value of j, because the compiler prints the value of !j. Some important details are that a test i < 10 would not be legal, as this compares a reference cell to an integer. Similarly, i := i+1 is not legal as a reference cell cannot be added to 1; only integers or real numbers can be added.

As illustrated in this example, two imperative expressions can be combined with a semicolon. Parentheses are used to keep the preceding while loop from parsing as a loop followed by j := !j+i. In fact, a semicolon can be used to combine any two expressions. The expression

```
e1; e2
```

is equivalent to

```
(fn x => e2) e1
```

where x is chosen not to appear in e2. As a result, the value of e1; e2 is the value of e2 after e1 has been evaluated.

Typing Imperative Operations. As previously mentioned, reference cells have a different type than the values they contain. Here is the typing rule:

If expression e has type τ, then the expression ref e has type τ ref.

The function ! can be applied to any argument of type τ ref, and assignment x := e is type correct only if x has type τ ref and e has type τ for some type τ. In summary,

---

x : int   — not assignable (like a constant in other languages)
y : int ref — assignable reference cell

5.4.6 ML Summary

ML is a programming language that encourages programming with functions. It is easy to define functions with function arguments and function return results. In addition, most data structures in ML programs are not assignable. Although it is possible to construct reference cells for any type of value and modify reference cells by assignment, side effects occur only when reference cells are used. Although most large ML programs do use reference cells and have side effects, the pure parts of ML are expressive enough that reference cells are used sparingly.

ML has an expressive type system. There are basic types for many common kinds of computable values, such as Booleans, integers, strings, and reals. There are also *type constructors*, which are type operators that can be applied to any type. The type constructors include tuples, records, and lists. In ML, it is possible to define tuples of lists of functions, for example. There is no restriction on the types of values that can be placed in data structures.

The ML type system is often called a *strong type system*, as every expression has a type and there are no mechanisms for subverting the type system. When the ML type checker determines that an expression has type int, for example, then any successful evaluation of that expression is guaranteed to produce an integer. There are no dangling pointers that refer to unallocated locations in memory and no casts that allow values of one type to be treated as values of another type without conversion.

ML has several forms that allow programmers to define their own types and type constructors. In this chapter, we looked at data-type declarations, which can be used to define ML versions of enumerated types (types consisting of a finite list of values), disjoint unions (types whose elements are drawn from the union of two or more types), and recursively defined types. Another important aspect of the ML type system is polymorphism, which we will study in the next chapter, along with other aspects of the ML type system. We will discuss additional type definition and module forms in Chapter 9.

5.5 CHAPTER SUMMARY

In this chapter, we discussed some of the basic properties of Algol-like languages and examined some of the advances and problem areas in Algol 60, Algol 68, Pascal, and C. The Algol family of languages established the command-oriented syntax, with blocks, local declarations, and recursive functions, that are used in most current programming languages. The Algol family of languages is all statically typed, as each expression has a type that is determined by its syntactic form and the compiler checks before running the program to make sure that the types of operations and operands agree. In looking at the improvements from Algol 60 to Algol 68 to Pascal, we saw improvements in the static type systems.

The C programming language is similar to Algol 60, Algol 68, and Pascal in some respects: command-oriented syntax, blocks, local declarations, and recursive functions. However, C also shares some features with its untyped precursor BCPL, such as pointer arithmetic. C is also more restricted than most Algol-based languages in that functions cannot be declared inside nested blocks: All functions are declared outside the main program. This simplifies storage management for C, as we will see in Chapter 7.

In the second half of this chapter, we looked at the ML programming language in more detail than we did the Algol family of languages. One reason to study ML is that this language combines many if the important features of the Algol family with features of Lisp; this language provides a good summary of the important language features that developed before 1980.

The part of ML that we covered in this chapter comes from what is called *core ML*. This is ML without the module features that were added in the 1980s. Core ML has the following types,

unit, Booleans, integers, strings, reals, tuples, lists, records
and the following constructs
patterns, declarations, functions, polymorphism, overloading, type declarations, reference cells, exceptions
We discussed most of these in this chapter, except polymorphism, which is covered in Chapter 6, and exceptions, which are studied in Chapter 8. The study of ML was summarized in this chapter in Subsection 5.4.6.

EXERCISES

5.1 Algol 60 Procedure Types

In Algol 60, the type of each formal parameter of a procedure must be given. However, *proc* is considered a type (the type of procedures). This is much simpler than the ML types of function arguments. However, this is really a type loophole; because calls to procedure parameters are not fully type checked, Algol 60 programs may produce run-time type errors.

Write a procedure declaration for Q that causes the following program fragment to produce a run-time type error:

```
proc P (proc Q)
    begin Q(true) end;
P(Q);
```

where true is a Boolean value. Explain why the procedure is statically type correct, but produces a run-time type error. (You may assume that adding a Boolean to an integer is a run-time type error.)

5.2 Algol 60 Pass-By-Name

The following Algol 60 code declares a procedure P with one pass-by-name integer parameter. Explain how the procedure call P(A[i]) changes the values of i and A by substituting the actual parameters for the formal parameters, according to the Algol

60 copy rule. What integer values are printed by tprogram? By using pass-by-name parameter passing?

The line integer x does not declare local variables – this is just Algol 60 syntax declaring the type of the procedure parameter:

```
begin
    integer i;
    integer array A[1:2];

    procedure P(x);
        integer x;
        begin
            i := x;
            x := i
        end

    i := 1;
    A[1] := 2; A[2] := 3;
    P (A[i]);
    print (i, A[1], A[2])
end
```

5.3 Nonlinear Pattern Matching

ML patterns cannot contain repeated variables. This exercise explores this language design decision.

A declaration with a single pattern is equivalent to a sequence of declarations using destructors. For example,

```
val p = (5,2);
val (x,y) = p;
```

is equivalent to

```
val p = (5,2);
val x = #1(p);
val y = #2(p);
```

where #1(p) is the ML expression for the first component of pair p and #2 similarly returns the second component of a pair. The operations #1 and #2 are called *destructors* for pairs.

A function declaration with more than one pattern is equivalent to a function declaration that uses standard if-then-else and destructors. For example,

```
fun f nil = 0
  |   f (x::y) = x;
```

is equivalent to

```
fun f(z) = if z=nil then 0 else hd(z);
```

where hd is the ML function that returns the first element of a list.
Questions:

(a) Write a function declaration that does not use pattern matching and that is equivalent to

```
fun f (x,0) = x
|    f (0,y) = y
|    f (x,y) = x+y;
```

ML pattern matching is applied in order, so that when this function is applied to an argument (a, b), the first clause is used if b = 0, the second clause if b≠0 and a=0, and the third clause if b≠0 and a≠0.

(b) Does the method you used in part (a), combining destructors and if-then-else, work for this function?

```
fun eq(x,x) = true
|    eq(x,y) = false;
```

(c) How would you translate ML functions that contain patterns with repeated variables into functions without patterns? Give a brief explanation of a general method and show the result for the function eq in part (b).

(d) Why do you think the designers of ML prohibited repeated variables in patterns? (*Hint:* If f, g : int → int, then the expression f = g is not type-correct ML as the test for equality is not defined on function types.)

5.4 ML Map for Trees

(a) The binary tree data type

```
datatype 'a tree = LEAF of 'a |
                  NODE of 'a tree * 'a tree;
```

describes a binary tree for any type, but does not include the empty tree (i.e., each tree of this type must have at least a root node).

Write a function maptree that takes a function as an argument and returns a function that maps trees to trees by mapping the values at the leaves to new values, using the function passed in as a parameter. In more detail, if f is a function that can be applied to the leaves of tree t and t is the tree on the left, then maptree f t should result in the tree on the right:

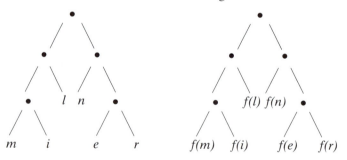

For example, if f is the function fun f(x)=x+1 then

maptree f (NODE(NODE(LEAF 1,LEAF 2),LEAF 3))

should evaluate to NODE(NODE(LEAF 2,LEAF 3),LEAF 4). Explain your definition in one or two sentences.

(b) What is the type ML gives to your function? Why is it not the expected type ('a → 'a) → 'a tree → 'a tree?

5.5 ML Reduce for Trees

Assume that the data type tree is defined as in problem 4. Write a function

$$\text{reduce} : ('a * 'a \to 'a) \to 'a\ \text{tree} \to 'a$$

that combines all the values of the leaves by using the binary operation passed as a parameter. In more detail, if oper : $'a * 'a \to 'a$ and t is the nonempty tree on the left in this picture,

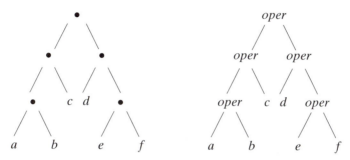

then reduce oper t should be the result we obtain by evaluating the tree on the right. For example, if f is the function,

```
fun f(x : int, y : int) = x + y;
```

then reduce f(NODE(NODE(LEAF 1, LEAF 2), LEAF 3)) $= (1 + 2) + 3 = 6$. Explain your definition of reduce in one or two sentences.

5.6 Currying

This problem asks you to show that the ML types $'a \to ('b \to 'c)$ and $('a * 'b) \to 'c$ are essentially equivalent.

(a) Define higher-order ML functions

$$\text{Curry: } (('a * 'b) \to 'c) \to ('a \to ('b \to 'c))$$

and

$$\text{UnCurry: } ('a \to ('b \to 'c)) \to (('a * 'b) \to 'c)$$

(b) For all functions f : $('a * 'b) \to 'c$ and g : $'a \to ('b \to 'c)$, the following two equalities should hold (if you wrote the right functions):

```
UnCurry(Curry(f)) = f
Curry(UnCurry(g)) = g
```

Explain why each is true for the functions you have written. Your answer can be three or four sentences long. Try to give the main idea in a clear, succinct way. (We are more interested in insight than in number of words.) Be sure to consider termination behavior as well.

5.7 Disjoint Unions

A *union type* is a type that allows the values from two different types to be combined in a single type. For example, an expression of type union(A, B) might have a value of type A or a value of type B. The languages C and ML both have forms of union types.

(a) Here is a C program fragment written with a union type:

```
...
union IntString {
    int i;
    char *s;
} x;
int y;
if ( ... ) x.i = 3 else x.s = "here, fido";
...
y = (x.i) + 5;
...
```

A C compiler will consider this program to be well typed. Despite the fact that the program type checks, the addition may not work as intended. Why not? Will the run-time system catch the problem?

(b) In ML, a union type union(A,B) would be written in the form datatype UnionAB = tag_a of A | tag_b of B and the preceding if statement could be written as

```
datatype IntString = tag_int of int | tag_str of string;
...
val x = if ... then tag_int(3) else tag_str("here, fido");
...
let val tag_int (m) = x in m + 5 end;
```

Can the same bug occur in this program? Will the run-time system catch the problem? The use of tags enables the compiler to give a useful warning message to the programmer, thereby helping the programmer to avoid the bug, even before running the program. What message is given and how does it help?

5.8 Lazy Evaluation and Functions

It is possible to evaluate function arguments at the time of the call (*eager evaluation*) or at the time they are used (*lazy evaluation*). Most programming languages (including ML) use eager evaluation, but we can simulate lazy evaluation in an eager language such as ML by using higher-order functions.

Consider a *sequence* data structure that starts with a known value and continues with a function (known as a *thunk*) to compute the rest of the sequence:

```
— datatype 'a Seq = Nil
                  | Cons of 'a * (unit -> 'a Seq);

— fun head (Cons (x, _)) = x;
val head = fn : 'a Seq -> 'a

— fun tail (Cons (_, xs)) = xs();
val tail = fn : 'a Seq -> 'a Seq

— fun BadCons (x, xs) = Cons (x, fn() =>xs);
val BadCons = fn : 'a * 'a Seq -> 'a Seq
```

Note that BadCons does not actually work, as xs was already evaluated on entering the function. Instead of calling BadCons(x, xs), you would need to use Cons(x, fn() =>xs) for lazy evaluation.

This lazy sequence data type provides a way to create infinite sequences, with each infinite sequence represented by a function that computes the next element in the sequence. For example, here is the sequence of infinitely many 1s:

```
— val ones = let fun f() = Cons(1,f) in f() end;
```

We can see how this works by defining a function that gets the *n*th element of a sequence and by looking at some elements of our infinite sequence:

```
— fun get(n,s) = if n=0 then head(s) else get(n-1,tail(s));
val get = fn : int * 'a Seq -> 'a
— get(0,ones);
val it = 1 : int
— get(5,ones);
val it = 1 : int
— get(245, ones);
val it = 1 : int
```

We can define the infinite sequence of all natural numbers by

```
— val natseq = let fun f(n)() = Cons(n,f(n+1)) in f(0) () end;
```

Using sequences, we can represent a function as a potentially infinite sequence of ordered pairs. Here are two examples, written as infinite lists instead of as ML code (note that $\sim$ is a negative sign in ML):

$$add1 = (0, 1) :: (\sim 1, 0) :: (1, 2) :: (\sim 2, \sim 1) :: (2, 3) :: \ldots$$
$$double = (0, 0) :: (\sim 1, \sim 2) :: (1, 2) :: (\sim 2, \sim 4) :: (2, 4) :: \ldots$$

Here is ML code that constructs the infinite sequences and tests this representation of functions by applying the sequences of ordered pairs to sample function arguments.

```
— fun make_ints(f)=
     let
        fun make_pos (n) = Cons( (n, f(n)), fn()=>make_pos(n + 1))
        fun make_neg (n) = Cons( (n, f(n)), fn()=>make_neg(n - 1))
     in
        merge (make_pos (0), make_neg(~1))
     end;
val make_ints = fn : (int -> 'a) -> (int * 'a) Seq

— val add1 = make_ints (fn(x) => x+1);
val add1 = Cons ((0,1),fn) : (int * int) Seq

— val double = make_ints (fn(x) => 2*x);
val double = Cons ((0,0),fn) : (int * int) Seq

— fun apply (Cons( (x1,fx1), xs) , x2) =
     if (x1=x2) then fx1
        else apply(xs(), x2);
val apply = fn : (''a * 'b) Seq * ''a -> 'b

— apply(add1, ~4);
val it = ~3 : int
```

— apply(double, 7);
val it = 14 : int

(a) Write *merge* in ML. Merge should take two sequences and return a sequence containing the values in the original sequences, as used in the make_ints function.

(b) Using the representation of functions as a potentially infinite sequence of ordered pairs, write *compose* in ML. Compose should take a function f and a function g and return a function h such that $h(x) = f(g(x))$.

(c) It is possible to represent a partial function whose domain is not the entire set of integers as a sequence. Under what conditions will your *compose* function not halt? Is this acceptable?

6

Type Systems and Type Inference

Programming involves a wide range of computational constructs, such as data structures, functions, objects, communication channels, and threads of control. Because programming languages are designed to help programmers organize computational constructs and use them correctly, many programming languages organize data and computations into collections called types. In this chapter, we look at the reasons for using types in programming languages, methods for type checking, and some typing issues such as polymorphism, overloading, and type equality. A large section of this chapter is devoted to type inference, the process of determining the types of expressions based on the known types of some symbols that appear in them. Type inference is a generalization of type checking, with many characteristics in common, and a representative example of the kind of algorithms that are used in compilers and programming environments to determine properties of programs. Type inference also provides an introduction to polymorphism, which allows a single expression to have many types.

6.1 TYPES IN PROGRAMMING

In general, a *type* is a collection of computational entities that share some common property. Some examples of types are the type int of integers, the type int→int of functions from integers to integers, and the Pascal subrange type [1 .. 100] of integers between 1 and 100. In concurrent ML there is the type int channel of communication channels carrying integer values and, in Java, a hierarchy of types of exceptions.

There are three main uses of types in programming languages:

- naming and organizing concepts,
- making sure that bit sequences in computer memory are interpreted consistently,
- providing information to the compiler about data manipulated by the program.

These ideas are elaborated in the following subsections.

Although some programming language descriptions will say things like, "Lisp is an untyped language," there is really no such thing as an untyped programming language. In Lisp, for example, lists and atoms are two different types: list operations can be applied to lists but not to atoms. Programming languages do vary a great deal, however, in the ways that types are used in the syntax and semantics (implementation) of the language.

6.1.1 Program Organization and Documentation

A well-designed program uses concepts related to the problem being solved. For example, a banking program will be organized around concepts common to banks, such as accounts, customers, deposits, withdrawals, and transfers. In modern programming languages, customers and accounts, for example, can be represented as separate types. Type checking can then check to make sure that accounts and customers are treated separately, with account operations applied to accounts but not used to manipulate customers. Using types to organize a program makes it easier for someone to read, understand, and maintain the program. Types therefore serve an important purpose in documenting the design and intent of the program.

An important advantage of type information, in comparison with comments written by a programmer, is that types may be checked by the programming language compiler. Type checking guarantees that the types written into a program are correct. In contrast, many programs contain incorrect comments, either because the person writing the explanation was careless or because the program was later changed but the comments were not.

6.1.2 Type Errors

A *type error* occurs when a computational entity, such as a function or a data value, is used in a manner that is inconsistent with the concept it represents. For example, if an integer value is used as a function, this is a type error. A common type error is to apply an operation to an operand of the wrong type. For example, it is a type error to use integer addition to add a string to an integer. Although most programmers have a general understanding of type errors, there are some subtleties that are worth exploring.

Hardware Errors. The simplest kind of type error to understand is a machine instruction that results in a hardware error. For example, executing a "function call"

```
x()
```

is a type error if x is not a function. If x is an integer variable with value 256, for example, then executing x() will cause the machine to jump to location 256 and begin executing the instructions stored at that place in memory. If location 256 contains data that do not represent a valid machine instruction, this will cause a hardware interrupt. Another example of a hardware type error occurs in executing an operation

```
float_add(3, 4.5)
```

where the hardware floating-point unit is invoked on an integer argument 3. Because the bit pattern used to represent 3 does not represent a floating-point number in the form expected by the floating-point hardware, this instruction will cause a hardware interrupt.

Unintended Semantics. Some type errors do not cause a hardware fault or interrupt because compiled code does not contain the same information as the program source code does. For example, an operation

```
int_add(3, 4.5)
```

is a type error, as int_add is an integer operation and is applied here to a floating-point number. Most hardware would perform this operation. Because the bits used to represent the floating-point number 4.5 represent an integer that is not mathematically related to 4.5, the operation it is not meaningful. More specifically, int_add is intended to perform addition, but the result of int_add(3, 4.5) is not the arithmetic sum of the two operands.

The error associated with int_add(3, 4.5) may become clearer if we think about how a program might apply integer addition to a floating-point argument. To be concrete, suppose a program defines a function f that adds three to its argument,

```
fun f(x) = 3+x;
```

and someplace within the scope of this definition we also declare a floating-point value z:

```
float z = 4.5;
```

If the programming language compiler or interpreter allows the call f(z) and the language does not automatically convert floating-point numbers to integers in this situation, then the function call f(z) will cause a run-time type error because int_add(3, 4.5) will be executed. This is a type error because integer addition is applied to a noninteger argument.

The reason why many people find the concept of type error confusing is that type errors generally depend on the concepts defined in a program or programming language, not the way that programs are executed on the underlying hardware. To be specific, it is just as much of a type error to apply an integer operation to a floating-point argument as it is to apply a floating-point operation to an integer argument. It does not matter which causes a hardware interrupt on any particular computer.

Inside a computer, all values are stored as sequences of bytes of bits. Because integers and floating-point numbers are stored as four bytes on many machines, some integers and floating-point numbers overlap; a single bit pattern may represent an integer when it is used one way and a floating-point number when it is used another. Nonetheless, a type error occurs when a pattern that is stored in the computer for the purpose of representing one type of value is used as the representation of another type of value.

6.1.3 Types and Optimization

Type information in programs can be used for many kinds of optimizations. One example is finding components of records (as they are called in Pascal and ML) or structs (as they are called in C). The component-finding problem also arises in object-oriented languages. A record consists of a set of entries of different types. For example, a student record may contain a student name of type string and a student number of type integer. In a program that also has records for undergraduate students, these might be represented as related type that also contains a field for the year in school of the student. Both types are written here as ML-style type expressions:

Student = {name : string, number : int}
Undergrad = {name : string, number : int, year : int}

In a program that manipulates records, there might be an expression of the form r.name, meaning the name field of the record r. A compiler must generate machine code that, given the location of record r in memory at run time, finds the location of the field name of this record at run time. If the compiler can compute the type of the record at compile time, then this type information can be used to generate efficient code. More specifically, the type of r makes it is possible to compute the location of r.name relative to the location r, at compile time. For example, if the type of r is Student, then the compiler can build a little table storing the information that name occurs before number in each Student record. Using this table, the compiler can determine that name is in the first location allocated to the record r. In this case, the expression r.name is compiled to code that reads the value stored in location r+1 (if location r is used for something else besides the first field). However, for records of a different type, the name field might appear second or third. Therefore, if the type of r is not known at compile time, the compiler must generate code to compute the location of name from the location of r at run time. This will make the program run more slowly. To summarize: Some operations can be computed more efficiently if the type of the operand is known at compile time.

In some object-oriented programming languages, the type of an object may be used to find the relative location of parts of the object. In other languages, however, the type system does not give this kind of information and run-time search must be used.

6.2 TYPE SAFETY AND TYPE CHECKING

6.2.1 Type Safety

A programming language is *type safe* if no program is allowed to violate its type distinctions. Sometimes it is not completely clear what the type distinctions are in a specific programming language. However, there are some type distinctions that are meaningful and important in all languages. For example, a function has a different type from an integer. Therefore, any language that allows integers to be used as functions is not type safe. Another action that we always consider a type error is to access memory that is not allocated to the program.

The following table characterizes the type safety of some common programming languages. We will discuss each form of type error listed in the table in turn.

Safety	Example languages	Explanation
Not safe	C and C++	Type casts, pointer arithmetic
Almost safe	Pascal	Explicit deallocation; dangling pointers
Safe	Lisp, ML, Smalltalk, Java	Complete type checking

Type Casts. Type casts allow a value of one type to be used as another type. In C in particular, an integer can be cast to a function, allowing a jump to a location that does not contain the correct form of instructions to be a C function.

Pointer Arithmetic. C pointer arithmetic is not type safe. The expression *(p+i) has type A if p is defined to have type A*. Because the value stored in location p+i might have any type, an assignment like x = *(p+i) may store a value of one type into a variable of another type and therefore may cause a type error.

Explicit Deallocation and Dangling Pointers. In Pascal, C, and some other languages, the location reached through a pointer may be deallocated (freed) by the programmer. This creates a *dangling pointer*, a pointer that points to a location that is not allocated to the program. If p is a pointer to an integer, for example, then after we deallocate the memory referenced by p, the program can allocate new memory to store another type of value. This new memory may be reachable through the old pointer p, as the storage allocation algorithm may reuse space that has been freed. The old pointer p allows us to treat the new memory as an integer value, as p still has type int. This violates type safety. Pascal is considered "mostly safe" because this is the only violation of type safety (after the variant record and other original type problems are repaired).

6.2.2 Compile-Time and Run-Time Checking

In many languages, type checking is used to prevent some or all type errors. Some languages use type constraints in the definition of legal program. Implementations of these languages check types at compile time, before a program is started. In these languages, a program that violates a type constraint is not compiled and cannot be run. In other languages, checks for type errors are made while the program is running.

Run-Time Checking. In programming languages with run-time type checking, the compiler generates code so that, when an operation is performed, the code checks to make sure that the operands have the correct type. For example, the Lisp language operation car returns the first element of a cons cell. Because it is a type error to apply car to something that is not a cons cell, Lisp programs are implemented so that, before (car x) is evaluated, a check is made to make sure that x is a cons cell. An advantage of run-time type checking is that it catches type errors. A disadvantage is the run-time cost associated with making these checks.

Compile-Time Checking. Many modern programming languages are designed so that it is possible to check expressions for potential type errors. In these languages, it is common to reject programs that do not pass the compile-time type checks. An advantage of compile-time type checking is that it catches errors earlier than run-time checking does: A program developer is warned about the error before the program is given to other users or shipped as a product. Because compile-time checks may eliminate the need to check for certain errors at run time, compile-time checking can make it possible to produce more efficient code. For a specific example, compiled ML code is two to four times faster than Lisp code. The primary reason for this speed increase is that static type checking of ML programs greatly reduces the need for run-time tests.

Conservativity of Compile-Time Checking. A property of compile-time type checking is that the compiler must be conservative. This mean that compile-time type checking will find all statements and expressions that produce run-time type errors, but also may flag statements or expressions as errors even if they do not produce run-time errors. To be more specific about it, most checkers are both sound and conservative. A type checker is sound if no programs with errors are considered correct. A type checker is conservative if some programs without errors are still considered to have errors.

There is a reason why most type checkers are conservative: For any Turing-complete programming language, the set of programs that may produce a run-time type error is undecidable. This follows from the undecidability of the halting problem. To see why, consider the following form of program expression:

```
if (complicated-expression-that-could-run-forever)
    then (expression-with-type-error)
    else (expression-with-type-error)
```

It is undecidable whether this expression causes a run-time type error, as the only way for expression-with-type-error to be evaluated is for complicated-expression-that-could-run-forever to halt. Therefore, deciding whether this expression causes a run-time type error involves deciding whether complicated-expression-that-could-run-forever halts.

Because the set of programs that have run-time type errors is undecidable, no compile-time type checker can find type errors exactly. Because the purpose of type checking is to prevent errors, type checkers for type-safe languages are conservative. It is useful that type checkers find type errors, and a consequence of the undecidability of the halting problem is that some programs that could execute without run-time error will fail the compile-time type-checking tests.

The main trade-offs between compile-time and run-time checking are summarized in the following table.

Form of Type Checking	Advantages	Disadvantages
Run-time	Prevents type errors	Slows program execution
Compile-time	Prevents type errors	May restrict programming
	Eliminates run-time tests	because tests are
	Finds type errors *before*	*conservative.*
	execution and run-time	
	tests	

Combining Compile-Time and Run-Time Checking. Most programming languages actually use some combination of compile-time and run-time type checking. In Java, for example, static type checking is used to distinguish arrays from integers, but array bounds errors (which are a form of type error) are checked at run time.

6.3 TYPE INFERENCE

Type inference is the process of determining the types of expressions based on the known types of some symbols that appear in them. The difference between type inference and compile-time type checking is really a matter of degree. A *type-checking* algorithm goes through the program to check that the types declared by the programmer agree with the language requirements. In *type inference*, the idea is that some information is not specified, and some form of logical inference is required for determining the types of identifiers from the way they are used. For example, identifiers in ML are not usually declared to have a specific type. The type system *infers* the types of ML identifiers and expressions that contain them from the operations that are used. Type inference was invented by Robin Milner (see the biographical sketch) for the ML programming language. Similar ideas were developed independently by Curry and Hindley in connection with the study of lambda calculus.

Although practical type inference was developed for ML, type inference can be applied to a variety of programming languages. For example, type inference could, in principle, be applied to C or other programming languages. We study type inference in some detail because it illustrates the central issues in type checking and because type inference illustrates some of the central issues in algorithms that find any kind of program errors.

In addition to providing a flexible form of compile-time type checking, ML type inference supports polymorphism. As we will see when we subsequently look at the type-inference algorithm, the type-inference algorithm uses *type variables* as placeholders for types that are not known. In some cases, the type-inference algorithm resolves all type variables and determines that they must be equal to specific types such as int, bool, or string. In other cases, the type of a function may contain type variables that are not constrained by the way the function is defined. In these cases, the function may be applied to any arguments whose types match the form given by a type expression containing type variables.

Although type inference and polymorphism are independent concepts, we discuss polymorphism in the context of type inference because polymorphism arises naturally from the way type variables are used in type inference.

6.3.1 First Examples of Type Inference

Here are two ML type-inference examples to give you some feel for how ML type inference works. The behavior of the type-inference algorithm is explained only superficially in these examples, just to give some of the main ideas. We will go through the type inference process in detail in Subsection 6.3.2.

Example 6.1

```
- fun f1(x) = x + 2;
val f1 = fn : int → int
```

The function f1 adds 2 to its argument. In ML, 2 is an integer constant; the real number 2 would be written as 2.0. The operator + is overloaded; it can be either integer addition or real addition. In this function, however, it must be integer addition because 2 is an integer. Therefore, the function argument x must be an integer. Putting these observations together, we can see that f1 must have type int → int.

Example 6.2

```
- fun f2(g,h) = g(h(0));
val f2 = fn : ('a → 'b) * (int → 'a) → 'b
```

The type ('a → 'b) * (int → 'a) → 'b inferred by the compiler is parsed as (('a → 'b) * (int → 'a)) → 'b.

The type-inference algorithm figures out that, because h is applied to an integer argument, h must be a function from int to something. The algorithm represents "something" by introducing a type variable, which is written as 'a. (This is unrelated to Lisp 'a, which would be syntax for a Lisp atom, not a variable.) The type-inference algorithm then deduces that g must be a function that takes whatever h returns (something of type 'a) and then returns something else. Because g is not constrained to return the same type of value as h, the algorithm represents this second something by a new type variable, 'b. Putting the types of h and g together, we can see that the first argument to f2 has type ('a → 'b) and the second has type (int → 'a). Function f2 takes the pair of these two functions as an argument and returns the same type of value as g returns. Therefore, the type of f2 is (('a → 'b) * (int → 'a)) → 'b, as shown in the preceding compiler output.

6.3.2 Type-Inference Algorithm

The ML type-inference algorithm uses the following three steps:

1. A assign a type to the expression and each subexpression. For any compound expression or variable, use a type variable. For known operations or constants, such as + or 3, use the type that is known for this symbol.
2. Generates a set of constraints on types, using the parse tree of the expression. These constraints reflect the fact that if a function is applied to an argument, for example, then the type of the argument must equal the type of the domain of the function.
3. Solve these constraints by means of unification, which is a substitution-based algorithm for solving systems of equations. (More information on unification appears in the chapter on logic programming.)

The type-inference algorithm is explained by a series of examples. These examples present the following issues:

- explanation of the algorithm
- a polymorphic function definition
- application of a polymorphic function
- a recursive function
- a function with multiple clauses
- type inference indicates a program error

Altogether, these six examples should give you a good understanding of the type-inference algorithm, except for the interaction between type inference and overloading. The interaction between overloading and type inference is not covered in this book.

Example 6.3 Explanation of the Algorithm

We can see how the type-inference algorithm works by considering this example function:

```
- fun g(x) = 5 + x;
val g = fn : int → int
```

The easiest way to see how the algorithm works is by drawing the parse tree of the expression. We use an abbreviated form of parse tree that lists only the symbols that occur in the expression, together with the symbol @ for an application of a function to an argument. For the preceding expression we use the following graph. This is a form of parse tree, together with a special edge indicating the binding lambda for each bound variable. Here, the link from x to λ indicates that x is lambda bound at the beginning of the expression:

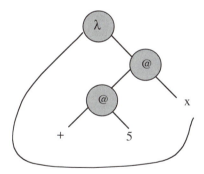

We use this graph to follow our type-inference steps:

1. We assign a type to the expression and each subexpression:

We illustrate this step by redrawing the graph, writing a type next to each node. To simplify notation, we use single letters *r, s, t, u, v,* . . . , for type variables instead of ML syntax 'a, 'b, and so on:

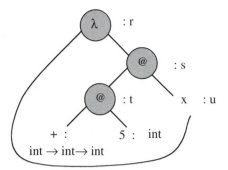

Recall that each node in a parse tree represents a subexpression. Repeating the information in the picture, the following table lists the subexpressions and their types:

Subexpression	Type
$\lambda x.\ ((+\ 5)\ x)$	r
$((+\ 5)\ x)$	s
$(+\ 5)$	t
$+$	int $\rightarrow$ (int $\rightarrow$ int)
5	int
x	u

Here we have written addition (+) as a Curried function and have chosen type int $\rightarrow$ int $\rightarrow$ int for this operation. The prefix notation for addition is not ML syntax, of course, but it is used here to make the pictures simpler. As we saw earlier, + can either be integer addition or real-number addition. Here we can see from context that integer addition is needed. The actual ML type-inference algorithm will require a few steps to figure this out, but we are not concerned with the mechanics of overloading resolution here.

2. We generate a set of constraints on types, using the parse tree of the expression.

Constraints are equations between type expressions that must be solved. The way we generate them depends on the form of each subexpression. For each function application, constraints are generated according to the following rule.

Function Application: If the type of f is a, the type of e is b, and the type of fe is c, then we must have $a = b \rightarrow c$.

This typing rule for function application can be used twice in our expression.

> Subexpression $(+5)$,   Constraint int $\rightarrow$ (int $\rightarrow$ int) $=$ int $\rightarrow t$,
>
> Subexpression $(+5)\,x$,   Constraint $t = u \rightarrow s$.

In the subexpression $(+\ 5)$, the type of the function $+$ is int $\rightarrow$ (int $\rightarrow$ int), the type of the argument 5 is int and the type of the application is t. Therefore, we must have int $\rightarrow$ (int $\rightarrow$ int), $=$ int $\rightarrow t$. The reasoning for subexpression $(+\ 5)\,x$ is similar: In the subexpression $(+\ 5)\,x$, the type of the function $(+\ 5)$ is t, the type of the argument x is u, and the type of the application is s. Therefore, we must have $t = u \rightarrow s$.

Lambda Abstraction (Function Expression): If the type of x is a and the type of e is b, then the type of $\lambda x.e$ must equal $a \rightarrow b$.

For our example expression, we have one lambda abstraction. This gives us the following constraint:

Subexpression $\lambda x.((+5)x)$,   Constraint $r = u \rightarrow s$.

In words, the type of the whole expression is r, the type of x is u, and the type of the subexpression $((+ 5) x)$ is s. This gives us the equation $r = u \rightarrow s$.

3. *We solve these constraints by means of unification.*
Unification is a standard algorithm for solving systems of equations by substitution. The general properties of this algorithm are not discussed here. Instead, the process is shown by example in enough detail that you should be able to figure out the types of simple expressions on your own.

For our example expression, we have the following constraints.

$$\text{int} \rightarrow (\text{int} \rightarrow \text{int}) = \text{int} \rightarrow t,$$
$$t = u \rightarrow s,$$
$$r = u \rightarrow s.$$

If there is a way of associating type expression to type variables that makes all of these equations true, then the expression is well typed. In this case, the type of the expression will be the type expression equal to the type variable r. If there is no way of associating type expression to type variables that makes all of these equations true, then there is no type for this expression. In this case, the type-inference algorithm will fail, resulting in an error message that says the expression is not well typed.

We can process these equations one at a time. The order is not very important, although it is convenient to put the equation involving the type of the entire expression last, as this is the output of the type-inference algorithm.

The first equation is true if $t = \text{int} \rightarrow \text{int}$. Because we need $t = \text{int} \rightarrow \text{int}$, we substitute int $\rightarrow$ int for t in the remaining equations. This gives us two equations to solve:

$$\text{int} \rightarrow \text{int} = u \rightarrow s,$$
$$r = u \rightarrow s.$$

The only way to have int $\rightarrow$ int $= u \rightarrow s$ is if $u = s = \text{int}$. Proceeding as before, we substitute int for both u and s in the remaining equation. This gives us

$$r = \text{int} \rightarrow \text{int},$$

which tells us that the type r of the whole expression is int $\rightarrow$ int. Because every constraint is solved, we know that the expression is typeable and we have computed a type for the expression.

Example 6.4 A Polymorphic Function Definition

```
- fun apply(f,x) = f(x);
val apply = fn : ('a → 'b) * 'a → 'b
```

This is an example of a function whose type involves type variables. The type-inference algorithm begins by assigning a type to each subexpression. Because this makes it easiest to understand the algorithm, we write the function as a lambda expression with a pair ⟨f,x⟩ instead of a variable as a formal parameter: apply is defined by the lambda expression λ⟨f,x⟩. f x that maps a pair ⟨f,x⟩ to the result f x of applying f to x.

Here is the parse graph of λ⟨f,x⟩. f x, in which a pairing node is used on the left to indicate that the argument ⟨f,x⟩ of the function is a pair, with links to f and x.

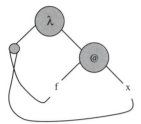

The first step of the algorithm is to assign types to each node in the graph, as shown here:

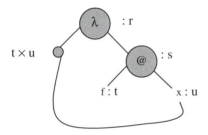

The same information is repeated in the following table, showing the subexpressions represented by each node and their types.

Subexpression	Type
λ⟨f,x⟩. fx	r
⟨f,x⟩.	t × u
fx	s
f	t
x	u

The second step of the algorithm is to generate a set of constraints. For this example, there is one constraint for the application and one for the lambda abstraction. The application gives us

$$t = u \to s.$$

In words, the type of the application f x has type s, provided that the type of the function f is equal to ⟨*type of argument*⟩ → s. Because the type of the argument is u, this gives us the constraint $t = u \to s$.

The second constraint, from the lambda abstraction, is

$$r = t * u \to s.$$

In words, the type of λ⟨f,x⟩. fx is r, where r must be equal to ⟨*type of argument*⟩ → s, as s is the type of the subtree representing the function result. Because the argument is the pair ⟨f,x⟩, the type of the argument is $t * u$.

The constraints can be solved in order. The first requires $t = u → s$, which we solve by substituting $u → s$ for t in the remaining constraint. This gives us

$$r = (u → s)^* u → s.$$

This tells us the type of the function. If we rewrite $(u → s) * u → s$ with 'a and 'b in place of u and s, then we get the compiler output previously shown. Because there are type variables in the type of the expression, the function may be used for many types of arguments. This is illustrated in the following example, which uses the type we have just computed for apply.

Example 6.5 Application of a Polymorphic Function

In the last example, we calculated the type of apply. The type of apply is ('a → 'b) * 'a → 'b, which contains type variables. The type variables in this type mean that apply is a *polymorphic* function, a function that may be applied to different types of arguments. In the case of apply, the type ('a → 'b) * 'a → 'b means that apply may be applied to a pair of arguments of type ('a → 'b) * 'a for any types 'a and 'b. In particular, recall that function fun g(x) = 5 + x from Example 6.3 has type int → int. Therefore, the pair (g,3) has type int → int.* int, which matches the form ('a → 'b) * 'a for function apply. In this example, we calculate the type of the application

---

apply(g,3);

Following the three steps of the type inference algorithm, we begin by assigning types to the nodes in the parse tree of this expression:

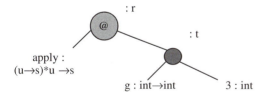

In this illustration, the smaller unlabeled circle is a pairing node. This node and the two below it represent the pair (g,3). In the previous example, we associated a product type with the pairing node. Here, to show that it is equivalent to use a type variable and constraint, we associate a type variable t with the pairing node and generate the constraint $t = (int → int) * int$.

There are two constraints, one for the pairing node and one for the application node. For pairing, we have

$$t = (int → int) * int.$$

For the application, we have

$$(u \to s)^* u \to s = t \to r.$$

In words, the type $(u \to s)^* u \to s$ of the function must equal $\langle type\ of\ argument \rangle \to r$, where r is the type of the application.

Now we must solve the constraints, The first constraint gives a type expression for t, which we can substitute for t in the second constraint. This gives us

$$(u \to s)^* u \to s = (\text{int} \to \text{int}) * \text{int} \to r.$$

This constraint has an expression on each side of the equal sign. To solve this constraint, corresponding parts of each expression must be equal. In other words, we can solve this constraint precisely by solving the following four constraints:

$$u = \text{int},\ s = \text{int},\ u = \text{int},\ s = r.$$

Because these require $u = s = \text{int}$, we have $r = \text{int}$. Because all of the constraints are solved, the expression apply(g,3) is typeable in the ML type system. The type of apply(g,3) is the solution for type variable r, namely int.

We can also apply apply to other types of arguments. If not : bool $\to$ bool, then

---

apply(not, false)

---

is a well-typed expression with type bool by exactly the same type-inference processes as those for apply(g,3). This illustrates the polymorphism of apply: Because the type ('a $\to$ 'b) * 'a $\to$ 'b of apply contains type variables, the function may be applied to any type of arguments that can be obtained if the type variables in ('a $\to$ 'b) * 'a $\to$ 'b are replaced with type names or type expressions.

Example 6.6 A Recursive Function

When a function is defined recursively, we must determine the type of the function body without knowing the type of recursive function calls. To see how this works, consider this simple recursive function that sums the integers up to a given integer. This function does not terminate, but it does type check:

```
- fun sum(x) = x+sum(x-1);
val sum = fn : int -> int
```

Here is a parse graph of the function, with type variables associated with each of the nodes except for $+$, $-$, and 1, as we ignore overloading and treat these as integer operations and integer constant. Because we are trying to determine the type of sum, we associate a type variable with sum and proceed:

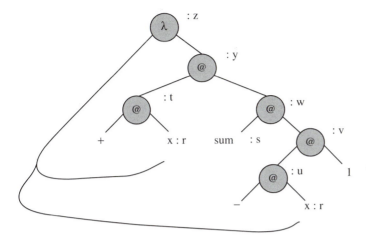

Starting with the applications of $+$ and $-$ and proceeding from the lower right up, the constraints associated with the function applications and lambda abstraction in this expression are

$$\text{int} \to (\text{int} \to \text{int}) = r \to t,$$
$$\text{int} \to (\text{int} \to \text{int}) = r \to u,$$

$$u = \text{int} \to v,$$
$$s = v \to w,$$
$$t = w \to y,$$
$$z = r \to y.$$

To this list we add one more because the type of sum must also be the type of the entire expression:

$$s = z.$$

The constraint $s = z$ is the one additional constraint associated with the fact that this is a recursive declaration of a function. Solving these in order, we have

$$r = \text{int}, \quad t = \text{int} \to \text{int},$$
$$u = \text{int} \to \text{int},$$
$$v = \text{int},$$
$$s = \text{int} \to w,$$
$$t = w \to y,$$
$$z = r \to y,$$
$$w = \text{int}, \quad y = \text{int},$$
$$z = \text{int} \to \text{int},$$
$$s = \text{int} \to \text{int}.$$

Because the constraints can be solved, the function is typeable. In the process of solving the constraints, we have calculated that the type of sum is int→int.

Example 6.7 A Function with Multiple Clauses

Type inference for functions with several clauses may be done by a type check of each clause separately. Then, because all clauses define the same function, we impose the constraint that the types of all clauses must be equal. For example, consider the append function on lists, defined as follows:

```
- fun append(nil, l) = l
  | append(x::xs, l) = x :: append(xs, l);
val append = fn : 'a list * 'a list → 'a list.
```

As the type : 'a list * 'a list → 'a list indicates, append can be applied to any pair of lists, as long as both lists contain the same type of list elements. Thus, append is a polymorphic function on lists.

We begin type inference for append by following the three-step algorithm for the first clause of the definition, then repeating the steps for the second clause. This gives us two types:

```
append : 'a list * 'b → 'b
append : 'a list * 'b → 'a list
```

Intuitively, the first clause has type 'a list * 'b → 'b because the first argument must match nil, but the second argument may be anything. The second clause has type 'a list * 'b → 'a list because the return result is a list containing one element from the list passed as the first argument.

If we impose the constraint

```
'a list * 'b → 'b = 'a list * 'b -> 'a list
```

then we must have 'b = a list. This gives us the final type for append:

```
append : 'a list * 'a list → 'a list
```

Example 6.8 Type Inference Indicates a Program Error

Here is an example that shows how type inference may produce output that indicates a programming error, even though the program may type correctly. Here is a sample (incorrect) declaration of a reverse function on lists:

```
- fun reverse (nil) = nil
  |    reverse (x::lst) = reverse (lst);
val reverse = fn : 'a list → 'b list
```

As the compiler output shows, this function is typeable; there is no type error in this declaration. However, look carefully at the type of reverse. The type 'a list → 'b list means that we can apply reverse to any type of list and obtain any type of list as a result. However, the type of the "reversed" list is not the same as the type of the list we started with!

Because it does not make sense for reverse to return a list that is a different type from its argument, there must be something wrong with this code. The problem is that, in the second clause, the first element x of the input list is not used as part of the output. Therefore, reverse always returns the empty list.

As this example illustrates, the type-inference algorithm may sometimes return a type that is more general than the one we expect. This does not indicate a type error. In this example, the faulty reverse can be used anywhere that a correct reverse function could be used. However, the type of reverse is useful because it tells the programmer that there is an error in the program.

6.4 POLYMORPHISM AND OVERLOADING

Polymorphism, which literally means "having multiple forms," refers to constructs that can take on different types as needed. For example, a function that can compute the length of any type of list is polymorphic because it has type 'a list → int for every type 'a.

There are three forms of polymorphism in contemporary programming languages:

- *parametric polymorphism*, in which a function may be applied to any arguments whose types match a type expression involving type variables;
- *ad hoc polymorphism*, another term for overloading, in which two or more implementations with different types are referred to by the same name;
- *subtype polymorphism*, in which the subtype relation between types allows an expression to have many possible types.

Parametric and ad hoc polymorphism (overloading) are discussed in this section. Subtype polymorphism is considered in later chapters in connection with object-oriented programming.

6.4.1 Parametric Polymorphism

The main characteristic of parametric polymorphism is that the set of types associated with a function or other value is given by a type expression that contains type variables. For example, an ML function that sorts lists might have the ML type

---

    sort : ('a * 'a → bool) * 'a list → 'a list

In words, sort can be applied to any pair consisting of a function and a list, as long as the function has a type of the form 'a * 'a -> bool, in which the type 'a must also be the type of the elements of the list. The function argument is a less-than operation used to determine the order of elements in the sorted list.

In parametric polymorphism, a function may have infinitely many types, as there are infinitely many ways of replacing type variables with actual types. The sort function, for example, may be used to sort lists of integers, lists of lists of integers, lists of lists of lists of integers, and so on.

Parametric polymorphism may be implicit or explicit. In *explicit parametric polymorphism*, the program text contains type variables that determine the way that a function or other value may be treated polymorphically. In addition, explicit polymorphism often involves explicit instantiation or type application to indicate how type variables are replaced with specific types in the use of a polymorphic value. C++ templates are a well-known example of explicit polymorphism. ML polymorphism is called *implicit parametric polymorphism* because programs that declare and use polymorphic functions do not need to contain types – the type-inference algorithm computes when a function is polymorphic and computes the instantiation of type variables as needed.

C++ Function Templates

For many readers, the most familiar type parameterization mechanism is the C++ template mechanism. Although some C++ programmers associate templates with classes and object-oriented programming, function templates are also useful for programs that do not declare any classes.

As an illustrative example, suppose you write a simple function to swap the values of two integer variables:

```
void swap(int& x, int& y){
    int tmp = x;  x = y;  y = tmp;
}
```

Although this code is useful for exchanging values of integer variables, the sequence of instructions also works for other types of variables. If we wish to swap values of variables of other types, then we can define a function template that uses a type variable T in place of the type name int:

```
template <typename T>
void swap(T& x, T& y){
    T tmp = x; x = y; y = tmp;
}
```

For those who are not familiar with templates, the main idea is to think of the type name T as a parameter to a function from types to functions. When applied to, or *instantiated* to, a specific type, the result is a version of swap that has int replaced with another type. In other words, swap is a general function that would work perfectly well for many types of arguments. Templates allow us to treat swap as a function with a type argument.

In C++, function templates are instantiated automatically as needed, with the types of the function arguments used to determine which instantiation is needed. This is illustrated in the following example lines of code.

```
int i,j;  ...     swap(i,j);  //  Use swap with T replaced with int
float a,b;  ...    swap(a,b);  //  Use swap with T replaced with float
String s,t;  ...   swap(s,t);  //  Use swap with T replaced with String
```

Comparison with ML Polymorphism

In ML polymorphism, the type-inference algorithm infers the type of a function and the type of a function application (as explained in Section 6.3). When a function is polymorphic, the actions of the type-inference algorithm can be understood as automatically inserting "template declarations" and "template instantiation" into the program. We can see how this works by considering an ML sorting function that is analogous to the C++ sort function previously declared:

```
fun insert(less, x, nil) = [x]
|   insert(less, x, y::ys) = if less(x,y) then x::y::ys
                                  else y::insert(less,x,ys);
fun sort(less, nil) = nil
|   sort(less, x::xs) = insert(less, x, sort(less,xs));
```

For sort to be polymorphic, a less-than operation must be passed as a function argument to sort.

The types of insert and sort, as inferred by the type-inference algorithm, are

```
val insert = fn : ('a * 'a -> bool) * 'a * 'a list -> 'a list
val sort = fn : ('a * 'a -> bool) * 'a list -> 'a list
```

In these types, the type variable 'a can be instantiated to any type, as needed. In effect, the functions are treated as if they were "templates." By use of a combination of C++ template, ML function, and type syntax, the functions previously defined could also be written as

```
template <type 'a>
fun insert(less : 'a * 'a -> bool, x : 'a, nil : 'a list) = [x]
|   insert(less, x, y::ys) = if less(x,y) then x::y::ys
                                  else y::insert(less,x,ys);
template <type 'a>
fun sort(less : 'a * 'a -> bool, nil : 'a list) = nil
|   sort(less, x::xs) = insert(less, x, sort(less,xs));
```

These declarations are the explicitly typed versions of the implicitly polymorphic ML functions. In other words, the ML type-inference algorithm may be understood as a program preprocessor that converts ML expressions without type information into expressions in some explicitly typed intermediate language with templates. From this point of view, the difference between explicit and implicit polymorphism is that a programming language processor (such as the ML compiler) takes the simpler implicit syntax and automatically inserts explicit type information, converting from implicit to explicit form, before programs are compiled and executed.

Finishing this example, suppose we declare a less-than function on integers:

```
- fun less(x,y) = x < y;
val less = fn : int * int -> bool
```

In the following application of the polymorphic sort function, the sort template is automatically instantiated to type int, so sort can be used to sort an integer list:

```
- sort (less, [1,4,5,3,2]);
val it = [1,2,3,4,5] : int list
```

6.4.2 Implementation of Parametric Polymorphism

C++ templates and ML polymorphic functions are implemented differently. The reason for the difference is not related to the difference between explicitly polymorphic syntax and implicitly polymorphic syntax. The need for different implementation techniques arises from the difference between data representation in C and data representation in ML.

C++ Implementation

C++ templates are instantiated at program link time. More specifically, suppose that the swap function template is stored in one file and compiled and a program calling swap is stored in another file and compiled separately. The so-called relocatable object files produced by compilation of the calling program will include information indicating that the compiled code calls a function swap of a certain type. The program linker is designed to combine the two program parts by linking the calls to swap in the calling program to the definition of swap in a separate compilation unit. It does so by instantiating the compiled code for swap in a form that produces code appropriate for the calls to swap.

If a program calls swap with several different types, then several different instantiated copies of swap will be produced. One reason that a different copy is needed for each type of call is that function swap declares a local variable tmp of type T. Space for tmp must be allocated in the activation record for swap. Therefore the compiled code for swap must be modified according to the size of a variable of type T. If T is a structure or object, for example, then the size might be fairly large. On the other hand, if T is int, the size will be small. In either case, the compiled code for swap must "know" the size of the datum so that addressing into the activation record can be done properly.

The linking process for C++ is relatively complex. We will not study it in detail. However, it is worth noting that if < is an overloaded operator, then the correct version of < must be identified when the compiled code for sort is linked with a calling program. For example, consider the following generic sort function:

```
template <typename T>
void sort( int count, T * A[count] ) {
    for (int i=0; i <count-1; i++)
        for (int j=i+1; j<count-1; j++)
            if (A[j] < A[i]) swap(A[i],A[j]);
}
```

If A is an array of type T, then sort(n, A) will work only if operator < is defined on type T. This requirement of sort is not declared anywhere in the C++ code. However, when the function template is instantiated, the actual type T must have an operator < defined or a link-time error will be reported and no executable object code will be produced.

ML Implementation

In ML, there is one sequence of compiled instructions for each polymorphic function. There is no need to produce different copies of the code for different types of arguments because related types of data are represented in similar ways. More specifically, pointers are used in parameter passing and in the representation of data structures such as lists so that when a function is polymorphic, it can access all necessary data in the same way, regardless of its type. This property of ML is called *uniform data representation*.

The simplest example of uniform data representation is the ML version of the polymorphic swap function:

```
– fun swap(x,y) = let val tmp = x in x := !y; y := !tmp end;
val swap = fn : 'a ref * 'a ref -> unit
```

As the type indicates, this swap function can be applied to any two references of the same type. Although ML references generally work like assignable variables in other languages, the value of a reference is a pointer to a cell that contains a value. Therefore, when a pair of references is passed to the swap function, the swap function receives a pair of pointers. The two pointers are the same size (typically 32 bits), regardless of what type of value is contained in the locations to which they point. In fact, we can complete the entire computation by doing only pointer assignment. As a result, none of the compiled code for swap depends on the size of the data referred to by arguments x and y.

Uniform data representation has its advantages and disadvantages. Because there is no need to duplicate code for different argument types, uniform data representation leads to smaller code size and avoids complications associated with C++-style linking. On the other hand, the resulting code can be less efficient, as uniform data representation often involves using pointers to data instead of storing data directly in structures.

For polymorphic list functions to work properly, all lists must be represented in exactly the same way. Because of this uniformity requirement, small values that would fit directly into the car part of a list cons cell cannot be placed there because large values do not fit. Hence we must store pointers to small values in lists, just as we store pointers to large values. ML programmers and compiler writers call the process of making all data look the same by means of pointers *boxing*.

Comparison

Two important points of comparison are efficiency and reporting of error messages. As far as efficiency, the C++ implementation requires more effort at link time and produces a larger code, as instantiating a template several times will result in several copies of the code. The ML implementation will run more slowly unless special optimizations are applied; uniform data representation involves more extensive use of pointers and these pointers must be stored and followed.

As a general programming principle, it is more convenient to have program errors reported at compile time than at link time. One reason is that separate program modules are compiled independently, but are linked together only when the entire system is assembled. Therefore, compilation is a "local" process that can be carried out by the designer or implementer of a single component. In contrast, link-time errors represent global system properties that are not known until the entire system is assembled. For this reason, C++ link-time errors associated with operations in templates can be irritating and a source of frustration.

Somewhat better error reporting for C++ templates could be achieved if the template syntax included a description of the operations needed on type parameters. However, this is relatively complicated in C++, because of overloading and other properties of the language. In contrast, the ML has simpler overloading and includes more information in parameterized constructs, allowing all type errors to be reported as a program unit is compiled.

6.4.3 Overloading

Parametric polymorphism can be contrasted with overloading. A symbol is *overloaded* if it has two (or more) meanings, distinguished by type, and resolved at compile time. In an influential historical paper, Christopher Strachey referred to ML-style polymorphism as *parametric polymorphism* (although ML had not been invented yet) and overloading as *ad hoc polymorphism*.

Example. In standard ML, as in many other languages, the operator + has two distinct implementations associated with it, one of type int $*$ int $\rightarrow$ int, the other of type real$*$real $\rightarrow$ real. The reason that both of these operations are given the name + is that both compute numeric addition. However, at the implementation level, the two operations are really very different. Because integers are represented in one way (as binary numbers) and real numbers in another (as exponent and mantissa, following scientific notation), the way that integer addition combines the bits of its arguments to produce the bits of its result is very different from the way this is done in real addition.

An important difference between parametric polymorphism and overloading is that parameter polymorphic functions use one algorithm to operate on arguments of many different types, whereas overloaded functions may use a different algorithm for each type of argument.

A characteristic of overloading is that overloading is *resolved* at compile time. If a function is overloaded, then the compiler must choose between the possible algorithms at compile time. Choosing one algorithm from among the possible algorithms associated with an overloaded function is called resolving the overloading. In many languages, if a function is overloaded, then only the function arguments are used to resolve overloading. For example, consider the following two expressions:

```
3 + 2;     /* add two integers */
3.0 + 2.0;  /* add two real (floating point) numbers */
```

Here is how the compiler will produce code for evaluating each expression:

- 3 + 2: The parsing phase of the compiler will build the parse tree of this expression, and the type-checking phase will compute a type for each symbol. Because the type-checking phase will determine that + must have type int $*$ int $\rightarrow$ int, the code-generation phase of the compiler will produce machine instructions that perform integer addition.
- 3.0 + 2.0: The parsing phase of the compiler will build the parse tree of this expression, and the type-checking phase will compute a type for each symbol. Because the type-checking phase will determine that + must have type real $*$ real $\rightarrow$ real, the code-generation phase of the compiler will produce machine instructions that perform integer addition.

Automatic conversion is a separate mechanism that may be combined with overloading. However, it is possible for a language to have overloading and not to have automatic conversion. ML, for example, does not do automatic conversion.

6.5 TYPE DECLARATIONS AND TYPE EQUALITY

Many kinds of type declarations and many kinds of type equality have appeared in programming languages of the past. The reason why type declarations and type equality are related is that, when a type name is declared, it is important to decide whether this is a "new" type that is different from all other types or a new name whose meaning is equal to some other type that may be used elsewhere in the program.

Some programming languages have used fairly complicated forms of type equality, leading to confusing forms of type declarations. Instead of discussing many of the historical forms, we simply look at a few rational possibilities.

6.5.1 Transparent Type Declarations

There are two basic forms of type declaration:

- *transparent*, meaning an alternative name is given to a type that can also be expressed without this name,
- *opaque*, meaning a new type is introduced into the program that is not equal to any other type.

In the ML form of transparent type declaration,

---

type <identifier> = <type_expression>

---

the identifier becomes a synonym for the type expression. For example,

---

type Celsius = real;
type Fahrenheit = real;

---

declare two type names, Celsius and Fahrenheit, whose meaning is the type real, just the way that the two value declarations

---

val x = 3;
val y = 3;

---

declare two identifiers whose value is 3. (Remember that ML identifiers are not assignable variables; the identifier x will have value 3 wherever it is used.) If we declare an ML function to convert Fahrenheit to Celsius, this function will have real $\rightarrow$ real:

– fun toCelsius(x) = ((x-32.0)* 0.555556);
val toCelsius = fn : real $\rightarrow$ real

This should not be surprising because there is no indication that the function argument or return value has any type other than real. If we want to specify the types of the argument and result, we can add them to the function declaration. This produces a function of type Fahrenheit $\rightarrow$ Celsius:

– fun toCelsius(x : Fahrenheit) = ((x-32.0)* 0.555556) : Celsius;
val toCelsius = fn : Fahrenheit $\rightarrow$ Celsius

This version of the toCelsius function is more informative to read, as the types indicate the intended purpose of the function. However, because Fahrenheit and Celsius are synonyms for real, this function can be applied to a real argument:

– toCelsius(74.5);
val it = 23.61113 : Celsius

The ML type checker gives the result type Celsius, but because Celsius=real, the result can be used in real expressions.

ML abstract types are an example of an opaque type declaration. These are discussed in Chapter 9. ML data type is another form of opaque type declaration; the opacity of ML data type declarations is discussed in Subsection 6.5.3.

Two historical names for two forms of type equality are *name type equality* and *structural type equality*. Intuitively, name equality means that two type names are considered equal in type checking only if they are the same name. Structural equality means that two type names are the same if the types they name are the same (i.e., have the same structure). Although these terms may seem simple and innocuous, there are lots of confusing phenomena associated with the use of name and structural type equivalence in programming languages.

6.5.2 C Declarations and Structs

The basic type declaration construct in C is typedef. Here are some simple examples:

```
typedef char byte;
typedef byte ten_bytes[10];
```

the first declaring a type byte that is equal to char and the second an array type ten_bytes that is equal to arrays of 10 bytes. Generally speaking, C typedef works similarly to the transparent ML type declaration discussed in the preceding subsection. However, when structs are involved, the C type checker considers separately declared type names to be unequal, even if they are declared to name the same struct type. Here is a short program example showing how this works:

```
typedef struct {int m;} A;
typedef struct {int m;} B;
A x;
B y;
x=y;   /* incompatible types in assignment */
```

Here, although the two struct types used in the two declarations are the same, the C type checker does not treat A and B as equal types. However, if we replace the two declarations with typedef int A; typedef int B;, using int in place of structs, then the assignment is considered type correct.

6.5.3 ML Data-Type Declaration

The ML data-type declaration, discussed in Subsection 5.4.4, is a form of type declaration that simultaneously defines a new type name and operations for building and making use of elements of the type. Because all of the examples in Subsection 5.4.4 were monomorphic, we take a quick look at a polymorphic declaration before discussing type equaliy.

Here is an example of a polymorphic data type of trees. You may wish to compare this with the monomorphic (nonpolymorphic) example in Subsection 5.4.4:

```
datatype 'a tree = LEAF of 'a | NODE of ('a tree * 'a tree);
```

This declaration defines a polymorphic type 'a tree, with instances int tree, string tree, and so on, together with polymorphic constructors LEAF and NODE:

```
- LEAF;
val it = fn : 'a -> 'a tree
- NODE;
val it = fn : 'a tree * 'a tree -> 'a tree
```

The following function checks to see if an element appears in a tree. The function uses an exception, discussed in Section 8.2, when the element cannot be found. ML requires an exception to be declared before it is used:

```
- exception NotFound;
exception NotFound

- fun inTree(x, EMPTY) = raise NotFound
|       inTree(x, LEAF(y)) = x = y
|       inTree(x, NODE(y,z)) = inTree(x, y) orelse inTree(x, z);

val inTree = fn : "a * "a tree → bool
```

Each ML data-type declaration is considered to define a new type different from all other types. Even if two data types have the same structure, they are not considered equivalent. The design of ML makes it hard to declare similar data types, as each constructor has only one type. For example, the two declarations

```
datatype A = C of int;
datatype B = C of int;
```

declare distinct types A and B. Because the second declaration follows the first and ML considers each declaration to start a new scope, the constructor C has type int → B after both declarations have been processed. However, we can see that A and B are considered different by writing a function that attempts to treat a value of one type as the other,

```
fun f(x:A) = x : B;
```

which leads to the message Error: expression doesn't match constraint [tycon mismatch].

6.6 CHAPTER SUMMARY

In this chapter, we studied reasons for using types in programming languages, methods for type checking, and some typing issues such as polymorphism, overloading, and type equality.

Reasons for Using Types

There are three main uses of types in programming languages:

- *Naming and organizing concepts:* Functions and data structures can be given types that reflect the way these computational constructs are used in a program. This helps the programmers and anyone else reading a program figure out how the program works and why it is written a certain way.
- *Making sure that bit sequences in computer memory are interpreted consistently:* Type checking keeps operations from being applied to operands in incorrect ways. This prevents a floating-point operation from being applied to a sequence of bits that represents a string, for example.
- *Providing information to the compiler about data manipulated by the program:* In languages in which the compiler can determine the type of a data structure, for example, the type information can be used to determine the relative location of a part of this structure. This compile-time type information can be used to generate efficient code for indexing into the data structure at run time.

Type Inference

Type inference is the process of determining the types of expressions based on the known types of some of the symbols that appear in them. For example, we saw how to infer that the function g declared by

```
fun g(x) = 5+x;
```

has type int $\rightarrow$ int. The difference between type inference and compile-time type checking is a matter of degree. A type-checking algorithm goes through the program to check that the types declared by the programmer agree with the language requirements. In type inference, the idea is that some information is not specified and some form of logical inference is required for determining the types of identifiers from the way they are used.

The following steps are used for type inference:

1. Assign a type to the expression and each subexpression by using the known type of a symbol of a type variable.
2. Generate a set of constraints on types by using the parse tree of the expression.
3. Solve these constraints by using unification, which is a substitution-based algorithm for solving systems of equations.

In a series of examples, we saw how to apply this algorithm to a variety of expressions. Type inference has many characteristics in common with the kind of algorithms that are used in compilers and programming environments to determine properties of programs. For example, some useful alias analysis algorithms that try to determine whether two pointers might point to the same location have the same general outline as that of type inference.

Polymorphism and Overloading

There are three forms of polymorphism: parametric polymorphism, ad hoc polymorphism (another term for overloading), and subtype polymorphism. The first two were examined in this chapter, with subtype polymorphism left for later chapters on object-oriented languages. Parametric polymorphism can be either implicit, as in ML, or explicit, as with C++ templates. There are also two ways of implementing parametric polymorphism, one in which the same data representation is used for many types of data and the other in which explicit instantiation of parametric code is used to match each different data representation.

The difference between parametric polymorphism and overloading is that parametric polymorphism allows one algorithm to be given many types, whereas overloading involves different algorithms. For example, the function + is overloaded in many languages. In an expression adding two integers, the integer addition algorithm is used. In adding two floating-point numbers, a completely different algorithm is used for computing the sum.

Type Declarations and Type Equality

We discussed opaque and transparent type declarations. In opaque type declarations, the type name stands for a distinct type different from all other types. In transparent type declarations, the declared name is a synonym for another type. Both forms are used in many programming languages.

EXERCISES

6.1 ML Types

Explain the ML type for each of the following declarations:

(a) fun a(x,y) = x+2*y;

(b) fun b(x,y) = x+y/2.0;

(c) fun c(f) = fn y => f(y);

(d) fun d(f,x) = f(f(x)));

(e) fun e(x,y,b) = if b(y) then x else y;

Because you can simply type these expressions into an ML interpreter to determine the type, be sure to write a short explanation to show that you understand why the function has the type you give.

6.2 Polymorphic Sorting

This function performing insertion sort on a list takes as arguments a comparison function less and a list l of elements to be sorted. The code compiles and runs correctly:

```
fun sort(less, nil) = nil   |
    sort(less, a : : l) =
        let
```

```
                    fun insert(a, nil) = a : : nil   |
                        insert(a, b : : l) = if less(a,b) then a : : (b : : l)
                                             else b : : insert(a, l)
            in
                insert(a, sort(less, l))
            end;
```

What is the type of this sort function? Explain briefly, including the type of the subsidiary function insert. You do not have to run the ML algorithm on this code; just explain why an ordinary ML programmer would expect the code to have this type.

6.3 Types and Garbage Collection

Language D allows a form of "cast" in which an expression of one type can be treated as an expression of any other. For example, if x is a variable of type integer, then $(string)x$ is an expression of type string. No conversion is done. Explain how this might affect garbage collection for language D.

For simplicity, assume that D is a conventional imperative language with integers, reals (floating-point numbers), pairs, and pointers. You do not need to consider other language features.

6.4 Polymorphic Fixed Point

A *fixed point* of a function f is some value x such that $x = f(x)$. There is a connection between recursion and fixed points that is illustrated by this ML definition of the factorial function factorial : int $\rightarrow$ int:

```
        fun Y f x = f (Y f) x;
        fun F f x = if x=0 then 1 else x*f(x-1);
        val factorial = Y F;
```

The first function, Y, is a fixed-point operator. The second function, F, is a function on functions whose fixed point is factorial. Both of these are curried functions; using the ML syntax fn x $\Rightarrow$ ... for λx ..., we could also write the function F as

```
        fun F(f) = fn x =>
                if x=0 then 1 else x*f(x-1)
```

This F is a function that, when applied to argument f, returns a function that, when applied to argument x, has the value given by the expression if x=0 then 1 else x*f(x-1).

(a) What type will the ML compiler deduce for F?

(b) What type will the ML compiler deduce for Y?

6.5 Parse Graph

Use the following parse graph to calculate the ML type for the function

```
        fun f(g,h) = g(h) + 2;
```

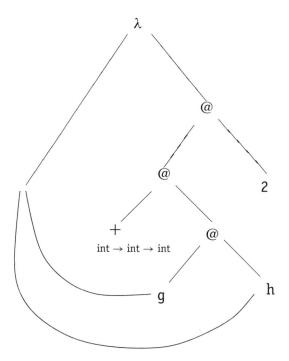

6.6 Parse Graph

Use the following parse graph to follow the steps of the ML type-inference algorithm on the function declaration

    fun f(g) = g(g) + 2;

What is the output of the type checker?

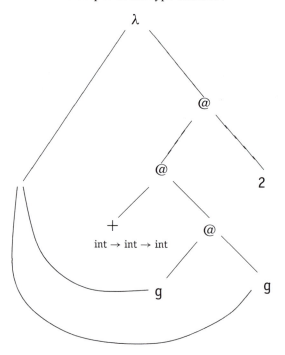

6.7 Type Inference and Bugs

What is the type of the following ML function?

```
fun append(nil, l) = l
|   append(x : : l, m) = append(l, m);
```

Write one or two sentences to explain succinctly and informally why append has the type you give. This function is intended to append one list onto another. However, it has a bug. How might knowing the type of this function help the programmer to find the bug?

6.8 Type Inference and Debugging

The reduce function takes a binary operation, in the form of a function f, and a list, and produces the result of combining all elements in the list by using the binary operation. For example;

```
reduce plus [1,2,3] = 1 + 2 + 3 = 6
```

if plus is defined by

```
fun plus (x, y : int) = x+y
```

A friend of yours is trying to learn ML and tries to write a reduce function. Here is his incorrect definition:

```
fun reduce(f, x) = x
|   reduce(f, (x : : y)) = f(x, reduce(f, y));
```

He tells you that he does not know what to return for an empty list, but this should work for a nonempty list: If the list has one element, then the first clause returns it. If the list has more than one element, then the second clause of the definition uses the function f. This sounds like a reasonable explanation, but the type checker gives you the following output:

```
val reduce = fn : (((′a * ′a list) -> ′a list) * ′a list) -> ′a list
```

How can you use this type to explain to your friend that his code is wrong?

6.9 Polymorphism in C

In the following C min function, the type void is used in the types of two arguments. However, the function makes sense and can be applied to a list of arguments in which void has been replaced with another type. In other words, although the C type of this function is not polymorphic, the function could be given a polymorphic type if C had a polymorphic type system. Using ML notation for types, write a type for this min function that captures the way that min could be meaningfully applied to arguments of various types. Explain why you believe the function has the type you have written.

```
int min (
    void *a[ ],              /* a is an array of pointers to data of unknown type */
    int n,                   /* n is the length of the array */
    int (*less)(void*, void*)    /* parameter less is a pointer to function */
    )                            /* that is used to compare array elements */
{
    int i;
    int m;
    m=0;
```

```
        for (i=1; i < n; i++)
            if (less(a[i], a[m])) m=i;
        return(m);
    }
```

6.10 Typing and Run-Time Behavior

The following ML functions have essentially identical computational behavior,

```
    fun f(x) = not f(x);
    fun g(y) = g(y) * 2;
```

because except for typing differences, we could replace one function with the other in any program without changing the observable behavior of the program. In more detail, suppose we turn off the ML type checker and compile a program of the form $\mathcal{P}[\text{fun } f(x) = \text{not } f(x)]$. Whatever this program does, the program $\mathcal{P}[\text{fun } f(y) = f(y) * 2]$ we obtain by replacing one function definition with the other will do exactly the same thing. In particular, if the first does not lead to a run-time type error such as adding an integer to a string, neither will the second.

(a) What is the ML type for f?

(b) What is the ML type for g?

(c) Give an informal explanation of why these two functions have the same run-time behavior.

(d) Because the two functions are equivalent, it might be better to give them the same type. Why do you think the designers of the ML typing algorithm did not work harder to make it do this? Do you think they made a mistake?

6.11 Dynamic Typing in ML

Many programmers believe that a run-time typed programming language like Lisp or Scheme is more expressive than a compile-time typed language like ML, as there is no type system to "get in your way." Although there are some situations in which the flexibility of Lisp or Scheme is a tremendous advantage, we can also make the opposite argument. Specifically, ML is more expressive than Lisp or Scheme because we can define an ML data type for Lisp or Scheme expressions.

Here is a type declaration for pure historical Lisp:

```
    datatype LISP = Nil
                  |  Symbol of string
                  |  Number of int
                  |  Cons of LISP * LISP
                  |  Function of (LISP -> LISP)
```

Although we could have used (Symbol "nil") instead of a primitive Nil, it seems convenient to treat nil separately.

(a) Write an ML declaration for the Lisp function atom that tests whether its argument is an atom. (Everything except a cons cell is an atom – The word atom comes from the Greek word *atomos*, meaning indivisible. In Lisp, symbols, numbers, nil, and functions cannot be divided into smaller pieces, so they are considered to be atoms.) Your function should have type LISP $\rightarrow$ LISP, returning atoms Symbol("T") or Nil.

(b) Write an ML declaration for the Lisp function islist that tests whether its argument is a *proper* list. A proper list is either nil or a cons cell whose cdr is a proper list. Note that not all listlike structures built from cons cells are proper lists. For instance, (Cons (Symbol("A"), Symbol("B"))) is not a proper list (it is instead what is known as a dotted list), and so (islist (Cons (Symbol("A"), Symbol("B")))) should evaluate to Nil. On the other hand, (Cons (Symbol("A"), (Cons (Symbol("B"), Nil)))) is a proper list, and so your function should evaluate to Symbol("T"). Your function should have type LISP → LISP, as before.

(c) Write an ML declaration for Lisp car function and explain briefly. The function should have type LISP → LISP.

(d) Write Lisp expression (lambda (x) (cons x 'A)) as an ML expression of type LISP → LISP. Note that 'A means something completely different in Lisp and ML. The 'A here is part of a Lisp expression, not an ML expression. Explain briefly.

7

Scope, Functions, and Storage Management

In this chapter storage management for block-structured languages is described by the run-time data structures that are used in a simple, reference implementation. The programming language features that make the association between program names and memory locations interesting are scope, which allows two syntactically identical names to refer to different locations, and function calls, which each require a new memory area in which to store function parameters and local variables. Some important topics in this chapter are parameter passing, access to global variables, and a storage optimization associated with a particular kind of function call called a *tail call*. We will see that storage management becomes more complicated in languages with nested function declarations that allow functions to be passed as arguments or returned as the result of function calls.

7.1 BLOCK-STRUCTURED LANGUAGES

Most modern programming languages provide some form of block. A *block* is a region of program text, identified by begin and end markers, that may contain declarations local to this region. Here are a few lines of C code to illustrate the idea:

```
outer     {int x = 2;
block        { int y = 3;  } inner
             x = y+2;       } block
          }
        }
```

In this section of code, there are two blocks. Each block begins with a left brace, {, and ends with a right brace, }. The outer block begins with the first left brace and ends with the last right brace. The inner block is nested inside the outer block. It begins with the second left brace and ends with the first right brace. The variable x is declared in the outer block and the variable y is declared in the inner block. A variable declared within a block is said to be *local* to that block. A variable declared in an enclosing block is said to be *global* to the block. In this example, x is local to the outer block, y is local to the inner block, and x is global to the inner block.

C, Pascal, and ML are all block-structured languages. In-line blocks are delineated by { . . . } in C, begin...end in Pascal, and let...in...end in ML. The body of a procedure or function is also a block in each of these languages.

Storage management mechanisms associated with block structure allow functions to be called recursively.

The versions of Fortran in widespread use during the 1960s and 1970s were not block structured. In historical Fortran, every variable, including every parameter of each procedure (called a subroutine in Fortran) was assigned a fixed-memory location. This made it *impossible* to call a procedure recursively, either directly or indirectly. If Fortran procedure P calls Q, Q calls R, and then R attempts to call P, the second call to P is not allowed. If P were called a second time in this call chain, the second call would write over the parameters and return address for the first call. This would make it impossible for the call to return properly.

Block-structured languages are characterized by the following properties:

■ New variables may be declared at various points in a program.
■ Each declaration is visible within a certain region of program text, called a block. Blocks may be nested, but cannot partially overlap. In other words, if two blocks contain any expressions or statements in common, then one block must be entirely contained within the other.
■ When a program begins executing the instructions contained in a block at run time, memory is allocated for the variables declared in that block.
■ When a program exits a block, some or all of the memory allocated to variables declared in that block will be deallocated.
■ An identifier that is not declared in the current block is considered global to the block and refers to the entity with this name that is declared in the closest enclosing block.

Although most modern general-purpose programming languages are block structured, many important languages do not provide full support for all combinations of block-structured features. Most notably, standard C and C++ do not allow local function declarations within nested blocks and therefore do not address implementation issues associated with the return of functions from nested blocks.

In this chapter, we look at the memory management and access mechanisms for three classes of variables:

■ *local variables*, which are stored on the stack in the activation record associated with the block
■ *parameters* to function or procedure blocks, which are also stored in the activation record associated with the block
■ *global variables*, which are declared in some enclosing block and therefore must be accessed from an activation record that was placed on the run-time stack before activation of the current block.

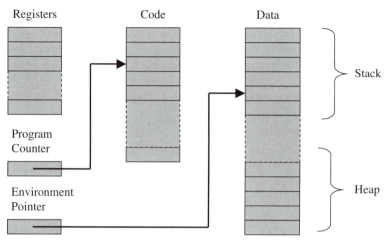

Figure 7.1. Program stack.

It may seem surprising that most complications arise in connection with access to global variables. However, this is really a consequence of stack-based memory management: The stack is used to make it easy to allocate and access local variables. In placing local variables close at hand, a global variable may be buried on the stack under any number of activation records.

Simplified Machine Model

We use the simplified machine model in Figure 7.1 to look at the memory management in block-structured languages.

The machine model in Figure 7.1 separates code memory from data memory. The program counter stores the address of the current program instruction and is normally incremented after each instruction. When the program enters a new block, an *activation record* containing space for local variables declared in the block is added to the run-time stack (drawn here at the top of data memory), and the environment pointer is set to point to the new activation record. When the program exits the block, the activation record is removed from the stack and the environment pointer is reset to its previous location. The program may store data that will exist longer than the execution of the current block on the heap. The fact that the most recently allocated activation record is the first to be deallocated is sometimes called the *stack discipline*. Although most block-structured languages are implemented by a stack, higher-order functions may cause the stack discipline to fail.

Although Figure 7.1 includes some number of registers, generally used for short-term storage of addresses and data, we will not be concerned with registers or the instructions that may be stored in the code segment of memory.

Reference Implementation. A reference implementation is an implementation of a language that is designed to define the behavior of the language. It need not be an efficient implementation. The goal in this chapter is to give you enough information about how blocks are implemented in most programming languages so that you can understand when storage needs to be allocated, what kinds of data are stored on the run-time stack, and how an executing program accesses the data locations it needs. We do this by describing a reference implementation. Because our goal is to understand programming languages, not build a compiler, this reference implementation will be simple and direct. More efficient methods for doing many of the things described in this chapter, tailored for specific languages, may be found in compiler books.

A Note about C

The C programming language is designed to make C easy to compile and execute, avoiding several of the general scoping and memory management techniques described in this chapter. Understanding the general cases considered here will give C programmers some understanding of the specific ways in which C is simpler than other languages. In addition, C programmers who want the effect of passing functions and their environments to other functions may use the ideas described in this chapter in their programs.

Some commercial implementations of C and C++ actually do support function parameters and return values, with preservation of static scope by use of closures. (We will discuss closures in Section 7.4.) In addition, the C++ Standard Template Library (covered in Subsection 9.4.3) provides a form of function closure as many programmers find function arguments and return values useful.

7.2 IN-LINE BLOCKS

An in-line block is a block that is not the body of a function or procedure. We study in-line blocks first, as these are simpler than blocks associated with function calls.

7.2.1 Activation Records and Local Variables

When a running program enters an in-line block, space must be allocated for variables that are declared in the block. We do this by allocating a set of memory locations called an *activation record* on the run-time stack. An activation record is also sometimes called a *stack frame*.

To see how this works, consider the following code example. If this code is part of a larger program, the stack may contain space for other variables before this block is executed. When the outer block is entered, an activation record containing space for x and y is pushed onto the stack. Then the statements that set values of x and y will be executed, causing values of x and y to be stored in the activation record. On entry into the inner block, a separate activation record containing space for z will be added to the stack. After the value of z is set, the activation record containing this value will be popped off the stack. Finally, on exiting the outer block, the activation record containing space for x and y will be popped off the stack:

```
{ int x=0;
  int y=x+1;
      { int z=(x+y)*(x-y);
        };
  };
```

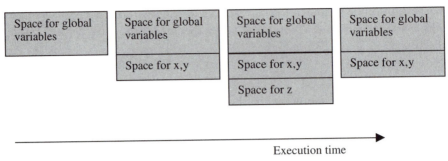

Execution time

Figure 7.2. Stack grows and shrinks during program execution.

We can visualize this by using a sequence of figures of the stack. As in Figure 7.1, the stack is shown growing downward in memory in Figure 7.2.

A simple optimization involves combining small nested blocks into a single block. For the preceding example program, this would save the run time spent in pushing and popping the inner block for z, as z could be stored in the same activation record as that of x and y. However, because we plan to illustrate the general case by using small examples, we do not use this optimization in further discussion of stack storage allocation. In all of the program examples we consider, we assume that a new activation record is allocated on the run-time stack each time the program enters a block.

The number of locations that need to be allocated at run time depends on the number of variables declared in the block and their types. Because these quantities are known at compile time, the compiler can determine the format of each activation record and store this information as part of the compiled code.

Intermediate Results

In general, an activation record may also contain space for intermediate results. These are values that are not given names in the code, but that may need to be saved temporarily. For example, the activation record for this block,

```
{ int z = (x+y)*(x-y);
}
```

may have the form

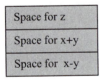

because the values of subexpressions x+y and x-y may have to be evaluated and stored somewhere before they are multiplied.

On modern computers, there are enough registers that many intermediate results are stored in registers and not placed on the stack. However, because register allocation is an implementation technique that does not affect programming language design, we do not discuss registers or register allocation.

Scope and Lifetime

It is important to distinguish the scope of a declaration from the lifetime of a location:

Scope: a region of text in which a declaration is visible.

Lifetime: the duration, during a run of a program, during which a location is allocated as the result of a specific declaration.

We may compare lifetime and scope by using the following example, with vertical lines used to indicate matching block entries and exits.

```
{ int x = ... ;
    { int y = ... ;
        { int x = ... ;
            ... .
        };
    };
};
```

In this example, the inner declaration of x hides the outer one. The inner block is called a *hole in the scope* of the outer declaration of x, as the outer x cannot be accessed within the inner block. This example shows that lifetime does not coincide with scope because the lifetime of the outer x includes time when inner block is being executed, but the scope of the outer x does not include the scope of the inner one.

Blocks and Activation Records for ML

Throughout our discussion of blocks and activation records, we follow the convention that, whenever the program enters a new block, a new activation record is allocated on the run-time stack. In ML code that has sequences of declarations, we treat each declaration as a separate block. For example, in the code

```
fun f(x) = x+1;
fun g(y) = f(y) +2;
g(3);
```

we consider the declaration of f one block and the declaration of g another block inside the outer block. If this code is not inside some other construct, then these blocks will both end at the end of the program.

When an ML expression contains declarations as part of the *let-in-end* construct, we consider the declarations to be part of the same block. For example, consider this example expression:

```
let fun g(y) = y+3
    fun h(z) = g(g(z))
in
      h(3)
end;
```

This expression contains a block, beginning with let and ending with end. This block contains two declarations, functions g and h, and one expression, h(x), calling one of these functions. The construct let ... in ... end is approximately equivalent to { ... ; ... } in C. The main syntactic difference is that declarations appear between the keywords let and in, and expressions using these declarations appear between keywords in and end. Because the declarations of functions g and h appear in the same block, the names g and h will be given values in the same activation record.

7.2.2 Global Variables and Control Links

Because different activation records have different sizes, operations that push and pop activation records from the run-time stack store a pointer in each activation record to the top of the preceding activation record. The pointer to the top of the previous activation record is called the *control link*, as it is the link that is followed when control returns to the instructions in the preceding block. This gives us a structure shown in Figure 7.3. Some authors call the control link the *dynamic link* because the control links mark the dynamic sequence of function calls created during program execution.

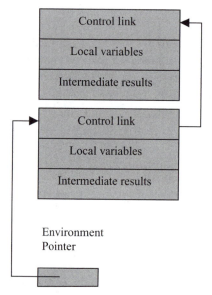

Figure 7.3. Activation records with control links.

When a new activation record is added to the stack, the control link of the new activation record is set to the previous value of the environment pointer, and the environment pointer is updated to point to the new activation record. When an activation record is popped off the stack, the environment pointer is reset by following the control link from the activation record.

The code for pushing and popping activation records from the stack is generated by the compiler at compile time and becomes part of the compiled code for the program. Because the size of an activation record can be determined from the text of the block, the compiler can generate code for block entry that is tailored to the size of the activation record.

When a global variable occurs in an expression, the compiler must generate code that will find the location of that variable at run time. However, the compiler can compute the number of blocks between the current block and the block where the variable is declared; this is easily determined from the program text. In addition, the relative position of each variable within its block is known at compile time. Therefore, the compiler can generate lookup code that follows a predetermined number of links

Example 7.1

```
{ int x=0;
  int y=x+1;
    { int z=(x+y)*(x-y);
    };
  };
```

When the expressions x+y and x-y are evaluated during execution of this code, the run-time stack will have activation records for the inner and outer blocks as shown below:

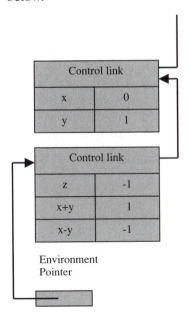

On a register-based machine, the machine code generated by the compiler will find the variables x and y, load each into registers, and then add the two values. The code for loading x uses the environment pointer to find the top of the current activation, then computes the location of x by adding 1 to the location stored in the control link of the current activation record. The compiler generates this code by analyzing the program text at compile time: The variable x is declared one block out from the current block, and x is the first variable declared in the block. Therefore, the control link from the current activation record will lead to the activation record containing x, and the location of x will be one location down from the top of that block. Similar steps can be used to find y at the second location down from the top of its activation record. Although the details may vary from one compiler to the next, the main point is that the compiler can determine the number of control links to follow and the relative location of the variable within the correct block from the source code. In particular, it is *not* necessary to store variable names in activation records.

7.3 FUNCTIONS AND PROCEDURES

Most block-structured languages have procedures or functions that include parameters, local variables, and a body consisting of an arbitrary expression or sequence of statements. For example, here are representative Algol-like and C-like forms:

```
procedure P(<parameters>)          <type> f(<parameters>)
begin                              {
    <local variables>;                 <local variables>;
    <procedure body>;              <function body>;
end;                               };
```

The difference between a *procedure* and a *function* is that a function has a return value but a procedure does not. In most languages, functions and procedures may have side effects. However, a procedure has only side effects; a procedure call is a statement and not an expression. Because functions and procedures have many characteristics in common, we use the terms almost interchangeably in the rest of this chapter. For example, the text may discuss some properties of functions, and then a code example may illustrate these properties with a procedure. This should remind you that the discussion applies to functions and procedures in many programming languages, whether or not the language treats procedures as different from functions.

7.3.1 Activation Records for Functions

The activation record of a function or procedure block must include space for parameters and return values. Because a procedure may be called from different call sites, it is also necessary to save the return address, which is the location of the next instruction to execute after the procedure terminates. For functions, the activation record must also contain the location that the calling routine expects to have filled with the return value of the function.

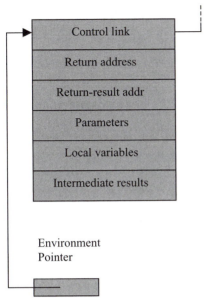

Figure 7.4. Activation record associated with funtion call.

The activation record associated with a function (see Figure 7.4) must contain space for the following information:

- *control link*, pointing to the previous activation record on the stack,
- *access link*, which we will discuss in Subsection 7.3.3,
- *return address*, giving the address of the first instruction to execute when the function terminates,
- *return-result address*, the location in which to store the function return value,
- *actual parameters* of the function,
- *local variables* declared within the function,
- *temporary storage* for intermediate results computed with the function executes.

This information may be stored in different orders and in different ways in different language implementations. Also, as mentioned earlier, many compilers perform optimizations that place some of these values in registers. For concreteness, we assume that no registers are used and that the six components of an activation record are stored in the order previously listed.

Although the names of variables are eliminated during compilation, we often draw activation records with the names of variables in the stack. This is just to make it possible for us to understand the figures.

Example 7.2

We can see how function activation records are added and removed from the run-time stack by tracing the execution of the familiar factorial function:

```
fun fact(n) = if n <= 1 then 1 else n * fact(n-1);
```

Suppose that some block contains the expression fact(3)+1, leading to a call of fact(3). Let us assume that the activation record of the calling block contains a location that will be used to store the value of fact(3) before computing fact(3)+1.

The next activation record that is placed on the stack will be an activation record for the call fact(3). In this activation record, shown after the list,

■ the control link points to the activation record of the block containing the call fact(3),
■ the return-result link points to the location in the activation record of the calling block that has been allocated for the intermediate value fact(3) of the calling expression fact(3)+1,
■ the actual parameter value 3 is placed in the location allocated for the formal parameter n,
■ a location is allocated for the intermediate value fact(n-1) that will be needed when n>0.

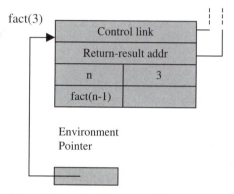

After this activation record is allocated on the stack, the code for factorial is executed. Because n>0, there is a recursive call fact(2). This leads to a recursive call fact(1), which results in a series of activation records, as shown in the subsequent figure.

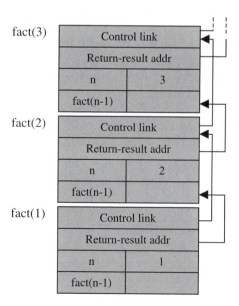

Note that in each of the lower activation records, the return-result address points to the space allocated in the activation record above it. This is so that, on return from fact(1), for example, the return result of this call can be stored in the activation record for fact(2). At that point, the final instruction from the calculation of fact(2) will be executed, multiplying local variable n by the intermediate result fact(1).

The final illustration of this example shows the situation during return from fact(2) when the return result of fact(2) has been placed in the activation record of fact(3), but the activation record for fact(2) has not yet been popped off the stack.

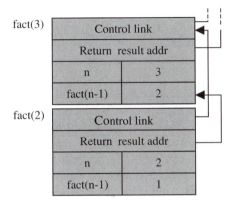

7.3.2 Parameter Passing

The parameter names used in a function declaration are called *formal parameters*. When a function is called, expressions called *actual parameters* are used to compute the parameter values for that call. The distinction between formal and actual parameters is illustrated in the following code:

```
proc p (int x, int y) {
    if (x > y) then ... else ... ;
    ...
    x := y*2 + 3;
    ...
}
p (z, 4*z+1);
```

The identifiers x and y are formal parameters of the procedure p. The actual parameters in the call to p are z and 4*z+1.

The way that actual parameters are evaluated and passed to the function depends on the programming language and the kind of parameter-passing mechanisms it uses. The main distinctions between different parameter-passing mechanisms are

■ the time that the actual parameter is evaluated
■ the location used to store the parameter value.

Most current programming languages evaluate the actual parameters before executing the function body, but there are some exceptions. (One reason that a language or program optimization might wish to delay evaluation of an actual parameter is that evaluation might be expensive and the actual parameter might not be used in some calls.) Among mechanisms that evaluate the actual parameter before executing the function body, the most common are

- *Pass-by-reference*: pass the L-value (address) of the actual parameter
- *Pass-by-value*: pass the R-value (contents of address) of the actual parameter

Recall that we discussed L-values and R-values in Subsection 5.4.5 in connection with ML reference cells (assignable locations) and assignment. We will discuss how pass-by-value and pass-by-reference work in more detail below. Other mechanisms such as *pass-by-value-result* are covered in the exercises.

The difference between pass-by-value and pass-by-reference is important to the programmer in several ways:

Side Effects. Assignments inside the function body may have different effects under pass-by-value and pass-by-reference.

Aliasing. Aliasing occurs when two names refer to the same object or location. Aliasing may occur when two parameters are passed by reference or one parameter passed by reference has the same location as the global variable of the procedure.

Efficiency. Pass-by-value may be inefficient for large structures if the value of the large structure must be copied. Pass-by-reference may be less efficient than pass-by-value for small structures that would fit directly on stack, because when parameters are passed by reference we must dereference a pointer to get their value.

There are two ways of explaining the semantics of call-by-reference and call-by-value. One is to draw pictures of computer memory and the run-time program stack, showing whether the stack contains a copy of the actual parameter or a reference to it. The other explanation proceeds by translating code into a language that distinguishes between L- and R-values. We use the second approach here because the rest of the chapter gives you ample opportunity to work with pictures of the run-time stack.

Semantics of Pass-by-Value

In pass-by-value, the actual parameter is evaluated. The value of the actual parameter is then stored in a new location allocated for the function parameter. For example, consider this function definition and call:

```
function f (x) = { x := x+1; return x };
....f(y)...;
```

If the parameter is passed by value and y is an integer variable, then this code has the same meaning as the following ML code:

```
fun f (z : int) = let   x = ref z   in   x := !x+1; !x   end;
...f(!y) ...;
```

As you can see from the type, the value passed to the function f is an integer. The integer is the R-value of the actual parameter y, as indicated by the expression !y in the call. In the body of f, a new integer location is allocated and initialized to the R-value of y.

If the value of y is 0 before the call, then the value of f(!y) is 1 because the function f increments the parameter and returns its value. However, the value of y is still 0 after the call, because the assignment inside the body of f changes the contents of only a temporary location.

Semantics of Pass-by-Reference

In pass-by-reference, the actual parameter must have an L-value. The L-value of the actual parameter is then bound to the formal parameter. Consider the same function definition and call used in the explanation of pass-by-value:

```
function f (x) = { x := x+1; return x };
. . . .f(y) . . . ;
```

If the parameter is passed by reference and y is an integer variable, then this code has the same meaning as the following ML code:

```
fun f (x : int ref) = ( x := !x+1; !x );
. . . f(y)
```

As you can see from the type, the value passed to the function f is an integer reference (L-value).

If the value of y is 0 before the call, then the value of f(!y) is 1 because the function f increments the parameter and returns its value. However, unlike the situation for pass-by-value, the value of y is 1 after the call because the assignment inside the body of f changes the value of the actual parameter.

Example 7.3

Here is an example, written in an Algol-like notation, that combines pass-by-reference and pass-by-value:

```
fun f(pass-by-ref x : int, pass-by-value y : int)
    begin
        x := 2;
        y := 1;
        if x = 1 then return 1 else return 2;
    end;
var z : int;
z := 0;
print f(z,z);
```

Translating the preceding pseudo-Algol example into ML gives us

```
fun f(x : int ref, y : int) =
    let val yy = ref y in
        x := 2;
        yy := 1;
        if (!x = 1) then 1 else 2
    end;
val z = ref 0;
f(z,!z);
```

This code, which treats L- and R-values explicitly, shows that for pass-by-reference we pass an L-value, the integer reference z. For pass-by-value, we pass an R-value, the contents !z of z. The pass-by-value is assigned a new temporary location.

With y passed by value as written, z is assigned the value 2. If y is instead passed by reference, then x and y are aliases and z is assigned the value 1.

Example 7.4
Here is a function that tests whether its two parameters are aliases:

```
function (y,z){
    y := 0;
    z :=0;
    y := 1;
    if z=1 then y :=0; return 1 else y :=0; return 0
}
```

If y and z are aliases, then setting y to 1 will set z to 1 and the function will return 1. Otherwise, the function will return 0. Therefore, a call f(x,x) will behave differently if the parameters are pass-by-value than if the parameters are pass-by-reference.

7.3.3 Global Variables (First-Order Case)

If an identifier x appears in the body of a function, but x is not declared inside the function, then the value of x depends on some declaration outside the function. In this situation, the location of x is outside the activation record for the function. Because x must be declared in some other block, access to a global x involves finding an appropriate activation record elsewhere on the stack.

There are two main rules for finding the declaration of a global identifier:

- *Static Scope*: A global identifier refers to the identifier with that name that is declared in the closest enclosing scope of the program text.
- *Dynamic Scope*: A global identifier refers to the identifier associated with the most recent activation record.

These definitions can be tricky to understand, so be sure to read the examples below carefully. One important difference between static and dynamic scope is that finding a declaration under static scope uses the static (unchanging) relationship between blocks in the program text. In contrast, dynamic scope uses the actual sequence of calls that are executed in the dynamic (changing) execution of the program.

Although most current general-purpose programming languages use static scope for declarations of variables and functions, dynamic scoping is an important concept that is used in special-purpose languages and for specialized constructs such as exceptions.

Dynamically Scoped	Statically Scoped
Older Lisps	Newer Lisps, Scheme
TeX/LaTeX document languages	Algol and Pascal
Exceptions in many languages	C
Macros	ML
	Other current languages

Example 7.5
The difference between static and dynamic scope is illustrated by the following code, which contains two declarations of x:

```
int x=1;
function g(z) = x+z;
function f(y) = {
    int x = y+1;
    return g(y*x)
};
f(3);
```

The call f(3) leads to a call g(12) inside the function f. This causes the expression x+z in the body of g to be evaluated. After the call to g, the run-time stack will contain activation records for the outer declaration of x, the invocation of f, and the invocation of g, as shown in the following illustration.

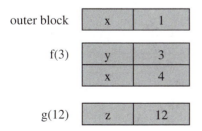

At this point, two integers named x are stored on the stack, one from the outer block declaring x and one from the local declaration of x inside f. Under dynamic scope, the identifier x in the expression x+z will be interpreted as the one from the most

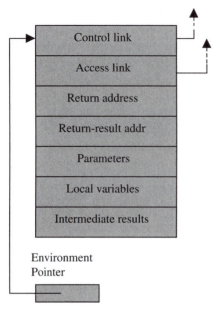

Figure 7.5. Activation record with access link for functions call with static scope.

recently created activation record, namely x=4. Under static scope, the identifier x in x+z will refer to the declaration of x from the closest program block, looking upward from the place that x+z appears in the program text. Under static scope, the relevant declaration of x is the one in the outer block, namely x=1.

Access Links are Used to Maintain Static Scope

The *access link* of an activation record points to the activation record of the closest enclosing block in the program. In-line blocks do not need an access link, as the closest enclosing block will be the most recently entered block – for in-line blocks, the control link points to the closest enclosing block. For functions, however, the closest enclosing block is determined by where the function is declared. Because the point of declaration is often different from the point at which a function is called, the access link will generally point to a different activation record than the control link. Some authors call the access link the *static link*, as the access links represent the static nesting structure of blocks in the source program.

The general format for activation records with an access link is shown in Figure 7.5.

Example 7.6

Let us look at the activation records and access links for the example code from Example 7.5, treating each ML declaration as a separate block.

Figure 7.6 shows the run-time stack after the call to g inside the body of f. As always, the control links each point to the preceding activation record on the stack.

The control links are drawn on the left here to leave room for the access links on the right. The access link for each block points to the activation record of the closest enclosing block in the program text. Here are some important points about

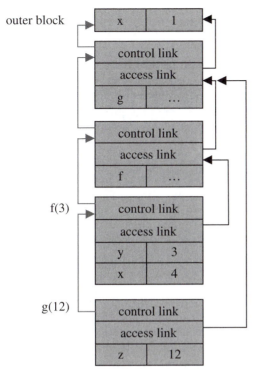

Figure 7.6. Run-time stack after call to g inside f.

this illustration, which follows our convention that we begin a new block for each ML declaration.

- The declaration of g occurs inside the scope of the declaration of x. Therefore, the access link for the declaration of g points to the activation record for the declaration of x.
- The declaration of f is similarly inside the scope of the declaration of g. Therefore, the access link for the declaration of f points to the activation record for the declaration of g.
- The call f(3) causes an activation record to be allocated for the scope associated with the body of f. The body of f occurs inside the scope of the declaration of f. Therefore, the access link for f(3) points to the activation record for the declaration of f.
- The call g(12) similarly causes an activation record to be allocated for the scope associated with the body of g. The body of g occurs inside the scope of the declaration of g. Therefore, the access link for g(12) points to the activation record for the declaration of g.
- We evaluate the expression x+z by adding the value of the parameter z, stored locally in the activation record of g, to the value of the global variable x. We find the location of the global variable x by following the access link of the activation of g to the activation record associated with the declaration of g. We then follow the access link in that activation record to find the activation record containing the variable x.

As for in-line blocks, the compiler can determine how many access links to follow and where to find a variable within an activation record at compile time. These properties are easily determined from the structure of the source code.

To summarize, the *control* link is a link to the activation record of the previous (calling) block. The *access link* is a link to the activation record of the closest enclosing block in program text. The control link depends on the dynamic behavior of program whereas the access link depends on only the static form of the program text. Access links are used to find the location of global variables in statically scoped languages with nested blocks at run time.

Access links are needed only in programming languages in which functions may be declared inside functions or other nested blocks. In C, in which all functions are declared in the outermost global scope, access links are not needed.

7.3.4 Tail Recursion (First-Order Case)

In this subsection we look at a useful compiler optimization called tail recursion elimination. For tail recursive functions, which are subsequently described, it is possible to reuse an activation record for a recursive call to the function. This reduces the amount of space used by a recursive function.

The main programming language concept we need is the concept of tail call. Suppose function f calls function g. Functions f and g might be different functions or f and g could be the same function. A call to f in the body of g is a *tail call* if g returns the result of calling f without any further computation. For example, in the function

```
fun g(x) = if x=0 then f(x) else f(x)*2
```

the first call to f in the body of g is a tail call, as the return value of g is exactly the return value of the call to f. The second call to f in the body of g is not a tail call because g performs a computation involving the return value of f before g returns.

A function f is *tail recursive* if all recursive calls in the body of f are tail calls to f.

Example 7.7
Here is a tail recursive function that computes factorial:

```
fun tlfact(n,a) = if n <= 1 then a else tlfact(n-1, n * a);
```

More specifically, for any positive integer n, tlfact(n,a) returns n!. We can see that tlfact is a tail recursive function because the only recursive call in the body of tlfact is a tail call.

The advantage of tail recursion is that we can use the same activation record for all recursive calls. Consider the call tlfact(3,1). Figure 7.7 shows the parts of each activation record in the computation that are relevant to the discussion.

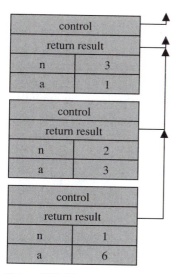

Figure 7.7. Three calls to tail recursive tlfact without optimization.

After the third call terminates, it passes its return result back to the second call, which then passes the return result back to the first call. We can simplify this process by letting the third call return its result to the activation that made the original call, tlfact(3,1). Under this alternative execution, when the third call finishes, we can pop the activation record for the second call as well, as we will no longer need it. In fact, because the activation record for the first call is no longer needed when the second call begins, we can pop the first activation record from the stack before allocating the second. Even better, instead of deallocating the first and then allocating a second activation record identical to the first, we can use one activation record for all three calls.

Figure 7.8 shows how the same activation record can be used used three times for three successive calls to tail recursive tlfact. The figure shows the contents of this activation record for each call. When the first call, tlfact(3,1), begins, an activation record with parameters (1,3) is created. When the second call, tlfact(2,3), begins, the parameter values are changed to (2,3). Tail recursion elimination reuses a single activation record for all recursive calls, using assignment to change the values of the function parameters on each call.

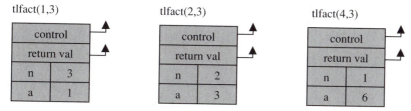

Figure 7.8. Three calls to tail recursive tlfact *with* optimization.

Tail Recursion as Iteration

When a tail recursive function is compiled, it is possible to generate code that computes the function value by use of an iterative loop. When this optimization is used, tail recursive functions can be evaluated by only one activation record for a first call and all resulting recursive calls, not one additional activation record per recursive call. For example, the preceding tail recursive factorial function may be compiled into the same code as that of the following iterative function:

```
fun itfact(n,a) = ( while !n > 0 do (a := !n * !a; n := !n - 1 ); !a );
```

An activation record for itfact looks just like an activation record for tlfact . If we look at the values of n and a on each iteration of the loop, we find that they change in exactly the same way is for tail recursive calls to tlfact. The two functions compute the same result by exactly the same sequence of instructions. Put another way, tail recursion elimination compiles tail recursive functions into iterative loops.

7.4 HIGHER-ORDER FUNCTIONS

7.4.1 First-Class Functions

A language has *first-class functions* if functions can be

- declared within any scope,
- passed as arguments to other functions, and
- returned as results of functions.

In a language with first-class functions and static scope, a function value is generally represented by a *closure*, which is a pair consisting of a pointer to function code and a pointer to an activation record.

Here is an example ML function that requires a function argument:

```
fun map (f, nil) = nil
 |   map(f, x::xs) = f(x) :: map(f, xs)
```

The map function take a function f and a list m as arguments, applying f to each element of m in turn. The result of map(f, m) is the list of results f(x) for elements x of the list m. This function is useful in many programming situations in which lists are used. For example, if we have a list of expiration times for a sequence of events and we want to increment each expiration time, we can do this by passing an increment function to map.

We will see why closures are necessary by considering interactions between static scoping and function arguments and return values. C and C++ do not support closures because of the implementation costs involved. However, the implementation of objects in C++ and other languages is related to the implementation of function values discussed in this chapter. The reason is that a closure and an object both combine data with code for functions.

Although some C programmers may not have much experience with passing functions as arguments to other functions, there are many situations in which this can be a useful programming method. One recognized use for functions as function arguments comes from an influential software organization concept. In systems programming, the term *upcall* refers to a function call up the stack. In an important paper called "The Structuring of Systems Using Upcalls," (ACM Symp. Operating Systems Principles, 1985) David Clark describes a method for arranging the functions of a system into layers. This method makes it easier to code, modularize, and reason about the system. As in the network protocol stack, higher layers are clients of the services provided by lower layers. In a layered file system, the file hierarchy layer is built on the vnode, which is in turn built over the inode and disk block layers. In Clark's method, which has been widely adopted and used, higher levels pass handler functions into lower levels. These handler functions are called when the lower level needs to notify the higher level of something. These calls to a higher layer are called upcalls. This influential system design method shows the value of language support for passing functions as arguments.

7.4.2 Passing Functions to Functions

We will see that when a function f is passed to a function g, we may need to pass the closure for f, which contains a pointer to its activation record. When f is called within the body of g, the environment pointer of the closure is used to set the access link in the activation record for the call to f correctly. The need for closures in this situation has sometimes been called the *downward funarg problem*, because it results from passing function as arguments downward into nested scopes.

Example 7.8
An example program with two declarations of a variable x and a function f passed to another function g is used to illustrate the main issues:

```
val x = 4;
fun f(y) = x*y;
fun g(h) = let val x=7 in h(3) + x;
g(f);
```

In this program, the body of f contains a global variable x that is declared outside the body of f. When f is called inside g, the value of x must be retrieved from the activation record associated with the outer block. Otherwise the body of f would be evaluated with the local variable x declared inside g, which would violate static scope. Here is the same program written with C-like syntax (except for the type expression int →int) for those who find this easier to read:

```
{ int x = 4;
      { int f(int y) {return x*y;}
            { int g(int ─→ int h) {
                  int x=7;
                  return h(3) + x;
                  }
            g(f);
}}}
```

The C-like version of the code reflects a decision, used for simplicity throughout this book, to treat each top-level ML declaration as the beginning of a separate block.

We can see the variable-lookup problem by looking at the run-time stack after the call to f from the invocation of g.

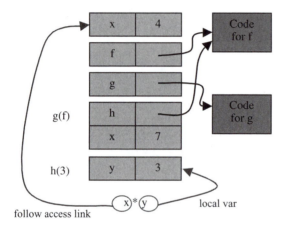

This simplified illustration shows only the data contained in each activation record. In this illustration, the expression x*y from the body of f is shown at the bottom, the activation record associated with the invocation of f (through formal parameter h of g). As the illustration shows, the variable y is local to the function and can therefore be found in the current activation record. The variable x is global, however, and located several activation records above the current one. Because we find global variables by following access links, the access link of the bottom activation record should allow us to reach the activation record at the top of the illustration.

When functions are passed to functions, we must set the access link for the activation record of each function so that we can find the global variables of that function correctly. We cannot solve this problem easily for our example program without extending some run-time data structure in some way.

Use of Closures
The standard solution for maintaining static scope when functions are passed to functions or returned as results is to use a data structure called a closure. A closure is a pair consisting of a pointer to function code and a pointer to an activation record. Because each activation record contains an access link pointing to the record for the

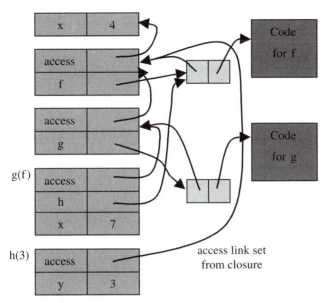

Figure 7.9. Access link set from closure.

closest enclosing scope, a pointer to the scope in which a function is declared also provides links to activation records for enclosing blocks.

When a function is passed to another function, the actual value that is passed is a pointer to a closure. The following steps are used for calling a function, given a closure:

- Allocate an activation record for the function that is called, as usual.
- Set the access link in the activation record by using the activation record pointer from the closure.

We can see how this solves the variable-access problem for functions passed to functions by drawing the activation records on the run-time stack when the program in Figure 7.8 is executed. These are shown in Figure 7.9.

We can understand Figure 7.9 by walking through the sequence of run-time steps that lead to the configuration shown in the figure.

1. *Declaration of* x: An activation record for the block where x is declared is pushed onto the stack. The activation record contains a value for x and a control link (not shown).
2. *Declaration of* f: An activation record for the block where f is declared is pushed onto the stack. This activation record contains a pointer to the run-time representation of f, which is a closure with two pointers. The first pointer in the closure points to the activation record for the static scope of f, which is the activation record for the declaration of f. The second closure pointer points to the code for f, which was produced during compilation and placed at some location that is known to the compiler when code for this program is generated.

3. *Declaration of* g: As with the declaration of f, an activation record for the block where g is declared is pushed onto the stack. This activation record contains a pointer to the run-time representation of g, which is a closure.

4. *Call to* g(f): The call causes an activation record for the function g to be allocated on the stack. The size and the layout of this record are determined by the code for g. The access link is set to the activation record for the scope where g is declared; the access link points to the same activation record as the activation record in the closure for g. The activation record contains space for the parameter h and local variable x. Because the actual parameter is the closure for f, the parameter value for h is a pointer to the closure for f. The local variable x has value 7, as given in the source code.

5. *Call to* h(3): The mechanism for executing this call is the main point of this example. Because h is a formal parameter to g, the code for g is compiled without knowledge of where the function h is declared. As a result, the compiler cannot insert any instructions telling how to set the access link for the activation record for the call h(3). However, the use of closures provides a value for the access link – the access link for this activation record is set by the activation record pointer from the closure of h. Because the actual parameter is f, the access link points to the activation record for the scope where f is declared. When the code for f is executed, the access link is used to find x. Specifically, the code will follow the access link up to the second activation record of the illustration, follow one additional access link because the compiler knew when generating code for f that the declaration of x lies one scope above the declaration of f, and find the value 4 for the global x in the body of f.

As described in step 5, the closure for f allows the code executed at run time to find the activation record containing the global declaration of x.

When we can pass functions as arguments, the access links within the stack form a tree. The structure is not linear, as the activation record corresponding to the function call h(3) has to skip the intervening activation record for g(f) to find the necessary x. However, all the access links point up. Therefore, it remains possible to allocate and deallocate activation records by use of a stack (last allocated, first deallocated) discipline.

7.4.3 Returning Functions from Nested Scope

A related but more complex problem is sometimes called the *upward funarg problem*, although it might be more accurate to call it the *upward fun-result problem* because it occurs when returning a function value from a nested scope, generally as the return value of a function.

A simple example of a function that returns a function is this ML code for function composition:

```
fun compose(f,g) = (fn x => g(f x));
```

Given two function arguments f and g, function compose returns the function composition of f and g. The body of compose is code that requires a function parameter x and then computes g(f(x)). This code is useful only if it is associated with some mechanism for finding values of f and g. Therefore, a closure is used to represent compose(f,g). The code pointer of this closure points to compiled code for "get function parameter x and then computes g(f(x))" and the activation record pointer of this closure points to the activation record of the call compose(f,g) because this activation record allows the code to find the actual functions f and g needed to compute their composition.

We will use a slightly more exciting program example to see how closures solve the variable-lookup problem when functions are returned from nested scopes. The following example may give some intuition for the similarity between closures and objects.

Example 7.9

In this example code, a "counter" is a function that has a stored, private integer value. When called with a specific integer increment, the counter increments its internal value and returns the new value. This new value becomes the stored private value for the next call. The followng ML function, make_counter, takes an integer argument and returns a counter initialized to this integer value:

```
fun make_counter (init : int) =
    let val count = ref init     (* private variable count *)
        fun counter(inc:int) = (count := !count + inc; !count)
    in
        counter     (* return function counter from make_counter *)
    end;
val c = make_counter(1); (* c is a new counter *)
c(2) + c(2);             (* call counter c twice *)
```

Function make_counter allocates a local variable count, initialized to the value of the parameter init. Function make_counter then returns a function that, when called, increments count's value by parameter inc, and then returns the new value of count.

The types and values associated with these declarations, as printed by the compiler, are

```
val make_counter = fn : int → (int → int)
val c = fn : int → int
8 : int
```

Here is the same program example written in a C-like notation for those who prefer this syntax:

```
{int→ int mk_counter (int init) {
        int count = init;
```

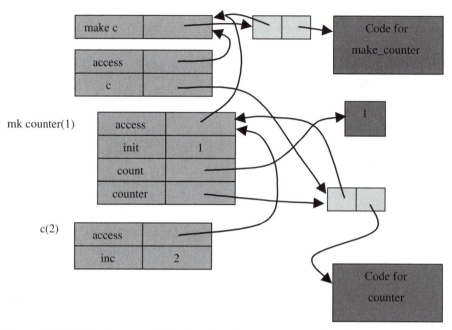

Figure 7.10. Activation records for function closure returned from function.

```
            int counter(int inc) { return count += inc;}
            return counter
        }
        int→ int c = mk_counter(1);
        print c(2) + c(2);
    }
```

If we trace the storage allocation associated with this compilation and execution, we can see that the stack discipline fails. Specifically, it is necessary to save an activation record that would be popped off the stack if we follow the standard last allocated–first deallocated policy.

Figure 7.10 shows that the records are allocated and deallocated in execution of the code from Example 7.9. Here are the sequence of steps involved in producing the activation records shown in Figure 7.10:

1. *Declaration of* make_counter: An activation record for the block consisting of the declaration of function make_counter is allocated on the run-time stack. The function name make_counter is abbreviated here as make_c so that the name fits easily into the figure. The value of make_counter is a closure. The activation record pointer of this closure points to the activation record for make_counter. The code pointer of this closure points to code for make_counter produced at compile time.

2. *Declaration of* c: An activation record for the block consisting of the declaration of function c is allocated on the run-time stack. The access pointer of this activation record points to the first activation record, as the declaration of

make_counter is the previous block. The value of c is a function, represented by a closure. However, the expression defining function c is not a function declaration. It is an expression that requires a call to make_counter. Therefore, after this activation record is set up as the program executes, it is necessary to call make_counter.

3. *Call to* make_counter: An activation record is allocated in order to execute the function make_counter. This activation record contains space for the formal parameter init of make_counter, local variable count and function counter that will be the return result of the call. The code pointer of the closure for counter points to code that was generated and stored at compile time. The activation record pointer points to the third activation record, because the global variables of the function reside here. The program still needs activation record three after the call to make_counter returns because the function counter returned from the call to make_counter refers to variables init and count that are stored in (or reachable through) the activation record for make_counter. If activation record three (used for the call to make_counter) is popped off the stack, the counter function will not work properly.

4. *First call to* c(2): When the first expression c(2) is evaluated, an activation record is created for the function call. This activation record has an access pointer that is set from the closure for c. Because the closure points to activation record three, so does the access pointer for activation record four. This is important because the code for counter refers to variable count, and count is located through the pointer in activation record three.

There are two main points to remember from this example:

- Closures are used to set the access pointer when a function returned from a nested scope is called.
- When functions are returned from nested scopes, activation records do *not* obey a stack discipline. The activation record associated with a function call cannot be deallocated when the function returns if the return value of the function is another function that may require this activation record.

The second point here is illustrated by the preceding example: The activation record for the call to make_counter cannot be deallocated when make_counter returns, as this activation record is needed by the function count returned from make_counter.

Solution to Storage Management Problem

You may have noted that, after the code in Example 7.9 is executed, following the steps just described, we have several activation records left on the stack that might or might not be used in the rest of the program. Specifically, if the function c is called again in another expression, then we will need the activation records that maintain its static scope. However, if the function c is not used again, then we do not need these activation records. How, you may ask, does the compiler or run-time system determine when an activation record can be deallocated?

There are a number of methods for handling this problem. However, a full discussion is complicated and not necessary for understanding the basic language design trade-offs that are the subject of this chapter. One solution that is relatively straightforward and not as inefficient as it sounds is simply to use a garbage-collection algorithm to find activation records that are no longer needed. In this approach, a garbage collector follows pointers to activation records and collects unreachable activation records when there are no more closure pointers pointing to them.

7.5 CHAPTER SUMMARY

A *block* is a region of program text, identified by begin and end markers, that may contain declarations local to this region. Blocks may occur inside other blocks or as the body of a function or procedure. Block-structured languages are implemented by activation records that contain space for local variables and other block-related information. Because the only way for one block to overlap another is for one to contain the other, activation records are generally managed on a run-time stack, with the most recently allocated activation record deallocated first (last allocated–first deallocated).

Parameters passed to functions and procedures are stored in the activation record, just like local variables. The activation record may contain the actual parameter value (in pass-by-value) or its address (in pass-by-reference). Tail calls may be optimized to avoid returning to the calling procedure. In the case of tail recursive functions that do not pass function arguments, this means that the same activation record may be used for all recursive calls, eliminating the need to allocate, initialize, and then deallocate an activation record for each call. The result is that a tail recursive function may be executed with the same efficiency as an iterative loop.

Correct access to statically scoped global variables involves three implementation concepts:

- Activation records of functions and procedures contain *access* (or *static scoping*) *links* that point to the activation record associated with the immediately enclosing block.
- Functions passed as parameters or returned as results must be represented as *closures*, consisting of function code together with a pointer to the correct lexical environment.
- When a function returns a function that relies on variables declared in a nested scope, static scoping requires a deviation from stack discipline: An activation record may need to be retained until the function value (closure) is no longer in use by the program.

Each of the implementation concepts discussed in this chapter may be tied to a specific language feature, as summarized in the following table.

Language Feature	Implementation construct
Block	Activation record with local memory
Nested blocks	Control link
Functions and procedures	Return address, return-result address
Functions with static scope	Access link
Function as arguments and results	Closures
Functions returned from nested scope	Failure of stack deallocation order for activation records

EXERCISES

7.1 Activation Records for In-Line Blocks

You are helping a friend debug a C program. The debugger gdb, for example, lets you set breakpoints in the program, so the program stops at certain points. When the program stops at a breakpoint, you can examine the values of variables. If you want, you can compile the programs given in this problem and run them under a debugger yourself. However, you should be able to figure out the answers to the questions by thinking about how activation records work.

(a) Your friend comes to you with the following program, which is supposed to calculate the absolute value of a number given by the user:

```
1:      int main( )
2:      {
3:              int num, absVal;
4:
5:              printf("Absolute Value\n");
6:              printf("Please enter a number:");
7:              scanf("%d",&num);
8:
9:              if (num <= 0)
10:             {
11:                     int absVal = num;
12:             }
13:             else
14:             {
15:                     int absVal = -num;
16:             }
17:
18:             printf("The absolute value of %d is %d.\n \n",num,absVal);
19:
20:             return 0;
21:     }
```

Your friend complains that this program just doesn't work and shows you some sample output:

```
cardinal:˜> gcc -g test.c
cardinal:˜> ./a.out
Absolute Value
Please enter a number: 5
The absolute value of 5 is 4.

cardinal:˜> ./a.out
Absolute Value
Please enter a number: -10
The absolute value of -10 is 4.
```

Being a careful student, your friend has also used the debugger to try to track down the problem. Your friend sets a breakpoints at line 11 and at line 18 and looks at the address of absval. Here is the debugger output:

```
cardinal:~> gdb a.out
(gdb) break test.c : 11
(gdb) break test.c : 18
(gdb) run
Starting program:
Absolute Value
Please enter a number: 5

Breakpoint 1, main (argc=1, argv=0xffbefb04) at test.c : 11
11              int absVal = num;
(gdb) print &absVal
$1 = (int *) 0xffbefa84
(gdb) c
Continuing.

Breakpoint 2, main (argc=1, argv=0xffbefb04) at test.c : 18
18                  printf("The absolute value of %d is %d.\n\n",num absVal);
(gdb) print &absVal
$2 = (int *) 0xffbefa88
```

Your friend swears that the computer must be broken, as it is changing the address of a program variable. Using the information provided by the debugger, explain to your friend what the problem is.

(b) Your explanation must not have been that good, because your friend does not believe you. Your friend brings you another program:

```
1:      int main( )
2:      {
3:              int num;
4:
5:              printf("Absolute Value\n");
6:              printf("Please enter a number:");
7:              scanf("%d",&num);
8:
9:              if (num >= 0)
10:             {
11:                     int absVal = num;
12:             }
13:             else
14:             {
15:                     int absVal = -num;
16:             }
17:
18:             {
19:             int absVal;
20:             printf("The absolute value of %d is %d.\n\n",num, absVal);
21:             }
22:     }
```

This program works. Explain why.

(c) Imagine that line 17 of the program in part (b) was split into three lines:

```
17a:            {
17b:            ...
17c:            }
```

Write a single line of code to replace the ... that would guarantee this program would NEVER be right. You may not declare functions or use the word absVal in this line of code.

(d) Explain why the change you made in part (c) breaks the program in part (b).

7.2 Tail Recursion and Iteration

The following recursive function multiplies two integers by repeated addition:

```
fun mult(a,b) =
    if a=0 then 0
        else if a = 1 then b
            else b + mult(a-1,b);
```

This is not tail recursive as written, but it can be transformed into a tail recursive function if a third parameter, representing the result of the computation done so far, is added:

```
fun mult(a,b) =
    let fun mult1(a,b,result) =
            if a=0 then 0
                else if a = 1 then b + result
                    else mult1(a-1, b, result+b)
    in
        mult1(a, b, 0)
    end;
```

Translate this tail recursive definition into an equivalent ML function by using a while loop instead of recursion. An ML while has the usual form, described in Subsection 5.4.5.

7.3 Time and Space Requirements

This question asks you to compare two functions for finding the middle element of a list. (In the case of an even-length list of $2n$ elements, both functions return the $n + 1$st.) The first uses two local recursive functions, len and get. The len function finds the length of a list and get(n,l) returns the nth element of list l. The second middle function uses a subsidiary function m that recursively traverses two lists, taking two elements off the first list and one off the second until the first list is empty. When this occurs, the first element of the second list is returned:

```
exception Empty;

fun middle1(l) =
    let fun len(nil) = 0
        |    len(x : : l) = 1+len(l)
        and get(n, nil) = raise Empty
        |    get(n, x : : l) = if n=1 then x else get(n-1, l)
    in
```

```
            get((len(l) div 2)+1, l)
        end;


    fun middle2(l) =
        let fun m(x, nil) = raise Empty
            |    m(nil,x : : l) = x
            |    m([y],x : : l) = x
            |    m(y::(z : : l1),x : : l2) = m(l1, l2)
        in
            m(l, l)
        end;
```

Assume that both are compiled and executed by a compiler that optimizes use of activation records or "stack frames."

(a) Describe the approximate running time and space requirements of middle1 for a list of length n. Just count the number of calls to each function and the maximum number of activation records that *must* be placed on the stack at any time during the computation.

(b) Describe the approximate running time and space requirements of middle2 for a list of length n. Just count the number of calls to m and the maximum number of activation records that *must* be placed on the stack at any time during the computation.

(c) Would an iterative algorithm with two pointers, one moving down the list twice as fast as the other, be significantly more or less efficient than middle2? Explain briefly in one or two sentences.

7.4 Parameter Passing

Consider the following procedure, written in an Algol/Pascal-like notation:

```
    proc power(x, y, z : int)
    begin
        z := 1
            while y > 0 do
                z := z*x
                y := y-1
            end
    end
```

The code that makes up the body of power is intended to calculate x^y and place the result in z. However, depending on the actual parameters, power may not behave correctly for certain combinations of parameter-passing methods. For simplicity, we only consider call-by-value and call-by-reference.

(a) Assume that a and c are assignable integer variables with distinct L-values. Which parameter-passing methods make $c = a^a$ *after* a call power(a, a, c). You may assume that the R-values of a and c are nonnegative integers.

(b) Suppose that a and c are formal parameters to some procedure P and that the preceding expression power(a, a, c) is evaluated inside the body of P. If a and c are passed to P by reference and become aliases, then what parameter-passing method(s) will make c = a^a *after* a call power(a, a, c)? If, after the call, c = a^a, does that mean that power actually performed the correct calculation?

7.5 Aliasing and Static Analysis

The designers of the systems programming language Euclid wanted programs written in Euclid to be easy to verify formally. They based the language on Pascal, changing those those features that made verification complicated. One set of changes eliminates *aliasing*, in which two different names denote the same location. Aliasing can arise in several ways in Pascal. For example, suppose that a program contains the declaration

    procedure P(var x,y: real);

Later in the body of the program the procedure call P(z,z) appears. While executing the body of P for this call, both x and y refer to the same location. In Pascal this call is perfectly legal, but in Euclid, the program is not considered syntactically correct.

(a) Explain briefly why aliasing might make it difficult to verify (reason about) programs.

(b) What problems do you think the designers of Euclid had to face in prohibiting aliasing? Would it be easy to implement a good compile-time test for aliasing?

7.6 Pass-by-Value-Result

In *pass-by-value-result*, also called call-by-value-result and copy-in/copy-out, parameters are passed by value, with an added twist. More specifically, suppose a function f with a pass-by-value-result parameter u is called with actual parameter v. The activation record for f will contain a location for formal parameter u that is initialized to the R-value of v. Within the body of f, the identifier u is treated as an assignable variable. On return from the call to f, the actual parameter v is assigned the R-value of u.

The following pseudo-Algol code illustrates the main properties of pass-by-value-result:

```
var x : integer;
x := 0;
procedure p(value-result y : integer)
    begin
        y := 1;
        x := 0;
    end;
p(x);
```

With pass-by-value-result, the final value of x will be 1: Because y is given a new location distinct from x, the assignment to x does not change the local value of y. When the function returns, the value of y is assigned to the actual parameter x. If the parameter were passed by reference, then x and y would be aliases and the assignment to x would change the value of y to 0. If the parameter were passed by value, the assignment to y in the body of p would not change the global variable x and the final value of x would also be 0.

Translate the preceding program fragment into ML (or pseudo-ML if you prefer) in a way that makes the operations on locations, and the differences between L-values and R-values, explicit. Your solution should have the form

```
val x = ref 0;
fun p(y' : int ref) =
    ... ;
p(x);
```

Note that, in ML, like C and unlike Algol or Pascal, a function may be called as a procedure.

7.7 Parameter-Passing Comparison

For the following Algol-like program, write the number printed by running the program under each of the listed parameter passing mechanisms. Pass-by-value-result, also sometimes called copy-in/copy-out, is explained in problem 6:

```
begin
    integer i;

    procedure pass ( x, y );
        integer x, y; // types of the formal parameters
        begin
            x := x + 1;
            y := x + 1;
            x := y;
            i := i + 1
        end

    i := 1;
    pass (i, i);
    print   i
end
```

(a) pass-by-value

(b) pass-by-reference

(c) pass-by-value-result

7.8 Static and Dynamic Scope

Consider the following program fragment, written both in ML and in pseudo-C:

```
1    let x = 2 in                    int x = 2; {
2        let val fun f(y) = x + y in     int f (int y) { return x + y; } {
3            let val x = 7 in                int x = 7; {
4                x +                             x +
5                    f(x)                            f(x);
6            end                             }
7        end                             }
8    end;                            }
```

The C version would be legal in a version of C with nested functions.

(a) Under static scoping, what is the value of x + f(x) in this code? During the execution of this code, the value of x is needed three different times (on lines 2, 4, and 5). For each line where x is used, state what numeric value is used when the value of x is requested and explain why these are the appropriate values under static scoping.

(b) Under dynamic scoping, what is the value of x + f(x) in this code? For each line in which x is used, state which value is used for x and explain why these are the appropriate values under dynamic scoping.

7.9 Static Scope in ML

ML uses static scope. Consider two functions of this form:

```
fun f(x) = ...;
fun g(x) = ...f...;
```

If we treat a sequence of declarations as if each begins a new block, static scoping implies that any mention of f in g will always refer to the declaration that precedes it, not to future declarations in the same interactive session.

(a) Explain how ML type inference relies on static scope. Would the current typing algorithm work properly if the language were changed to use dynamic scope?

(b) Suppose that, instead of using the language interactively, we intend to build a "batch" compiler. This compiler should accept any legal interactive session as input. The difference is that the entire program will be read and compiled before printing any type information or output. Will the problem with type inference and dynamic scope become simpler in this context?

7.10 Eval and Scope

Many compilers look at programs and eliminate any unused variables. For example, in the following program, x is unused so it could be eliminated:

```
let x = 5 in f(0) end
```

Some languages, including Lisp and Scheme, have a way to construct and evaluate expressions at run time. Constructing programs at run time is useful in certain kinds of problems, such as symbolic mathematics and genetic algorithms.

The following program evaluates the string bound to s, inside the scope of two declarations:

```
let s = read_text_from_user( ) in
    let x = 5 and y = 3 in eval s end
end
```

If s were bound to 1+x*y then eval would return 16. Assume that eval is a special language feature and not simply a library function.

(a) The "unused variable" optimization and the "eval" construct are not compatible. The identifiers x and y do not appear in the body of the inner let (the part between in and end), yet an optimizing compiler cannot eliminate them because the eval *might* need them. In addition to the values 5 and 3, what information does the language implementation need to store for eval that would not be needed in a language without eval?

(b) A clever compiler might look for eval in the scope of the let. If eval does *not* appear, then it may be safe to perform the optimization. The compiler could eliminate any variables that do not appear in the scope of the let declaration. Does this optimization work in a statically scoped language? Why or why not?

(c) Does the optimization suggested in part (b) work in a dynamically scoped language? Why or why not?

7.11 Lambda Calculus and Scope

Consider the following ML expression:

```
fun foo(x : int) =
    let fun bar(f) = fn x => f (f (x))
    in
        bar(fn y => y + x)
    end;
```

In β reduction on lambda terms, the function argument is substituted for the formal parameter. In this substitution, it is important to rename bound variables to avoid capture. This question asks about the connection between names of bound variables and static scope. Using a variant of substitution that does not rename bound variables, we can investigate dynamic scoping.

(a) The following lambda term is equivalent to the function foo:

$$\lambda x.((\lambda f.\lambda x. f(fx)) (\lambda y.y + x))$$

Use β reduction to reduce this lambda term to normal form.

(b) Using the example reduction from part (a), explain how renaming bound variables provides static scope. In particular, say which preceding variable (x, f, or y) must be renamed and how some specific variable reference is therefore resolved statically.

(c) Under normal ML static scoping, what is the value of the expression foo(3)(2)?

(d) Give a lambda term in normal form that corresponds to the function that the expression in part (a) would define under dynamic scope. Show how you can reduce the expression to get this normal form by *not* renaming bound variables when you perform substitution.

(e) Under dynamic scoping, what is the value of the expression foo(3)(2)?

(f) In the usual statically scoped lambda calculus, α conversion (renaming bound variables) does not change the value of an expression. Use the example expression from part (a) to explain why α conversion may change the value of an expression if variables are dynamically scoped. (This is a general fact about dynamically scoped languages, not a peculiarity of lambda calculus.)

7.12 Function Calls and Memory Management

This question asks about memory management in the evaluation of the following statically scoped ML expression:

```
val x = 5;
fun f(y) = (x+y) -2;
fun g(h) = let val x = 7 in h(x) end;
let val x = 10 in g(f) end;
```

(a) Fill in the missing information in the following illustration of the run-time stack after the call to h inside the body of g. Remember that function values are represented by closures and that a closure is a pair consisting of an environment (pointer to an activation record) and compiled code.

In this figure, a bullet (•) indicates that a pointer should be drawn from this slot to the appropriate closure or compiled code. Because the pointers to activation records cross and could become difficult to read, each activation record is numbered at the far left. In each activation record, place the number of the activation record of the statically enclosing scope in the slot labeled "access link." The first two are done for you. Also use activation record numbers for the environment pointer part of each closure pair. Write the values of local variables and function parameters directly in the activation records.

	Activation Records		*Closures*	*Compiled Code*
(1)	access link	(0)		
	x			
(2)	access link	(1)		
	f	●		
(3)	access link	( )	⟨ ( ), ● ⟩	
	g	●		|code for f |
(4)	access link	( )	⟨ ( ), ● ⟩	
	x			
(5) g(f)	access link	( )		
	h	●		|code for g |
	x			|... ...|
(6) h(x)	access link	( )		
	y			

(b) What is the value of this expression? Why?

7.13 Function Returns and Memory Management

This question asks about memory management in the evaluation of the following statically scoped ML expression:

```
val x = 5;
fun f(y) =
    let val z = [1, 2, 3]    (* declare list *)
        fun g(w) = w+x+y (* declare local function *)
    in
        g                    (* return local function *)
    end;
val h = let val x=7 in f(3) end;
h(2);
```

(a) Write the type of each of the declared identifiers (x, f, and h).

(b) Because this code involves a function that returns a function, activation records cannot be deallocated in a last-in/first-out (LIFO) stacklike manner. Instead, let us just assume that activation records will be garbage collected at some point. Under this assumption, the activation record for the call f in the expression for h will still be available when the call h(2) is executed.

Fill in the missing information in the following illustration of the run-time stack after the call to h at the end of this code fragment. Remember that function values are represented by closures and that a closure is a pair consisting of an environment (pointer to an activation record) and compiled code.

In this figure, a bullet (•) indicates that a pointer should be drawn from this slot to the appropriate closure, compiled code, or list cell. Because the pointers to activation records cross and could become difficult to read, each activation record is numbered at the far left. In each activation record, place the number of the activation record of the statically enclosing scope in the slot labeled "access link." The first two are done for you. Also use activation record numbers for the environment pointer part of each closure pair. Write the values of local variables and function parameters directly in the activation records.

Activation Records　　　　*Heap Data and Closures*　　　*Compiled Code*

(1)	access link	(0)	
	x		
(2)	access link	(1)	⟨ ( ), • ⟩
	f	•		code for f	
(3)	access link	( )	⟨ ( ), • ⟩
	h	•	
(4)	access link	( )		code for g	
	x		
(5) f(3)	access link	( )	
	y		1 • ⟶ 2 • ⟶ 3
	z	•	
	g		
(6) h(2)	access link	( )	
	w		

(c) What is the value of this expression? Explain which numbers are added together and why.

(d) If there is another call to h in this program, then the activation record for this closure cannot be garbage collected. Using the definition of garbage given in the Lisp chapter (see Chapter 3), explain why, as long as h is reachable, mark-and-sweep will fail to collect some garbage that will never be accessed by the program.

7.14 Recursive Calls and Memory Management

This question asks about memory management in the evaluation of the following ML expression (with line numbers):

```
1>    fun myop(x,y) = x*y;
2>    fun recurse(n) =
3>        if n=0 then 1
4>        else myop(n, recurse(n-1));
5>    let
6>        fun myop(x,y) = x + y
7>    in
8>        recurse(1)
9>    end;
```

(a) Assume that expressions are evaluated by static scope. Fill in the missing information in the following illustration of the run-time stack after the last call to myop on line 4 of this code fragment. Remember that function values are represented by closures and that a closure is a pair consisting of an environment (pointer to an activation record) and compiled code. Remember also that in ML function arguments are evaluated before the function is called.

In this figure, a bullet (•) indicates that a pointer should be drawn from this slot to the appropriate closure, compiled code, or list cell. Because the pointers to activation records cross and could become difficult to read, each activation record is numbered at the far left. In each activation record, place the number of the activation record of the statically enclosing scope in the slot labeled "access link" and the number of the activation record of the dynamically enclosing scope in the slot labeled "control link." The first two are done for you. Also use activation record numbers for the environment pointer part of each closure pair. Write the values of local variables and function parameters in the activation records. Write the line numbers of code inside the brackets [ ].

Activation Records			*Closures*	*Compiled Code*
(1)	access link	(0)		
	control link	(0)		
	myop	•		
(2)	access link	(1)	⟨ ( ), • ⟩	code for myop
	control link	(1)		defined line [ ]
	recurse	•		
(3)	access link	( )	⟨ ( ), • ⟩	code for recurse
	control link	( )		
	myop	•		
(4) recurse(1)	access link	( )		
	control link	( )		
	n		⟨ ( ), • ⟩	code for myop
(5) myop(1,0)	access link	( )		defined line [ ]
	control link	( )		
	x			
	y			
(6) recurse(0)	access link	( )		
	control link	( )		
	n			

(b) What is the value of this expression under static scope? Briefly explain how your stack diagram from part (a) allows you to find which value of myop to use.

(c) What would be the value if dynamic scope were used? Explain how the stack diagram would be different from the one you have drawn in part (a) and briefly explain why.

7.15 Closures

In ANSI C, we can pass and return pointers to functions. Why does the implementation of this language not require closures?

7.16 Closures and Tail Recursion

The function f in this declaration of factorial is formally tail recursive: The only calls in the body of f are tail calls:

```
fun fact(n) =
    let f(n, g) = if n=0 then g(1)
                  else let h(i) = g(i*n)
                       in
                           f(n-1, h)
                       end
    in
        f(n, fn x => x)
    end
```

This question asks you to consider the problem of applying the ordinary tail recursion elimination optimization to this function.

(a) Fill in the missing information in the following outline of the activation records resulting from the unoptimized execution of f(2, fn x => x). You may want to draw closures or other data.

f(2, fn x => x)	access link	
	n	
	g	
f(1, h)	access link	
	n	
	g	
f(0, h)	access link	
	n	
	g	

(b) What makes this function more difficult to optimize than the other examples discussed in this chapter? Explain.

7.17 Tail Recursion and Order of Operations

This asks about the order of operations when converting a function to tail recursive form and about passing functions from one scope to another. Here are three versions of our favorite recursive function, *factorial*:

$$\text{Normal recursive version}$$
$$\textbf{fact}_A\ (n) =\quad (\text{if } n=0 \text{ then } 1 \text{ else } n*\text{fact}_A(n-1))$$

$$\text{Tail-recursive version}$$
$$\textbf{fact}'(n,a) =\quad (\text{if } n=0 \text{ then } a \text{ else } \text{fact}'(n-1,(n*a)))$$
$$\textbf{fact}_B(n) =\quad \text{fact}'(n,1)$$

$$\text{Another tail-recursive version}$$
$$\textbf{fact}''(n,rest) =\quad (\text{if } n=0 \text{ then } rest(1)$$
$$\text{else } \text{fact}''(n-1,(\text{fn}(r)\Rightarrow rest(n*r))))$$
$$\textbf{fact}_C(n) =\quad \text{fact}''(n,\text{fn(answer)}\Rightarrow \text{answer})$$

Here is the evaluation of $\textbf{fact}_A$ (3) and $\textbf{fact}_B$ (3):

$$\textbf{fact}_A(3) =\quad (\text{if } 3=0 \text{ then } 1 \text{ else } 3*\text{fact}_A(2))$$
$$=\quad (\text{if false then } 1 \text{ else } 3*\text{fact}_A(2))$$
$$=\quad (3*\text{fact}(2))$$
$$=\quad (3*(\text{if } 2=0 \text{ then } 1 \text{ else } 2*\text{fact}_A(1)))$$
$$=\quad (3*(2*\text{fact}(1)))$$

$$= \quad (3*(2*(\text{if } 1=0 \text{ then } 1 \text{ else } 1*\text{fact}_A(0)))))$$
$$= \quad (3*(2*(1*\text{fact}(0)))))$$
$$= \quad (3*(2*(1*(\text{if } 0=0 \text{ then } 1 \text{ else } 0*\text{fact}_A(-1))))))$$
$$= \quad (3*(2*(1*(1))))$$
$$\mathbf{fact}_B(3) = \quad \text{fact}'(3,1)$$
$$= \quad (\text{if } 3=0 \text{ then } 1 \text{ else } \text{fact}'(2,(3*1)))$$
$$= \quad (\text{fact}'(2,(3*1)))$$
$$= \quad (\text{if } 2=0 \text{ then } (3*1) \text{ else } \text{fact}'(1,(2*(3*1))))$$
$$= \quad (\text{fact}'(1,(2*(3*1))))$$
$$= \quad (\text{if } 1=0 \text{ then } (2*(3*1)) \text{ else } \text{fact}'(0,(1*(2*(3*1)))))$$
$$= \quad (\text{fact}'(0,(1*(2*(3*1)))))$$
$$= \quad (\text{if } 0=0 \text{ then } (1*(2*(3*1))) \text{ else } \text{fact}'(-1,(0*(1*(2*(3*1))))))$$
$$= \quad (1*(2*(3*1)))$$

The multiplications are not carried out in these symbolic calculations so that we can compare the order in which the numbers are multiplied. The evaluations show that $\mathbf{fact}_A$ (3) multiplies by 1 first and by 3 last; $\mathbf{fact}_B$ (3) multiplies by 3 first and 1 last. The order of multiplications has changed.

(a) Show that $\mathbf{fact}_C$ (3) multiplies the numbers in the correct order by a symbolic calculation similar to those above that does not carry out the multiplications.

(b) We can see that $\mathbf{fact}''$ is tail recursive in the sense that there is nothing left to do after the recursive call. If these functions were entered into a compiler that supported tail recursion elimination, would $\mathbf{fact}_C$ (n) be closer in efficiency to $\mathbf{fact}_A$ (n) or $\mathbf{fact}_B$ (n)? First, ignore any overhead associated with creating functions, then discuss the cost of passing functions on the recursive calls.

(c) Do you think it is important to preserve the order of operations when translating an arbitrary function into tail recursive form? Why or why not?

8

Control in Sequential Languages

After looking briefly at the history of jumps and structured control, we will study exceptions and continuations. Exceptions are a form of jump that exits a block or function call, returning to some previously established point for handling the exception. Continuations are a more general form of "return" based on calling a function that is passed into a block for this purpose. The chapter concludes with a discussion of *force* and *delay*, complimentary techniques for delaying computation by placing it inside a function and forcing delayed computation with a function call.

8.1 STRUCTURED CONTROL

8.1.1 Spaghetti Code

In Fortran or assembly code, it is easy to write programs with incomprehensible control structure. Here is a short code fragment that illustrates a few of the possibilities. The fragment includes a Fortran CONTINUE statement, which is an instruction that does nothing but is used for the purpose of placing a label between two instructions. If you scan the code from top to bottom, you might get the idea that the instructions between labels 10 and 20 act together to perform some meaningful task. However, then as you scan downward, you can see that it is possible later to jump to instruction 11, which is in the middle of this set of instructions:

```
10 IF (X .GT. 0.000001) GO TO 20
   X = -X
11 Y = X*X - SIN(Y)/(X+1)
   IF (X .LT. 0.000001) GO TO 50
20 IF (X*Y .LT. 0.00001) GO TO 30
   X = X-Y-Y
30 X = X+Y
   . . .
50 CONTINUE
```

GUY STEELE

An energetic man with sincere conviction and a sense of humor, Guy Lewis Steele, Jr., is a Distinguished Engineer at Sun Microsystems, Inc. He received his A.B. in applied mathematics from Harvard College (1975) and his S.M. and Ph.D. in computer science and artificial intelligence from MIT (1977, 1980). He is known for his seminal work on Scheme, including the revolutionary continuation-based Rabbit compiler described in his S.M. thesis, and subsequent years of work on Common Lisp, parallel computing, and Java. In addition to reference books on Common Lisp, Fortran, C, and Java, Guy was the original lead author of *The Hacker's Dictionary*, now revised as *The New Hacker's Dictionary*.

Guy Steele's interests also include chess and music. A Life Member of the United States Chess Federation, he has sung in the bass section of the MIT Choral Society, the Masterworks Chorale, and in choruses with the Pittsburgh Symphony Orchestra and the Boston Concert Opera. Guy composed The Telnet Song, published in the April 1984 ACM, which pokes lighthearted fun at the exponential explosion of `ctrl-Q` keystrokes needed to exit cascaded telnet sessions.

In a masterful 1998 plenary address at the Object-Oriented Programming: Systems, Languages, and Applications (OOPSLA) conference, Guy illustrated the difficulty of growing a language by starting with words of one syllable and defining every longer word in his talk from one-syllable words and previously defined words of two or more syllables. You can find the text of this speech on the web. Guy Steele was awarded the ACM Grace Murray Hopper Award in 1988.

```
X = A
Y = B-A + C*C
GO TO 11

...
```

Although no short sequence can begin to approximate the Byzantine control flow of many archaic Fortran programs, this example may give you some feel for the kind of confusing control flow that was used in many programs in the early days of computing.

8.1.2 Structured Control

In the 1960s, programmers began to understand that unstructured jumps could make it difficult to understand a program. This was partly a realization about programming style and partly a realization about programming languages: If incomprehensible control flow is bad programming style, then programming languages should provide mechanisms that make it easy to organize the control structure of programs. This led to the development of some constructs that structure jumps:

```
if ... then ... else ... end
while ... do ... end
for ... { ... }
case ...
```

These are now adopted in virtually all modern languages.

In modern programming style, we group code in logical blocks, avoid explicit jumps except for function returns, and cannot jump *into* the middle of a block or function body.

The restriction on jumps into blocks illustrates the value of leaving a construct out of a programming language. If a label is placed in the middle of a function body and a program executes a jump to this label, what should happen? Should an activation record be created for the function call? If not, then local variables will not be meaningful. If so, then how will function parameters stored in the activation record be set? Without executing a call to the function, there are no parameter values to use in the call. Because these questions have no good, convincing, clear answers, it is better to design the compiler to reject programs that might jump into the middle of a function body.

Although most introductory programming books and courses today emphasize the importance of clean control structure and discourage the use of go to (if the language even allows it), it took many years of discussion and debate to reach this modern point of view. One reason for the change in perspective over the years is the decreasing importance of instruction-level efficiency. In 1960 and even 1970, there were many applications in which it was useful to save the cost of a test, even if it meant complicating the control structure of the program. Therefore, programmers considered it important to be able to jump out of the middle of a loop, avoiding another test at the top of the loop.

In the 1980s and 1990s, as computer speed increased, the number of applications in which a small change in efficiency would truly matter decreased significantly, to the point at which, in the 1990s, Java was introduced without any go to statement. Those interested in history may enjoy reading E.W. Dijkstra's March 1968 letter to the editor of *Communications of the ACM*, "Go To Considered Harmful," later posted on the Association for Computing Machinery web site as the October 1995 "Classic of the Month." The letter begins with these sentences:

> For a number of years I have been familiar with the observation that the quality of programmers is a decreasing function of the density of **go to** statements in the programs they produce. More recently I discovered why the use of the **go to** statement has such disastrous effects, and I became convinced that the **go to** statement should be abolished from all "higher level" programming languages. . . .

Simple control structures such as if-then-else have now been in common use since the rise of Pascal in the late 1970s. Exceptions and continuations, discussed in the remainder of this chapter, are more recent innovations in programming languages.

8.2 EXCEPTIONS

8.2.1 Purpose of an Exception Mechanism

Exceptions provide a structured form of jump that may be used to exit a construct such as a block or function invocation. The name *exception* suggests that exceptions are to be used in exceptional circumstances. However, programming languages cannot enforce any sort of intention like this. Exceptions are a basic mechanism that can be used to achieve the following effects:

- jump out of a block or function invocation
- pass data as part of the jump
- return to a program point that was set up to continue the computation.

In addition to jumping from one program point to another, there is also some memory management associated with exceptions. Specifically, unnecessary activation records may be deallocated as the result of the jump. We subsequently see how this works.

Exception mechanisms may be found in many programming languages, including Ada, C++, Clu, Java, Mesa, ML, and PL/1. Every exception mechanism includes two constructs:

- a statement or expression form for *raising* an exception, which aborts part of the current computation and causes a jump (transfer of control),
- a *handler* mechanism, which allows certain statements, expressions, or function calls to be equipped with code to respond to exceptions raised during their execution.

Another term for raising an exception is *throwing* an exception; another term for handling an exception is *catching* an exception.

There are several reasons why exceptions have become an accepted language construct. Many languages do not otherwise have a clean mechanism for jumping out of a function call, for example, aborting the call. Rather than using go tos, which can be used in unstructured ways, many programmers prefer exceptions, which can be used to jump only out of some part of a program, not into some part of the program that has not been entered yet. Exceptions also allow a programmer to pass data as part of the jump, which is useful if the program tries to recover from some kind of error condition. Exceptions provide a useful dynamic way of determining to where a jump goes. If more than one handler is declared, the correct handler is determined according to dynamic scoping rules. This effect would not be easy to achieve with other forms of control jumps.

The importance of dynamic scoping is illustrated in the following example.

Example 8.1

This example involves computing the inverse of a matrix. For the purpose of this example, a matrix is an array of real numbers. We compute matrix multiplication, used in linear algebra, by multiplying the entries of two matrices together in a certain way. If A is a matrix and I is the identity matrix (with ones along the diagonal and zeros elsewhere), then the inverse A^{-1} of A is a matrix such that the product $AA^{-1} = I$. A square matrix has an inverse if and only if something called the *determinant* of A is not zero. It is approximately as much computational work to find the determinant of a matrix as it is to invert a matrix.

Suppose we write a function for inverting matrices that have real-number entries. Because only matrices with nonzero determinants can be inverted, we cannot correctly compute the inverse of a matrix if the determinant turns out to be zero. One way of handling this difficulty might be to check the determinant before calling the invert function. This is not a good idea, however, as computing the determinant of a matrix is approximately as much work as inverting it. Because we can easily check the determinant as we try to convert the inverse, it makes more sense to try to invert the matrix and then raise an exception in the event that we detect a zero determinant. This leads to code structured as follows:

```
exception Determinant; (* declare Determinant exception *)
fun invert(aMatrix) =
    . . .
    if . . .
    then raise Determinant (* if matrix determinant is zero *)
        else . . .
    end;
invert(myMatrix) handle Determinant . . .;
```

In this example, the function invert raises an exception if the determinant of aMatrix turns out to be zero. If the function raises this exception as a result of the call invert(myMatrix), then because of the associated handler declaration, the call to invert is aborted and control is transferred to the code immediately following handle Determinant.

In this example, the exception mechanism is used to handle a condition that makes it impossible to continue the computation. Specifically, if the determinant is zero, the matrix has no inverse, and it is impossible for the invert function to return the inverse of the matrix.

If you think about it, this example illustrates the need for some kind of dynamic scoping mechanism. More specifically, suppose that there are several calls to invert in a program that does matrix calculations. Each of these calls could cause the Determinant exception to be raised. When a call raises this exception, where would we like the exception to be handled?

The main idea behind dynamic scoping of exception handlers is that the code in which the invert function is called is the best place to decide what to do if the determinant is zero. If exceptions were statically scoped, then raising an exception would jump to the exception handler that is declared lexically before the definition of the invert function. This handler would be in the program text before the invert function. If invert is in a program library, then the handler would have to be in the library. However, the person who wrote the library has no idea what to do in the cases in which the exception occurs. For this reason, exceptions are dynamically scoped: When an exception is raised, control jumps to the handler that was most recently established in the dynamic call history of the program. We will see how this works in more detail in after looking at some specific exception mechanisms.

8.2.2 ML Exceptions

The ML mechanism has three parts:

- Exceptions *declarations*, which declare the name of an exception and specify the type of data passed when this exception is raised,
- A *raise* expression, which raises an exception and passes data to the handler,
- *Handler* declarations, which establish handlers.

An ML exception declaration has the form

exception ⟨name⟩ of ⟨type⟩

where ⟨name⟩ is the name of the exception and ⟨type⟩ is the type of data that are passed to an exception handler when this exception is raised. The last part of this declaration, of ⟨type⟩, is optional. For example, the exception Ovflw below does not pass data, but the exception Signal requires an integer value that is passed to the receiving handler:

exception Ovflw;
exception Signal of int;

An ML raise expression has the form

raise ⟨name⟩   ⟨arguments⟩

where ⟨name⟩ is a previously declared exception name and ⟨arguments⟩ have a type that matches the exception declaration. For example, the exceptions previously declared can be raised with the following expressions:

```
raise Ovflw;
raise Signal (x+4);
```

An ML handler is part of an expression form that allows a handler to be specified. An expression with handler has the form

```
⟨exp1⟩ handle ⟨pattern⟩ => ⟨exp2⟩;
```

We evaluate this expression by evaluating ⟨exp1⟩. If the evaluation of ⟨exp1⟩ terminates normally, then this is the value of the larger expression. However, if ⟨exp1⟩ raises an exception that matches ⟨pattern⟩, then any values passed in raising the exception are bound according to ⟨pattern⟩ and ⟨exp2⟩ is evaluated. In this case, the value of ⟨exp2⟩ becomes the value of the entire expression. If ⟨exp2⟩ raises an exception or ⟨exp2⟩ raises an exception that does not match ⟨pattern⟩, then ⟨exp1⟩ handle ⟨pattern⟩ => ⟨exp2⟩ has an uncaught exception that can be caught by the handler established by an enclosing expression or function call. A more general form involving multiple patterns is described below.

Examples

Here is a simple example that uses the "overflow" exception previously mentioned:

```
exception Ovflw;         (* Declare exception name *)
fun f(x) = if x <= Min   (* Function with exception *)
                then raise Ovflw
                else 1/x;
(* – Expression that handles Ovflw in two ways – *)
( f(x) handle Ovflw => 0 ) / (f(x) handle Ovflw => 1)
```

Note that the final expression has two different handlers for the Ovflw exception. In the numerator, the handler returns value 0, making the fraction zero if overflow occurs. In the denominator, it would cause division by zero if the handler returns zero; the handler therefore returns 1 if the Ovflw exception is raised. This example shows how the choice of handler for an exception raised inside a function depends on how the function is called.

Here is another example, illustrating the way that data may be passed and used:

```
exception Signal of int;
fun f(x) = if x=0 then raise Signal(0)
            else if x=1 then raise Signal(1)
            else if x 10 then raise Signal(x-8)
            else (x-2) mod 4;
```

```
f(10) handle Signal(0) => 0
       |   Signal(1) => 1
       |   Signal(x) => x+8;
```

The handler in this expression uses pattern matching, which follows the form established for ML function declarations. More specifically, the meaning of an expression of the form

```
<exp> handle <pattern₁> => <exp₁>
        |   <pattern₂> = <exp₂>
                . . .
        |   <patternₙ> => <expₙ>
```

is determined as follows:

1. The expression to the left of the handle keyword is evaluated.
2. If this expression terminates normally, its value is the value of the entire expression with handler declaration; the handler is never invoked. (If evaluation of this expression does not terminate, then evaluation of the enclosing expression cannot terminate either.) If the expression raises an exception that matches $<pattern_i>$ (and there is no matching handler declared within $<exp>$), then the handler is invoked.
3. If the handler is invoked, pattern matching works just as an ordinary ML function call. The value passed by exception is matched against $<pattern_1>$, $<pattern_2>$, ..., $<pattern_n>$ in order until a match is found. If the value matches $<pattern_i>$, this causes any variables in $<pattern_i>$ to be bound to values. The corresponding expression $<exp_i>$ is evaluated with the bindings created by pattern matching.

8.2.3 C++ Exceptions

C++ exceptions are similar in spirit to exceptions in ML and other languages. The C++ syntax involves try blocks, a throw statement, and a catch block to handle exceptions that have been thrown within the associated try block. C++ exceptions are slightly less elegant than ML exceptions because C++ exceptions are not a separate kind of entity recognized by the type system.

The try block surrounds statements in which exceptions may be thrown. Here is a code fragment showing the form of a try block:

```
try {
       // statements that may throw exceptions
}
```

A throw statement may be executed within a try block, either directly by a statement in the try block or from a function called directly or indirectly from the block. A throw statement contains an expression and passes the value of the expression. Here is an example in which a character value is thrown:

```
throw "This generates a char * exception";
```

A catch block may immediately follow a try block and receive any thrown exceptions. Here is an example a catch-block receiving char * exceptions:

```
catch (char *message) {
        // statements that process the thrown char * exception
}
```

C++ uses types to distinguish between different kinds of exceptions. The throw statement may be used to throw different types of values:

```
throw "Hello world";        // throws a char *
throw 18;                    // throws an int
throw new String("hello"); // throws a String *
```

In a block that may throw more than one type of exceptions, multiple catch blocks may be used:

```
try {
        // code may throw char pointers and other pointers
}
catch (char *message) {
        // code processing the char pointers thrown as exceptions
}
catch (void *whatever) {
        // code processing all other pointers thrown as exceptions
}
```

Although it is possible to throw objects, some care is required because local objects are deallocated when an exception is thrown. More discussion of objects and storage allocation in C++ appears in Chapter 12.

Here is a more complete C++ example, combining try, throw, and catch:

```
void f(char * c) {
    ... if (c == 0) throw exception("Empty string argument");
}
main() {
```

```
try {
... f(x); ...
}
catch (exception) {
 exit(1);
}
}
```

As in ML and other languages, throwing a C++ exception causes a control transfer to the most recently established handler that is appropriate for the exception. Whereas ML uses pattern matching to determine whether a handler is appropriate for an exception, C++ uses type matching.

As is generally the case for C/C++, the type-matching issues are a little more complicated that we would like. To be specific, a handler of the form

```
catch(T t)
catch(const T t)
catch(T& t)
catch(const T& t)
```

can catch exception objects of type E if

- T and E are the same type, or
- T is an accessible base class of E at the throw point, or
- T and E are pointer types and there exists a standard pointer conversion from E to T at the throw point.

The rules for standard pointer conversion are also a little complicated, but we do not discuss them here because they are not critical for understanding the basic idea of exceptions.

One significant difference between ML and C++ that is important when programming with exceptions is that ML is garbage collected and C++ is not. In both languages, raising or throwing an exception will cause all run-time stack activation records between the point of the throw and the point of the catch to be deallocated. However, storage that is reachable from activation records may no longer be reachable after the exception, as the activation records with pointers no longer exist. This problem is discussed at the end of Subsection 8.2.4. There are also some details regarding the way exceptions work in constructors and destructors of objects that will be of interest to C++ programmers.

8.2.4 More about Exceptions

This section contains some additional examples of exceptions, with ML used as an illustrative syntax, and we discuss the interaction between exceptions, storage management, and static type checking. If you have used exceptions in a language different from ML, you might think about how the exception mechanism you have used is different and whether the difference is a consequence of some basic difference between the underlying programming languages.

Exceptions for Error Conditions

Exceptions arose as a mechanism for handling errors that occur when a program is running. One common form of run-time error occurs when an operation is not defined on some particular arguments. For example, division by zero raises an exception in many languages that have exception mechanisms. Here is a simple ML example, involving the left-subtree function that is not meaningful for trees that have only one node:

```
datatype 'a tree = Leaf of 'a | Node of 'a tree * 'a tree;
exception No_Subtree;
fun lsub ( Leaf x ) = raise No_Subtree
|   lsub (Node(x,y)) = x;
```

In this example, a function lsub(t) returns the left subtree of t if the tree has two subtrees (left and right). However, if there is no left subtree, then the No_Subtree exception is raised.

Exceptions for Efficiency

Sometimes it is useful to terminate a computation when the answer is evident. Exceptions can be useful for this purpose, as an exception terminates a computation. Consider the following code for computing the product of the integers stored at the leaves of a tree. This is written for the tree data type previously defined:

```
fun prod (Leaf x) = x : int
|   prod (Node(x,y)) = prod(x) * prod(y);
```

This correctly computes the product of all the integers stored at the leaves of a tree, but is inefficient in the case that some of the leaves are zero. If we are frequently computing the product for large trees that have zero at one or more leaves, then we might want to optimize this function as follows:

```
fun prod(aTree) =
    let exception Zero
        fun p(Leaf x) = if x = 0 then raise Zero else x
        |   p(Node(x,y)) = p(x) * p(y)
    in
        p(aTree) handle Zero => 0
    end;
```

In this function, a test is performed at each leaf to see if the value is zero. If it is, then an exception is raised and no other leaves of the tree are examined. This function is less efficient than the preceding one for trees without a zero, but is more efficient if zero is found. Even if the last leaf is zero, raising an exception avoids all the multiplications that would otherwise be performed.

Static and Dynamic Scope

We look at two ML code fragments that use identifier X in analogous ways. In the first example, X is an expression variable and hence is accessed according to static scoping rules. In the second, X is the name of an exception, and so its handlers are used according to dynamic scoping rules. The point of these two code fragments is to see the differences between the two scoping rules and to clearly illustrate that exception handlers are determined by dynamic scope.

The following code illustrates static scoping:

```
val x = 6;
let fun f(y) = x
and g(h) = let val x = 2 in h(1) end
in
        let val x = 4 in g(f) end
end;
```

Under static scoping, the value returned by the call to g(f) is the value of x in the scope where f is declared, which is 6.

If we rewrite this code making X an exception, we will see what value we get under dynamic scoping. One thing to remember when looking at the following code is that ML exceptions use a postfix notation, so although the code is structurally quite similar, it looks somewhat different at first glance:

```
exception X;
(let fun f(y) = raise X
and g(h) = h(1) handle X => 2
in
        g(f) handle X => 4
end ) handle X => 6;
```

Here, the value of the g(f) expression is 2. The handler X that is used is the latest one at the time the function raising the exception is called.

The following illustration shows the run-time stack for each code fragment, following the style explained in Chapter 7, with the exception code on the left and the corresponding code with values in place of exceptions on the right. For brevity, only the handler (or identifier) values and the access links are shown in each activation record, except that the parameter value is also shown in the activation record for each function call. If you begin at the bottom of the stack and search up the stack for the most recent handler, which is the rule for dynamic scope, this is the one with value 2. On the other hand, static scoping according to access links leads to value 6.

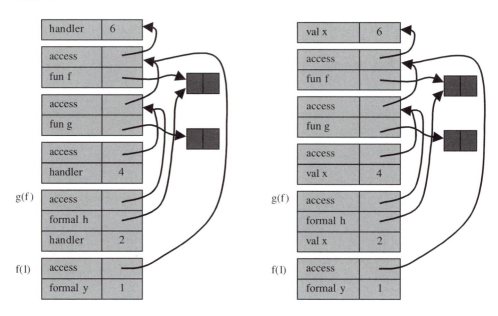

This illustration also clearly shows which activation records will be popped off the run-time stack when an exception is raised. Specifically, when the exception X is raised in the code associated with the stack on the left, control transfers to the handler identified in the top activation record. At this point, all of the activation records below the activation record with handler X and value 6 are removed from the run-time stack because they are not needed to continue the computation.

Typing and Exceptions
In ML, the expression

```
e1 handle A => e2;
```

returns either the value of e1 or the value of e2. This suggests that the types of e1 and e2 should be the same. To see why in more detail, look at this expression, which contains the preceding one:

```
1 + (e1 handle A => e2);
```

Here, the value of e1 handle A => e2 is added to 1, so both e1 and e2 must be integer expressions. More generally, the type system can assign only one type to the expression (e1 handle A => e2). Because (e1 handle A => e2) can return either the value of e1 or the value of e2, both e1 and e2 must have the same type.

The situation for raise is very different, as raise <exception> does not have a value. To see how this works, consider the expression

```
1 + raise No_Value
```

where No_Value is a previously declared exception. In this expression, the addition will never be performed because raising the exception jumps to the nearest handler, which is outside the expression shown. In ML, the type of raise <exception> is a type variable 'a, which allows the type-inference algorithm to give raise <exception> any type.

Exceptions and Resource Allocation

Raising an exception may cause a program to jump out of any number of in-line blocks and function invocations. In each of these blocks, the program may have allocated data on the stack or heap. In ML, C++, and other contemporary languages, all data allocated on the run-time stack will be reclaimed after an exception is raised. This occurs when the handler is located and intervening activation records are popped off the run-time stack.

Data allocated on the heap are treated differently in different languages. In ML, data on the heap that is no longer reachable after the exception will become garbage. Because ML is garbage collected, the garbage collector will reclaim this unreachable data. The situation is illustrated by the following code:

```
exception X;
(let
    val y = ref [1,2,3]
in
    ... raise X
end) handle X => ... ;
```

The local declaration let val x= ... in ... end causes a list [1,2,3] to be built in the heap. When raise X raises an exception inside the scope of this declaration, control is transferred to the handler outside this scope. The reference y, stored in the activation record associated with the local declaration, is popped off the stack. The list [1,2,3] remains in the program heap and is later collected whenever the garbage collector happens to run.

In C++, storage that is reachable from activation records may no longer be reachable after an exception is thrown. Because C++ is not garbage collected, it is up to the programmer to make sure that any data stored on the heap are explicitly deallocated. However, it may be impossible to explicitly deallocate memory that was previously allocated by the program if the only pointers to the data were those on the run-time stack. In particular, in the C++ version of the preceding program, with a linked list created in the heap, the only pointer to the list is the pointer y on the run-time stack. After the exception is thrown, the pointer y is gone, and there is no way to reach the data. There are two general solutions: Either make sure there is some way of reaching all heap data from the handler or accept the phenomenon and live with the memory leak. The C++ implementation provides some assistance for this problem by invoking the destructor of each object on the run-time stack as the containing activation record is popped off the stack. This solves the list problem if we build the list by placing one list object on the stack and by including code in the list destructor that follows the list pointer and invokes the destructor of any reachable list nodes.

The general problem with managing unreachable memory also occurs with other resources. For example, if a file is opened between the point of the handler and the point where an exception is thrown, there may be no way to close the open file. The same problem may occur with synchronization locks on concurrently accessible data areas. There is no systematic language solution that seems effective for handling these situations cleanly. Resource management is simply a complication that must be handled with care when one is programming with exceptions.

8.3 CONTINUATIONS

Continuations are a programming technique, based on higher-order functions, that may be used directly by a programmer or may be used in program transformations in an optimizing compiler. Programming with continuations is also related to the systems programming concepts of *upcall* or *callback* functions. As mentioned in Section 7.4, a callback is a function that is passed to another function so that the second function may call the first at a later time.

The concept of continuation originated in denotational semantics in the treatments of jumps (goto) and various forms of loop exit and in systems programming in the notion of upcall discussed in Section 7.4. Continuations have found application in continuation-passing-style (CPS) compilers, beginning with the groundbreaking Rabbit compiler for Scheme, developed by Guy Steele and Gerald Sussman in the mid-1970s. Since that time, continuations have been essential to many of the competitive optimizing compilers for functional languages.

8.3.1 A Function Representing "The Rest of the Program"

The basic idea of a continuation can be illustrated with simple arithmetic expressions. For example, consider the function

```
fun f(x,y) = 2.0*x + 3.0*y + 1.0/x + 2.0/y;
```

Assume that this body of the function is evaluated from left to right, so that if we stop evaluation just before the first division, we will have computed 2.0*x + 3.0*y and, when the quotient 1.0/x is completed, the evaluation will proceed with an addition, another division, and a final addition. The *continuation* of the subexpression 1.0/x is the rest of the computation to be performed *after* this quotient is computed. We can write the computation completed before this division and the continuation to be invoked afterward explicitly as follows:

```
fun f(x,y) = let val befor = 2.0*x + 3.0*y
                 fun continu(quot) = befor + quot + 2.0/y
             in
                 continu(1.0/x)
             end;
```

The evaluation order and result for the second definition of f will be the same as the first; we have just given names to the part to be computed before and the part to be computed after the division. The function called continu is the continuation of 1.0/x; it is exactly what the computer will do after dividing 1.0 by x. The continuation of the subexpression 1.0/x is a function, as the value of f(x,y) depends on the value of the subexpression 1.0/x.

Let us suppose that, if x is zero, it makes sense to return before/5.2 as the value of the function, and that otherwise we know that y should be nonzero and we can proceed to compute the function normally. Rather than change the function in a special-purpose way, we can illustrate the general idea by defining a division function that is passed the continuation, applying the continuation only in the case in which the divisor is nonzero:

```
fun divide(numerator,denominator,continuation,alternate_value) =
    if denominator > 0.0001
       then continuation(numerator/denominator)
       else alternate_value;

fun f(x,y) = let val befor = 2.0*x + 3.0*y
                 fun continu(quot) = befor + quot + 2.0/y
             in
                 divide(1.0, x, continu, befor/5.2)
             end;
```

This version of f now uses an error-avoiding version of division that can exit in either of two ways, the normal exit applying the continuation to the result of division and an error exit returning some alternative value passed as a parameter. This is not the most general version of division, however, because, in general, we might have one computation we might wish to perform when division is possible and another to perform when division is not. We can represent the computation on error as a function also, leading to the following revision. Here we have assumed, for simplicity, that computation after error is a function that need not be passed any of the other arguments:

```
fun divide(numerator,denominator,normal_cont,error_cont) =
    if denominator > 0.0001
        then normal_cont(numerator/denominator)
        else error_cont()

fun f(x,y) = let val befor = 2.0*x + 3.0*y
                 fun continu(quot) = befor + quot + 2.0/y
                 fun error_continu() = befor/5.2
             in
                 divide(1.0, x, continu, error_continu)
             end
```

For this specific computation, it is a relatively minor point that the division befor/5.2 is now done only if error_continu is invoked. However, in general, it is far more useful to have normal continuation and error continuation both presented as functions, as error handling may require some computation after the error has been identified.

The preceding example can be handled more simply with exceptions. Ignoring the precomputation of (2.0*x + 3.0*y), which a compiler could identify as a common subexpression anyway, we can write the function as follows:

```
exception Div;
fun f(x,y) = (2.0*x + 3.0*y +
              1.0/(if x > 0.001 then x else raise Div) + 2.0/y
             ) handle Div => (2.0*x + 3.0*y)/5.2
```

In general, continuations are more flexible than exceptions, but also may require more programming effort to get exactly the control you want.

8.3.2 Continuation-Passing Form and Tail Recursion

There is a program form called *continuation-passing form* in which each function or operation is passed a continuation. This allows each function or operation to terminate by calling a continuation. As a consequence, no function needs to return to the point from which it was called. This property of continuation-passing form may remind you of tail calls, discussed in Subsection 7.3.4, as a tail call need not return to the calling function. We will investigate the correspondence after looking at an example.

There are systematic rules for transforming an expression or program to CPS. The main idea is that each function or operation should take a continuation representing the remaining computation after this function completes. If we begin with a program that does not contain exceptions or other jumps, then each operation will be expected to terminate normally. Because each function or operation will therefore terminate by calling the function passed to it as a continuation, each function or operation will terminate by executing a tail call to another function.

We can transform the standard factorial function

```
fun fact(n) = if (n=0) then 1 else n*fact(n-1);
```

to continuation-passing form by first examining the continuation of each call. Consider the computation of fact(9), for example. This computation begins with an activation record for fact(9), then a recursive call to fact(8). The activation record for fact(8) points to the activation record for fact(9), as the multiplication associated with fact(9) must be performed after the call for fact(8) returns. The chain of activation records is shown in the following illustration:

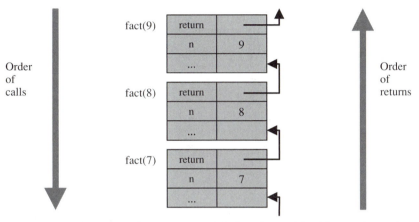

Because the invocation fact(9) multiplies the result of fact(8) by 9, the continuation of fact(8) is $\lambda x.\ 9*x$.

Similarly, after fact(7) returns, the invocation of fact(8) will multiply the result by 8 and then return to fact(9), which will in turn multiply by 9. Written as a function in lambda notation, the continuation of fact(7) is $\lambda y.(\lambda x.\ 9*x)\ (8*y)$.

By similar reasoning, the continuation of fact(6) is $\lambda z.(\lambda y.\ (\lambda x.\ 9*x)\ (8*y))\ (7*z)$.

Generalizing from these examples, the continuation of fact(n-1) is the composition of $(\lambda x.\ n*x)$ with the continuation of fact(n).

Using this insight, we can write a general CPS function to compute factorial. The function

```
f(n, k) = if n=0 then k(1) else f(n-1, λx. k (n*x) )
```

takes a number n and a continuation k as arguments. If n=0, then the function passes 1 to the continuation. If n>0, then the function makes a recursive call. Because the recursive call is to a CPS function, the continuation passed to the call must be the continuation of factorial of n-1. Given factorial x of n-1, the continuation multiplies by n and then passes the result to the continuation k of the factorial of n. Here is a sample calculation, with initial continuation the identity function, illustrating how the continuation-passing function works:

$$f(3, \lambda x.x) = f(2, \lambda y.((\ \lambda x.x)\ (3*y)))$$
$$= f(1, \lambda x.((\ \lambda y.3*y)(2*x)))$$
$$= \lambda x.((\ \lambda y.3*y)(2*x))\ 1$$
$$= 6$$

Intuitively, the continuation-passing form of factorial performs a sequence of recursive calls, accumulating a continuation. When the recursion terminates by reaching n=0, the continuation is applied to 1 and that produces the return value n!. When the continuation is applied, the continuation consists of a sequence of multiplications that compute factorial. This is exactly the same sequence of multiplications as would be done in the ordinary recursive factorial. However, in the case of ordinary recursive factorial, each multiplication would be done by a separate invocation of the factorial function.

Continuations and Tail Recursion. The following ML continuation-passing factorial function appears to use a tail recursive function f to do the calculation: fun factk(n) = let fun:

```
    f(n, k) = if n=0 then k(1) else f(n-1, fn x => k (n*x) )
in
    f(n, fn x => x)
end
```

The inner function f is tail recursive in the sense that the recursive call to f is the entire value of the function in the case n>0. Therefore, there is no need for the recursive call to return to the calling invocation. However, this does *not* mean that the continuation-passing function factk runs in constant space. The reason has to do with closures and scoping of variables. Specifically, the continuation

```
fn x => k (n*x)
```

contains the identifier x that is a parameter of the function. The continuation is therefore represented as a closure, with a pointer to the activation record of the calling invocation of f. Because the activation record is needed as part of the closure, it is not possible to use tail recursion optimization to eliminate the need for a new activation record.

Factorial can, however, be written in a tail recursive form:

```
fun fact1(n) = let fun
              f(n,k) = if n=0 then k else f(n-1, n*k)
         in
             f(n,1)
         end;
```

As discussed in Subsection 7.3.4, the tail recursive form is more efficient, as the compiler can generate code that does not allocate a new activation record for each call. Instead, the same activation record can be used for all invocations of the function f, with each call effectively assigning new values to local variables n and k.

We can derive the tail recursive form from the continuation-passing form by using a little insight. The main idea is that each continuation in the continuation-passing form will be a function that multiplies its argument by some number. We can therefore achieve the same effect by passing the number instead of the function. Although there is no standard, systematic way of transforming an arbitrary function into a tail recursive function that can be executed by use of constant space, there is a systematic transformation to continuation-passing form and, in some instances, a clever individual can produce a tail recursive function from the continuation-passing form.

8.3.3 Continuations in Compilation

Continuations are commonly used in compilers for languages with higher-order functions. The main steps in a continuation-based compiler follow the design pioneered by Steele and Sussman for Scheme (MIT AI MEMO 474, MIT, 1978):

1. lexical analysis, parsing, type checking
2. translation to lambda calculus form
3. conversion to CPS
4. optimization of CPS
5. closure conversion – eliminate free variables
6. elimination of nested scopes
7. register spilling – no expression with more than n free vars
8. generation of target-assembly language program
9. Assembly to produce target-machine program

The core step that makes continuations useful is step 4, optimizing the continuation-passing form of a program. The merit of continuations is that continuations make control flow explicit – each part of the computation explicitly calls a function to do the next part of the computation.

Furthermore, because a continuation-passing operation terminates with a call instead of a return, it is possible to compile calls directly into jumps. Arranging the target code in the correct order can eliminate many of these jumps. Although additional discussion of continuation-based compilation is beyond the scope of this book, there are several compiler books that address this subject in detail and many additional articles and web sources.

8.4 FUNCTIONS AND EVALUATION ORDER

Exceptions and continuations are forms of jumps that are used in high-level programming languages. A final technique for manipulating the order of execution in programs is to use function definitions and calls. More specifically, if a calculation can be put off until later, it may be placed inside a function and passed to code that will eventually decide when to do the calculation. This is most useful if the calculation might not be needed at all. In our brief survey of this simple technique, we look at controlling the order of evaluation for efficiency.

Delay and force are programming forms that can be used together to optimize program performance. Delay and Force are explicit program constructs in Scheme, but the main idea can be used in any language with functions and static scope. To see how Delay and Force are used, we start with an example. Consider a function declaration and call of the following form:

```
fun f(x,y) =
    ... x ... y ...
...
f(e1, e2)
```

Suppose that

- the value of y is needed only if the value of x has some property, and
- the evaluation of e2 is expensive.

In these circumstances, it is a good idea to delay the evaluation of e2 until we determine (inside the body of f) that the value of e2 is actually needed. If and when we make this determination, we may then force the evaluation of e2. In other words, we would like to be able to write something like the following, in which Delay(e) causes the evaluation of e to be delayed until we call Force(Delay(e)):

```
fun f(x,y) =
    ... x ... Force(y) ...
...
f(e1, Delay(e2))
```

If Force(y) occurs only where the value of y is needed and y is needed at most only once in the body of f, then it should be clear that this form is more efficient than the preceding one. Specifically, if many calls do not require the value of y, then each of these calls will run much more quickly, as we avoid evaluating e2 and we are assuming that evaluation of e2 is expensive. In cases in which the value of e2 is needed, we do the same amount of work as before, plus the presumably small overhead we introduced by adding Delay and Force to the computation.

We discuss two remaining questions: How can we express Delay and Force in a conventional programming language and what should happen if a delayed value is needed more than once?

Let us begin with the first problem, expressing Delay and Force in a conventional language, assuming for simplicity that there will only be one reference to the delayed value. Delay *cannot* be an ordinary function. To see this, suppose briefly that Delay(e) is implemented as a function Delay applied to the expression e. In most languages, the semantics of function calls requires that we evaluate the arguments to a function before invoking the function. Then in evaluating Delay(e) we will evaluate e first.

However, this defeats the purpose of Delay, which was to avoid evaluating e unless its value was actually needed.

Because Delay cannot be a normal function, we are left with two options:

- make Delay a built-in operation of the programming language where we wish to delay evaluation, or
- implement the conceptual construct Delay(e) as some program expression or sequence of commands that is not just a function applied to e.

The first option works fine, but only if we are prepared to modify the implementation of a programming language. Scheme, for example, inherits the concept of special form, a function that does not evaluate its arguments, from Lisp. When special forms are used, a Delay operation that does not evaluate its argument can be defined.

In other languages, we can think of Delay(e) as an abbreviation that gets expanded in some way before the program is compiled. An implementation of Delay and Force that works in ML is

```
Delay(e) == λ().e , which is actually written fn() => e
Force(e) == e()
```

where == means "macro expand to this form before compiling the program."

Here Delay(e) makes e into a parameterless function. The notation λ ().e indicates a function that takes no parameters and that returns e when called. This delays evaluation because the body of a functions is not evaluated until the function is called.

Force evaluates expressions that have previously been delayed. Because delayed expressions are zero-argument functions, Force calls a zero-argument function to cause the function body to be evaluated.

Example 8.2

Here is an example in which the Takeuchi function, tak, is used. The function tak runs for a *very* long time, without using so much stack space that the run-time stack overflows. (Try it!) Because of this characteristic of tak, it is often used as benchmark for testing the speed of function calls in a compiler or interpreter. In this example, the function f has two arguments; the second argument is used only if the first is odd. The purpose of Force and Delay in this example is to make f(fib(9), time_consuming(9)) run more quickly; fib is the Fibonacci function and time_consuming uses tak:

```
fun time_consuming(n) =
    let fun tak(x,y,z) = if x <= y then y
                else tak(tak(x-1,y,z), tak(y-1,z,x), tak(z-1,x,y))
    in
        tak(3*n, 2*n, n)
    end;
fun fib(n) = if n=0 orelse n = 1 then 1 else fib(n-1) + fib(n-2);
fun odd(n) = (n mod 2 ) = 1;
fun f(x,y) = if odd(x) then 1 else fib(y);
```

If we evaluate the following expression directly, it will run for a very long time:

```
f(fib(9), time_consuming(9));
```

Instead we rewrite the function f to expect a Delay-ed value as the second argument, and Force evaluation only if needed:

```
fun lazy_f(x,y) = if odd(x) then 1 else fib( y() );
```

Here is the corresponding call, with calculation of time_consuming(9) delayed:

```
lazy_f( fib(9), fn () => (time_consuming(9)));
```

Because fib(9) is odd, this expression terminates much more quickly than the expression without Delay.

The versions of Delay and Force described in Example 8.2 rely on static scoping and save time only if the delayed function argument is used at most once. Static scoping is necessary to preserve the semantics of the program. Without static scoping, placing an expression inside a function and passing it to another function might change the values of identifiers that appear in the expression. The reason why Delay and Force do not help if the expression is used twice or more is that each occurrence would involve evaluating the delayed expression. This will take extra time and may give the wrong result if the expression has side effects.

It is a relatively simple programming exercise to write versions of Delay and Force that work when the delayed value is needed more than once. The main idea is to store a flag that indicates whether the expression has been evaluated once or not. If not, and the value is needed, then the expression is evaluated and stored so that it can be retrieved without further evaluation when it is needed again. This trick is a form of evaluation that is referred to as *call-by-need* in the literature.

Here is a simple ML version of the code needed to delay a value that may be needed more than once. A delayed value will be a reference cell containing an " unevaluated delay":

```
Delay ( e ) == ref(UN(fn () => e ))
```

where the constructor UN and the type of "delays" are defined by

```
datatype 'a delay = EV of 'a | UN of unit -> 'a;
```

Intuitively, a delayed value is an assignable cell that will contain an unevaluated value until it is evaluated. After that, the assignable cell will contain an evaluated value. The type delay is a union of the two possibilities. A "delay" is either an evaluated value, tagged with constructor EV, or an unevaluated delay, tagged with constructor UN. The tagged unevaluated delay is a function of no arguments that can be called to get an evaluated value.

The corresponding force function,

```
fun force(d) = let val v = ev(!d) in (d := EV(v); v) end;
```

uses assignment and a subsidiary function ev that evaluates a delay:

```
fun ev(EV(x)) = x
  |   ev(UN(f)) = f();
```

In words, if a delay is already evaluated, then ev has nothing to do. Otherwise, ev calls the function of no arguments to get an evaluated delay. To give a concrete example, here is the code for a delayed evaluation of time_consuming(9), followed by a call to force to evaluate it:

```
val d = ref(UN(fn () => time_consuming(9)));
force(d);
```

This call to force evaluates the delayed expression and has a side effect so that, on subsequent calls to force, no further evaluation is needed.

8.5 CHAPTER SUMMARY

We looked at several ways of controlling the order of execution and evaluation in sequential (nonconcurrent) programs. Here are the main topics of the chapter:

- structured programming without go to,
- exceptions,
- continuations,
- Delay and Force.

Control and Go to. Because structured programming is commonly accepted and taught, we did not look at the entire historical controversy surrounding go to statements. The main conclusion in the "Go to considered harmful" debate is that, in the end, program clarity is often more important than absolute efficiency. This has always been true to some degree, but as computer speed has increased, the relation between programmer time and program execution time has shifted. In modern software development, it is not worth several days of programmer time to reduce the execution time of a large application by one or two instruction cycles. Programmer time is expensive, and clever programming can lead to costly mistakes and increased debugging time. An instruction or two takes so little time that for most applications noone will notice the difference.

Exceptions. Exceptions are a structured form of jump that may be used to exit a block or function call and pass a return value in the process. Every exception mechanism includes a statement or expression form for *raising* an exception and a mechanism for defining *handlers* that respond to exceptions. When an exception is raised and several handlers have been established, control is transferred to the handler associated with the most recent activation record on the run-time stack. In other words, handlers are selected according to dynamic scope, not the static scope rules used for most other declarations in modern general-purpose programming languages.

Continuations. Continuation is a programming technique based on higher-order functions that may be used directly in programming or in program transformations in an optimizing compiler. Some mostly functional languages, such as Scheme and ML, provide direct support for capturing and invoking continuations.

Intuitively, the continuation of a statement or expression is a function representing the computation remaining to be performed after this statement or expression is evaluated. There is a general, systematic method for transforming any program into continuation-passing form. A function in continuation-passing form does not return, but calls a continuation (passed as an argument to the function) in order to continue after the function is complete. Continuation-passing form is related to tail recursion (see Subsection 7.3.4). Formally, a continuation-passing function appears to be tail recursive, as all calls are tail calls. However, continuation-passing functions may pass functions are arguments.

This makes it impossible to perform tail recursion elimination – the function created and passed out of a function call may need the activation record of the function in order to maintain the value of statically scoped global variables. However, a clever programmer can sometimes use the continuation-passing version of a function to devise a tail recursive function that will be compiled as efficiently as an iterative loop.

Continuation-passing form is used in a number of contemporary compilers for languages with higher-order functions.

Delay and Force. Delay and Force may be used to delay a computation until it is needed. When the delayed computation is needed, Force is used. Delay and Force may be implemented in conventional programming languages by use of functions: The delayed computation is placed inside a function and Force is implemented by calling this function. This technique is simplest to apply if functions can be declared anywhere in a program. If a delayed value may be needed more than once, this value may be stored in a location that will be used in every subsequent call to Force.

EXERCISES

8.1 Exceptions

Consider the following functions, written in ML:

```
exception Excpt of int;
fun twice(f,x) = f(f(x)) handle Excpt(x) => x;
fun pred(x) = if x = 0 then raise Excpt(x) else x-1;
fun dumb(x) = raise Excpt(x);
fun smart(x) = 1 + pred(x) handle Excpt(x) => 1;
```

What is the result of evaluating each of the following expressions?

(a) twice(pred,1);

(b) twice(dumb,1);

(c) twice(smart,0);

In each case, be sure to describe which exception gets raised and where.

8.2 Exceptions

ML has functions hd and tl to return the head (or first element) and tail (or remaining elements) of a list. These both raise an exception Empty if the list is empty. Suppose that we redefine these functions without changing their behavior on nonempty lists, so that hd raises exception Hd and tl raises exception Tl if applied to the empty list nil:

```
– hd(nil);
uncaught exception Hd
– tl(nil);
uncaught exception Tl
```

Consider the function

```
fun g(l) = hd(l) :: tl(l) handle Hd => nil;
```

that behaves like the identity function on lists. The result of evaluating g(nil) is nil. Explain why. What makes the function g return properly without handling the exception Tl?

8.3 Exceptions

The following two versions of the closest function take an integer x and an integer tree t and return the integer leaf value from t that is closest in absolute value to x. The first is a straightforward recursive function, the second uses an exception:

```
datatype 'a tree = Leaf of 'a | Nd of ('a tree) * ('a tree);

fun closest(x, Leaf(y))  = y:int
|    closest(x, Nd(y, z)) = let val lf = closest(x, y) and rt = closest(x, z) in
                            if abs(x-lf) < abs(x-rt) then lf else rt end;

fun closest(x, t) =
    let
        exception Found
        fun cls (x, Leaf(y)) = if x=y then raise Found else y:int
        |    cls (x, Nd(y, z)) = let val lf = cls(x, y) and rt = cls(x, z) in
                                 if abs(x-lf) < abs(x-rt) then lf else rt end
    in
        cls(x, t) handle Found => x
    end;
```

(a) Explain why both give the same answer.

(b) Explain why the second version may be more efficient.

8.4 Exceptions and Recursion

Here is an ML function that uses an exception called Odd.

```
fun f(0) = 1
  |   f(1) = raise Odd
  |   f(3) = f(3-2)
  |   f(n) = (f(n-2) handle Odd => ~n)
```

The expression ~n is ML for $-n$, the negative of the integer n.

When f(11) is executed, the following steps will be performed:

```
call f(11)
call f(9)
call f(7)
      . . .
```

Write the remaining steps that will be executed. Include only the following kinds of steps:

- function call (with argument)
- function return (with return value)
- raise an exception
- pop activation record of function off stack without returning control to the function
- handle an exception

Assume that if f calls g and g raises an exception that f does not handle, then the activation record of f is popped off the stack without returning control to the function f.

8.5 Tail Recursion and Exception Handling

Can we use tail recursion elimination to optimize the following program?

```
exception OddNum;
let fun f(0,count) = count
      | f(1, count) = raise OddNum
      | f(x, count) = f(x-2, count+1) handle OddNum => -1
```

Why or why not? Explain. This is a tricky situation – try to explain succinctly what the issues are and how they might be resolved.

8.6 Evaluation Order and Exceptions

Suppose we add an exception mechanism similar to the one used in ML to pure Lisp. Pure Lisp has the property that if every evaluation order for expression e terminates, then e has the same value under every evaluation order. Does pure Lisp with exceptions still have this property? [*Hint:* See if you can find an expression containing a function call $f(e_1, e_2)$ so that evaluating e_1 before e_2 gives you a different answer than evaluating the expression with e_2 before e_1.]

8.7 Control Flow and Memory Management

An *exception* aborts part of a computation and transfers control to a handler that was established at some earlier point in the computation. A *memory leak* occurs when memory allocated by a program is no longer reachable, and the memory will not be deallocated. (The term "memory leak" is used only in connection with languages that are not garbage collected, such as C.) Explain why exceptions can lead to memory leaks in a language that is not garbage collected.

8.8 Tail Recursion and Continuations

(a) Explain why a tail recursive function, as in

```
fun fact(n) =
    let fun f(n, a) = if n=0 then a
                      else f(n-1, a*n)
    in f(n, 1) end;
```

can be compiled so that the amount of space required for computing fact(n) is independent of n.

(b) The function f used in the following definition of factorial is "formally" tail recursive: The only recursive call to f is a call that need not return:

```
fun fact(n) =
    let fun f(n,g) = if n=0 then g(1)
                     else f(n-1, fn x=>g(x)*n)
    in f(n, fn x => x) end;
```

How much space is required for computing fact(n), measured as a function of argument n? Explain how this space is allocated during recursive calls to f and when the space may be freed.

8.9 Continuations

In addition to continuations that represent the "normal" continued execution of a program, we can use continuations in place of exceptions. For example, consider the following function f that raises an exception when the argument x is too small:

```
exception Too_Small;
fun f(x) = if x<0 then raise Too_Small else x/2;
(1 + f(y)) handle Too_Small => 0;
```

If we use continuations, then f could be written as a function with two extra arguments, one for normal exit and the other for "exceptional exit," to be called if the argument is too small:

```
fun f(x, k_normal, k_exn) = if x<0 then k_exn() else k_normal(x/2);
f(y, (fn z => 1+z), (fn () => 0));
```

(a) Explain why the final expressions in each program fragment will have the same value for any value of y.

(b) Why would tail call optimization be helpful when we use the second style of programming instead of exceptions?

PART 3

Modularity, Abstraction, and Object-Oriented Programming

Data Abstraction and Modularity

Computer programmers have long recognized the value of building software systems that consist of a number of program modules. In an effective design, each module can be designed and tested independently. Two important goals in modularity are to allow one module to be written with little knowledge of the code in another module and to allow a module to be redesigned and reimplemented without modifying other parts of the system. Modern programming languages and software development environments support modularity in different ways.

In this chapter, we look at some of the ways that programs can be divided into meaningful parts and the way that programming languages can be designed to support these divisions. Because in Chapters 10–13 we explore object-oriented languages in detail, in this chapter we are concerned with modularity mechanisms that do not involve objects. The main topics are structured programming, support for abstraction, and modules. The two examples used to describe module systems and generic programming are the standard ML module system and the C++ Standard Template Library (STL).

9.1 STRUCTURED PROGRAMMING

In an influential 1969 paper called Structured Programming, E.W. Dijkstra argued that one should develop a program by first outlining the major tasks that it should perform and then successively refining these tasks into smaller subtasks, until a level is reached at which each remaining task can be expressed easily by basic operations. This produces subproblems that are small enough to be understood and separate enough to be solved independently.

In Example 9.1, the data structures passed between separate parts of the program are simple and straightforward. This makes it possible to identify the main data structures early in the process. Because the data structures remain invariant through most of the design process, Dijkstra's example centers on refinement of procedures into smaller procedures. In more complex systems, it is necessary to refine data structures as well as procedures. This is illustrated in Example 9.2.

EDSGER W DIJKSTRA

An exacting and fundamentally warm-hearted person, Edsger W. Dijkstra has made many important contributions to the field of computing science. He is known for semaphores, which are commonly used for concurrency control, algorithms such as his method for finding shortest paths in graphs, his "guarded command" language, and methods for reasoning about programs.

Over the years, Dijkstra has written a series of carefully handwritten articles, known commonly as the EWDs. As of the early 2002, he had written over 1309 EWDs, scanned and available on the web. As Dijkstra now says on his web page,

My area of interest focuses on the streamlining of the mathematical argument so as to increase our powers of reasoning, in particular, by the use of formal techniques.

His interest in streamlining mathematical argument is evident in the EWDs, each developing an elegant solution to an intriguing problem in a few pages.

Like many old-school Europeans, and unlike most Americans, Dijkstra has impeccable handwriting. In part as a joke and in part as a tribute to Dijkstra, a programming language researcher named Luca Cardelli carefully copied the handwriting from a set of EWDs and produced the EWD font. If you can find the font on the web, you can try writing short notes in Dijkstra's famous handwriting.

Example 9.1

Dijkstra considered the problem of computing and printing the first 1000 prime numbers. The first version of the program contains a little bit of syntax to get us thinking about writing a program. Otherwise, it just looks like an English description of the problem we want to solve.

Program 1:

```
begin
    print first thousand prime numbers
end
```

This task can now be refined into subtasks. To divide the problem in two, some data structure must be selected for passing the result of the first subtask onto the second. In Dijkstra's example, the data structure is a table, which will be filled with the first 1000 primes.

Program 2:

```
begin variable table p
    fill table p with first thousand primes
    print table p
end
```

In the next refinement, each subtask is further elaborated. One important idea in structured programming is that each subtask is considered independently. In the example at hand, the problem of filling the table with primes is independent of the problem of printing the table. Therefore, each subtask could be assigned to a different programmer, allowing the problems to be solved at the same time by different people. Even if the program were going to be written by a single person, there is an important benefit of separating a complex problem into independent subproblems. Specifically, a single person can think about only so many details at once. Dividing a task into subtasks makes it possible to think about one task at a time, reducing the number of details that must be considered at any one time.

Program 3:

```
begin integer array p[1:1000]
    make for k from 1 through 1000
        p[k] equal to the kth prime number
    print p[k] for k from 1 through 1000
end
```

At this point, the basic program structure has been determined and the programmer can concentrate on the algorithm for computing successive primes. Although this example is extremely simple, it should give some idea of the basic idea of programming by stepwise refinement. Stepwise refinement generally leads to programs with a tree-like conceptual structure.

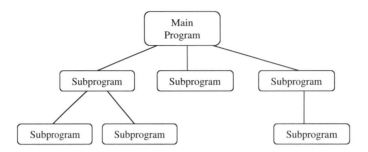

One difficult aspect of top-down program development is that it is important to make the problem simpler on each refinement step. Otherwise, it might be possible to refine a task and produce a list of programming problems that are each more difficult than the original task. This means that a designer who uses stepwise refinement must have a good idea in advance of how tasks will eventually be accomplished.

9.1.1 Data Refinement

In addition to refining tasks into simpler subtasks, evolution in a system design may lead to changes in the data structures that are used to combine the actions of independent modules.

Example 9.2

Consider the problem of designing a simple banking program. The goal of this program is to process account deposits, process withdrawals, and print monthly bank statements. In the first pass, we might formulate a system design that looks something like this:

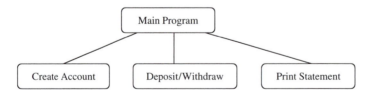

In this design, the main program receives a list of input transactions and calls the appropriate subprograms. If we assume that statements only contain the account number and balance, then we could represent a single bank account by an integer value and store all bank accounts in a single integer array.

If we later refine the task "Print Statement" to include the subtask "Print list of transactions," then we will have to maintain a record of bank transactions. For this refinement, we will have to replace the integer array with some other data structure that records the sequence of transactions that have occurred since the last statement. This may require changes in the behavior of all the subprograms, as all of them perform operations on bank accounts.

9.1.2 Modularity

Divide and conquer is one of the fundamental techniques of computer science. Because software systems can be exceedingly complex, it is important to divide programs into separate parts that can be treated independently. Top-down program development, when it works, is one method for producing programs that consist of separable parts. In some cases, it is also useful to work bottom-up, designing basic parts that will be needed in a large software system and then combining them into larger subsystems. Since the 1970s, a number of other program-development methods have been proposed.

One useful development method, sometimes called *prototyping*, involves implementing parts of a program in a simple way to understand if the design will really work. Then, after the design has been tested in some way, one can improve parts of the program independently by reimplementing them. This process can be carried out incrementally by a series of progressively more elaborate prototypes to develop a satisfactory system. There are also related object-oriented design methods, which we will discuss in Chapter 10.

One important way for programming languages to support modular programming methods is by helping programmers keep track of the dependencies between different parts of a system. For the purposes of discussion, we call a meaningful part of a program that is meant to be partially independent of other parts a program *component*.

Two important concepts in modular program development are interfaces and specifications:

- *Interface:* A description of the parts of a component that are visible to other program components.
- *Specification:* A description of the behavior of a component, as observable through its interface.

When a program is designed modularly, it should be possible to change the internal structure of any component, as long as the behavior visible through the interface remains the same.

A simple example of a program component is a single function. The interface of a function consists of the function name, the number and types of parameters, and the type of the return result. A function interface is also called a *function header*.

A function specification usually describes the relationship between function arguments and the corresponding return result. If a function will work properly on only certain arguments, then this restriction should be part of the function specification. For example, the interface of a square-root function might be

> function sqrt (float x) returns float

A specification for this function can be written as

> If x>0, then sqrt(x)*sqrt(x) $\approx$ x.

where the squiggly approximation sign, $\approx$, is used to mean "approximately equal," as computation with floating-point numbers is carried out to only limited precision.

In some forms of modular programming, system designers write a specification for each component. When a component is implemented, it should be designed to work correctly when all of the components it interacts with satisfy their specifications. In other words, the correctness of one component should not depend on any hidden implementation details of any other component. One reason for striving to achieve this degree of independence is that it allows components to be reimplemented independently. Specifically, in a system in which each component relies on only stated specifications of other components, we can replace any component with another that satisfies the same specification. This allows us to optimize components independently or to add functionality that does not violate the original specification.

There are many different languages and methods for writing specifications, ranging from English and graphical notations that have little structure to formal languages that can be manipulated by specification tools. A basic problem associated with program specification is that there is no algorithmic method for testing that a module satisfies its specification. This is a consequence of a fundamental mathematical limitation, similar to the undecidability of the halting problem. As a result, programming with specifications requires substantial effort and discipline.

To illustrate the use of data structures and specifications, we look at a sorting algorithm that uses a general data structure that also serves other purposes.

Example 9.3 A Modular Sorting Algorithm

An integer priority queue is a data structure with three operations:

```
empty : pqueue
insert : int * pqueue → pqueue
deletemax: pqueue → int * pqueue
```

In words, there is a way of representing an empty priority queue, an insert operation that adds an integer to a priority queue, and a deletemax operation that removes an element from a priority queue. These three operations form the interface to priority queues. To give more detail, we have the following specifications:

- Each priority queue has a multiset of elements. There must be an ordering $\leq$ on the elements that may be placed in a priority queue. (For integer priority queues, we may use the ordinary $\leq$ ordering on integers.)
- An empty priority queue has no elements.
- insert(elt, pq) returns a priority queue whose elements are elt plus the elements of pq.
- deletemax(pq) returns an element of pq that is $\geq$ all other elements of pq, together with a data structure representing the priority queue obtained when this element is removed.

These specifications do not impose any restrictions on the implementation of priority queues other than properties that are observable through the interface of priority queues.

Knowing in advance that we would like to use priority queues in our sorting algorithm, we can begin the top-down design process by stating the problem in a program form:

Program 1:

```
function sort
    begin
        sort an array of integers
    end
```

The next step is to refine the statement sort an array of integers into subtasks. One way to do this, using priority queues, is to transfer the elements of the array into a priority queue and then remove them one at a time. In addition, we can make the decision at this point that the function will take an array and its integer length as separate arguments.

Program 2:

```
function sort(n:int, A : array [1..n] of int)
    begin
        place each element of array A in a priority queue
        remove elements in decreasing order and place in array A
    end
```

Finally, we can translate these English descriptive statements into some form of program code. (Here, the program is written in a generic Algol- or Pascal-like notation.)

Program 3:

```
function sort(n:int, A : array [1..n] of int)
    begin priority queue s;
        s := empty;
        for i := 1 to n do s := insert(A[i], s);
        for i := n downto 1 do (A[i],s) := deletemax(s);
    end
```

One advantage of this sorting algorithm is that there is a clear separation between the control structure of the algorithm and the data structure for priority queues. We could implement priority queues inefficiently to begin with, by using an algorithm that is easy to code, and then optimize the implementation later if this turns out to be needed.

As written, it seems difficult to sort an array in place by this algorithm. However, it is possible to come close to the conventional heapsort algorithm.

9.2 LANGUAGE SUPPORT FOR ABSTRACTION

Programmers and software designers often speak about "finding the right abstraction" for a problem. This means that they are looking for general concepts, such as data structures or processing metaphors, that will make a complex, detailed problem seem more orderly or systematic. One way that a programming language can help programmers find the right abstraction is by providing a variety of ways to organize data and computation. Another way that a programming language can help with finding the right abstraction is to make it possible to build program components that capture meaningful patterns in computation.

9.2.1 Abstraction

In programming languages, an abstraction mechanism is one that emphasizes the general properties of some segment of code and hides details. Abstraction mechanisms generally involve separating a program into parts that contain certain details and parts where these details are hidden. Common terms associated with abstraction are

- *client:* the part of a program that uses program component
- *implementation:* the part of a program that defines a program component.

The interaction between the client of an abstraction and the implementation of the abstraction is usually restricted to a specific interface.

Procedural Abstraction

One of the oldest abstraction mechanisms in programming languages is the procedure or function. The client of a function is a program making a function call. The implementation of a function is the function body, which consists of the instructions that will be executed each time the function is called.

If we have a few lines of code that store the square root of a variable x in the variable y, for example, then we can *encapsulate* this code into a function. This accomplishes several things:

1. The function has a well-defined interface, made explicit in the code. The interface consists of the function name, which is used to call the function, the input parameters (and their types, if it is a typed programming language) and the type of the output.
2. If the code for computing the function value uses other variables, then these can be made local to the function. If variables are declared inside the function body, then they will not be visible to other parts of the program that use the function. In other words, no assignment or other use of local variables has any effect on other parts of the program. This provides a form of *information hiding*: information about how the function computes a result is contained in the function declaration, but hidden from the program that uses the function.
3. The function may be called on many different arguments. If code to carry out a computation is written in-line, then the computation is performed on specific variables. By enclosing the code in a function declaration, we obtain an *abstract*

entity that makes sense apart from its specific use on these specific variables. In grandiose terms, enclosing code inside a function makes the code generic and reusable.

This is an idealistic description of the advantages of enclosing code inside a function. In most programming languages, a function may read or assign to global variables. These global variables are not listed in the function interface. Therefore, the behavior of a function is not always determined by its interface alone. For this reason, some purists in program design recommend against using global variables in functions.

Data Abstraction

Data abstraction refers to hiding information about the way that data are represented. Common language mechanisms for data abstractions are abstract data-type declarations (discussed in Subsection 9.2.2) and modules (discussed in Section 9.3).

We saw in Subsection 9.1.2 how a sorting algorithm can be defined by using a data structure called a priority queue. If a program uses priority queues, then the writer of that program must know what the operations are on priority queues and their interfaces. Therefore, the set of operations and their interfaces is called the interface of a data abstraction. In principle, a program that uses priority queues should not depend on whether priority queues are represented as binary search trees or sorted arrays. These implementation details are best hidden by an encapsulation mechanism.

As for procedural abstraction, there are three main goals of data abstraction:

1. Identifying the interface of the data structure. The interface of a data abstraction consists of the operations on the data structure and their arguments and return results.
2. Providing *information hiding* by separating implementation decisions from parts of the program that use the data structure.
3. Allowing the data structure to be used in many different ways by many different programs. This goal is best supported by generic abstractions, discussed in Section 9.4.

9.2.2 Abstract Data Types

Interest in data abstraction came to prominence in the 1970s. This led to the development of a programming language construct call the *abstract data-type* declaration.

This is a common short definition of an abstract data type:

An *abstract data type* consists of a type together with a specified set of operations.

Good languages for programming with abstract data types not only allow a programmer to group types and operations, but also use type checking to limit access to the representation of a data structure. In other words, not only does an abstract data type have a specific interface that can be used by other parts of a program, but access is also restricted so that *the only use of an abstract data type is through its interface*.

If a stack is implemented with an array, then programs that use a stack abstract data type can use only the stack operations (push and pop, say), not array operations such as indexing into the array at arbitrary points. This hides information about the implementation of a data structure and allows the implementer of the data structure to make changes without affecting parts of a program that use the data structure.

We can appreciate some aspects of abstract data types by understanding a historical idea that was in the air at the time of their development. In the early 1970s, there was a movement to investigate "extensible" languages. The goal of this movement was to produce programming languages in which the programmer would be able to define constructs with the same flexibility as a language designer. For example, if some person or group of programmers wanted to write programs by using a new form of iterative loop, they could use a "loop declaration" to define one and use it in their programs. This idea turned out to be rather unsuccessful, as programs littered with all kinds of programmer-defined syntactic conventions can be extremely difficult to read or modify. However, the idea that programmers should be able to define types that have the same status as the types that are provided by the language did prove useful and has stood the test of time.

A potential confusion about abstract data types is the sense in which they are abstract. A simple distinction is that a data type whose representation and operational details are hidden from clients is abstract. In contrast, a data type whose representation details are visible to clients may be called a transparent type. ML abstype, discussed in the next subsection, defines abstract data types, whereas ML data type, discussed in Subsection 6.5.3, is a transparent type-declaration form.

9.2.3 **ML** abstype

We use the historical ML abstract data-type construct, called abstype, to discuss the main ideas associated with abstract data-type mechanisms in programming languages.

As discussed in the preceding subsection, an abstract data-type mechanism associates a type with a data structure in such a way that a specific set of functions has direct access to the data structure but general code in other parts of a program does not. We will see how this works in ML by considering a simple example, complex numbers.

We can represent a complex number as a pair of real numbers. The first real is the "real" part of the complex number, and the second is the "imaginary" part of the complex number. If we are going to compute with complex numbers, then we need to have a way of forming a complex number from two reals and ways of getting the real and imaginary parts of a complex number. Computation with complex numbers may also involve complex addition, multiplication, and other standard operations. Here, simply providing complex addition is discussed. Other operations could be included in the abstract data type in similar ways.

An ML declaration of an abstract data type of complex numbers may be written as follows:

```
abstype cmplx = C of real * real with
    fun cmplx(x,y: real) = C(x,y)
    fun x_coord(C(x,y)) = x
    fun y_coord(C(x,y)) = y
    fun add(C(x1, y1), C(x2, y2)) = C(x1+x2, y1+y2)
end
```

This declaration binds five identifiers for use outside the declaration: the type cmplx and the functions cmplx, x_coord, y_coord, and add. The declaration also binds the name C to a constructor that can be used only within the bodies of the functions that are part of the declaration. Specifically, C may appear in the code for cmplx, x_coord, y_coord, and add but not in any other part of the program.

The type name cmplx is the type of complex numbers. When a program uses complex numbers, each complex number will be represented internally as a pair of real numbers. However, because the type name cmplx is different from the ML type real*real for a pair of real numbers, a function that is meant to operate on a pair of real numbers cannot be applied to a value of type cmplx: The ML type checker will not allow this. This restriction is one of the fundamental properties of any good abstract data-type mechanism: Programs should be restricted so that only the declared operations of the abstract type can be applied.

Within the data-type declaration, however, the functions that are part of the abstract data type must be able to treat complex numbers as pairs of real numbers. Otherwise, it would not be possible to implement many operations. In ML, a constructor is used to distinguish "abstract" from "concrete" uses of complex numbers. Specifically, if z is a complex number, then matching z against the pattern C (x,y) will bind x to the real part of z and y to the imaginary part of z. This form of pattern matching is used in the implementation of complex addition, for example, in which add combines the real parts of its two arguments and the imaginary parts of its two arguments. The pair representing the complex sum is then identified as a complex number by application of the constructor C.

When ML is presented with this declaration of complex numbers, it returns the following type information:

```
type cmplx
val cmplx = fn : real * real → cmplx
val x_coord = fn : cmplx → real
val y_coord = fn : cmplx → real
val add = fn : cmplx * cmplx → cmplx
```

The first line indicates that the declaration introduces a new type, named cmplx. The next four lines list the operations allowed on expressions with type cmplx. The types of these operations involve the type cmplx, not the type real*real that is used to represent complex numbers. Be sure you understand the code for add, for example, and why the type checker gives add the type cmplx * cmplx → cmplx.

In general, an ML abstype declaration has the form

```
abstype t = <constructor> of <type>
    with
        val <pattern> = <body>
        ...
        fun f(<pattern>) = <body>
        ...
    end
```

The syntax

```
t = <constructor> of <type>
```

is the same notation used to define data types. The identifier t is the name of the new type, <constructor> is the name of the constructor for the new type t, and <type> gives the type used to represent elements of the abstract type. The difference between an abstype and a data type lies with the rest of the preceding syntax. The value and function declarations that occur between the with and the end keywords are the only operations that may be written with the constructor. Other parts of the program may refer to the type name t and the functions and values declared between with and end. However, other parts of the program are outside the scope of the declaration of the constructor and therefore may not convert between the abstract type and its representation. The operations declared in an abstype declaration are called the *interface* of the abstract type, and the hidden data type and associated function bodies are called its *implementation*.

As many readers know, there are two common ways of representing complex numbers. The preceding abstract type uses rectangular coordinates – each complex number is represented by a pair consisting of its real and imaginary coordinates. The other standard representation is called polar coordinates. In the polar representation, each complex number is represented by its distance from the origin and an angle indicating the direction (relative to the real axis) used to reach the point from the origin. Because the implementation of the abstract data type cmplx is hidden, a program that uses a rectangular implementation can be replaced with one that uses a polar representation without changing the behavior of any program that uses the abstract data type.

A polar representation of complex numbers is used in this abstract data-type declaration:

```
abstype cmplx = C of real * real with
    fun cmplx(x,y: real) = C(sqrt(sq(x)+sq(y)), arctan(y/x))
    fun x_coord(C(r,theta)) = r * cos(theta)
    fun y_coord(C(r,theta)) = r * sin(theta)
    fun add(C(x1,y1), C(x2,y2)) = C(..., ...)
end
```

where the implementation of add is filled in as appropriate.

Example 9.4 Set Abstract Type

We can also create polymorphic abstypes, as the following abstype declaration illustrates:

```
abstype 'a set = SET of 'a list with
    val empty = SET(nil)
    fun insert(x, SET(elts)) = . . .
    fun union(SET(elts1), SET(elts2)) = . . .
    fun isMember(x, SET(elts)) = . . .
end
```

Assuming the preceding . . . 's are filled in with the appropriate code to implement insert, union, and isMember, ML returns as the result of evaluating this declaration:

```
type 'a set
val empty = - : 'a set
val insert = fn : 'a * ('a set) → ('a set)
val union = fn : ('a set) * ('a set) → ('a set)
val isMember = fn : 'a * ('a set) → bool
```

Note that the value for empty is written as -, instead of nil. This hiding prevents users of the 'a set abstype from using the fact that the abstype is currently implemented as a list.

Clu Clusters

The first language with user-declared abstract types was Clu. In Clu, abstract types are declared with the cluster construct. Here is an example declaration of complex numbers:

```
complex = cluster is make_complex, real_part, imaginary_part, plus, times
    rep = struct [ re, im : real ]
    make_complex = proc (x, y : real) returns (cvt)
            return (rep${re:x, im:y})
    real_part = proc (z : cvt) returns (real)
            return (x.re)
    imaginary_part = proc (z : cvt) returns (real)
            return (x.im)
    plus = proc (z, w : cvt) returns (cvt)
            return (rep${re: z.re + w.re, z.im + w.im})
    mult = . . .
end complex
```

BARBARA LISKOV

Barabara Liskov's research and teaching interests include programming languages, programming methodology, distributed computing, and parallel computing. She was the developer of the programming language Clu, which was described this way when it was developed in the 1970s: "The programming language Clu is a practical vehicle for study and development of approaches in structured programming. It provides a new linguistic mechanism, called a cluster, to support the use of data abstractions in program construction."

When I was a graduate student at MIT, Barbara had huge piles of papers, many three or four feet high, covering the top of her desk. Whenever I went in to talk with her, I imagined I might find her unconscious under a fallen heap of printed matter.

In this code, the line rep = struct [re, im : real] specifies that each complex number is represented by a struct with two real (float) parts, called re and im. Inside the implementations of operations of the cluster, the keywords cvt and rep are used to convert between types complex and struct [re, im : real], in the same way that pattern matching and the constructor C are used in the ML abstype declaration for cmplex.

9.2.4 Representation Independence

We can understand the significance of abstract type declarations by considering some of the properties of a typical built-in type such as int:

- We can declare variables x : int of this type.
- There is a specific set of built-in operations on the type +, -, *, etc.
- Only these built-in operations can be applied to values of type int; it is not type correct to apply string or other types of operations to integers.

Because ints can be accessed only by means of the built-in operations, they enjoy a property called *representation independence*, which means that different computer representations of integers do not affect program behavior. One computer could represent ints by using 1's complement, and another by using 2's complement, and the same program run on the two machines will produce the same output (assuming all else is equal).

A type has the *representation-independence* property if different (correct) underlying representations or implementations for the values of that type are indistinguishable by clients of the type. This property implies that implementations for such types may be changed without breaking any client code, a useful property for software engineering.

In a type-safe programming language with abstract data types,

- we can declare variables of an abstract type,
- we define operations on any abstract type,
- the type-checking rules guarantee that only these specified operations can be applied to values of the abstract type.

For the same reasons as those for built-in types such as int, these properties of abstract data types imply representation independence for user-defined type. Representation independence means that we can change the representation for our abstract type without affecting the clients of our abstraction.

In practice, different programming languages provide different degrees of representation independence. In Clu, ML, and other type-safe programming languages with an abstract data-type mechanism, it is possible to prove a form of representation independence as a theorem about the ideal implementation of the language. The proof of this theorem relies on the way the programming language restricts access to implementation of an abstract data type. In languages like C or C++ that have type loopholes, representation independence is an ideal that can be achieved through good programming style. More specifically, if a program uses only a specific set of operations on some data structure, then the data structure and implementations of these operations can be changed in various ways without changing the behavior of the program that uses them. However, C does not enforce representation independence. This is true for built-in types as well as for user-declared types. For example, C code that examines the bits of an integer can distinguish 1's complement from 2's complement implementations of integer operations.

9.2.5 Data-Type Induction

Data-type induction is a useful principle for reasoning about abstract data types. We are not interested here in the formal aspects of this principle, only the intuition that it provides for thinking about programming and data-type equivalence. Data-type equivalence is an important relation between abstract data types: We can replace a data type with any equivalent one without changing the behavior of any client program. This principle is used informally in program development and maintenance. In particular, it is common to first build a software system with potentially inefficient prototype implementations of a data type and then to replace these with more efficient implementations as time permits.

Partition Operations

For many data types, it is possible to partition the operations on the type into three groups:

1. *Constructors*: operations that build elements of the type.
2. *Operators*: operations that map elements of the type that are definable only

with constructors to other elements of the type that are definable with only constructors.

3. *Observers*: operations that return a result of some other type.

The main idea is that all elements of the data type can be defined with constructors; operators are useful for computing with elements of the type, but do not define any new values. Observers are the functions that let us distinguish one element of the data type from another. They give us a notion of *observable equality*, which is usually different from equality of representation.

Example 9.5 Equivalence of Integer Sets Implementations
For the data type of integer sets with the signature

```
empty : set
insert : int * set  →  set
union : set * set  →  set
isMember: int * set  →  bool
```

the operations can be partitioned as follows:

1. *Constructors*: empty and insert
2. *Operator*: union
3. *Observer*: isMember

We may understand some of the intuition behind this partitioning of the operations by thinking about how sets might be used in a program. Because there is no print operation on sets, a program cannot produce a set directly as output. Instead, if any printable output of a program depends on the value of some set expression, it can be only because of some membership test on sets. Therefore, if two sets, s_1 and s_2, have the property that

For all integers n, isMember(n,s_1) = isMember(n,s_2)

then no program will be able to distinguish one from the other in any observable way. This actually gives us a useful equivalence relation on sets: Two sets s_1 and s_2 are *equivalent* if isMember(n,s_1) = isMember(n,s_2) for every integer n. For sets, this equivalence principle is actually the usual *extensionality axiom* from set theory: Two sets are equal if they have precisely the same elements.

Given extensionality of sets, it is easy to see that any set can be defined by insertion of some number of elements into the empty set. More specifically, for every set s, there is a sequence of elements $n_1, n_2, \ldots, n_k$, with

$$s \approx insert(n_1, insert(n_2, \ldots insert(n_k, empty) \ldots)).$$

This demonstrates that insert and empty are in fact constructors for the data type of sets: Every set can be defined with only these two operations.

To formally show that a given method is an operator, we need to demonstrate that, for any given use of an operator, there exists a sequence of constructor calls that produces the same result. As we expect, union is a useful operation on sets, but if s_1 and s_2 are definable with the operations of this data type, then union(s_1,s_2) can be defined with only insert and empty. For this reason, union is classified as an operator, not a constructor.

In practice, it is not always easy to partition the operations of a data type into these three groups. Some functions might appear to fit into two groups. However, the principle of data-type induction still provides a useful guide for reasoning about arbitrary abstract data types.

Induction over Constructors

Because all elements of a given abstract type are given by a sequence of constructor operations, we may prove properties of all elements of an abstract type by induction on the number of uses of constructors necessary to produce a given element. Once we show that some function of the signature is an operator, we can generally eliminate it from further consideration.

Example 9.6

As an illustration of data-type induction, we will go through the outline of a proof that two different implementations of integer sets are equivalent. The term equivalent means that, if we replace one implementation with another, then no client program can detect the change.

Let us begin with a definition of equivalence, the property we are trying to prove:

Two implementations set and set' are equivalent if, for all values of all parameters, all corresponding applications of observers to set expressions are equal.

We refer to the operations of set by empty, insert, union, and isMember and the operations of set' by empty', insert', union', and isMember'. Some examples of corresponding applications of observers are

isMember(6, insert(n1, ... insert(nk, empty) ...)) and
isMember'(6, insert'(n1, ... insert'(nk, empty') ...))

These expressions correspond in the sense that all the nonset arguments are the same, but we have replaced the operations of one implementation with another.

The intuition behind this definition of data-type equivalence is similar to the equivalence relation on set expressions we previously discussed. Specifically, suppose we have two different implementations of sets. The only way a client program can use one of them to produce a printable (or observable) output is to use the set constructors and operators to build up some potentially complicated sets and then to "observe" the resulting sets by using the observer operations.

Because we have established that union is an operator, not a constructor, and the only observer function is isMember, proving the equivalence of two different implementations of sets boils down to showing that

for all z, isMember(z, aSet) = isMember'(z, aSet')

where aSet and aSet' are corresponding expressions in which only the constructors empty and insert (or empty' and insert') are used.

We have now reduced the problem of establishing data-type equivalence to the problem of showing that

isMember(n, insert(n1, ... insert(nk, empty) ...))
= isMember′(n, insert′(n1, ... insert′(nk, empty′) ...))

for all sequences of natural numbers n, n1, ... , nk. We can do this by induction on k, the number of insert operations required for constructing the sets.

The inductive proof proceeds as follows.

Base Case: Zero Insert Operations. In this case, we must show that

for all n, isMember(n, empty) = isMember′(n, empty′)

We must do this by looking at the actual implementations of the data type. However, in a correct implementation of sets, the empty set has no elements. Therefore, if both implementations are correct, then isMember(n, empty) = isMember′(n, empty′) = false.

Induction Step. We assume that equivalence holds when k insert operations are used and consider the case of k+1 insert operations. This reduces to showing that, for all n, m, we have

isMember(n, insert(m, s)) = isMember′(n, insert′(m, s′))

under the assumption that for all n we have isMember(n,s) = isMember′(n,s′). Again, we must do this by looking at the actual implementations. However, if both implementations are correct, then we should have isMember(n,s) = isMember′(n,s′).

An interesting aspect of this argument is that we have proved something about all possible programs that use a data type by using only ordinary induction over the constructors. The reason this is possible is the assumption that, in a language with abstract data types, only the operations of the data type can be applied to values of the type. It would be impossible to use this form of proof if type-checking rules did not guarantee that only set operations may be applied to a set. In practice, however, the ideas illustrated here may be useful for programming in languages such as C that do not enforce data abstraction, as long as the actual programs that are built do not operate on data structures except through operations designed for this purpose.

The "proof" previously described is actually just a proof outline that assumes some properties of each implementation of sets. To understand how data-type induction really works, you may work through the equivalence proof with two specific implementations in mind. For example, you may use data-type induction to prove the equivalence of a linked-list implementation and a doubly linked-list implementation of sets.

9.3 MODULES

Early abstract data-type mechanisms, like Clu clusters, declared only one type. If you want only an abstract data type of stacks, queues, trees, or other common data structures, then this form is sufficient: In each of these examples, there is one kind of data structure that is being defined, and this can be the abstract type. However, there are situations in which it is useful to define several related structures. More generally, a set of types, functions, exceptions, and other user-definable entities may be conceptually related and have implementations that depend on each other.

A *module* is a programming language construct that allows a number of declarations to be grouped together. Early forms of modules, such as in the language Modula, provide minimal information hiding. However, a good module mechanism will allow a programmer to control the visibility of items declared in a module. In addition, parameterized modules, as discussed in the next subsection and in more detail in Section 9.4, make it possible to generalize a set of declarations and instantiate them together in different ways for different purposes.

9.3.1 Modula and Ada

As mentioned briefly in Subsection 5.1.4, the Modula programming language was a descendent of Pascal, developed by Pascal designer Niklaus Wirth in Switzerland in the late 1970s. The main innovation of Modula over Pascal is a module system. We will use Modula-2, a successful version of the language, to discuss Modula modules.

The basic form for Modula-2 modules is

```
module <module_name>;
    import specifications;
    declarations;
begin
    statements;
end <module_name>.
```

The declarations may be constant, type and procedure declarations, as in Pascal. The statements are Pascal-like statements. An import specification lists another module name and lists the constants, types, and procedures used from that other module; for example,

```
from Trig import sin, cos, tan
```

It is also possible to write the module name only, importing all declarations from that module.

The basic form of the preceding module may be used as a main program, with the statements performing some task. However, the basic form does not have any parts that are visible externally. To make declarations of one module visible to another, a module interface must be given.

In Modula terminology, a module interface is called a *definition module* and an implementation an *implementation module*. An implementation module has the form given at the beginning of this section, and a definition module contains only the names and types of the parts of an implementation module that are to be visible to other modules.

Example 9.7 Modula-2 Definition of Fractions

```
definition module Fractions;
    type fraction = ARRAY [1 .. 2] OF INTEGER;
    procedure add (x, y : fraction) : fraction;
    procedure mul (x, y : fraction) : fraction;
end Fractions.
implementation module Fractions;
    procedure Add (x, y : Fraction) : Fraction;
        VAR temp : Fraction;
        BEGIN
            temp [1] := x [1] * y [2] + x [2] * y [1];
            temp [2] := x [2] * y [2]; RETURN temp;
        END Add;
    procedure Mul (x, y : Fraction) : Fraction;
        . . .
    END Mul;
end Fractions.
```

In this example, a complete type declaration is included in the interface. As a result, the client code can see that a fraction is an array of integers. The following example hides the implementation of a type. In Modula terminology, the type declaration in Example 9.7 is *transparent* whereas the declaration in Example 9.8 is abstract or *opaque*.

Example 9.8 Modula-2 Stack Module

```
definition module Stack_module
    type stack (* an abstract type *)
    procedure create_stack ( ) : stack
    procedure push( x:integer, var s:stack ) : stack
    . . .
end Stack_module

implementation module Stack_module
    type stack =array [1..100] of integer
    . . .
end Stack_module
```

This example code defines stacks of integers. For stacks of various kinds, we would either need to repeat this definition with other types of elements or to build a generic stack module that takes the element type as a parameter. Mechanisms for defining generic modules are included in Modula-2, Ada, and most modern languages (except Java!). As representative examples, we discuss C++ templates and ML functors in Section 9.4.

Ada Packages

The Ada programming language was designed in the late 1970s and early 1980s as the result of an initiative by the U.S. Department of Defense (DoD). The DoD wanted to standardize its software procurement around a common language that would provide program structuring capabilities and specific features related to real-time programming. A competitive process was used to design the language. Four teams, each assigned a color as its code name, were each funded to produce a tentative "strawman" design. One of these designs, selected by a process of elimination, eventually led to the language Ada.

By some measures, Ada has been a successful language. Many Ada programs have been written and used. Some Ada design issues led to research studies and improvements in the state of the art of programming language design. However, in spite of some practical and scientific success, adoption of the language outside of suppliers of the U.S. government has been limited. One limitation was the lack of easily available implementations. Most companies who produced Ada compilers, especially at the height of the language's popularity, expected to sell them for high prices to military contractors. As a result, the language received little acceptance in universities, research laboratories, or in companies concerned primarily with civilian rather than military markets.

Ada modules are called *packages*. Packages can be written with a separate interface, called a package specification, and implementation, called a package body. Here is a sketch of how the fraction package in Example 9.7 would look if translated into Ada:

```
package FractionPkg is
    type fraction is array ... of integer;
    procedure Add_. . .
end FractionPkg;
package body FractionPkg is
    procedure Add ...
end FractionPkg;
```

9.3.2 ML Modules

The standard ML module system was designed in the mid-1980s as part of a redesign and standardization effort for the ML programming language. The principal architect of the ML module system was David MacQueen, who drew on concepts from type theory as well as his experience with previous programming languages.

The three main parts of the standard ML module system are *structures*, *signatures*, and *functors*. An ML structure is a module, which is a collection of type, value, and structure declarations. Signatures are module interfaces. In standard ML, signatures behave as a form of "type" for a structure, in the sense that a module may have more than one signature and a signature may have more than one associated module. If a structure satisfies the description given in a signature, the structure "matches" the signature.

Functors are functions from structures to structures. Functors are used to define generic modules. Because ML does not support higher-order functors (functors taking functors as arguments or yielding functors as results), there is no need for functor signatures.

Structures are defined with structure expressions, which consist of a sequence of declarations between keywords struct and end. Structures are not "first class" in that they may only be bound to structure identifiers or passed as arguments to functors. The following declaration defines a structure with one type and one value component:

```
structure S =
    struct
        type t = int
        val x : t = 3
    end
```

In this example, the structure expression following the equal sign has type component t equal to int and value component x equal to 3. In standard ML this structure is "time stamped" when the declaration is elaborated, marking it with a unique name that distinguishes it from any other structure with the same type and value components. Structure expressions are therefore said to be "generative" because each elaboration may be thought of as "generating" a new one. The reason for making structure expressions generative is that the module language provides a form of version control based on specifying that two possibly distinct structures or types must be equal.

The components of a structure are accessed by qualified names, written in a form used for record access in many languages. For instance, given our preceding structure declaration for S, above, the name S.x refers to the x component of S, and hence has value 3. Similarly, S.t refers to the t component of S and is equivalent to the type int during type checking. In other words, type declarations in structures are transparent by default. As in Modula and Ada, the distinction between transparent and opaque type declarations appears in the interface.

ML signatures are structure interfaces and may declared as follows:

```
signature SIG =
    sig
        type t
        val x : t
    end
```

This signature describes structures that have a type component t and a value component x, whose type is the type bound to t in the structure. Because the structure S previously introduced satisfies these conditions, it is said to *match* the signature SIG. The structure S also matches the following signature SIG':

```
signature SIG' =
    sig
        type t
        val x : int
    end
```

This signature is matched by any structure providing a type t and a value x of type int such as the structure S. However, there are structures that match SIG, but not SIG', namely any structure that provides a type other than int and a value of that type. In addition to ambiguities of this form, there is another, more practically motivated, reason why a given structure may match a variety of distinct signatures: Signatures may be used to provide distinct views of a structure. The main idea is that the signature may specify fewer components than are actually provided. For example, we may introduce the signature

```
signature SIG" =
    sig
        val x : int
    end
```

and subsequently define a view T of the structure S by declaring

```
structure T : SIG" = S
```

It should be clear that S matches the signature SIG" because it provides an x component of type int. The signature SIG" in the declaration of T causes the t component of S to be hidden, so that subsequently only the identifier T.x is available.

Example 9.9 ML Geometry Signatures and Structures

This example gives signatures and structures for a simple geometry program. An associated functor, for which structure parameterization is used, appears in Example 9.11. The three following signatures describe points, circles, and rectangles, with each signature containing a type name and names of associated operations. Two signatures use the SML include statement to include a previous signature. The effect of include is the same as copying the body of the named signature and placing it within the signature expression containing the include statement:

```
signature Point =
    sig
        type point
        val mk_point : real * real → point
        val x_coord : point - real
```

```
            val y_coord : point - real
            val move_p : point * real * real → point
        end;
    signature Circle =
        sig
            include Point
            type circle
            val mk_circle : point * real → circle
            val center : circle → point
            val radius : circle → real
            val move_c : circle * real * real → circle
        end;
    signature Rect =
        sig
            include Point
            type rect
    (* make rectangle from lower right, upper left corners *)
            val mk_rect : point * point → rect
            val lleft : rect → point
            val uright : rect → point
            val move_r : rect * real * real → rect
        end;
```

Here is the code for the Point, Circle, and Rect structures:

```
    structure pt : Point =
        struct
            type point = real*real
            fun mk_point(x,y) = (x,y)
            fun x_coord(x,y) = x
            fun y_coord(x,y) = y
            fun move_p((x,y):point,dx,dy) = (x+dx, y+dy)
        end;
    structure cr : Circle =
        struct
            open pt
            type circle = point*real
            fun mk_circle(x,y) = (x,y)
            fun center(x,y) = x
            fun radius(x,y) = y
            fun move_c(((x,y),r):circle,dx,dy) = ((x+dx, y+dy),r)
        end;
    structure rc : Rect =
        struct
            open pt
```

```
type rect = point * point
fun mk_rect(x,y) = (x,y)
fun lleft(x,y) = x
fun uright (x,y) = y
fun move_r(((x1,y1),(x2,y2)):rect,dx,dy) =
    ((x1+dx,y1+dy),(x2+dx,y2+dy))
end;
```

9.4 GENERIC ABSTRACTIONS

Abstract data types such as stacks or queues are useful for storing many kinds of data. In typed programming languages, however, the code for stacks of integers is different from the code for stacks of strings. The two different versions of stacks are written with different type declarations and may be compiled to code that allocates different amounts of space for local variables. However, it is time consuming to write different versions of stacks for different types of elements and essentially pointless because the code for the two cases is almost identical. Thus, over time, most typed languages that emphasize abstraction and encapsulation have incorporated some form of type parameterization.

9.4.1 C++ Function Templates

For many readers, the most familiar type-parameterization mechanism is the C++ template mechanism. Although some C++ programmers associate templates with classes and object-oriented programming, function templates are also useful for programs that do not declare any classes. We look at function templates briefly before considering module-parameterization mechanisms from other languages.

Simple Polymorphic Function
Suppose you write a simple function to swap the values of two integer variables:

```
void swap(int& x, int& y){
    int tmp = x; x = y; y = tmp;
}
```

Although this code is useful for exchanging values of integer variables, it is not written in the most general way possible. If you wish to swap values of variables of other types, then you can define a function template that uses a type variable T in place of the type name int:

```
template<typename T>
void swap(T& x, T& y){
    T tmp = x; x = y; y = tmp;
}
```

The main idea is to think of the type name T as a parameter to a function from types to functions. When applied, or *instantiated*, to a specific type, the result is a version of swap that has int replaced with another type. In other words, swap is a general function that would work perfectly well for many types of arguments, except for the fact that the code contains the specific type int. Templates allow us to treat swap as a function with a type argument.

In C++, function templates are instantiated automatically as needed, using the types of the function arguments to determine which instantiation is needed. This is illustrated in the following lines of code:

```
int i,j; ...        swap(i,j);      // Use swap with T replaced by int
float a,b; ... ... swap(a,b); // Use swap with T replaced by float
String s,t; ... swap(s,t);       // Use swap with T replaced by String
```

You may have noticed that the C++ keyword associated with a type variable is class. In C++, some types are classes and some, like int and float, are not. As illustrated here, the keyword class is misleading, because a template may be used with nonclass types such as int and float.

C++ templates are instantiated at program link time. More specifically, suppose that the swap function template is stored in one file and compiled and a program calling swap is stored in another file and compiled separately. The so-called relocatable object files produced when the calling program is compiled will include information indicating that the compiled code calls a function swap of a certain type. The program linker is designed to combine the two program parts by linking the calls to swap in the calling program to the definition of swap in a separate compilation unit. It does so by instantiating the compiled code for swap in a form that produces code appropriate for the calls to swap. If the calling program calls swap with several different types, then several different instantiated copies of swap will be produced. A different copy is needed for each type of call because swap declares a local variable tmp of type T. Space for tmp must be allocated in the activation record for swap. Therefore, the compiled code for swap must be modified according to the size of a variable of type T. If T is a structure or object, for example, then the size might be fairly large. On the other hand, if T is int, the size will be small. In either case, the compiled code for swap must "know" the size of the datum so that addressing into the activation record can be done properly.

Operations on Type Parameters

The swap example is simpler than most generic functions in several respects. The most important is that the body of swap does not require any operations on the type parameter T, other than variable declaration and assignment. A more representative example of a function template is the following generic sort function:

```
template <typename T>
void sort( int count, T * A[count] ) {
for (int i=0; i<count-1; i++)
```

```
        for (int j=i+1; j<count-1; j++)
            if (A[j] < A[i]) swap(A[i],A[j]);
}
```

If A is an array of type T, then sort(n, A) will work only if operator < is defined on type T. This property of sort is not declared anywhere in the C++ code. However, when the function template is instantiated at link time, the actual type T must have an operator < defined or a link-time error will be reported and no executable object code will be produced.

The linking process for C++ is relatively complex. We will not study it in detail. However, it is worth noting that if < is an overloaded operator, then the correct version of < must be identified when compiled code for sort is linked with a calling program.

As a general programming principle, it is more convenient to have program errors reported at compile time than at link time. One reason is that separate program modules are compiled independently, but linked together only when the entire system is assembled. Therefore, compilation is a "local" process that can be carried out by the designer or implementer of a single component. In contrast, link-time errors represent global system properties that may not be known until the entire system is assembled. For this reason, C++ link-time errors associated with operations in templates can be irritating and a source of frustration.

Somewhat better error reporting for C++ templates could be achieved if the template syntax included descriptions of the operations needed on type parameters. However, this is relatively complicated in C++ because of overloading and other properties of the language. In contrast, ML has simpler overloading and includes more information in parameterized constructs, as described in Subsection 9.4.2.

Comparison with ML Polymorphism

Here is the ML code for a polymorphic sort function. The algorithm used in this code is insertion sort, which uses the subsidiary function insert that appears first:

```
fun insert(less, x, nil) = [x]
   |   insert(less, x, y::ys) = if x<y then x::y::ys
                                else y::insert(less,x,ys)
   fun sort(less, nil) = nil
   |   sort(less, x::xs) = insert(less, x, sort(less,xs))
```

In the ML polymorphic sort function, the less-than operation is passed as a function argument to sort. No instantiation is needed because all lists are represented in the same way (with cons cells, as in Lisp).

Uniform data representation has its advantages and disadvantages. Because there is no need to repeat code for different argument types, uniform data representation leads to smaller code size and avoids complications associated with C++-style linking. On the other hand, the resulting code can be less efficient, as uniform data representation often involves using pointers to data instead of storing data directly in structures.

9.4.2 Standard ML Functors

In the ML module system, structures may be parameterized in very flexible ways. We look at this part of the ML module system as a good example of the ways that modules can usefully be parameterized in programming languages. Module parameterization is different from ML polymorphism and is essentially independent of it. More specifically, the ML module design could be adapted to languages that do not have polymorphism or type inference.

In standard ML, a parameterized structure is called a functor. Functors are written in a functionlike form, with a parameter list containing structure names and signatures. Here is an example that uses the signature SIG defined in Subsection 9.3.2:

```
functor F ( S : SIG ) : SIG =
    struct
        type t = S.t * S.t
        val x : t = (S.x,S.x)
    end
```

This code declares a functor F that takes as argument a structure matching the signature SIG and yields a structure matching the same signature. When applied to a suitable structure S, the functor F yields as its result the structure whose type component t, is bound to the product of S.t with itself and whose value component x, is the pair whose components evaluate to the value of S.x.

When free structure variables in signatures are used, certain forms of dependency of functor results on functor arguments may be expressed. For example, the following declaration specifies the type of y in the result signature of G in terms of the type component t of the argument S:

```
functor G ( S : SIG ) : sig val y : S.t * S.t end =
    struct
        val y = (S.x,S.x)
    end
```

The rest of this section consists of examples that show how SML module parameterization can be used to solve some programming problems. Example 9.10 discusses a form of container structure and Example 9.11 completes the geometry example started in Example 9.9.

Example 9.10 Parameterized Priority Queue Module

Container structures such as sets, queues, dictionaries, and so on are used in many programs. This example shows how to define a container structure, priority queues, when one or more container operations require some operation on the type of objects stored in the container. Because priority queues require an ordering on the elements stored in a queue, our definition of priority queues is parameterized by a structure consisting of a type and order relation.

We begin by defining the signature of a type with an order relation:

```
signature Ordered =
  sig
      type t;
      val lesseq : t * t ⟶ bool;
  end;
```

Any structure that matches signature Ordered must have a type t and a binary relation lesseq. We assume in the definition of priority queue that this relation is a total order on the type t. In this functor definition, we declare a type-implementing priority queue operations and a set of operations on priority queues. Because the insert or deletemax operations must test whether an element is less than other elements, at least one of these operations will use the operation elem.lesseq provided by the parameter structure elem:

```
functor PQ(elem:Ordered) =
  struct
      type pq = ... elem.t ... ;           (* representation uses element type
*)
      val empty : pq              = ...;
      fun insert: elem.t * pq ⟶ pq   = ...; (* operations may use elem.lesseq
*)
      fun deletemax: pq ⟶ elem.t * pq = ...;
  end;
```

Example 9.11 Completion of Geometry Example

This example shows how the Point, Circle, and Rect structures in Example 9.9 can be combined to form a geometry structure with operation on all three kinds of geometric objects. To show how additional operations can be added when modules are combined, the Geom signature contains all of the geometric types and operations, plus a bounding box function, bbox, intended to map a circle to the smallest rectangle containing it:

```
signature Geom =
  sig
      include Circle
(* add signature of Rect, except Point since Point is already defined in Circle*)
      type rect
      val mk_rect : point * point ⟶ rect
      val lleft : rect ⟶ point
      val uright : rect - ⟶ point
```

```
val move_r : rect * real * real → rect
(* include function computing bounding box of circle *)
    val bbox : circle → rect
end;
```

The geometry structure is constructed with a functor that takes Circle and Rect structures as arguments. The signatures Circle and Rect both name a type called point. The two point types must be implemented in the same way. Otherwise, operations that involve both circles and rectangles will not work properly. The constraint that two structures (Circle and Rect) must share a common substructure (point) is stated explicitly in the sharing constraint in the parameter list of this functor:

```
functor geom(
    structure c:Circle
    structure r:Rect
    sharing type r.point = c.point (*constraint requires same type in both
structures *)
) : Geom =
    struct
        type point = c.point
        val mk_point = c.mk_point
        val x_coord = c.x_coord
        val y_coord = c.y_coord
        val move_p = c.move_p
        type circle = c.circle
        val mk_circle = c.mk_circle
        val center = c.center
        val radius = c.radius
        val move_c = c.move_c
        type rect = r.rect
        val mk_rect = r.mk_rect
        val lleft = r.lleft
        val uright = r.uright
        val move_r = r.move_r
(* Bounding box of circle *)
        fun bbox(c) =
            let val x = x_coord(center(c))
            and y = y_coord(center(c))
            and r = radius(c)
            in
                mk_rect(mk_point(x-r,y-r),mk_point(x+r,y+r))
            end
    end;
```

9.4.3 C++ Standard Template Library

The C++ Standard Template Library (STL) is a large program library developed by Alex Stepanov and collaborators and adopted as part of the C++ standard. The STL provides a collection of container classes, such as lists, vectors, sets, and maps, and a collection of related algorithms and other components. Because STL is a good example of a large, practical library with generic structures, we survey some of the main concepts. The goal in this section is not to teach you enough about STL so that you can use it easily, but rather to explain the concepts so you can appreciate some of the design ideas and the power of the system.

One striking feature of STL is the run-time efficiency of the code that is generated. STL not only makes it easy to write certain programs by providing useful structures, STL makes it possible to write library-based code that is as fast or faster than the code you might produce if you worked much harder and did not use STL. One reason for the efficiency of STL is that C++ templates are expanded at compile/link time, with a separate code generated (and optimized) for each instantiation. Another reason is the use of overloading, which is resolved at compile time, similarly allowing the compiler to optimize code that is selected for exactly the type of data manipulated in the program. On the other hand, because of code duplication resulting from template expansion, the compiled code of programs that use STL may be large.

In this subsection, the term *object* is used to mean a value stored in memory. This is consistent with the use of the term in C, C++, and STL documentation. STL relies on C++ templates, overloading, and the typing algorithms that figure out type parameters to templates. STL does not use virtual functions and, according to its developer, is not an example of object-oriented programming.

There are six kinds of entities in STL:

- *Containers*, each a collection of typed objects.
- *Iterators*, which provide access to objects of a container. Intuitively, an iterator is a generalization of pointer or address to some position in a container.
- *Algorithms*.
- *Adapters*, which provide conversions between one form of entity and another. An example is a reverse iterator, which reverses the direction associated with an iterator.
- *Function objects*, which are a form of closure (function code and associated environment). These are used extensively in a form that allows function arguments to templates to be in-lined. More specifically, a function object is passed as two separate arguments, a template argument carrying the code and a run-time argument carrying the state of the function. The type system is used to make sure that the code and state match.
- *Allocators*, which encapsulate the memory pool. Different allocators may provide garbage-collected memory, reference-counted memory, persistent memory, and so on.

An example will give you some feel for how STL works.

Example 9.12 STL Lists

List is one of the simplest container types defined in STL. Here is sample code that declares a list of strings called wordlist:

```
#include <string>
#include <list>
int main (void) {
    list<string> wordlist;
}
```

The code list<string> wordlist instantiates a template class list<string> and then creates an object of that type. STL gives you operations for putting elements on the front or back of a list. Here is sample code to add words to our word list:

```
wordlist.push_back("peppercorn");
wordlist.push_back("funnybone");
wordlist.push_front("nosegay");
wordlist.push_front("supercilious");
```

We now have a list with four strings in it. As the names suggest, the list member function push_back() places an object onto the back of the list and push_front() puts one on the front. We can print the words in our list by using an iterator. Here is the declaration of an iterator for lists of strings:

```
list<string>::iterator wordlistIterator;
```

As suggested earlier in this section, an STL iterator is like a pointer – an iterator points to an element of a container, and dereferencing a nonnull iterator produces an object from the container. An STL iterator is declared to have a specific container type; this is important because moving a "pointer" through a container works differently for different types of containers. Here is sample code that prints the words in the list:

```
for (wordlistIterator=wordlist.begin();
    wordlistIterator!=wordlist.end();
    ++wordlistIterator) {
// dereference the iterator to get the list element
    cout << *wordlistIterator << endl;
}
```

We determine the bounds of this for loop by calling wordlist.begin(), which returns an iterator pointing to the beginning of the container, and wordlist.end(), which returns an iterator pointing to the position one past the end of the container. The loop variable is incremented by the operator ++, which is defined on each iterator and moves the iterator from one list element to the next. In the body of the loop, we dereference the iterator to obtain the list element at the current position.

As Example 9.12 shows, iterators are essential for programming with STL containers. Most STL algorithms use iterators of some kind, and there are several different kinds of iterators. The simplest form, so-called *trivial iterators*, may be dereferenced to refer to some object, but operations such as increment and comparison are not guaranteed to be supported. Input iterators may be dereferenced to refer to some object and may be incremented to obtain the next iterator in a container. Output iterators are a fairly restricted form of iterator that may be used for storing (but not necessarily accessing) a sequence of values. The other forms of iterators are forward iterator, bidirectional iterator, and random-access iterator. Specific STL algorithms may require specific kinds of iterators, depending on whether the algorithm reads from a container or stores values into a container and whether the access is sequential (like reading or writing a tape) or random access.

Another basic concept in STL is a *range*. A range is the portion of a container defined by two iterators. The elements of a range are all the objects that may be reached by incrementing the first interator until it reaches the value of the second iterator. If you think of an array as an example container, then a range is a pair of integers, the first less than the second and both less than the length of the array, representing the portion of the array lying between the first index and the second.

The following example discusses the STL merge function, which uses ranges as inputs and outputs. In general, a merge operation combines two sorted sequential structures and produces a third. In merge sort, for example, the merge phase combines two sorted lists into a longer sorted list that contains all the elements of the two input lists.

Example 9.13 Generic Merge Function
The generic STL merge function takes two ranges as inputs and returns another range. Conceptually, the type of merge is

$$\text{merge} : \text{range(s)} \times \text{range(t)} \times \text{comparison(u)} \longrightarrow \text{range(u)}$$

where range(s) means a range of a container that contains objects of type s. Because C++ has subtyping (explained in Chapters 10 and 12), the types s, t, and u need not be identical. However, types s and t must be subtypes of u, meaning that every object of type s or t can be viewed as or converted to an object of type u. The informal notation comparison(u) means that merge requires a comparison operation (less-than-or-equal) on type u, so that merge can combine structures in order.

In fact, each input range in STL is passed as two iterators and an output range is passed as one iterator. The reason we need two iterators for each input range is that we need to know how many elements in the range. Because the output of merge is determined by the input, the output range is represented by a single output iterator that marks the place to begin writing the merged container. Therefore, merge has the following parameters:

```
merge(InputIterator1 first1, InputIterator1 last1,
          InputIterator2 first2, InputIterator1 last2,
          OutputIterator result, Compare comp)
```

In words, the first two arguments provide the first input range, the next two arguments the second input range, the fifth argument the output range, and the sixth argument must provide a comparison function.

Merge is a polymorphic function, merging ranges that contain any types of objects, as long as the types are consistent with each other. The polymorphism of merge is implemented by a template with four parameters. The template requires two iterator types, one for each of the two sequential structures that will be merged, together with the type of output structure and the type of the comparison. This brings us to the full header of merge:

```
template<typename InputIterator1,
         typename InputIterator2,
         typename OutputIterator,
         typename Compare> inline
OutputIterator merge( InputIterator1 first1,
            InputIterator1 last1,
            InputIterator2 first2,
            InputIterator2 last2,
            OutputIterator result,
            Compare comp)
```

It is possible to call merge without supplying a comparison function object. In this case, operator< is used by default. Here is a short program that uses merge, taken from the *Standard Template Library Programmer's Guide*:

```
int main()
{
int A1[ ] = { 1, 3, 5, 7 };
int A2[ ] = { 2, 4, 6, 8 };
const int N1 = sizeof(A1) / sizeof(int);
const int N2 = sizeof(A2) / sizeof(int);

merge(A1, A1 + N1, A2, A2 + N2,
    ostream_iterator<int>(cout, " "));
// The output is "1 2 3 4 5 6 7 8"
}
```

As you can see from this sample code, even though the concepts and design of STL are subtle and complex, using STL can be very easy and direct once the concepts are understood.

9.5 CHAPTER SUMMARY

In this chapter, we studied some of the ways that programs can be divided into meaningful parts and the way that programming languages support these divisions. The main topics were structured programming, support for abstraction, and modules. Two examples were used to investigate module systems and generic programming: the standard ML module system and the C++ Standard Template Library.

Structured Programming

Historically, interest in program organization grew out of the movement for structured programming. In the late 1960s, Dijkstra and others advocated a top-down approach. Although most programs of that day were small, currently many of the early ideas continue to be influential. Most important, we are still concerned with the decomposition of a complex programming task into smaller subproblems that can be solved independently.

Top-down programming has its limitations. Top-down design is difficult when the interfaces and data structures used to communicate between modules must be changed. In addition, the concept of top-down programming does not provide any help when programmers discover that the initial design must be modified to account for phenomena that were not fully appreciated in the initial design. As other design methods have emerged, the principle of decomposing a design problem into separable parts remains central to managing large software development projects.

Two important concepts in modular program development are interfaces and specifications:

Interface:

A description of the parts of a component that are visible to other program components.

Specification:

A description of the behavior of a component, as observable through its interface.

When a program is designed modularly, it should be possible to change the internal structure of any component as long as the behavior visible through the interface remains the same.

Language Support for Abstraction

Procedural abstraction and data abstraction are programming language concepts that allow sequences of statements, or data structures and code to manipulate them, to be grouped into meaningful program units. Here are three features of data-abstraction mechanisms:

- Identifying the interface of the data structure. The interface of a data abstraction consists of the operations on the data structure and their arguments and return results.

■ Providing *information hiding* by separating implementation decisions from parts of the program that use the data structure.

■ Allowing the data structure to be used in different ways by many different programs.

In typed programming languages, the typing rules associated with abstract data types guarantee *representation independence*, which means that changing the implementation of a data type does not affect the observable behavior of client programs. Another principle associated with abstract data types is *data-type induction*, which may be used to reason about the behavior of abstract data types or their equivalence.

Modules and Generic Programming

A *module* is a programming language construct that allows a number of declarations to be grouped together. Early forms of modules provided minimal information hiding. However, good module mechanisms allow a programmer to control the visibility of items declared in a module. In addition, parameterized modules make it possible to instantiate a set of declarations in different ways for different purposes.

The three main parts of the standard ML module system are *structures*, *signatures*, and *functors*. An ML structure is a module, which is a collection of type, value, and structure declarations. Signatures are module interfaces that behave as a form of "type" for a structure. Functors are parameterized modules, requiring one or more types or structures for producing a structure. We looked at a set of structures that provide points, circles, and rectangles, and a functor Geom that combines circles and rectangles into a geometry structure. One interesting aspect of this example is that the circle and the rectangle structures that are combined must have the same point representation. In standard ML, this is enforced by a sharing constraint in the parameter list of the Geom functor.

The C++ Standard Template Library is a large program library, adopted as part of the C++ standard, that provides container classes, such as lists, vectors, sets, and maps. The main concepts in STL are *Containers*, *Iterators*, *Algorithms*, *Adapters*, *Function objects*, and *Allocators*. We looked at lists, as an example container, and a merge function that combines two ranges from sorted collections into a single range. In STL, a range is represented as a pair of iterators, indicating a starting and ending "address" inside a collection.

Polymorphic functions such as merge are represented as function templates, instantiated and optimized before program execution. Function objects, which we did not study, are a form of closure used to pass functions to generic STL algorithms. A function object is passed as two separate arguments, a template argument carrying the code and a run-time argument carrying the state of the function. The type system is used to make sure that the code and the state match.

The concept explored in this chapter can be used in the design of general-purpose programming languages or special-purpose languages developed to solve specialized programming problems (such as specifying a chemical simulation or specifying the security policy of a large organization). Because you are much more likely to design a special-purpose input language in your career as a practicing computer scientist than you are to design a general-purpose object-oriented language, the non-object-oriented methods explained here may be useful to you in the future.

EXERCISES

9.1 Efficiency vs. Modularity

The text describes the following form of heapsort:

```
function heapsort1(n:int, A:array[1..n])
begin
    s := empty;
    for i := 1 to n do          s := insert(A[i], s);
    for i := n downto 1 do      (A[i],s) := deletemax(s);
end
```

where heaps (also known as priority queues) have the following signature

```
empty : heap
insert : elt * heap -> heap
deletemax: heap -> elt * heap
```

and specification:

- Each heap has an associated multiset of elements. There is an ordering < on the elements that may be placed in a heap.

- empty has no elements.

- insert(elt, heap) returns a heap whose elements are elt plus the elements of heap.

- deletemax(heap) returns an element of heap that is ≥ all other elements of heap, together with a heap obtained when this element is removed. If heap is empty, deletemax(heap) raises an exception.

This problem asks you to reformulate the signature of heaps and the sorting algorithm so that the algorithm is more efficient, without destroying the separation between the sorting algorithm and the implementation of heaps. You may assume in this problem that we use pass-by-reference everywhere.

The standard nonmodular heapsort algorithm uses a clever way of representing a binary tree by an array. Specifically, we can think of an array A of length n as a tree by regarding A[1] as the root of the tree and elements A[2*k] and A[2*k+1] as the left and the right children of A[k]. One efficient aspect of this representation is that the links between tree nodes do not need do be stored; we only need memory locations for the data stored at the tree nodes.

We say a binary tree is a *heap* if the value of the root of any subtree is the maximum of all the node values in that subtree. For example, the following tree is a heap and can be represented by the array next to it:

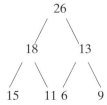

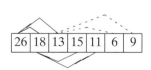

The standard heapsort algorithm has the form

```
function heapsort2(n:int, A:array[1..n])
begin
    variable heap_size:int := n;
```

```
build_heap(n,A);
for i := n downto 2 do
    swap(A[1], A[i]);
    heap_size := heap_size - 1;
    heapify(heap_size,A);
end
```

where the procedure build_heap(n,A) reorders the elements of array A so that they form a heap (binary search tree) and procedure heapify(k,A) restores array elements $A[1], \ldots, A[k]$ to heap form, assuming that only $A[1]$ was out of place.

(a) Assume that procedures insert, deletemax, and heapify all take time $O(\log n)$, i.e., time proportional to the logarithm of the number of elements in the heap, and that build_heap takes time $O(n)$, i.e., time linear in the number of elements in the heap.* Compare the time and space requirements of the two algorithms, heapsort1 and heapsort2, and explain what circumstances might make you want to choose one over the other.

(b) Suppose we change the signature of heaps to

    make_heap : array * int -> heap
    deletemax : heap -> elt

where deletemax may have a side effect on the heap and there is no longer empty or insert.

In addition to the specification of a return value, which is needed for a normal function, a function f with side effects should specify the before and after values of any variables that change, using the following format:

f: If x_{before} is ... then x_{after} is ...

The idea here is that the behavior of a function that may change the values of its arguments can be specified by describing the relationship between values before the call and values after the call. This "if ... then ... " form also allows you to state any preconditions you might need, such as that the array A has at least n elements.

Write a specification for this modified version of heaps.

(c) Explain in words (or some kind of pseudocode if you prefer) how you might implement the modified form of heap with imperative operations described in part(b). You may assume that procedures such as build_heap, heapify, and swap are available. Assume that you will use your heaps for some form of heapsort. Try to make your operations efficient, at least for this application if not for all uses of heaps in general.

[*Hint*: You will need to specify a representation for heaps and an implementation of each function. Try representing a heap by a pair $\langle i, A \rangle$, where A is an array and $0 < i \leq \text{length}(A)$.]

(d) Write a heapsort algorithm (heapsort3) using the modified form of heap with imperative operations described in part (b). How will the time and the space compare with the other two algorithms?

---

* Function build_heap works by a form of iterated insertion. This might require $O(n \log n)$, but analysis of the actual code for heapify allows us to show that it takes $O(n)$ time. If this interests or puzzles you, see *Introduction to Algorithms*, by Cormen, Leiserson, and Rivest (MIT Press, 1990), Section 7.3.

(e) In all likelihood, your algorithm in part (d) (heapsort3) is not as time and space efficient as the standard heapsort algorithm (heapsort2). See if you can think of some way of modifying the definition or implementation of heaps that would let you preserve modularity and meet the optimum efficiency for this algorithm, or explain some of the obstacles for achieving this goal. (Alternatively, argue that your algorithm *is* as efficient as the standard heapsort.)

9.2 Equivalence of Abstract Data Types

Explain why the following two implementations of a point abstract data type are equivalent. More explicitly, explain why any program using the first would give exactly the same result (except possibly for differences in the speed of computation and any consequences of round-off error) as the other.

Appeal to the principle of data-type induction, or related ideas, from this chapter. You need not give a detailed formal inductive proof; a simple informal argument referring to the principles discussed in class will be sufficient. You may explain what needs to be calculated or what conditions need to be checked without doing the calculations. The point of this problem is not to review trigonometry. An answer consisting of three to five sentences should suffice.

```
(* ————————— Trig function for arctan(y/x) ————————— *)
fun atan(x,y) =
                    let val pi = 3.14159265358979323844
                    in
                      if (x > 0.0) then arctan(y / x)
                                    else (if (y > 0.0) then (arctan(y / x) + pi)
                                                       else (arctan(y / x) - pi))
                      handle Div ⟹ (if (y > 0.0) then pi/2.0 else ~pi/2.0)
                    end;
(* ————————— Two point abstract types ————————— *)
abstype point = Pt of (real ref)*(real ref) (* rectilinear coordinates *)
      with fun mk_Point(x,y) = Pt(ref x, ref y)
      and x_coord (Pt(x, y)) = !x
      and y_coord (Pt(x, y)) = !y
      and direction (Pt(x, y)) = atan(!x, !y)
      and distance (Pt(x, y)) = sqrt(!x * !x + !y * !y)
      and move (Pt (x, y), dx, dy) = (x := !x + dx; y := !y + dy)
end;

abstype point = Pt of (real ref)* (real ref) (* polar coordinates *)
with fun mk_Point(x,y) = Pt(ref (sqrt(x*x + y*y)), ref (atan(x,y)))
      and x_coord (Pt(r, t)) = !r * cos(!t)
      and y_coord (Pt(r, t)) = !r * sin(!t)
      and direction (Pt(r, t)) = !t
      and distance (Pt(r, t)) = !r
      and move (Pt(r, t), dx, dy) =
                let val x = !r * cos(!t) + dx
                    and y = !r * sin(!t) + dy
                in r := sqrt(x*x + y*y); t := atan(x,y) end
end;
```

The types of the functions given in either declaration are listed in the following output from the ML compiler:

```
type point
val mk_Point = fn : real * real -> point
val x_coord = fn : point -> real
val y_coord = fn : point -> real
val direction = fn : point -> real
val distance = fn : point -> real
val move = fn : point * real * real -> unit
```

9.3 Equivalence of Closures

Explain why the following two functions that return a form of point "objects," represented as ML closures of the same type, are equivalent. More explicitly, explain why any program using the first would give exactly the same result (except possibly for differences in the speed of computation and any consequences of round-off error) as the other.

We did not cover any induction or equivalence principle for closures, but you might think about whether you can use the same sort of reasoning you used for abstract data types in Problem 9.2.

```
(* ————— Two point objects (as closures) ————— *)
fun mk_point(xval,yval) =
    let val x = ref xval and y = ref yval
    in {
            x_coord = fn () ⇒ !x,
            y_coord = fn () ⇒ !y,
            direction = fn () ⇒ atan(!x, !y),
            distance = fn () ⇒ sqrt(!x * !x + !y * !y),
            move = fn (dx, dy) ⇒ (x := !x + dx; y := !y + dy)
        }
    end;

fun mk_point(x,y) =
    let val r = ref (sqrt(x*x + y*y)) and t = ref (atan(x,y))
    in {
            x_coord = fn () ⇒ !r * cos(!t),
            y_coord = fn () ⇒ !r * sin(!t),
            direction = fn () ⇒ !t,
            distance = fn () ⇒ !r,
            move = fn (dx, dy) ⇒
                let val x = !r * cos(!t) + dx
                    and y = !r * sin(!t) + dy
                in r := sqrt(x*x + y*y); t := atan(x,y) end
        }
    end;
```

9.4 Modularity of Concrete Data Types

Given a grammar for a language, we can define ML data types for parse trees of expressions in that language. Consider a grammar for expressions involving binary (base 2) numbers and the left shift operator (<<) from C. We will use 0^b and 1^b to distinguish the syntax of bits from the numerals 0 and 1.

$$B ::= 0^b \mid 1^b$$
$$N ::= B \mid N\,B$$
$$E ::= N \mid E \ll E$$

In ML, we can create one data type for each nonterminal in the grammar:

```
datatype B = zero | one
datatype N = bit of B | many of N * B
datatype E = num of N | leftshift of E * E
```

A parse tree for an expression in our language can be written in ML with the appropriate constructors. For example, the expression $0^b 1^b \ll 1^b 1^b$ would be written leftshift(many(num(bit(zero), one)), many(num(bit(one), one))).

We may have a denotational semantics for expressions in this language. For example, a function to evaluate binary expressions could be written as

$$\text{eval}\,[\![0^b]\!] = 0,$$
$$\text{eval}\,[\![1^b]\!] = 1,$$
$$\text{eval}\,[\![nb]\!] = 2 \cdot \text{eval}\,[\![n]\!] + \text{eval}\,[\![b]\!],$$
$$\text{eval}\,[\![e_1 \ll e_2]\!] = \text{eval}\,[\![e_1]\!] \cdot 2^{\text{eval}[\![e_2]\!]}.$$

In ML, we would have to write one function per data type:

```
fun evalB(zero) = 0
  | evalB(one) = 1
fun evalN(bit(b)) = evalB(b)
  | evalN(many(n,b)) = 2 * evalN(n) + evalB(b)
```

(a) Write evalE, which has type E $\longrightarrow$ int. Assume you can use the power function in ML, e.g. power(2,3) will return 8.

If you want to try your program in SML, you may define power by

```
fun power(b,0) = 1
  | power(b,e) = b*power(b,e-1)
```

(b) Discuss what has to be changed to add an operator (such as >>) to expressions. Do not worry about how >> actually works.

(c) Discuss what has to be changed to add a new denotational semantics function (such as odd, a function that takes a binary expression and returns true if there are an odd number of 1^b bits in it). Do not worry about how odd actually works.

(d) If Alice modified the program to add a function bitcount and Bob modified it to add a function odd, how hard is it to combine the two modifications into the same program? What has to be changed? Explain.

(e) If instead, Alice modified the program to add an operator >> and at the same time Bob modified the program to add the odd function, how hard is it to combine the two modifications into the same program? What has to be changed? Explain.

(f) If instead, Alice modified the program to add an operator >> and Bob modified the program to add an operator xor, how hard is it to combine the two modifications into the same program? What has to be changed? Explain.

In your discussion of changes, assume that the parts of the program can be classified as one of four kinds:

■ data-type declarations for binary expressions

■ functions that perform pattern matching on binary expressions

■ functions that use binary expressions but do not perform pattern matching

■ functions that do not use binary expressions

For each kind of program component, you should discuss whether it has to be changed, what has to be changed, and why. If it does not have to be changed, explain why it can be left unchanged.

9.5 Templates and Polymorphism

ML and C++ both have mechanisms for creating a generic stack implementation that can be used for stacks with any type of element. In ML, polymorphic stacks could be written as

```
datatype 'a stack = Empty | Push of 'a * 'a stack
```

```
fun top(Empty) = raise EmptyStack
|    top(Push(x,s)) = x
```

```
fun pop(Empty) = raise EmptyStack
|    pop(Push(x,s)) = x
```

To achieve a similar effect in C++, we could write a template for stack objects of the following form:

```
template <typename A> class node {
public:
    node(A v,node<A>* n) {val=v; next=n;}
    A val;
    node<A>* next;
};

template <typename A> class stack {
    node<A>* first;
public:
    stack () { first=0; }
    void push(A x) { node<A>* n = new node<A>(x,first); first=n; }
    void pop() { node<A>* n=first; first=first->next; delete n; }
    A top() { return(first->val); }
};
```

Assume we are writing a program that uses five or six different types of stacks.

(a) For which language will the compiler generate a larger amount of code for stack operations? Why?

(b) For which language will the compiler generate more efficient run-time representations of stacks? Why?

10

Concepts in Object-Oriented Languages

Over the past 30 years, object-oriented programming has become a prominent software design and implementation strategy. The topics covered in this chapter are object-oriented design, four key concepts in object-oriented languages, and the way these language concepts support object-oriented design and implementation.

An *object* consists of a set of operations on some hidden data. An important characteristic of objects is that they provide a uniform way of encapsulating almost any combination of data and functionality. An object can be as small as a single integer or as large as a file system or database. Regardless of its size, all interactions with an object occur by means of simple operations that are called *messages* or *member-function calls*.

If you look in magazines or research journals, you will find the adjective *object-oriented* applied to a variety of languages. As object orientation has become more popular and gained wider commercial acceptance, advocates of specific languages have decided that their favorite language is now object oriented. This has created some amount of confusion about the meaning of object oriented. In this book, we are interested in making meaningful distinctions between different language features and understanding how specific features support different kinds of programming. Therefore, the term *object-oriented language* is used to refer to programming languages that have objects and the four features highlighted in this chapter: dynamic lookup, abstraction, subtyping, and inheritance.

10.1 OBJECT-ORIENTED DESIGN

Object-oriented design involves identifying important concepts and using objects to structure the way that these concepts are embodied in a software system. The following list of steps is taken from one overview of object-oriented design, written by object-oriented design proponent Grady Booch (Object-Oriented Design with Applications, Benjamin/Cummings, 1991):

- Identify the objects at a given level of abstraction.
- Identify the semantics (intended behavior) of these objects.

- Identify the relationships among the objects.
- Implement the objects.

Object-oriented design is an iterative process based on associating objects with components or concepts in a system. The process is iterative because typically we implement an object by using a number of subobjects, just as we typically implement a procedure by calling a number of finer-grained procedures. Therefore, after the important objects in a system are identified and implemented at one level of abstraction, the next iteration will involve identifying additional objects and implementing them. The "relationships among objects" mentioned here might be relationships between their interfaces or relationships between their implementations. Modern object-oriented languages provide mechanisms for using relationships between interfaces and relationships between implementations in the design and implementation process.

The data structures used in the early examples of top-down programming (see Section 9.1) were very simple and remained invariant under successive refinements of the program. When refinement involves replacing a procedure with more detailed procedures, older forms of structured programming languages such as Algol, Pascal, and C are adequate. For more complex tasks, however, both the procedures and the data structures of a program need to be refined together. Because objects are a combination of functions and data, object-oriented languages support the joint refinement of functions and data more effectively than do procedure-oriented languages.

10.2 FOUR BASIC CONCEPTS IN OBJECT-ORIENTED LANGUAGES

All object-oriented languages have some form of object. As mentioned in the preceding section, an object consists of functions and data, accessible only through a specific interface. In common object-oriented languages, including Smalltalk, Modula-3, C++, and Java, the implementation of an object is determined by its *class*. In these languages, we create objects by creating an *instance* of their classes.

The function parts of an object are called *methods* or *member functions*, and the data parts of an object are called *instance variables*, fields, or data members.

Programming languages with objects and classes typically provide dynamic lookup, abstraction, subtyping, and inheritance. These are the four main language concepts for object-oriented programming. They may be summarized in the following manner:

- *Dynamic lookup* means that when a message is sent to an object, the function code (or *method*) to be executed is determined by the way that the object is implemented, not some static property of the pointer or variable used to name the object. In other words, the object "chooses" how to respond to a message, and different objects may respond to the same message in different ways.
- *Abstraction* means that implementation details are hidden inside a program unit with a specific interface. For objects, the interface usually consists of a set of public functions (or *public methods*) that manipulate hidden data.
- *Subtyping* means that if some object a has all of the functionality of another object b, then we may use a in any context expecting b.
- *Inheritance* is the ability to reuse the definition of one kind of object to define another kind of object.

These terms are defined and these features are explored in more detail in the following subsections.

There are several forms of object-oriented languages that are not covered directly in this book. One form is the *delegation-based language*. Two delegation-based languages are Dylan, originally designed to program Apple Newton personal digital assistants, and Self, a general-purpose language evolving out of research on implementation of object-oriented languages. In delegation-based languages, objects are defined directly from other objects when new methods are added by means of *method addition* and old methods are replaced by means of *method override*. Although delegation-based languages do not have classes, they do have the four essential characteristics required for object-oriented languages.

10.2.1 Dynamic Lookup

In any object-oriented language, there is some way to invoke the operations associated with an object. A general syntax for invoking an operation on an object, possibly with additional arguments, is

object $\longrightarrow$ operation (arguments)

In Smalltalk, this is called "sending a message to an object," whereas in C++ it is called "calling a member function of an object." To avoid switching back and forth between different choices of terminology, we will use the Smalltalk terminology for the remainder of this section. In Smalltalk terminology, a *message* consists of an operation name and set of additional arguments. When a message is sent to an object, the object responds to the message by executing a function called a *method*.

Dynamic lookup means that a method is selected dynamically, at run time, according to the implementation of the object that receives a message. The important property of dynamic lookup is that different objects may implement the same operation differently. For example, the statement

x $\longrightarrow$ add(y)

sends the message add(y) to the object x. If x is an integer, then the method (code implementing this operation) may add integer y to x. If x is a set, then the add method may insert y into the set x. These operations have different effects and are implemented differently. However, a single line of code x $\longrightarrow$ add(y) inside a loop could cause integer addition the first time it is executed and set insertion the second time if the value of the variable x changes from an integer to a set between one pass through the loop and another.

Dynamic lookup is sometimes confused with overloading, which is a mechanism based on static types of operands. However, the two are very different, as we will see.

Dynamic lookup is a very useful language feature and an important part of object-oriented programming. Consider, for example, a simple graphics program that manipulates pictures containing shapes such as squares, circles, and triangles. Each square object may contain a draw method with code to draw a square, each circle a draw method that contains code to draw a circle, and so on. When the program wants to display a given picture, sending a draw message to each shape in the picture can do this. The part of the program that sends the draw message does not have to know which kind of shape will receive the message. Instead, each shape receiving a draw message will know how to draw that shape. This makes sense because the implementer of a specific shape is in the best position to figure out how to draw that kind of shape.

We can understand some aspects of dynamic lookup and scoping by using a brief comparison with abstract data types. Using an abstract data-type mechanism, we might define matrices as follows:

```
abstype matrix = ...
    with
        create(...) = ...
        update(m, i, j, x) = ... set m(i, j) = x...
        add(m1, m2) = ...
        ...
    end;
```

A characteristic of this implementation of matrices is that the add function takes two matrices as arguments, with call of the form

```
add(x, y)
```

The declaration of type matrix and associated operations has a specific scope. Within this scope, add refers specifically to the function declared for matrices. Therefore, in an expression add(x,y), both x and y must be matrices. If add were defined for complex numbers in some outer scope, then either the inner declaration hides the outer one or the language must provide some static overloading mechanism.

With objects in a class-based language, we might instead declare matrices as follows:

```
class matrix
    ...      (representation)
    update(i, j, x) = ... set (i, j) of *this* matrix ...
    add(m) = ... add m to *this* matrix ...
end
```

The add method of a matrix requires one matrix as an argument. The method might be invoked by an expression such as

$$x \longrightarrow add(y)$$

In this expression, the operation add appears to have only one argument, the matrix that is to be added to the matrix x receiving the message add(y).

There are several ways that dynamic lookup may be implemented. In one implementation, each object contains a pointer to a method lookup table that associates a method body with each message defined for that object. When a message is sent to an object at run time, the corresponding method is retrieved from that object's method table. Because different objects may have different method lookup tables, sending the same message to different objects may result in the execution of different code.

It is also possible to think of dynamic lookup as a run-time form of overloading. More specifically, we can think of each method name as the name of an overloaded function. When a message m is sent to an object named by variable x, then x is treated as the first argument of an overloaded function named m. Unlike traditional overloading, though, the code to execute must be chosen according to the run-time value of x. In contrast, traditional overloading uses the static type of a variable x to decide which code to use.

Dynamic lookup is an important part of Smalltalk, C++, and Java. In Smalltalk and Java, method lookup is done dynamically by default. In C++, only *virtual* member functions are selected dynamically.

There is a family of object-oriented languages that is based on the "run-time overloading" view of dynamic lookup. The most prominent design of this form is the common Lisp object system, sometimes referred to by the acronym CLOS. In CLOS, an expression corresponding to

$$x \longrightarrow f(y,z)$$

is treated as a call f(x, y, z) to an overloaded function with three arguments. Although ordinary dynamic lookup would select a function body for f based on the implementation of x alone, CLOS method lookup uses all three arguments. This feature is sometimes called *multiple dispatch* to distinguish it from more conventional single-dispatch languages in which only one of the arguments of a function (the object receiving the message) determines the function body that is called at run time.

Multiple dispatch is useful for implementing operations such as equality, in which the appropriate comparisons to use depend on the dynamic type of both the receiver object and the argument object. Although multiple dispatch is in some ways more general than the single dispatch found in Smalltalk, C++, and Java, there is also some loss of encapsulation. Specifically, to define a function on different kinds of arguments, that function must have access to the internal data of each function argument.

Because single-dispatch languages are the object-oriented mainstream, we focus on single-dispatch languages in this book.

10.2.2 Abstraction

As discussed in Chapter 9, abstraction involves restricting access to a program component according to its specified interface. In most modern object-oriented languages, access to an object is restricted to a set of public operations that are chosen by the designer and implementer of the object. For example, in a program that manipulates geometric shapes, each shape could be represented by an object. We could implement an object representing a circle by storing the center and radius of the circle. The designer of circle objects could choose to make a function that changes the center of the circle part of the interface or choose not to put such a function in the interface. If there is no public function for changing the center of a circle, then no client code could change the center of a circle, as client code can manipulate objects only through their interface.

Abstraction based on objects is similar in many ways to abstraction based on abstract data types: Objects and abstract data types both combine functions and data, and abstraction in both cases involves distinguishing between a public interface and private implementation. However, other features of object-oriented languages make abstraction in object-oriented languages more flexible than abstraction in which abstract data types are used. One way of understanding the flexibility of object-oriented languages is by looking at the way that relationships between similar abstractions can be used to advantage.

Consider the following two abstract data types, written in ML syntax. The first is an abstract data type of queues, the second an abstract data type of priority queues. For simplicity, both queues and priority queues are defined for only integer data:

```
exception Empty;
abstype queue = Q of int list
    with
        fun mk_Queue() = Q(nil)
        and is_empty(Q(l)) = l=nil
        and add(x,Q(l)) = Q(l @ [x])
        and first (Q(nil)) = raise Empty | first (Q(x::l)) = x
        and rest (Q(nil)) = raise Empty | rest (Q(x::l)) = Q(l)
        and length (Q(nil)) = 0          | length (Q(x::l))= 1 + length (Q(l))
    end;
```

In this abstract data type, a queue is represented by a list. The add operation uses the ML append operator @ to add a new element to the end of a list. The first and the rest operations read and remove an element from the front of a list. Because client code cannot manipulate the representation of a queue directly, the implementation maintains an invariant: List elements appear in first-in/first-out order, regardless of how queues are used in client programs.

A priority queue is similar to a queue, except that elements are removed according to some preference ordering. More specifically, some priority is given to elements, and the first and the remove operations read and remove the queue elements that have highest priority:

```
abstype pqueue = Q of int list
    with
        fun mk_PQueue() = Q(nil)
        and is_empty(Q(l)) = l=nil
        and add(x,Q(l)) =
                let fun insert(x,nil) = [x:int]
                |   insert(x,y::l) = if x<y then x::y::l else y::insert(x,l)
                in Q(insert(x,l)) end
        and first (Q(nil)) = raise Empty | first (Q(x::l)) = x
        and rest (Q(nil)) = raise Empty | rest (Q(x::l)) = Q(l)
        and length (Q(nil)) = 0          | length (Q(x::l))= 1 + length (Q(l))
    end;
```

The interface of an abstract data type is the list of public functions and their types. Queues and priority queues have the same interface: Both have the same number of operations, the operations have the same names, and each operation has the same type in both cases, except for the difference between the type names pqueue and queue. The point of this example is that, although the interfaces of queues and priority queues are identical, this correspondence is not used in traditional languages with abstract data types. In contrast, if we implement queues and priority queues in an object-oriented language, then we can take advantage of the similarity between the interfaces of these data structures.

A drawback to the kind of abstract data types used in ML and similar languages becomes apparent when we consider a program that uses both queues and priority queues. For example, suppose that we build a system with several wait queues, such as a hospital. In a hospital billing department, customers are served on a first-come, first-serve basis. However, in a hospital emergency room, patients are treated in order of the severity of their injuries or ailments. In a hospital program, we might like to treat priority queues and ordinary queues uniformly. For example, we might wish to count the total number of people waiting in any line in the hospital. To write this code, we would like to have a list of all the queues (both priority and ordinary) in the hospital and sum the lengths of all the queues in the list. However, if the length operation is different for queues and priority queues, we have to decide whether to call q_length or pq_length, even though the correct operation is uniquely determined by the data. This shortcoming of ordinary abstract data types is eliminated in object-oriented programming languages by a combination of subtyping (see Subsection 10.2.3) and dynamic lookup.

The implementation of priority queues shows us another drawback of traditional abstract data types. Although the priority queue add function is different from the queue add function, the other five functions have identical implementations. In an object-oriented language, we may use inheritance (see Subsection 10.2.4) to define priority_queue from queue (or vice versa), giving only the new add function and reusing the other functions.

10.2.3 Subtyping

Subtyping is a relation on types that allows values of one type to be used in place of values of another. Although it is simplest to describe subtyping in the context of statically typed programming languages, there is also an implicit subtyping relation in untyped languages. We will discuss subtyping assuming that we are in a typed language, in most of this section, turning to untyped languages in the final paragraphs.

In most typed languages, the application of a function f to an argument x requires some relation between the type of f and the type of x. The most common case is that f must be a function from type A to type B, for some A and B, and x must be a variable or expression of type A. We can think of this type comparison as a comparison for equality: The type checker finds a type $A \rightarrow B$ for function f and a type C for x, and checks that $A=C$.

In languages with subtyping, there is a subtype relation on types. The basic principle associated with subtyping is *substitutivity*: If A is a subtype of B, then any expression of type A may be used without type error in any context that requires an expression of type B. We write A <: B to indicate that A is a subtype of B.

With subtyping, the subtype relation is used in place of equality in type checking. Specifically, to type the application of f to argument x, the type checker finds a type $A \rightarrow B$ for function f and a type C for x, and checks that C is a subtype of A.

The primary advantage of subtyping is that it permits uniform operations over various types of data. For example, subtyping makes it possible to have heterogeneous data structures that contain objects that belong to different subtypes of some common type. Consider as an example a queue containing various bank accounts to be balanced. These accounts could be savings accounts, checking accounts, investment accounts, and so on. However, if each type of account is a subtype of bank_account, then a queue of elements of type bank_account can contain all types of accounts.

Subtyping in an object-oriented language also allows functionality to be added without modifying general parts of a system. If objects of a type B lack some desired behavior, then we may wish to replace objects of type B with objects of another type A that have the desired behavior. In many cases, the type A will be a subtype of B. By designing the language so that substitutivity is allowed, one may add functionality in this way without any other modification to the original program.

This use of subtyping helps in building a series of prototypes of an airport scheduling system. In an early prototype, one would define a class airplane with methods such as position, orientation, and acceleration that would allow a control-tower object to affect the approach of an airplane. In a later prototype, it is likely that different types of airplanes would be modeled. If we add classes for Boeing 757s and Beechcrafts, these would be subtypes of airplane, containing extra methods and fields reflecting features specific to these aircraft. By virtue of the subtyping relation, Beechcrafts and Boeings are subtypes of airplane, and the general control algorithms that apply to all airplanes can be used for Beechcrafts and Boeings without modification.

10.2.4 Inheritance

Inheritance is a language feature that allows new objects to be defined from existing ones. We discuss the form of inheritance that appears in most class-based object-oriented languages by using a neutral notation. The following class A defines objects with private data v and public methods f and g. We define the class B by inheriting the declarations of A, redefining g, and adding a private variable w:

```
class A =
      private
          val v = ...
      public
          fun f(x) = ... g(...) ...
          fun g(y) = ... original definition ...
      end;
class B = extend A with
      private
          val w = ...
      public
          fun g(y) = ... new definition ...
      end;
```

In principle, inheritance can be implemented by code duplication. For every object or class of objects defined by inheritance, there is a corresponding definition that does not use inheritance; it is obtained by expansion of the definition so that inherited code is duplicated. The importance of inheritance is that it saves the effort of duplicating (or reading duplicated) code and that, when one class is implemented by inheriting from another, changes to one affect the other. This has a significant impact on code maintenance and modification.

A straightforward implementation of inheritance that avoids code duplication is to build linked data structures of method lookup tables. More specifically, for each class, a lookup table can contain the list of operations associated with the class. When one class inherits from another, then the second class can contain a pointer to the lookup table of the first. If a method is inherited, it can be found in the method lookup table of the class in which it was originally defined. A scheme of this form is used in the implementation of Smalltalk, as we will see in Subsection 11.5.3.

A significant optimization may be made in statically typed languages such as C++, in which the set of possible messages to each object can be determined at compile time. If lookup tables can be constructed so that all subclasses of a given class store repeated pointers in the same relative positions, then the offset of a method within a lookup table can be computed at compile time. This reduces the cost of method lookup to a simple indirection without a search, followed by an ordinary function call. We will look at this implementation of inheritance in more detail in Subsection 12.3.3.

Inheritance and Abstraction

In ordinary modules or abstract data types, there are two views of an abstraction: the client view and the implementation view. With inheritance, there are three views of classes: the implementation view, the client view, and the inheritance view. The inheritance view is the view of classes that inherit from a class. Because object definitions have two external clients, there are two interfaces to the outside: The *public* interface lists what the general client may see, whereas the *protected* interface lists what inheritors may see. (This terminology comes from C++.) In most languages, the public interface is a subset of the protected one. In Smalltalk, these interfaces are generated automatically: The public interface includes all the methods of an object, whereas the protected interface is all methods and all instance variables (data). In C++, the programmer explicitly declares which components of an object are public, which are protected, and which are *private* and visible only in the class definition itself. We will discuss this in more detail in Section 12.3.

10.2.5 Closures as Objects

The first characteristic of objects, dynamic lookup, is also provided by records (in Pascal or ML terminology) or structs (in C terminology). In a language with closures, we can simulate objects by using records that have function components. If an object has private data (or functions), then we can hide them by using static scoping. This leads us to look at record closures as a simple first model of objects. It turns out to be instructive to see how useful this notion of object is and where it falls short.

To see the similarities, consider the following ML code:

```
exception Empty;
fun newStack(x) =
  let val store = ref [x]
  in
      {push = fn(y) => store := y ::(!store),
       pop = fn() => case !store of
                      nil = raise Empty
                  |  (y::ys) = (store := ys; y)
      }
      end;
val myStack = newStack(0);
#push(myStack)(1);
#pop(myStack)( );
```

The notation #field_name(record_value) is ML notation for field selection. In Pascal-like syntax, this expression would be written as record_value.field_name.

The function newStack returns a record with two function components, the first called push, the second called pop. Because the fields of this record contain functions, they are represented at run time as closures. The environment pointers for these closures point to the activation record for the newStack function, which stores the local data store. The initial value of store is a list containing only the initial element passed as an argument to newStack. If you draw out the activation records and closures, you will obtain a diagram that is very similar to the ones we will be drawing to represent objects. However, most object-oriented languages optimize the representation in one or more ways.

Because closures and objects have essentially the same functionality, it is reasonable to wonder why we talk about "object-oriented" programming, instead of "closure-oriented" programming. In other words, what do object-oriented programming languages have that languages like ML lack? The answer is subtyping and inheritance. If you try to translate an object-oriented program into a non-object-oriented language, you will appreciate the language support for subtyping and inheritance.

10.2.6 Inheritance Is Not Subtyping

Perhaps the most common confusion surrounding object-oriented languages is the difference between subtyping and inheritance. The simplest distinction between subtyping and inheritance is this: *Subtyping is a relation on interfaces, inheritance is a relation on implementations.*

One reason subtyping and inheritance are often confused is that some class mechanisms combine the two. A typical example is C++, in which A will be recognized by the compiler as a subtype of B only if B is a public base class of A. Combining subtyping and inheritance is an elective design decision, however; C++ could have been designed differently without linking subtyping and public base classes in this way.

We may see that, in principle, subtyping and inheritance do not always go hand-in-hand by considering an example suggested by object-oriented researcher, Alan Snyder. Suppose we are interested in writing a program that requires dequeues, stacks, and queues. These are three similar kinds of data structures, with the following basic characteristics:

- *Queues*: Data structures with insert and delete operations, such that the first element inserted is the first one removed (first-in, first-out),
- *Stacks*: Data structures with insert and delete operations, such that the first element inserted is the last one removed (last-in, first-out),
- *Dequeues*: Data structures with two insert and two delete operations. A dequeue, or doubly ended queue, is essentially a list that allows insertion and deletion from each end. If an element is inserted at one end, then it will be the first one returned by a series of removes from that end and the last one returned by a series of removes from the opposite end.

An important part of the relationship among stacks, queues, and dequeues is that a dequeue can serve as both a stack and a queue. Specifically, suppose a dequeue d has insert operations insert_front and insert_rear and delete operations delete_front and delete_rear. If we use only insert_front and delete_rear, we have a queue. However, if we use insert_front and delete_front, we have a stack.

One way to implement these three classes is first to implement dequeue and then implement stack and queue by appropriately restricting (and perhaps renaming) the operations of dequeue. For example, we may obtain stack from dequeue by limiting access to those operations that add and remove elements from one end of a dequeue. Similarly, we may obtain queue from dequeue by restricting access to those operations that add elements at one end and remove them from the other. This method of defining stack and queue by inheriting from dequeue is possible in C++ through the use of private inheritance. (This is not a recommended style of implementation; this example is used simply to illustrate the differences between subtyping and inheritance.)

Although stack and queue may be implemented from dequeue, they are not subtypes of dequeue. Consider a function f that takes a dequeue d as an argument and then adds an element to both ends of d. If stack or queue were a subtype of dequeue, then function f should work equally well when given a stack s or a queue q. However, adding elements to both ends of either a stack or a queue is not legal; hence, neither stack nor queue is a subtype of dequeue. In fact, the reverse is true. Dequeue is a subtype of both stack and queue, as any operation valid for either a stack or a queue would be a legal operation on a dequeue. Thus, inheritance and subtyping are different relations in principle: it makes perfect sense to define stack and queue by inheriting from dequeue, but dequeue is a subtype of stack and queue, not the other way around.

A more detailed comparison of the two mechanisms appears in Section 11.7, in which the inheritance and subtyping relationships among Smalltalk collection classes are analyzed.

10.3 PROGRAM STRUCTURE

There are some systematic differences between the structure of function-oriented (or procedure-oriented) programs and object-oriented programs. One of the main differences is in the organization of functions and data. In a function-oriented program, data structures and functions are declared separately. If a function will be applied to many types of data, then it is common to use some form of case or switch statement within the function body. In an object-oriented program, functions are associated with the data they are designed to manipulate. Using dynamic lookup, the programming language implementation will select the correct function for each kind of data. This basic difference between function-oriented and object-oriented programs is illustrated by a comparison of Example 10.1 and Example 10.2. A longer example illustrating this point, written in C and C++, appears in Appendix B.1.

In both Examples 10.1 and 10.2, we consider a hospital simulation. The data in these examples represent doctors, nurses, and orderlies. The functions that will be applied to these data include a function to display information about a hospital employee and a function to set or determine the pay of an employee.

Example 10.1 Conventional Function-Oriented Organization

In a conventional function-oriented program, operations are grouped into function. If we want a single function to display information about all types of hospital employees, then we may use run-time tests to determine how to apply each operation to the given data. In outline, codes for display and pay functions might look like this:

```
display(x) =
  case type(x) of
        Doctor  : ["display Doctor" ]
        Nurse   : ["display Nurse" ]
        Orderly : ["display Orderly" ]
    end;
```

```
            end;
        pay(x) =
            case type(x) of
                Doctor  : ["pay Doctor a lot" ]
                Nurse   : ["pay Nurse less" ]
                Orderly : ["pay Orderly less than that" ]
            end;
        end;
```

Example 10.2 Object-Oriented Organization

In an object-oriented program, functions are grouped with the data they are designed to manipulate. For the hospital example, the doctor, nurse, and orderly classes will contain the code for the two functions. In outline, this produces the following program organization:

```
        class Doctor =
            display = "Display Doctor";
            pay = "pay Doctor a lot ";
        end;
        class Nurse =
            display = "display Nurse";
            pay = "pay Nurse less";
        end;
        class Orderly =
            display = "display Orderly";
            pay = "pay Orderly less than that";
        end;
```

Comparison of Examples 10.1 and 10.2

The data and operations used in Examples 10.1 and 10.2 may be arranged into the following matrix. In the conventional function-oriented organization, the code is arranged by row into functions that work for all kinds of data. In the object-oriented organization, the code is arranged by column, grouping each function case with the data it is designed for.

Operation	Doctor	Nurse	Orderly
Display	Display Doctor	Display Nurse	Display Orderly
Pay	Pay Doctor	Pay Nurse	Pay Orderly

In the function-oriented organization, it is relatively easy to add a new operation, such as PayBonus or Promote, but difficult to add a new kind of data, such as Administrator or Intern. In the object-oriented organization, it is easy to add new data, such as Administrator or Intern, but more cumbersome to add new operations such as PayBonus or Promote because this involves changes to every class.

10.4 DESIGN PATTERNS

The design pattern method is a popular approach to software design that has developed along with the rise in popularity of object-oriented programming. In basic terms, a *design pattern* is a general solution that has come from the repeated addressing of similar problems. Design patterns are not solutions developed from first principles or generic code that can simply be instantiated for a variety of purposes. Instead, a design pattern is a guideline or approach to solving a kind of problem that occurs in a number of specific forms. Solutions based on a design pattern can be similar; applying a design pattern to a specific situation can require some thought.

The concept of a design pattern can be used in any design discipline, such as mechanical design or architecture. The work of architect Christopher Alexander is often cited as an inspiration for software design patterns. Here is an architectural example, excerpted from one of Alexander's books (*A Pattern Language: Towns, Buildings, Construction, Oxford Univ. Press, 1977*). This passage includes both a description of the problem context and a solution developed as a result of experience:

> *Sitting Circle*
> *... A group of chairs, a sofa and a chair, a pile of cushions – these are the most obvious things in everybody's life – and yet to make them work, so people become animated and alive in them, is a very subtle business. Most seating arrangements are sterile, people avoid them, nothing ever happens there. Others seem somehow to gather life around them, to concentrate and liberate energy. What is the difference between the two?*
> *... Therefore, place each sitting space in a position which is protected, not cut by paths or movements, roughly circular, made so that the room itself helps suggest the circle – not too strongly – with paths and activities around it, so that people naturally gravitate toward the chairs when they get into the mood to sit. Place the chairs and cushions loosely in the circle, and have a few too many.*

When programmers find that they have solved the same kind of problem over and over again in slightly different ways but using essentially the same design ideas, they may try to identify the general design pattern of their solutions. The popularity of this process has led to the identification of a large number of software design patterns. To quote pattern advocate Jim Coplien, a *good* pattern does the following:

- *It solves a problem*: Patterns capture solutions, not just abstract principles or strategies.
- *It is a proven concept*: Patterns capture solutions with a track record, not theories or speculation.
- *The solution isn't obvious*: Many problem-solving techniques (such as software design paradigms or methods) try to derive solutions from first principles. The best patterns *generate* a solution to a problem indirectly – a necessary approach for the most difficult problems of design.
- *It describes a relationship*: Patterns don't just describe modules, but describe deeper system structures and mechanisms.

■ *The pattern has a significant human component (minimize human intervention).* All software serves human comfort or quality of life; the best patterns explicitly appeal to aesthetics and utility.

Beyond reading about general principles of design patterns, the best way to learn about patterns is to study some examples and use patterns in your programming. Here are a couple of examples. You can find many more in the books and web pages devoted to design patterns. A widely used book is *Design Patterns: Elements of Reusable Object-Oriented Software* by E. Gamma, R. Helm, R. Johnson, and J. Vlissides (Addison-Wesley, 1994).

Example 10.3 Singleton Design Pattern

The singleton design pattern is a *creational* design pattern, meaning that it is a pattern that is used for creating objects in a certain way. Here is a brief overview of the singleton pattern, that uses the kind of subject headings that are commonly used in books and other presentations of design patterns.

Motivation

The singleton pattern is useful in situations in which there should be a single instance (object) of a class. This pattern gives a class direct control over how many instances can be created. This is better than making the programmer responsible for creating only one instance, as the restriction is built into the program.

Implementation

Only one class needs to be written to implement the singleton pattern. The class uses encapsulation to keep the class constructor (the function that returns new objects of the class) hidden from client code. The class has a public method that calls the constructor only if an object of the class has not already been created. If an object has been created, then the public function returns a pointer to this object and does not create a new object.

Sample Code

Here is how a generic singleton might be written in C++. Readers who are not familiar with C++ may wish to scan the explanation and return to this example after reading Chapter 12. The interface to class Singleton provides a public method that lets client code ask for an instance of the class:

```
class Singleton {
    public:
        static Singleton* instance(); // function that returns an instance
    protected:
        Singleton();                  // constructor is not made public
    private:
        static Singleton* _instance;  // private pointer to single object
};
```

Here is the implementation. Initially, the private pointer _instance is set to 0. In the implementation of public method instance(), a new object is created and assigned to _instance only if a previous call has not already created an object of this class:

```
Singleton* Singleton::_singleton = 0
Singleton* Singleton::instance() {
    if (_instance == 0){ _instance = new Singleton; }
    return _instance;
}
```

Example 10.4 Façade

Façade is a *structural object* pattern, which means it is a pattern related to composing objects into larger structures containing many objects.

Motivation

The *façade* pattern provides a single object for accessing a set of objects that have been combined to form a structure. In effect, the façade provides a higher-level interface to a collection of objects, making the collection easier to use.

Implementation

There is a façade class, defined for a set of classes that are used to make up a structure "behind" the facade. In a typical use, a façade object has relatively little actual code, passing most calls to objects in the structure behind the façade.

Example of Façade Pattern

Façade is a very common pattern when a task is accomplished by a combination of the results of a number of subtasks. For example, a compiler might be constructed by implementation of a lexical scanner, parser, semantic analyzer, and other phases indicated in the figure in Subsection 4.1.1. If each phase is implemented as an object with methods that perform its main functions, then the compiler itself will be a façade object that takes a program as input and uses the separate objects that are implementing each phase to compile the program. A user of the compiler may see the interface presented by the compiler object. This is a more useful interface than the more detailed interfaces to the constituent objects that are hidden behind the façade.

10.5 CHAPTER SUMMARY

This chapter contains a short overview of object-oriented design and summarizes the four basic concepts associated with object-oriented languages: dynamic lookup, abstraction, subtyping, and inheritance.

- *Dynamic lookup* means that when a message is sent to an object, the function code (or *method*) that is executed is determined by the way that the object is implemented. Different objects may respond to the same message in different ways.

■ *Abstraction* means that implementation details are hidden inside a program unit with a specific interface. The interface of an object is usually a set of public functions (or *public methods*) that manipulate hidden data.

■ *Subtyping* means that if some object a has all of the functionality of another object b, then we may use a in any context expecting b.

■ *Inheritance* is the ability to reuse the definition of one kind of object to define another kind of object.

In conventional languages that implement closures and allow records to contain functions, records provide a form dynamic lookup and abstraction. Subtyping and inheritance, in the form needed to support object-oriented programming, are generally not found in conventional languages.

Many people confuse subtyping and inheritance. As the term is used in this book, subtyping is a relation on types that allows values of one type to be used in place of values of another. (In Section 11.7, Smalltalk is used to discuss subtyping in a language that does not have a static type system.) As the term is used in this book, inheritance allows new objects to be defined from existing ones. In class-based languages, inheritance allows the implementation of one class to be reused as part of the implementation of another. The simplest way to keep subtyping and inheritance straight is to remember this: *Subtyping is a relation on interfaces* and *inheritance is a relation on implementations.*

In Section 10.3, the difference between the organizational structure of object-oriented programs and the organizational structure of conventional programs is summarized. In conventional languages, functions are designed to operate on many types of data. In object-oriented programs, functions can be written to operate on a single type of data, with dynamic lookup finding the right function at run time.

In Section 10.4, we looked at the basic idea behind design patterns and saw two examples, singleton and façade. A design pattern is a general solution that has come from the repeated addressing of similar problems. The design pattern method is a popular approach to software design that has evolved along with object-oriented programming.

10.6 LOOKING FORWARD: SIMULA, SMALLTALK, C++, JAVA

In the next three chapters, we will look at four object-oriented languages:

■ *Simula*, the first object-oriented language. The object model in Simula was based on procedure activation records, with objects originally described as procedures that return a pointer to their own activation record. There was no abstraction in Simula 67, but a later version incorporated abstraction into the object system. Simula was an important inspiration for C++.

■ *Smalltalk*, a dynamically typed object-oriented language. Many object-oriented ideas originated or were popularized by the Smalltalk group, which built on Alan Kay's then-futuristic idea of the Dynabook. The Dynabook, which was never built by this group, was intended to be a small portable computer capable of running a user-friendly programming language. We will look at the Smalltalk implementation of method lookup and later compare this with C++.

■ C++, a widely used statically typed object-oriented language. This language is designed for efficiency around the principle that programs that do not use a certain feature should run as efficiently as programs written in a language without that feature. A significant design constraint was backward compatibility with C.

■ *Java*, a modern language design in which security and portability are valued as much as efficiency. Some interesting features are interfaces, which provide explicit support for abstract base classes, and run-time class loading, intended for use in a distributed environment.

Because there is not enough time to study all aspects of each language, we will concentrate on a few important or distinctive features of each one. One general theme in our investigation of these languages is the trade-off between language features and implementation complexity.

Simula is primarily important as a historical language and for the way it illustrates the relationship between objects and activation records. Of the remaining three languages, Smalltalk represents one extreme and C++ the other. Smalltalk is extremely flexible and based on the notion that everything is an object. C++, on the other hand, is defined to favor efficiency over conceptual simplicity. Although C++ provides objects, many features of C++ are inherited from C and are not based on objects. Java is a compromise between Smalltalk and C++ in the sense that the flexibility of the implementation and organization around objects are closer to Smalltalk than to C++. Java also contains features not found in either of the other languages, such as dynamic class loading and a typed intermediate language.

EXERCISES

10.1 Expression Objects

We can represent expressions given by the grammar

$$e \quad ::= \quad num \mid e + e$$

by using objects from a class called expression. We begin with an "abstract class" called expression. Although this class has no instances, it lists the operations common to all kinds of expressions. These are a predicate telling whether there are subexpressions, the left and right subexpressions (if the expression is not atomic), and a method computing the value of the expression:

```
class expression() =
    private fields:
        (* none appear in the _interface_ *)
    public methods:
        atomic?()    (* returns true if no subexpressions *)
        lsub()       (* returns "left" subexpression if not atomic *)
        rsub()       (* returns "right" subexpression if not atomic *)
        value()      (* compute value of expression *)
    end
```

Because the grammar gives two cases, we have two subclasses of expression, one for numbers and one for sums:

```
class number(n) = extend expression() with
    private fields:
```

```
                val num = n
            public methods:
                atomic?()  = true
                lsub    () = none (* not allowed to call this, *)
                rsub    () = none (* because atomic?() returns true *)
                value   () = num
        end
        class sum(e1, e2) = extend expression() with
            private fields:
                val left = e1
                val right = e2
            public methods:
                atomic?()  = false
                lsub    () = left
                rsub    () = right
                value   () = ( left.value() ) + ( right.value() )
        end
```

(a) *Product Class:* Extend this class hierarchy by writing a prod class to represent product expressions of the form

$$e \quad ::= \quad \ldots \mid e * e.$$

(b) *Method Calls:* Suppose we construct a compound expression by

```
val a = number(3);
val b = number(5);
val c = number(7);
val d = sum(a,b);
val e = prod(d,c);
```

and send the message value to e. Explain the sequence of calls that are used to compute the value of this expression: e.value(). What value is returned?

(c) *Unary Expressions:* Extend this class hierarchy by writing a square class to represent squaring expressions of the form

$$e \quad ::= \quad \ldots \mid e^2.$$

What changes will be required in the expression interface? What changes will be required in subclasses of expression? What changes will be required in functions that use expressions?* What changes will be required in functions that do not use expressions? (Try to make as few changes as possible to the program.)

(d) *Ternary Expressions:* Extend this class hierarchy by writing a cond class to represent conditionals[†] of the form

$$e \quad ::= \quad \ldots \mid e?e : e$$

What changes will be required if we wish to add this ternary operator? [As in part (c), try to make as few changes as possible to the program.]

---

[*] Keep in mind that not all functions simply want to evaluate entire expressions. They may call the other methods as well.

[†] In C, conditional expressions a?b:c evaluate a and then return the value of b if a is nonzero or return the value of c if a is zero.

(e) *N-Ary Expressions:* Explain what kind of interface to expressions we would need if we would like to support atomic, unary, binary, ternary and n-ary operators without making further changes to the interface. In this part of the problem, we are not concerned with minimizing the changes to the program; instead, we are interested in minimizing the changes that may be needed in the future.

10.2 Objects vs. Type Case

With object-oriented programming, classes and objects can be used to avoid "type-case" statements. Here is a program in which a form of case statement is used that inspects a user-defined type tag to distinguish between different classes of shape objects. This program would not statically type check in most typed languages because the correspondence between the tag field of an object and the class of the object is not statically guaranteed and visible to the type checker. However, in an untyped language such as Smalltalk, a program like this could behave in a computationally reasonable way:

```
enum shape_tag {s_point, s_circle, s_rectangle };
class point {
  shape_tag tag;
  int x;
  int y;

  point (int xval, int yval)
     { x = xval; y = yval; tag = s_point; }
  int x_coord () { return x; }
  int y_coord () { return y; }
  void move (int dx, int dy) { x += dy; y += dy; }
};
class circle {
  shape_tag tag;
  point c;
  int r;

  circle (point center, int radius)
     { c = center; r = radius; tag = s_circle }
  point center () { return c; }
  int radius () { return radius; }
  void move (int dx, int dy) { c.move (dx, dy); }
  void stretch (int dr) { r += dr; }
};
class rectangle {
  shape_tag tag;
  point tl;
  point br;

  rectangle (point topleft, point botright)
     { tl = topleft; br = botright; tag = s_rectangle; }
  point top_left () { return tl; }
  point bot_right () { return br; }
  void move (int dx, int dy) { tl.move (dx, dy); br.move (dx, dy); }
  void stretch (int dx, int dy) { br.move (dx, dy); }
```

```
    };
    /* Rotate shape 90 degrees. */
    void rotate (void *shape) {
      switch ((shape_tag *) shape) {
        case s_point:
        case s_circle:
          break;
        case s_rectangle:
          {
            rectangle *rect = (rectangle *) shape;
            int d = ((rect->bot_right ().x_coord ()
                    - rect->top_left ().x_coord ()) -
                    (rect->top_left ().y_coord ()
                    - rect->bot_right ().y_coord ()));
            rect->move (d, d);
            rect->stretch (-2.0 * d, -2.0 * d);
          }
      }
    }
```

(a) Rewrite this so that, instead of rotate being a function, each class has a rotate method and the classes do not have a tag.

(b) Discuss, from the point of view of someone maintaining and modifying code, the differences between adding a triangle class to the first version (as previously written) and adding a triangle class to the second [produced in part (a) of this question].

(c) Discuss the differences between changing the definition of rotate (say, from 90° to the left to 90° to the right) in the first and the second versions. Assume you have added a triangle class so that there is more than one class with a nontrivial rotate method.

10.3 Visitor Design Pattern

The extension and maintenance of an object hierarchy can be greatly simplified (or greatly complicated) by design decisions made early in the life of the hierarchy. This question explores various design possibilities for an object hierarchy representing arithmetic expressions.

The designers of the hierarchy have already decided to structure it as subsequently shown, with a base class Expression and derived classes IntegerExp, AddExp, MultExp, and so on. They are now contemplating how to implement various operations on Expressions, such as printing the expression in parenthesized form or evaluating the expression. They are asking you, a freshly minted language expert, to help.

The obvious way of implementing such operations is by adding a method to each class for each operation. The Expression hierarchy would then look like:

```
    class Expression
    {
        virtual void parenPrint();
        virtual void evaluate();
        //...
```

```
    }
class IntegerExp : public Expression
{
    virtual void parenPrint();
    virtual void evaluate();
    //...
}
class AddExp : public Expression
{
    virtual void parenPrint();
    virtual void evaluate();
    //...
}
```

Suppose there are *n* subclasses of Expression altogether, each similar to IntegerExp and AddExp shown here. How many classes would have to be added or changed to add each of the following things?

(a) A new class to represent product expressions.

(b) A new operation to graphically draw the expression parse tree.

Another way of implementing expression classes and operations uses a pattern called the visitor design pattern. In this pattern, each operation is represented by a visitor class. Each visitor class has a visitCLS method for each expression class CLS in the hierarchy. The expression class CLS is set up to call the visitCLS method to perform the operation for that particular class. Each class in the expression hierarchy has an accept method that accepts a visitor as an argument and "allows the visitor to visit the class and perform its operation." The expression class does not need to know what operation the visitor is performing.

If you write a visitor class ParenPrintVisitor to print an expression tree, it would be used as follows:

```
Expression *expTree = ...some code that builds the expression tree...;
Visitor *printer = new ParenPrintVisitor();
expTree->accept(printer);
```

The first line defines an expression, the second defines an instance of your ParenPrintVisitor class, and the third passes your visitor object to the accept method of the expression object.

The expression class hierarchy that uses the visitor design pattern has this form, with an accept method in each class and possibly other methods:

```
class Expression
{
    virtual void accept(Visitor *vis) = 0; //Abstract class
    //...
}
class IntegerExp : public Expression
{
    virtual void accept(Visitor *vis) {vis->visitIntExp(this);};
    //...
}
```

```
class AddExp : public Expression
{
    virtual void accept(Visitor *vis)
    { lhs->accept(vis); vis->visitAddExp(this); rhs->accept(vis); }
    //...
}
```

The associated Visitor abstract class, naming the methods that must be included in each visitor and some example subclasses, have this form:

```
class Visitor
{
    virtual void visitIntExp(IntegerExp *exp) = 0;
    virtual void visitAddExp(AddExp *exp) = 0;   // Abstract class
}
class ParenPrintVisitor : public Visitor
{
    virtual void visitIntExp(IntegerExp *exp) {// IntExp print code};
    virtual void visitAddExp(AddExp *exp) {// AddExp print code};
}
class EvaluateVisitor : public Visitor
{
    virtual void visitIntExp(IntegerExp *exp) {// IntExp eval code};
    virtual void visitAddExp(IntegerExp *exp) {// AddExp eval code};
}
```

Suppose there are n subclasses of Expression and m subclasses of Visitor. How many classes would have to be added or changed to add each of the following things by use of the visitor design pattern?

(c) A new class to represent product expressions.

(d) A new operation to graphically draw the expression parse tree.

The designers want your advice.

(e) Under what circumstances would you recommend using the standard design?

(f) Under what circumstances would you recommend using the visitor design pattern?

11

History of Objects: Simula and Smalltalk

Objects were invented in the design of Simula and refined in the evolution of Smalltalk. In this chapter, we look at the origin of object-oriented programming in Simula, based on the concept of a procedure that returns a pointer to its activation record, and the development of a purely object-oriented paradigm in the Smalltalk project and programming language. Twenty years after its development, Smalltalk provides an important contrast with C++ and Java both in simplicity of concept and in the way that its implementation provides maximal programming flexibility.

11.1 ORIGIN OF OBJECTS IN SIMULA

As the name suggests, the *Simula* programming language was originally designed for the purpose of simulation. The language was designed by O.-J. Dahl and K. Nygaard at the Norwegian Computing Center, Oslo, in the 1960s. Although the designers began with a specific interest in simulation, they eventually produced a general-purpose programming language with widespread impact on the field of computing.

Simula has been extremely influential as the first language with classes, objects, dynamic lookup, subtyping, and inheritance. It was an inspiration to the Xerox Palo Alto Research Center (PARC) group that developed Smalltalk and to Bjarne Stroustrop in his development of C++. Although Simula 67 had important object-oriented concepts, much of the popular mystique surrounding objects and object-oriented design developed later as a result of other efforts, most notably the Smalltalk work of Alan Kay and his collaborators at Xerox PARC.

11.1.1 Object and Simulation

You may wonder what objects have to do with simulation. A partial answer may be seen in the outline of an event-based simulation program. An event-based simulation is one in which the operation of a system is represented as a sequence of events. Here is pseudocode representing a generic event-based simulation program:

KRISTEN NYGAARD

A driving force behind Simula was Kristen Nygaard, an operations research specialist and a political activist. He wanted a general modeling language that could be used to describe complex dynamic social and industrial systems in a simple way. Nygaard's interest in modeling motivated the development of innovative computing techniques, including objects, classes, inheritance, and quasi-parallel program execution allowing every object to have an optional action thread.

Nygaard was concerned by the social consequences of computing and expressed some of his reservations as follows:

I could see that SIMULA was being used to organize work for people and I could see that it would contribute to major changes in this area: More routine work, less demand for knowledge and a skilled labor force, less flexibility at the work place, more pressure. ... I gradually came to face a moral dilemma. ... I realized that the technology I had helped to develop had serious consequences for other people...The question was what to do about it? I had no desire to un-invent SIMULA .. because I was convinced that in the society I wanted to help build, computers would come to play an immensely important role. [Translation by J.R. Holmevik]

In addition to the ACM Turing Award and the IEEE John von Neumann Medal, Kristen Nygaard, received the 1990 Norbert Wiener Award for Professional and Social Responsibility from Computer Professionals for Social Responsibility (CPSR), "For his pioneering work in Norway to develop 'participatory design,' which seeks the direct involvement of workers in the development of the computer-based tools they use." Historical information about Nygaard and the development of Simula can be found in an article by J.R. Holmevik, (*Annals of the History of Computing* Vol. 16, Number 4, 1994; pp. 25–37). More recent information may be found on Nygaard's home page.

```
Q := make_queue(first_event);
repeat
    remove next event e from Q
    simulate event e
    place all events generated by e on Q
until Q is empty
```

This form of simulation requires a data structure (some form of queue or priority queue) that may contain a variety of kinds of events. In a typed language, the most natural way to obtain such a structure is through subtyping. In addition, the operation simulate e must be written in some generic way or involve case statements that branch according to the kind of event that e actually represents. Objects help because dynamic lookup for simulate e can determine the correct code automatically. Inheritance arises when we consider ways of implementing related kinds of events.

As this quick example illustrates, event-based simulations can be programmed in a general-purpose object-oriented language. The designers of Simula discovered this when they tried to make a special-purpose language, one tailored to simulation only. Apparently, when someone once asserted that Simula was not a general-purpose language, Nygaard's response was that, because Simula had all of the features of Fortran and Algol, and more, what would he need to remove before Simula could be called general purpose?

11.1.2 Main Concepts in Simula

Simula was designed as an extension and modification of Algol 60. Here are short lists of the main features that were added to and removed from Algol 60:

- *Added to Algol 60:*
  - class concepts and reference variables (pointers to objects),
  - pass-by-reference,
  - char, text, and input–output features,
  - coroutines, a mechanism for writing concurrent programs.
- *Removed from Algol 60:*
  - changed default parameter passing mechanism from pass-by-name to a combination of pass-by-value and pass-by-result,
  - some initialization requirements on variables,
  - own variables (which are analogous to C static variables),
  - the Algol 60 string type (in favor of a text type).

In addition to objects, concurrency was an important development in Simula. This arose from an interest in simulations that had several independent parts, each defining a sequence of events. Before representing events by objects, the designers experimented with representing independent sequences of events by independent processes, with the main simulation loop alternating between these processes to allow the simulation to progress. Here is a short quote from Nygaard on the incorporation of processes into the language:

> In the spring of 1963, we were almost suffocated by the single-stack structure of Algol. Then Ole-Johan developed a new storage management scheme [the multistack scheme] in the summer and autumn of 1963. The preprocessor idea was dropped, and we got a new freedom of choice. In Feb, 1964 the process concept was created, which [led to] Simula 67's class and object concept.

This quote appears in "The Development of the Simula Languages" by K. Nygaard and O.-J. Dahl (published in *History of Programming Languages*, R. L. Wexelblat, ed., Academic, New York, 1981.)

11.2 OBJECTS IN SIMULA

Objects arise from a very simple idea: After a procedure call is executed, it is possible to leave the procedure activation record on the run-time stack and return a pointer to it. A procedure of this modified form is called a *class* in Simula and an activation record left on the stack is an *object*:

Class: A procedure returning a pointer to its activation record.

Object: An activation record produced by call to a class, called an instance of the class.

Because a Simula activation record contains pointers to the functions declared in the block and their local variables, a Simula object *is* a closure! Pointers, missing from Algol 60, were needed in Simula because a class returns a pointer to an activation record. In Simula terminology, a pointer is called a ref.

Although the concept of object begins with the idea of leaving activation records on the stack, returning a pointer to an activation record means that the activation record cannot be deallocated until the activation record (object) is no longer used by the program. Therefore, Simula implementations place objects on the heap, not the run-time stack used for procedure calls. Simula objects are deallocated by the garbage collector, which deallocates objects only when they are no longer reachable from the program that created them.

11.2.1 Basic Object-Oriented Features in Simula

Simula contains most of the main object-oriented features that we use today. In addition to classes and objects, mentioned in the preceding subsection, Simula has the following features:

- *Dynamic lookup*, as operations on an object are selected from the activation record of that object,
- *Abstraction* in later versions of Simula, although not in Simula 67,

- *Subtyping,* arising from the way types were associated with classes,
- *Inheritance*, in the form of class prefixing, including the ability to redefine parts of a class in a subclass.

Although Simula 67 did not distinguish between public and private members of classes, a later version of the language allowed attributes to be made "protected," which means that they are accessible for subclasses (but not other classes), or "hidden," in which case they are not accessible to subclasses either.

In addition to the features just listed, Simula contains a few object-related features that are not found in most object-oriented languages:

- Inner, which indicates that the method of a subclass should be called in combination with execution of superclass code that contains the inner keyword,
- Inspect and qua, which provide the ability to test the type of an object at run time and to execute appropriate code accordingly. Inspect is a class (type) test, and qua is a form of type cast that is checked for correctness at run time.

All of these features are discussed in the following subsections. Some features that are found in other languages but not in early Simula are multiple inheritance, class variables (as in Smalltalk), and the self / super mechanism found in Smalltalk.

11.2.2 An Example: Points, Lines, Circles

Here is a short program example, taken from a classic book describing early Simula (Birtwistle, Dahl, Myhrhaug, and Nygaard, *Simula Begin*, Auerbach, 1973). This example illustrates some characteristics of Simula and shows how closely early object-oriented programming in Simula resembles object-oriented programming today.

Problem
Given three distinct points p, q, and r in the plane, find the center and the radius of the circle passing through p, q, and r. The situation is drawn in Figure 11.1.

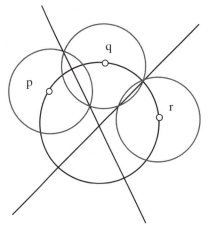

Figure 11.1. Points, circles, and their lines of intersection.

Algorithm

An algorithm for solving this problem is suggested by 11.1. The algorithm has the following steps:

1. Draw intersecting circles Cp and Cq, centered at points p and q, respectively.
2. Draw intersecting circles Cq' and Cr, centered at q and r, respectively. For simplicity, we assume that Cq and Cq' are the same circle.
3. Draw line $L1$ through the points of intersection of Cp and Cq.
4. Draw line $L2$ through the points of intersection of Cq and Cr.
5. The intersection of $L1$ and $L2$ is the center of the desired circle.

This method will fail if the three points are colinear, as there is no circle passing through three colinear points.

Methodology

We can code this algorithm by representing points, lines, and circles as objects and equipping each class of objects with the necessary operations. Here is a sketch of the classes and operations we need:

Point

Representation
   x, y coordinates
Operations

```
equality(anotherPoint) : boolean
distance(anotherPoint) : real
```

Line

Representation
   All lines have the form $ax + by + c = 0$. We may store a, b, and c, normalized so that all three numbers are not too large. When we call the Line class to build a Line object, we will normalize the values of a, b, and c.
Operations

```
parallelto(anotherLine) : boolean
meets(anotherLine) : ref(Point)
```

The parallelto operation is used to see if two lines will intersect. The meets operation is used to find the intersection of two lines that are not parallel.

Circle

Representation

```
center : ref(Point)
```

Operations

---

intersects(anotherCircle) : ref(Line)

It should be clear how to solve the problem with these classes of objects. Given two points, we can pass one to the distance function of the other and obtain the distance between the two points. This lets us calculate the radius for intersecting circles centered at the two points. Given two circles, the intersects function finds the line passing through the two points of intersection, and so on.

11.2.3 Sample Code and Representation of Objects

In Simula, the Point class can be written and used to create a new point, as follows:

```
class Point(x,y); real x,y;
begin
    boolean procedure equals(p); ref(Point) p;
        if p =/= none then
            equals := abs(x - p.x) + abs(y - p.y) < 0.00001;
    real procedure distance(p); ref(Point) p;
        if p == none then error else
            distance := sqrt(( x - p.x )**2 + (y - p.y) ** 2);
end ***Point***
p :- new Point(1.0, 2.5);
```

Because all objects are manipulated by refs (the Simula term for pointers), the type of an object variable has the form ref(Class), where Class is the class of the object. Because the equals procedure requires another point as an argument, the formal parameter p is declared to have type ref(Point). Simula references are initialized to a special value none and :- is used for pointer assignment. The test p =/= none (read "p not-equal none") tests whether the pointer p refers to an object.

In the body of the Point class, we access parts of the object, which are locally declared variables and procedures, simply by naming them. Parts of other objects, such as the object passed as a parameter to distance, are accessed with a dot notation, as in p.x and p.y.

When the statement at the bottom of the code example above is executed, it produces a run-time structure that we may draw as follows:

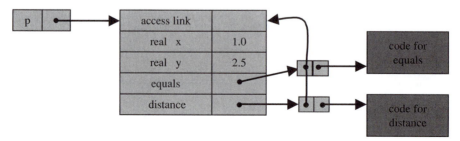

This Point object contains pointers to the closures for Point class procedures and the environment pointer of each closure points to the activation record that is the object. (This means the codes for equals and distance can be shared among all points, but the closure pairs must be different for each object.) When one of these procedures is called, as in p.equals(q), an activation record for the call is created and its access link is set according to the closure for the procedure. This way, when the code for equals refers to x, the x that will be used is the x stored inside the object p.

There are several ways that this representation of objects may be optimized; you should assume only that this representation captures the behavior of Simula objects, not that every Simula compiler actually uses precisely this storage layout. Some useful optimizations are shown in the chapters on Smalltalk and C++, in which each object stores only a pointer to a table storing pointers to the methods.

To give a little more sample code, the line class may be written in Simula as follows:

```
class Line(a,b,c); real a,b,c;
begin
    boolean procedure parallelto(l); ref(Line) l;
        if l =/= none then
            parallelto := abs(a*l.b - b* l.a) < 0.00001;
    ref(Point) procedure meets(l); ref(Line) l;
    begin real t;
        if l =/= none and ~parallelto(l) then
            begin
            t := 1/(l.a * b - l.b * a);
            meets :- new Point(..., ...);
            end;
    end; ***meets***
    real d;
    d := sqrt(a**2 + b**2);
    if d = 0.0 then error else
        begin
        d := 1/d;
        a := a * d; b := b * d; c := c * d;
        end;
end *** Line***
```

The procedure meets invokes another procedure of the same object, parallelto. The code following the procedure meets is initialization code; it is executed whenever a Line object is instantiated. You might want to think about how this initialization code, which is written as if a class were an ordinary procedure, corresponds to constructor code in object-oriented languages you are familiar with.

11.3 SUBCLASSES AND SUBTYPES IN SIMULA

11.3.1 Subclasses and Inheritance

The classes in a Simula program are arranged in a hierarchy. One class is a *superclass* of a second if the second is defined by inheritance from the first. We also say that a class is a *subclass* of its superclass.

Simula syntax for a class C1 with subclasses C2 and C3 is

```
class C1
     <declarations_1> ;
C1 class C2
     <declarations_2>
C1 class C3
     <declarations_3>
```

When we create a C2 object, for example, we do this by first creating a C1 object (activation record) and then appending a C2 object (activation record). In a picture, a C2 object looks like this:

```
C1 parts of object
C2 parts of object
```

The structure is essentially the same as if procedure called C2 was declared and called within C1: The access links of the second activation record refer to the first.

Here is an example code that uses Simula class prefixing to define a colored point subclass of the Point class defined in Subsection 11.2.3:

```
Point class ColorPt(c); color c;        ! List new parameter only
begin
     boolean procedure equals(q); ref(ColorPt) q;
         . . . ;
end ***ColorPt***
ref(Point) p;                           ! Class reference variables
ref(ColorPt) cp;
p :- new Point(2.7, 4.2);
cp :- new ColorPt(3.6, 4.9, red);       ! Include parent class parameters
```

The ColorPt class adds a color field c to points. Because Simula 67 did not hide fields, the c field of a ColorPt object can be accessed and changed directly by use of the dot notation. For example, cp.c := green changes to color of the point named by cp. The ColorPt class redefines equals so that cp.equals can compare color as well as x and y.

The statement p :- New Point(2.7, 4.2) causes an activation record to be created with locations for parameters x and y. These are set to 2.7 and 4.2, respectively and then the body of the Point class is executed. Because the body of the Point} class is empty, nothing happens at this stage for points. After the body is executed, a pointer to the activation record is returned. The activation record contains pointers to function values (closures) equals and distance.

A prefixed class object is created by a similar sequence of steps that involves calls to the parent class before the child class. More specifically, an activation record is created for the parent class and an activation record is created for the child class. Then parameter values are copied to the activation records, parent class first, and the class bodies are executed, parent class first. Some additional details are considered in the exercises.

11.3.2 Object Types and Subtypes

All instances of a class are given the same type. The name of this type is the same as the name of the class. For example, if p and q are variables referring to objects created by the Point class, then they will have type ref(Point). As mentioned in Section 11.2, ref arises because all Simula objects are manipulated through pointers.

The class names (types of objects) are arranged in a *subtype* hierarchy corresponding exactly to the subclass hierarchy. In other words, the only subtype relations that are recognized in Simula 67 are exactly those that arise from inheritance: If class A is derived from class B, then the Simula type checker treats type A as a subtype of type B.

There are some interesting subtleties regarding assignment and subtyping that also apply to other languages. For example, look carefully at the following legal Simula code, in which Simula syntax :- is used for reference (pointer) assignment:

```
class A;
A class B;    /* B is a subclass of A */
ref (A) a;
ref (B) b;
a :- b;       /* legal since B is a subclass of A */
...
b :- a;       /* also legal but checked at run-time to make sure a points to a B
                 object*/
```

Both assignments are accepted at compile time and satisfy Simula's notion of type compatibility. However, a run-time check is needed for the second assignment to guarantee type safety. The same run-time checking also appears in Beta, a cultural descendant of Simula, and in Java array array assignment. The reason for the run-time test is that the object reference a might point to an object of class B or it might point to an object of class A that is not an object of class B. In the first case, the assignment is OK; in the second case, it is not. If an assignment causes an object reference b with static type ref(B) to point to an object that is *not* from class B or some subclass of B, this is a type error.

It is possible to rewrite the assignment to b in the code we just looked at by using Simula inspect:

```
inspect a
    when B do b :- a
    otherwise .../* some appropriate action */
```

If a does not refer to a B object, then the otherwise clause will catch the error and let the programmer take appropriate action. However, in the case in which the programmer knows that a refers to a B object, the syntax with an implicit run-time test is obviously simpler.

There was an error in the original Simula type checker surrounding the relationship between subtyping and inheritance. This is illustrated in the following code, extracted from a running DEC-20 Simula program written by Alan Borning. (The DEC-20 version of Simula uses := instead of :- for pointer assignment.)

```
class A;
A class B; /* B is a subclass of A */
ref (A) a;
ref (B) b;
proc assignA (ref (A) x)
    begin
    x := a
    end;
assignA(b);
```

In the terminology of Chapter 10, Simula subclassing produces the subtype relation B <: A. Simula also uses the semantically incorrect principle that, if B <: A, then ref (B) <: ref (A). Therefore, this code will statically type check, but will cause a type error at run time. The same type error occurs in the original implementation of Eiffel, a language designed many years later.

11.4 DEVELOPMENT OF SMALLTALK

The Smalltalk project at Xerox PARC in the 1970s streamlined the object metaphor and drew attention to object-oriented programming. Although the central object-oriented concepts in Smalltalk resemble their Simula ancestors, Smalltalk was not an incremental modification of any previously existing language. It was a completely new language, with new terminology and an original syntax.

This is a list of some of the main advances of Smalltalk over Simula:

- The object metaphor was extended and refined
  - In Smalltalk, everything is an object, even a class.
  - All operations are therefore messages to objects.

- □ Objects and classes were shown to be useful organizing concepts for building an entire programming environment and system.
- ■ Abstraction was added, using the distinction between
  - □ private *instance variables* (data associated with an object) and
  - □ public *methods* (code for performing operations)

These short lists, however, do not do justice to the Smalltalk project. Smalltalk was conceived as part of an innovative and forward-looking effort that designed an entire computing system around a new programming language.

Smalltalk is more flexible and more powerful than Simula or other languages that preceded it, and many Smalltalk fans consider it a better language than most that followed. Smalltalk is untyped, allowing greater flexibility in the modification of programs and greater flexibility in the use of general-purpose algorithms on a variety of data objects. In addition, the importance of treating everything as an object cannot be underestimated. This is the source of much of the flexibility of Smalltalk. Smalltalk has many interesting and powerful facilities, including a mechanism that allows objects to detect a message they do not understand and to respond to the message.

Dynabook

Part of the inspiration for the Smalltallk language and system came from Alan Kay's concept of a *Dynabook*. The Dynabook was to be a small portable computer that was capable of storing useful and interesting personal information and running programs for a variety of applications. It was a laptop computer with business and entertainment software, and sufficient storage space to store telephone numbers, business data, or a copy of a popular novel. It is almost impossible to explain, in the present day, how utterly improbable this sounded in the 1970s. At the end of the 1970s, a minicomputer, typically shared by 15 or 20 people, required the same floor space as a small laundromat and had roughly the same appearance – rows of machines, some with visible spinning drums. Very-large-scale integrated (VLSI) circuits were not a reality until the late 1970s, so there was really no way the Dynabook could conceivably have been manufactured at the time it was imagined. To give another historical data point, the Xerox Alto of the 1970s was an advanced personal computer that cost $32,000 at the time, more than the annual salary of a computer professional. It had removable disks, which each person would use to store personal working data. Each disk was 2ft in diameter, a couple inches thick, and weighed 5–10 lb! Hardly the sort of thing you could carry around in your pocket or even imagine inserting into a portable computer. Not only was Kay's prediction of hardware miniaturization revolutionary, but the idea that people would use a computer for a wide range of personal activities was shocking.

Smalltalk was intended to be the operating system interface as well as the standard programming language for Dynabook; all of a user's interaction with the Dynabook would be through Smalltalk. With this in mind, the syntax of Smalltalk was designed to be used with a special-purpose Smalltalk editor. Because the Xerox group believed that hardware would eventually catch up with the need for computing power, the Smalltalk implementation emphasized flexibility and ease of use over efficiency.

11.5 SMALLTALK LANGUAGE FEATURES

11.5.1 Terminology

The Smalltalk project developed precise terminology for the main Smalltalk concepts and constructs. Here is a list of the main object-related terms and brief descriptions:

- *Object*: A combination of private data and functions. Each object is an *instance* of some class.
- *Class*: A template defining the implementation of a set of objects.
- *Subclass*: Class defined by inheriting from its superclass.
- *Selector*: The name of a message (analogous to a function name).
- *Message:* A selector together with actual parameter values (analogous to a function call).
- *Method*: The code in a class for responding to a message.
- *Instance Variable*: Data stored in an individual object (instance of a class).

The way these terms were used in the Smalltalk language and documentation is close to current informal use among many object-oriented professionals, but not entirely universal. For example, some people use "method" to refer to both the name of a method (which Smalltalk would call a selector) and the code used to respond to a message.

11.5.2 Classes and Objects

The Smalltalk environment included a special editor designed for the Smalltalk language. With this editor, classes were defined by filling in a table of a certain form, illustrated with the definition of a Point class in Figure 11.2.

In Smalltalk terminology, a class variable is a variable that is defined in the class and shared among all objects of the class. In this example, the value of pi may be used in geometric calculations involving points. Therefore, the class includes a variable called pi. An instance variable is a variable that is repeated for each object. Each point object, for example, will have two instance variables, x and y, as each point may

class name	Point
super class	Object
class var	pi
instance var	x y
class messages and methods	
〈...names and code for methods...〉	
instance messages and methods	
〈...names and code for methods...〉	

Figure 11.2. Definition of Point class.

be located at a different position in the x–y plane. Methods are functions that may be used to manipulate objects, and messages contain the names and parameters of methods.

Here are some example class messages and methods for point objects (subsequently explained):

```
newX:xvalue Y:yvalue ||
                ^ self new x: xvalue y: yvalue
    newOrigin ||
                ^ self new x: 0 y: 0
                initialize ||
                    pi <- 3.14159
```

and some example instance messages and methods:

```
x: xcoord y: ycoord ||
        x <- xcoord
        y <- ycoord
    moveDx: dx Dy: dy ||
        x <- dx + x
        y <- dy + y
    x || ^x
    y || ^y
    draw ||< < ... code to draw point ... > >
```

These are written with Smalltalk syntax, which includes the following:

```
||    −place to list local declarations for method body
^ - unary prefix operator giving return value of method
<- - assignment
```

Smalltalk message names include positions for message arguments, indicated by colons.

The first class method, newX:Y:, is a two-argument method that creates a new point. The two arguments are the x coordinate and the y coordinate of the new point. A new point at coordinates (3, 2) is created when the message

```
newX: 3 Y:2
```

is sent to the Point class, with x coordinate 3 following the first colon and y coordinate 2 following the second coordinate. When we look at inheritance and other situations in which the name of a method is important, it will be useful to remember that the official Smalltalk name of a message contains all the words and colons, as in "newX:Y:."

The newX:Y: method is a class method of the Point class, which means that if you want to create a new point with specific *x* and *y* coordinates, you may send a newX:Y: message to the Point class (which is itself an object). The newX:Y: method has no local variables, as any local declarations would appear between the vertical bars following the name. The effect of the method is indicated by the expression

```
^ self new x: xvalue y: yvalue
```

As previously mentioned, the first symbol, ^, means "return." The value that is returned is the object produced when the message new x: xvalue y: yvalue is sent to the Point class. (Self refers to the object that contains the method; this is discussed in Subsection 11.6.3.) This message is handled by a predefined class method, provided by the system, that allows any class to create instances of it.

To continue the example, suppose we execute the following code:

```
p <- Point newOrigin
p moveDx: 3 Dy: 4
```

This will create a point at the origin, $(0, 0)$, and then move the point to position $(3, 4)$. Thereafter, the value of expression

```
p x
```

that sends the message x to the object p will be the object 3 and the value of

```
p y
```

that sends the message y to the object p will be the object 4.

Run-Time Representation of Objects

The run-time representation of a Smalltalk object has a number of parts. Each point object, for example, may have a different *x* coordinate and *y* coordinate. Therefore, each object must contain space for an *x* coordinate and a *y* coordinate. The methods, on the other hand, are shared among all point objects. To save space and take advantage of the similarity between objects of the same class, each object contains a pointer to a data structure containing information associated with its class. The basic run-time structure for points is illustrated in Figure 11.3. This illustration is intended to show the basic functionality of Smalltalk classes and objects; actual implementations might store things differently or perform various optimizations to improve performance.

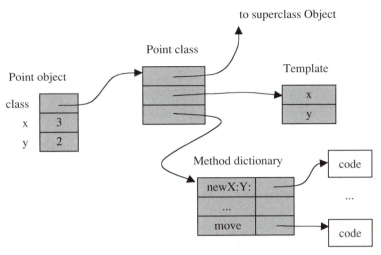

Figure 11.3. Run-time representation of Point object and class.

When a message, such as move, is sent to a point object, the code for move is located by following a pointer to the class of the object, following another pointer to the method dictionary, and then looking up the code in this data structure. If the code for a method is not found in the method dictionary for the class, the method dictionaries of superclasses are searched, as described in the next subsection on inheritance.

11.5.3 Inheritance

We look at Smalltalk inheritance by considering a subclass of Point that implements colored points. The main difference between ColoredPoint and Point is that each colored point has an associated color. If we want to provide methods for the same geometric calculations, then we can make colored points a subclass of points. In Smalltalk, the ColoredPoint class can be defined as shown in Figure 11.4.

class name	ColoredPoint	
super class	Point	
class var		
instance var	color	
class messages and methods		
newX:xv Y:yv C:cv	⟨ ... code ... ⟩	
instance messages and methods		
color	|| ^color	
draw	⟨ ... code ... ⟩	

Figure 11.4. Definition of ColoredPoint class.

The second line of Figure 11.4 shows that Point is the superclass of ColoredPoint. As a result, all instance variables and methods of Point become instance variables and methods of ColoredPoint by default. In Smalltalk terminology, ColoredPoint *inherits* instance variables x and y, methods x:y:, moveDx:Dy:, and so on. In addition, ColoredPoint adds an instance variable color and a method color to return the color of a ColoredPoint.

Although ColoredPoint inherits the draw method from Point, the draw method for ColoredPoint must be implemented differently. When we draw a ColoredPoint, the point should be drawn in color. Therefore, Figure 7.1 shows a draw method, overriding the one inherited from Point. (Redefinition of a method is sometimes called *overriding* the method.) An option that is available in Smalltalk, but not in most other object-oriented languages, is to specify that a superclass method should be undefined on a subclass.

Because colored points should have a color specified when they are created, the ColoredPoint class will have a class method that sets the color of a colored point:

```
newX: xvalue Y:yvalue C:cvalue ||
        ^ self new x: xvalue y:yvalue color:cvalue
```

As an example use of ColoredPoint, suppose we execute the following code:

```
cp <- ColoredPoint newX:1 Y:2 C:red
cp moveDx: 3 Dy: 4
```

Then the value of the expression

```
cp x
```

that sends the message x to object cp will be the object 4, and the value of the expression

```
cp color
```

that sends the message color to the object cp will be the object red. Note that even though move is an inherited method, defined originally for points without color, the result of moving a ColoredPoint is a ColoredPoint.

Run-Time Structure to Support Inheritance

The run-time structures for a ColoredPoint object and ColoredPoint class are illustrated in Figure 11.5. The illustration shows a ColoredPoint object, with the object's class pointer pointing to the ColoredPoint class object. The ColoredPoint class contains a superclass pointer that points to the Point class object. Like the Point class, the

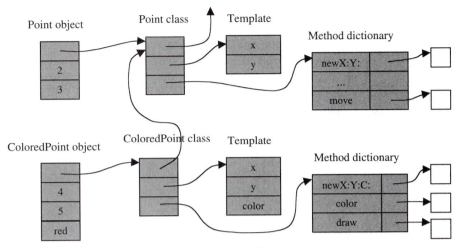

Figure 11.5. Run-time representation of ColoredPoint object and classs.

ColoredPoint class also has a pointer to a template, which contains the names of the instance variables, and a method dictionary, which contains pointers to code that implements each of the methods. Like Figure 11.3, this figure is schematic. An actual compiler could store things slightly differently or perform optimizations to improve performance.

If a draw message is sent to a ColoredPoint object, then we find the code for executing this method by following the pointer in the object to the ColoredPoint class structure and by following the pointer there to the method dictionary for the ColoredPoint class. The dictionary is then searched for a method with the right name. If a message other than new, color, and draw is sent, then the method name will not be found in the ColoredPoint method dictionary. In this case, the superclass pointer in the ColoredPoint class is used to locate the Point class and the Point method dictionary. Then the search continues as if the object were an instance of its superclass.

It should be clear from these data structures that looking up a method at run time can involve a large number of steps. If class A inherits from class B and class B inherits from class C, for example, then searching for an inherited method could involve searching all three method dictionaries at run time. If the operation performed by this method is simple, then it might take more time to find a method than to execute it.

This run-time cost of Smalltalk method lookup illustrates one of the basic principles of programming language design: *You can't get something for nothing.* Dynamic lookup is a powerful programming feature, but it has its costs. Fortunately, there are optimizations that reduce the cost of method lookup in practice. One common optimization (also used in Java) is to cache recently found methods at the method invocation site in a program. If this is done, then a second invocation of the same method can be executed by a jump directly to the code location stored in the cache. As discussed in the next chapter, static type information can also be used to significantly reduce the cost of method lookup. This makes lookup more efficient in C++. However, optimizations based on static type information do not work in Smalltalk because Smalltalk has no static type system.

There are some interesting details surrounding the way that instance variables are accessed by methods. Because the code for the draw method in the ColoredPoint class is compiled at the same time that the layout of ColoredPoint objects is determined, the ColoredPoint method can be compiled so that if it needs to access instance variables of a ColoredPoint object, it can locate them easily (given a pointer to the object). Specifically, the offset of the x coordinate, y coordinate, and color, relative to the starting address of the ColoredPoint object, is known at compile time and can be used in any ColoredPoint method. The same is true for Point methods. However, because a Point method can be inherited by ColoredPoint and invoked on a ColoredPoint object, it is necessary for Point instance variables to appear at the same relative offset in both Point and ColoredPoint objects. More generally, accessing instance variables by use of offsets known at compile time requires the layout of a subclass object to resemble the layout of a superclass object. You might want to think about the advantages and disadvantages of compiling methods in this way compared with run-time search for instance variables by using the class templates. One consequence of using compile-time offsets is that, when a superclass is changed and a new instance variable is added, all subclasses must be recompiled. (This was the case for the Xerox PARC Smalltalk compiler.)

11.5.4 Abstraction in Smalltalk

In most object-oriented languages, a programmer can decide which parts of an object are visible to clients of the class and which parts are not. Smalltalk makes this decision for the programmer by using particularly simple rules:

- *Methods are Public:* Any code with a pointer to an object may send any message to that object. If the corresponding method is defined in the class of the object, or any superclass, the method will be invoked. This makes all methods of an object visible to any code that can access the object.
- *Instance Variables are Protected:* The instance variables of an object are accessible only to methods of the class of the object and to methods of its subclasses.

This is not a fully general approach to abstraction. In particular, there are practical situations in which it would be useful to have private methods, accessible only to other methods of the same class. However, the Smalltalk visibility rules are simple, easy to remember, and sufficient in many situations.

11.6 SMALLTALK FLEXIBILITY

11.6.1 Dynamic Lookup and Polymorphism

Advocates of object-oriented languages often speak about the "polymorphism" inherent in object-oriented code. When they say this, they mean that the same message name invokes different code, depending on the object that receives the message. In this book, we refer to this phenomenon as dynamic lookup, as explained in Chapter 10.

Here is an example that illustrates the value of dynamic lookup. Consider a list of objects, some of which are points and others of which are colored points. If we want to display every point on the list, we may traverse the list, sending each object the draw method. Because of dynamic lookup, the Point objects will execute the Point draw method and the ColoredPoint objects will execute the ColoredPoint draw method. Dynamic lookup supports code reuse, as one routine will display lists of Points, lists of ColoredPoint, and lists that have both Points and ColoredPoints.

The run-time structures used for Smalltalk classes and objects support dynamic lookup in two ways. First, methods are selected through the receiver object. Second, method lookup starts with the method dictionary of the class of the receiver and then proceeds upward. The first method found with the appropriate name is selected.

The following code sends a draw message to a Point and a ColoredPoint:

```
p <- Point newOrigin
p draw
p <- ColoredPoint newX:1 Y:2 C:red
p draw
```

Be sure you understand how and why different code is used in lines two and four to draw the two different kinds of objects.

11.6.2 Booleans and Blocks

An assumption that many people make when learning about Smalltalk is that it has the same kind of syntax, with specific reserved words and special forms, as other languages.

However, many constructs that would be handled with a special-purpose statement form in other languages can be handled uniformly in Smalltalk with the principle that *everything is an object*. A good example is the Smalltalk treatment of Booleans, which uses the built-in construct of blocks.

A Smalltalk Boolean object (true or false) has a selector named ifTrue:ifFalse:. The method associated with this selector requires two parameters, one to be executed if the object is true and the other if the object is false. The arguments to this method are generally Smalltalk *blocks*, which are objects that have a message, "execute yourself." Although blocks may be defined by special in-line syntax, for convenience, they are not essentially different from other Smalltalk objects.

The reason for using blocks in Smalltalk Booleans is easy to understand if we think about conditionals in other languages. In general, the construct

```
if ... then ... else ...
```

cannot be defined as an ordinary function, as an ordinary function call would involve evaluating all arguments before calling the function. If we evaluated A, B, and C first in

```
if A then B else C
```

this is inefficient and incorrect if B and C have side effects or fail to terminate. We want to evaluate B only in the case that A is true and evaluate C only in the case that A is false.

For example, consider the following expression:

```
i < j ifTrue: [i add: 1] ifFalse: [j subtract: 1]
```

This is the Smalltalk way of writing

```
if i < j then i+1 else j-1
```

The first part of the expression, i < j, is a < j message to object i, asking it to compare itself with j. The result will be either the object true or the object false, in either case an object that understands an ifTrue:ifFalse: message. Therefore, after the comparison, i < j, one of the two subsequent blocks will be executed, depending on the result of the comparison.

The way Smalltalk actually works is that the class Boolean has two subclasses, True and False, each with one instance, called true and false, respectively. In these classes, the ifTrue:ifFalse: method is implemented as follows:

```
True class . . .
    ifTrue: trueBlock ifFalse: falseBlock
        trueBlock value
False class . . .
    ifTrue: trueBlock ifFalse: falseBlock
        falseBlock value
```

where value is the message you send to a block if you want it to evaluate itself and return its value.

There is a little bit of "special treatment" here in that the system will not allow more instances of classes True and False to be created. This is to guarantee correctness of an optimization. For efficiency, the standard idiom ifTrue: [. . .] ifFalse: [. . .] is optimized by the compiler in most Smalltalk implementation. However, this is again simply an optimization for efficiency. In principle, Booleans could be defined within the language. In addition, the unoptimized methods previously given are called if any arguments are variables that might hold blocks.

11.6.3 Self and Super

The special symbol self may be used in the body of a Smalltalk method. The special property of self is that it always refers to the object that contains this method, whether directly or by inheritance. The way this works is most easily explained by example.

There are several classes of numbers in Smalltalk. Three are arranged in the following hierarchy:

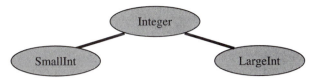

Even if the Integer class does not create any objects, we can define the following method in the Integer class:

```
factorial ||
    self <= 1
        ifTrue: [^ 1]
        ifFalse: [^(self - 1) factorial * self]
```

This method computes the factorial of the integer object to which it belongs. The method first asks the object to compare itself with the predefined number object 1. If it is less-than-or-equal, the result will be the object true and the block [^1] will be evaluated, giving the result 1. If the object is greater than 1, then the second block [^(self - 1) factorial * self] will be evaluated, causing a recursive call to the factorial method on a smaller integer.

There are two operations in the ifFalse case of the factorial method that could be implemented in different ways in the two subclasses of Integer. The first is - (minus). Because small integers may have a different representation from large integers, subtraction may be implemented differently in the two classes. Multiplication, *, may also be implemented differently in the two classes. These methods do not have to return objects of the same class. For example, n*m could be a SmallInt if n and m are both small, or could be a LargeInt if both are SmallInts and their product is larger than the maximum size for SmallInt.

In Smalltalk, we begin a message to self by beginning the search for each method at the object where the first message is received. For example, suppose we want to compute the factorial of a small integer n. The computation will begin by sending the factorial message to n. Because the first step of factorial is self <= 1, the message <= 1 will be sent to the object n. It is important that dynamic lookup is used here, as the correct method for comparing n with 1 is the <= method defined in the SmallInt class. In fact, the Integer class does not need to have a <= method defined in order for the calculation of factorial to work properly. To appreciate the value of self, you might think about whether you could write a factorial method in class Integer that would work properly on SmallInt and LargeInt without using self.

The special symbol super is similar to self, except that, when a message is sent to super, the search for the appropriate method body starts with the superclass of the object instead of the class of the object. This mechanism provides a way of accessing a superclass version of a method that has been overidden in a subclass.

11.6.4 System Extensibility: The Ingalls Test

Dan Ingalls, a leader of the Smalltalk group, proposed the following test for determining whether a programming language is truly object oriented:

Can you define a new kind of integer, put your new integers into rectangles, ask the system to blacken a rectangle, and have everything work?

This test is probably the most extreme test of an object-oriented language. Essentially he is asking "Is *everything* an object?" Or, more specifically, "Is every operation determined by dynamic lookup through objects?"

Why is This Important?

The main issue addressed by this test is the extensibility of programs and systems. If we build a graphic-oriented system that manipulates and displays various kinds of objects, then the design and implementation of basic objects like points and coordinates might be determined very early in the design process. If a complex system is built around one basic construct, like standard language-supplied integers, then how easy will it be to modify the system to use another form of integers?

The answer, of course, is that it depends on how you build the system. In Smalltalk, however, the only way of building a system is by representing basic concepts as objects. Because all operations in Smalltalk are done by sending messages and every message results in run-time lookup of the appropriate method body, a lot of flexibility is inherently built into any system. In C++ and Java, by contrast, it is possible to build a system with integers that are not objects. As a result, it is possible to build systems that will not immediately accept other forms of integer without some change to the code. In particular, most Java or C++-based systems will not be able to handle a rectangle that has some coordinates given by built-in integers that are not objects and some coordinates given by objects.

What Are the Implementation Costs?

If a system is built so that every operation on integers is accompanied by method lookup, then an expression x add y sending a message to an integer cannot be safely optimized to a static function call such as integer_add(x,y). If the compiler or programmer replaces x add y with integer_add(x,y), then we cannot replace a built-in integer x with a user-defined integer object x.

If a program uses integers repeatedly and each integer operation involves a run-time search for an appropriate method, this is a *substantial run-time cost*, even if the best-known optimizations are used to reduce running time as much as possible. In fact, for essentially this reason, the efficiency of many Smalltalk programs is 5 to 10 times less than corresponding programs in C. Of course, program running time is not everything. If a system will be used in many ways, and flexibility and adaptability are important, then flexibility and adaptability may be more important than running speed.

11.7 RELATIONSHIP BETWEEN SUBTYPING AND INHERITANCE

11.7.1 Interfaces as Object Types

Although the Smalltalk language does not use any static type checking, there is an implicit form of type that every Smalltalk programmer uses in some way. The type of an object in Smalltalk is its interface, the set of messages that can be sent to the object without receiving the error "message not understood." The interface of an object is determined by its class, as a class lists the messages that each object will answer. However, different classes may implement the same messages, as there are no Smalltalk rules to keep different classes from using the same selector names.

The Smalltalk library contains a number of implemented classes for a variety of purposes. One part of the library that provides interesting examples of interfaces and inheritance is the collection-class library. The collection classes implement general collections like Set, Bag, Dictionary, LinkedList, and a number of more specialized kinds of collections. Some example interfaces from the collection classes are the following sets of selector names:

Set_Interface = {isEmpty, size, includes:, removeEvery:}
Bag_Interface = {isEmpty, size, includes:, occurrencesOf:, add:, remove:}
Dictionary_Interface = {at:put:, add:, values, remove:}
Array_Interface = {at:put:, atAllPut:, replaceFrom:to:with:}

Remember that a colon indicates a position for a parameter. For example, if s is a set object, then s includes:3 sends the message includes:3 to s. The result will be true or false, depending on whether the set s contains the element 3.

Here is a short explanation of the intended meaning of each of the selectors:

isEmpty: return true if the collection is empty, else false
size: return number of elements in the collection
includes:x: return true if x is in the collection, false otherwise
removeEvery:x: remove all occurrences of x from the collection
occurrencesOf:x: return a number telling how many occurrences of x are in the
    collection
add:x: add x to the collection
remove:x: remove x from the collection
at:x put:y: insert value y into an indexed collection at position indexed by x
values: return the set of indexed values in the indexed collection (e.g., list all the
    words in a dictionary)
atAllPut:x: in finite updateable collection such as an array, set every value to x
replaceFrom:x t:y with:v: in range from x to y, set every indexable value to v (e.g.,
    for array A, set A[x]=A[x+1]= ... =A[y]=v)

11.7.2 Subtyping

Because Smalltalk is an untyped language, it may not seem relevant to compare subtyping and inheritance. However, if we recall the definition of a subtype,

Type A is a subtype of a type B if any context expecting an expression of type
B may take any expression of type A without introducing a type error,

we can see that subtyping is about substitutivity. If we build a Smalltalk program by using one class of objects and then try to use another class in its place, this can work if the interface of the second class contains all of the methods of the first, but not necessarily otherwise. Therefore, it makes sense to associate subtyping with the *superset* relation on Smalltalk class interfaces. Subtyping is sometimes called conformance when discussing interfaces instead of types of some typed programming language.

An example of subtyping arises if we consider extensible collections. To be specific, let us define ExtensibleCollection_Interface by

---

ExtensibleCollection_Interface = {isEmpty, size, includes:, add:, removeEvery:}

This is the same as Set_Interface, with the method add: added. Using <: for subtyping, we have

---

ExtensibleCollection_Interface <: Set_Interface

In words, this means that every object that implements the ExtensibleCollection interface also implements the Set interface. Semantically, this makes sense because a program that uses Set objects can send any of the messages listed in the Set interface to Set objects. Because each one of these messages is also implemented in every ExtensibleCollection object, we can substitute ExtensibleCollection objects for Set objects without obtaining "message not understood" errors.

11.7.3 Subtyping and Inheritance

In Smalltalk, the interface of a subclass is often a subtype of the interface of its superclass. The reason is that a subclass will ordinarily inherit all of the methods of its superclass, possibly adding more methods. This is certainly the case for Point and ColoredPoint, as described earlier in this chapter. Points have the five methods x:y:, moveDx:Dy:, x,y, and draw. Colored points have these five methods and a color method, so every colored point has all of the point methods.

In general, however, subclassing does not always lead to subtyping in Smalltalk. The simplest way that subtyping may fail is when a subclass does not implement all of the methods of the superclass. In Smalltalk, there is simply a way of saying, in a subclass, that one or more superclass methods should not be defined on subclass objects. Because it is possible to delete a method from a superclass, a subclass may not produce a subtype.

On the other hand, it is easy to have subtyping without inheritance. Because subtyping, as we have defined it, is based only on the names of methods, two classes could be defined independently (neither a subclass of the other) but have exactly the same methods. Then, according to our definitions, each is a subtype of the other. But there is no inheritance.

William Cook, a researcher at Hewlett-Packard Labs and later a developer at Apple Computer, did an empirical study of the collection classes in the Smalltalk-80 class library to determine which relationships between subtyping and inheritance arise in Smalltalk practice (Interfaces and Specifications for the Smalltalk-80 Collection Classes, ACM Conf. Object.Oriented Programming: Systems, Languages, and Applications, ACM SIGPLAN Notices 27(10), 1992). Among a relatively small number of classes, he found all possible relationships between subtyping and inheritance. A diagram from his study is shown in Figure 11.6. In this diagram, solid lines indicate subtyping between interfaces, and dotted curves show actual places where inheritance is used in the construction of the collection classes of the Smalltalk-80 library. In studying this diagram, it is important to keep in mind that there are more interfaces listed here than were actually implemented in the library. To show the structural relationship between classes more clearly, Cook included some interfaces that are intersections of the interfaces of classes in the library.

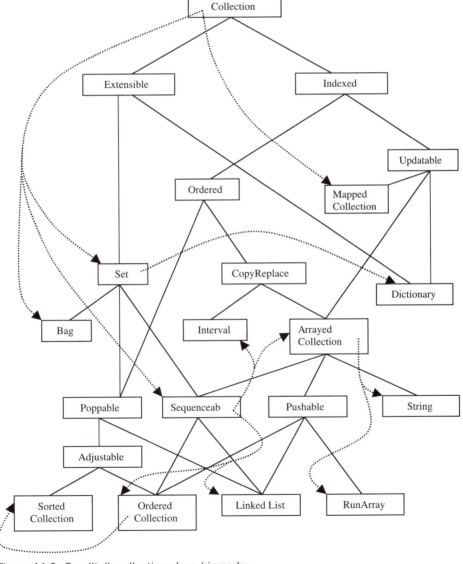

Figure 11.6. Smalltalk collection class hierarchy.

Generally speaking, the subtyping relation between a set of classes is independent of how the classes are implemented, but the inheritance relation is not. Subtyping is a relation between types, which is a property that is important to users of an object, whereas inheritance is a property of implementations. Imagine a group of people sitting down to design the Smalltalk collection classes. Once they have agreed on the names of the classes and the operations on each class, they have agreed on the subtyping relation between the classes. However, the inheritance relation is not determined at this point. If each person implemented one of the classes independently, then all of the classes could be built without using inheritance at all. At the other extreme, it is often possible to factor the functionality of a set of related classes so that inheritance is used extensively. To give a specific example, arrays and dictionaries are similar kinds of collections. Abstractly, both are a form of function from a finite set to an arbitrary set. Therefore, it is conceivable that a programmer could build a general finite-function class and use this as the dictionary class. This programmer can inherit from dictionary to produce the special case of arrays in which the index set is always a range of integers. On the other hand, a different programmer could first build arrays and then use arrays to implement dictionaries by hashing each index word to an integer value and using this to store the indexed value in a specific array location. This illustrates the independence of subtyping and inheritance in Smalltalk.

11.8 CHAPTER SUMMARY

In this chapter, we studied Simula, the first object-oriented language, and Smalltalk, an influential language that generalized and popularized object-oriented programming.

Simula was designed in Norway, beginning as part of a project to develop a simulation language. Smalltalk was designed at Xerox PARC (in Palo Alto, California) and was intended to accompany a futuristic concept called the Dynabook. An important unifying concept in Smalltalk is that everything should be an object.

Simula

- *Objects:* A Simula object is an activation record produced by call to a class.
- *Classes:* A Simula class is a procedure that returns a pointer to its activation record. The body of a class may initialize the object it creates.
- *Abstraction:* Hiding was not provided in 1967, but was added later and used as the basis for C++.
- *Subtyping:* Objects are typed according to the classes that create them. Subtyping is determined by class hierarchy.
- *Inheritance:* A Simula class may be defined as an extension of a class that has already been defined.

Smalltalk

- *Objects:* A Smalltalk object is created by a class. At run time, an object stores its instance variables and a pointer to the instantiating class.
- *Classes:* A Smalltalk class defines class variables, class methods, and the instance methods that are shared by all objects of the class. At run time, the class data

structure contains pointers to an instance variable template, a method dictionary, and the superclass.

■ *Abstraction:* Abstraction is provided through protected instance variables. All methods are public but instance variables may be accessed only by the methods of the class and methods of subclasses.

■ *Subtyping:* Smalltalk does not have a compile-time type system. Subtyping arises implicitly through relations between the interfaces of objects. Subtyping depends on the set of messages that are understood by an object, not the representation of objects or whether inheritance is used.

■ *Inheritance:* Smalltalk subclasses inherit all instance variables and methods of their superclasses. Methods defined in a superclass may be redefined in a subclass or deleted.

Because Smalltalk has no compile-time type system, a variable may point to any object of any type at run time. This makes it more difficult to implement efficient method lookup algorithms for Smalltalk than for some other object-oriented languages. You may wish to review the data structure and algorithms for locating a method of an object as illustrated in Subsection 11.5.3. Be sure you understand how search for a method proceeds from subclass to superclass in the event that the method is not defined in the subclass.

EXERCISES

11.1 Simula Inheritance and Access Links

In Simula, a class is a procedure that returns a pointer to its activation record. Simula prefixed classes were a precursor to C++ -derived classes, providing a form of inheritance. This question asks about how inheritance might work in an early version of Simula, assuming that the standard static scoping mechanism associated with activation records is used to link the derived class part of an object with the base class part of the object.

Sample Point and ColorPt classes are given in the text. For the purpose of this problem, assume that if cp is a ColorPt object, consisting of a Point activation record followed by a ColorPt activation record, the access link of the parent-class (Point) activation record points to the activation record of the scope in which the class declaration occurs, and the access link of the child-class (ColorPt) activation record points to activation record of the parent class.

(a) Fill in the missing information in the following activation records, created by execution of the following code:

```
ref(Point) p;
ref(ColorPt) cp;
r :- new Point(2.7, 4.2);
cp :- new ColorPt(3.6, 4.9, red);
cp.distance(r);
```

Remember that function values are represented by closures and that a closure is a pair consisting of an environment (pointer to an activation record) and a compiled code.

In the following illustration, a bullet (•) indicates that a pointer should be drawn from this slot to the appropriate closure or compiled code. Because the pointers to activation records cross and could become difficult to read, each activation record is numbered at the far left. In each activation record, place the number of the activation record of the statically enclosing scope in the slot labeled "access link." The first two are done for you. Also use activation record numbers for the environment pointer part of each closure pair. Write the values of local variables and function parameters directly in the activation records.

Activation Records			*Closures*	*Compiled Code*
(0)	x			
	y			
(1) r →	access link	(0)		
	x			code for
	y		⟨( ), • ⟩	equals
	equals	•		
	distance	•	⟨( ), • ⟩	
(2) Point part of cp	access link	(0)		
	x			code for
	y		⟨( ), • ⟩	distance
	equals	•		
	distance	•	⟨( ), • ⟩	
(3) cp →	access link	( )		
	c		⟨( ), • ⟩	code for
	equals	•		cpt equals
(4) cp.distance(r)	access link	( )		
	q	(r)		

(b) The body of distance contains the expression

$$sqrt((\ x - q.x\ )**2 + (y - q.y)\ **\ 2)$$

that compares the coordinates of the point containing this distance procedure to the coordinate of the point q passed as an argument. Explain how the value of x is found when cp.distance(r) is executed. Mention specific pointers in your diagram. What value of x is used?

(c) This illustration shows that a reference cp to a colored point object points to the ColorPt part of the object. Assuming this implementation, explain how the expression cp.x can be evaluated. Explain the steps used to find the right x value on the stack, starting by following the pointer cp to activation record (3).

(d) Explain why the call cp.distance(r) needs access to only the Point part of cp and not the ColorPt part of cp.

(e) If you were implementing Simula, would you place the activation records representing objects r and cp on the stack, as shown here? Explain briefly why you might consider allocating memory for them elsewhere.

11.2 Loophole in Encapsulation

A priority queue (also known as a heap) is a form of queue that allows the minimum element to be retrieved. Assuming that Simula has a list type, a Simula pq class might look something like this:

```
class pq();
begin
    (int list) contents;
    bool procedure isempty();
        < ... return true if pq empty, else false ... >
    procedure insert(x); int x;
        < ... put x at appropriate place in list ... >
    int procedure deletemin();
        < ... delete first list elt and return it ... >
    contents := nil
end
```

where the sections <...> would be filled in with appropriate executable Simula code. We would create a priority queue object by writing

```
h :- new pq();
```

and access the components by writing something like

```
h.contents;
h.isempty;
h.insert(x);
h.deletemin();
```

In ML we can write a function that produces a closure with essentially the same behavior as that of a Simula priority queue object. This is subsequently written, together with the associated exception declaration:

```
exception Empty;

fun new_pq() =
    let val contents = (ref nil) : int list ref
        fun insert(x,nil)  = [x]
        |   insert(x, y::l) = if x<y then x::(y::l)
                                     else y::insert(x, l)
    in
        {
        emp_meth = fn () => !contents = nil,
        ins_meth = fn x => (contents := insert(x, !contents)),
        del_meth = fn () => case !contents of
                            nil => raise Empty
                            |   y::l => (contents := l; y)
        }
    end;
```

This question asks you to think about a "loophole" in the Simula object system that allows a client program to interfere with the correct behavior of a priority queue object.

(a) The main property of a priority queue is that if n elements are inserted and k are removed (for any $k < n$), then these k elements are returned in increasing order. Explain in two or three sentences why both the Simula and ML forms of priority queue objects should exhibit this behavior in a "reasonable" program.

(b) Explain in a few sentences how a "devious" program that uses a Simula priority queue object h could cause the following behavior: After 0 and 1 are inserted into the priority queue by calls h.insert(0) and h.insert(1), the first deletemin operation on the priority queue returns some number other than 0. (This will not be possible for an ML priority queue object.) Do not use any pointer arithmetic or other operations that would not be allowed in a language like Pascal.

(c) Write a short sequence of priority queue operations of the form

```
h :- new pq();
h.insert(0);
h.insert(1);
...
h.deletemin();
```

where the ellipsis (...) may contain h operations, but not insert or deletemin, demonstrating the behavior you described in part (b).

11.3 Subtyping of Refs in Simula

In Simula, the procedure call assignA(b) in the following context is considered statically type correct:

```
class A ... ;    /* A is a class */
A class B ... ;  /* B is a subclass of A */

ref (A) a;       /* a is a variable pointing to an A object */
ref (B) b;       /* b is a variable pointing to a B object */

proc assignA (ref (A) x)
   begin
      x := a
   end;

assignA(b);
```

(a) Assume that *if* $B <: A$ *then* $ref (B) <: ref (A)$. Using this principle, explain why both the procedure assignA and the call assignA(b) can be considered statically type correct.

(b) Explain why actually executing the call assignA(b) and performing the assignment given in the procedure may lead to a type error at run time.

(c) The problem is that the "principle," *if* $B <: A$ *then* $ref (B) <: ref (A)$, is not semantically sound. However, we can make type checking by using this principle sound by inserting run-time tests. Explain the run-time test you think a Simula compiler should insert in the compiled code for procedure assignA. Can you think of a reason why the designers of Simula might have decided to use run-time tests instead of disallowing ref subtyping in this situation? (You do not have to agree with them; just try to imagine what rationale might have been used at the time.)

11.4 Smalltalk Run-Time Structures

Here is a Smalltalk Point class whose instances represents points in the two-dimensional Cartesian plane. In addition to accessing instance variables, an instance method allows point objects to be added together.

Class name	Point
Superclass	Object
Class variables	*Comment: none*
Instance variables	*x y*
Class messages and methods	*Comment: instance creation* newX: xValue Y: yValue | | ↑ self new x: xValue y: yValue
Instance messages and methods	*Comment: accessing instance vars* x: xCoordinate y: yCoordinate | | x ← xCoordinate y ← yCoordinate x | | ↑ x y | | ↑ y *comment: arithmetic* + aPoint | | ↑ Point newX: (x + aPoint x) Y: (y + aPoint y)

(a) Complete the top half of the illustration of the Smalltalk run-time structure shown in Figure P.11.4.1 for a point object with coordinates (3, 4) and its class. Label each of the parts of the top half of the figure, adding to the drawing as needed.

(b) A Smalltalk programmer has access to a library containing the Point class, but she cannot modify the Point class code. In her program, she wants to be able to create points by using either Cartesian or polar coordinates, and she wants to calculate both the polar coordinates (radius and angle) and the Cartesian coordinates of points. Given a point (x, y) in Cartesian coordinates, the radius is ((x * x) + (y * y)) squareRoot and the angle is (x/y) arctan. Given a point (r, θ) in polar coordinates, the x coordinate is r * (θ cos) and the y coordinate is r * (θ sin).

    i. Write out a subclass PolarPoint, of Point and explain how this solves the programming problem.

    ii. Which parts of Point could you reuse and which would you have to define differently for PolarPoint?

(c) Complete the drawing of the Smalltalk run-time structure by adding a PolarPoint object and its class to the bottom half of the figure you already filled in with Point structures. Label each of the parts and add to the drawing as needed.

11.5 Smalltalk Implementation Decisions

In Smalltalk, each class contains a pointer to the class template. This template stores the names of all the instance variables that belong to objects created by the class.

(a) The names of the methods are stored next to the method pointers. Why are the names of instance variables stored in the class, instead of in the objects (next to the values for the instance variables)?

(b) Each class's method dictionary stores the names of only the methods explicitly written for that class; inherited methods are found by searching up the super-class pointers at run time. What optimization could be done if each subclass

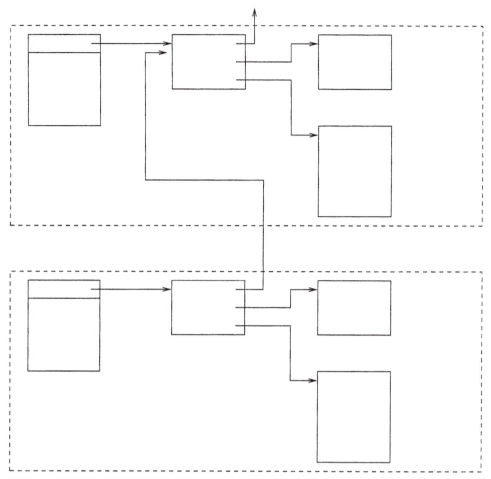

Figure P.11.4.1. Smalltalk run-time structures for Point and PolarPoint.

contained all of the methods of its superclasses in its method dictionary? What are some of the advantages and disadvantages of this optimization?

(c) The class template stores the names of all the instance variables, even those inherited from parent classes. These are used to compile the methods of the class. Specifically, when a subclass is added to a Smalltalk system, the methods of the new class are compiled so that, when an instance variable is accessed, the method can access this directly without searching through the method dictionary and without searching through superclasses. Can you see some advantages and disadvantages of this implementation decision compared with looking up the relative position of an instance variable in the appropriate class template each time the variable is accessed? Keep in mind that in Smalltalk, a set of classes could remain running for days, while new classes are added incrementally and, conceivably, existing classes could be rewritten and recompiled.

11.6 Protocol Conformance

We can compare Smalltalk interfaces to classes that use *protocols*, which are lists of operation names (selectors). When a selector allows parameters, as in at: put: , the selector name includes the colons but not the spaces. More specifically, if dict is an updatable collection object, such as a dictionary, then we could send dict a message by writing dict at:'cross' put:'angry'. (This makes our dictionary definition of "cross" the single word "angry.") The protocol for updatable collections will therefore contain the seven-character selector name at:put: . Here are some example protocols:

$$\text{stack} : \{\text{isEmpty, push:, pop} \}$$
$$\text{queue} : \{\text{isEmpty, insert:, remove} \}$$
$$\text{priority\_queue} : \{\text{isEmpty, insert:, remove} \}$$
$$\text{dequeue} : \{\text{isEmpty, insert:, insertFront:, remove, removeLast} \}$$
$$\text{simple\_collection} : \{\text{isEmpty} \}$$

Briefly, a stack can be sent the message isEmpty, returning true if empty, false otherwise; push: requires an argument (the object to be pushed onto the stack), pop removes the top element from the stack and returns it. Queues work similarly, except they are first-in, first-out instead of first-in, last-out. Priority queues are first-in, minimum-out and dequeues are doubly ended queues with the possibility of adding and removing from either end. The simple_collection class just collects methods that are common to all the other classes. We say that the protocol for A *conforms* to the protocol for B if the set of A selector names contains the set of B selector names.

(a) Draw a diagram of these classes, ordered by protocol conformance. You should end up with a graph that looks like William Cook's drawing shown in Figure 11.6.

(b) Describe briefly, in words, a way of implementing each class so that you make B a subclass of A only if the protocol for B conforms to the protocol set for A.

(c) For some classes A and B that are unrelated in the graph, describe a strategy for implementing A as a subclass of B in a way that keeps them unrelated.

(d) Describe implementation strategies for two classes A and B (from the preceding set of classes) so that B is a subclass of A, but A conforms to B, not the other way around.

11.7 Removing a Method

Smalltalk has a mechanism for "undefining" a method. Specifically, if a class A has method m, then a programmer may cancel m in subclass B by writing

```
m:
    self shouldNotImplement
```

With this declaration of m in subclass B, any invocation of m on a B object will result in a special error indicating that the method should not be used.

(a) What effect does this feature of Smalltalk have on the relationship between inheritance and subtyping?

(b) Suppose class A has methods m and n, and method m is canceled in subclass B. Method n is inherited and not changed, but method n sends the message m to self. What do you think happens if a B object b is sent a message n? There are two possible outcomes. See if you can identify both, and explain which one you think the designers of Smalltalk would have chosen and why.

11.8 Subtyping and Binary Methods

This question is about the relationship between subtyping and inheritance. Recall that the main principle associated with subtyping is substitutivity: If A is a subtype of B, then wherever a B object is required in a program, an A object may be used instead without producing a type error. For the purpose of this question, we will use *Message not understood* as our Smalltalk type error. This is the most common error message resulting from a dynamic type failure in Smalltalk; it is the object-oriented analog of the error *Cannot take car of an atom* that every Lisp programmer has generated at some time. Remember that Smalltalk is a dynamically typed language. This question asks you to show how substitutivity can fail, using the fact that a method given in a superclass can be redefined in a subclass.

If there are no restrictions on how a method (member function) may be redefined in a subclass, then it is easy to redefine a method so that it requires a different number of arguments. This will make it impossible to meaningfully substitute a subclass object for a superclass object. A more subtle fact is that subtyping may fail when a method is redefined in a way that appears natural and (unless you've seen this before) unproblematic. This is illustrated by the following Point class and ColoredPoint subclass:

Class name	Point
Class variables	
Instance variables	xval yval
Instance messages and methods	xcoord ↑ xval
	ycoord ↑ yval
	origin
	xval ← 0
	yval ← 0
	movex: dx movey: dy
	xval ← xval + dx.
	yval ← yval + dy
	equal: pt
	↑ (xval = pt xcoord & yval = pt ycoord)

Class name	ColoredPoint
Class variables	
Instance variables	color
Instance messages and methods	color ↑ color
	changecolor: newc color ← newc
	equal: cpt
	↑ (xval = cpt xcoord & yval = cpt ycoord & color = cpt color)

The important part here is the way that equal is redefined in the colored point class. This change would not be allowed in Simula or C++, but is allowed in Smalltalk. (The C++ compiler does not consider this an error, but it would not treat it as redefinition of a member function either.) The intuitive reason for redefining equal is that two colored points are equal only if they have the same coordinates and are the same color.

Problem: Consider the expression p1 equal:p2, where p1 and p2 are either Point objects or ColoredPoint objects. It is guaranteed not to produce *Message not understood* if both p1 and p2 are either Points or ColoredPoints, but may produce an error if one is a Point and the other a ColoredPoint. Consider all four combinations of p1 and p2 as Points and ColoredPoints, and explain briefly how each message is interpreted.

11.9 Delegation-Based Object-Oriented Languages

In this problem, we explore a delegation-based object-oriented language, SELF, in which objects can be defined directly from other objects. Classes are not needed and not supported. SELF has run-time type checking and garbage collection.

Here is the SELF language description:

(extracted from D. Ungar and R. B. Smith, Self: The power of simplicity, ACM SIGPLAN Notices 22(12), 1987, pp. 227–242.)

> In Smalltalk,... everything is an object and every object contains a pointer to its class, an object that describes its format and holds its behavior. In SELF too, everything is an object. But, instead of a class pointer, a SELF object contains named slots with may store either state or behavior. If an object receives a message and it has no matching slot, the search continues via a *parent* pointer. This is how SELF implements inheritance. Inheritance in SELF allows objects to share behavior, which in turn allows the programmer to alter the behavior of many objects with a single change. For instance, a [Cartesian] point object would have slots for its non-shared characteristics: x and y. Its parent would be an object that held the behavior shared among all points: +, etc.
>
> In SELF, there is no direct way to access a variable: instead, objects send messages to access data residing in name slots. So to access its "x" value, a point sends itself the "x" message. The message finds the "x" slot, and evaluates the object found therein.... In order to change contents of the "x" slot to, say, 17, instead of performing an assignment like "x←17," the point must send itself the "x:" message with 17 as the argument. The point object must contain a slot named "x:" containing the assignment [function].

(a) Using this description, draw the run-time data structure of the SELF version of a (3,4) Point object, as described in the last two sentences of the first paragraph, and it parent object. Assume that assignments to the x and y characteristics are permitted.

(b) SELF's lack of classes and instance variables make inheritance more powerful. For example, to create two points sharing the same x coordinate, the x and x: slots can be put in a separate object that is a parent of each of the two points. Draw a picture of the run-time data structures for two points sharing the same x coordinate.

(c) To create a new Point object, the clone message is sent to an existing point. The language description continues:

> Creating new objects...is accomplished by a simple operation, copying.... [In Smalltalk,] creating new objects from classes is accomplished by instantiation, which includes the interpretation of format information in a class. Instantiation is similar to building a house from a plan.

Cloning an object does not clone its parent, however.

If a *point* object contains fields x and y and methods x:, y:, move, then cloning the object will create another object with two fields and three methods. Each point will have a parent pointer, two fields, and three methods – six entries in all. The SELF point will be twice the size of the corresponding Smalltalk point.

Explain how you would structure your SELF program so that each point can be cloned without cloning its methods.

(d) SELF also allows a *change-parent* operation on an object. The parent pointer of an object can be set to point to any other object. (An exception is that the first object must not be an ancestor of the second – we do not want a cycle.)

The change-parent operation is useful for objects that change behavior in different states. For example, a window can be in the *visible* or *iconified* (minimized) state. When iconified, mouse clicks and window display work differently than when the window is visible. A window's parent pointer can be set to VisibleWindow initially, then changed to IconifiedWindow when the "minimized" button is pressed. Another example is a file object that can be in the *open* or *closed* state. The open method changes the parent pointer from ClosedFile to OpenFile.

The change-parent operation adds a lot of flexibility to SELF. Can you think of disadvantages of this feature?

12

Objects and Run-Time Efficiency: C++

C++ is an object-oriented extension of the C language. It was originally called *C with classes*, with the name C++ originating around 1984. A Bell Laboratories researcher interested in simulation, Bjarne Stroustrup began the C++ project in the early 1980s. His goal was to add objects and classes to C, using his experience with Simula as the basis for the design. The design and implementation of C++ was originally a one-person effort, with no apparent intent to produce a commercial product. However, as interest in objects and program structure grew over the course of the 1980s, C++ became popular and widely used. In the 1990s, C++ became the most widely used object-oriented language, with good compilers and development environments available for the Macintosh, PC, and Unix-based workstations.

C, discussed in Section 5.2, was originally designed by Dennis Ritchie. The C programming language was used for writing the Unix operating system at Bell Laboratories. The original implementation of C++ was a preprocessor that converted C++ to C.

12.1 DESIGN GOALS AND CONSTRAINTS

The main goal of C++ is to provide object-oriented features in a C-based language without compromising the efficiency of C. In the process of adding objects to C, some other improvements were also made. In more detail, the main design goals of C++ may be summarized as follows:

- data abstraction and object-oriented features,
- better static type checking,
- backwards compatibility with C. In other words, most C code should compile as legal C++, without requiring significant changes to the code,
- efficiency of compiled code, according to the principle "If you do not use a feature, you should not pay for it."

The principle stated in the final goal is significant and may require some thought to appreciate. This principle suggests that C programs should compile as efficiently under the C++ compiler as under the C compiler. It would violate this principle to

BJARNE STROUSTRUP

Bjarne Stroustrup is the pricipal designer of C++. Bjarne came to Bell Laboratories in 1979 after finishing his M.S. degree in Aarhus, Denmark, and his Ph.D. on design of distributed systems in Cambridge, U.K.

Working on distributed computing, in the same Computing Science Center as C and Unix designers Ritchie and Thompson, Stroustrup decided to add object-oriented features from Simula to C. His goal was to further his personal research objectives, which involved simulation.

An occasionally reserved but essentially gregarious and friendly person, Stroustrup was catapulted into the technological limelight by the success of C++, first within AT&T and later in the wider community of practicing software developers. He has written several books on C++, including *The Design and Evolution of C++* (Addison-Wesley, 1994), which contains an interesting history, explanation, and commentary on the language. Bjarne's nonresearch interests include reading books that are not about computer science, photography, hiking and running, travel, and music.

implement C integers as objects, for example, and use dynamic method lookup to find integer functions at run time as in Smalltalk, as this would significantly reduce the performance of C integer calculations. The principle does not mean that C++ statements that also appear in C must be implemented in exactly the same way in both languages, but whatever changes are adopted in C++, they must not slow down execution of compiled code unless some slower features of C++ are also used in the program.

12.1.1 Compatibility with C

The decision to maintain compatibility with C has a pervasive effect on the design of C++. Those familiar with C know that C has a specific machine model, revealing much of the structure of the underlying computer architecture. In particular, C operations that return the address of a variable and place any bit pattern in any location make it possible for C programs to rely on the exact representation of data. Therefore C++ must adhere to the same data representations as C.

Most other object-oriented languages, including those designed before C++ and those designed after, use garbage collection to relieve programmers from the task of identifying inaccessible objects and deallocating the associated memory locations. However, there is no inherent reason why objects must be garbage collected. The strongest connection is that with the increased emphasis on abstraction and type correctness, it would have been consistent with other goals of C++ to offer some form of garbage collection where feasible in a form that does not affect the running time of programs that do not use garbage-collected objects. However, because there are features of C that make garbage collection extremely difficult, it would have been difficult to base C++ objects on garbage collection. Not only is garbage collection counter to the C philosophy of providing programmer control over memory, but the similarity between pointers and integers makes it effectively impossible to build a garbage collector that works on C++ programs that use pointer arithmetic or cast integers to pointers.

An important specific decision is to treat C++ objects as a generalization of C structs. This makes it necessary to allow objects to be declared and manipulated in the same way as structs. In particular, objects can be allocated in the activation records of functions or local blocks, as well as on the heap, and can be manipulated directly (i.e., not through pointers). This is one place where C++ deviates from Simula, as Simula objects can be manipulated only through pointers. More specifically, C++ allows a form of object assignment that copies one object into the space previously occupied by another, whereas most other object-oriented languages allow only pointer assignment for objects. Some aspects of C++ objects on the stack are explored in the homework exercises.

12.1.2 Success of C++

C++ is a very carefully designed language that has succeeded admirably, in spite of difficult design constraints. Measured by the number of users, C++ is without question the most successful language of the decade from its development in the mid-1980s until the release of Java in the mid-1990s. However, the design goals and backward compatibility with C do not allow much room for additional aesthetic consideration. Some aspects of C++ have become complex and difficult for many programmers to understand. On the other hand, many C programmers use the C++ compiler and appreciate the benefits of better type checking. Perhaps a fair summary of the success of C++ is that it is widely used, with most users choosing to program in some subset of the language that they feel they understand and that they find suitable for their programming tasks. In other words, C++ is a useful programming tool that allows designers to craft good object-oriented programs, but it does not enforce good programming style in the way that other language designs have attempted to do. This is intended to be a statement of fact and not a count against C++. In fact, much of its success seems attributable to the way that C++ is designed to give programmers choices and not to restrict programmers to a particular style.

There are many published style guides that advocate use of certain features of C++ and caution against the use of others. Those interested in serious C++ programming or interested in understanding how many programmers view the language may wish to visit their library or bookstore and take a look at some of the current guides.

12.2 OVERVIEW OF C++

Before looking at the object-oriented features of C++ in Subsection 12.2.2, we will take a quick tour of some of the additions to C that are not related to objects. Evaluation and commentary on C++ appear in Subsection 12.2.3.

12.2.1 Additions to C Not Related to Objects

There are a number of differences between C++ and C that are not related to objects. Although we are primarily interested in the C++ object system, it is worth considering a few of the more significant changes. The most interesting additions are

- type bool
- reference types and pass-by-reference
- user-defined overloading
- function templates
- exceptions

There are also changes in memory management calls (new and delete instead of malloc and free), changes in stream and file input and output, addition of default parameter values in function declarations, and more minor changes such as the addition of end-of-line comments and elimination of the need for typedef keyword with struct/union/enum declarations.

   The first three additions, bool, pass-by-reference, and overloading, are discussed in the remainder of this subsection. Function templates are discussed in Subsection 9.4.1 and a general discussion of exceptions appears in Subsection 8.2.

Type bool

In C, the value of a logical test is an integer. For example, the *C Reference Manual* defines the comparison operator < and logical operator && as follows:

- The operator < (less than) returns 1 if the first operand is less than the second and 0 otherwise.
- The && operator returns 1 if both its operands are nonzero and 0 otherwise.

   This makes it possible to write C statements with expressions such as

```
if ((5 < 3) + 1 && 2 ==3) { ... }
```

which combine comparison operations and arithmetic.

   To make a syntactic distinction between Booleans and integers, C++ has a separate type: bool with values true and false. Because of conversions, this does not completely separate integers and Booleans. In particular, integer values may be assigned to variables of type bool, with implicit conversion of nonzero numbers to true and 0 to false. However, the type bool does improve the readability of many programs by indicating that a variable or return value of a function will be used as a Boolean value rather than an integer.

The C++ changes can be mimicked in C by the declarations

```
typedef int bool;
#define false 0
#define true 1
```

which define the type bool and values true and false. One difference between built-in Booleans of C++ and Booleans in C is that when C++ Booleans are printed, they print as true and false, not 1 and 0.

Because of all the implicit conversions, a separate Boolean type does not help with one of the most common simple programmer mistakes in C. At least for beginners, conditional statements such as

```
if (a=b) c;
```

are often the result of typographic error; the programmer meant to write

```
if (a==b) c;
```

The reason why the first statement type checks and compiles in C is that an integer assignment a=b has type int and has the value of b. Because a C conditional statement requires an integer (not a Boolean), there is no warning associated with this statement. In most languages with bool different from integer, it would be a type error to write if (a=b) c. However, because C++ Booleans are automatically converted to integers, the statement if (a=b) c remains legal in C++.

Because the introduction of bool into C++ has very little effect in the end, you might wonder why this was done. Before a Boolean type was added, C/C++ often contained definitions of bool, true, and false by macro, as previously illustrated. However, bool could be defined in different ways, with the resulting types having slightly different semantics. For example, bool could be defined as int, unsigned int, or short int. This caused problems when libraries that use slightly different definitions were combined. Therefore it was useful to standardize code by adding a built-in Boolean type.

Reference Type and Pass-By Reference

In C, all parameters are passed by value. If you wish to modify a value that is passed as a parameter, you must pass a pointer to the value. For example, here is C code for a function that increments an integer:

```
void increment(int *p) { /* parameter is pointer to int */
  (*p)++; }                /* modify value pointed to by p */
main() {
  int k = 0;
```

```
increment(&k);        /* pass address of variable k */
k;                    /* value of k is now 1 */
...
}
```

In C++, it is possible to pass-by-reference, as shown here:

```
void increment(int & n) { /* parameter is reference to int */
  n++; }                   /* modify reference param */
main() {
  int k = 0;
  increment(k);           /* no need to explicitly compute address */
  k;                      /* value of k is now 1 */
  ...
}
```

The effect is similar to C's pointer argument, but the calling function does not have to provide the address of an argument and the called function does not have to dereference pointers. A mild inconvenience with C pointer arguments is that the programmer must remember whether a given function uses pass-by-value or the pointer in its parameter list. If pointer arguments are changed to C++ pass-by-reference, then no address calculation needs to be written as part of the call and a programmer using functions from a library can avoid this issue entirely.

A benefit of explicit references is sometimes called *pass-by-constant-reference*. If a function argument is not to be changed by the function, then it is possible to specify that the argument is to be a constant, as in void f (const int &x). In the body of a function with parameter x passed this way, it is illegal to assign to x.

User-Defined Overloading

As discussed in Chapter 6, overloading allows one name to be used for more than one value. In C++, it is possible to declare several functions with the same name, as long as the functions have a different number and type of parameters. For example, here is a C++ program with three types of print function, each called show:

```
#include <stdio.h>
void show(int val) {
    printf("Integer: %d\n", val);
}
void show(double val) {
    printf("Double: %lfn", val);
}
void show(char *val) {
    printf("String: %s\n", val);
}
int main( ) {
```

```
        show(12);
        show(3.1415);
        show("Hello World\n!");
}
```

Because the three functions have different types of arguments, the compiler can determine which function to call by the type of the actual parameter used in the function call.

C++ does not allow overloaded functions that have the same number and types of arguments but differ only in their return value because C and C++ functions can be called as statements. When a function is called as a statement, ignoring the return value of the function, the compiler would not have any way of determining which function to call.

One source of potential confusion in C++ arises from combinations of overloading and automatic conversion. In particular, if the actual parameters in a function call do not match any version of a function exactly, the compiler will try to produce a match by promoting and/or converting types. In this example code,

```
void f(int)
void f(int *)
...
f('a')
```

the call f('a') will result in f(int) instead of f(int *) because a char can be promoted to be an int. When a function is overloaded and there are many possible implicit conversions, it can be difficult for a programmer to understand which conversions and call will be used.

12.2.2 Object-Oriented Features

The most significant part of C++ is the set of object-oriented concepts added to C; these are the main concepts:

- *Classes*, which declare the type associated with all objects constructed from the class, the data members of each object, and the member functions of the class.
- *Objects*, which consist of private data and public functions for accessing the hidden data, as in other object-oriented languages.
- *Dynamic lookup*, for member functions that are declared virtual. A virtual function in a derived class (subclass) may be implemented differently from virtual functions of the same name in a base class (superclass).
- *Encapsulation*, based on programmer designations public, private, and protected that determine whether data and functions declared in a class are visible outside the class definition.
- *Inheritance*, using subclassing: One class may be defined by inheriting the data and functions declared in another. C++ allows single inheritance, in which a class

has a single base class (superclass) or multiple inheritance in which a class has more than one base class.

■ *Subtyping*, based on subclassing. For one class to define a subtype of the type defined by another class, inheritance must be used. However, the programmer may decide whether inheritance results in a subtype or not.

This is only a brief summary; there are many more features, and it would take an entire book to explain all of the interactions between features of C++. Further description of classes, inheritance, and objects appear in Section 12.3.

C++ Terminology. Although C++ terminology differs from Smalltalk (and Java) terminology, there is a fairly close correspondence. The terms class and object are used similarly. Smalltalk instance variables are called member data and methods are called member functions. The term subclass is not usually used in connection with C++. Instead, a superclass is called a base class and a subclass a derived class. The term inheritance has the same meaning in both languages.

12.2.3 Good Decisions and Problem Areas

C++ is the result of an extensive effort involving criticism and suggestions from many experienced programmers. In many respects, the language is as good a design as possible, given the goals of adding objects and better compile-time type checking to C, without sacrificing efficiency or backwards compatibility. Some particularly successful parts of the design are

■ *encapsulation:* careful attention to visibility and hiding, including *public, protected,* and *private* levels of visibility and *friend* functions and classes,
■ *separation of subtyping and inheritance:* classes may have public or private base classes, giving the programmer some explicit control over the resulting subtype hierarchy,
■ *templates* (described in Section 9.4),
■ *exceptions* (described in Section 8.2)
■ *better static type checking* than C.

There are also a number of smaller successful design decisions in C++. One example is the way the scope resolution operator (written as ::) is used in connection with inheritance and multiple inheritance to resolve ambiguities that are problematic in other languages.

Problem Areas

There are a number of aspects of C++ that programmers occasionally find difficult. Some of the main problem areas are

■ *casts and conversions*, which can be complex and unpredictable in certain situations,
■ *objects allocated on the stack* and other aspects of object memory management,
■ *overloading*, a complex code selection mechanism in C++ that can interact unpredicatably with dynamic lookup (virtual function lookup),
■ *multiple inheritance*, which is more complex in C++ than in other languages because of the way objects and virtual function tables are configured and accessed.

These problem areas exist not because of oversight but because the goals of C++, followed to their logical conclusion, led to a design with these properties. In other words, these problems were not the result of carelessness or inattention, but a consequence of decisions that were made with other objectives in mind. To be fair, most of them have their roots in C, not the C++ extensions to C. Nonetheless, these features might reasonably lead programmers to prefer other languages when compatibility with C and absolute efficiency of compiled code are not essential to an application.

Some programmers might also say that lack of garbage collection, or lack of a standard interface for writing concurrent programs, is a problem in C++. However, these are facilities that simply lie outside the scope of the language design.

Casts and Conversions. A cast instructs the compiler to treat an expression of one type as if it is an expression of another. For example, (float) i instructs the compiler to treat the variable i as a float, regardless of its type otherwise, and (int *)x causes x to be treated as pointer to an integer. In certain situations, C and C++ compilers perform implicit type conversions. For example, when a variable is assigned the value of an expression, the expression may be converted to the type associated with the variable, if needed. In most object-oriented languages, the automatic conversion of an object from one type to another does not change the representation of the object. For example, we have seen from the description of subtyping in Smalltalk in Chapter 11 that Point objects can be treated as ColoredPoint objects without changing the representation of objects because ColoredPoint objects are represented in a way that is compatible with the representation of Point objects. If multiple inheritance is used in C++, however, converting an object from a subtype to a supertype may require some change in the value of a pointer to the object. This happens in a way that may introduce hard-to-find bugs and forces programmers to understand the underlying representation of objects. More generally, Stroustrup himself says, "Syntactically and semantically, casts are one of the ugliest features of C and C++" in *The Design and Evolution of C++* (Addison-Wesley, 1994).

Objects Allocated on the Stack. Simula, Smalltalk, and Java allow objects to be created only on the heap, not on the run-time stack. In these other languages, objects can be accessed through pointers, but not through ordinary stack variables that contain space for an object of a certain size. Although C++ on-the-stack objects are efficiently allocated and deallocated as part of entry and exit from local blocks, there are also some disadvantages. The most glaring rough spot is the way that assignment works in combination with subtyping, truncating an object to the size that fits when an assignment is performed. This can change the behavior of an object, as eliminating some of its member data forces the compiler to change the way that virtual functions are selected. Although the C++ language definition explains what happens and why, the behavior of object assignment can be confusing to programmers.

Overloading. Overloading in itself is not a bad programming language feature, but C++ user-defined overloading can be complex. In addition, the interaction with dynamic lookup (virtual functions) can be unpredictable. Because overloading is a compile-time code selection mechanism and dynamic lookup is a run-time code selection mechanism, the two behave very differently. This causes confusion for many programmers.

Multiple Inheritance. There are some inherent complications associated with multiple inheritance that are difficult to avoid. These are discussed in Section 12.5. The C++ language design compounds these problems with a tricky object and method lookup table (vtable) format. Unfortunately, the details of the implementation of multiple inheritance seem to intrude on ordinary programming, sometimes forcing a programmer who is interested in using multiple inheritance to learn some of the implementation details. Even a programmer not using multiple inheritance may be affected if a derived class is defined using multiple inheritance.

12.3 CLASSES, INHERITANCE, AND VIRTUAL FUNCTIONS

The main object-oriented features of C++ are illustrated by a repeat of the point and colored-point classes from Chapter 11.

12.3.1 C++ Classes and Objects

We can define point objects in C++ by declaring the point class, here called Pt, and separately declaring the member functions of class Pt. The class declaration without implementation defines both the interface of point objects and the data used to implement points, but need not include the code for member functions. The declarations that appear in the Pt class are divided into three parts, public members, protected members, and the private members of the class.

For simplicity, Pt is a class of one-dimensional points, each point having only an *x* coordinate:

```
/* ---------- Point Class Interface -------------------*/
class Pt {
  public:
    Pt(int xv);
    Pt(Pt* pv);
    int getX();
    virtual void move(int dx);
  protected:
    void setX(int xv);
  private:
    int x;
  };
/* ---------- Declarations of Constructors --------*/
Pt::Pt(int xv) { x = xv; }
Pt::Pt(Pt* pv) { x = pv->x; }
/* ---------- Declarations of Member Functions --------*/
int Pt::getX() { return x; }
void Pt::setX(int xv) { x = xv; }
```

Constructors. A constructor is used to initialize the member data of an object when a program contains a statement or expression indicating that a new object is to be created. When a new point is created, space is allocated, either on the heap or in an activation record on the stack, depending on the statement creating the object. A constructor is then called to initialize the locations allocated for the object. Constructors are declared with the same syntax as that of member functions, except that the "function" name is the same as the class name. In the point class, two constructors are declared. The result is an overloaded function Pt, with one constructor called if the argument is an integer and the other called if the argument is a Pt.

In Smalltalk terminology, constructors are "class methods," not "instance methods," as a constructor is called without referring to any object that is an instance of the class. In particular, constructors are not member functions.

Visibility. As previously mentioned, the declarations that appear in the Pt class are divided into three parts, public members, protected members, and private members of the class. These designations, which affect the visibility of a declaration, may be summarized as follows:

- *public:* members that are visible in any scope in which an object of the class can be created or accessed,
- *protected:* members that are visible within the class and in any derived classes,
- *private:* members visible only within the class in which these members are declared.

The Pt class is written following one standard visibility convention that is used by many C++ programmers. Member data is made private, so that if a programmer wishes to change the way that objects of the class are represented, this may be done without affecting the way that other classes (including derived classes) depend on this class. Members that modify private data are made protected, so that derived classes may change the value of member data, but external code is not allowed to do so. Finally, member functions that read the value of member data and provide useful operations on objects are declared public, so that any code with access to an object of this class can manipulate these objects in useful ways.

A feature of C++ that is not illustrated in this example is the *friend* designation, which is used to allow visibility to the private part of a class. A class may declare friend functions and friend classes. If the Pt class contained the declaration friend class A, then code written as part of class A (such as member functions of class A) would have access to the private part of class Pt. The friend mechanism is used when a pair of classes is closely related, such as matrices and vectors.

Virtual Functions. Member functions may be designated *virtual* or left *nonvirtual*, which is the default for member functions that are not preceded by the keyword virtual. If a method is virtual, it may be redefined in derived classes. Because different objects will then have different member functions of the same name, selection of virtual member functions is by dynamic lookup: There is a run-time code selection mechanism that is used to find and invoke the correct function. These extra steps make calls to virtual functions less efficient than calls to nonvirtual functions.

Nonvirtual methods may not be redefined in derived classes. As a result, calls to nonvirtual methods are compiled and executed in the same way as ordinary function calls not associated with objects or classes.

A common point of confusion is that, syntactically, a redeclaration of a nonvirtual function may appear in a derived class. However, this produces an overloaded function, with code selection done at compile time. We will discuss this phenomenon in Subsection 12.3.3.

12.3.2 C++ Derived Classes (Inheritance)

The following ColorPt class defines an extension of the one-dimensional points defined in the Pt class. As the name suggests, ColorPt objects have a color added. For simplicity, we assume that colors are represented by integers. In addition, to illustrate virtual function definition, moving a colored point causes the color to darken a little:

```
/* ---------- Color Point Class Interface -------------------*/
class ColorPt: public Pt {
  public:
    ColorPt(int xv,int cv);
    ColorPt(Pt* pv,int cv);
    ColorPt(ColorPt* cp);
    int getColor();
    virtual void darken(int tint);
    virtual void move(int dx);
  protected:
    void setColor(int cv);
  private:
    int color;
  };
/* ---------- Declarations of Constructors --------*/
  ColorPt::ColorPt(int xv,int cv)
    : Pt(xv)        /* call parent's constructor */
    { color = cv; }   /* then initialize color */
  ColorPt::ColorPt(Pt* pv,int cv): Pt(pv) { color = cv; }
/* ---------- Declarations of Member Functions --------*/
  int ColorPt::getColor() { return color; }
  void ColorPt::darken(int tint) { color += tint; }
  void ColorPt::move(int dx) {Pt::Move(dx); this->darken(1); }
  void ColorPt::setColor(int cv) { color=cv; }
```

Inheritance. The first line of code declares that the ColorPt class has Pt as a public base class; this is the meaning of the clause : public Pt following the name of the ColorPt class. If the keyword public is omitted, then the base class is called a private base class.

When a class has a base class, the class inherits all of the members of the base class. This means that ColorPt objects have all of the public, protected, and private members of the Pt class. In particular, although the ColorPt class declares only member data color, ColorPt objects also have member data x, inherited from Pt.

The difference between public base classes and private base classes is that, when a base class is public, then the declared (derived) class is declared to be a subtype of the base class. Otherwise, the C++ compiler does not treat the class as a subtype, even though it has all the members of the base class. This is discussed in more detail in Section 12.4.

Constructors. The ColorPt class has three constructors. As in the Pt class, the result is an overloaded function ColorPt, with selection between the three functions completed at compile time according to the type of arguments to the constructor.

The two constructor bodies previously discussed illustrate how a derived-class constructor may call the constructor of a base class. As with points, when a new colored point is created, space is allocated, either on the heap or in an activation record on the stack, depending on the statement creating the object, and a constructor is called to initialize the locations allocated for the object. Because the derived class has all of the data members of the base class, most derived-class constructors will call the base class constructor to initialize the inherited data members. If the base class has private data members, which is the case for Pt, then the only way for the derived class ColorPt to initialize the private members is to call the base-class constructor.

Visibility. When one class inherits from another, the members have essentially the same visibility in the derived class as in the base class. More specifically, public members of the base class become public members of the derived class, protected members of the base class are accessible in the derived class and its derived classes, which is the same visibility as if the member were declared protected in the derived class. Inherited private members exist in the derived class, but cannot be named directly in code written as part of the derived class. In particular, every ColorPt object has an integer member x, but the only way to assign to or read the value of this member is by calling the protected and public functions from the Pt class.

Virtual Functions. As previously mentioned, virtual functions in a base class may be redefined in a derived class. The member function move is declared virtual in the Pt class and redefined above for ColorPt. In this example, the move function for points just changes the x coordinate of the point, whereas the move function on colored points changes the x coordinate and the color. If the implementation of ColorPt::move were omitted, then the move function from Pt would be inherited on ColorPt. The implementation of virtual functions is discussed in the next subsection.

12.3.3 Virtual Functions

Dynamic lookup is used for C++ virtual functions. A virtual function f defined on an object o is called by the syntax o.f(...) or p->f(...) if p is a pointer to object o. When a virtual function is called, the code for that function is located by a sequence of run-time steps. These steps are similar to the lookup algorithm for Smalltalk, but simpler because of some optimizations that are made possible by the C++ static type system. Each object has a pointer to a data structure associated with its class, called the *virtual function table*, or *vtable* for short (sometimes written as vtbl). The relationship among an object, the vtable of its class, and code for virtual functions is shown in Figure 12.1 with points and colored points.

Virtual Function on Base Class. Suppose that p is a pointer to the Pt object in Figure 12.1. When an expression of the form p->move(...) is evaluated, the code

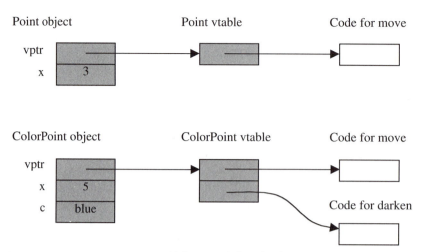

Figure 12.1. Representation of Point and ColoredPoint in C++.

for move must be found and executed. The process begins by following the vtable pointer in p to the vtable for the Pt class. The vtable for Pt is an array of pointers to functions. Because move is the first (and only) virtual function of the Pt class, the compiler can determine that the first location in this array is a pointer to the code for move. Therefore, the run-time code for finding move simply follows the first pointer in the Pt vtable and calls the function reached by this pointer. Unlike in Smalltalk, here there is no need to search the vtable at run time to determine which pointer is the one for move. The C++ type system lets the compiler determine the type of the object pointer at compile time, and this allows the compiler to find the relative position of the virtual function pointer in the vtable at compile time, eliminating the need for run-time search of the vtable.

Virtual Function on Derived Class. Suppose that cp is a pointer to the ColorPt object in Figure 12.1. When an expression of the form cp->move(. . .) is evaluated, the algorithm for finding the code for move is exactly the same as for p->move(. . .): The vtable for ColorPt is an array containing two pointers, one for move and the other for darken. The compiler can determine at compile time that cp is a pointer to a ColorPt object and that move is the first virtual function of the class, so the run-time algorithm follows the first pointer in the vtable without Smalltalk-style run-time search.

Correspondence Between Base- and Derived-Class Vtables. As a consequence of subtyping, a program may assign a colored point to a pointer to a point and call move through the base-class pointer, as in

```
p = cp;
p-> move(...);
```

Because p now points to a colored point, the call p->move(. . .) should call the move function from the ColorPt class. However, the compiler does not know at compile time that p will point to a ColorPt object. In fact, the same statement can be executed many times (if this is inside a loop, for example) and p may point to a Pt object on some executions and a ColorPt object on others. *Therefore, the code that the compiler produces for finding* move *when* p *points to a* Pt *must also work correctly when* p *points to a* ColorPt. The important issue is that because move is first in the Pt vtable, move must also be first in the ColorPt vtable. However, the compiler can easily arrange this, as the compiler will first compile the base class Pt before compiling the derived-class ColorPt. In summary, when a derived class is compiled, the virtual functions are ordered in the same way as the base class. This makes the first part of a derived-class vtable look like a base class vtable. Because member data can be accessed by inherited functions, member data in a derived class are also arranged in the same order as member data in a base class.

Unlike in Smalltalk, here there is no link from ColorPt to Point; the derived-class vtable contains a copy of the base-class vtable. This causes vtables to be slightly larger than Smalltalk method dictionaries might be for corresponding programs, but the space cost is small compared with the savings in running time.

Note that nonvirtual functions do not appear in a vtable. Because nonvirtual functions cannot be redefined from base class to derived class, the compiler can determine the location of a nonvirtual function at compile time (just like normal function calls in C).

12.3.4 Why is C++ Lookup Simpler than Smalltalk Lookup?

At run-time, C++ lookup uses indirection through the vtable of the class, with an offset (position in the vtable) that is known at compile time. In contrast, Smalltalk method lookup does a run-time search of one or more method dictionaries. The C++ lookup procedure is much faster than the Smalltalk procedure. However, the C++ lookup procedure would not work for Smalltalk. Let's find out why.

Smalltalk has no static type system. If a Smalltalk program contains the line

```
p selector : parameters
```

sending a message to an object p, then the compiler has no compile-time information about the class of p. Because any object can be assigned to any Smalltalk pointer, p could point to any object in the system. The compiler knows that selector must refer to some method defined in the class of p, but different classes could put the same selector (method name) in different positions of their method dictionaries. As a consequence, the compiler must generate code to perform a run-time search for the method.

The C++ static type system makes all the difference. When a call such as p->move(. . .) is compiled, the compiler can determine a static type for the pointer p. This static type must be a class, and that class must declare or inherit a function called move. The compiler can examine the class hierarchy to see what location a virtual function move will occupy in the vtable for this class. A call

```
p->move(x)
```

compiles to the equivalent of the C code

```
(*(p->vptr[1]))(p,x)
```

where the index 1 in the array reference vptr[1] indicates that move is first function in the vtable (represented by the array vptr) for the class of p. The reason why p is passed as an argument to the function (*(p->vptr[1])) is explained in the next subsection.

Arguments to Member Functions and this

There are several issues related to calls to member function, function parameters, and the this pointer. Consider the following code, in which one virtual function calls another:

```
class A {
   public:
       virtual int f (int x);
       virtual int g(int y);
};
int A::f(int x) { ... g(i) ...;}
int A::g(int y) { ... f(j) ...;}
```

If virtual function f is redefined in a derived class B, then a call to the inherited g on class B objects should invoke the new function B::f, not the original function A::f defined for class A. Therefore, calls to one virtual function inside another must use a vtable. However, the call to f inside A::g does not have the form p->f(...), and it is not clear at first glance what object p we would use if we wanted to change the call from the simple f(...) that appears above to p->f(...).

One way of understanding the solution to this problem is to rewrite the code as it is compiled. In other words, the preceding function A::g is compiled as if it were written as

```
int A::g(A* this, int x) { ... this->f(j) ...;}
```

with a new first parameter this to the function, called this, and the call f(j) replaced with this->f(j). Now the call this->f(j) can be compiled in the usual way, by use of the vtable pointer of this to find the code for f, provided that when g is called, the appropriate object is passed as the value of this.

The calling sequence for a member function, whether it is virtual or not, passes the object itself as the this pointer. For example, returning to the Pt and ColorPt example, in code such as

```
ColorPt* q = new ColorPt(3,4);
q->darken(5);
```

the call to darken is compiled as if it were a C function call:

```
(*(q->vptr[2]))(q,5);
```

This call shows the offset of darken in the vtable (assumed here to be 2) and the call with the pointer to q passed as the first argument to the compiled code for the member function.

There are several ways that the this pointer is used. As previously illustrated, the this pointer is used to call virtual functions on the object. The this pointer is also used to access data members of the object, whether there are virtual functions or not. The this pointer is also used to resolve overloading, as described in the next subsection.

Scope Qualifiers

Because some of the calling conventions may be confusing, it is worth saying clearly how names are interpreted in C++. There are three *scope qualifiers*. They are :: (double colons), -> (right arrow, consisting of two ASCII characters – and >), and . (period or dot). These are used to qualify a member name with a class name, a pointer to an object, or an object name, respectively.

The following rules are for resolving names:

■ A name outside a function or class, not prefixed by :: and not qualified, refers to global object, function, enumerator, or type.
■ Suppose C is a class, p is a pointer to an object of class C, and o is an object of class C. These might be declared as follows:

```
Class C : ... { .... }; /* C is a class */
C *p = new C( ...);   /* p is a pointer to an object of class C */
C o( ...)                   /* o is an object of class C */
```

Then the following qualified names can be formed with ::, ->, and .:

```
C::n    /* Class name C followed by member name n */
p->n   /* pointer p to object of class C followed by member name n */
o.n       /* pointer p to object of class C followed by member name n */
```

These refer to a member n of class C, or a base class of C if n is not declared in C but is inherited from a base class.

Nonvirtual and Overloaded Functions

The C++ virtual function mechanism does not affect the way that the address of a nonvirtual or overloaded function is determined by the C++ compiler. For nonvirtual functions, the C++ calls work in exactly the same way as in C, except for the way that the object itself is passed as the this pointer, as described in the preceding subsection.

There are also some situations in which overloading and virtual function lookup may interact or be confusing.

Recall that, if a function is not a virtual function, the compiler will know the address of the function at compile time. (Those familiar with linking may realize that this is not strictly true for separately compiled program units. However, linkers effectively make it possible for compilers to be written as if the location of a function is known at compile time.) Therefore, if a C++ program contains a call f(x), the compiler can generate code that jumps to an address associated with the function f.

If f is an overloaded function and a program contains a call f(x), then the compile-time type associated with the parameter x will be used to decide, at compile time, which function code for f will be called when this expression is executed at run time.

The difference between overloading and virtual function lookup is illustrated by the following code. Here, we have two classes, a parent and a child class, with two member functions in each class. One function, called printclass, is overloaded. The other, called printvirtual, is a virtual function that is redefined in the derived class:

```
class parent {
public:
    void printclass() {printf("parent");};
    virtual void printvirtual() {printf("parent");};
};
class child : public parent {
public:
    void printclass() {printf("child");};
    void printvirtual() {printf("child");}; };
main() {
    parent p; child c; parent *q;
    p.printclass(); p.printvirtual(); c.printclass(); c.printvirtual();
    q = &p; q->printclass(); q->printvirtual();
    q = &c; q->printclass(); q->printvirtual();
}
```

The program creates two objects, one of each class. When we invoke the member functions of each class directly through the object identifiers c and p, we get the expected output: The parent class functions print "parent" and the child class functions print "child." When we refer to the parent class object through a pointer of type *parent, then we get the same behavior. However, something else happens when we refer to the child class object through the pointer of type *parent. The call q->printclass() always causes the parent class member to be called; the printclass function is not virtual so the type of the pointer q is used. The static type of q is *parent, so overloading resolution leads to the parent class function. On the other hand, the call q->printvirtual() will invoke a virtual function. Therefore, the output of this program is

```
parent parent child child parent parent parent child.
```

The call q->printclass() is effectively compiled as a call printclass(q), passing the object q as the this pointer to printclass. Although the printclass function does not need the this pointer in order to print a string, the argument is used to resolve overloading. More specifically, q->printclass() calls the parent class function because this call is compiled as printclass(q) and the type of the implicit argument q is used by the compiler to choose which version of the overloaded printclass function to call.

12.4 SUBTYPING

In principle, subtyping and inheritance are independent concepts. However, subtyping as implemented in C++ occurs only when inheritance is used. In this section, we look at how subtyping-in-principle might work in C++ and compare this with the form of subtyping used by the C++ type checker. Although the C++ type checker is not as flexible as it conceivably could be, there are also some sound and subtle reasons for some central parts of the C++ design.

12.4.1 Subtyping Principles

Subtyping for Classes. The main principle of subtyping is that, if A <: B, then we should be able to use an A value when a B is required. For classes, subtyping requires a superset relation between public members of the class. For example, we can see that the colored-point class ColorPt defined in Subsection 12.3.2 is a subtype of the point class Pt defined in Subsection 12.3.1 by a comparison of the public members of the classes:

```
Pt:      int getX();
         void move(int);
ColorPt: int getX();
         int getColor();
         void move(int);
         void darken(int tint);
```

The superset relation between sets of public members is guaranteed by C++ inheritance: Because ColorPt inherits from Pt, ColorPt has all of the public members of Pt. Because Pt is a public base class of ColorPt, the C++ type checker will allow ColorPt objects to be assigned to Pt class pointers.

Subtyping for Functions. One type of function is substitutable for another if there is a certain correspondence between the types of arguments and the types of results. More specifically, if functions f and g return the same kind of result and function f can be applied to every kind of argument to which function g can be applied, then we can use function f in place of function g without type error. Similarly, if functions f and g are applicable to the same type of arguments and the result type of f is a subtype of the result type of g, then f can be used in place of g without type error. These two subtyping ideas for functions can be combined in a relatively simple-looking rule that is hard for most people to understand and remember:

The function type A → B is a subtype of C → D whenever C <: A and B <: D.

It helps to look at a few examples. Let us assume that circle <: shape and consider some function types involving circle and shape.

One reasonably straightforward relation is (circle → circle) <: (circle → shape): You can understand this by assuming you have a program that calls a circle → shape function f:

```
shape f (circle x) { ... return(y) ;}
main {
  ... f(circ) ...
}
```

The assertion that circle → circle is a subtype of circle → shape means that it is type safe to replace this f with another function that returns a circle instead of a shape. In other words, where a program requires an circle → shape function, we would not create a type error if we used a circle → circle function instead.

When we change the argument type of a function, the subtyping relation is reversed. For example, (shape → circle) <: (circle → circle): The reasoning involved here is similar to the case we just discussed. If a program uses a function f of type circle → circle correctly, then it may apply f to a circle argument. However, it would work just as well to use a shape → circle function g instead, as our assumption circle <: shape means that g could be applied to any circle argument without causing a type error.

When these two basic ideas are combined, there are four function types involving circle and shape. They are ordered as shown in the following illustration, in which each type shown is a subtype of those above it:

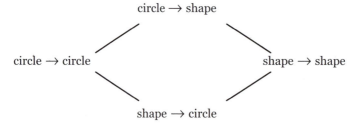

It is worth taking some time to be sure you understand all of the relationships implied by this diagram.

12.4.2 Public Base Classes

When a derived class B has public base class A, the rules of C++ inheritance guarantee that the type of B objects will be a subtype of the type of A objects. The following basic rule guarantees that a derived class defines a subtype of its public base class:

> *Standard C++ Inheritance:* A derived class may redefine virtual members of the base class and may add new members that are not defined in the base class. However, the type and visibility (public, protected or private) of any redefined member must be exactly the same in the base and the derived classes.

This rule was originally used in most implementations of C++, except for the clause about maintaining visibility, which is added here to eliminate some awkward cases.

In principle, if the compiler follows systematic rules for setting the order of member data in objects and the order of virtual function pointers in the vtable, it is possible to define compatible classes of objects without using inheritance. For example, consider the following two classes. The one on the left is the Pt class defined in Subsection 12.3.1, with protected and private members elided for brevity. The class on the right is equivalent (for most compilers) to the ColorPt class defined in Subsection 12.3.2.

```
class Point {              class ColorPoint {
  public:                    public:
    int getX();                int getX();
    void move(int);            int getColor();
  protected:   ...             void move(int);
  private:     ...             void darken(int);
};                           protected:   ...
                             private:     ...
                           } :
```

It has exactly the same public, private and protected members, in exactly the same order, producing exactly the same object layout and exactly the same vtable. However, the C++ type checker will not recognize subtyping between this ColorPt class and this Pt class because ColorPt does not use Pt as a public base class.

12.4.3 Specializing Types of Public Members

A more permissive rule than the *standard C++ inheritance* rule stated in Subsection 12.4.2 allows virtual functions to be given subtypes of their original types:

> *Permissive Inheritance:* A derived class may redefine virtual members of the base class and may add new members that are not defined in the base class. The derived-class type of any redefined public member must be a *subtype* of the type of this member in the base class. The visibility (public, protected, or private) of each member must be the same in the derived class as in the base class.

Although early C++ used *standard C++ inheritance*, contemporary implementations of C++ use a rule that is halfway between the standard and the permissive inheritance rules:

> *Contemporary C++ Inheritance:* A derived class may redefine virtual members of the base class and may add new members that are not defined in the

base class. The visibility (public, protected, or private) of any redefined member must be the same in the base and the derived classes. If a virtual member function f has type $A \rightarrow B$ in a base class, then f may be given type $A \rightarrow C$ in a derived class, provided $C <: B$.

This allows the return type to be replaced with a subtype, but does not allow changes in the argument types of member functions. Because the argument types of functions are used to resolve overloading, but the return types are not, this inheritance rule does not interact with the C++ overloading algorithm.

12.4.4 Abstract Base Classes

In many object-oriented programs, it is useful to define general concepts, such as container, account, shape, or vehicle, that are not implemented themselves, but are useful as generalizations of some set of implemented classes. For example, in the Smalltalk container class library discussed in Section 11.7, all of the classes define the methods of the container interface, but the implemented containers come from more specialized classes such as dictionary, array, set, or bag. Because subtyping follows inheritance in C++, there is a specific C++ construct developed to meet the need for classes that serve an organizational purpose but do not have any implemented objects of their own.

An *abstract class* is a class that has at least one pure virtual member function. A pure virtual member function is one whose implementation is declared empty. It is not possible to construct objects of an abstract class. The purpose of an abstract class is to define a common interface for one or more derived classes that are not abstract.

For example, an abstract-class file can be used to define the operations open and read that must be implemented in every kind of file class that uses file as a base class:

```
class file {
public:
    void virtual Open() = 0; /* pure virtual member function */
    void virtual Read() = 0; /* pure virtual member function */
//..
};
```

Another example appears in the geometry classes in Appendix B.1.5. The class shape is abstract, defining the common interface of various kinds of shapes. Two derived classes of shape are circle and rectangle.

Although it is not possible to create an instance of an abstract class like file or shape, it is possible to declare a pointer with type file* or shape*. If pointer f has type file*, then f can be assigned any object from any derived class of file. Another way that abstract classes are used is as the argument types of functions. If some function can be applied to any type of file, its argument can be declared to have type file*.

In addition to defining an interface, an abstract class establishes a layout for a virtual function table (vtable). In particular, if textFile and streamFile have file as a base class, then both classes will have open and read in the same positions in their respective vtables.

The use of "abstract" in the term "abstract class" is not the same as in "abstract data type." In particular, an abstract class is not a class with a stronger form of information hiding.

12.5 MULTIPLE INHERITANCE

Multiple inheritance is a controversial part of object-oriented programming. Once we have adopted the idea of using inheritance to build new classes, it seems natural to allow a class to be implemented by inheriting from more than one base class.

Unfortunately, multiple inheritance brings with it a set of problems that does not have simple, elegant solutions. For this reason, many language designers tried to avoid putting multiple inheritance in their language (like Java) or postponed adding multiple inheritance as long as possible (like Smalltalk and C++).

Some of the most compelling examples of multiple inheritance involve combining two or more independent kinds of functionality. For example, suppose we are doing some geometric calculations and want to manage the memory allocated to various geometric objects in various ways. We might have a class hierarchy of geometric objects, such as shapes, circles, and rectangles, and a hierarchy of classes of memory management mechanisms. For example, we might have ordinary C++ heap objects that require users to call their destructors and garbage-collected objects that are automatically reclaimed when some function invoking the garbage collector is called. Another possibility that might be useful for some objects would be to associate a reference count with each object (maintaining a count of the number of pointers that refer to this object). This is a simple form of garbage collection that works more efficiently when it is easy to maintain a count accurately. If we have separate geometry and memory management hierarchies, then it will be possible to implement many combinations of shape and memory by multiple inheritance. An example is shown in Figure 12.2.

Here, reference-counted rectangles are implemented by inheriting the geometric aspects of rectangles from the rectangle class and the mechanism for reference counting from the reference-counted class.

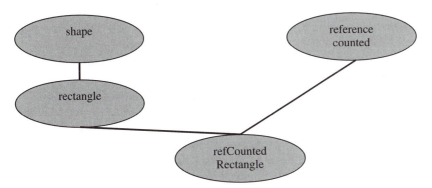

Figure 12.2. Multiple inheritance.

12.5.1 Implementation of Multiple Inheritance

The fundamental property of C++ class implementation is that if class B has class A as a public base class, then the initial segment of every B object must look like an A object, and similarly for the B and A virtual function tables. This property makes it possible to access an inherited A member of a B object in exactly the same way we would access the same member of an A object. Although it is fairly easy to guarantee this property with only single inheritance, the implementation of objects and classes with multiple inheritance is more complex.

The implementation issues are best illustrated by example. Suppose class C is defined by inheriting from classes A and B, as in the following code:

```
class A {
  public:
    int x;
    virtual void f();
};
class B {
  public:
    int y;
    virtual void g();
    virtual void f();
};
class C: public A, public B {
  public:
    int z;
    virtual void f();
};
  C *pc = new C;
  B *pb = pc;
  A *pa = pc;
```

In the final three lines of the sample code, we have three pointers to the same object. However, the three pointers have three different static types.

The representation of the C object created from the preceding example class C and the values of the associated pointers are illustrated in Figure 12.3. The illustration shows three pointers to the class C object. Pointers pa and pc point to the top of the object and pointer pb points to a position δ locations below the top of the object. The class C object has two virtual function table pointers and three sections of member data, one for member data declared in the A class, one for member data declared in the B class, and one for member data declared in the C class. The two virtual function table pointers point to two different vtables whose use is subsequently explained. The top vtable, labeled C-as-A, is used when a C object is used as an object of type C or as an object of type A. The lower vtable, labeled C-as-B, is used when a C object is used as an object of type B and to call C member functions that are inherited from B (in this case, function g).

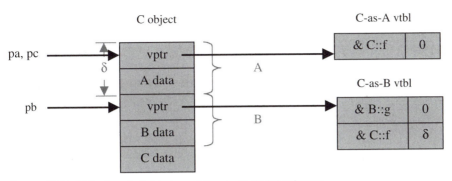

Figure 12.3. Object and vtable layout for multiple inheritance.

Figure 12.3 shows three complications associated with the implementation of multiple inheritance in C++:

■ There are multiple virtual function tables for class C, not just one.
■ A pointer of static type B points to a different place in the object than an A or C pointer.
■ There are some extra numbers stored in the vtable, shown here to the right of the address & C::f of a virtual function.

There are two vtables for class C because a C object may be used as an A object or as a B object. In symbols, we want C <: A and C <: B. For this to work, the C virtual function table must have an initial segment that looks like an A virtual function table and an initial segment that looks like a B virtual function table. However, because A and B are independent classes, there is no reason why A and B should have similar vtables. The solution is to provide two vtables, one that allows a C object to be used as an A object, and another that allows a C object to be used as a B object. In principle, if a derived class has n base classes, the class will have n+1 vtables, one for each base class and one for the derived class itself. However, in practice, only n vtables are needed, as the vtable for the derived class can follow the order of the vtable for one of the base classes, allowing the vtable for the derived class to be the same as the vtable used for viewing objects of the derived class as objects of one of the base classes.

There is a similar issue surrounding the arrangement of data members within a C object. As we can see from Figure 12.3, the pointer pb, referring to a C object as a B object, points to a different place in the object than pa and pc. When a C object is used as a B object, the member data must be accessed in exactly the same way as if the object had been created as a B object. This is accomplished when the member data inherited from B are arranged in a contiguous part of the object, below the A data. When a pointer to a C object is converted or cast to type B, the pointer must be incremented by some amount δ to skip over the A part and point directly to the B part of the object.

The number δ, which is the numeric difference pb – pa, is stored in the B table, as it is also used in calling some of the member functions. The offset δ in this vtable is used in call to pb->f(), as the virtual function f defined in C may refer to A member data that are above the pointer pb. Therefore, on the call to inherited member function f, the this pointer passed to the body of f must be δ less than the pointer pb.

12.5.2 Name Clashes, Diamond Inheritance, and Virtual Base Classes

Some interesting and troubling issues arise in connection with multiple inheritance. The simplest and most pervasive problem is the problem of name clashes, which arises when two base classes have members of the same name. A variant of the name clash problem arises when a class C inherits from two classes, A and B, that inherit the same member from a common base class, D. In this case, the inherited members of C with the same name will have the same definition. This eliminates some problems. However, there is still the issue of deciding whether to place two copies of doubly inherited member data in a derived class. By default, C++ duplicates members that are inherited twice. The virtual base-class mechanism provides an alternative way of sharing common base classes in which doubly inherited members occur only once in the derived class.

Name Clashes

If class C inherits from classes A and B and A and B have members of the same name, then there is a *name clash*. There are three general ways of handling name clashes:

- *Implicit resolution:* The language resolves name conflicts with an arbitrary rule.
- *Explicit resolution:* The programmer must explicitly resolve name conflicts in the code in some way.
- *Disallow name clashes:* Programs are not allowed to contain name clashes.

There is no systematic best solution to the problem of name clashes. The simplest solution is to disallow name clashes. However, there are some situations, such as the diamond inheritance patterns subsequently described, for which this seems unnecessarily restrictive.

Implicit resolution also has its problems. Python and the CLOS, for example, have mechanisms that give priority to one base class over another. This approach does not work well in some situations. For example, suppose class C inherits from classes A and B and suppose that both A and B have a member function named f. If class C is declared so that A has priority over B, then class C will inherit the member function f from A and not inherit the member f from B. However, suppose that class B has another member function g that calls member function f and relies on a particular definition of f in order to work properly. Then, in effect, inheriting f from class A will cause the inherited member g from B not to work properly.

C++ allows name clashes and requires explicit resolution in the program. If a data member m is inherited from two bases classes A and B, then there will be two data members in the derived class. If a member m is inherited from two bases classes A and B, then the only way to refer to member m is by a fully qualified name. This is illustrated in the following C++ code samples.

The following code contains a compile-time error because the call to an inherited member function is ambiguous:

```
class A {
   public:
      virtual void f() { ... }
};
class B {
   public:
      virtual void f() { ... }
};
class C : public A, public B { };
...
      C* p;
      p->f();   // error since call to member function is ambiguous
```

In C++, it is not an error to inherit from two classes containing the same member names. The error occurs only when the compiler sees a reference to the doubly inherited member. The preceding program fragment can be rewritten to avoid the error, by use of fully qualified names. Classes A and B remain the same; only the definition of class C needs to be changed to specify which inherited member function f should be called:

```
class C : public A, public B {
public:
      virtual void f( ) {
            A::f( );   // Call member function f from A, not B::f();
      }
...
};
```

Here, class C explicitly defines a member function f. However, the definition of C::f is simply to call A::f. This makes the definition of C::f unambiguous and has the same effect as inheriting A::f by some other name resolution rule.

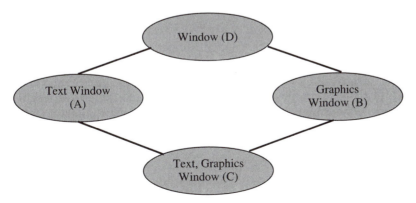

Figure 12.4. Diamond inheritance.

Diamond Inheritance

An interesting kind of name clash occurs when two classes share a common base class. In this situation, a member that is inherited twice will have the same definition in both classes. The complications associated with this situation are commonly called the *diamond inheritance problem*, as this situation involves a diamond-shaped inheritance graph. For example, consider the four classes shown in Figure 12.4.

The classes are labeled A, B, C, and D because these shorter labels fit better in subsequent illustrations.

Under ordinary multiple inheritance, there are two copies of window members in a text graphics window. More specifically, the data members of a class C object have the following form:

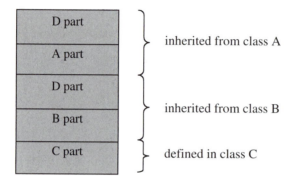

A class C object has all of these parts because a class C object has parts for both of the base classes, A and B. However, classes A and B both inherit from D, so A objects have a copy of each data member inherited from D and B objects have a copy of each data member inherited from D.

For window classes, it does not make sense for a text and graphics window to have two copies of each window-class member. In a windowing system with this design, the window class might contain data members to store the bounding box of the window, data members to determine the background color and border color of the window, and so on. The text window class might have additional data members and member functions to store and display text inside a window, and similarly the graphics window class would contain declarations and code for displaying graphics inside a window. If we want a window that can contain graphics and text within the same window, then C++ multiple inheritance as described so far will not work. Instead, the C++ implementation of multiple inheritance will produce objects that consist of two windows, one capable of displaying text and the other capable of displaying graphics.

The diamond inheritance problem is the basic problem that there is no "right" way to handle multiple inheritance when two base classes of a class C both have the same class D as a base class. This is called the diamond inheritance problem because the classes A, B, C, and D form a diamond shape, as shown in Figure 12.4. The biggest problem with diamond inheritance is what to do with member data. One option is to duplicate the D class data members. This can give useful behavior in some cases, but is undesirable in situations like the window classes in Figure 12.4. If data members are duplicated, then there is also a naming problem: If you select an inherited D member

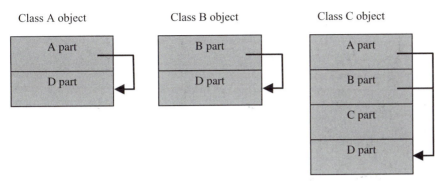

Figure 12.5. Virtual base class.

by name, which copy should you get? The C++ solution is to require a fully qualified name.

The alternative to duplicating data members is to put only one copy of each D member into a C object and have the inherited A and B class member functions both refer to the shared copy. This also can lead to problems if the A and B classes may use D data members differently. For example, some A member function may be written assuming an inherited D class data member is an even number, whereas some B class member function may set it to an odd number. Diamond inheritance leads to problems that do not have a simple, generally applicable solution.

Virtual Base Classes

C++ has a mechanism for eliminating multiple copies of duplicated base-class members, called *virtual base classes*. If D is declared a virtual base class of A and B, and class C has A and B as base classes, then A, B, and C class objects will have the form illustrated in Figure 12.5.

The main idea is that if class A has a virtual base class D, then access to D data members of an A object is by indirection through a pointer in the object. As a result, the location of the D part does not matter. The D part could immediately follow the A part of the object or reside someplace else in memory. This indirection through a pointer allows C objects to have an A part and a B part that share a common D part.

Inheritance with virtual base classes has its complications. One annoyance is that the choice between virtual and nonvirtual base classes is made once for all uses of a class. More specifically, suppose that one class, A, has another class, D, as a base class. Then the designer of A must decide whether D should be a virtual base class or not, even though this affects only other classes that inherit from A. Moreover, if some classes that inherit from A need D to be a virtual base class of A and others require the opposite, then the only solution is to make two versions of the A class, one with D as a virtual base class and the other with D as a nonvirtual base class. An oddity of virtual base classes is that it is possible to convert a pointer to an instance of a class that has a virtual base class to a pointer to an object of that virtual base class. However, the opposite conversion is not allowed, making this form of type conversion irreversible. For this reason, some style guides recommend against casts when virtual base classes are used. This can be a complex guideline to follow, as users of a class library must pay careful attention to when virtual base classes are used in the implementation of the library.

12.6 CHAPTER SUMMARY

The main goal of C++ is to provide object-oriented features in a C-based language without compromising the efficiency of C. C++ is a very carefully designed language that has succeeded admirably in spite of difficult design constraints.

Some features of C++ that are not part of the object system are type bool, reference types and pass-by-reference, user-defined overloading, function templates, and exceptions. C++ also has better static type checking than C.

The focus on C++ efficiency is articulated in the design principle, "If you do not use a feature, you should not pay for it." This principle suggests that C programs should compile as efficiently under the C++ compiler as under the C compiler. It would violate this principle to implement C integers as objects, for example, and use dynamic method lookup to find integer functions at run-time as in Smalltalk, as this would significantly reduce the performance of C integer calculations.

The most significant part of C++ is the set of object-oriented concepts added to C; these are the main concepts:

- *Classes*, which declare the type associated with all objects constructed from the class, the data members of each object, and the member functions of the class.
- *Objects*, which consist of private data and public functions for accessing the hidden data, as in other object-oriented languages.
- *Dynamic lookup*, for member functions that are declared virtual. A virtual function in a derived class (subclass) may be implemented differently from virtual functions of the same name in a base class (superclass).
- *Encapsulation*, based on programmer designations public, private, and protected that determine whether data and functions declared in a class are visible outside the class definition.
- *Inheritance*, using subclassing, in which one class may be defined by inheriting the data and functions declared in another. C++ allows single inheritance, in which a class has a single base class (superclass) or multiple inheritance in which a class has more than one base class.
- *Subtyping*, based on subclassing. For one class to define a subtype of the type defined by another class, inheritance must be used. However, the programmer may decide whether inheritance results in a subtype or not by specifying that the base class is public or not.

At run time, C++ virtual function lookup uses indirection through the virtual function table (vtable) of the class. The C++ static type system makes it possible to determine the offset (position of a pointer in the vtable) of virtual function at compile time. When a call like p->move(...) is compiled, the compiler can determine a static type for the pointer p. This static type must be a class, and this class must declare or inherit a function called move. The compiler can examine the class hierarchy to see what location the virtual function move will occupy in the vtable for the class.

A fundamental property of C++ class implementation is that if class B has class A as a public base class, then the initial segment of every B object must look like an

A object, and similarly for the B and A virtual function tables. This property makes it possible to access an inherited A member of a B object in exactly the same way we would access the same member of an A object. Although it is fairly easily to guarantee this property with only single inheritance, the implementation of objects and classes with multiple inheritance is more complex.

There are a number of aspects of C++ that programmers occasionally find difficult. Some of the main problem areas are

- *casts and conversions* that can be complex and unpredictable in certain situations,
- *objects allocated on the stack* and other aspects of object memory management,
- *overloading*, a complex code selection mechanism in C++ that can interact unpredicatably with dynamic lookup (virtual function lookup),
- *multiple inheritance*, which is more complex in C++ than in other languages because of the way objects and virtual function tables are configured and accessed.

These problem areas exist not because of oversights but because the goals of C++, followed to their logical conclusion, led to a design with these properties.

EXERCISES

12.1 Assignment and Derived Classes

This problem exams the difference between two forms of object assignment. In C++, local variables are stored on the run-time stack, whereas dynamically allocated data (created with the new keyword) are stored on the heap. A local object variable allocated on the stack has an object L-value and an R-value. Unlike many other object-oriented languages, C++ allows object assignment into object L-values.

A C++ programmer writes the following code:

```
class Vehicle {
public:
    int x;
    virtual void f();
    void g();
};

class Airplane : public Vehicle {
public:
    int y;
    virtual void f();
    virtual void h();
};

void inHeap() {
    Vehicle *b1 = new Vehicle;      // Allocate object on the heap
    Airplane *d1 = new Airplane;    // Allocate object on the heap
    b1->x = 1;
    d1->x = 2;
    d1->y = 3;
    b1 = d1;                        // Assign derived class object to base class pointer
```

```
        }

        void onStack() {
            Vehicle b2;                   // Local object on the stack
            Airplane d2;                  // Local object on the stack
            b2 . x = 4;
            d2 . x = 5;
            d2 . y = 6;
            b2 = d2;                      // Assign derived class object to base class variable
        }

        int main() {
            inHeap();
            onStack();
        }
```

(a) Draw a picture of the stack, heap, and vtables that result after objects b1 and d1 have been allocated (but *before* the assignment b1=d1) during the call to inHeap. Be sure to indicate where the instance variables and vtable pointers of the two objects are stored before the assignment b1=d1 and to which vtables the respective vtable pointers point.

(b) Redraw your diagram from (a), showing the changes that result after the assignment b1=d1. Be sure to clearly indicate where b1's vtable pointer points after the assignment b1=d1. Explain why b1's vtable pointer points where it does after the assignment b1=d1.

(c) Draw a picture of the stack, heap, and vtables that result after objects b2 and d2 have been allocated (but *before* the assignment b2=d2) during the call to onStack. Be sure to indicate where the instance variables and vtable pointers of the two objects are stored before the assignment b2=d2 and to which vtables the respective vtable pointers point.

(d) In C++, assignment to objects (such as b2=d2) is performed by copying into all the left object's data members (b2's in our example) from the right object's (d2's) corresponding data members. If the right object contains data members not present in the left object, then those data simply are not copied. In b2=d2 this means overwriting all b2's data members with the corresponding value from d2.

    i. Re-draw your diagram from (c), showing the changes that result after the assignment b2=d2.

    ii. Explain why it is not sensible to copy all of d2's member data into b2's record.

    iii. Explain why b2's vtable pointer is not changed by the assignment.

(e) We have used assignment statements b1=d1 and b2=d2. Why are the opposite statements d1=b1 and d2=b2 not allowed?

12.2 Function Objects

The C++ Standard Template Library (STL) was discussed in an earlier chapter. In STL terminology, a *function object* is any object that can be called as if it is a function. Any object of a class that defines operator() is a function object. In addition, an ordinary function may be used as a function object, as f() is meaningful is f is a function and similarly if f is a function pointer.

Here is a C++ template for combining an argument type, return type, and operator() together into a function object. Every object from every subclass of FuncObj<A,B>, for any types A and B is a function object, but not all function objects come from such classes:

```
template <typename Arg, typename Ret>
class FuncObj {
public:
    typedef Arg argType;
    typedef Ret retType;
    virtual Ret operator()(Arg) = 0;
};
```

Here are two example classes of function objects. In the first case, the constructor stores a value in a protected data field so that different function objects from this class will divide by different integers. In a sense to be explored later in this problem, instances of DivideBy are similar to closures as they may contain hidden data:

```
class DivideBy : public FuncObj<int, double> {
protected:
    int divisor;
public:
    DivideBy(int d) {
        this->divisor = d;
    }
    double operator()(int x) {
        return x/((double)divisor);
    }
};

class Truncate : public FuncObj<double, int> {
public:
    int operator()(double x) {
        return (int) x;
    }
};
```

Because DivideBy uses the FuncObj template as a public base class, DivideBy is a subtype of FuncObj<int, double>, and similarly for Truncate.

(a) Fill in the blanks to complete the following Compose template. The Compose constructor takes two function objects f and g and creates a function object that computes their composition λx. f(g(x)).

You will need to fill in type declarations on lines 9 and 13 and code on lines 10, 11, and 14. If you do not know the correct C++ syntax, you may use short English descriptions for partial credit. (We have double-checked the parentheses to make sure they are correct.)

To give you a better idea of how Compose is supposed to work, you may want to look at the following sample code that uses Compose to compose DivideBy and Truncate:

```
1:    template < typename Ftype , typename Gtype >
2:    class Compose :
3:      public FuncObj < typename Gtype : : argType,
4:                       typename Ftype : : retType > {
5:    protected:
6:      Ftype *f;
7:      Gtype *g;
8:    public:
9:      Compose( _____ f, _____ g) {
10:            _____ = f ;
11:            _____ = g ;
12:      }
13:      _____ operator()( _____ x) {
14:        return ( _____ )(( _____ )( _____ ));
15:      }
16:    };
```

```
void main() {
  DivideBy *d = new DivideBy(2);
  Truncate *t = new Truncate();
  Compose<DivideBy, Truncate> *c1
    = new Compose<DivideBy, Truncate>(d,t);
  Compose<Truncate, DivideBy> *c2
    = new Compose<Truncate, DivideBy>(t,d);

  cout << (*c1)(100.7) << endl; // Prints 50.0
  cout << (*c2)(11) << endl;    // Prints 5
}
```

(b) Consider code of the following form, in which A, B, C, and D are types that might not all be different (i.e., we could have A = B = C = D = int or A, B, C, and D might be four different types):

```
class F : public FuncObj<A, B> {
  . . .
};
class G : public FuncObj<C, D> {
  . . .
};
F *f = new F( . . . );
G *g = new G( . . . );
Compose<F, G> *h
  = new Compose<F, G>(f,g);

cout << (*h)( . . . ) << endl; // call compose function
```

What will happen if the return type D of g is not the same as the argument type A of f? If it is possible for an error to occur and possible for an error not to occur, say which conditions will cause an error and which will not. If it is possible for an error to occur at compile time or at run time, say when the error will occur and why.

(c) Our Compose template is written assuming that Ftype and Gtype are classes
     that have argType and retType type definitions. If you wanted to define a
     Compose template that works for all function objects, what arguments would
     your template have and why? Your answer should be in the form of "the
     types of variables ..., the arguments of functions ..., and the return values
     of...." Assume that the code in lines 10, 11, and 14 stays the same. All we
     want to change are the template parameters on line 1 and possibly the parts
     of the body of the template that refer to template parameters.

     The rest of this problem asks about the similarities and differences between
     C++ function objects and function closures in languages like Lisp, ML, and
     Scheme. In studying scope and activation records, we looked at a function
     makeCounter that returns a counter, initialized to some integer value. Here is
     makeCounter function in Scheme:

```
(define makeCounter
  (lambda (val)
    (let (( counter (lambda (inc) (set! val (+ val inc)) val)) )
      counter)))
```

Here is part of an interactive session in which makeCounter is used:

```
==> (define c (makeCounter 3))
#<unspecified>
==> (c 2)
5
==> (c 2)
7
```

The first input defines a counter c, initialized to 3. The second input line adds
2, producing value 5, and the third input line adds 2 again, producing value 7.
     A general idea for translating Lisp functions into C++ function objects
is to translate each function f into a class A so that objects from class A are
function objects that behave like f. If f is defined within some nested scope,
then the constructor for A will put the global variables of f into the function
object, so that an instance of A behaves like a closure for f.
     Because makeCounter does not have any free variables, we can translate
makeCounter into a class MAKECOUNTER that has a constructor with no parameters:

```
class MAKECOUNTER {
    public:
        class COUNTER {
            protected:
                int val;
            public:
                COUNTER(int init){val = init;}
                int operator()(int inc) {
                    val = val + inc;
                    return val;
                }
        };
        MAKECOUNTER(){}
```

```
                    COUNTER* operator()(int val) {
                        return new COUNTER(val);
                    }
            };
```

We can create a MAKECOUNTER function object and use it to create a COUNTER function object as follows:

```
MAKECOUNTER *m = new MAKECOUNTER();
MAKECOUNTER::COUNTER * c = (*m)(3);
```

```
cout << (*c)(2) << endl; // Prints 5
```

(d) Thinking generally about Lisp closures and C++ function objects, describe one way in which C++ function objects might serve some programming objectives better than Lisp closures.

(e) Thinking generally about Lisp closures and C++ function objects, describe one way in which Lisp closures might serve some programming objectives better than C++ function objects.

(f) Do you think this approach sketched in this problem will allow you to translate an arbitrary nesting of Lisp or ML functions into C++ function objects? You may want to consider the following variation of MAKECOUNTER in which the counter value val is placed in the outer class instead of in the inner class:

```
class MAKECOUNTER {
protected:
    int val;

public:
    class COUNTER {
    private:
        MAKECOUNTER *mc;

    public:
        COUNTER(MAKECOUNTER* mc, int init) {
            this->mc = mc;
            mc->val = init;
        }

        int operator()(int inc) {
            mc->val = mc->val + inc;
            return mc->val;
        }
    };
    friend class COUNTER;

    MAKECOUNTER(){}
    COUNTER* operator()(int val) {
        return new COUNTER(this,val);
    }
};
```

12.3 Function Subtyping

Assume that A <: B and B <: C. Which of the following subtype relationships involving the function type B $\longrightarrow$ B hold in principle?

  (i) (B $\longrightarrow$ B) <: (B $\longrightarrow$ B)
 (ii) (B $\longrightarrow$ A) <: (B $\longrightarrow$ B)
(iii) (B $\longrightarrow$ C) <: (B $\longrightarrow$ B)
 (iv) (C $\longrightarrow$ B) <: (B $\longrightarrow$ B)
  (v) (A $\longrightarrow$ B) <: (B $\longrightarrow$ B)
 (vi) (C $\longrightarrow$ A) <: (B $\longrightarrow$ B)
(vii) (A $\longrightarrow$ A) <: (B $\longrightarrow$ B)
(viii) (C $\longrightarrow$ C) <: (B $\longrightarrow$ B)

12.4 Subtyping and Public Data

This question asks you to review the issue of specializing the types of public member functions and consider the related issue of specializing the types of public data members. To make this question concrete, we use the example of circles and colored circles in C++. Colored circles get darker each time they are moved. We assume there is a class Point of points and class ColPoint of colored points with appropriate operations. Class Point is a public base class of ColPoint. The basic definition for circle is:

```
class Circle {
public:
    Circle(Point* c, float r) { center=c; radius=r; }

    Point* center;
    float radius;
    virtual Circle* move(float dx, float dy)
            {center->move(dx,dy); return(this);}
};
```

For each of the following definitions of colored circle, explain why a colored circle should or should not be considered a subtype of a circle, in principle. If a colored circle should not be a subtype, give some fragment of code that would be type correct if we considered colored circles to be a subtype of circles, but would lead to a type error at run time:

  (a) class ColCircle : public Circle {
       public:
           ColCircle(Point* c, float r, color cl) : Circle(c,r) { col=cl; }

           color col;
           virtual Circle* move(float dx, float dy)
                   {center->move(dx,dy); darken(); return(this);}
           virtual void darken()
                   {if (col==green) col=darkgreen;}
       };

  (b) Suppose we change the definition of ColCircle so that move returns a colored circle:

       class ColCircle : public Circle {

```
public:
    ColCircle(Point* c, float r, color cl) : Circle(c,r) { col=cl; }

    color col;
    virtual ColCircle* move(float dx, float dy)
                {center->move(dx,dy); darken(); return(this);}
    virtual void darken()
                {if (col==green) col=darkgreen;}
};
```

(c) Suppose that instead of representing the color of a circle by a separate data member, we replace points with colored points and use a colored point for the center of the circle. One advantage of doing so is that we can use all of the color operations provided for colored points, as illustrated by the darken member function below. This could be useful if we wanted to have the same color operations on a variety of geometric shapes:

```
class ColCircle : public Circle {
public:
    ColCircle(ColPoint* c, float r) : Circle(c,r) { }

    ColPoint* center;

    virtual ColCircle* move(float dx, float dy)
                {center->move(dx,dy); darken(); return(this);}
    virtual void darken()
                {center->darken();}
};
```

The important issue is the redefinition of the type of center. Assume that each ColCircle object has center and radius data fields at the same offset as the center and radius fields of a Circle object. In the modified version of C++ considered in this question, the declaration ColPoint* center does *not* mean that a ColCircle object has two center data fields.

12.5 Phantom Members

A C++ class may have virtual members that may be redefined in derived classes. However, there is no way to "undefine" a virtual (or nonvirtual) member. Suppose we extend C++ by adding another kind of member, called a *phantom* member, that is treated as virtual, but only defined in derived classes if an explicit definition is given. In other words, a "phantom" function is not inherited unless its name is listed in the derived class. For example, if we have two classes

```
class A {
...
public:
    phantom void f(){...}
    ...
};
class B : public A {
...
```

```
public:
    .../* no definition of f */
};
```

then f would appear in the vtbl for A objects and, if x is an A object, x . f() would be allowed. However, if f is not declared in B, then f might not need to appear in the vtbl for B objects and, if x is a B object, x . f() would not be allowed. Is this consistent with the design of C++, or is there some general property of the language that would be destroyed? If so, explain what this property is and why it would be destroyed.

12.6 Subtyping and Visibility

In C++, a virtual function may be given a different access level in a derived class. This produces some confusing situations. For example, this is legal C++, at least for some compilers:

```
class Base {
    public:
        virtual int f();
};
class Derived: public Base {
    private:
        virtual int f();
};
```

This question asks you to explain why this program conflicts with some reasonable principles, yet somehow does not completely break the C++ type system.

(a) In C++, a derived class D with public base class B is treated as a subtype of B. Explain why this is generally reasonable, given the definition of subtyping from class.

(b) Why would it be reasonable for someone to argue that it is *incorrect* to allow a public member inherited from a public base class to be redefined as private?

(c) A typical use of subtyping is to apply a function that expects an B argument to a D when D <: B. For example, here is a simple "toy" program that applies a function defined for base-class objects to a derived-class object. Explain why this program *compiles* and *executes* for the preceding Base and Derived classes (assuming we have given an implementation for f):

```
int g(Base &x) {
  return(x.f()+1);
}

int main() {
  Base b;
  cout << "g(b) = " << g(b) << endl;
  Derived d;
  cout << "g(d) = " << g(d) << endl;
}
```

(d) Do you think there is a mistake here in the design of C++ ? Briefly explain why or why not.

12.7 Private Virtual Functions

At first thought, the idea of a private virtual function might seem silly: Why would you want to redefine a function that is not visible outside the class? However, there is a programming idiom that makes use of private virtual functions in a reasonable way. This idiom is illustrated in the following code, which uses a public function to call a private virtual function:

```
class Computer {
  public:
  void retailPrice(void) {
     int p = 2 * manufactureCost();
     printf("$ %d \ n", p); // Print p
  }
  private:
  virtual int manufactureCost(void) {return 1000;}
};

class IBMComputer: public Computer {
  private:
  virtual int manufactureCost(void) {return 1500;}
};

int main(void) {
  Computer *cPtr = new Computer();
  IBMComputer *ibmPtr = new IBMComputer();
  Computer *cibmPtr = new IBMComputer();

  cPtr->retailPrice();
  ibmPtr->retailPrice();
  cibmPtr->retailPrice();
  return 0;
}
```

This question asks about how the function calls to retailPrice() are evaluated.

(a) Explain which version of manufactureCost() is used in the call cibmPtr-> retailPrice() and why.

(b) If the virtual keyword is omitted from the declaration of manufactureCost in the derived class IBMComputer, the preceding code will still compile without error and execute. Will manufactureCost be implemented as a virtual function in class IBMComputer? Use your knowledge of how C++ is implemented to explain why or why not.

(c) It is possible for the private base-class function to be declared public in the derived class. Does this conflict with subtyping principles? Explain why or why not in a few words.

12.8 "Like Current" in Eiffel

Eiffel is a statically typed object-oriented programming language designed by Bertrand Meyer and his collaborators. The language designers did not intend the language to have any type loopholes. However, there are some problems surrounding an Eiffel type expression called like current. When the words like current appear as a type in a method of some class, they mean, "the class that contains this method." To give an example, the following classes were considered statically type correct in the language Eiffel.

```
Class Point
    x : int
    method equals (pt : like current) : bool
        return self.x == pt.x

class ColPoint inherits Point
    color : string
    method equals (cpt : like current) : bool
        return self.x == cpt.x and self.color == cpt.color
```

In Point, the expression like current means the type Point, whereas in ColPoint, like current means the type ColPoint. However, the type checker accepts the redefinition of method equals because the declared parameter type is like current in both cases. In other words, the declaration of equals in Point says that the argument of p.equals should be of the same type as p, and the declaration of equals in ColPoint says the same thing. Therefore the types of equals are considered to match.

(a) Using the basic rules for subtyping objects and functions, explain why ColPoint should not be considered a subtype of Point "in principle."

(b) Give a short fragment of code that shows how a type error can occur if we consider ColPoint to be a subtype of Point.

(c) Why do you think the designers of Eiffel decided to allow subtyping in this case? In other words, why do you think they wanted like current in the language?

(d) When this error was pointed out (by W. Cook after the language had been in use for several years), the Eiffel designers decided not to remove like current, as this would "break" lots of existing code. Instead, they decided to modify the type checker to perform whole-program analysis. More specifically, the modified Eiffel type checker examined the whole Eiffel program to see if there was any statement that was likely to cause a type error.

i. What are some of the disadvantages of whole-program analysis? Do not just say, "it has to look at the whole program." Instead, think about trying to debug a program in a language in which the type checker uses whole-program analysis. Are there any situations in which the error messages would not be as useful as in traditional type checking in which the type of an expression depends only on the types of its parts?

ii. Suppose you were trying to design a type checker that allows safe uses of like current. What kind of statements or expressions would your type checker look for? How would you distinguish a type error from a safe use of like current?

12.9 Subtyping and Specifications

In the Eiffel programming language, methods can have preconditions and post-conditions. These are Boolean expressions that must be true before the method is called and true afterwards. For example, the pop method in the following Stack class has a precondition size > 0. This means that in order for the pop method to execute properly, the stack should be nonempty beforehand. The postcondition size′ = size - 1 means that the size after executing pop will be one less than the size before this method is called. The syntactic convention here is that a "primed variable," such as size′, indicates the value of that variable after execution of the method:

```
class Stack {
    ...
    int size
    ...
    void pop() pre: size > 0
                post: size′ = size - 1 {
        ...
    }
    ...
}
```

This question asks you about subtyping when preconditions and postconditions are considered part of the type of a method.

(a) In an implementation of stacks in which each stack has a maximum size, given by a constant MAX_SIZE, the push method might have the following form:

```
class FixedStack {
    ...
    int size
    ...
    void push() pre: size < MAX_SIZE {
        ...
    }
    ...
}
```

whereas without this size restriction, we could have a stack class

```
class Stack {
    ...
    int size
    ...
    void push() pre: true {
        ...
    }
    ...
}
```

with the precondition of push always satisfied. (For simplicity, there are no postconditions in this example.) If this is the only difference between the two classes, which one should be considered a subtype of the other? Explain briefly.

(b) Suppose that we have two classes that are identical except for the preconditions and postconditions on one method:

```
class A {
  ...
  int size
  ...
  void f() pre: PA, post: TA {
      ...
  }
  ...
}
class B {
  ...
  int size
  ...
  void f() pre: PB, post: TB {
      ...
  }
  ...
}
```

What relationships among PA, TA, PB, and TB should hold in order to have
B <: A? Explain briefly.

12.10 C++ Multiple Inheritance and Casts

An important aspect of C++ object and virtual function table (vtbl) layout is that if
class D has class B as a public base class, then the initial segment of every D object
must look like a B object, and similarly for the D and B virtual function tables.
The reason is that this makes it possible to access any B member data or member
function of a D object in exactly the same way we would access the B member data
or member function of a B object. Although this works out fairly easily with only
single inheritance, some effort must be put into the implementation of multiple
inheritance to make access to member data and member functions uniform across
publicly derived classes.

Suppose class C is defined by inheriting from classes A and B:

```
class A {
   public:
        int x;
        virtual void f();
};
class B {
   public:
        int y;
        virtual void f();
        virtual void g();
};
class C : public A, public B {
   public:
        int z;
        virtual void f();
};
C *pc = new C;   B *pb = pc;   A *pa = pc;
```

and pa, pb, and pc are pointers to the same object, but with different types. The representation of this object of class C and the values of the associated pointers are illustrated in this chapter.

(a) Explain the steps involved in finding the address of the function code in the call pc->f(). Be sure to distinguish what happens at compile time from what happens at run time. Which address is found, &A::f(), &B::f(), or &C::f()?

(b) The steps used to find the function address for pa->f() and to then call it are the same as for pc->f(). Briefly explain why.

(c) Do you think the steps used to find the function address for and to call pb->f() have to be the same as the other two, even though the offset is different? Why or why not?

(d) How could the call pc->g() be implemented?

12.11 Multiple Inheritance and Thunks

Suppose class C is defined by inheriting from classes A and B:

```
class A {
    public:
        virtual void g();
        int x;
};
class B {
    public:
        int y;
        virtual B* f();
        virtual void g();
};
class C : public A, public B {
    public:
        int z;
        virtual C* f();
        virtual void g();
};
C *pc = new C;   B *pb = pc;   A *pa = pc;
```

and pa, pb, and pc are pointers to the same object, but with different types.

Then, pa and pc will contain the same value, but pb will contain a different value; it will contain the address of the B part of the C object. The fact that pb and pc do not contain the same value means that in C++, a cast sometimes has a run-time cost. (In C this is never the case.)

Note that in our example B::f and C::f do not return the same type. Instead, C::f returns a C* whereas B::f returns a B*. That is legal because C is derived from B, and thus a C* can always be used in place of a B*.

However, there is a problem: When the compiler sees pb->f() it does not know whether the call will return a B* or a C*. Because the caller is expecting a B*, the compiler must make sure to return a valid pointer to a B*. The solution is to have the C-as-B vtable contain a pointer to a *thunk*. The thunk calls C::f, and then adjusts the return value to be a B*, before returning.

(a) Draw all of the vtables for the classes in these examples. Show to which function each vtable slot points.

(b) Does the fact that casts in C++ sometimes have a run-time cost, whereas C never does, indicate that C++ has not adhered to the principles given in class for its design? Why or why not?

(c) Because thunks are expensive and because C++ charges programmers only for features they use, there must be a feature, or combination of features, that are imposing this cost. What feature or features are these?

12.12 Dispatch on State

One criticism of dynamic dispatch as found in C++ and Java is that it is not flexible enough. The operations performed by methods of a class usually depend on the state of the receiver object. For example, we have all seen code similar to the following file implementation:

```
class StdFile {
    private:
        enum { OPEN, CLOSED } state; /* state can only be either OPENor CLOSED */

    public:
        StdFile() { state = CLOSED; }          /* initial state is closed */
        void Open() {
            if (state == CLOSED) {
                /* open file ... */
                state = OPEN;
            } else {
                error "file already open";
            }
        }
        void Close() {
            if (state == OPEN ) {
                /* close file ... */
                state = CLOSED;
            } else {
                error "file not open";
            }
        }
    }
}
```

Each method must determine the state of the object (*i.e.,* whether or not the file is already open) before performing any operations. Because of this, it seems useful to extend dynamic dispatch to include a way of dispatching not only on the class of the receiver, but also on the state of the receiver. Several object-oriented programming languages, including BETA and Cecil, have various mechanisms to do this. In this problem we examine two ways in which we can extend dynamic dispatch in C++ to depend on state. First, we present dispatch on three pieces of information:

- the name of the method being invoked
- the type of the receiver object
- the explicit state of the receiver object

As an example, the following declares and creates objects of the File class with the new dispatch mechanism:

```
class File {
    state in { OPEN, CLOSED };    /* declare states that a File object may be in */

    public:
        File() { state = CLOSED; }    /* initial state is closed */
        switch(state) {

        case CLOSED: {
            void Open() {         /* 1 */
                /* open file ... */
                state = OPEN;
            }
            void Close() {
                error "file not open";
            }
        }

        case OPEN: {
            void Open() {         /* 2 */
                error "file already open";
            }
            void Close() {
                /* close file ... */
                state = CLOSED;
            }
        }
    }
}

File* f = new File();
f->Open();    /* calls version 1 */
f->Open();    /* calls version 2 */
...
```

The idea is that the programmer can provide a different implementation of the same method for each state that the object can be in.

(a) Describe one advantage of having this new feature, i.e., are there any advantages to writing classes like File over classes like StdFile. Describe one disadvantage of having this new feature.

(b) For this part of the problem, assume that subclasses cannot add any new states to the set of states inherited from the base class. Describe an object representation that allows for efficient method lookup. Method call should be as fast as virtual method calls in C++, and changing the state of an object should be a constant time operation. (*Hint*: you may want to have a different vtable for each state). Is this implementation acceptable according to the C++ design goal of only paying for the features that you use?

(c) What problems arise if subclasses are allowed to extend the set of possible states? For example, we could now write a class such as

```
class SharedFile: public File {
    state in { OPEN, CLOSED, READONLY };    /* extend the set of states */
    ...
}
```

Do not try to solve any of these problems. Just identify several of them.

(d) We may generalize this notion of dispatch based on the state of an object to dispatch based on any predicate test. For example, consider the following Stack class:

```
class Stack {
private:
    int n;
    int elems[100];

public:
    Stack() { n = 0; }

    when(n == 0) {
        int Pop() {
            error "empty";
        }
    }

    when(n > 0) {
        int Pop() {
            return elems[--n];
        }
    }
    ...
}
```

Is there an easy way to extend your proposed implementation in part (b) to handle dispatch on predicate tests? Why or why not?

13

Portability and Safety: Java

The Java programming language was designed by James Gosling and others at Sun Microsystems. The language, arising from a project that began in 1990, was originally called *Oak* and was intended for use in a device affectionately referred to as a *set-top box*. The set-top box was intended to be a small computational device, attached to a network of some kind, and placed on top of a television set. There are various features a set-top box might provide. You can imagine some of your own by supposing that a web browser is displayed on your television set and, instead of a keyboard, you click on icons by using some buttons on your remote control. You might want to select a television program or movie or download a small computer simulation that could be executed on the computational device and displayed on your screen. A television advertisement for an automobile might allow you to download an interactive visual tour of the automobile, giving each viewer a personalized simulation of driving the car down the road. Whatever scenario might appeal to you, the computing environment would involve graphics, execution of simple programs, and communication between a remote site and a program executed locally.

At some point in the development of Oak, engineers and managers at Sun Microsystems realized that there was an immediate need for an Internet-browser programming language, a language that could be used to write small applications that could be transmitted over the network and executed under the control of any standard browser on any standard platform. The need for a standard is a result of the intrinsic desire of companies and individuals with web sites to be able to reach as large an audience as possible. In addition to portability, there is also a need for security so that someone downloading a small application can execute the program without fear of computer viruses or other hazards.

The Oak language started as a reimplementation of C++. Although language design was not an end goal of the project, language design became an important focus of the group. Some of the reasons for designing a new language are given in this overly dramatic but still informative quote from "The Java Saga" by David Bank in *Hot Wired* (December 1995):

Photo by Mast Photography

JAMES GOSLING

James Gosling was the lead engineer and key architect behind the Java programming language and platform. He is now back in Sun's research laboratories, working on software development tools. His first project at Sun was the NeWS window system, distributed for Sun workstations in the 1980s. Before joining Sun, Gosling built a multiprocessor version of UNIX; the original Andrew window system and toolkit; and several compilers and mail systems. He is known to many as the author of the original UNIX 'Emacs.'

A techie with a sense of humor, Gosling is shown in the right-hand photograph about to put a pie in the face of a stagehand wearing a Bill Gates mask, in a picture from his partially politicized web page at http://java.sun.com/people/jag/.

James Gosling received a B.S. in Computer Science from the University of Calgary, Canada, and a Ph.D. in Computer Science from Carnegie-Mellon University for a dissertation entitled, "The Algebraic Manipulation of Constraints."

Gosling quickly concluded that existing languages weren't up to the job. C++ had become a near-standard for programmers building specialized applications where speed is everything... But C++ wasn't reliable enough for what Gosling had in mind. It was fast, but its interfaces were inconsistent, and programs kept on breaking. However, in consumer electronics, reliability is more important than speed. Software interfaces had to be as dependable as a two-pronged plug fitting into an electrical wall socket. "I came to the conclusion that I needed a new programming language," Gosling says.

For a variety of reasons, including a tremendous marketing effort by Sun Microsystems, Java became surprisingly successful a short time after it was released as an Internet communication language in mid-1995.

The main parts of the Java system are

- the Java programming language,

- Java compilers and run-time systems (Java virtual machine),
- an extensive library, including a Java toolkit for graphic display and other applications, and sample Java applets.

Although the library and toolkit helped with early adoption, we will be primarily interested in the programming language, its implementation, and the way language design and implementation considerations influenced each other. Gosling, more modest in real life than the preceding quote might suggest, has this to say about languages that influenced Java: "One of the most important influences on the design of Java was a much earlier language called *Simula*. It is the first OO language I ever used (on a CDC 6400!).... [and] where the concept of a 'class' was invented."

13.1 JAVA LANGUAGE OVERVIEW

13.1.1 Java Language Goals

The Java programming language and execution environment were designed with the following goals in mind:

- *Portability:* It must be easy to transmit programs over the network and have them run correctly in the receiving environment, regardless of the hardware, operating system, or web browser used.
- *Reliability:* Because programs will be run remotely by users who did not write the code, error messages and program crashes should be avoided as much as possible.
- *Safety:* The computing environment receiving a program must be protected from programmer errors and malicious programming.
- *Dynamic Linking:* Programs are distributed in parts, with separate parts loaded into the Java run-time environment as needed.
- *Multithreaded Execution:* For concurrent programs to run on a variety of hardware and operating systems, the language must include explicit support and a standard interface for concurrent programming.
- *Simplicity and Familiarity:* The language should appeal to your average website designer, typically a C programmer or a programmer partially familiar with C/C++.
- *Efficiency:* This is important, but may be secondary to other considerations.

Generally speaking, the reduced emphasis on efficiency gave the Java designers more flexibility than the C++ designers had.

13.1.2 Design Decisions

Some of the design goals and global design decisions are listed in Table 13.1, in which + indicates that a decision contributes to this goal, − indicates that a decision detracts from this goal, and +/− indicates that there are advantages and disadvantages of the decision. Some squares are left blank, indicating that a design decision has little or no effect on the goal. We can see the relative importance of efficiency in the Java design process by looking down the rightmost column. This does not mean that efficiency

Table 13.1. Java design decisions

	Portability	Safety	Simplicity	Efficiency
Interpreted	+	+		−
Type safe	+	+	+/−	+/−
Most values are object	+/−	+/−	+	−
Objects by means of pointers	+		+	−
Garbage collection	+	+	+	−
Concurrency support	+	+		

was sacrificed needlessly, only that relative to other goals, efficiency was not the primary objective.

Interpreted. The initial and most widely used implementations of Java are based on interpreted bytecode. This is discussed in more detail in Section 13.4. In brief, Java programs are compiled to a simplified form of lower-level language. This language, called *Java bytecode*, is the form that is usually used when Java programs are sent across the network as parts of web pages. Java bytecode is executed by an interpreter called the *Java virtual machine* (JVM). One advantage of this architecture is that once a JVM is implemented for a particular hardware and operating system, all Java programs can be run on that platform without change. In addition to portability, interpreted bytecode facilitates safe execution, as commands that violate the semantics of the Java language can be recognized just before they are executed. A good example is array-bounds checking. It is not feasible to tell at compile time whether a program will access arrays out of bounds. However, the JVM does run-time tests to make sure that no Java program accesses memory incorrectly through out-of-bounds array indexing.

Type Safety. There are three levels of type safety in Java. The first is compile-time type checking of Java source code. The Java type checker works like other conventional type checkers (as in Pascal, C++, and so on), preventing compilation of programs that do not conform to the Java type discipline. There is no pointer arithmetic, there are no unchecked type casts, and the language is garbage collected, proving a greater degree of type safety than C++, for example. The second level of type safety is provided by type-checking Java bytecode programs before they are executed. The third level is provided by run-time type checks, such as the array-bounds checks described in the preceding subsection. In addition to safety, the Java type system simplifies the language to some degree by eliminating constructs that would complicate the language semantics or run-time system. There are some efficiency costs associated with run-time checking, however.

Objects and References. In Java, many things are objects but not all things. In particular, values of certain basic types such as integers, Booleans, and strings are not objects. This is a compromise between simplicity and efficiency. In particular, if all integer operations required dynamic method lookup, this would slow down integer arithmetic considerably. A simplifying decision associated with objects is that all objects are accessed by pointer, and pointer assignment is the only form of assignment provided for all objects. This simplifies programs by eliminating some special cases, but in some situations reduces program efficiency.

All parameters to Java methods are passed by value. When the parameter has a reference type (including all objects and arrays), though, it is the reference itself that is copied and passed by value. In effect, this means that values of primitive types are passed by value and objects are passed by reference.

Garbage Collection. As discussed in Subsection 6.2.1, garbage collection is necessary for complete type safety. Garbage collection also simplifies programming by eliminating the need for code that determines whether memory can be deallocated, but has a run-time cost. Java garbage collection takes advantage of concurrency. Specifically, the Java garbage collector is implemented as a low priority background thread, allowing garbage collection to occur during times when it might not affect a user's perception of running speed.

Dynamic Linking. The classes defined and used in a Java program may be loaded into the JVM incrementally, as they are needed by the running program. This shortens the elapsed time between the beginning of transmission of a program across the network and the beginning of program execution, as the program can begin executing before all of the related code is transmitted. Moreover, if a program terminates without needing some classes, these classes never need to be transmitted or loaded into the virtual machine. Dynamic linking does not have a large effect on the language design, other than to require clear interfaces that can be used to check one part of a program under assumptions about the code provided by another part of the program.

Concurrency Support. Java has a concurrency model based on threads, which are independent concurrent processes. This is a significant part of the language, both because the design is substantial and because of the importance of having standardized concurrency primitives as part of the Java language. Clearly, if Java programs relied on operating system specific concurrency mechanisms, Java programs would not be portable across different operating system platforms.

Simplicity. Although Java has grown over the years, and features like reflection and inner classes may not seem "simple," the language is still smaller and simpler in design than most production-quality general-purpose programming languages. One way to see the relative simplicity of Java is to list the C++ features that do not appear in Java. These include the following features:

- *Structures and unions:* Structures are subsumed by objects, and some uses of unions can be replaced with classes that share a common superclass.
- *Functions* can be replaced with static methods.
- *Multiple inheritance* is complex and most cases can be avoided if the simpler interface concept of Java is used.
- *Goto* is not necessary.
- *Operator overloading* is complex and deemed unnecessary; Java functions can be overloaded.
- *Automatic coercions* are complex and deemed unnecessary.
- *Pointers* are the default for objects and are not needed for other types. As a result a separate pointer type is not needed.

Some of these features appear in C++ primarily because of the C++ design goal of backward compatibility with C. Others were omitted from Java after some discussion, because it was decided that complexity of including them was more significant than the functionality they would provide. The most significant omissions are multiple inheritance, automatic conversions, operator overloading, and pointer operations of the forms found in C and C++.

13.2 JAVA CLASSES AND INHERITANCE

13.2.1 Classes and Objects

Java is written in a C++-like syntax so that programming is more accessible to C and C++ programmers. This makes the C++ one-dimensional point class used in Subsection 12.3.1 look similar when translated into Java. Here is an abbreviated version of the class, with the move method omitted:

```
class Point {
    public int getX() { ... }
    protected void setX (int x) { ... }
    private int x;
    Point(int xval) {x = xval;}
};
```

Like other class-based languages, Java classes declare the data and functions associated with all objects created by this class. When a Java object is created, space is allocated to store the data fields of the object and the constructor of the class is called to initialize the data fields. As in C++, the constructor has the same name as the class. Also following C++, the Point class has public, private, and protected components. Although public, private, and protected are keywords of Java, these visibility specifications do not mean exactly the same thing in the two languages, as explained in Subsection 13.2.2.

Java terminology is slightly different from that of Simula, Smalltalk and C++. Here is a brief summary of the most important terms used to discuss Java:

■ *Class* and *object* have essentially the same meaning as in other class-based object-oriented languages, *field:* data member
■ *Method:* member function, *static member:* analogous to Smalltalk class field or class method, *this:* like C++ this or Smalltalk self, the identifier this in the body of a Java method refers to the object on which this method was invoked
■ *Native Method:* method written in another language, such as C
■ *Package:* set of classes in shared name space.

We will look at several characteristics of classes and objects in Java, including static fields and methods, overloading, finalize methods, main methods, toString methods used to produce a print representation of an object, and the possibility of defining native methods. We will discuss the Java run-time representation of objects and the implementation of method lookup in Section 13.4 in connection with other aspects of the architecture of the run-time system.

Initialization. Java guarantees that a constructor is called whenever an object is created. Because some interesting issues arise with inheritance, this is discussed in Subsection 13.2.3.

Static Fields and Methods. Java static fields and methods are similar to Smalltalk class variables and class methods. If a field is declared to be static, then there is one field for the entire class, instead of one per object. If a method is declared static, the method may be called without using an object of the class. In particular, static methods may be called before any objects of the class are created. Static methods can access only static fields and other static methods; they cannot refer to this because they are not part of any specific object of the class. Outside a class, a static member is usually accessed with the class name, as in class_name.static_method(args), rather than through an object reference.

Static fields may be initialized with initialization expressions or a *static initialization block*. Both are illustrated in the following code:

```
class ... {
  /* --- static variable with initial value --- */
  static int x = initial_value;
  /* --- static initialization block      --- */
  static { /* code to be executed once, when class is loaded */
  }
}
```

As indicated in the program comment, the static initialization block of a class is executed once, when the class is loaded. Class loading is discussed in Section 13.4 in connection with the JVM. There are specific rules governing the order of static initialization, when a class contains both initialization expressions and a static initialization block. There are also restrictions on the form of static initialization blocks. For example, a static block cannot raise an exception, as it is not certain that a corresponding handler will be installed at class-loading time.

Overloading. Java overloading is based on the signature of a method, which consists of the method name, the number of parameters, and the type of each parameter. If two methods of a class (whether both declared in the same class, or both inherited, or one declared and one inherited) have the same name but different signatures, then the method name is overloaded. As in other languages, overloading is resolved at compile time.

Garbage Collection and Finalize: Because Java is garbage collected, it is not necessary to explicitly free objects. In addition, programmers do not need to worry about dangling references created by premature deallocation of objects. However, garbage collection reclaims only the space used by an object. If an object holds access to another sort of resource, such as a lock on shared data, then this must be freed when the object is no longer accessible. For this reason, Java objects may have finalize methods, which are called under two conditions, by the garbage collector just before the space is reclaimed and by the virtual machine when the virtual machine exits. A useful convention in finalize methods is to call super.finalize, as subsequently illustrated, so that any termination code associated with the superclass is also executed:

```
class ... {
  ...
  protected void finalize () {
    super.finalize();
    close(file);
  }
};
```

There is an interesting interaction between finalize methods and the Java exception mechanism. Any uncaught exceptions raised while a finalize method is executed are ignored.

A programming problem associated with finalize methods is that the programmer does not have explicit control over when a finalize method is called. This decision is left to the run-time system. This can create problems if an object holds a lock on a shared resource, for example, as the lock may not be freed until the garbage collector determines that the program needs more space. One solution is to put operations such as freeing all locks or other resources in a method that is explicitly called in the program. This works well, as long as all users of the class know the name of the method and remember to call this method when the object is no longer needed.

Some other interesting aspects of Java objects and classes are main methods used to start program execution, toString methods used to produce a print representation of an object, and the possibility of defining native methods:

- main: A Java application is invoked with the name of the class that drives the application. This class must have a main method, which must be public, static, must return void, and must accept a single argument of type String[]. The main method is called with the program arguments in a string array. Any class with a main method can be invoked directly as if it were a stand-alone application, which can be useful for testing.
- toString: A class may define a toString method, which is called when a conversion to string type is needed, as in printing an object.
- native methods: A native method is one written in another language, such as C. Portability and safety are reduced with native methods: Native code cannot be shipped over the network on demand, and controls incorporated into the JVM are ineffective because the method is not interpreted by the virtual machine. The reasons for using native methods are (1) efficiency of native object code and (2) access to utilities or programs that have already been written in another language.

13.2.2 Packages and Visibility

Java has four visibility distinctions for fields and methods, three corresponding to C++ visibility levels and a fourth arising from packages.

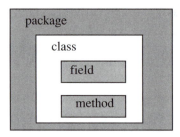

Figure 13.1. Java package and class visibility.

Java *packages* are an encapsulation mechanism similar to C++ name space that allows related declarations to be grouped together, with some declarations hidden from other packages. In a Java program, every field or method belongs to a specific class and every class is part of a package, as shown in Figure 13.1. A class can belong to the unnamed default package, or some other package if specified in the file containing the class.

The visibility distinctions in Java are

- *public:* accessible anywhere the class is visible,
- *protected:* accessible to methods of the class and any subclasses, as well as to other classes in the same package,
- *private:* accessible only in the class itself,
- *package:* accessible only to code in the same package; not visible to subclasses in other packages. Members declared without an access modifier have package visibility.

Put another way, a method can refer to the private members of the class it belongs to, nonprivate members of all classes in the same package, protected members of superclasses (including superclasses in a different package), and public members of all classes in any visible package.

Names declared in another package can be accessed with import, which imports declarations from another package, or with qualified names of the following form, which indicate the package containing the name explicitly:

$$\underbrace{\text{java.lang}}_{\text{package}} . \underbrace{\text{String}}_{\text{class}} . \underbrace{\text{substring()}}_{\text{method}}$$

13.2.3 Inheritance

In Java terminology, a *subclass* inherits from its *superclass*. The Java inheritance mechanism is essentially similar to that of Smalltalk, C++, and other class-based object-oriented languages. The syntax associated with inheritance is similar to C++, with the keyword extends, as shown in this example ColorPoint class extending the Point class from Subsection 13.2.1:

```
class ColorPoint extends Point {
    // Additional fields and methods
    private Color c;
    protected void setC (Color d) {c = d;}
    public Color getC() {return c;}
    // Define constructor
    ColorPoint(int xval, Color cval) {
        super(xval); // call Point constructor
        c = cval; }   // initialize ColorPoint field
};
```

Method Overriding and Field Hiding. As in other languages, a class inherits all the fields and methods of its superclass, except when a field or method of the same name is declared in the subclass. When a method name in the subclass is the same as a method name in the superclass, the subclass definition *overrides* the superclass method with the same signature. An overriding method must not conflict with the definition that it overrides by having a different return type. An overridden method of the superclass can be accessed with the keyword super. For fields, a field declaration in a subclass hides any superclass field with the same name. A hidden field can be accessed by use of a qualified name (if it is static) or by use of a field access expression that contains a cast to a superclass type or the keyword super.

Constructors. Java guarantees that a constructor is called whenever an object is created. In compiling the constructor of a subclass, the compiler checks to make sure that the superclass constructor is called. This is done in a specific way that programmers generally want to take into consideration. In particular, if the first statement of a subclass constructor is not a call to super, then the call super() is inserted automatically by the compiler. This does not always work well, because, if the superclass does not have a constructor with no arguments, the call super() will not match a declared constructor, and a compiler error results. An exception to this check occurs if one constructor invokes another. In this case, the first constructor does not need to call the superclass constructor, but the second one must. For example, if the constructor declaration ColorPoint() { ColorPoint(0,blue);} is added to the preceding ColorPoint class, then this constructor is compiled without inserting a call to the superclass Point constructor.

A slight oddity of Java is that the inheritance conventions for finalize are different from the conventions for constructors. Although a call to the superclass is required for constructors, the compiler does not force a call to the superclass finalize method in a subclass finalize method.

Final Methods and Classes. Java contains an interesting mechanism for restricting subclasses of a class: A method or an entire class can be declared final. If a method is declared final, then the method cannot be overridden in any subclass. If a class is declared final, then the class cannot have any subclasses. The reason for this feature is that a programmer may wish to define the behavior of all objects of a certain type. Because subclasses produce subtypes, as discussed in Section 13.3, this requires some restriction on subclasses. To give an extreme example, the singleton pattern discussed in Section 10.4 shows how to design a class so that only one object of the class can be created. The pattern hides the constructor of the class and makes public only a function that will call the constructor once during program execution. This pattern solves the problem of restricting the number of objects of the class, but only if no subclass overrides the public method with a method that can create more than one object. If a programmer really wants to enforce the singleton pattern, there must be a way to keep other programmers from defining subclasses of the singleton class.

The Java class java.lang.System is another example of a final class. This class is final so that programmers do not override system methods.

In a loose sense, Java final is the opposite of C++ virtual: Java methods can be overridden until they are marked final, whereas C++ member functions can be overridden only if they are virtual. The analogy is not exact, though, as a C++ member function cannot be virtual in one class and nonvirtual in a base class or derived class, because that would violate the requirement that base- and derived-class vtables must have the same layout.

Class *Object*. In principle, every class declared in a Java program extends another class, as a class without an explicit superclass is interpreted as a subclass of the class Object. The class Object is the one class that has no superclasses. Class Object contains the following methods, which can be overridden in derived classes:

- GetClass, which returns the Class object that represents the class of the object. This can be used to discover the fully qualified name of a class, its members, its immediate superclass, and any interfaces that it implements.
- ToString, which returns a String representation of an object.
- equals, which defines a notion of object equality based on value, not reference, comparison.
- hashCode, which returns an integer that can be used to store the object in a hash table.
- clone, which is used to make a duplicate of an object.
- Methods wait, notify, and notifyAll used in concurrent programming.
- finalize, which is run just before an object is destroyed (discussed in Subsection 13.2.1 in connection with garbage collection),

Because all classes inherit the methods of class Object, every object has these methods.

13.2.4 Abstract Classes and Interfaces

The Java language has an *abstract-class* mechanism that is similar to C++. As we discussed in Chapter 12, an abstract class is a class that does not implement all of its methods and therefore cannot have any instances. Java uses the keyword abstract instead of the C++ "=0" syntax, as shown in the following code:

```
abstract class Shape {
   . . .
   abstract point center();
   abstract void rotate(degrees d);
   . . .
}
```

Java also has a "pure abstract" form of class called an interface. An interface is defined in a manner similar to that of a class, except that all interface members must be constants or abstract methods. An interface has no direct implementation, but classes may be declared to implement an interface. In addition, an interface may be declared as an extension of another, providing a form of interface inheritance.

One reason that Java programmers use interfaces instead of pure abstract classes when a concept is being defined but not implemented is that Java allows a single class to implement several interfaces, whereas a class can have only one superclass. The following interfaces and class illustrate this possibility. The Shape interface identifies some properties of simple geometric shapes, namely, each has a center point and a rotate method. Drawable similarly identifies properties of objects that can be displayed on a screen. If circles are geometric shapes that can be displayed on a screen, then the Circle class can be declared to implement both Shape and Drawable, as subsequently shown.

Interfaces are often used as the type of argument to a method. For example, if the windows system has a method for drawing items on a screen, then the argument type of this method could be Drawable, allowing every object that implements the Drawable interface to be displayed:

```
interface Shape {
    public Point center();
    public void rotate(float degrees);
}
interface Drawable {
    public void setColor(Color c);
    public void draw();
}
class Circle implements Shape, Drawable {
    // does not inherit any implementation
    // but must define Shape, Drawable methods
}
```

Unlike C++ multiple inheritance (discussed in Section 12.5), there is no name clash problem for Java interfaces. More specifically, suppose that the preceding two interfaces Shape and Circle also both define a Size method. If the two Size methods both have the same number of arguments and the same argument types, then class Circle must implement one Size method with this number of arguments and the argument types given in both interfaces. On the other hand, if the two Size methods have a different number of arguments or the arguments can be distinguished by type, then these are considered two different method names and Circle must define an implementation for each one. Because Java method lookup uses the method name and number and types of arguments to select the method code, the two methods with the same name will be treated separately at method lookup time.

13.3 JAVA TYPES AND SUBTYPING

13.3.1 Classification of Types

The Java types are divided into two categories: primitive types and reference types. The eight primitive types are the boolean type and seven numeric types. The seven numeric types are the forms of integers byte, short, int, long, and char and the floating-point types float and double. The three forms of reference types are class types, interface types (subsequently discussed), and array types. There is also a special null type. The values of a reference type are references to objects (which include arrays). All objects, including arrays, support the methods of class Object.

The subtyping relationships between the main families of types are illustrated in Figure 13.2, which includes a Shape interface and Circle and Square classes to show how user-defined classes and interfaces fit into the picture. Other predefined types such as String, ClassLoader, and Thread occupy positions similar to that of Exception in this figure. Object[] is the type of arrays of objects, and similarly for array types Shape[], Circle[], and Square[].

Although it is standard Java terminology to call Object and its subtypes reference types, this may be slightly confusing. Although C++ distinguishes Object from Object *, there are no explicit pointer types in Java. Instead, the difference between a pointer to an object and an object itself is implicit, with pointer dereferencing combined with operations like method invocation and field access. If T is a reference type, then a variable x of type T is a reference to T objects; in C++ the variable x would have type T*. Because there is no explicit way to dereference x to get a value of type T, Java does not have a separate type for objects not referred to by pointer.

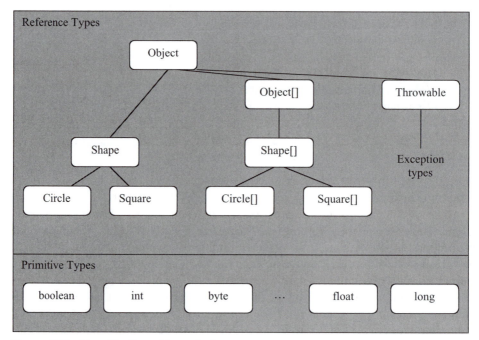

Figure 13.2. Classification of types in Java.

Because every class is a subtype of Object, variables of type Object can refer to objects or arrays of any type.

13.3.2 Subtyping for Classes and Interfaces

Subtyping for classes is determined by the class hierarchy and the interface mechanism. Specifically, if a class A extends class B, then the type of A objects is a subtype of the type of B objects. There is no other way for one class to define a subtype of another, and no private base classes (as in C++) to allow inheritance without subtyping.

A class may be declared to implement one or more interfaces, meaning that any instance of the class implements all the abstract methods specified in the interface. This (multiple) interface subtyping allows objects to support (multiple) common behaviors without sharing any common implementation.

Run-Time Type Conversion. Java does not allow unchecked casts. However, objects of a supertype may be cast to a subtype by a mechanism that includes a run-time type test. If you want to make a list class in Java, you make it hold objects of type Object. Objects of any class can then be put onto a list, but, to take them off the list and use them nontrivially, they must be converted back to their original type (or some supertype). In Java, type conversion is checked at run time, raising an exception if the object does not have the designated type.

Implementation. Java uses different bytecode instructions for member lookup by interface and member lookup by class or subclass. In a high-performance compiler, lookup by class could be implemented as in C++, with offset known at compile time. However, lookup by interface cannot, because a class may implement many interfaces and the interfaces may list members in different orders. This is discussed in detail in Subsection 13.4.4.

13.3.3 Arrays, Covariance, and Contravariance

For any type T, Java has an *array* type T[ ] of arrays whose elements have type T. Although array types are grouped with classes and interfaces, it is not possible to inherit from an array type. In Java terminology, array types are final.

Array types are subtypes of Object, and therefore arrays support all of the methods associated with class Object. Like other reference types, an array variable is a pointer to an array and can be null. It is common to create arrays when an array reference is declared, as in

```
Circle[ ] x = new Circle[array_size]
```

However, it is also possible to create array objects "anonymously," in much the same way that we can create other Java objects. For example,

```
new int[ ] {1,2,3, ... 10}
```

is an expression that creates an integer array of length 10, with values 1, 2, 3, . . . , 10. Because a variable of type T[ ] can be assigned an array of any length, the length of an array is not part of its static type.

There are some complications surrounding the way that Java array types are placed in the subtype hierarchy. The most significant decision is that if A <: B then the Java type checker also uses the subtyping A[ ] <: B[ ]. This introduces a problem often referred to as the *array covariance problem*. Consider the following class and array declarations:

```
class A { ... }
class B extends A { ... }
B[ ] bArray = new B[10]
A[ ] aArray = bArray        // considered OK since B[ ] <: A[ ]
aArray[0] = new A()    // allowed but run-time type error; raises
ArrayStoreException
```

In this code, we have B <: A because class B extends class A. The array reference bArray refers to an array of B objects, initially all null, and the array reference aArray refers to the same array. The declaration A[ ] aArray = bArray is allowed by the Java type checker (although semantically it should not be allowed) because of the Java design decision that if B <: A then B[ ] <: A[ ]. The problem with allowing the A[ ] array reference aArray to refer to an array of B objects is illustrated by the last statement. The assignment aArray[0] = new A() looks perfectly reasonable: aArray is an array with static type A[ ], suggesting that it is acceptable to assign an A object to any location in the array. However, because aArray actually refers to an array of B objects, this assignment would violate the type of bArray. Because this assignment would cause a typing problem, the Java implementation does not allow the assignment to be executed. A run-time test will determine that the value being assigned to an array of B objects is not a B object and the ArrayStoreException exception will be raised.

Although the Java designers considered array covariance advantageous for some specific purposes (writing some binary copy routines), array covariance in Java leads to some confusion and many run-time tests. It does not seem to be a successful language design decision.

13.3.4 Java Exception Class Hierarchy

Java programs may declare, raise, and handle exceptions. The Java exception mechanism has the general features we discussed in Section 8.2. Java exceptions may be the result of a throw statement in a user program or the result of some error condition detected by the virtual machine such as an attempt to index outside the bounds of an array. In Java terminology, an exception is said to be *thrown* from the point where it occurred and is said to be *caught* at the point to which control is transferred. As in other languages, throwing an exception causes the Java implementation to halt every expression, statement, method or constructor invocation, initializer, and field initialization expression that has started but not completed execution. This process continues until a handler is found that matches the class of the exception that is thrown.

One interesting aspect of the Java exception mechanism is the way that it is integrated into the class and type hierarchy. Every Java exception is represented by an instance of the class Throwable or one of its subclasses. An advantage of representing exceptions as objects is that an exception object can be used to carry information from the point at which an exception occurs to the handler that catches it. Subtyping can also be used in handling an exception: A handler matches the class of an exception if it explicitly names the class of the exception that is thrown or names some superclass of the class of the exception.

The Java exception mechanism is designed to work well in multithreaded (concurrent) programs. When an exception is thrown, only the thread in which the throw occurs is affected. The effect of an exception on the concurrent synchronization mechanism is that locks are released as synchronized statements and invocations of synchronized methods complete abruptly. We will return to this topic in Chapter 14.

Java exceptions are caught inside a construct called a *try-finally block*. Here is an example outline, showing a block with two handlers, each identified by the catch keyword. Intuitively, a try-finally block tries to execute a sequence of statements. If the sequence of statements terminates normally, then that is the end result of the block. However, if an exception is raised, it may be caught inside the block. If an exception is raised and caught, then the sequence of statements following the keyword finally will be executed after the exception handler has finished:

```
try {
        ⟨statements⟩
} catch ((⟨ex-type1⟩ ⟨identifier1⟩)) {
        ⟨statements⟩
} catch ((⟨ex-type2⟩ ⟨identifier2⟩)) {
        ⟨statements⟩
} finally {
        ⟨statements⟩
}
```

Although it may not be apparent why, there is some complication in the JVM associated with try-finally blocks. Specifically, a significant fraction of the complexity of the Java bytecode verifier is a result of the way finally clauses are implemented as a form of "local subroutine" (called jsr) in the Java bytecode interpreter. We will discuss the JVM in Section 13.4.

The classes of exceptions are shown in Figure 13.3. Every exception is, by definition, an object of some subclass of Throwable. The class Throwable is a direct subclass of Object. Programs can use the preexisting exception classes in throw statements or define additional exception classes. Additional exceptions classes must be subclasses of Throwable or one of its subclasses. To take advantage of the Java platform's compile-time checking for exception handlers, it is typical to define most new exception classes as checked exception classes. These are subclasses of Exception that are not subclasses of RuntimeException.

The phrases checked exceptions and "unchecked exceptions" refer to compile-time checking of the set of exceptions that may be thrown in a Java program. The

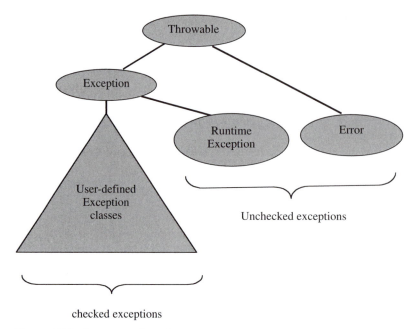

Figure 13.3. Java exception classes.

Java compiler checks, at compile time, that a program contains handlers for every checked exception. We accomplish this by analyzing the checked exceptions that can be thrown during execution of a method or constructor. These checks are based on the declared set of exceptions that a Java method could throw, called the throws clause of the method. For each checked exception that is a possible result of a method call, the throws clause for the method must mention the class of that exception or one of the superclasses of the class of that exception. This compile-time checking for the presence of exception handlers is designed to reduce the number of exceptions that are not properly handled.

Because Error and RuntimeException exceptions are generally thrown by the Java run-time system and not by the user code, it is not necessary for a programmer to declare these exceptions in the throws clause of a method. More specifically, the run-time exception classes (RuntimeException and its subclasses) are exempt from compile-time checking because, in the judgment of the designers of the Java programming language, declaring such exceptions would not aid significantly in establishing the correctness of programs. Many of the operations and constructs of the Java programming language can result in run-time exceptions. The information available to a compiler and the level of analysis the compiler performs are usually not sufficient to establish that such run-time exceptions cannot occur, even though this may be obvious to the programmer.

Ordinary programs do not usually recover from exceptions from the class Error or its subclasses. The class Error is a separate subclass of Throwable, distinct from Exception in the class hierarchy, to allow programs to use the idiom

```
} catch (Exception e) {
```

to catch all exceptions from which recovery may be possible without catching errors from which recovery is typically not possible.

13.3.5 Subtype Polymorphism and Generic Programming

In Section 9.4, we discussed some approaches to generic programming based on templates and related mechanisms such as generic modules and packages. The main idea is that we can define a generic data structure, such as a list or binary search tree, so that any type of data can be inserted into or retrieved from the data structure, provided that a few required operations, such as equality test or a linear ordering, are defined and implemented on the data. Generic algorithms such as sorting, applicable to any list or array of data, can be defined similarly by use of templates or related mechanisms. Templates and generic modules are useful in generic programming because they provide a form of polymorphism: The same code may be instantiated and executed on a variety of types of data.

In object-oriented programming, the term polymorphism is often used to refer to a specific kind of polymorphism that we call *subtype polymorphism*. In subtype polymorphism, a single piece of code, typically a set of functions or methods, can be applied to more than one type of argument. However, the language mechanism for allowing this is not through implicit type parameters (as in ML type-inference polymorphism) or explicit type parameters (as in C++ templates or Ada generic packages), but through subtyping. Specifically, in a language with subtyping, if a method m will accept any argument of type A, then m may also be applied to any argument from any subtype of A. This works almost as well as parametric polymorphism (polymorphism based on type parameters), except that typically the compile-time type checker has less information about the types of arguments. This either leads to run-time type checking or some sacrifice in type safety. The general phenomenon is illustrated in the following Java example.

Example 13.1 Java Subtype Polymorphism
Let us consider the problem of defining a general class of stacks. We would like to be able to build stacks of any type of object. We will implement stacks as linked lists of stack nodes, each node containing a stack element.

Because Object is a supertype of all reference types (including all references to objects and arrays), we can let stack cells contain references of type Object. Let us begin with a subsidiary class definition, the class of stack nodes:

```
class Node {
  Object element;   // Any object can be placed in a stack
  Node next;
  Node (Node n, int e) {
    next=n;
    element=e;
  }
}
```

This class is intended to belong to the same package as that of the Stack class. Because there are no access qualifiers here (public, private, or protected) the fields and methods are accessible only to methods in the same package.

Here is the outline of a Stack class in which Node objects are used to store elements of a linked list of stack elements. The methods shown here are empty, which tells whether a stack is empty, push, which adds a new element to the top of a stack, and pop, which removes the top node and returns the object stored in that node. The class is declared public so that it is visible outside the package in which it is defined:

```
public class Stack {
    private Node top=null;           // top of the stack, starts as empty
    public Stack(){
    }
    public boolean empty(){          // determine whether stack is empty
        return top == null;
    }
    public void push(Object val) {   // push element on top of stack
        top = new Node(top,val);
    }
    public Object pop() {            // Remove first node and return value.
        if (top==null) return -1;
        Node temp = top;
        top = top.next;
        return temp.element;
    }
}
```

Most of the code here is entirely straightforward. The important limitation, for the purpose of generic programming, is the type of the node elements and the return type of pop. Because the argument type of push is Object, any object can be pushed onto a stack. However, the return type of pop is also Object, meaning that, when an object is removed from a stack, the static type of the expression removing the object is Object. Therefore, if a program pushes strings onto a stack and then pops them off the stack, the Java type checker will not be able to determine that the objects removed from the stack are strings.

Here is an example of the way that stacks might be used in a Java program:

```
String s = "Hello";
Stack st = new Stack();
...
st.push(s);
...
s = (String) st.pop;
```

In this code fragment, a String object is pushed onto a stack. When the String object is popped off the stack, the static type of st.pop() is Object, not string. Therefore, to assign st.pop() to a string variable, it is necessary to cast the Object to String. This cast generates a run-time test. If the top element on the stack is not a string when this assignment is executed, the run-time test will throw an exception and prevent the assignment from occurring.

In comparison, a C++ stack class template may be defined by the following form:

```
template <typename t> class Stack {
    private: Node<t> top;
    public: boolean empty() { ... };
            void    push (t* x) { ... }
            t*      pop ( ) { ... }
};
```

If Java had a template mechanism similar to this, then we could define a generic stack class like this,

```
class Stack<A> {
    public Boolean empty(){ ... }
    public void push(A a) { ... }
    public A pop() { ... }
}
```

and use generic stacks as follows:

```
String s = "Hello";
Stack<String> st = new Stack<String>();
st.push(s);
...
s = st.pop();
```

There are several important points of comparison between the two styles illustrated here. In the template-based code, the stack st has type Stack<string> instead of Stack. As a result, st.pop() has static type String. Two advantages are clarity and efficiency. The programmer's intent is clearer, as the stack st is explicitly declared to be a stack of strings. The efficiency advantage is that there is no need for a cast and run-time test.

There have been several research projects aimed at adding a template mechanism to Java. Although the basic goals of such a mechanism seem clear, there are a number of details that need to be addressed. One issue is implementation. One approach is to simply translate Java with templates into Java without templates. This allows programmers to write code with templates and provides a relatively simple implementation. However, the result of the translation is code that contains many run-time-checked type conversions, so it may not be as efficient as other implementation techniques. An alternative is to compile a generic class such as Stack<t> into a form of class file that has type parameters and load class Stack<String> by instantiating this class file at class-load time. This produces more efficient code, but might involve loading more classes. Because class loading is slow, the overall program may run more slowly in some cases. There is also the problem of instantiating class templates for primitive types such as boolean, int, float, and so on. The first implementation method will not work for primitive types, as these are stored differently from object types. The second method, instantiating class files at load time, can be made to work, although handling primitive types adds some complexity to the mechanism. In either case, there are some additional subtleties in the design of the type-checking mechanism for generic classes that we have not discussed.

13.4 JAVA SYSTEM ARCHITECTURE

13.4.1 Java Virtual Machine

There are several implementations of Java. This section discusses the implementation architecture used in the Sun Java compiler and the JVM. The biggest difference between this architecture and some others is that some optimized implementations generate native code for the underlying hardware instead of interpreted code. However, because the "just-in-time" or (JIT), compilers that generate native code on the fly are significantly more complicated than the standard JVM architecture, we use the JVM architecture as the basis for our discussion and analysis of Java implementation issues.

The Java compiler produces a form of machine code called *bytecode*. The origin of the name bytecode, which is a standard term that predates Java, is that bytecodes are instructions for a *virtual machine* that may be 1 byte long. Many compilers for high-level languages actually produce bytecode instead of native machine code. For example, the influential UCSD Pascal compiler produces a form of bytecode called P-code, which is then interpreted by a virtual machine. Common ML and Smalltalk implementations also generate virtual machine bytecode.

Figure 13.4 shows the main parts of the JVM and some of the steps involved in compiling and executing Java source code. The main parts of the JVM are the class loader, the bytecode verifier, the linker, and the bytecode interpreter.

The top of Figure 13.4 shows a Java source code file A.java compiled to produce a *class file* A.class. The class file is in a specific format, containing bytecode instructions and some auxiliary data structures, including a symbol table called a *constant pool*. The class loader reads the class file and arranges the bytecode instructions in a form suitable for the verifier. The Java bytecode language contains type information, allowing the verifier to check that bytecode is type correct before it is executed by the virtual machine. The linker resolves interfile references, and the bytecode interpreter executes the bytecode instructions.

The box labeled B.class in Figure 13.4 is meant to show that Java classes are loaded incrementally, as needed during program execution, and may be loaded over

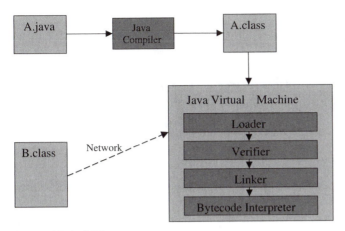

Figure 13.4. JVM.

the network as well as from the local file system. More specifically, if class A has a main method, then class A may be loaded as a main program and executed. If some method of class A refers to class B, then class B will be loaded when this method is called. The class loader then attempts to find the appropriate class file and load it into the virtual machine so that program execution may continue.

The JVM may run several threads (processes) concurrently; it terminates when either all nondaemon threads terminate or some thread runs the exit method of the class Runtime or class System.

13.4.2 Class Loader

The Java run-time system loads classes, as they are needed, searching compiled byte-codes for any class that is referenced but not already loaded. There is a default loading mechanism, which we can replace by defining an alternative ClassLoader object. One reason to define an alternative ClassLoader is to obtain bytecodes from some remote source and load them at run time.

We define a class loader by extending the abstract ClassLoader class and implementing its loadClass method. Here is a possible form of a class-loader definition:

```
class Load_My_Classes extends ClassLoader {
    private Hashtable loaded_classes = new Hashtable();
    public Class loadClass(string name, boolean resolve)
        throws ClassNotFoundException {
        /* Code to try to load class "name" and add to "loaded_classes".
           If boolean arg "resolve" is true, then invoke "resolveClass"
           method to ensure that all classes referred to by class are
           loaded. Raise exception if class cannot be found and loaded. */
    }
    ...
}
```

When loadClass finds the bytecodes of the class to be loaded, it may invoke the inherited defineClass method, which takes a byte array, a start position, and a number of bytes. This method installs this sequence of bytes as the implementation of the desired class.

The return type of method loadClass is Class. Classes are objects, and we may be able to find the class loader for a given class by invoking the getClassLoader method of the class. If the class has no class loader, the method returns null.

13.4.3 Java Linker, Verifier, and Type Discipline

The linker takes a binary form of class or interface as input and adds it to the run-time state of the JVM.

Each class is verified before it is linked and made available for execution. Java bytecode verification is a specific process that checks to make sure that every class has certain properties:

- Every instruction must have a valid operation code.
- Every branch instruction must branch to the start of some other instruction, rather than the middle of some instruction.
- Every method has a structurally correct signature.
- Every instruction obeys the Java type discipline.

If an error occurs in verification, then an instance of the class VerifyError will be thrown at the point in the Java program that caused the class to be verified.

Linking involves creating the static fields of a class or interface and initializing them to the standard default (typically 0). Names are also resolved, which involves checking symbolic references and replacing them with direct references that can be processed more efficiently if the reference is used repeatedly.

Classes are not explicitly unloaded. If no instance of class is reachable, the class may be removed as part of garbage collection.

13.4.4 Bytecode Interpreter and Method Lookup

The bytecode interpreter executes the Java bytecode and performs run-time tests such as array-bound tests to make sure that every array access is within the declared bounds of the array. The basic run-time architecture of the bytecode interpreter is similar to the simple machine architecture outlined in Section 7.1, with a program counter, instruction area, stack, and heap.

A running Java program consists of one or more sequential threads. When a new thread is created, it is given a program counter and a stack. The program counter indicates the next instruction to execute. The Java stack is composed of activation records, each storing the local variables, parameters, return value, and intermediate calculations for a Java method invocation. The JVM has no registers to hold inter-mediate data values; these are stored on the Java stack. This approach was taken by the Java designers to keep the JVM instruction set compact and to facilitate imple-mentation on a variety of underlying machine architectures. When an object or array is created, it is stored on the heap. All threads running within a single JVM share the same heap.

A Java activation record has three parts: local variable area, operand stack, and data area. The sizes of the local variable area and operand stack, which are measured in words, depend on the needs of the method and are determined at compile time. The local variable area of a Java activation record is organized as an array of words, with different types of data occupying different numbers of words. The operand stack is used for intermediate calculations and passing parameters to other methods. Instead of accessing data from memory by using a memory address, most Java bytecode instructions operate by pushing, popping, or replacing values from the top of this stack-within-a-stack. An add instruction with two operands, for example, pops its two operands off the operand stack and pushes their sum onto the operand stack. This kind of architecture leads to shorter instruction codes because an instruction with several operands needs to identify only the operation – it is not necessary to give an address or register number for the operands because the operands are always the top few data items on the stack. The data area of an activation record stores data used to support constant pool resolution (which we discuss in the next paragraph), normal method return, and exception dispatch.

Compiled Java bytecode instructions are stored in a file format that includes a data structure called the constant pool. The constant pool is a table of symbolic names, such as class names, field names, and methods names. When a bytecode instruction refers to a field, for example, the reference will actually be a number, representing an index into the constant pool. In the instruction to get a field, for example, the instruction may contain the number 27, indicating the 27th symbolic name in the constant pool. This approach stores symbolic names from the source code in the bytecode file, but saves space by storing each symbolic name only once.

When executing programs, the bytecode interpreter makes the following run-time tests to prevent type errors and preserve the integrity of the run-time system:

- All casts are checked to make sure they are type safe.
- All array references are checked to make sure the array index is within the array bounds.
- References are tested to make sure they are not null before they are dereferenced.

In addition, the absence of pointer arithmetic (see Section 5.2) and the use of automatic garbage collection (programmers cannot explicitly free allocated memory) contribute to type-safe execution of Java programs.

When instructions that access a field or method are executed, there is often a search for the appropriate location in an object template or method lookup table, by use of the symbolic name of the field or method from the constant pool. This is inefficient if access through the constant pool occurs frequently. Search through the constant pool is also an execution bottleneck for concurrent programs, as this may require a lock on the constant pool and locking the constant pool restricts execution of other threads.

The JVM implementation optimizes the search for object fields and methods by modifying bytecode during program execution. More specifically, bytecode instructions that refer to the constant pool are modified to an equivalent so-called *quick* bytecodes, which refers to the absolute address of a field or method. For example, the bytecode instruction

```
getfield #18 <Field Obj var>
```

pushes the value of an object field onto the operand stack. (The object whose field is retrieved is the object that is on top of the operand stack before the operation is performed.) When the getfield instruction is executed, the constant pool is searched for the symbolic field name that matches the string stored at position #18 in the constant pool. If this field is found, and it is located 6 bytes below the first location of the object, then the preceding instruction is replaced with the following quick version,

```
getfield_quick 6
```

which uses the calculated offset of the field from the top of the object. If the program passes through this instruction again, as when the instruction appears inside a loop, for example, the quick instruction is used. You do not need to understand all of the parts of the getfield instruction – the important issue here is the way that modifying a bytecode instruction the first time it is executed can make the program run more quickly if this instruction is executed again.

Finding a Virtual Method by Class

There are four different bytecodes for invoking a method:

- invokevirtual: used when a superclass of the object is known at compile time,
- invokeinterface: used when only an interface of the object is known at compile time,
- invokestatic: used to invoke static methods,
- invokespecial: used in some special cases that will not be discussed.

In simplest terms, invokevirtual is used in situations that resemble C++ virtual function calls, as Java is a statically typed programming language and all subclasses of a class can be implemented with the same method table (vtable) order. Invokeinterface similarly corresponds to Smalltalk method lookup, as an interface implemented by the class of an object does not determine the relative position of the method in a method table. We will look at invokevirtual before considering properties of invokeinterface.

Like getfield, invokevirtual involves searching for a symbolic name the first time the instruction is executed. More specifically, suppose we have a Java source code declaring an object reference x and invoking a method of x:

```
Object x;
...
x.equals("test");
```

For concreteness, and because this affects the way the code is compiled, let us assume that x is the first local variable in this block. The call x.equals("test") is compiled into something like the following sequence of bytecodes, in which the phrases to the right of ";" are comments:

```
aload_1    ; push local variable 1 (which is 'x') onto the operand stack
ldc "test" ; push the string "test" onto the operand stack
invokevirtual java/lang/Object/equals(Ljava/lang/Object;)Z
```

The string java/lang/Object/equals(Ljava/lang/Object;)Z is called a method specification. This string is not literally located in the bytecode, but is stored in the constant pool, as previously described.

When invokevirtual is executed, the virtual machine looks at method specification and related information in the class file and determines how many arguments the method requires. For our example equals method, there is one argument. The argument and the object reference, in this case the number 1 indicating the first local variable in the current scope, are popped off the operand stack. Using the information stored in the object reference (local variable x), the virtual machine retrieves the Java class for the object, searches the list of methods defined by that class and then its superclasses, looking for a method matching the method specification. When the correct method is located, the method is called in the same way that function calls are executed in most block-structured programming languages.

Bytecode Rewriting for *Invokevirtual.* Although this method lookup process will find and correctly call a method, it does not take advantage of the static type information computed by the Java compiler at compile time. More specifically, the Java compiler can arrange every subclass method table in the same way as the superclass table, just as the C++ compiler does. By doing this, the compiler can guarantee that each method is located at the same relative position in all method tables associated with all subclasses of any class. Therefore, once method lookup is used to find a method in a method table, the offset of this method will be the same for all future executions of this instruction.

Figure 13.5 shows how bytecode can be modified so that on subsequent executions of an invokevirtual instruction, the correct method can be found immediately within the method table (called "mtable" in the illustration) of the object.

The part of Figure 13.5 above the dotted line shows the invokevirtual command in the instruction stream, followed by a pointer to the method specification in the constant pool. After the method is found, the instruction stream can be modified as shown below the dotted line. In the modified instruction stream, invokevirtual is replaced with the "quick" version invokevirtual_quick and the method specification pointer is replaced with the offset of the method in the method table. When invokevirtual_quick is executed, the virtual machine will use the object reference on the operand stack to locate the class and method table and then use the mtable offset in the instruction stream to find the appropriate method without further search.

It is important to realize that if the method invocation is in a loop, for example, then different objects may be on the operand stack for different executions of the

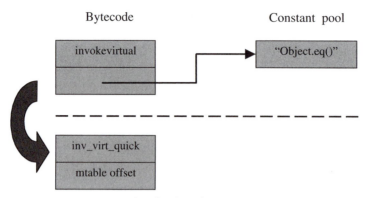

Bytecode   Constant pool

Figure 13.5. Optimizing invokevirtual by rewriting bytecode.

method call. As a result, the class of the object may change from one call to the next. However, the offset of the method in the method table will be the same on each call, as each class is a subclass of the static type of the object reference in the Java source code.

A short summary of this optimization is that the first time a method call instruction is executed, Smalltalk-style method search is used to find the position of the method in a method table. After the search succeeds, the code is changed so that if this method call instruction is executed again, C++-style lookup will find the method quickly.

Finding a Virtual Method by Interface

The situation is similar for finding a method when an interface of the object is known at compile time. The difference is that the optimization involving invokevirtual_quick will not work correctly. Therefore, another technique is used.

Suppose a compiled Java program contains a method declaration

```
void add2(Incrementable x) { x.inc(); x.inc(); }
```

where Incrementable is an interface guaranteeing that the argument x will have an inc method when add2 is called at run time. There may be several classes that implement the Incrementable interface. For example, there could be classes IntCounter and FloatCounter of the following form:

```
interface Incrementable {
   public void inc();
}
class IntCounter implements Incrementable {
   public void add(int);
   public void inc();
   public int value();
}
class FloatCounter implements Incrementable {
   public void inc();
```

```
        public void add(float);
        public float value();
    }
```

Because the classes implementing Incrementable might be declared in different packages, neither referring to the other, there is no reason to believe that the method inc
is located at the same offset in the two method tables. (In fact, it is easy to construct
a set of interfaces and classes for which there is no way of making all classes that
implement each interface compatible in this way.)

When the add2 method is compiled, the Java compiler generates code of the
following form (with method specification from the constant pool written in the
code for clarity):

```
    aload_1 ; push local variable 1 (i.e. x) onto the stack
    invokeinterface package/inc()Z 1
```

When invokeinterface is executed, the class of the object is found and the method table
for this class is searched to find the method with the given method specification. When
the method is located, the method is called as for invokevirtual.

Because the offset of the method in the method table may be different on the
next execution of this instruction, it is not correct to rewrite invokeinterface to in-
vokevirtual_quick. However, there is some possibility that the next execution of this
instruction will be for an object from the same class, so it seems wasteful to discard
the offset and other information. Figure 13.6 shows the bytecode modification used
for invokeinterface.

The part of Figure 13.6 above the dotted line shows the initial instruction sequence, with the invokeinterface instruction followed by a pointer to the method
specification in the constant pool and an unused empty location. After execution of invokeinterface, the instruction is replaced with invokeinterface_quick and a
pointer to the class and method is stored below the method specification. When

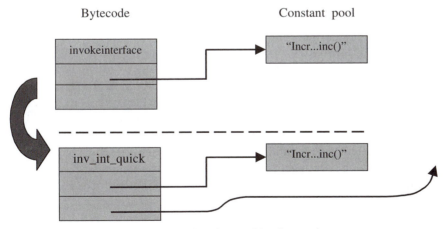

Figure 13.6. Optimizing invokeinterface by rewriting bytecode

invokinterface_quick is executed on another pass through this instruction sequence, the class of the object operand is compared with the cached class. If the object is from the same class, then the same method is used. If the object is from a different class, then, because the method specification is still available in the instruction sequence, the same search process can be followed as if the instruction were invokeinterface again.

Efficiency Summary. In Java, the method call overhead is high the first time an instruction is executed and potentially much lower on subsequent executions. On the first lookup that uses invokevirtual there are two indirections (one to look up the constant table of the class this method is in and one to look up the method table of the class of the object), two array indexes (in the constant table and the method list), and the cost of rewriting some bytecode. On subsequent calls, there is one indirection and one array index. For invokeinterface, there is a search through the method table the first time an instruction is executed. On subsequent calls, there is either one array index or another search through a method table if the class is changed.

13.5 SECURITY FEATURES

Computer security involves preventing unauthorized use of computational resources. Some computer security topics are network security, which provides methods for preserving the secrecy and integrity of information transmitted on the network, and operating system security, which is concerned with preventing an attacker from gaining access to a system. In this section, we look at ways that programming languages can help and hinder our efforts to build secure systems, with particular attention to how Java is designed to improve the security of systems that use Java.

One way that attackers may try to gain access to a system is to send data over the network to a program that processes network input. For example, many attacks against the e-mail program Sendmail have been devised over the years. These attacks typically take advantage of some error or oversight in a particular implementation of Sendmail. Sendmail is a target because this program accepts network connections and runs with superuser privileges. In Subsection 13.5.1 we will look at buffer overflow attacks, which are an important example of the kind of attack that is often mounted against network programs.

Because Java code is sometimes transmitted over the network, a computer user may run code that comes from another site, such as a web page. *Mobile code,* a general term for code transmitted over the network before it is executed, provides another way for an attacker to try to gain access to a system or cause damage to a system. The two main mechanisms for managing risks raised by mobile code are called *sandboxing* and *code signing.* The idea behind sandboxing, which was invented before the development of Java, is to give a program a restricted execution environment. This restricted environment, called a sandbox, may contain certain functions (analogous to certain toys you might give a child to play with in a sandbox), but the program cannot call functions or perform actions that are outside the sandbox.

Code signing is used to determine which person or company produced a class file. With digital signatures, it is possible for the producer of code to sign it in a way that any recipient can verify the signature. The JVM uses digital signatures to identify the producer of a file that contains Java bytecode. The user of a computer system can specify a set of trusted producers and allow code from these producers to execute on their computer. With the Java security manager, it is also possible to assign different access permissions to different code producers.

After looking at buffer overflow, we will discuss some of the main features of the Java sandbox. If you want to learn more about the Java security model, you can read one of the books on Java security or find additional information on the web.

13.5.1 Buffer Overflow Attack

In *a buffer overflow attack*, an attacker sends network messages that cause a program to read data into a buffer in memory. If the program does not check the number of bytes placed in the buffer, then the attacker may be able to write past the allocated memory. By writing over the return address that is stored in the activation record of a function, the attacker may cause the program to misbehave and "return" by jumping to instructions chosen by the attacker. This is a powerful form of attack. The vast majority of security advisories issued by the Computer Emergency Response Team (CERT) over the past decade or two have been security problems related to buffer overflow.

Java code is not vulnerable to buffer overflow attacks because the JVM checks array bounds at run time. This prevents a function from writing more data into an array than the array can hold. To show how important this feature is for Java security, we look at how a buffer overflow attack may be designed against C code.

Here is a very simple C function that illustrates the principle, taken from an article called "Smashing the Stack for Fun and Profit," written by someone called Aleph One (Phrack 49(14), 1996):

```
void f (char *str) {
char buffer[16];
    . . .
    strcpy(buffer,str);
}
```

This function copies a character string, passed by pointer, into the array buffer on the run-time stack. The C function strcpy() copies the contents of *str into buffer[ ] until a null character is found in the string. Because the function does not check the length of the string, careful C programmers would consider the use of strcpy() a coding error. The similar function strncpy(), which has an additional parameter n and copies at most n characters, should be used instead.

If the function f is called from this main program,

```
void main() {
    char large_string[256];
    int i;
    for( i = 0; i < 255; i++)
        large_string[i] = 'A';
```

```
        large_string[255]=0;
        f(large_string);
    }
```

---

then the call to strcpy in function f will write over locations on the stack. Because buffer[ ] is 16 bytes long and large_string is 256 bytes, the copy will write 240 bytes beyond the end of the array. This will change the return address of f, which is sitting in the activation record for f a few memory locations away from buffer[ ]. Because large_string contains the character 'A', with hex character value 0x41, the return address of f is set to 0x41414141. Because this address is outside of the process address space, a segmentation fault will occur when function f tries to "return" to location 0x41414141. However, if we change 'A' to a value that is the address of a meaningful instruction, the buffer overflow will cause function f to jump to that location.

Several steps are needed to turn this simple idea into an attack. First, the attacker needs to choose a function that reads data that the attacker can control. Next, the attacker must figure out what data will cause the function to misbehave in a way that is of interest to the attacker. On some computer architectures, an attacker can fill a buffer with code the attacker wants to execute and then cause the function to jump into the buffer. This allows the attacker to execute any instructions.

13.5.2 The Java Sandbox

The JVM executes Java bytecode in a restricted environment called the Java sandbox. The term sandbox is metaphorical – there is no literal data structure or code called the sandbox. The word sandbox is used to indicate that, when bytecode is executed, some operations that can be written in the Java language might not be allowed to proceed, just the way that, when a child plays in a sandbox, an adult supervisor may give the child only those toys that the supervisor considers safe.

The JVM restricts the operation of a Java bytecode program by using four interrelated mechanisms: the class loader, the Java bytecode verifier, run-time checks performed by the JVM, and the actions of the security manager. Although the class loader, bytecode verifier, and virtual machine run-time checks perform general functions related to type correctness and preserving the integrity of the run-time system, the security manager is a specific object designed specifically for security functions. We take a quick look at how each of these mechanisms contributes to Java security. If you are interested in learning more, you may want to read *Securing Java* by Gary McGraw and Ed Felten (Wiley, 1999) or other books on Java security or the JVM.

Class Loader

The class loader, discussed in Subsection 13.4.2, contributes to the Java sandbox in three ways:

- The class-loader architecture separates trusted class libraries from untrusted packages by making it possible to load each with different class loaders.
- The class-loader architecture provides separate name spaces for classes loaded by different class loaders.

■ The class loader places code into categories (called *protection domains*) that let the security manager restrict the actions that specific code will be allowed to take.

The Bytecode Verifier and Virtual Machine Run-Time Tests

The Java bytecode verifier checks Java bytecode programs before they are executed, as discussed in Subsection 13.4.3. Complimentary run-time checks, such as array-bounds checks, are performed by the JVM. Together, these checks provide the following guarantees:

■ *No Stack Overflow or Underflow:* The verifier examines the way that bytecode manipulates data on the operand stack and guarantees that no method will overflow the operand stack allocated to it.
■ *All Methods are Called with Parameters of the Correct Type:* This type-correctness guarantee prevents the kind of type-confusion attacks discussed in Subsection 13.5.3.
■ *No Illegal Data Conversions (Casts) Occur:* For example, treating an integer as a pointer is not allowed. This is also essential to prevent the kind of type-confusion attacks discussed in Subsection 13.5.3.
■ *Private, Public, Protected, and Default Accesses must be Legal:* In other words, no improper access to restricted classes, interfaces, variables, and methods will be allowed.

The Security Manager

The security manager is a single Java object that answers at run time. The job of the security manager is to keep track of which code is allowed to do which dangerous operations. The security manager does its job by examining the protection domain associated with a class. Each protection domain has two attributes – a signer and a location. The signer is the person or organization that signed the code before it was loaded into the virtual machine. This will be null if the code is not signed by anyone. The location is the URL where the Java classes reside. These attributes are used to determine which operations the code is allowed to perform. A standard security manager will disallow most operations when they are requested by untrusted code and may allow trusted code to do whatever it wants.

A running virtual machine can have only one security manager installed at a time. In addition, once a security manager has been installed, it cannot be uninstalled without restarting the virtual machine. Java-enabled applications such as web browsers install a security manager as part of their initialization, thus locking in the security manager before any potentially untrusted code has a chance to run.

The security manager does not observe the operation of other running bytecode. Instead, the security manager uses the system policy to answer questions about access permissions. It is up to library code that has access to important resources to consult the security manager. In outline, the standard Java library uses the security manager according to the following steps:

■ If a Java program makes a call to a potentially dangerous operation in the Java API, the associated Java API code asks the security manager whether the operation should be allowed.
■ If the operation is permitted, the call to the security manager returns normally

(without throwing an exception) and the Java API performs the requested operation.

■ If the operation is not permitted, the security manager throws a SecurityException. This exception propagates back to the Java program.

One limitation of this mechanism is that a hostile applet or other untrusted code may catch a security exception by using a try-finally block. Therefore, although the security manager may prevent an action by raising an exception, this exception might not be noticed by the user of a system under attack.

13.5.3 Security and Type Safety

Type safety is the cornerstone of Java security, in the sense that all of the sandbox mechanisms rely on type safety. To understand the importance of type safety, we discuss some of the ways that type errors can allow code to perform arbitrary and potentially dangerous actions. We begin with a C example, as C has many type loopholes. It is then shown how similar problems could occur in Java code if it were possible to create two pointers with different types that point to the same object.

One way for a C/C++ program to call an arbitrary function is through a function pointer. For example, suppose a C/C++ program contains lines of the following form:

```
int (*fp)()  /* variable "fp" is a function pointer                  */
...
fp = addr;  /* assign fp an address stored in an integer variable    */
(*fp)(n);   /* call the function at this address                      */
```

Using casts, code like this can call a function at virtually any address. Therefore, if a program may cast integers to function pointers, it is impossible to tell in advance which functions the program calls.

Similar type confusion between object types would also allow a program to perform dangerous actions. Here is an example from *Securing Java* by McGraw and Felten. Suppose that it is possible to create a Java program with two pointers to the same object o, one pointer with type T and one with type U. Let us further suppose that classes T and U are defined as follows:

```
class T {
    SecurityManager x;
}
class U {
    MyObject x;
}
```

where MyObject is some class that we can write in whatever way we want. Here is a program that uses the two pointers to object o to change the security manager, even though the fields of the security manager are declared private and should not be subject to alteration by arbitrary code:

```
T t = (the pointer to object o with type T);
U u = (the pointer to object o with type U);
t.x = System.getSecurity(); // the Security Manager
MyObject m = u.x;
```

The first two lines of this code segment create two references to object o with types T and U, respectively. The next line assigns the security manager to the field x of object o. This assignment is allowed because the type of field x is SecurityManager. The final line then gives us a reference m to the security manager, where the type of m is MyObject, a class that we can declare in any way we wish. By changing the fields of m, the program can change the private fields of the security manager.

Although this example shows how type confusion can be used to corrupt the security manager, the basic tactic may be used to corrupt almost any part of the running Java system.

An early type-confusion attack on Java was made possible by a buggy class loader and linker. The incorrect system aborted class loading if an exception was raised but did not remove the class name and associated class methods. More specifically, the first step in class loading was to add the class name and constructor to the table of defined references, then load the byte code for the class. If an exception was raised during the second step, the first step was not undone. This made it possible to then successfully load another class with a different interface and to use the first class name for objects of the second class.

13.6 JAVA SUMMARY

The Java programming language and execution environment were designed with portability, reliability, and safety in mind. These goals took higher priority than efficiency, although many engineers and implementers have worked hard to make Java implementations run efficiently.

Java programs are compiled from Java source code (in the Java programming language) to Java bytecode, an interpreted language that is executed on a simple stack-based virtual machine. The run-time environment provides dynamic linking, allowing classes to be loaded into the virtual machine as they are needed. The Java language contains specific concurrency primitives (discussed in Chapter 14), and the virtual machine runs multiple threads simultaneously.

Java is a modern general-purpose object-oriented language that is used in many academic, educational, and commercial projects. We studied the object-oriented features of Java, the Java Virtual Machine and implementation of method lookup, and Java security features.

Objects and Classes

A Java object has fields, which are data members of the object, and methods, which are member functions. All objects are allocated on the run-time heap (not the run-time stack), accessible through pointers, and garbage collected.

Every Java object is an instance of a class. Classes can have static (class) fields that are initialized when the class is loaded into the virtual machine. A constructor of the class is used to create and initalize objects, and objects may have a finalize method that is called when the garbage collector reclaims the space occupied by the object.

Dynamic Lookup

Method lookup in Java is more efficient than in Smalltalk, because the static type system gives the compiler more information, but often is less efficient than in C++. When instructions that access a field or method are executed the first time, there is a search for the appropriate location in an object template or method lookup table. After the first execution of a reference inside a program, the virtual machine optimizes the search for object fields and methods by modifying bytecode. Bytecode instructions that refer to the constant pool are modified to an equivalent so-called *quick* bytecode, which refers to the absolute address of a field or method.

Encapsulation

Java has four visibility distinctions for fields and methods:

- *Public:* accessible anywhere the class is visible.
- *Protected:* accessible to methods of the class and any subclasses as well as to other classes in the same package.
- *Private:* accessible only in the class itself.
- *Package:* accessible only to code in the same package; not visible to subclasses in other packages. Members declared without an access modifier have package visibility.

Names declared in another package can be accessed by import or by qualified names.

Java type checking, applied when source code is compiled and again when byte-code is loaded into the virtual machine, together with run-time tests performed by the bytecode interpreter, guarantees that private fields are truly private and similarly for other visibility levels.

Inheritance

In Java terminology, a *subclass* inherits from its *superclass*. The Java inheritance mechanism is essentially similar to that of Smalltalk, C++, and other class-based object-oriented languages. Java provides single inheritance for classes and multiple inheritance for interfaces.

Java individual methods of a class or an entire class can be declared final. If a method is declared final, then the method cannot be overridden in any subclass. If a class is declared final, then the class cannot have any subclasses. This gives the designer of a class the ability to fix the implementation of a method (or the entire class) by keeping designers of subclass from overriding the method.

In principle, every class declared in a Java program inherits from another class. The class Object is the one class that has no superclasses.

Subtyping

Subtyping for classes is determined by the class hierarchy and the interface mechanism. Specifically, if class A extends class B, then the type of A objects is a subtype of the type of B objects. There is no other way for one class to define a subtype of another, and no private base classes (as in C++) to allow inheritance without subtyping.

A class may be declared to implement one or more interfaces, meaning that any instance of the class implements all the abstract methods specified in the interface. This (multiple) interface subtyping allows objects to support (multiple) common behaviors without sharing any common implementation.

The Java types are divided into two categories, called primitive types and reference types. The primitive types include boolean and seven numeric types. The three forms of reference types are class types, interface types, and array types. All class, interface, and array types are considered subtypes of Object. Java exception types are subclasses of Throwable, which is a subtype of Object.

Virtual Machine Architecture

The main parts of the Java Virtual Machine are the class loader, the bytecode verifier, the linker, and the bytecode interpreter. A Java source code file is compiled to produce a *class file*. Class files are in a specific format that contains bytecode instructions and some auxiliary data structures, including a symbol table called a *constant pool*. The class loader reads the class file and arranges the bytecode instructions in a form suitable for the verifier. The Java bytecode language contains type information, allowing the verifier to checks that bytecode is type correct before it is executed by the virtual machine. The linker resolves interfile references, and the bytecode interpreter executes the bytecode instructions.

When instructions that access a field or method are executed, there is a search for the appropriate location, based on the symbolic name of the field or method in the constant pool. The JVM implementation optimizes this search by modifying bytecode during program execution. Bytecode instructions that initially refer to the constant pool are modified to an equivalent so-called quick bytecode, which refers to the absolute address after the name has been resolved. Different degrees of optimization are possible for method invocation when the class is known and method invocation when the interface is guaranteed to be the same for all executions of the instruction.

Security

Java security is provided by type-correct compilation and execution and by access control through the security manager. The JVM restricts the operation of a Java bytecode program by using four interrelated mechanisms: the class loader, the Java bytecode verifier, run-time checks performed by the JVM, and the actions of the security manager. Whereas the class loader, bytecode verifier, and virtual machine run-time checks perform general functions related to type correctness and preserving the integrity of the run-time system, the security manager is a specific object designed specifically for security functions. The techniques used to restrict execution of a bytecode program are collectively called the Java sandbox.

Code signing is used to determine which person or company produced a class file. The security manager uses the producer of a class and the URL from which it was obtained to decide whether it can perform potentially hazardous operations such as creating, opening, or writing into a file.

Without type safety, Java programs could be susceptible to the buffer overflow attacks and could carry out the type-confusion attacks we discussed in Section 13.5.

EXERCISES

13.1 Initializing Static Fields

Why do static fields of a class have to be initialized when the class is loaded? Why can't we initialize static fields when the program starts? Give an example of what goes wrong if, instead of static fields being initialized too early, they are initialized too late.

13.2 Java final **and** finalize

Java has keywords final and finalize.

(a) Describe one situation in which you would want to mark a class final, and another in which you would want a final method but not a final class.

(b) Describe the similarity and differences between Java final and the C++ use of nonvirtual in similar situations.

(c) Why is Java finalize (the other keyword!) a useful feature?

13.3 Subtyping and Exceptions

In Java, a method that can throw an exception (other than from a subclass of Error or RuntimeException) must either catch the exception or specify the types of possible exceptions with a throws clause in the method declaration. For example, a method declaration might have the form

        public void f(int x) throws Exception1, Exception2

meaning that a call to f may either terminate normally or raise one of the listed exceptions (without catching them internally).

Assuming that the type of the method f in B is a subtype of the method f in A, class declarations of the following form are type correct in principle:

            class A {
              ...
              public Returntype1 f(Argtype1 x) ...
            }
            class B extends A {
              ...
              public Returntype2 f(Argtype2 x) ...
            }

This example of function subtyping Argtype2 $\rightarrow$ Returntype2 <: Argtype1 $\rightarrow$ Returntype1 requires Returntype2 <: Returntype1 and Argtype1 <: Argtype2.

Suppose we keep the argument and return types the same, but vary the set of exceptions, as in the following code:

            class A {
              ...
              public Returntype f(Argtype x) throws Exception1, Exception2, ...

```
        }
        class B extends A {
            . . .
            public Returntype f(Argtype x) throws Exception1, Exception2, . . .
        }
```

(a) What relation between the two sets of exceptions is required for the subclass B to be a subtype of class A? Do the sets have to be the same? Or would it be alright for one to be a subset of the other? Explain briefly. In this part, do not worry about subtyping of exception types – we are concerned with only the *sets* of types.

(b) Now suppose that we allow for the possibility that the exceptions in one set could be subtypes of exceptions in the other set. What is the relation we require for class B to be a subtype of class A?

13.4 Java Interfaces and Multiple Inheritance

In C++, a derived class may have multiple base classes. In contrast, a Java derived class may only have one base class but may implement more than one interface. This question asks you to compare these two language designs.

(a) Draw a C++ class hierarchy with multiple inheritance using the following classes:

> *Pizza*, for a class containing all kinds of pizza,
> *Meat*, for pizza that has meat topping,
> *Vet*, for pizza that has vegetable topping,
> *Sausage*, for pizza that has sausage topping,
> *Ham*, for pizza that has ham topping,
> *Pineapple*, for pizza that has pineapple topping,
> *Mushroom*, for pizza that has mushroom topping,
> *Hawaiian*, for pizza that has ham and pineapple topping.

For simplicity, treat sausage and ham as meats and pineapple and mushroom as vegetables.

(b) If you were to implement these classes in C++ for some kind of pizza-manufacturing robot, what kind of potential conflicts associated with multiple inheritance might you have to resolve?

(c) If you were to represent this hierarchy in Java, which would you define as interfaces and which as classes? Write your answer by carefully redrawing your picture, identifying which are classes and which are interfaces. If your program creates objects of each type, you may need to add some additional classes. Include these in your drawing.

(d) Give an advantage of C++ multiple inheritance over Java classes and interfaces and one advantage of the Java design over C++.

13.5 Array Covariance in Java

As discussed in this chapter, Java array types are covariant with respect to the types of array elements (i.e., if B <: A, then B[] <: A[]). This can be useful for creating functions that operate on many types of arrays. For example, the following function takes in an array and swaps the first two elements in the array.

```
1:    public swapper (Object[] swappee){
2:        if (swappee.length > 1){
3:          Object temp = swappee[0];
4:          swappee[0] = swappee[1];
5:          swappee[1] = temp;
6:        }
7:    }
```

This function can be used to swap the first two elements of an array of objects of any type. The function works as is and does not produce any type errors at compile time or run time.

(a) Suppose a is declared by Shape[] a to be an array of shapes, where Shape is some class. Explain why the principle if B <: A, then B[ ] <: A[ ] allows the type checker to accept the call swapper(a) at compile time.

(b) Suppose that Shape[] a is as in part (a). Explain why the call swapper(a) and execution of the body of swapper will not cause a type error or exception at run time.

(c) Java may insert run-time checks to determine that all the objects are of the correct type. What run-time checks are inserted in the compiled code for the swapper function and where? List the line number(s) and the check that occur on that line.

(d) A friend of yours is aghast at the design of Java array subtyping. In his brilliance, he suggests that Java arrays should follow contravariance instead of covariance (i.e., if B <: A, then A[ ] <: B[ ]). He states that this would eliminate the need for run-time type checks. Write three lines or fewer of code that will compile fine under your friend's new type system, but will cause a run-time type error (assuming no run-time type tests accompany his rule). You may assume you have two classes, A and B, that B is a subtype of A, and that B contains a method, foo, not found in A. Here are two declarations that you can assume before your three lines of code:

```
B b[];
A a[] = new A[10];
```

(e) Your friend, now discouraged about his first idea, decides that covariance in Java is all right after all. However, he thinks that he can get rid of the need for run-time type tests through sophisticated compile-time analysis. Explain in a sentence or two why he will not be able to succeed. You may write a few lines of code similar to those in part (d) if it helps you make your point clearly.

13.6 Java Bytecode Analysis

One property of a Java program that is checked by the verifier is that each object must be properly initialized before it is used. This property is fairly difficult to check. One relatively simple part of the analysis, however, is to guarantee that each subclass constructor must call the superclass constructor. The reason for this check is to guarantee that the inherited parts of every object will be initialized properly. If we were designing our own bytecode verifier, there are two ways we might consider designing this check:

(i) The verifier can analyze the bytecode program to make sure that on every execution of a subclass constructor, there is some call to a superclass constructor.

(ii) The verifier can check that the first few bytecode instructions of a subclass constructor contain a call to the superclass constructor, before any loop or jump inside the subclass constructor.

In design (i), the verifier should accept every bytecode program that satisfies this condition and reject every bytecode program that allows some subclass constructor to complete without calling the superclass constructor. In design (ii), some subclass constructors that would be acceptable according to condition (i) will be rejected by the bytecode verifier. However, it may be possible to design the Java source code compiler so that every correct Java source code program is compiled to bytecode that meets the condition described in design (ii).

(a) If you were writing a Java compiler and another person on your team was writing the bytecode verifier, which design would you prefer? Explain briefly.

(b) If you were writing a Java compiler and your manager told you that the standard verifier used design (ii) instead of (i), could you still write a decent compiler? Explain briefly.

(c) If you were writing a bytecode verifier and your manager offered to double your salary if you satisfied design condition (i) instead of (ii) but would fire you if you failed, would you accept the offer? Explain in one sentence.

13.7 Exceptions, Memory Management, and Concurrency

This question asks you to compare properties of exceptions in C++ and Java.

(a) In C++, objects may be reside in the activation records that are deallocated when an exception is thrown. As these activation records are deallocated, all of the destructors of these stack objects are called. Explain why this is a useful language mechanism.

(b) In Java, objects are allocated on the heap instead of the stack. However, an activation record that is deallocated when an exception is raised may contain a pointer to an object. If you were designing Java, would you try to call the finalize methods of objects that are accessible in this way? Why or why not?

(c) Briefly explain one programming situation in which the C++ treatment of objects and exceptions is more convenient than Java and one situation in which Java is more convenient than C++.

(d) In languages that allow programs to contain multiple threads, several threads may be created between the point where an exception handler is established and the point where an exception is thrown. In the spirit of trying to abort any computation that is started between these two points, a programming language might try to abort all such threads when an exception is raised. In other words, there are two possible language designs:

■ raising an exception affects only the current thread, or

■ raising an exception aborts all threads that were started between the point where the exception handler is established and the point where the exception is thrown.

Which design would be easier to implement? Explain briefly.

(e) Briefly explain one programming situation in which you would like raising an exception to abort all threads that were started between the point where the exception handler is established and the point where the exception is thrown. Can you think of a programming situation in which you would prefer not to have these threads terminated?

13.8 Adding Pointers to Java

Java does not have general pointer types. More specifically, Java has primitive types (Booleans, integers, floating-point numbers ...) and reference types (objects and arrays). If a variable has a primitive type, then the variable is associated with a location and a value of that type is stored in that location. When a variable of primitive type is assigned a new value, a new value is copied into the location. In contrast, variables of reference type are implemented as pointers. When a variable referring to an object is assigned a value, the location associated with the variable will contain a pointer to the appropriate object.

Imagine that you were part of the Java design team and you believe strongly in pointers. You want to add pointers to Java, so that, for every type A, there is a type A* of pointers to values of type A. Gosling is strongly opposed to adding an address-of operator (like & in C), but you think there is a useful way of adding pointers without adding address-of.

One way of designing a pointer type for Java is to consider A* equivalent to the following class:

```
class A* {
    private A data=null;
    public void assign(A x) {data=x;};
    public A deref(){return data;}
    A*(){};
};
```

Intuitively, a pointer is an object with two methods, one assigning a value to the pointer and the other dereferencing a pointer to get the object it points to. One pointer, p, can be assigned the object reached by another, q, by writing p.assign(q.deref()). The constructor A* does not do anything because the initialization clause sets every new pointer by using the null reference.

(a) If A is a reference type, do A* objects seem like pointers to you? More specifically, suppose A is a Java class with method m that has a side effect on the object and consider the following code:

```
A x = new A(...);
A* p = new A*();
p.assign(x);
(p.deref()).m();
```

Here, pointer p points to the object named by x and p is used to invoke a method. Does this modify the object named by x? Answer in one or two sentences.

(b) What if A is a primitive type, such as int? Do A* objects seem like pointers to you? [*Hint:* Think about the code in part (a).] Answer in one or two sentences.

(c) If A <: B, should A* <: B*? Answer this question by comparing the type of A*::assign with the type of B*::assign and comparing the type of A*::deref with the type of B*::deref.

(d) If Java had templates, then you could define a pointer template Ptr, with Ptr⟨ A ⟩ defined as A* above. One of the issues that arises in adding templates to Java is subtyping for templates. From the Ptr example, do you think it is correct to assume that, for every class template Template, if A <: B then Template ⟨ A ⟩ <: Template ⟨ B ⟩? Explain briefly.

13.9 Stack Inspection

One component of the Java security mechanism is called *stack inspection*. This problem asks you some general questions about activation records and the run-time stack then asks about an implementation of stack inspection that is similar to the one used in Netscape 3.0. Some of this problem is based on the book *Securing Java*, by Gary McGraw and Ed Felten (Wiley, 1999).

Parts of this problem ask about the following functions, written in a Java-like pseudocode. In the stack used in this problem, activation records contain the usual data (local variables, arguments, control and access links, etc.) plus a *privilege flag*. The privilege flag is part of our security implementation and will be subsequently discussed. For now, SetPrivilegeFlag() sets the privilege flag for the current activation record:

```
void url.open(string url) {
    int urlType = GetUrlType(url); // Gets the type of URL

    SetPrivilegeFlag();

    if (urlType == LOCAL_FILE)
        file.open(url);
}
void file.open(string filename) {
    if (CheckPrivileges())
    {
        // Open the file
    }
    else
    {
        throw SecurityException;
    }
}
void foo() {
    try {
        url.open("confidential.data");
    } catch (SecurityException) {
        System.out.println("Curses, foiled again!\n");
    }
    // Send file contents to evil competitor corporation
}
```

(a) Assume that the URL confidential.data is indeed of type LOCAL_FILE and that sys.main calls foo(). Fill in the missing data in the following illustration of the activation records on the run-time stack just before the call to CheckPrivileges().

For convenience, ignore the activation records created by calls to GetUrlType() and SetPrivilegeFlag(). (They would have been destroyed by this point anyway.)

	Activation Records		Closures	Compiled Code
(1)	Principal	SYSTEM		
(2)	Principal	UNTRUSTED		
(3)	control link	(2)		
	access link	(1)		
	url.open	•	⟨( ), • ⟩	
(4)	control link	(3)		∣code for url.open∣
	access link	(3)		
	file.open	•	⟨( ), • ⟩	
(5)	control link	(4)		∣code for file.open∣
	access link	(2)		
	foo	•	⟨( ), • ⟩	
(6) sys.main	control link	(5)		∣code for foo ∣
	access link	(1)		
	privilege flag	NOT SET		
(7) foo	control link	( )		
	access link	( )		
	privilege flag			
(8) url.open	control link	( )		
	access link	( )		
	privilege flag			
	url	"____"		
(9) file.open	control link	( )		
	access link	( )		
	privilege flag			
	url	"____"		

(b) As part of stack inspection, each activation record is classified as either SYSTEM or UNTRUSTED. Functions that come from system packages are marked SYSTEM. All other functions (including user code and functions coming across the network) are marked UNTRUSTED. UNTRUSTED activation records are not allowed to set the privilege flag.

Effectively, every package has a global variable Principal that indicates whether the package is SYSTEM or UNTRUSTED. Packages that come across the network have this variable set to UNTRUSTED automatically on transfer. Activation records are classified as SYSTEM or UNTRUSTED based on the value of Principal, which is determined according to static scoping rules.

List all activation records (by number) that are marked SYSTEM and list all activation records (by number) that are marked UNTRUSTED.

(c) CheckPrivileges() uses a dynamic scoping approach to decide whether the function corresponding to the current activation record is allowed to perform privileged operations. The algorithm looks at all activation records on the stack, from most recent on up, until one of the following occurs:

■ It finds an activation record with the privilege flag set. In this case it returns TRUE.

■ It finds an activation record marked UNTRUSTED. In this case it returns FALSE. (Remember that it is not possible to set the privilege flag of an untrusted activation record.)

■ It runs out of activation records to look at. In this case it returns FALSE.

What will CheckPrivileges() return for the preceding stack [resulting from the call to foo() from sys.main]? Please answer True or False.

(d) Is there a security problem in this code? (That is, will something undesirable or "evil" occur when this code is run?)

(e) Suppose that CheckPrivileges() returned FALSE and thus a SecurityException was thrown. Which activation records from part (a) will be popped off the stack before the handler is found? List the numbers of the records.

PART 4

Concurrency and Logic Programming

14

Concurrent and Distributed Programming

A concurrent program defines two or more sequences of actions that may be executed simultaneously. Concurrent programs may be executed in two general ways:

- *Multiprogramming.* A single physical processor may run several processes simultaneously by interleaving the steps of one process with steps of another. Each individual process will proceed sequentially, but actions of one process may occur between two adjacent steps of another.
- *Multiprocessing.* Two or more processors may share memory or be connected by a network, allowing processes on one processor to interact with processes running simultaneously on another.

Concurrency is important for a number of reasons. Concurrency allows different tasks to proceed at different speeds. For example, multiprogramming allows one program to do useful work while another is waiting for input. This makes more efficient use of a single processor. Concurrency also provides programming concepts that are important in user interfaces, such as window systems that display independent windows simultaneously and for networked systems that need to send and receive data to other computers at different times. Multiprocessing makes more raw processing power available to solve a computational problem and introduces additional issues such as unreliability in network communication and the possibility of one processor proceeding while another crashes. Interaction between sequential program segments, whether they are on the same processor or different processors, raises significant programming challenges.

Concurrent programming languages provide control and communication abstractions for writing concurrent programs. In this chapter, we look at some general issues in concurrent programming and three language examples: the actor model, Concurrent ML, and Java concurrency. Some constructs we consider are more appropriate for multiprogramming, some for multiprocessing, and some are useful for both.

Historically, many concurrent systems have been written in languages that do not support concurrency. For example, concurrent processes used to implement a network router can be written in a language like C, with system calls used in place of concurrency constructs. Concurrently executed sequential programs can

TONY HOARE

A buoyant, inquisitive person with a twinkle in his eye, Charles Anthony Richard Hoare began his career in computing in 1960 as a programmer for Elliott Brothers, a small scientific computer manufacturer. He became Professor of Computer Science at the Queen's University in Belfast in 1968 and moved to Oxford University in 1977. Professor Hoare retired from Oxford at the mandatory age in 1999 but continues to be active in computing at Microsoft Research Labs in Cambridge, U.K.

Midway through his career, Hoare received the ACM Turing Award in 1980, "For his fundamental contributions to the definition and design of programming languages." At the time he was recognized for his work on methods for reasoning about programs, clever algorithms such as Quicksort, data structuring techniques, and the study of monitors. In 1980, he was also beginning his study of concurrency through the development of Communicating Sequential Processes (CSP). Along with Milner's Calculus of Communicating Systems (CCS), CSP has been a highly influential system for specifying and analyzing certain types of concurrent systems. The standard method for proving properties of imperative programs by using loop invariants, defined in his 1969 journal article, is now commonly called Hoare Logic.

The picture on this page shows Tony Hoare and his wife Jill standing outside Buckingham Palace, holding the medal he received when he was knighted by Queen Elizabeth II.

communicate by reading and writing to a shared structure or by using abstractions provided by the operating system. Programs can send or receive data from a Unix pipe, for example, by function calls that are handled by the operating system. C programs can also create processes and terminate them by using system calls.

There are several reasons why a concurrent programming language can be a better problem-solving tool for concurrent programming than a sequential language. One is that a concurrent programming language can provide abstractions and control structures that are designed specifically for concurrent programming. We look at several examples in this chapter. Another is that a programming language may provide "lighter-weight" processes. Operating systems generally give each process its own address space, with a separate run-time stack, program counter, and heap. Although this protects one process from another, there are significant costs associated with setting up a process and in switching the flow of control from one process to another. Programming language implementations may provide lightweight processes that run in the same operating system address space but are protected by programming language properties. With lightweight processes, there is less cost associated with concurrency, allowing a programmer to use concurrency more freely. Finally, there is the issue of portability across operating systems. Although it is possible to do concurrent programming with C and Unix system calls, for example, programs written for one version of Unix may not run correctly under other versions of Unix and may not be easy to port to other operating systems.

14.1 BASIC CONCEPTS IN CONCURRENCY

Before looking at some specific language designs, we discuss some of the basic issues in concurrent programming and some of the traditional operating system mechanisms used to allow concurrent processes to cooperate effectively.

A sequence of actions may be called a *process*, *thread*, or *task*. Although some authors use these terms interchangeably, they can have different connotations. The word process is often used to refer to an operating system process, which generally runs in its own address space. Threads, in specific languages like Concurrent ML and Java, may run under control of the language run-time system, sharing the same operating system address space. Some authors define thread to mean "lightweight process," which means a process that does not run in a separate operating system address space. The term process is used in the rest of Section 14.1, as many of the mechanisms we discuss are used in operating systems. In discussing Concurrent ML and Java, we use the term thread because this is the standard term for these languages and because threads defined in a Concurrent ML or Java program are lightweight processes that all run in the same operating system address space.

14.1.1 Execution Order and Nondeterminism

Concurrent programs may have many possible execution orders. An elementary and historical concurrent programming construct is the cobegin/coend form used in Concurrent Pascal. This language was developed by P. Brinch Hansen at Caltech in the 1970s. Here is an example Concurrent Pascal program that has several execution orders:

```
x := 0;
cobegin
    begin x := 1; x := x+1 end;
    begin x := 2; x := x+1 end;
coend;
print(x);
```

This program executes sequentially, as usual in Pascal, except that, within the cobegin/coend statement, all of the independent blocks are executed concurrently. Concurrent blocks may interact by reading or assigning to global variables. The cobegin/coend statement terminates when all of the concurrent blocks inside it terminate. After the cobegin/coend statement terminates, the program continues sequentially with the statement following coend.

Here is a diagram showing how our sample Concurrent Pascal program can be executed on a single processor. Each assignment statement is executed *atomically*, meaning that even though an assignment statement might be carried out with a sequence of more elementary machine-language steps, once the processor starts executing an assignment statement, the processor continues and completes the assignment

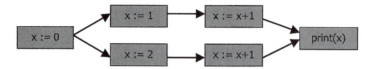

before allowing another process to execute. In other words, only one assignment statement runs at a time. However, the order between assignments may be different on different executions of the program. Each arrow in this figure illustrates a constraint on execution order: The statement at the left end of the arrow must finish before the statement on the right can start. However, there is no necessary ordering between statements that are not connected by a sequence of arrows. In particular, the assignment x:=1 could be executed before or after the assignment x:=2. Here are some possible execution orders for this program:

```
x:=0; x:=1; x:=2; x:=x+1; x:=x+1; print(x) // Output 4
x:=0; x:=2; x:=1; x:=x+1; x:=x+1; print(x) // Output 3
x:=0; x:=1; x:=x+1; x:=2; x:=x+1; print(x) // Output 3
x:=0; x:=2; x:=x+1; x:=1; x:=x+1; print(x) // Output 2
```

This program illustrates one of the main difficulties in designing and testing concurrent systems: nondeterminism. A program is *deterministic* if, for each sequence of program inputs, there one sequence of program actions and resulting outputs. In contrast, a program is *nondeterministic* if there is more than one possible sequence of actions corresponding to a single input sequence. Our sample Concurrent Pascal program is nondeterministic because the order of execution of the statements inside the cobegin/coend construct is not determined. There are several possible execution orders and, if the program is run several times on the same computer, it is possible for the program to produce different outputs on different runs.

Nondeterminism makes it difficult to design and debug programs. In a complex software system, there may be many possible execution orders. It is difficult for program designers to think carefully about millions of possible execution orders and identify errors that may occur in only a small number of them. It also may be impractical to test program behavior under all possible execution orders. Even if there is some way to cause the system to try all possible orders (a difficult task for distributed systems involving many computers connected by a network), there could be so many orders that it would take years to try them all.

One example that illustrates the complexity of nondeterminism is the design of cache coherency protocols for multiprocessors. In a modern shared-memory multiprocessor, several processors share common memory. Because access to shared memory takes time and can be a bottleneck when one processor needs to wait for another process, each processor maintains a local cache. Each cache is a small amount of memory that duplicates values stored in main memory. The job of the cache coherence protocol is to maintain the processor caches and to guarantee some form of memory consistency, e.g., the value returned by every load/store sequence must be consistent with what could have happened if there were no caches and all load/store instructions operated directly on shared memory in some order. Cache coherence protocols are notoriously difficult to design and many careful designs contain flaws that surface only under certain conditions. Because of their subtlety, many cache coherence protocols are analyzed by automated tools that are designed to detect errors in nondeterministic systems. In Subsection 14.4.3 we look at the Java virtual machine memory model, which involves some of the same issues as cache coherency protocols for multiprocessors.

14.1.2 Communication, Coordination, and Atomicity

Every programming language for explicit concurrency provides some mechanism to initiate and terminate independent sequential processes. The programming languages we consider in this chapter also contain mechanisms for some or all of the following general purposes:

■ *communication* between processes, achieved by mechanisms such as buffered or synchronous communication channels, broadcast, or shared variables or objects,
■ *coordination* between processes, which may explicitly or implicitly cause one process to wait for another process before continuing,
■ *atomicity*, which affects both interaction between processes and the handling of error conditions.

When we compare concurrent programming languages, we always look at the way processes are defined, how they communicate and coordinate activities, and how programmers may define atomic actions within the language (if the language provides explicit support for atomicity).

The most elementary form of interprocess communication, as illustrated in the Concurrent Pascal example in Subsection 14.1.1, is through shared variables. Processes may also communicate through shared data structures or files. Another form of interprocess communication is called *message passing*. Here are some of the main distinctions among various forms of message-passing mechanisms:

■ *Buffering*. If communication is *buffered*, then every data item that is sent remains available until it is received. In *unbuffered* communication, a data item sent before the receiver is ready to accept that it may be lost.
■ *Synchronicity*. In *synchronous* communication, the sender cannot transmit a data item unless the receiver is ready to receive it. With *asynchronous* communication,

the sending process may transmit a data item and continue executing even if the receiver is not ready to receive the data.

■ *Message Order.* A communication mechanism may preserve transmission order or it may not. If a mechanism preserves transmission order, then a sequence of messages will be received in the order that they are sent.

Coordination mechanisms allow one process to wait for another or notify a waiting process that it may proceed. Concurrent Pascal cobegin/coend provides a rudimentary form of process coordination as all processes started at the same cobegin must finish before the statement following coend may proceed. Locking and semaphores, discussed in Subsections 14.1.3 and 14.1.4, provide more sophisticated forms of concurrency control.

An action is *atomic* if every execution will either complete successfully or terminate in a state that is indistinguishable from the state in which the action was initiated. A nonatomic action may involve intermediate states that are observable by other processes. A nonatomic action may also halt in error before the entire action is complete, leaving some trace of its partial progress. Generally speaking, any concurrent programming language must provide some atomic actions, because, without some guarantee of atomicity, it is extremely difficult to predict the behavior of any program.

14.1.3 Mutual Exclusion and Locking

There are many programming situations in which two or more processes share some data structure, and some coordination is needed to maintain consistency of the data structure. Here is a simple example that illustrates some of the issues.

Example 14.1

Suppose we have a system that allows people to sign up for mailing lists. This system may involve a number of lists of people, and some of these lists may be accessed by more than one process. Here is a procedure to add a person to a list:

```
procedure sign_up(person)
    begin
        n := n + 1;
        list[n] := person;
    end;
```

This procedure uses an array to store the names in the list and an integer variable to indicate the position of the last person added to the list. There may be other procedures to read names from the list or remove them.

The sign_up procedure works correctly if only one process adds to the list at a time, but not if two processes add to the list concurrently. For example, consider the following program section:

```
cobegin
    sign_up(fred);
    sign_up(bill);
end;
```

As discussed in Subsection 14.1.1, there are several possible execution orders for the assignments to number and list. The ordering between assignments is shown in this illustration:

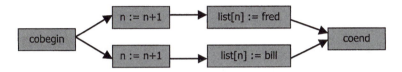

One possible execution order increments n twice, then writes names fred and bill into the same location. This is not correct: Instead of adding both names to the list, we end up with an empty location, and only one of the two names in the list. The state resulting from the sequence of assignments

```
n := n+1; n := n+1; list[n] := fred; list[n] := bill;
```

is called an *inconsistent state* because it is not consistent with the intended behavior of the operations on lists. An invariant for list and integer variable n is that for every integer i up to n there are data stored in list[i]. This invariant is preserved by sign_up, if it is called sequentially. However, if it is called concurrently, the data structure invariant may be destroyed.

Mutual Exclusion

Example 14.1 shows that, for certain operations, it is important to restrict concurrency so that only one process proceeds at a time. This leads to the notion of *critical section*. A critical section is a section of a program that accesses shared resources. Because a process in a critical section may disrupt other processes, it may be important to allow only one process into a critical section at a time. Mechanisms for preventing conflicting actions in independent processes are called *mutual-exclusion* mechanisms.

Mutual-exclusion mechanisms may be designed to satisfy some or all of the following criteria:

- *Mutual exclusion*: Only one process at a time may be in its critical section.
- *Progress:* If no processes are in their critical section and some process wants to enter a critical section, it becomes possible for one waiting process to enter its critical section.
- *Bounded waiting:* If one process is waiting, there must be a bound on the number of times that other processes are allowed to enter the critical section before this process is allowed to enter. In other words, no waiting process should have to wait indefinitely.

It is also desirable to ensure that, if one process halts in a critical section, other processes will eventually be able to enter the critical section.

Locks and Busy Waiting

A general approach to mutual exclusion is shown in the following pseudocode, which uses the sign_up procedure from Example 14.1. The main idea is that each process executes some kind of *wait* action before calling sign_up and executes some kind of *signal* action afterward. The wait action should check to see if any other process is calling sign_up or executing any other procedure that might interfere with sign_up. If so, the action should make the process wait, only allowing the call to sign_up to occur when this is acceptable. The signal action allows a waiting process to proceed.

```
<initialze concurrency control>
cobegin
    begin
        <wait>           // wait for access
        sign_up(fred);   // critical section
        <signal>         // allow waiting process to proceed
    end;
    begin
        <wait>           // wait for access
        sign_up(bill);   // critical section
        <signal>         // allow waiting process to proceed
    end;
end;
```

Although the ideas behind *wait* and *signal* actions may seem straightforward, implementing these actions is tricky. In fact, in the early days of concurrent programming, several incorrect implementations were proposed before a good solution was finally discovered. We can understand some of the subtlety by examining a plausible but imperfect implementation.

Example 14.2

Let us try to implement wait and signal by using an ordinary integer variable as a "lock." Each process will test the variable before it enters its critical section. If another process is already in its critical section, then the lock will indicate that the process must wait. If the value of the lock indicates that the process may enter, then the process sets the lock to keep other processes out. This approach is shown in the following code:

```
lock := 0;
cobegin
    begin
        while lock=1 do end;   // loop doing nothing until lock is 0
```

```
        lock:=1;                // set lock to enter critical section
        sign_up(fred);          // critical section
        lock:=0;                // release lock
    end;
    begin
        while lock=1 do end;    // loop doing nothing until lock is 0
        lock:=1;                // set lock to enter critical section
        sign_up(bill);          // critical section
        lock := 0;              // release lock
    end;
end;
```

Each process (each of the two blocks) tests the lock before entering the critical section (i.e., before calling sign_up). If the lock is 1, indicating that another process is using sign_up, then the process loops until the lock is 0. When the lock is 0, the process enters the critical section, setting lock:=1 on entry and lock:=0 on exit. Using a loop to wait for some condition is called *busy waiting*.

The problem with using a shared variable for mutual exclusion is that the operation that reads the value of the variable is different from the operation that sets the variable. With the method shown in this code, it is possible for one process to test the variable and see that the lock is open, but before the process can lock other processes out, another process can also see that the lock is open and enter its critical section. This allows two processes to call sign_up at the same time.

A fundamental idea is concurrency control is atomic test-and-set. An atomic test-and-set, sometimes called TSL for Test and Set Lock, copies the value of the lock variable and sets it to a nonzero (locked) value, all in one atomic step. Although the value of the lock variable is being tested, no other process can enter its critical section. Most modern processors provide some form of test-and-set in their instruction set.

Deadlock

Deadlock occurs if a process can never continue because the state of another process. Deadlock can easily occur if there are two processes and two locks. Suppose that Process 1 first sets Lock 1 and then wait for Lock 2. If Process 2 first sets Lock 2 and then waits for Lock 1, then both processes are waiting for the lock held by the other process. In this situation, neither process can proceed and deadlock has occurred.

One technique that prevents deadlock is called *two-phase locking*. In two-phase locking, a process is viewed as a sequence of independent tasks. For each task, the process must first acquire all locks that are needed (or could be needed) to perform the task. Before proceeding from one task to the next, a process must release all locks. Thus there are two phases in the use of locks, a locking phase in which all locks are acquired and a release phase in which all locks are released. To avoid deadlock in the locking phase, all processes agree on an ordering of the locks and acquire locks in that order. You may find more information about locking policies and deadlock in books on operating systems and database transactions.

14.1.4 Semaphores

Semaphores, first proposed by Edsger W. Dijkstra in 1968, provide a way for an operating system to guarantee mutual exclusion without busy waiting. There are several different detailed implementations of semaphores. All use a counter or Boolean flag and require the operating system to execute the entire wait or signal procedure atomically. Atomicity prevents individual statements of one wait procedure from being interleaved with individual statements of another wait on the same semaphore.

A standard *semaphore* is represented by an integer variable, an integer maximum, and a queue of waiting processes. Initially, the integer variable is set to the maximum. The maximum indicates the number of processes that may enter a critical section at the same time; in many situations the maximum is one. If a program contains several shared resources, the program may use a separate semaphore for each resource.

When a process waits on a semaphore, the wait operation checks the integer value of the semaphore. If the value is greater than 0, this indicates that a process may proceed. The value is decremented before proceeding to limit the number of processes that are allowed to proceed. (If the maximum is 1, then the semaphore is decremented to 0 and no other process can proceed.)

If a wait is executed on a semaphore whose integer value is 0, then the process is suspended and placed on a queue of waiting processes. Suspending a process is an operating system operation that keeps the process from continuing until the process is resumed. Here is a pseudocode showing how semaphore wait may be implemented:

```
procedure wait (s : Semaphore)
begin                              // This procedure must be executed atomically
    if s.value > 0 then
            s.value:= s.value - 1;   // Enter section and decrement counter
    else
            suspend_on (s.queue); // Wait for other processes to finish
    end;
```

When a process leaves a critical section, it must allow other processes waiting on the associated semaphore to proceed. The signal operation checks the semaphore queue to see if any process is suspended. If the queue is not empty, one of the suspended waiting processes is allowed to run. If no process is waiting, then the integer value of the semaphore is incremented. Here is a pseudocode showing how semaphore signal might be implemented:

```
procedure signal (s : Semaphore)
begin                              // This procedure must be executed atomically
    if length (s.queue) = 0 then
        s.value := s.value + 1;   // Increase count allowing other processes to enter
    else
        allow_one_process (s.queue);   // Wake up one suspended process
end
```

If allow_one_process wakes up the first process on the queue, then each waiting process will have to wait only for the processes ahead of it in the queue. This achieves bounded waiting, as defined in Subsection 14.1.3.

Originally, Dijkstra, used P() for Wait() because P is the first letter of the Dutch word *passeren*, which means to pass, and V() for Signal() because V is the first letter of the Dutch word *vrijgeven*, which means to release.

14.1.5 Monitors

Semaphores provide mutual exclusion, but only if used properly. If a process calls wait before entering a critical section, but fails to call signal afterwards, this error may cause the program to deadlock. This kind of program error can be hard to find. Monitors, developed in the early 1970s, place the responsibility for synchronization on the operations that access data. Monitors are similar to abstract data types, with all synchronization placed in the operations of the data type. This makes it easier to write correct client code.

A *monitor* consists of one or more procedures, an initialization sequence, and local data. The local data are accessible only by the monitor procedures, which are responsible for all synchronization associated with concurrent access to the data. In traditional terminology, a process *enters* the monitor by invoking one of its procedures. The synchronization code is generally designed so that only one process may be in the monitor at a time; any other process that calls a monitor procedure is suspended and waits for the monitor to become available.

In modern terminology, a monitor might be called a *synchronized object*. In an important early paper (Monitors: An Operating System Structuring Concept, Comm. ACM 17(10) 1974, pp. 549–557), C.A.R. Hoare showed that monitors can be implemented by use of semaphores and, conversely, semaphores can be implemented by use of monitors. In this sense, the two constructs are equally powerful synchronization constructs. However, monitors have proven to be a more useful program-structuring concept. We look at the main programming issues associated with monitors in Section 14.4 in our discussion of Java synchronized objects.

14.2 THE ACTOR MODEL

Actors are a general approach to concurrent computation. Each actor is a form of reactive object, executing some computation in response to a message and sending out a reply when the computation is done. Actors do not have any shared state, but use buffered asynchronous message passing for all communication. Although pure actor systems have not been widely successful, actors are an appealing metaphor and an interesting point on the spectrum of concurrent language design alternatives.

Actors originated through Carl Hewitt's work on the artificial intelligence system Planner in the early 1970s. The concept evolved as a result of approximately 20 years of subsequent effort by Hewitt and many others, influencing a range of concurrent object-oriented systems. There is no one actor system that embodies all of the concepts that have been developed in the literature. As a result, our discussion of actor systems is more a discussion of a point of view, with possible alternatives and embellishments, than an evaluation of a specific, concrete system.

An *actor* is an object that carries out its actions in response to communications it receives. There are three basic actions that an actor may perform:

- It may send communication to itself or other actors,
- It may create actors,
- It may specify a replacement behavior, which is essentially another actor that takes the place of the actor that creates it for the purpose of responding to later communication.

Actor computation is reactive, which means that computation is performed only in response to communication. An actor program does not explicitly create new processes and control their execution. Instead, an actor program creates some number of actors and sends them messages. All of these actors can react to messages concurrently, but there is no explicit concept of thread.

An actor is dormant until it receives communication. When an actor receives a message, the script of the actor may specify subsequent communication and a set of new actors to create. After executing its script, the actor returns to its dormant state. The replacement behavior specifies how the actor will behave when it receives another message. For example, if an actor representing the number 3 receives a communication *increment by* 1, its replacement behavior will be to represent the number 4. There is no assignment to local variables in the actor model; the only side effect of an actor is to specify a replacement behavior, which is an atomic state change that takes effect only after the other activities are complete.

In any computation, each actor receives a linearly ordered sequence of messages. However, messages are not guaranteed to arrive in the order in which they are sent. If one actor, A, sends two communications to another, B, then B may not receive them in the same order that A sent them. This is consistent with the idea that actors may be physically located in different places, connected by a communication network that might route different messages along different paths.

An important part of the actor model is the *mail system*, which routes and buffers messages between actors. Every message must be sent to a *mail address*; one actor may communicate with another if it knows its mail address. When an actor A specifies a replacement behavior, the replacement behavior will be the script for a new actor that receives all messages addressed to the mail address of A.

A message from one actor to another is called a *task*. A task has three parts:

- A unique tag, distinguishing it from other tasks in the system,
- A target, which is the mail address of the intended receiver,
- A communication, which is the data contained in the message.

Figure 14.1 shows a finite set represented by an actor. The actor in the upper left of the figure represents the set with elements 1, 4, and 7. This actor receives a task Insert 2. In response, the actor becomes the actor on the right that has elements 1, 2, 4, and 7. This actor receives the task Get_min. As a result, the actor sends the message 1, which is the minimum element in the set, and becomes an actor that represents the set with elements 2, 4, and 7.

The configuration of an actor system consists of a finite set of actors and a finite set of pending or undelivered tasks. Because each task has a single, specified destination,

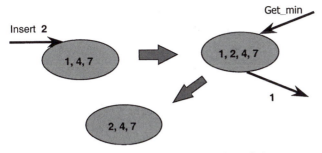

Figure 14.1. Messages and state change for a finite-set actor.

we may visualize the system as a set of actors and task queues, with one queue per actor and each task on exactly one queue.

Although we will not look at the syntactic structure of actor programs in any detail, here is a short example to give some feel for the language. The code subsequent is something called a behavior definition, which defines a behavior and gives it a name but does not create an actor. A program that uses this behavior definition creates one or more stack_node actors and sends them tasks. As this example illustrates, a behavior may be defined as a function of parameters, which are called *acquaintances:*

```
a stack_node with acquaintances content and link
    if operation requested is push(new_content) then
        let P=new stack_node with current acquaintances
        become stack_node with acquaintances new_content and P
    if operation requested is a pop and content != nil then
        become forwarder to link
        send content to customer
```

A stack_node actor with the behavior defined by this code has two data fields (determined by acquaintances), content and link. This actor sits and waits for a task. The two tasks that the actor will process are push and pop. If the operation requested is a push, then the push task will include a content value called new_content. The actor creates a copy P of itself, as indicated by the expression new stack_node with current acquaintances and becomes a stack node with data new_content and link to the copy P of the actor's previous state. The reason why the actor "becomes" the new actor, instead of keeping its original state and creating a new actor linked to it, is that future tasks sent to this actor should reach the new stack with new_content added, not the old stack without these data.

The pop operation uses an actor-specific concept called a forwarder. A forwarder actor does nothing itself, except forward all tasks to another actor. The reason for having forwarders is illustrated by the pop operation, in which the actor that receives the pop task would like to disappear and let another actor take its place. Instead of "disappearing," the actor becomes a forwarded to the actor it is linked to.

We can see how forwarders work by looking at some pictures. Suppose that three actors represent a stack, with data 3, 4, and 5, as shown here:

If the actor on the left, representing the top of the stack, receives a pop task, then the actor sends content 3 to the actor that sent the pop task and becomes a forwarder. This produces a stack of three actors, as shown here.

The forwarder has the same mail address as that of the actor with content 3, so any task sent to the top of the stack will now be forwarded to the actor with content 4. In effect, the forwarder node is invisible to any user of the stack. In fact, an actor implementation may garbage-collect forwarders and handle forwarding in the mail system.

Two interesting general aspects of actors are the concepts of replacement behavior and the use of buffered asynchronous communication. An actor changes state only by becoming another actor after it completes processing input. This is a very clean idea that eliminates state change within an actor while computing a response to a task.

The motivation for using asynchronous communication is that it is easily implemented on a wide-area network. When actors are on different computers connected by a slow network, it is easier to implement asynchronous communication by means of standard IP-based protocols than it is to devise some form a synchronous communication. With asynchronous communication, it is important either to use some form of buffering or to use some kind of resend protocol to handle lost messages. Although buffers may overflow in practice, buffered communication is a convenient abstraction for many programming situations.

The actor design does not guarantee the order of message delivery. This is inconvenient in many situations. For example, consider an actor traversing a graph, using another stack actor to keep track of graph nodes to revisit. If there is no guarantee on the order of messages that push graph nodes onto the stack, the algorithm will not necessarily traverse the graph in depth-first order. The design rationale for basing actors on communication without guaranteed order is that order can be imposed by adding sequence numbers to messages.

There are also some pragmatic issues associated with programming when message delivery may take arbitrarily long. Returning to the example of searching a graph, using a stack to keep track of nodes that must be revisited, it seems difficult to tell whether the graph search is finished. The usual algorithm continues to visit nodes of the graph until the stack of remaining nodes is empty. However, if an actor representing a stack sends a message saying that the stack is empty, this may mean only that all push messages are still in the mail system somewhere and have not yet been delivered to the stack.

Although the simplicity of the actor model is appealing, these problems with message order, message delivery, and coordination between sequences of concurrent actions also help us appreciate the programming value of more complex concurrent languages.

14.3 CONCURRENT ML

Concurrent ML is a concurrent extension of Standard ML that provides dynamic thread creation and synchronous message passing on typed channels. The language was designed by John Reppy, who was interested in concurrency in user interfaces and distributed systems. A motivating application was Exene, a multithreaded *X Window System* toolkit written by Emden Gansner and Reppy. The language implementation, as an extension of Standard ML of New Jersey, is available on the web from several sources and a book describing the language has been published (J. H. Reppy, *Concurrent Programming in ML*, Cambridge Univ. Press, New York, 1999). In the uniprocessor implementation, Concurrent ML threads are implemented with continuations.

The most interesting aspects of Concurrent ML, also referred to as CML, are the ways that communication and coordination are combined and the way that CML allows programmers to define their own communication and synchronization abstractions. The main programming language concept that gives CML this power is a first-class value representing a synchronization called an *event*. We look at some aspects of CML in some detail to study the way that synchronous communication can work as a basic language primitive. Whereas Actors provide too little synchronization, CML, with only threads and channels, provides too much synchronization. This problem is solved with an interesting event mechanism.

14.3.1 Threads and Channels

A CML process is called a *thread*. When a CML program begins, it consists of a single thread. This thread may create additional threads by using the spawn primitive:

```
spawn : (unit → unit) → thread_id
```

where unit is the SML type with only one element (similar to C void, as discussed in Subsection 5.4.2), and thread_id is the CML type used to identify and refer to threads.

When spawn f is evaluated, the function call f() is executed as a separate thread. The return value of the function is discarded, but the function may communicate with other threads by using channels. The thread that evaluates spawn f is called the *parent thread* and the thread running f() is called the *child thread*. In CML, the parent–child relation does not have any impact on thread execution – either thread may terminate without affecting the other.

Here is an expression that spawns two child threads, each printing a message by using the CIO.print function for concurrent input/output:

```
let  val pr = CIO.print
in   pr "begin parent\n";
     spawn (fn () => (pr "child 1\n";));
     spawn (fn () => (pr "child 2\n";));
     pr "end parent\n"
end;
```

When evaluated, this expression will always print "begin parent" first and then print the other three strings, "child 1", "child 2", and "end parent" in arbitrary order. Unlike cobegin/coend, each child thread may finish before or after the parent thread.

Another CML primitive, which we can define by combining spawn with looping or tail recursion, is forever. This function takes an initial value and a function that can be repeatedly applied to this value:

---

forever : 'a $\rightarrow$ ('a $\rightarrow$ 'a) $\rightarrow$ unit

---

The expression forever init f computes x1 = f(init), followed by x2 = f(x1), x3 = f(x2), and so on, indefinitely. The values x1, x2, x3, ..., are discarded, but the function f may communicate with other threads. Other features of CML can be used to terminate a thread that loops indefinitely.

An important communication mechanism in CML is called a *channel*. For each CML type 'a, there is a type 'a chan of channels that communicate values of type 'a. Two useful operations on channels are send and receive:

---

recv : 'a chan $\rightarrow$ 'a
send : ('a chan * 'a) $\rightarrow$ unit

As you would expect, if c is an int chan, for example, then recv c returns an int. The type of send is a little more complicated, but makes sense if you think about it: If c is an int channel, then send(c,3) sends the integer 3 on channel c. There is no obvious value for send(c,3) to return, so the type of send(c,3) is unit.

CML message passing is synchronous, meaning that communication occurs only when both a sender and a receiver are ready to communicate. If one thread executes a send and no thread is ready to execute recv on the same channel, the sending thread *blocks* (stops and waits) for a thread to execute recv. Similarly, if a thread executes recv and no thread is sending, the receiving thread blocks and waits for a thread to send. Although standard CML channels are point-to-point, meaning that each send reaches one receiver, CML also has multicast channels that allow one send to reach many receivers.

Channels are created by the channel constructor,

---

channel : unit $\rightarrow$ 'a chan

---

which creates a channel of arbitrary type. Type inference will generally replace the type variable in the type of channel() with the type of values sent or received from the channel. It is not possible to use the same channel to send and receive different types of values, except by using ML datatype to create a type that is a union of several types.

Here is a simple example that uses a channel to synchronize two threads:

```
- fun child_talk () =
    let val ch = channel ()
        val pr = CIO.print
    in
        spawn (fn () => (pr "begin 1\n";   send(ch,0); pr "end 1\n"));
        spawn (fn () => (pr "begin 2\n";   recv ch; pr "end 2\n"));
    end;
> val child_talk = fn: unit → unit
```

This can be run (by RunCML.doit), with the following output:

```
begin 1
begin 2
end 2
end 1
```

The ordering between the two begins is arbitrary – they could appear in either order – and similarly for the ends. However, synchronous communication between the two threads causes the two begins to be printed before either of the ends.

Functions Using Threads and Channels

Because channels are "just another type" in CML, we can define functions that take channel arguments and return channel results. For example, it is easy to write a thread that takes integers off an input channel and sends their squares on an output channel. Because we may want to create threads that do squaring for different channels, it is useful to write a function that creates a squaring thread, given an input channel and an output channel:

```
fun square (inCh, outCh) =
    forever () (fn () =>
        send (outCh, square(recv(inCh))));
```

One useful programming technique in CML involves defining functions that create threads, then assembling a network of communicating threads by applying the functions to particular channels. Assuming that numbers(ch) creates a thread that outputs numbers on channel ch, here is a function that creates a thread that outputs squares on a channel and returns that channel:

```
fun mkSquares () =
let
    val outCh = channel()
    and c1 = channel()
in
    numbers(c1);
    square(c1, outCh);
    outCh
end;
```

If a CML thread has the name of a channel, then the thread can send messages on the channel, receive messages on the channel, or both. If a channel is passed to more than one thread, then each thread can send messages and receive messages on the channel.

14.3.2 Selective Communication and Guarded Commands

A basic problem with synchronous communication is that when only one thread is ready to communicate, it blocks and cannot do any other useful work. To see why this is a problem, think about a concurrent system in which several "producer" processes place items onto a queue and several "consumer" processes remove items from the queue.

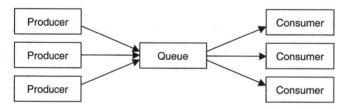

A natural way to implement the queue is by some thread that runs forever, taking input from a producer channel and sending output to a consumer channel. When the queue is not empty, it should be ready to either send or receive, depending on whether a producer or consumer is ready. We can define the indefinitely looping thread by using forever and build the queue internal data structure by using the nonconcurrent part of CML, but choosing between producer and consumer cannot be done with synchronous channels and sequential control structures. The problem is that, if the queue thread executes a recv and a consumer is ready but no producer is ready, the system will wait for a producer to send, even though we would like the queue to send to the waiting consumer. A similar problem occurs if the queue process tries to send when it would be better to receive.

The solution to this problem is a concurrent control structure that chooses among available actions. A historically important notation for selective choice is Dijkstra's *guarded command language*. A guarded command, which has historically been written in the form

```
Condition ⇒ Command
```

consists of a predicate and an action. The intent of Condition ⇒ Command is that, if the Condition is true, then the Command may be executed. Dijkstra's guarded command language includes constructs such as

```
if
    Condition ⇒ Command
    Condition ⇒ Command
    · · ·
    Condition ⇒ Command
fi
```

which executes one of the commands whose condition is true, and

```
do
    Condition ⇒ Command
    Condition ⇒ Command
    · · ·
    Condition ⇒ Command
od
```

which loops indefinitely, on each iteration selecting one of the conditions that is true and executing the corresponding command. The if . . . fi construct is *not* the same as Lisp cond. Lisp cond is a sequential conditional. Each condition is tested in turn, starting with the first one, until a true condition is found. In Dijkstra's guarded command language, an if . . . fi statement may nondeterministically choose any guarded command whose condition is true.

The solution to the queue programming problem in CML is to build a form of do . . . od out of CML control structures, in effect writing the queue as

```
do
    Producer is ready to send ⇒ Receive input and store in queue
    Consumer is ready to receive and queue is not empty ⇒ Send to waiting consumer
od
```

We will see how to do this in the next subsection.

14.3.3 First-Class Synchronous Operations: Events

The most innovative and novel feature of CML is a synchonization value that is called an *event*. (The word event generally means "something that happens" in other languages, but in CML the word has a very specific meaning.) Intuitively, we can decompose send into two parts: the code executed when the send occurs and the act of executing this code. In a sense, the code that will cause a send to occur is the *send event*, and doing the send is called *synchronizing on this event*. We can similarly represent the ability to execute recv as an event and synchronize on this event to synchronously receive a value. By grouping send and receive events together in the type of events and defining operations on events CML provides some very interesting programming possibilities.

In case the idea behind CML events seems completely baffling, here is another way to think about events. Suppose that the send command is implemented as a function call. Then, in a language in which we can pass functions as arguments, return them as results, and store them in reference cells, it is possible to do various kinds of computation with the function that implements send, without actually sending. For example, you could build a function that sends twice in parallel out of one send function. You can think of the "send event" as the function that performs a send and "synchronizing on a send event" as calling the function that performs a send.

CML uses the type

```
'a event
```

as the type of all synchronous operations that return a value of type 'a when a thread synchronizes on them. The sync function takes an event and synchronizes on it, returning a value of the appropriate type:

```
sync : 'a event ⟶ 'a
```

One kind of synchronous event is a receive event,

```
recvEvt : 'a chan ⟶ 'a event
```

When a thread synchronizes on a receive event by executing sync(recvEvt c) on a channel c of type 'a chan, the result is a value of type 'a. The recv function previously defined for synchronously receiving a value from a channel is definable as

```
fun recv(ch) = sync (recvEvt (ch));
```

In words, a thread can synchronously receive from a channel by synchronizing on a receive event for that channel.

The relation between a send event and send discussed in Subsection 14.3.1 is similar. A send event produces only a value of type unit, so the basic event operator sendEvt has type

```
sendEvt : ('a chan * 'a) ⟶ unit event
```

The functions sendEvt and recvEvt are called base-event constructors because they create event values that produce a single primitive synchronous operation.

The power of CML events comes from operators that build more complicated events from base events, including an operator select for selective communication, which we will discuss shortly. A simpler operator on events is the wrap function,

wrap : ('a event * ('a → 'b)) → 'b event

which combines an event that produces an 'a with a function 'a → 'b to get an event that produces a 'b. The idea is that if event e will produce a value x of type 'a and f: 'a → 'b, then wrap(e,f) will produce the value f(x).

Selective Communication with Events

The select operator for selective communication can be defined from a primitive function on events that chooses an event out of a list. The function

choose : 'a event list → 'a event

takes a list of events and returns one event from the list. (If the list is empty, then a special event that can never be used is returned.) Choose does not have to return the first event in the list or the last event from the list, or the event from any other specific position in the list. However, choose must return an event that can be synchronized on if there is one in the list. We will see how this works by discussing select.

The select function is defined as

fun select(evs) = sync(choose (evs))

In words, selecting from a list of events chooses an event from the list and synchronizes on it. This is the function we need to solve the programming problem described in Subsection 14.3.2.

Here is a simple example that uses select. The add function creates a thread that repeatedly reads a pair of numbers, one from each of two input channels, and sends the sum of each pair out on an output channel:

```
fun add ( inCh1, inCh2, outCh) =
    forever () (fn () = > let
        val (a,b) = select [
                    wrap (recEvt inCh1, fn a => (a, recv inCh2)),
                    wrap (recEvt inCh2, fn b => (recv inCh1, b))
                ]
        in
            send (outCh, a+b)
        end
    )
```

Let us read through the code and see how this works. Given three integer channels, the add function creates a looping thread by using forever. Each time through the body of the loop, add binds (a, b) to a pair of integers. The way it gets the pair of integers is determined by select. Select is applied to a list containing two events, the first involving recEvt(inCh1) and the second recEvt(inCh2). If some thread is ready to send an integer on inCh1, then the first event may be selected. Similarly, if some thread is ready to send an integer on inCh2, then the second event may be selected. Moreover, if there is a thread ready to send on either channel, then the select will choose a receive that can proceed; it will not choose the event that has to block and wait for another thread to send. If select chooses to receive an integer on inCh1, then the add thread may block and wait for an integer on the other channel, inCh2, as one integer from each channel is needed in order to proceed. Once a pair (a, b) is received, then add sends the sum a+b on the output channel outCh.

The programming technique used in add can also be used to implement a queue, as described in Subsection 14.3.2. The main idea is to use select to choose between send and receive events, depending on whether producer or consumer threads are ready to communicate. Here is the outline of a thread like the queue that selects between sending and receiving:

```
fun queue ( inCh, outCh) =
    forever () (fn () = >let
        val x = ...
        in
            select [
                wrap (recvEvt(inCh) , fn a => ( ... )),
                ...
                wrap (sendEvt(outCh, x) , fn () => ( ... )),
                ...
            ]
        end
)
```

The event mechanism of CML can be used to define and implement other communication abstractions such as a remote procedure call (RPC) style communication mechanism or a multicast channel.

Example 14.3 Synchronized Shared Memory

CML allows threads to share reference cells; because CML is an extension of Standard ML, it would be awkward to prevent this. However, assignment to shared variables can have anomalous results if the threads doing the assignment do not coordinate their effects. A good way to coordinate assignment to shared memory is through the concept of synchronized shared memory. There are several possible forms of synchronized memory. We look at one example both to understand the concept and as an example of how communications abstractions can be defined in CML.

An M-structure is a memory cell that has two states, empty and full. When an M-structure is empty, a value can be placed in the structure. When it is full, a thread can read the value, which leaves the structure empty. (The name M-structure comes from the parallel language ID, designed by R. Nikhil at MIT.) An M-structure is initially empty and can be given a value by calling a put function. If the M-structure is not empty then a take function will get its value. There are two error conditions, one arising if a thread tries to put into a full structure and the other if a thread tries to take from an empty structure. The reason why M-structures cannot be written into when they are full is to avoid losing the value that is in the structure.

In our CML definition of M-structures, taken from Reppy's book (mentioned at the beginning of Section 14.3), we use the type 'a mvar for M-variables that hold a value of type 'a. Initially, an M-variable is empty. M-variables have operations mPut, which assign a value to an M-variable, and mTake, which read a value from an M-variable. Following the pattern established for channel send and recv, we find that it is more useful to define an event form of mTake, as this allows us to use select and other event operations and we can define mTake from mTakeEvt in the same way we defined recv from recvEvt. This gives us the following interface for M-variables:

```
type 'a mvar
val mVar : unit ⟶ 'a mvar
exception Put
val mTakeEvt : 'a mvar ⟶ 'a event
val mPut : ('a mvar * 'a) ⟶ unit
```

Here is the implementation of M-variables so you can see how channels may be used to build interesting data structures and events may be used to build interesting control mechanisms:

```
datatype 'a mvar = MV of {
    takeCh : 'a chan,
    putCh : 'a chan
    ackCh : bool chan
};
fun mVar() = let
    val takeCh = channel();
    val putCh = channel();
    val ackCh = channel();
    fun empty() = let val x = recv putCh in send (ackCh, true); full x end;
    and full x = select [
            wrap (sendEvt(takeCh, x) , empty),
            wrap (recvEvt(putCh) , fn _ => (send(ackCh, false); full x))
        ]
    in
        spawn empty;
        MV{ takeCh = takeCh, putCh = putCh, ackCh = ackCh }
```

```
        End;
fun mTakeEvt (MV{takeCh, ... }) = recvEvt takeCh;
exception Put;
fun mPut (MV{takeCh, putCh, ... }, x) = (
    send(putCh, x);
    if (recv ackCh) then () else raise Put);
```

The main idea is to spawn a thread for each M-variable and use channels for communicating with this thread to implement the operations mPut and mTake. Because the operations mPut and mTake send messages to the thread representing the M-variable, most of the work is actually done by the M-variable thread, not the functions mPut and mTake.

The most complicated part of the implementation is the function mVar for creating an empty M-variable. Because the representation of an M-variable is a record of three channels, the function mVar creates three new channels at the beginning of the function body and returns the record of them at the end of the function body. The three channels are used to send and receive messages to a thread that is spawned in the body of the function. The function empty, defining the operation of the thread, first waits for a value to be put into the M-variable by synchronously receiving on channel putCh used by the mPut function. Once the M-variable has been given a value, the thread sends an acknowledgement that the variable has a value on channel ackCh, then continues by executing the function call full x, where x is the value stored in the M-variable. The function full, which is executed when the M-variable is full, will either send the value of the M-variable or receive an attempt to put a new value in the variable. However, the mPut function sends a new value and then the thread sends false on ackCh, causing mPut to raise the exception Put.

One question you might want to think about is why full sends a message on ackCh that causes mPut to raise an exception, instead of raising the exception itself. If you understand this from reading the code, then you have really understood this program. The reason full does not raise an exception is that full is executing inside the thread that is used to implement the M-variables. By sending a message to mPut, which is executed in the thread that is attempting to store a value in the M-variable, the exception is raised in the calling thread. This allows the calling thread to handle the exception and proceed with some other task.

14.4 JAVA CONCURRENCY

Java concurrency is an integral part of the Java language and run-time system. We create a Java thread object by defining a class with a run() method, either by extending the Thread class or implementing the Runnable interface directly. When a thread object is activated, the run method runs as a separate thread inside the Java virtual machine (JVM). Java communication and synchronization are provided by separate mechanisms.

Java threads may communicate by calling methods of shared objects. For example, a producer thread may communicate with a consumer thread by using a queue object. When the producer thread wants to send its output to the consumer, the producer calls an enqueue method that places its output in the queue. When the consumer is ready for another item, the consumer thread may call a dequeue method, drawing another item off the queue.

Communication through a shared object does not synchronize the threads involved – each thread may attempt to execute a method independently. To avoid problems associated with shared resources (see Subsection 14.1.3), Java provides various synchronizations primitives. The Java language provides a semaphore primitive (maintaining a queue of waiting processes) and supports monitors directly in the form of synchronized objects, which are objects that allow only one thread to invoke a method at a time.

A second form of Java concurrency, which we discuss briefly in Subsection 14.4.4, arises when Java programs running in one VM communicate with programs running in another. The Java remote method invocation (RMI) mechanism allows an object running in one JVM to invoke methods of an object running in another JVM. Java RMI is used for distributed Java programming, with distributed programming infrastructures such as JINI and JXTA relying on RMI to varying degrees.

The Java thread design is a successful language feature. Java makes concurrent programs portable across a variety of computing platforms, as concurrency is a standardized part of the language and run-time system. Java threads are used in the execution of many Java programs, as the Java garbage collector runs as a separate thread in the JVM.

Although Java has been adopted widely, there remain some difficulties in programming with Java threads. In part, these are just general problems associated with the difference between sequential and concurrent programming. Classes designed for use in sequential programs generally do not use synchronization and may not work well in multithreaded programs. Conversely, code with synchronization may be unnecessarily inefficient in serial programs – synchronization imposes a locking overhead that is wasteful in a single-threaded program.

14.4.1 Threads, Communication, and Synchronization

We can create a Java thread by extending the class Thread, which implements the Runnable interface. When a class extends Thread, it inherits methods to start the thread and throw an exception to the thread:

start: A method that spawns a new thread by causing the virtual machine to execute the run method in parallel with the thread that creates the object.

interrupt: A method that suspends and throws an exception to the thread.

Here is an example subclass of Thread:

```
class PrintMany extends Thread {
    private String msg;
    public PrintMany (String m) {msg = m;}
    public void run() {
        try { for (;;){ System.out.print(msg + " ");
            sleep(10);
```

```
                    }
             } catch (InterruptedException e) {
                    return;
             }
      }
}
```

Suppose a program creates an object pm = new PrintMany("Hi"). When pm.start is called, a thread is created that prints the string "Hi" over and over. This continues until the thread is interrupted by a call to pm.interrupt.

Originally, Java threads had additional methods that affect their execution, including the following two methods:

suspend: A method that stops execution of the thread until it is later resumed.

stop: A method that forcibly causes the thread to halt.

However, these have now been deprecated because programmers have found that these methods often cause more problems than they solve. The problem with Thread.suspend is that it can contribute to deadlock. If a thread holding a lock on a critical section is suspended, then no other thread can enter the critical section until the target thread is resumed. The problem with Thread.stop is related but almost the opposite. When a thread is stopped by Thread.stop, this causes all the locks it holds to be released. If any of the objects protected by these locks is in an inconsistent state, then other threads may now have access to damaged objects. This can cause the program to behave in unexpected and incorrect ways.

Threads running inside the same virtual machine are scheduled according to their priority. Threads with higher priority are generally executed in preference to threads with lower priority, but there is no guarantee that the highest priority thread will always be run. A Java thread inherits the priority of the thread that creates it and may be changed with the setPriority method.

Communication between threads

In a sense, Java does not make any special provisions for communication: Java threads communicate by assigning to shared variables or calling the methods of shared objects. By themselves, shared variables and shared objects can be problematic, as discussed in Subsection 14.1.3. Java does provide specific synchronization mechanisms that make access to shared objects safe.

Synchronization Primitives

Java synchronization is based on three basic mechanisms:

- Locks: Every object has a lock, used for mutual exclusion.
- Wait sets: Every object has a wait set, providing a form of semaphore.
- Thread termination: A process can pause until another thread terminates.

Locks are tested and set by synchronized blocks and methods, wait sets are used by methods wait, notify, and notifyAll that are defined on all objects, and thread termination is used by the join method on thread objects.

Locks are used by the synchronized statement, which has the form

```
synchronized( object ) {
    statements
}
```

When executed, this statement computes a reference to the indicated object and locks its associated lock before executing the body of the statement. If the lock is already locked by another thread, the thread waits for the lock to become available. After executing the body of the statement, the thread releases the lock. Inside a method, it is common to use this as the lock object. However, it is possible to synchronize on the lock of any object.

Java locks are a *reentrant*, meaning that a thread may acquire a lock multiple times. This may occur if a thread executes one synchronized statement inside another or with synchronized methods that call each other. For example, the synchronized method f in the following class calls the synchronized method g:

```
public class LockTwice {
    public synchronized void f() { g(); }
    public synchronized void g() { System.out.println("Method g() called");}
}
```

When f is called, the calling thread acquires the lock for the LockTwice object. When f calls g, the thread attempts to acquire the same lock again. Because Java locks are reentrant, the calling thread may acquire the LockTwice object's lock again and both methods terminate and return. In systems that do not support reentrant locks, a second call to a synchronized method would deadlock. The semaphore implementation discussed in Subsection 14.1.4 is *not* reentrant.

The methods wait, notify, and notifyAll of class Object use the wait set of an object to provide concurrency control. A thread may suspend itself by using wait. A suspended thread does not execute any statements until another thread awakens it by using notify. The wait/notify combination can be used when threads have a producer–consumer relationship, for example. Because wait notifies the virtual machine scheduler that a process should be suspended, wait and notify are more efficient than busy waiting, which would involve a loop that repeatedly tests to see if a thread should proceed.

The notifyAll method is similar to notify, except that every thread in the wait set for the object is removed and reenabled for thread scheduling. Most Java books recommend calling the notify or notifyAll method of an object only after the calling thread has locked the object's lock.

The third form of synchronization, pausing until another thread terminates, is provided by the join method. Here is a short code example illustrating its use:

```
class Compute_thread extends Thread {
        private int result;
        public void run() { result = f(...); }
        public int getResult() { return result;}
}
...
Compute_thread t = new Compute_thread;
t.start()                // start compute thread
...
t.join(); x = t.getResult();   // wait and get result
...
```

In this code, a Compute_thread object does some kind of computation to determine some result. The program creates a Compute_thread object and starts the thread running so that it will compute a useful result. Later, when the result is needed, the program calls t.join() to wait for the Compute_thread to finish before requesting the result.

14.4.2 Synchronized Methods

Java threads typically communicate by calling methods on shared objects, with synchronization used to provide mutual exclusion. For example, if a transaction manager allows only one thread to commit at a time, the class defining a transaction manager might look like this:

```
class TransactionManager { ...
    public synchronized void commitTransaction(...) {...}
...
}
```

When a method is declared synchronized, the effect is the same as placing the body of the method inside a synchronized statement, using the lock on the object that contains the method. Therefore, even if several threads have access to a Transaction-Manager object m, only one thread can execute m.commitTransaction(...) at a time. If one thread invokes m.commitTransaction(...) while another thread is in the process of doing so, the second thread will block and wait until the lock on object m is free.

A class may have some synchronized methods and some methods that are not synchronized. If a method is not declared synchronized, then more than one thread may call the unsynchronized method simultaneously. If two threads call an unsynchronized method at the same time, then each thread will have an activation record for a method call on its own run-time stack. However, the two activation records will point to the same (shared) object fields on the run-time heap, in effect allowing the threads to interact through shared variables. In general, a programmer may wish to leave as many methods unsynchronized as possible, allowing for maximal concurrency. However, care must be taken to synchronize enough methods to avoid placing an object in an inconsistent state.

Here is a simple example of a class with two synchronized methods and an unsynchronized method (similar LinkedCell classes appear in various books and articles on Java threads and on web pages with Java program examples):

```
class LinkedCell {   // Lisp-style cons cell containing
    protected double value;   // value and link to next cell
    protected LinkedCell next;
    public LinkedCell (double v, LinkedCell t) {
        value = v; next = t;
    }
    public synchronized double getValue() {
        return value;
    }
    public synchronized void setValue(double v) {
        value = v;   // assignment not atomic
    }
    public LinkedCell next() {   // no synch needed
        return next;
    }
}
```

This class implements a standard linked cell, as might be used to implement stacks, queues, or singly linked lists, with one data field and a next field that can be used to link one linked cell to the next. Note that the data has type double. This is important (for illustrating the need for synchronization) because assignment of doubles is not atomic. Because doubles are represented by 8 bytes and 32-bit processors normally move 4 bytes at a time, it takes two separate instructions to set or read a double.

If setValue were not synchronized and two threads called value setValue simultaneouosly, this could put the LinkedCell object in an *inconsistent state*. Specifically, consider two calls, c.setValue(x) and c. setValue(y), where x and y are doubles. One possible interleaving of steps in the two assignments to c.value is

Set first half of c.value to first half of x
Set first half of c.value to first half of y
Set second half of c.value to second half of y
Set first half of c.value to second half of x

After execution in this order, c.value does not contain either x or y, but rather contains some strange number it determined by combining some bits from the representation of x with some bits from the representation of y. Because the intended effect of setValue(z) is to place the value z in the cell, interleaved execution is inconsistent with the intended semantics of the method. It is necessary to synchronize calls to setValue.

The reason for synchronizing getValue is similar. If one thread calls getValue while another calls setValue, then the double returned by the call to getValue could contain half of the bits that were in the cell before setValue took effect and half of the bits after. To prevent getValue and setValue from running simultaneously, we synchronize both. More generally, although it is possible for two threads to read a data structure simultaneously, errors can occur if a read occurs during a write. The simplest way to prevent these errors is to lock out reads while a write is occurring. A more sophisticated approach, which may be worth the effort in some applications, is to use separate read and write locks, with one read allowing any number of other reads to proceed, but preventing any write.

The next method is not synchronized because, when two threads call next simultaneously, they both get the same correct answer. There is no method to change the next link of a cell, and pointer assignment is atomic in Java anyway.

Synchronized Methods and Inheritance

The synchronized designation is not part of the method signature, and therefore a subclass may override a synchronized method with an unsynchronized method. This programmer flexibility can be useful. However, it is also possible to destroy completely the locking policy of a class through inheritance and subtyping. Therefore, programmers must be very careful when extending classes in multithreaded programs.

14.4.3 Virtual Machine and Memory Model

General properties of the JVM are discussed in Section 13.4. In the Java architecture, Java source code is compiled to an intermediate form called the Java bytecode, which is then interpreted by the JVM. When a Java program creates a new thread, this thread runs inside the JVM. As mentioned in Section 13.4, each Java thread has its own stack, but all threads share same heap. Therefore, when two threads call a method of the same object, the activation records associated with the method calls are on separate stacks, but the fields of the shared object reside in a single heap accessible to both threads. Although the basic Java virtual machine is designed to run on a single processor, multiprocessor implementations have also been developed and used.

In this subsection, we discuss two aspects of the JVM that are relevant to concurrency: concurrent garbage collection and the memory model used to manage reads and writes to shared locations.

Concurrent Garbage Collection

The JVM uses concurrent garbage collection. One advantage is performance. In sequential garbage collection, the program must stop long enough for the garbage collector to identify and reclaim unused memory. With concurrent garbage collection, the garbage collector is designed to run as other threads execute, keeping accessible memory in a consistent state so that other threads can do useful work. When properly tuned, this approach may keep an interactive program from exhibiting long pauses. Instead of pausing long enough to do a complete collection, the scheduler can switch back and forth between the garbage collector and a thread interacting with a user in a way that keeps the user from noticing any long garbage-collection pauses.

The actual design and implementation of concurrent garbage collectors is complicated and involves concepts that are not covered in this book. If you want to gain some appreciation for the issues involved, imagine running a mark-and-sweep algorithm in parallel with a program that modifies memory. As the garbage collector searches for reachable locations, starting from pointers stored on the stack, the program may modify the stack and modify pointers in reachable data. This makes it difficult to understand whether a cell that has not been marked as reachable is truly garbage. In fact, most garbage-collection algorithms, once started, must either finish the task or abandon all their work. Incremental and concurrent garbage collectors generally involve a concept called a *barrier*, which prevents threads from writing to areas of memory that are in use by the garbage collector.

Java Memory Model

The Java memory model is a specification of how shared memory can be cached and accessed by multiple threads. The specification is called a memory *model* because there are many possible implementations of the JVM. The memory model is a set of properties that every implementation must have, including both single-processor and multiprocessor implementations. The original memory model, presented in the *Java Language Specification*, has proven difficult to understand and unsatisfactory for implementers in various ways. Although it is likely that the memory model will eventually be revised to correct some of the known problems, we discuss the original design briefly in order to understand some of the subtle basic issues involved in concurrent memory access.

In the JVM, all threads share the same heap, which will be referred to as *shared memory* for the rest of this section. The virtual machine specification allows each thread to have a local memory, which will be referred to as the *thread cache*. The reason for each thread cache is to avoid coordinated reads and writes to shared memory when possible. If each thread can proceed independently, reading and writing to its own cache, this reduces the need for synchronization between threads.

Because there are several kinds of reads and writes in the memory model, it is useful to establish some precise terminology:

- *use* and *assign* are actions that read and write the thread cache,
- *load* and *store* are actions that transfer values between shared memory and cache,
- *read* and *write* are actions that read and write shared memory.

Bytecode programs execute instructions like getfield, which loads the value stored in a field of an object onto the operand stack (see Subsection 13.4.4) and putfield, which stores a value in the field of an object. In our discussion of the Java memory model, we do not need to distinguish among a getfield instruction, a getstatic instruction (which loads a value from a static field of a class), and array load instructions; we refer to all of these as *use* actions. Similarly, *assign* may be putfield, putstatic, or an array store instruction.

For example, consider a thread executing a compiled bytecode from this source code:

```
r.i = r.i+1;
```

In general, six memory actions will occur as a result of executing this statement. These actions may be interleaved with other actions by the same thread, as long as the order of actions conforms to the memory model. Here is an illustration showing only the six actions directly related to this assignment, in their expected order:

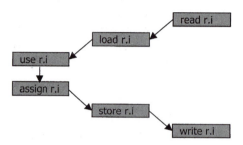

Before the thread computes the sum r.i+1, the value of field i of object r must be read from shared memory, loaded into the local cache of the thread, and used (placed on the operand stack of the thread). Similar steps occur in reverse order to place the value of r.i in shared memory. In the drawing, the left column shows actions that read and write the thread cache, the center column shows actions that transfer values between the thread cache and shared memory, and the right column shows actions that read and write shared memory. Although the effect of *store* r.i, for example, is to place a value in shared memory, the memory model includes separate *store* and *write* actions because the steps that transfer data may not take place atomically. The *store* action indicates the point when the value is read from the thread cache, and the *write* action indicates the point at which the value is actually placed shared memory. If another *assign* occurs after the *store* but before the *write*, it will change the value in the thread cache, but not the value that is placed in shared memory. An important goal in the design of the Java memory model is called *coherence*: For each variable, the uses and assigns to the variable should appear as if they acted directly on shared memory in an order that matches the order within each thread. In other words, threads may proceed independently. In the absence of synchronization, an assignment to a variable in one thread may occur before or after an assignment or use in another thread. However, the cache must be essentially invisible; the program should behave as if the actions operated on shared memory directly. Although coherence is a goal, it is not clear that the goal is actually achieved by the design.

The memory model specifies that each new thread starts with an empty local cache and, when a new variable is created, the variable is created in shared memory, not the thread cache. Here are the main constraints relating *use*, *assign*, *load*, and *store*:

- *Use* and *assign* actions by a thread must occur in the order specified by the program.
- A thread is not permitted to lose its most recent assign (more precisely, a *store*

action by thread T on variable V must occur between an *assign* by T of V and a subsequent *load* by T of V).

■ A thread is not permitted to write data from its cache to shared memory for no reason (more precisely, an *assign* action by thread T on variable V must be scheduled to occur between a *load* or *store* by T of V and a subsequent *store* by T of V).

There are similar constraints relating *load*, *store*, *read*, and *write*:

■ For every *load*, there must be a preceding *read* action.
■ For every *store*, there must be a following *write* action,
■ Actions on master copy of a variable are performed by the shared memory in the order requested by thread.

The *Java Language Specification* gives the implementer complete freedom beyond these constraints, stating that "Provided that all the constraints are obeyed, a *load* or *store* action may be issued at any time by any thread on any variable, at the whim of the implementation."

A complication in the Java memory model is a provision for so-called *prescient stores*, which are *store* actions that occur earlier than would otherwise be permitted. The purpose of allowing a prescient store is to allow Java compilers to perform certain optimizations that make properly synchronized programs run faster, but might allow some memory actions to execute out of order in programs that are not properly synchronized. In other words, the memory model lets some compilers choose to execute store actions early under conditions that are intended to preserve coherence for properly structured programs.

Here is the outline of a simple program (devised by William Pugh). The Java Memory Model is Futally Flawed, *Concurrency: Practice and Experience*, 12(6) 2000, pp. 445–455), whose behavior is affected by the relaxed prescient store rule (this is obviously not Java syntax; the idea is that we have a program that initializes x and y to 0, and then spawns two threads that each execute two assignments):

```
x = 0; y = 0;
Thread 1:    a = x; y = 1;
Thread 2:    b = y; x = 1;
```

Without prescient stores, the two assignments in each thread must occur in the order shown. As a result, after both threads are executed, variables a and b can both be 0, or one can be 0 and the other 1. With prescient stores, the store actions can be done before the assign actions. This makes it legal for the write actions for both x and y to come before either of the read actions, and the threads can finish with a==b==1. The prescient store rule does not allow the load and store actions for a particular variable to be reordered, but a store involving variable y can be done before an assignment involving a and x.

William Pugh has studied the Java memory model (see paper mentioned above) Here is a simple program that, by his analysis, shows that the memory model is more restrictive than necessary:

```
// p & q are aliased
i = r.y;
j = p.x;
// concurrent write to p.x from another thread occurs here
k = q.x;
p.x = 42;
```

When executed in a manner consistent with the Java memory model, Pugh's analysis shows that the Java memory model *forces* a write to p.x from another thread to change the value of q.x in the thread cache, giving j and k different values in this program.

Here is a drawing showing the ordering of events required by the Java memory model. All of the actions in the drawing come from the preceding code, except for the write action halfway down the right-hand column, which comes from another thread:

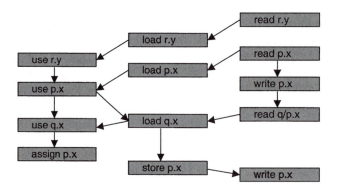

Although it takes a little time, it is possible to check that this ordering between actions satisfies the constraints that make up the Java memory model. For example, all use and assign actions, which are in the left-hand column, are in the order corresponding to the assignments in the Java source code. Each use is preceded by a load that initializes the local cache, and similarly each load has a preceding read from shared memory.

The problem with this situation is that it forces a change in a thread cache that does not seem intuitively necessary. A programmer who writes this code and knows that p and q are aliases would be perfectly happy to have j and k get the same value. However, the implementation is forced to do extra work, setting the thread cache after the write from another thread. This requirement makes it more difficult to implement the Java memory model than it needs to be. The problem is particularly significant for multiprocessor implementations, as multiprocessors may reorder instructions for efficiency in situations like this. In fact, common single-processor implementations also appear not to enforce the full Java memory model correctly.

Although the details of the Java memory model are complicated, it should be clear from our brief discussion that it is difficult to design a good memory model. The two problems are that the memory model for any concurrent programming language with shared variables must be easy for programmers to understand so they can write correct and efficient programs that take advantage of concurrency. At the same time, the memory model must be implementable. This is particularly tricky for multiprocessors that may have their own form of processor caches and shared memory. Because Java is the first programming language that integrates concurrency and is widely used for general programming, it is likely that further experience with Java will lead to better understanding of memory models for concurrent languages.

14.4.4 Distributed Programming and Remote Method Invocation

RMI allows a thread running on one JVM to call a method of an object on another virtual machine across the network. This communication mechanism is one of the basic building blocks of distributed Java programming. Because RMI is an asymmetric operation (one thread executes a method call, the other does not), it is convenient to refer to the two threads by two different names. We will refer to the caller as the *client* and the thread providing the remote object as the *server*.

A typical server application creates some remote objects, makes references to them accessible, and waits for clients to invoke methods on these remote objects. There is a basic chicken-and-egg problem, however. Once we have some established connection between client and server, we can use this connection to pass references to objects. But how do we make the first connection between two systems? A solution used in distributed Java programming is the RMI registry, which is a remotely accessible directory of available objects.

Java provides three general facilities for distributed programming:

- *Locating remote objects*: A server can register its remote objects by using the RMI registry or the server can pass object references through other connections already established by the programs.
- *Communicating with remote objects*: Communication between remote objects is handled by RMI, which looks like standard Java method invocation to the programmer.
- *Transmitting objects across the network*: An object can be sent as an argument to a remote call or as the return value of such a call. When a Java object is transmitted, one virtual machine transmits the bytecode to execute the object and associated data to another. The receiving virtual machine loads the bytecode and creates the object.

Creating Remote Objects

There are several steps involved in creating an object that can be accessed remotely. The first step is to define a class that implements a *remote interface*, which is an interface that extends the interface java.rmi.Remote. Each method of the remote interface must declare java.rmi.RemoteException in its throws clause, in addition to any other exceptions. This allows a remote client to throw a remote exception to any object of this class.

When an object from a class that implements a remote interface is passed from the server virtual machine to a client virtual machine, RMI passes a remote *stub* for the object. The stub object has the same methods as the original object sitting on the server, but calls to methods on the stub object are sent across the network and executed on the server object. In the client program, all of this looks like regular Java programming: A call to an object that happens to be remote returns the stub of another object, and subsequent calls to methods on that object are transmitted across the network and executed on the server.

Compiling the server code requires two steps. The first step is to use the regular Java compiler to compile the source files, which contain the implementation of the remote interfaces and implementations and the server classes. The second step uses a second compiler to create stubs for the remote objects.

Dynamic Class Loading

An important feature of Java RMI is the way that the bytecode is transmitted across the network. This is possible because Java provides a uniform execution environment, the JVM, that runs standard bytecode regardless of the kind of hardware or operating system used. When RMI is used to pass an object from one virtual machine to another, the bytecode for the class of the object is transmitted and loaded, if the class has not already been installed on the receiving machine. This allows new types to be introduced into a remote virtual machine, extending the behavior of a program dynamically.

The RMI Registry

The RMI registry, running on a server, allows remote clients to get a reference to a remote object. The registry is typically used to locate only the first remote object that a client needs, as methods of the first object can return other remote objects.

The RMI system allows a programmer to bind a URL-formatted name of the form //host/objectname to a remote object. Once a remote object is registered on the server, callers can look up the object by name, obtain a remote object reference, and then remotely invoke methods on the object. For example, if helo is an object that can be called remotely to say "hello world," the following code binds the name HelloWorld to a reference to the helo object:

```
Naming.rebind("//machine.stanford.edu/HelloWorld", helo);
```

This will allow a client program to get a stub for helo by a network access to the host (in this case machine.stanford.edu). There are several details involved in setting this all up properly that need not concern us. The main point is that a Java thread can get an object from a server across the network by using a symbolic name for the server and the object, and this is enough to let a client thread get more remote objects from this server.

14.5 CHAPTER SUMMARY

In this chapter, we discussed some general aspects of concurrent and distributed programming and looked at three example languages: Actor systems, CML, and Java features providing threads, synchronization, and RMI. These three languages were chosen to illustrate different general approaches to communication and synchronization. Actors and CML are based on message passing, whereas Java threads communicate by shared variables and shared objects that may have one or more synchronized methods. Threads are implicit in actor systems, arising from concurrently sending more than one message to a set of concurrently reactive actors, whereas CML and Java programs must explicitly create threads.

General Issues in Concurrency

Concurrent programming languages define concurrent actions that may be executed simultaneously on several processors or in an interleaved fashion on a single processor. Concurrent programs generally have nondeterministic behavior, as the order of execution may depend on the speed of communication or the order in which process are scheduled. Independent threads may communicate in order to compute a useful result and coordinate to avoid problems associated with shared resources. When two threads attempt to update a shared data structure, for example, some coordination may be needed to keep the actions of each thread from interfering with the other. Without coordination, assignments by one thread may cancel assignments of another and leave the data structure in a state that is not meaningful to the program.

Locking, semaphores, and monitors are traditional operating systems mechanisms for coordinating the actions of independent processes. A lock is a kind of shared variable that may be set to indicate that a resource is locked or unlocked. When one process locks a resource, other processes should not access the resource. One problem with locking is that testing and setting a lock must be atomic. For this reason, locks with atomic test-and-set are often provided by hardware.

Semaphores structure a set of waiting processes into a list that may be given access to the shared resource when it becomes available. Processes using a semaphore must call *wait* before accessing the protected resource and *signal* when they are done. Both *wait* and *signal* are atomic actions that may be implemented by the operating system (or programming language run-time system) using locks. Monitors group synchronization with operations on data, eliminating the need for the calling process to call *wait* and *signal*.

Concurrent programs communicate by using shared resources or message passing. In principle, message-passing mechanisms can be synchronous or asynchronous, buffered or unbuffered, and preserve or not preserve transmission order. Actors and CML differ in all three ways, illustrating two very different sets of communication assumptions. As explored in the exercises, some of the remaining combinations are sensible language design choices and some are either not sensible or too weak for many programming problems.

	Synchronous		Asynchronous	
	Ordered	Unordered	Ordered	Unordered
Buffered				Actors
Unbuffered	CML			

Actor Systems

An actor is a form of reactive object that performs a computation in response to a message and may perform one or more of the following basic actions:

- Sending communication to itself or other actors,
- Creating actors,
- Specifying a replacement behavior.

Actors do not have any shared state, but use buffered asynchronous message passing for all communication. Actors change state atomically. There are no changes in the internal state of an actor while it is responding to a message. Instead, an actor changes state atomically as it completes its computation and specifies a replacement behavior. Some interesting aspects of the actor model are the mail system, which buffers and delivers messages, and the challenges of programming with only asynchronous communication without order guarantees.

Concurrent ML

CML is a concurrent extension of Standard ML that provides dynamic thread creation and synchronous message passing on typed channels. The most interesting aspects of CML, are the ways that communication and coordination are combined and the way that CML allows programmers to define their own communication and synchronization abstractions by using events. Events represent synchronous actions that are performed when a program synchronizes on them. CML event primitives can be used to implement selective computation, as illustrated by Dijkstra's guarded commands, and a variety of communication mechanisms such as multicast channels and various forms of protected shared variables.

Java Threads and Synchronization

Java makes concurrent programs portable across a variety of computing platforms. We create a Java thread object by defining a class with a run() method, either by extending the Thread class or by implementing the Runnable interface directly. When a thread object is activated, the run method runs as a separate thread inside the JVM. Java threads generally communicate by calling methods of shared objects. The Java language provides several synchronization primitives and supports monitors directly through objects with synchronized methods.

Java synchronization is achieved through three basic mechanisms:

- Locks: Every object has a lock, used for mutual exclusion.
- Wait sets: Every object has a wait set, providing a form of semaphore.
- Thread termination: A process can pause until another thread terminates.

Locks are tested and set by synchronized blocks and methods, wait sets are used by methods wait, notify, and notifyAll that are defined on all objects, and thread termination is used by the join method on thread objects.

The Java memory model is a specification of how shared memory can be cached and accessed by multiple threads. The original memory model, presented in *Java Language Specification*, has proven difficult to understand and unsatisfactory for implementers in various ways. Although it is likely that the memory model will eventually be revised to correct some of the known problems, we discussed the memory model briefly in order to understand some of the subtle basic issues involved in concurrent memory access.

Distributed Java Programming and Remote Method Invocation

RMI allows a thread running on one JVM to call a method of an object on another virtual machine across the network. A typical server application creates some remote objects, makes references to them accessible, and waits for clients to invoke methods on these remote objects. A server may make objects accessible by using the RMI registry, which is a remotely accessible directory of available objects. When RMI is used to pass an object from one virtual machine to another, the bytecode for the class of the object is transmitted and loaded if the class has not already been installed on the receiving machine. This allows new types to be introduced into a remote virtual machine, extending the behavior of a program dynamically.

EXERCISES

14.1 Mutual Exclusion

Example 14.2 gives an incorrect implementation of *wait* and *signal* by using an ordinary integer variable lock as a "lock." Describe an execution of the code in Example 14.2 that leads to an inconsistent state. Support your description by giving the initial values of the variable n and array list and list in order the assignments and tests that occur in executing the code. Explain why atomic implementations of *wait* and *signal* would prevent this execution sequence.

14.2 Fairness

The guarded-command looping construct

```
do
    Condition ⇒ Command
    ...
    Condition ⇒ Command
od
```

involves nondeterministic choice, as explained in the text. An important theoretical concept related to potentially nonterminating nondeterministic computation is *fairness*. If a loop repeats indefinitely, then a fair nondeterministic choice must eventually select each command whose guard is true. For example, in the loop

```
do
    true ⇒ x := x+1
    true ⇒ x := x-1
od
```

both commands have guards that are always true. It would be *unfair* to execute x := x+1 repeatedly without ever executing x := x-1. Most language implementations are designed to provide fairness, usually by providing a bounded form. For example, if there are n guarded commands, then the implementation may guarantee that each enabled command will be executed at least once in every $2n$ or $3n$ times through the loop. Because the number $2n$ or $3n$ is implementation dependent, though, programmers should assume only that each command with a true guard will eventually be executed.

(a) Suppose that an integer variable x can contain an integer value with only absolute value less than INTMAX. Will the preceding do . . . od loop cause overflow or underflow under a fair implementation? What about an implementation that is not fair?

(b) What property of the following loop is true under a fair implementation but false under an unfair implementation?

```
go := true;
n := 0;
do
    go => n := n+1
    go => g := false
od
```

(c) Is fairness easier to provide on a single-processor language implementation or on a multiprocessor? Discuss briefly.

14.3 Actor Computing

The actor mail system provides asynchronous buffered communication and does not guarantee that messages (*tasks* in actor terminology) are delivered in the order they are sent. Suppose actor A sends tasks $t_1, t_2, t_3, \ldots$, to actor B and we want actor B to process tasks in the order A sends them.

(a) What extra information could be added to each task so that B can tell whether it receives a task out of order? What should B do with a task when it first receives it before actually performing the computation associated with the task?

(b) Because the actor model does not impose any constraints on how soon a task must be delivered, a task could be delayed an arbitrary amount of time. For example, suppose actor A sends tasks $t_1, t_2, t_3, \ldots, t_{100}$ and actor B receives the tasks $t_1, t_3, \ldots, t_{50}$ without receiving task t_2. Because B would like to proceed with some of these tasks, it makes sense for B to ask A to resend task t_2. Describe a protocol for A and B that will add resend requests to the approach you described in part (a) of this problem.

(c) Suppose B wants to do a final action when A has finished sending tasks to B. How can A notify B when A is done? Be sure to consider the fact that if A sends *I'm done* to B after sending task t_{100}, the *I'm done* message may arrive before t_{100}.

14.4 Message Passing

There are eight message-passing combinations involving synchronization, buffering, and message order, as shown in the following table.

	Synchronous		Asynchronous	
	Ordered	**Unordered**	**Ordered**	**Unordered**
Buffered				
Unbuffered				

For each combination, give a programming language that uses this combination and explain why the combination makes some sense, or explain why you think the combination is either meaningless or too weak for useful concurrent programming.

14.5 CML Events

The CML recv function can be defined from recvEvt by

```
fun recv(ch) = sync (recvEvt (ch));
```

as shown in the text. Give a similar definition of send by using sendEvt and explain your definition in a few sentences.

14.6 Concurrent Access to Objects

This question asks about synchronizing methods for stack and queue objects.

(a) Bounded stacks can be defined as objects, each containing an array of up to *n* items. Here is a pseudocode for one form of stack class.

```
class Stack
  private
    contents : array[1..n] of int
    top : int
  constructor
    stack () = top := 0
  public
    push (x:int) : unit =
        if top < n then
          top := top + 1;
          contents[top] := x
        else raise stack_full;
      pop ( ) : int =
        if top > 0 then
          top := top - 1;
          return contents[top+1]
        else raise stack_empty;
  end Stack
```

If stacks are going to be used in a concurrent programming language, what problem might occur if two threads invoke push and pop simultaneously? Explain.

(b) How would you solve this problem by using Java concurrency concepts? Explain.

(c) Suppose that, instead of stacks, we have queues:

```
class Queue
  private
    contents : array[1..n] of int
    front, back : int
  constructor
    queue() = front := back := 1
  public
    insert (x:int) : unit =
        if back+1 mod n != front then
          back := back+1 mod n;
          contents[back] := x
        else raise queue_full;
      remove ( ) : int =
        if front != back then
          front := front+1 mod n;
          return contents[front]
        else raise queue_empty;
  end Queue
```

Suppose that five elements have been inserted into a queue object and none of them have been removed. Do we have the same concurrency problem as we did with push and pop when one thread invokes insert and another thread simultaneously invokes remove? Assume that n is 10. Explain.

14.7 Java Synchronized Objects

This question asks about the following Java implementation of a bounded buffer. A bounded buffer is a FIFO data structure that can be accessed by multiple threads:

```
class BoundedBuffer {
    // designed for multiple producer threads and
    // multiple consumer threads
    protected int numSlots = 0;
    protected int[] buffer = null;
    protected int putIn = 0, takeOut = 0;
    protected int count = 0;
    public BoundedBuffer(int numSlots) {
        if (numSlots <= 0)
            throw new IllegalArgumentException("numSlots <= 0");
        this.numSlots = numSlots;
        buffer = new int[numSlots];
    }
    public synchronized void put(int value)
            throws InterruptedException {
        while (count == numSlots) wait();
        buffer[putIn] = value;
        putIn = (putIn + 1) % numSlots;
        count++;
        notifyAll();
    }
    public synchronized int get()
            throws InterruptedException {
        int value;
        while (count == 0) wait();
        value = buffer[takeOut];
        takeOut = (takeOut + 1) % numSlots;
        count--;
        notifyAll();
        return value;
    }
}
```

(a) What is the purpose of while (count == numSlots) wait() in put?

(b) What does notifyAll() do in this code?

(c) Describe one way that the buffer would fail to work properly if all synchronization code is removed from put.

(d) Suppose a programmer wants to alter this implementation so that one thread can call put at the same time as another calls get. This causes a problem in some situation but not in others. Assume that some locking may be done at entry to put and get to make sure the concurrent-execution test is satisfied. You may also assume that increment or decrement of an integer variable is atomic and that only one call to get and one call to put may be executed at any given time. What test involving putIn and takeOut can be used to decide whether put and get can proceed concurrently?

(e) The changes in part (d) will improve performance of the buffer. List one reason that leads to this performance advantage. Despite this win, some programmers may choose to use the original method anyway. List one reason why they might make this choice.

14.8 Resources and Java Garbage Collection

Suppose we are writing an application that uses a video camera that is attached to the computer. Our application, written in Java, has multiple threads, which means that separate parts of the application may run concurrently. The camera is a shared resource that can be used by only one thread at a time, and our multithreaded application may try to use the camera concurrently from multiple threads.

The camera library (provided by the camera manufacturer) contains methods that will ensure that only one thread can use the camera at a time. These methods are called

```
camera.AcquireCamera()
camera.ReleaseCamera()
```

A thread that tries to acquire the camera while another object has acquired it will be blocked until camera.ReleaseCamera() has been called. When a thread is blocked, it simply stops without executing any further commands until it becomes unblocked.

You decide to structure your code so that you create a MyCamera object whenever a thread wants to use the camera, and you "delete" the object (by leaving the scope that contains a pointer to it) when that thread is done with the camera. The object calls camera.AcquireCamera() in the constructor and calls camera.ReleaseCamera() in the finalize method:

```
import camera    // imports the camera library
class MyCamera {
    ...
    MyCamera() {
        ...
        camera.AcquireCamera();
        ...
    }
    ...              // (other methods that use the camera go here)
    finalize() {
        ...
        camera.ReleaseCamera();
        ...
    }
}
```

Here is a sample code that would use the Mycamera object:

```
{
...
MyCamera c = new MyCamera();
...  // (code that uses the camera)
}    // end of scope so object is no longer reachable
```

In this question, we will say that a *deadlock* occurs if all threads are waiting to acquire the camera, but camera.ReleaseCamera is never called.

(a) When does camera.ReleaseCamera actually get called?

(b) This code can cause a deadlock situation in some Java implementations. Explain how.

(c) Does calling the garbage collector by using Runtime.getRuntime().gc() after leaving the scope where the camera is reachable solve this problem?

(d) How can you fix this problem by modifying your program (without trying to force garbage collection or by using synchronized) so deadlock will not occur?

(e) Suppose you have a multithreaded Java implementation with the garbage collector running concurrently as a separate thread. Assume the garbage collector is always running, but it may run slowly in the background if the program is active. This will eventually garbage collect every unreachable object, but not necessarily as soon as it becomes unreachable. Does deadlock, as previously defined, occur (in the preceding original code) in this implementation? Why or why not?

14.9 Separate read and write Synchronization

For many data structures, it is possible to allow multiple reads to occur in parallel, but reads cannot be safely performed while a write is in progress and it is not safe to allow multiple writes simultaneously. Rewrite the Java LinkedCell class given in this chapter to allow multiple simultaneous reads, but prevent reads and writes while a write is in progress. You may want to use more than one lock. For example, you could assume objects called ReadLock and WriteLock and use synchronized statements involving these two objects. Explain your approach and why it works.

14.10 Java Memory Model

This program with two threads is discussed in the text:

```
x = 0; y = 0;
Thread 1: a = x;   y = 1;
Thread 2: b = y;   x = 1;
```

Draw a box-and-arrow illustration showing the order constraints on the memory actions (*read, load, use, assign, store, write*) associated with the four assignments that appear in the two threads (you do not need to show these actions for the two assginments setting x and y to 0):

(a) Without prescient stores.

(b) With prescient stores.

15

The Logic Programming Paradigm and Prolog

Krzysztof R. Apt

15.1 HISTORY OF LOGIC PROGRAMMING

The logic programming paradigm has its roots in automated theorem proving from which it took the notion of a deduction. What is new is that in the process of deduction some values are computed. The creation of this programming paradigm is the outcome of a long history that for most of its course ran within logic and only later inside computer science. Logic programming is based on the syntax of first-order logic, which was originally proposed in the second half of nineteenth century by Gottlob Frege and later modified to the currently used form by Giuseppe Peano and Bertrand Russell.

In the 1930s, Kurt Gödel and Jacques Herbrand studied the notion of computability based on derivations. These works can be viewed as the origin of the "computation as deduction" paradigm. Additionally, Herbrand discussed in his doctoral thesis a set of rules for manipulating algebraic equations on terms that can be viewed now as a sketch of a unification algorithm. Some 30 years later, in 1965, Alan Robinson published his fundamental paper (Robinson 1965) that lies at the foundation of the field of automated deduction. In this paper, he introduced the resolution principle, the notion of unification, and a unification algorithm. Using the resolution method, one can prove theorems of first-order logic, but another step was needed to see how one could compute within this framework.

This was eventually achieved in 1974 by Robert Kowalski (Predicate logic as a programming language, North-Holland, 1974.) Proc. IFIP'74, in which logic programs with a restricted form of resolution were introduced. The difference between this form of resolution and the one proposed by Robinson is that the syntax is more restricted, but proving now has a side effect in the form of a satisfying substitution. This substitution can be viewed as a result of a computation and consequently certain logical formulas can be interpreted as programs. In parallel, Alain Colmerauer and his colleagues worked on a programming language for natural language processing based on automated theorem proving. This ultimately led to creation of Prolog in 1973. Kowalski and Colmerauer with his team interacted in the period from 1971 to 1973. This influenced their views and helped them to crystallize the ideas.

Prolog can be seen as a practical realization of the idea of logic programs. It started as a programming language for applications in natural language processing, but soon after it was found that it can also be used as a general purpose programming language. A number of other attempts to realize the computation as deduction paradigm were proposed about the same time, notably by Cordell Green and Carl Hewitt, but the logic programming proposal, probably because it was the simplest and most versatile, became most successful.

Originally, Prolog was implemented by Philippe Roussel, a colleague of Colmerauer, in the form of an interpreter written in Algol-W. An important step forward was achieved by David H. Warren, who proposed in 1983 an abstract machine, now called Warren Abstract Machine (WAM), which consists of a machine architecture with an instruction set that serves as a target for machine independent Prolog compilers. WAM became a standard basis for implementing Prolog and other logic programming languages.

The logic programming paradigm influenced a number of developments in computer science. As early as the 1970s, it led to the creation of deductive databases that extend the relational databases by providing deduction capabilities. A further impetus to the subject came unexpectedly from the Japanese Fifth Generation Project for intelligent computing systems (1982–1991), in which logic programming was chosen as its basis. More recently, this paradigm led to constraint logic programming that realizes a general approach to computing in which the programming process is limited to a generation of constraints (requirements) and a solution of them, and to inductive logic programming, a logic-based approach to machine learning.

The above account of history of logic programming and Prolog shows its roots in logic and automated deduction. In fact, Colmerauer and Roussel (1996) write "There is no question that Prolog is essentially a theorem prover à la Robinson. Our contribution was to transform that theorem prover into a programming language." This origin of the logic paradigm probably impeded its acceptance within computer science in times when imperative programming got impetus thanks to the creation of Pascal and C, the fields of verification and semantics of imperative programs gained ground, and when the artificial intelligence community already adopted Lisp as their language of choice.

Here, we offer an alternative presentation of the subject by focusing on the ordinary programming concepts (often implicitly) present in logic programming and by relating various of its ideas to those present in the imperative and functional programming paradigms.

15.2 BRIEF OVERVIEW OF THE LOGIC PROGRAMMING PARADIGM

The logic programming paradigm differs substantially from other programming paradigms. When stripped to the bare essentials, it can be summarized by the following three features.

■ Computing takes place over the domain of all terms defined over a "universal" alphabet.

■ Values are assigned to variables by means of automatically generated substitutions, called *most general unifiers*. These values may contain variables, called *logical variables*.

■ The control is provided by a single mechanism: automatic backtracking.

In our exposition of this programming paradigm, we shall stress the above three points. Even such a brief summary shows both the strength and weakness of the logic programming paradigm. Its strength lies in an enormous simplicity and conciseness; its weakness has to do with the restrictions to one control mechanism and the use of a single data type.

This framework has to be modified and enriched to accommodate it to the customary needs of programming, for example by providing various control constructs and by introducing the data type of integers with the customary arithmetic operations. This can be done and, in fact, Prolog and constraint logic programming languages are examples of such a customization of this framework.

15.2.1 Declarative Programming

Two additional features of logic programming are important to note. First, in its pure form it supports *declarative programming*. A declarative program admits two interpretations. The first one, called a *procedural interpretation*, explains *how* the computation takes place, whereas the second one, called a *declarative interpretation*, is concerned with the question *what* is being computed.

Informally, the procedural interpretation is concerned with the *method*, whereas the declarative interpretation is concerned with the *meaning*. In the procedural interpretation, a declarative program is viewed as a description of an algorithm that can be executed. In the declarative interpretation, a declarative program is viewed as a formula, and one can reason about its correctness without any reference to the underlying computational mechanism. This makes declarative programs easier to understand and to develop.

As we shall see, in some situations the specification of a problem in the logic programming format already forms an algorithmic solution to the problem. So logic programming supports declarative programming and allows us to write *executable specifications*. It should be added, however, that in practice the Prolog programs obtained in this way are often inefficient, so this approach to programming has to be combined with various optimization techniques, and an appropriate understanding of the underlying computation mechanism is indispensable. To clarify this point, we shall present here a number of Prolog programs that are declarative and eliminate from them various sources of inefficiency.

This dual interpretation of declarative programs also accounts for the double use of logic programming as a formalism for programming and for knowledge representation, and explains the importance of logic programming in the field of artificial intelligence.

15.2.2 Interactive Programming

Another important feature of logic programming is that it supports *interactive programming*. In other words, the user can write a single program and interact with it by means of various queries of interest to which answers are produced. The Prolog systems greatly support such an interaction and provide simple means to compute one or more solutions to the submitted query, to submit another query, and to trace the execution by setting up, if desired, various check points, all within the same "interaction loop." This leads to a flexible style of programming.

This is completely analogous to the way functional programs are used where the interaction is achieved by means of expressions that need to be evaluated using a given collection of function definitions.

In what follows, we shall introduce Prolog, the best known programming language based on the logic programming paradigm. Prolog is then based on a subset of first-order logic. We explain here how Prolog uses this syntax in a novel way (this characteristic is called *ambivalent syntax*) and extends it by a number of interesting features, notably by supporting infix notation and by providing so-called *anonymous* and *meta-variables*. These extensions amount to more than syntactic sugar. In fact, they make it possible to realize in Prolog higher-order programming and meta-programming in a simple way.

When discussing Prolog, it is useful to abstract from the programming language and first consider the underlying conceptual model provided by logic programming.

15.3 EQUATIONS SOLVED BY UNIFICATION AS ATOMIC ACTIONS

We begin by explaining how computing takes place at the "atomic level." In logic programming, the atomic actions are equations between terms (arbitrary expressions). They are executed by means of the unification process that attempts to solve such equations. In the process of solving, values are assigned to variables. These values can be arbitrary terms. In fact, the variables are all of one type that consists of the set of all terms.

This informal summary shows that the computation process in logic programming is governed by different principles than in the other programming paradigms.

15.3.1 Terms

In a more rigorous explanation, let us start by introducing an alphabet that consists of the following disjoint classes of symbols:

- *variables*, denoted by $x, y, z, \ldots$ possibly with subscripts
- *function symbols*
- parentheses, "("and")"
- comma, ","

We also postulate that each function symbol has a fixed *arity*, that is the number of arguments associated with it. 0-ary function symbols are called *constants*, and are usually denoted by $a, b, c, d, \ldots$. Below we denote function symbols of positive arity by $f, g, h, \ldots$.

Finally, *terms* are defined inductively as follows:

- a variable is a term,

- if f is an n-ary function symbol and $t_1, \ldots, t_n$ are terms, then $f(t_1, \ldots, t_n)$ is a term.

In particular every constant is a term. Variable-free terms are usually called *ground terms*. Below we denote terms by $s, t, u, w, \ldots$.

For example, if a is a constant, x and y are variables, f is a binary function symbol and g a unary function symbol, then $f(f(x, g(b)), y)$ is a term.

Terms are fundamental concepts in mathematical logic, but at first sight they seem to be less common in computer science. However, they can be seen as a generalization of the concept of a string familiar from the theory of formal languages. In fact, strings can be viewed as terms built out of an alphabet the only function symbols of which are the concatenation operations in each arity (or alternatively, out of an alphabet the only function symbol of which is the binary concatenation operation assumed to be associative, say to the right). Another familiar example of terms are arithmetic expressions. These are terms built out of an alphabet in which, as the function symbols, we take the usual arithmetic operations of addition, subtraction, multiplication, and, say, integer division, and as constants $0, -1, 1, \ldots$.

In logic programming, no specific alphabet is assumed. In fact, it is convenient to assume that in each arity an infinite supply of function symbols exists and that all terms are written in this "universal alphabet." These function symbols can be, in particular, the denotations of arithmetic operations, but no meaning is attached to these function symbols. This is in contrast to most of the imperative programming languages, in which for example the use of "$+$" in an expression implies that we refer to the addition operation. The other consequence of this choice is no types are assigned to terms. In fact, no types are assumed and consequently there is no distinction between, say, arithmetic expressions, Boolean expressions, and terms denoting lists. All these terms are considered as being of one type.

15.3.2 Substitutions

Unlike in imperative programming, in logic programming the variables can be uninitialized. Moreover, the possible values of variables are terms. So to properly explain the computation process we need to reexamine the notion of a state.

At any moment during the computation there will be only a finite number of variables that are *initialized* – these are variables to which, in the considered computation, some value was already assigned. Since these values are terms, we are naturally led to consider *substitutions*. These are finite mappings from variables to terms such that no variable is mapped to itself. So substitution provides information about which variables are initialized. (Note that no variable can be initialized to itself, which explains the restriction that no variable is mapped to itself.)

Substitutions then form a counterpart of the familiar notion of a *state* used in imperative programming. We denote a substitution by $\{x_1/t_1, \ldots, x_n/t_n\}$. This notation implies that $x_1, \ldots, x_n$ are different variables, $t_1, \ldots, t_n$ are terms and that no term t_i equals the variable x_i. We say then that the substitution $\{x_1/t_1, \ldots, x_n/t_n\}$ *binds* the variable x_i to the term t_i.

Using a substitution, we can evaluate a term in much the same way as using a state we can evaluate an expression in imperative programming languages. This process of evaluation is called an *application* of a substitution to a term. It is the outcome of a simultaneous replacement of each variable occurring in the domain of the substitution by the corresponding term. So, for example, the application of the substitution $\{x/f(z), y/g(z)\}$ to the term $h(x, y)$ yields the term $h(f(z), g(z))$. Here the variable x was replaced by the term $f(z)$ and the variable y by the term $g(z)$. In the same way, we define an application of a substitution to an atom, query, or a clause.

So an evaluation of a term using a substitution yields again a term. This is in contrast to imperative programming where an evaluation of an expression using a state yields a value that belongs to the type of this expression.

15.3.3 Most General Unifiers

As already mentioned, in logic programming the atomic actions are equations between terms and the unification process is used to determine their meaning. Before we discuss these matters in detail, let us consider some obvious examples of how solving equations can be used as an assignment.

We assume that all mentioned variables are uninitialized. By writing $x = a$, we assign the constant a to the variable x. Because in logic programming the equality "=" is symmetric, the same effect is achieved by writing $a = x$. More interestingly, by writing $x = f(y)$ (or, equivalently, $f(y) = x$) we assign the term $f(y)$ to the variable x. Since $f(y)$ is a term with a variable, we assigned to the variable x an expression with a variable in it. Recall that a variable that occurs in a value assigned to another variable is called a logical variable. Therefore, y is a logical variable here. The use of logical variables is an important distinguishing feature of logic programming and we devote the whole subsection 15.5.2 to an explanation of their use. Finally, by writing $f(y) = f(g(a))$, we assign the term $g(a)$ to the variable y, as this is the way to make these two terms equal.

These examples show that the equality "=" in logic programming and the assignment in C, also written using "=", are totally different concepts.

Intuitively, *unification* is the process of solving an equation between terms (i.e., of making two terms equal) in a least constraining way. The resulting substitution (if it exists) is called a *most general unifier* (*mgu*). For example, the equation $x = f(y)$ can be solved (i.e., the terms x and $f(y)$ *unify*) in a number of ways, for instance, by means of each of the substitutions $\{x/f(y)\}, \{x/f(a), y/a\}, \{x/f(a), y/a, z/g(b)\}$, Clearly, only the first one is "least constraining." In fact, out of these three substitutions the first one is the only most general unifier of the equation $x = f(y)$. The notion of a least constraining substitution can be made precise by defining an order on substitutions. In this order, the substitution $\{x/f(y)\}$ is more general than $\{x/f(a), y/a\}$, etc.

Note that we made the terms x and $f(y)$ equal by instantiating only one of them. Such a special case of the unification is called *matching*, which is the way of assigning values in functional programming languages. Unification is more general than matching as the following, slightly less obvious, example shows. Consider the equation $f(x, a) = f(b, y)$. Here, the most general unifier is $\{x/b, y/a\}$. In contrast to the previous example, it is now not possible to make these two terms equal by instantiating only one of them.

The problem of deciding whether an equation between terms has a solution is called the *unification problem*. Robinson (JACM, 12(1): 23–41, 1965) showed that the unification problem is decidable. More precisely, he introduced a unification algorithm with the following property. If an equation between terms has a solution, the algorithm produces an mgu, otherwise it reports a failure. An mgu of an equation is unique up to renaming of the variables.

15.3.4 A Unification Algorithm

In what follows, we discuss the unification process in more detail using an elegant unification algorithm introduced in Martelli and Montanari (An efficient unification algorithm, ACM Trans. Prog. Lang. and Systems; vol 4, 1982, pp. 258–282). This algorithm takes as input a finite set of term equations $\{s_1 = t_1, \ldots, s_n = t_n\}$ and tries to produce an mgu of them.

MARTELLI–MONTANARI ALGORITHM

Nondeterministically choose from the set of equations an equation of a form below and perform the associated action.

(1) $f(s_1, \ldots, s_n) = f(t_1, \ldots, t_n)$ *replace by the equations* $s_1 = t_1, \ldots, s_n = t_n$,

(2) $f(s_1, \ldots, s_n) = g(t_1, \ldots, t_m)$ where $f \neq g$ *halt with failure,*

(3) $x = x$ *delete the equation,*

(4) $t = x$ where t is not a variable   *replace by the equation* $x = t$,

(5) $x = t$ where x does not occur in t *apply the substitution* $\{x/t\}$ and x occurs elsewhere   *to all other equations*

(6) $x = t$ where x occurs in t and x differs from t *halt with failure.*

The algorithm terminates when no action can be performed or when failure arises. In case of success, by changing in the final set of equations all occurrences of "=" to "/" we obtain the desired mgu. Note that action (1) includes the case $c = c$ for every constant c which leads to deletion of such an equation. In addition, action (2) includes the case of two different constants.

To illustrate the operation of this algorithm, reconsider the equation $f(x, a) = f(b, y)$. Using action (1) it rewrites to the set of two equations, $\{x = b, a = y\}$. By action (4) we now get the set $\{x = b, y = a\}$. At this moment, the algorithm terminates and we obtain the mgu $\{x/b, y/a\}$.

So by interpreting the equality symbol as the request to find a most general unifier of the considered pair of terms, each equation is turned into an atomic action that either produces a substitution (a most general unifier) or *fails*. This possibility of a failure at the level of an atomic action is another distinguishing feature of logic programming.

By writing a sequence of equations, we can create very simple logic programs that either succeed and produce as output a substitution or fail. It is important to understand how the computation then proceeds. We illustrate it by means of three progressively more complex examples.

First, consider the sequence

$$f(x, a) = f(g(z), y), h(u) = h(d).$$

The first equation yields first the intermediate substitution $\{x/g(z), y/a\}$ and the second one the substitution $\{u/d\}$. By combining these two substitutions we obtain the substitution $\{x/g(z), y/a, u/d\}$ produced by this logic program.

As a slightly less obvious example, consider the sequence

$$f(x, a) = f(g(z), y), h(x, z) = h(u, d).$$

Here the intermediate substitution $\{x/g(z), y/a\}$ binds the variable x that also occurs in the second equation. This second equation needs to be evaluated first in the "current state," here represented by the substitution $\{x/g(z), y/a\}$, before being executed. This evaluation produces the equation $h(g(z), z) = h(u, d)$. This equation yields the most general unifier $\{u/g(d), z/d\}$ and the resulting final substitution is here $\{x/g(d), y/a, u/g(d), z/d\}$.

What happened here is that the substitution $\{u/g(d), z/d\}$ was *applied* to the intermediate substitution $\{x/g(z), y/a\}$. The effect of an application of one substitution, say δ, to another, say γ, (or of *composition* of the substitutions) is obtained by

- applying δ to each of the terms that appear in the range of γ
- adding to the resulting substitution the bindings to the variables that are in the domain of δ but not in the domain of γ

In the above example, the first step yields the substitution $\{x/g(d), y/a\}$, and the second step adds the bindings $u/g(d)$ and z/d to the final substitution. This process of substitution composition corresponds to an *update of a state* in imperative programming, and that is how we shall refer to it in the sequel.

As a final example consider the sequence

$$f(x, a) = f(g(z), y), h(x, z) = h(d, u).$$

It yields a failure. Indeed, after executing the first equation the variable x is bound to $g(z)$, so the evaluation of the second equation yields $h(g(z), z) = h(d, u)$ and no substitution makes equal (unifies) the terms $h(g(z), z)$ and $h(d, u)$.

It is useful to compare solving equations by unification with the assignment command. First, note that, in contrast to assignment, unification can assign an arbitrary term to a variable. Also, it can fail, something the assignment cannot do. On the other hand, using assignment one can modify the value of a variable, something unification can perform in a very limited way: by further instantiating the term used as a value. Thus, these atomic actions are incomparable.

15.4 CLAUSES AS PARTS OF PROCEDURE DECLARATIONS

Logic programming is a rule based formalism and Prolog is a rule based language. In this context, the rules are called *clauses*. To better understand the relationship between logic programming and imperative programming, we proceed in two steps and introduce a restricted form of clauses first.

15.4.1 Simple Clauses

Using unification, we can execute only extremely simplistic programs that consist of sequences of equations. We now enrich this framework by adding procedures. In logic programming they are modelled by means of *symbols*, sometimes called *predicates*. Below, we denote relation symbols by $p, q, r, \ldots$. As in the case of the function symbols, we assume that each relation symbol has a fixed arity associated with it. When the arity is 0, the relation symbol is usually called a *propositional symbol*.

If p is an *n*-ary relation symbol and $t_1, \ldots, t_n$ are terms, then we call $p(t_1, \ldots, t_n)$ an *atom*. When $n = 0$ the propositional symbols coincide with atoms. Interestingly, as we shall see, such atoms are useful. Intuitively, a relation symbol corresponds to a *procedure identifier* and an atom to a *procedure call*. The equality symbol "=" is a binary relation symbol written in an infix form, so each equation is also an atom. However, the meaning of equality is determined, so it can be viewed as a built-in procedure, i.e., a procedure with a predefined meaning.

We still need to define the procedure declarations and to clarify the parameter mechanism used. Given an *n*-ary relation symbol p and atoms $A_1, \ldots, A_k$ we call an expression of the form

$$p(x_1, \ldots, x_n) :\text{-} A_1, \ldots, A_k.$$

a *simple clause*. $p(x_1, \ldots, x_n)$ is called the *head* of the clause and $A_1, \ldots, A_k$ its *body*. The fullstop "." at the end of the clause is important: it signals to the compiler (or interpreter) that the end of the clause is encountered.

The procedural interpretation of a simple clause $p(x_1, \ldots, x_n) :\text{-} A_1, \ldots, A_k$ is: "to establish $p(x_1, \ldots, x_n)$ establish $A_1, \ldots, A_k$", while the declarative interpretation is: "$p(x_1, \ldots, x_n)$ is true if $A_1, \ldots, A_k$ is true". The declarative interpretation explains why in the logic programming theory the reversed implication symbol "$\leftarrow$" is used instead of ":-".

Finally, a *simple logic program* is a finite set of clauses. Such a program is activated by providing an initial *query*, which is a sequence of atoms. In the imperative programming jargon a query is then a program and a simple logic program is a set of procedure declarations. Intuitively, given a simple program, the set of its simple clauses with the same relation symbol in the head corresponds to the procedure declaration in the imperative languages. One of the syntactic confusions is that in logic programming the comma "," is used as a separator between the atoms constituting a query, whereas in the imperative programming the semicolon ";" is used for this purpose.

15.4.2 Computation Process

A nondeterminism is introduced into this framework by allowing *multiple clauses* with the same relation symbol in the head. In the logic programming theory, this form of nondeterminism (called *don't know nondeterminism*) is retained by considering all computations that can be generated by means of multiple clauses and by retaining the ones that lead to a success. "Don't know" refers to the fact that in general we do not know which computation will lead to a success.

In Prolog, this computation process is made deterministic by ordering the clauses by the textual ordering and by employing automatic backtracking to recover from failures. Still, when designing Prolog programs, it is useful to have the don't know nondeterminism in mind. In fact, in explanations of Prolog programs phrases like "this program nondeterministically guesses an element such that . . ." are common. Let us explain now more precisely how the computing takes place in Prolog. To this end, we need to clarify the procedure mechanism used and the role played by the use of multiple clauses.

The procedure mechanism associated with the simple clauses introduced above is *call-by-name* according to which the formal parameters are simultaneously substituted by the actual ones. So this procedure mechanism can be simply explained by means of substitutions: given a simple clause $p(x_1, \ldots, x_n) :- A_1, \ldots, A_k.$ a procedure call $p(t_1, \ldots, t_n)$ leads to an execution of the statement $(A_1, \ldots, A_k)\{x_1/t_1, \ldots, x_n/t_n\}$ obtained by applying the substitution $\{x_1/t_1, \ldots, x_n/t_n\}$ to the statement $A_1, \ldots, A_k$. (We assume here that the variables of the clauses are appropriately renamed to avoid variable clashes.) Equivalently, we can say that the procedure call $p(t_1, \ldots, t_n)$ leads to an execution of the statement $A_1, \ldots, A_k$ in the state (represented by a substitution) updated by the substitution $\{x_1/t_1, \ldots, x_n/t_n\}$.

The clauses are tried in the order they appear in the program text. The depth-first strategy is implied by the fact that a procedure call leads directly to an execution of the body of the selected simple clause. If at a certain stage a failure arises, the computation backtracks to the last choice point (a point in the computation at which one out of more applicable clauses was selected) and the subsequent simple clause is selected. If the selected clause was the last one, the computation backtracks to the previous choice point. If no choice point is left, a failure arises. Backtracking implies that the state is restored, so all the state updates performed since the creation of the last choice point are undone.

Let us illustrate now this definition of Prolog's computation process by considering the most known Prolog program the purpose of which is to append two lists. In Prolog, the empty list is denoted by [] and the list with head h and tail t by [h | t]. The term [a | [b | s]] abbreviates to a more readable form [a,b | s], the list [a | [b | []]] abbreviates to [a,b] and similarly with longer lists. This notation can be used both for lists and for arbitrary terms that start with the list formation operator [.|..].

Then the following logic program defines by induction w.r.t. the first argument how to append two lists. Here and elsewhere we follow Prolog's syntactic conventions and denote variables by strings starting with an upper case letter. The names ending with "s" are used for the variables meant to be instantiated to lists.

```
% append(Xs, Ys, Zs) :- Zs is the result of concatenating the lists Xs and Ys.
append(Xs, Ys, Zs) :- Xs = [], Zs = Ys.
append(Xs, Ys, Zs) :- Xs = [H | Ts], Zs = [H | Us], append(Ts, Ys, Us).
```

In Prolog, the answers are generated as substitutions written in an equational form (as in the Martelli–Montanari algorithm presented above). In what follows, we display a query $Q.$ as ?- $Q.$. Here "?-" is the system prompt and the fullstop "." signals the end of the query.

One can check then that the query

?- append([jan,feb,mar], [april,may], Zs).

yields Zs = [jan,feb,mar,april,may] as the answer and that the query

?- append([jan,feb,mar], [april,may], [jan,feb,mar,april,may]).

succeeds and yields the empty substitution as the answer.

In contrast, the query

?- append([jan,feb,mar], [april,may], [jan,feb,mar,april]).

fails. Indeed, the computation leads to the subsequent procedure calls

```
append([feb,mar], [april,may], [feb,mar,april]),
append([mar], [april,may], [mar,april]) and
append([], [april,may], [april]),
```

and the last one fails because the terms [april,may] and [april] don't unify.

15.4.3 Clauses

The last step in defining logic programs consists of allowing arbitrary atoms as heads of the clauses. Formally, given atoms $H, A_1, \ldots, A_k$, we call an expression of the form

$$H :- A_1, \ldots, A_k.$$

a *clause*. If $k = 0$, that is if the clause's body is empty, such a clause is called a *fact* and the ":-" symbol is then omitted. If $k > 0$, that is, if the clause's body is nonempty, such a clause is called a *rule*. A *logic program* is then a finite set of clauses and a *pure Prolog program* is a finite sequence of clauses.

Given a pure Prolog program, we call the set of its clauses with the relation p in the head the *definition of p*. Definitions correspond to the procedure declarations in imperative programming and to the function definitions in functional programming. Variables that occur in the body of a clause but not in its head are called *local*. They correspond closely to the variables that are local to the procedure bodies in the imperative languages with the difference that in logic programs their declaration is implicit. Logic programming, like Pascal, does not have a block statement.

To explain how the computation process takes place for pure Prolog programs, we simply view a clause of the form

$$p(s_1, \ldots, s_n) :- A_1, \ldots, A_k.$$

as a shorthand for the simple clause

$$p(x_1, \ldots, x_n) :\text{-} (x_1, \ldots, x_n) = (s_1, \ldots, s_n), A_1, \ldots, A_k.$$

where $x_1, \ldots, x_n$ are fresh variables. We use here Prolog's syntactic facility according to which given a sequence $s_1, \ldots, s_n$ of terms $(s_1, \ldots, s_n)$ is also a term.

So given a procedure call $p(t_1, \ldots, t_n)$ if the above clause $p(s_1, \ldots, s_n) :\text{-} A_1, \ldots, A_k$ is selected, an attempt is made to unify $(t_1, \ldots, t_n)$ with $(s_1, \ldots, s_n)$. (As before, we assume here that no variable clashes arise; otherwise the variables of the clause should be appropriately renamed.) If the unification succeeds and produces a substitution θ, the state (represented by a substitution) is updated by applying to it θ and the computation continues with the statement $A_1, \ldots, A_k$ in this new state. Otherwise, a failure arises and the next clause is selected.

Therefore, by using clauses instead of simple clauses, unification is effectively lifted to a parameter mechanism. As a side effect, this makes the explicit use of unification, modelled by means of "=", superfluous. As an example, reconsider the above program appending two lists. Using the clauses it can be written in a much more succinct way, as the following program APPEND:

```
% append(Xs, Ys, Zs) :- Zs is the result of concatenating the lists Xs and Ys.
append([], Ys, Ys).
append([X | Xs], Ys, [X | Zs]) :- append(Xs, Ys, Zs).
```

Here, the implicit case analysis present in the previous program is in effect moved into the heads of the clauses. The use of terms in the heads of the clauses is completely analogous to the use of *patterns* in function definitions in functional programming.

To summarize, the characteristic elements of procedure declarations in logic programming, in contrast to imperative programming, are: the use of multiple rules and use of patterns to select among these rules.

15.5 PROLOG'S APPROACH TO PROGRAMMING

The power and originality of the Prolog programming style lies in the combination of automatic backtracking with the use of relations and logical variables.

15.5.1 Multiple Uses of a Single Program

As a first illustration of the novelty of Prolog's approach to programming, we illustrate the possibility of using the same program for different purposes. The perhaps simplest example involves the following program MEMBER. We use in it a useful feature of Prolog, so-called anonymous variable, written as an "underscore" character "_." Each occurrence of "_" in a query or in a clause is interpreted as a *different* variable. Anonymous variables are analogous to the *wildcard pattern* feature of the ML or Haskell language.

% member(X, Xs):- X is a member of the list Xs.
member(X, [X | _]).
member(X, [_ | Xs]):- member(X, Xs).

MEMBER can be used both for testing and for computing:

?- member(wed, [mon, wed, fri]).
yes
?- member(X, [mon, wed, fri]).
Xs = mon ;
Xs = wed ;
Xs = fri ;
no

Here ";" is the user's request to produce the next answer. If this request fails, the answer "no" is printed.

Consequently, given a variable X and two lists s and t, the query member(X, s), member(X, t). generates all elements that are present both in s and t. Operationally, the first call generates all members of s and the second call tests for each of them the membership in t.

Also the APPEND program can be used for a number of purposes, in particular to concatenate two lists and to split a list in all possible ways. For example, we have

?- append(Xs, Ys, [mon, wed, fri]).
Xs = []
Ys = [mon, wed, fri];
Xs = [mon]
Ys = [wed, fri];
Xs = [mon, wed]
Ys = [fri];
Xs = [mon, wed, fri]
Ys = [];
no

This cannot be achieved with any functional programing version of the APPEND. The difference comes from the fact that in logic programming procedures are defined by means of the relations, whereas in functional programming functions are used. In fact, there is no distinction between input and output arguments in the procedures in logic programs.

To see two uses of append in a single program, consider a program that checks whether one list is a consecutive sublist of another one. The one line program SUBLIST

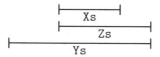

Figure 15.1. Xs is a sublist of the list Ys

that follows formalizes the following definition of a sublist:

- the list Xs is a sublist of the list Ys if Xs is a prefix of a suffix of Ys.

% sublist(Xs, Ys) :- Xs is a sublist of the list Ys.
sublist(Xs, Ys) :- append(_, Zs, Ys), append(Xs, _, Zs).

Here, both anonymous variables and Zs are local. In this rule Zs is a suffix of Ys and Xs is a prefix of Zs. This relation is illustrated in Figure 15.1.

Operationally, given two lists, as and bs, the query sublist(as, bs). leads to a generation of splits of the list bs through the call append(_, Zs, bs). Then for each generated suffix Zs of bs it is checked whether for some list, denoted by the anonymous variable _, the call append(as, _, Zs) succeeds. This happens when as is a prefix of Zs. So a typical use of this program involves backtracking.

15.5.2 Logical Variables

Let us return now to the logical variables. They are an important feature of logic programming, but it is easy to overlook their use. For example, they already appear in the computations involving the first version of the list concatenation program, and consequently, because of the way we defined the computation process, in the computations of the APPEND program. Indeed, given the query append ([jan,feb,mar], [april,may], Zs). the rule

---

append(Xs, Ys, Zs) :- Xs = [H | Ts], Zs = [H | Us], append(Ts, Ys, Us).

---

leads to the binding of the variable Zs to the term [jan | Us]. The value of the variable Us is computed later, by means of the call append([feb,mar], [april,may], Us). This call first binds Us to the term [feb | U1s], where U1s is a fresh variable, and hence Zs to the term [jan, feb | U1s]. This progressive building of the output using the logical variables is typical for Prolog. The real power of logical variables should become apparent after considering the following three original Prolog programs.

A type assignment

The typed lambda calculus and Curry's system of type assignment involves statements of the form $s : \tau$, which should be read as "term s has type τ." Finite sequences of such statements with s being a variable are called *environments* are denoted below by E. A statement of the form $E \vdash s : \tau$ should be read as "in the environment E the term s has type τ". The following three rules define by induction on the structure of lambda terms how to assign types to lambda terms:

$$\frac{x : t \in E}{E \vdash x : t}$$

$$\frac{E \vdash m : s \to t, \quad E \vdash n : s}{E \vdash (m\ n) : t}$$

$$\frac{E, \ x : s \vdash m : t}{E \vdash (\lambda x.m) : s \to t}$$

To encode the lambda terms as usual "first-order" terms, we use the unary function symbol var and two binary function symbols, lambda and apply. The lambda term x (a variable) is translated to the term var(x), the lambda term $(m\ n)$ to the term apply (m, n), and the lambda term $\lambda x.m$ to the term lambda(x, m). For example, the lambda term $\lambda x. (x\ x)$ translates to lambda(x, apply(var(x), var(x))). The subtle point is that according to Prolog convention, lower case letters stand for constants, so for example var(x) is a ground term (i.e., a term without variables).

The above rules directly translate into the following Prolog program that refers to the previously defined member relation.

```
:- op(1100, yfx, arrow).
% type(E, S, T):- lambda term S has type T in the environment E.
type(E, var(X), T):- member([X, T], E).
type(E, apply(M, N), T):- type(E, M, S arrow T), type(E, N, S).
type(E, lambda(X, M), (S arrow T)):- type([[X, S] | E], M, T).
```

For readability, we use here arrow as a binary function symbol written in infix notation. The first line declares this use of arrow together with a certain associativity and priority information (The details of this archaic, though useful, Prolog notation are not relevant here.)

As expected, the above program can be used to check whether a given (representation of a) lambda term has a given type. Less expected is that this program can also be used to compute a type assignment to a lambda term, if such an assignment exists, and to report a failure if no such assignment exists. To this end, given a lambda term s, it suffices to use the query type([], t, T)., where the empty list [] denotes the empty environment and where t is the translation of s to a first-order term. For instance, the query

```
?- type([], lambda(x, apply(var(x), var(x))), T).
```

fails. In fact, no type can be assigned to the lambda term $\lambda x. (x\ x)$. The computation first leads to the call type([[x, S]], apply(var(x), var(x)), T)

and then to the call

type([[x, S]], var(x), S arrow T).

This in turn leads to the call

member([x, S arrow T], [[x, S]])

which fails, because the terms S arrow T and S do not unify. In the above computation, T is used as a logical variable.

The problem of computing a type assignment for lambda terms was posed and solved by Curry and Feys (1958). It is an important topic in the theory of lambda calculus that is of relevance for type inference in functional programming. The solution in Prolog given above is completely elementary. A typical use of this program does not involve backtracking. In fact, its power relies on unification.

A Sequence Program
Next, consider the following problem: arrange three 1s, three 2s, ..., three 9s in sequence so that for all $i \in [1,9]$ there are exactly i numbers between successive occurrences of i. An example of such a sequence is

1, 9, 1, 2, 1, 8, 2, 4, 6, 2, 7, 9, 4, 5, 8, 6, 3, 4, 7, 5, 3, 9, 6, 8, 3, 5, 7.

The desired program is an almost verbatim formalization of the problem in Prolog.

```
% sequence(Xs) :- Xs is a list of 27 variables.
sequence([_,_,_,_,_,_,_,_,_,_,_,_,_,_,_,_,_,_,_,_,_,_,_,_,_,_,_]).
% question(Ss) :- Ss is a solution to the problem.
question(Ss) :-
    sequence(Ss),
    sublist([9,_,_,_,_,_,_,_,_,_,9,_,_,_,_,_,_,_,_,_,9], Ss),
    sublist([8,_,_,_,_,_,_,_,_,8,_,_,_,_,_,_,_,_,8], Ss),
    sublist([7,_,_,_,_,_,_,_,7,_,_,_,_,_,_,_,7], Ss),
    sublist([6,_,_,_,_,_,_,6,_,_,_,_,_,_,6], Ss),
    sublist([5,_,_,_,_,_,5,_,_,_,_,_,5], Ss),
    sublist([4,_,_,_,_,4,_,_,_,_,4], Ss),
    sublist([3,_,_,_,3,_,_,_,3], Ss),
    sublist([2,_,_,2,_,_,2], Ss),
    sublist([1,_,1,_,1], Ss).
```

Note how the anonymous variables dramatically improve the readability of the program.

Operationally, the query ?- question(Ss). leads to the procedure call sequence(Ss) that instantiates the variable Ss to the list of 27 anonymous (so different) variables. Then each of the nine calls of the sublist procedure enforces an existence of a specific sublist pattern on Ss. Each pattern involves syntactically anonymous variables, each of them representing operationally a logical variable.

In spite of the fact that the program is simple and transparent, the resulting computation is involved because of a extensive use of backtracking. The query generates all six solutions to the problem.

Difference lists

One of the drawbacks of the concatenation of lists performed by the APPEND program is that for lists s and t the execution of the query append(s, t, Z) takes the number of steps that is proportional to the length of the first list, s. This is obviously inefficient. In an imperative setting, if one represents a list as a link list, to concatenate two lists it suffices to adjust one pointer.

Difference list is a generalization of the concept of a list that allows us to perform concatenation in constant time. The fact that many programs rely explicitly on list concatenation explains the importance of this concept.

In what follows, we use the subtraction operator "-" written in the infix form. Its use has nothing to do with arithmetic, though intuitively one should read it as the "difference." Formally, a *difference list* is a construct of the form $[a_1, \ldots, a_m | x] - x$, where x is a variable and where we used the notation introduced in Subsection 15.4.2. It *represents* the list $[a_1, \ldots, a_m]$ in a form amenable to a different definition of concatenation. Namely, consider two difference lists $[a_1, \ldots, a_m | x] - x$ and $[b_1, \ldots, b_n | y] - y$. Then their concatenation is the difference list $[a_1, \ldots, a_m, b_1, \ldots, b_n | y] - y2$.

This concatenation process is achieved by the following one line APPEND_DL program:

```
% append(Xs, Ys, Zs) :- the difference list Zs is the result of concatenating
%              the difference lists Xs and Ys.
append_dl(X-Y, Y-Z, X-Z).
```

For example, we have:

```
?- append_dl([a,b|X]-X, [c,d|Y]-Y, U).
U = [a,b,c,d|Y]-Y,
X = [c,d|Y]
```

which shows that U became instantiated to the difference list representing the list [a,b,c,d].

We shall illustrate the use of difference lists in Subsection 15.6.2.

15.6 ARITHMETIC IN PROLOG

The Prolog programs presented so far are *declarative* since they admit a dual reading as a formula. The treatment of arithmetic in Prolog compromises to some extent its declarative underpinnings. However, it is difficult to come up with a better solution than the one offered by the original designers of the language. The shortcomings of Prolog's treatment of arithmetic are overcome in the constraint logic programming languages.

15.6.1 Arithmetic Operators

Prolog provides integers and floating point numbers as built-in data structures, with the typical operations on them. These operations include the usual arithmetic operators such as +, -, * (multiplication), and // (integer division).

Now, according to the usual notational convention of logic programming and Prolog, the relation and function symbols are written in the *prefix form*, that is in front of the arguments. In contrast, in accordance with their usage in arithmetic, the binary arithmetic operators are written in *infix form*, that is between the arguments. Moreover, negation of a natural number can be written in the *bracketless prefix form*, that is, without brackets surrounding its argument.

This discrepancy in the syntax is resolved by considering the arithmetic operators as built-in function symbols written in the infix or bracketless prefix form with information about their associativity and binding power that allows us to disambiguate the arithmetic expressions.

Actually, Prolog provides a means to declare an *arbitrary* function symbol as an infix binary symbol or as a bracketless prefix unary symbol, with a fixed *priority* that determines its binding power and a certain *mnemonics* that implies some (or no) form of associativity. An example of such a declaration was the line :- op(1100, yfx, arrow). used in the above-type assignment program. Function symbols declared in this way are called *operators*. Arithmetic operators can be thus viewed as operators predeclared in the language "prelude."

In addition to the arithmetic operators we also have at our disposal infinitely many integer constants and infinitely many floating point numbers. In what follows, by a *number*, we mean either an integer constant or a floating point number. The arithmetic operators and the set of all numbers uniquely determine a set of terms. We call terms defined in this language *arithmetic expressions* and introduce the abbreviation *gae* for ground (i.e., variable free) arithmetic expressions.

15.6.2 Arithmetic Comparison Relations

With each gae, we can uniquely associate its *value*, computed in the expected way. Prolog allows us to compare the values of gaes by means of the customary six *arithmetic comparison relations*

<, =<, =:= ("equal"), =\=, ("different"), >=, and >.

The "equal" relation "=:=" should not be confused with the "is unifiable with" relation "=" discussed in Section 15.3.

The arithmetic comparison relations work on gaes and produce the expected outcome. For instance, > compares the values of two gaes and succeeds if the value of the first argument is larger than the value of the second and fails otherwise.

Thus, for example

```
?- 6*2 =:= 3*4.
yes
?- 7 > 3+4.
no
```

However, when one of the arguments of the arithmetic comparison relations is not a gae, the computation *ends in an error*.

For example, we have

```
?- [] < 5.
error in arithmetic expression: [] is not a number.
```

As a simple example of the use of the arithmetic comparison relations, consider the following program, which checks whether a list of numbers is ordered.

```
% ordered(Xs) :- Xs is an =<-ordered list of numbers
ordered([]).
ordered([_]).
ordered([X, Y | Xs]) :- X =< Y, ordered([Y | Xs]).
```

Recall that [X, Y | Xs]) is the abbreviated Prolog notation for [X | [Y | Xs]]).

We now have

```
?- ordered([1,1,2,3]). yes
```

but also

```
?- ordered([1,X,1]).
instantiation fault in 1 =< X
```

Here, a run-time error took place because at a certain stage the comparison relation "=<" was applied to an argument that is not a number.

As another example, consider Prolog's version of the *quicksort* procedure of C.A.R. Hoare. According to this sorting procedure, a list is first partitioned into two sublists using an element X of it, one consisting of the elements smaller than X and the other consisting of the elements larger or equal than X. Then each sublist is quicksorted and the resulting sorted sublists are appended with the element X put in the middle. This can be expressed in Prolog by means of the following QUICKSORT program, where X is chosen to be the first element of the given list:

```
% qs(Xs, Ys) :- Ys is an ordered permutation of the list Xs.
qs([], []).
qs([X | Xs], Ys) :-
      part(X, Xs, Littles, Bigs),
      qs(Littles, Ls),
      qs(Bigs, Bs),
      append(Ls, [X | Bs], Ys).
% part(X, Xs, Ls, Bs) :- Ls is a list of elements of Xs which are < X,
%                   Bs is a list of elements of Xs which are >= X.
part(_, [], [], []).
part(X, [Y | Xs], [Y | Ls], Bs) :- X > Y, part(X, Xs, Ls, Bs).
part(X, [Y | Xs], Ls, [Y | Bs]) :- X =< Y, part(X, Xs, Ls, Bs).
```

We now have, for example

```
?- qs([7,9,8,1,5], Ys).
Ys = [1, 5, 7, 8, 9]
```

and also

```
?- qs([7,9,8,1,5], [1,5,7,9,8]).
no
```

The QUICKSORT program uses the append relation to concatenate the lists. Consequently, its efficiency can be improved using the difference lists introduced in Subsection 15.5.2. Conceptually, the calls of the append relation are first replaced by the corresponding calls of the append_dl relation. This yields a program defining the qs_dl relation. Then unfolding the calls of append_dl leads to a program that does not use the APPEND_DL program anymore and performs the list concatenation "on the fly." This results in the program QUICKSORT_DL in which the definition of the qs relation is replaced by

```
% qs(Xs, Ys) :- Ys is an ordered permutation of the list Xs.
qs(Xs, Ys) :- qs_dl(Xs, Ys - []).
% qs_dl(Xs, Y) :- Y is a difference list representing the
%            ordered permutation of the list Xs.
qs_dl([], Xs - Xs).
```

```
qs_dl([X | Xs], Ys - Zs) :-
    part(X, Xs, Littles, Bigs),
    qs_dl(Littles, Ys - [X | Y1s]),
    qs_dl(Bigs, Y1s - Zs).
```

The first rule links the qs relation with the qs_dl relation.

15.6.3 Evaluation of Arithmetic Expressions

So far we have presented programs that use ground arithmetic expressions but have not yet introduced any means of evaluating them. For example, no facilities have been introduced so far to evaluate 3+4. All we can do at this stage is to check that the outcome is 7 by using the comparison relation =:= and the query 7 =:= 3+4. However, using the comparison relations it is not possible to *assign* the value of 3+4, that is 7, to a variable, say X. Note that the query X =:= 3+4. ends in an error, while the query X = 3+4. instantiates X to the term 3+4.

To overcome this problem, the binary *arithmetic evaluator* is is used in Prolog. is is an infix operator defined as follows.

Consider the call s is t.

Then t has to be a ground arithmetic expression (gae).

The call of s is t results in the unification of the *value* of the gae t with s.

If t is not a gae then a run-time error arises.

Thus, for example, we have

```
?- 7 is 3+4.
yes
8 is 3+4.
no
?- X is 3+4.
X = 7
?- X is Y+1.
! Error in arithmetic expression: not a number
```

As an example of the use of an arithmetic evaluator, consider the proverbial factorial function. It can be computed using the following program FACTORIAL:

```
% factorial(N, F) :- F is N!.
factorial(0, 1).
factorial(N, F) :- N > 0, N1 is N-1, factorial(N1, F1), F is N*F1.
```

Note the use of a local variable N1 in the atom N1 is N-1 to compute the decrement of N and the use of a local variable F1 to compute the value of N1 factorial. The atom N1 is N-1 corresponds to the assignment command N := N-1 of imperative programming. The difference is that a new variable needs to be used to compute the value of N-1. Such uses of local variables are typical when computing with integers in Prolog.

As another example consider a Prolog program that computes the length of a list.

```
% length(Xs, N) :- N is the length of the list Xs.
length([], 0).
length([_ | Ts], N) :- length(Ts, M), N is M+1.
```

We then have

```
?- length([a,b,c], N).
N = 3
```

An intuitive but incorrect version would use as the second clause

```
length([_ | Ts], N+1) :- length(Ts, N).
```

With such definition we would get the following nonintuitive outcome:

```
?- length([a,b,c], N).
N = 0 + 1 + 1 + 1
```

The point is that the generated ground arithmetic expressions are not automatically evaluated in Prolog.

We conclude that arithmetic facilities in Prolog are quite subtle and require good insights to be properly used.

15.7 CONTROL, AMBIVALENT SYNTAX, AND META-VARIABLES

In the framework discussed so far, no control constructs are present. Let us see now how they could be simulated by means of the features explained so far. Consider the customary **if** B **then** S **else** T **fi** construct. It can be modelled by means of the following two clauses:

```
p(x) :- B, S.
p(x) :- not B, T.
```

where p is a new procedure identifier and all the variables of B, S and T are collected in **x**. To see how inefficiency creeps into this style of programming, consider two cases.

First, suppose that the first clause is selected and that B is true (i.e., succeeds). Then the computation continues with S. But in general B is an arbitrary query and because of the implicit nondeterminism present B can succeed in many ways. If the computation of S fails, these alternative ways of computing B will be automatically tried even though we know already that B is true.

Second, suppose that the first clause is selected and that B is false (that is fails). Then backtracking takes place and the second clause is tried. The computation proceeds by evaluating not B. This is completely unneeded, since we know at this stage that not B is true (that is, succeeds).

Note that omitting not B in the second rule would cause a problem in case a success of B were followed by a failure of S. Then upon backtracking T would be executed.

15.7.1 Cut

To deal with such problems, Prolog provides a low level built-in nullary relation symbol called *cut* and denoted by "!". To explain its meaning we rewrite first the above clauses using cut:

p($\mathbf{x}$) :- B, !, S.
p($\mathbf{x}$) :- T.

In the resulting analysis, two possibilities arise, akin to the above case distinction. First, if B is true (i.e., succeeds), then the cut is encountered. Its execution

- discards all alternative ways of computing B,
- discards the second clause, p($\mathbf{x}$) :- T., as a backtrackable alternative to the current selection of the first clause.

Both items have an effect that in the current computation some clauses are not available anymore.

Second, if B is false (i.e., fails), then backtracking takes place and the second clause is tried. The computation proceeds now by directly evaluating T.

So using the cut and the above rewriting we achieved the intended effect and modelled the **if B then S else T fi** construct in the desired way.

The above explanation of the effect of cut is a good starting point to provide its definition in full generality.

Consider the following definition of a relation p:

p($\mathbf{s}_1$) :- $\mathbf{A}_1$.
. . .
p($\mathbf{s}_i$) :- $\mathbf{B}$,!,$\mathbf{C}$.
. . .
p($\mathbf{s}_k$) :- $\mathbf{A}_k$.

Here, the ith clause contains a cut atom. Now, suppose that during the execution of a query, a call p($\mathbf{t}$) is encountered and eventually the ith clause is used and the indicated occurrence of the cut is executed. Then the indicated occurrence of ! succeeds immediately, but additionally

1. all alternative ways of computing **B** are discarded, and
2. all computations of p(**t**) using the ith to k^{th} clause for p are discarded as back-trackable alternatives to the current selection of the *i*-clause.

The cut was introduced to improve the implicit control present through the combination of backtracking and the textual ordering of the clauses. Because of the use of patterns in the clause heads, the potential source of inefficiency can be sometimes hidden somewhat deeper in the program text. Reconsider for example the QUICKSORT program of Section 15.6 and the query ?- qs([7,9,8,1,5], Ys). To see that the resulting computation is inefficient, note that the second clause defining the part relation fails when 7 is compared with 9 and subsequently the last, third, clause is tried. At this moment 7 is again compared with 9. The same redundancy occurs when 1 is compared with 5. To avoid such inefficiencies the definition of part can be rewritten using cut as follows:

```
part(_, [], [], []).
part(X, [Y | Xs], [Y | Ls], Bs) :- X > Y, !, part(X, Xs, Ls, Bs).
part(X, [Y | Xs], Ls, [Y | Bs]) :- part(X, Xs, Ls, Bs).
```

Of course, this improvement can be also applied to the QUICKSORT_DL program.

Cut clearly compromises the declarative reading of the Prolog programs. It has been one of the most criticized features of Prolog. In fact, a proper use of cut requires a good understanding of Prolog's computation mechanism and a number of thumb rules were developed to help a Prolog programmer to use it correctly. A number of alternatives to cut were proposed. The most interesting of them, called *commit*, entered various constraint and parallel logic programming languages but is not present in standard Prolog.

15.7.2 Ambivalent Syntax and Meta-variables

Before we proceed, let us review first the basics of Prolog syntax mentioned so far.

1. Variables are denoted by strings starting with an upper case letter or "_" (underscore). In particular, Prolog allows so-called anonymous variables, written as "_" (underscore).
2. Relation symbols (procedure identifiers), function symbols, and nonnumeric constants are denoted by strings starting with a lower case letter.
3. Binary and unary function symbols can be declared as infix or bracketless prefix operators.

Now, in contrast to first-order logic, in Prolog the *same* name can be used both for function symbols and for relation symbols. Moreover, the same name can be used for function or relation symbols of different arity. This facility is called *ambivalent syntax*. A function or a relation symbol f of arity n is then referred to as f/n. Thus, in a Prolog program, we can use both a relation symbol p/2 and function symbols p/1 and p/2 and build syntactically legal terms or atoms like p(p(a,b),c,p(X)).

In presence of the ambivalent syntax, the distinction between function symbols and relation symbols and between terms and atoms disappears, but in the context of queries and clauses, it is clear which symbol refers to which syntactic category.

The ambivalent syntax together with Prolog's facility to declare binary function symbols (and thus also binary relation symbols) as infix operators allows us to pass queries, clauses and programs as arguments. In fact, ":-/2" is declared internally as an infix operator and so is the comma ",/2" between the atoms, so each clause is actually a term. This facilitates *meta-programming*, that is, writing programs that use other programs as data.

In what follows, we shall explain how meta-programming can be realized in Prolog. To this end, we need to introduce one more syntactic feature. Prolog permits the use of variables in the positions of atoms, both in the queries and in the clause bodies. Such a variable is called then a *meta-variable*. Computation in the presence of the meta-variables is defined as before since the mgus employed can also bind the meta-variables. Thus, for example, given the legal, albeit unusual, Prolog program (that uses the ambivalent syntax facility)

```
p(a).
a.
```

the execution of the Prolog query p(X), X. first leads to the query a. and then succeeds. Here, a is both a constant and a nullary relation symbol.

Prolog requires that the meta-variables are properly instantiated before they are executed. In other words, they need to evaluate to a nonnumeric term at the moment they are encountered in an execution. Otherwise, a run-time error arises. For example, for the above program and the query p(X), X, Y., the Prolog computation ends up in error once the query Y. is encountered.

15.7.3 Control Facilities

Let us now see how the ambivalent syntax in conjunction with meta-variables supports meta-programming. In this section we limit ourselves to (meta-)programs that show how to introduce new control facilities. We discuss here three examples, each introducing a control facility actually available in Prolog as a built-in. More meta-programs will be presented in the next section once we introduce other features of Prolog.

Disjunction
To start with, we can define *disjunction* by means of the following simple program:

```
or(X,Y) :- X.
or(X,Y) :- Y.
```

A typical query is then or(Q,R), where Q and R are "conventional queries." Disjunction is a Prolog's built-in declared as an infix operator ";/2" and defined by means of the above two rules, with "or" replaced by ";". So instead of or(Q,R) one writes Q ; R.

If-then-else

The other two examples involve the cut operator. The already discussed **if** B **then** S **else** T **fi** construct can be introduced by means of the now-familiar program

```
if_then_else(B, S, T) :- B,!,S.
if_then_else(B, S, T) :- T.
```

In Prolog, if_then_else is a built-in defined internally by the above two rules. if_then_else(B, S, T) is written as B -> S;T, where "→ /2" is a built-in declared as an infix operator. As an example of its use, let us rewrite yet again the definition of the part relation used in the QUICKSORT program, this time using Prolog's B -> S;T. To enforce the correct parsing, we need to enclose the B -> S;T statement in brackets:

```
part(_, [], [], []).
part(X, [Y | Xs], Ls, Bs) :-
  ( X > Y ->
  Ls = [Y | L1s], part(X, Xs, L1s, Bs)
  ;
  Bs = [Y | B1s], part(X, Xs, Ls, B1s)
  ).
```

Note that here we had to dispense with the use of patterns in the "output" positions of part and reintroduce the explicit use of unification in the procedure body. By introducing yet another B -> S;T statement to deal with the case analysis in the second argument, we obtain a definition of the part relation that very much resembles a functional program:

```
part(X, X1s, Ls, Bs) :-
  ( X1s = [] ->
  Ls = [], Bs = []
  ;
  X1s = [Y | Xs],
  ( X > Y ->
  Ls = [Y | L1s], part(X, Xs, L1s, Bs)
  ;
  Bs = [Y | B1s], part(X, Xs, Ls, B1s)
  )
  ).
```

In fact, in this program all uses of unification boil down to matching and its use does not involve backtracking. This example explains how the use of patterns often hides an implicit case analysis. By making this case analysis explicit using the **if-then-else** construct we end up with longer programs. In the end the original solution with the cut seems to be closer to the spirit of the language.

Negation

Finally, consider the negation operation not that is supposed to reverse failure with success. That is, the intention is that the query not Q. succeeds iff the query Q. fails. This operation can be easily implemented by means of meta-variables and cut as follows:

```
not(X) :- X, !, fail.
not(_).
```

fail/0 is Prolog's built-in with the empty definition. Thus, the call of the parameterless procedure fail always fails.

This cryptic two-line program employs several discussed features of Prolog. In the first line, X is used as a meta-variable. Now consider the call not(Q), where Q is a query. If Q succeeds, then the cut is performed. This has the effect that all alternative ways of computing Q are discarded and also the second clause is discarded. Next, the built-in fail is executed and a failure arises. Because the only alternative clause was just discarded, the query not(Q) fails. If, on the other hand, the query Q fails, then backtracking takes place and the second clause, not(_), is selected. It immediately succeeds and so the initial query not(Q) succeeds. So this definition of not achieves the desired effect.

not/1 is defined internally by the above two line definition augmented with the appropriate declaration of it as a bracketless prefix unary symbol.

Call

Finally, let us mention that Prolog also provides an indirect way of using meta-variables by means of a built-in relation call/1. call/1 is defined internally by this rule:

```
call(X) :- X.
```

call/1 is often used to "mask" the explicit use of meta-variables, but the outcome is the same.

15.7.4 Negation as Failure

The distinction between successful and failing computations is one of the unique features of logic programming and Prolog. In fact, no counterpart of failing computations exists in other programming paradigms.

The most natural way of using failing computations is by employing the negation operator not that allows us to turn failure into success, by virtue of the fact that the query not Q. succeeds iff the query Q. fails. This way we can use not to represent negation of a Boolean expression. In fact, we already referred informally to this use of negation at the beginning of Section 15.7.

This suggests a declarative interpretation of the not operator as a classical negation. This interpretation is correct only if the negated query always terminates and is ground. Note, in particular, that given the procedure p defined by the single rule p :- p. the query not p. does not terminate. Also, for the query not(X = 1)., we get the following counterintuitive outcome:

```
?- not(X = 1).
no
```

Thus, to generate all elements of a list Ls that differ from 1, the correct query is member(X, Ls), not(X = 1). and not not(X = 1), member(X, Ls). One usually refers to the way negation is used in Prolog as "negation as failure." When properly used, it is a powerful feature as testified by the following jewel program. We consider the problem of determining a winner in a two-person finite game. Suppose that the moves in the game are represented by a relation move. The game is assumed to be finite, so we postulate that given a position pos the query move(pos, Y). generates finitely many answers, which are all possible moves from pos. A player loses if he is in a position pos from which no move exists, i.e., if the query move(pos, Y). fails.

A position is a winning one when a move exists that leads to a losing, i.e., non-winning position. Using the negation operator, this can be written as

```
% win(X) :- X is a winning position in the two-person finite game
%          represented by the relation move.
win(X) :- move(X, Y), not win(Y).
```

This remarkably concise program has a simple declarative interpretion. In contrast, the procedural interpretation is quite complex: the query win(pos). determines whether pos is a winning position by performing a minimax search on the 0–1 game tree represented by the relation move. In this recursive procedure, the base case appears when the call to move fails. Then the corresponding call of win also fails.

15.7.5 Higher-Order Programming and Meta-Programming in Prolog

Thanks to the ambivalent syntax and meta-variables, higher-order programming and another form of meta-programming can be easily realized in Prolog. To explain this, we need two more built-ins. Each of them belongs to a different category.

Term Inspection Facilities

Prolog offers a number of built-in relations that allow us to inspect, compare, and decompose terms. One of them is =../2 (pronounced *univ*) that allows us to switch between a term and its representation as a list. Instead of precisely describing its meaning, we just illustrate one of its uses by means the following query:

```
?- Atom =.. [square, [1,2,3,4], Ys].
Atom = square([1,2,3,4], Ys).
```

The left-hand side, here Atom, is unified with the term (or, equivalently, the atom), here square([1,2,3,4], Ys), represented by a list on the right-hand side, here [square, [1,2,3,4], Ys]. In this list representation of a term, the head of the list is the leading function symbol and the tail is the list of the arguments.

Using *univ*, one can construct terms and pass them as arguments. More interestingly, one can construct atoms and execute them using the meta-variable facility. This way it is possible to realize higher-order programming in Prolog in the sense that relations can be passed as arguments. To illustrate this point, consider the following program MAP:

```
% map(P, Xs, Ys) :- the list Ys is the result of applying P
%        elementwise to the list Xs.
map(P, [], []).
map(P, [X | Xs] , [Y | Ys]) :- apply(P, [X, Y]), map(P, Xs, Ys).
% apply(P, [X1, ... , Xn]) :- execute the atom P(X1, ... , Xn).
apply(P, Xs) :- Atom =.. [P|Xs], Atom.
```

In the last rule, *univ* is used to construct an atom. Note the use of the meta-variable Atom. MAP is Prolog's counterpart of the familiar higher-order functional program and it behaves in the expected way. For example, given the program % square(X, Y) :- Y is the square of X. square(X, Y) :- Y is X*X. we get

```
?- map(square, [1,2,3,4], Ys).
Ys = [1, 4, 9, 16]
```

Program manipulation facilities

Another class of Prolog built-ins makes it possible to access and modify the program during its execution. We consider here a single built-in in this category, clause/2 , that allows us to access the definitions of the relations present in the considered program. Again, consider first an example of its use in which we refer to the program MEMBER of Subsection 15.5.1.

```
?- clause(member(X,Y), Z).
Y = [X|_A],
Z = true ;
Y = [_A|_B],
Z = member(X,_B) ;
no
```

In general, the call clause(head, body) leads to a unification of the term head :- body with the successive clauses forming the definition of the relation in question. This relation, here member, is the leading symbol of the first argument of clause/2 that has to be a non-variable.

This built-in assumes that true is the body of a fact, here member(X, [X | _]). true/0 is Prolog's built-in that succeeds immediately. Thus, its definition consists just of the fact true. This explains the first answer. The second answer is the result of unifying the term member(X,Y) :- Z with (a renaming of) the second clause defining member, namely member(X, [_ | Xs]):- member(X, Xs).

Using clause/2, we can construct Prolog interpreters written in Prolog, that is, *meta-interpreters*. Here is the simplest one:

```
% solve(Q) :- the query Q succeeds for the program accessible by clause/2.
solve(true) :- !.
solve((A,B)) :- !, solve(A), solve(B).
solve(A) :- clause(A, B), solve(B).
```

Recall that (A,B) is a legal Prolog term (with no leading function symbol). To understand this program, one needs to know that the comma between the atoms is declared internally as a right associative infix operator, so the query A,B,C,D actually stands for the term (A,(B,(C,D))), etc.

The first clause states that the built-in true succeeds immediately. The second clause states that a query of the form A, **B** can be solved if A can be solved and **B** can be solved. Finally, the last clause states that an atomic query A can be solved if there exists a clause of the form A :- **B** such that the query **B** can be solved. The cuts are used here to enforce the a "definition by cases": either the argument of solve is true or a nonatomic query or else an atomic one.

To illustrate the behavior of the above meta-interpreter, assume that MEMBER is a part of the considered program. We then have

```
?- solve(member(X, [mon, wed, fri])).
X = mon ;
X = wed ;
X = fri ;
no
```

This meta-program forms a basis for building various types of interpreters for larger fragments of Prolog or for its extensions.

15.8 ASSESSMENT OF PROLOG

Prolog, because of its origin in automated theorem proving, is an unusual programming language. It leads to a different style of programming and to a different view of programming. A number of elegant Prolog programs presented here speak for themselves. We also noted that the same Prolog program can often be used for different purposes – for computing, testing or completing a solution, or for computing all solutions. Such programs cannot be easily written in other programming paradigms. Logical variables are a unique and, as we saw, very useful feature of logic programming. Additionally, pure Prolog programs have a dual interpretation as logical formulas. In this sense, Prolog supports declarative programming.

Both through the development of a programming methodology and ingenious implementations, great care was taken to overcome the possible sources of inefficiency. On the programming level, we already discussed cut and the difference lists. Programs such as FACTORIAL of Subsection 15.6.3 can be optimized by means of tail recursion. On the implementation level, efficiency is improved by such techniques as the last call optimization that can be used to optimize tail recursion, indexing that deals with the presence of multiple clauses, and a default omission of the occur-check (the test "x does not occur in t" in clause (5) of the Martelli–Montanari algorithm) that speeds up the unification process (although on rare occasions makes it unsound).

Prolog's only data type, the terms, is implicitly present in many areas of computer science. In fact, whenever the objects of interest are defined by means of grammars, for example first-order formulas, digital circuits, programs in any programming language, or sentences in some formal language, these objects can be naturally defined as terms. Prolog programs can then be developed starting with this representation of the objects as terms. Prolog's support for handling terms by means of unification and various term inspection facilities becomes handy. In short, symbolic data can be naturally handled in Prolog.

The automatic backtracking becomes very useful when dealing with search. Search is of paramount importance in many artificial intelligence applications and backtracking itself is most natural when dealing with the NP-complete problems. Moreover, the principle of "computation as deduction" underlying Prolog's computation process facilitates formalization of various forms of reasoning in Prolog. In particular, Prolog's negation operator not can be naturally used to support nonmonotonic reasoning. All this explains why Prolog is a natural language for programming artificial intelligence applications, such as automated theorem provers, expert systems, and machine learning programs where reasoning needs to be combined with computing, game playing programs, and various decision support systems.

Prolog is also an attractive language for computational linguistics applications and for compiler writing. In fact, Prolog provides support for so-called definite clause grammars (DCG). Thanks to this, a grammar written in the DCG form is already a Prolog program that forms a parser for this grammar. The fact that Prolog allows one to write executable specifications makes it also a useful language for rapid prototyping, in particular in the area of meta-programming.

For the sake of a balanced presentation let us discuss now Prolog's shortcomings.

Lack of Types

Types are used in programming languages to structure the data manipulated by the program and to ensure its correct use. In Prolog, one can define various types like binary trees and records. Moreover, the language provides a notation for lists and offers a limited support for the type of all numbers by means of the arithmetic operators and arithmetic comparison relations. However, Prolog does not support types in the sense that it does not check whether the queries use the program in the intended way.

Because of this absence of type checking, type errors are easy to make but difficult to find. For example, even though the APPEND program was meant to be used to concatenate two lists, it can also be used with nonlists as arguments:

```
?- append([a,b], f(c), Zs).
Zs = [a, b|f(c)]
```

and no error is reported. In fact, almost every Prolog program can be misused. Moreover, because of lack of type checking some improvements of the efficiency of the implementation cannot be carried out and various run-time errors cannot be prevented.

Subtle Arithmetic

We discussed already the subtleties arising in presence of arithmetic in Section 15.6. We noted that Prolog's facilities for arithmetic easily lead to run-time errors. It would be desirable to discover such errors at compile time but this is highly nontrivial.

Idiosyncratic Control

Prolog's control mechanisms are difficult to master by programmers accustomed to the imperative programming style. One of the reasons is that both bounded iteration (the for statement) and unbounded iteration (the while statement) need to be implemented by means of the recursion. For example, a nested for statement is implemented by means of nested tail recursion that is less easy to understand. Of course, one can introduce both constructs by means of meta-programming, but then their proper use is not enforced because of the lack of types. Additionally, as already mentioned, cut is a low-level mechanism that is not easy to understand.

Complex Semantics of Various Built-ins

Prolog offers a large number of built-ins. In fact, the ISO Prolog Standard describes 102 built-ins. Several of them are quite subtle. For example, the query not(not Q). tests whether the query Q. succeeds and this test is carried out without changing the state, i.e., without binding any of the variables. Moreover, it is not easy to describe precisely the meaning of some of the built-ins. For example, in the ISO Prolog Standard the operational interpretation of the **if-then-else** construct consists of 17 steps.

No Modules and No Objects

Finally, even though modules exist in many widely used Prolog versions, neither modules nor objects are present in ISO Prolog Standard.as This makes it difficult to properly structure Prolog programs and reuse them as components of other Prolog programs. It should be noted that thanks to Prolog's support for meta-programming, the object-programming style can be mimicked in Prolog in a simple way. But no compile-time checking of its proper use is then enforced then and errors in the program design will be discovered at best at the run-time. The same critique applies to Prolog's approach to higher-order programming and to meta-programming.

Of course, these limitations of Prolog were recognized by many researchers who came up with various good proposals on how to improve Prolog's control, how to add to it (or how to infer) types, and how to provide modules and objects. Research in the field of logic programming also has dealt with the precise relation between the procedural and declarative interpretation of logic programs and a declarative account of various aspects of Prolog, including negation and meta-programming. Also verification of Prolog programs and its semantics were extensively studied.

However, no single programming language proposal emerged yet that could be seen as a natural successor to Prolog in which the above shortcomings are properly solved. The language that comes closest to this ideal is Mercury (see http://www.cs.mu.oz.au/research/mercury/). Colmerauer designed a series of successors of Prolog, Prolog II, III, and IV that incorporated various forms of constraint processing into this programming style.

When assessing Prolog, it is useful to have in mind that it is a programming language designed in the early 1970s (and standardized in the 1990s). The fact that it is still widely used and that new applications for it keep being found testifies to its originality. No other programming language succeeded to embrace first-order logic in such an effective way.

15.9 BIBLIOGRAPHIC REMARKS

For those interested in learning more about the origins of logic programming and of Prolog, the best place to start is Colmerauer and Roussel's account (The Birth of Prolog, in Bergin and Gibson, History of Programming Languages, ACM Press/Addison-Wesley, 1996, pp. 331–367). There a number of excellent books on programming in Prolog. The two deservedly most successful are Bratko (*PROLOG Programming for Artificial Intelligence*, Addison-Wesley, 2001) and Sterling and Shapiro (*The Art of Prolog*, MIT Press, 1994). The work by O'Keefe (*The Craft of Prolog*, MIT Press, 1990) discusses in depth the efficiency and pragmatics of programming in Prolog. The work by Aït-Kaci (*Warrens' Abstract Machine*, MIT Press, 1991. Out of print. Available at http://www.isg.sfu.ca/~hak/documents/wam.html) is an outstanding tutorial on the implementation of Prolog.

15.10 CHAPTER SUMMARY

We discussed the logic programming paradigm and its realization in Prolog. This paradigm has contributed a number of novel ideas in the area of programming languages. It introduced unification as a computation mechanism and it realized the

Table 15.1.

Logic Programming	Imperative Programming
equation solved by unification	assignment
relation symbol	procedure identifier
term	expression
atom	procedure call
query	program
definition of a relation	procedure declaration
local variable of a rule	local variable of a procedure
logic program	set of procedure declarations
"," between atoms	sequencing (";")
substitution	state
composition of substitutions	state update

concept of "computation as deduction". Additionally, it showed that a fragment of first-order logic can be used as a programming language and that declarative programming is an interesting alternative to structured programming in the imperative programming style.

Prolog is a rule-based language but thanks to a large number of built-ins it is a general purpose programming language. Programming in Prolog substantially differs from programming in the imperative programming style. Table 15.1 may help to relate the underlying concepts used in both programming styles.

Acknowledgements

Maarten van Emden and Jan Smaus provided K.R. Apt with useful comments on this chapter.

Additional Program Examples

A.1 PROCEDURAL AND OBJECT-ORIENTED ORGANIZATION

This appendix uses an extended example to illustrate some of the differences between object-oriented and conventional program organization. Sections A.1.1 and A.1.2 contain two versions of a program to manipulate geometric shapes, the second with classes and objects, the first without. The object-oriented code is written in C++, the conventional code in C. To keep the examples short, the only shapes are circles and rectangles.

The non-object-oriented code uses C structs to represent geometric shapes. For each operation on shapes, there is a function that tests the type of shape passed as an argument and branches accordingly. We refer to this program as the *typecase* version of the geometry example, as each function is implemented by a case analysis on the types of shapes.

In the object-oriented code, each shape is represented by an object. Circle objects are implemented by the circle class, which groups circle operations with the data needed to represent a circle. Similarly, the rectangle class groups the data used to represent rectangles with code to implement operations on rectangles. When an operation is done on a shape, the correct code is invoked by dynamic lookup.

Here are some general observations that you may wish to keep in mind when reading the code:

■ An essential difference between the two program organizations is illustrated in the following matrix. For each function, center, move, rotate, and print, there is code for each kind of geometric shape, in this case circle and rectangle. Thus we have eight different pieces of code:

| | Function | | | |
Class	Center	Move	Rotate	Print
Circle	c_center	c_move	c_rotate	c_print
Rectangle	r_center	r_move	r_rotate	r_print

In the typecase version, these functions are arranged by column: the Center function contains code c_center and r_center for finding the center of a circle and a rectangle, respectively. In the object-oriented program, functions are arranged by row: The circle class contains code c_center, c_move, c_rotate, and c_print for manipulating circles. Each arrangement has some advantages when it comes to program maintenance and modification. In the object-oriented approach, adding a new shape is straightforward. The code that details how the new shape should respond to the existing operations all goes in one place: the class definition. Adding a new operation is more complicated, as the appropriate code must be added to each of the class definitions, which could be spread throughout the system. In the typecase version, the opposite is true: Adding a new operation is relatively easy, but adding a new shape is difficult.

- There is a loss of abstraction in the typecase version, as the data manipulated by rotate, print, and the other functions have to be publicly accessible. In contrast, the object-oriented solution encapsulates the data in *circle* and *square* objects. Only the methods of these objects may access this data.

- The typecase version cannot be statically type checked in C. It could be type checked in a language with a built-in typecase statement that tests the type of a struct directly. An example of such a language feature is the Simula inspect statement. Adding such a statement would require that every struct be tagged with its type, a process that requires about the same amount of space overhead as making each struct into an object.

- In the typecase version, subtyping is used in an ad hoc manner. The example is coded so that circle and rectangle have a shared field in their first location. This is a hack to implement a tagged union that could be avoided in a language providing disjoint (as opposed to C unchecked) unions.

- The running time of the two programs is roughly the same. In the typecase version, there is the space cost of an extra data field (the type tag) and the time cost, in each function, of branching according to type. In the object-oriented version, there is a hidden class or vtbl pointer in each object, requiring essentially the same space as a type tag. In the optimized C++ approach, there is one extra indirection in determining which method to invoke, which corresponds to the switch statement in the typecase version. A Smalltalk-like implementation would be less efficient in general, but for methods that are found immediately in the subclass method dictionary (or by caching), the run-time efficiency may be comparable.

A.1.1 Shape Program: Typecase Version

```
#include <stdio.h>
#include <stdlib.h>

/* We use the following enumeration type to "tag" shapes.  */
/* The first field of each shape struct stores what particular */
/* kind of shape it is.                                    */

enum shape_tag {Circle, Rectangle};
```

```
/* The following struct pt and functions new_pt and copy_pt are */
/* used in the implementations of the circle and rectangle    */
/* shapes below.                                          */

struct pt {
  float x;
  float y;
};

struct pt* new_pt(float xval, float yval) {
    struct pt* p = (struct pt *)malloc(sizeof(struct pt));
    p->x = xval;
    p->y = yval;
    return p;
};

struct pt* copy_pt(struct pt* p) {
    struct pt* q = (struct pt *)malloc(sizeof(struct pt));
    q->x = p->x;
    q->y = p->y;
    return q;
};

/* This struct is used to get some static type checking in the   */
/* operation functions (center, move, rotate, and print) below. */

struct shape {
    enum shape_tag tag;
};

/* The following circle struct is our representation of a circle. */
/* The first field is a type tag to indicate that this struct   */
/* represents a circle. The second field stores the circle's     */
/* center and the third its radius.                         */

struct circle {
    enum shape_tag tag;
    struct pt* cnter;
    float radius;
};
```

```
/* The function new_circle creates a circle struct from a given */
/* center point and radius. It sets the type tag to "Circle".*/

struct circle* new_circle(struct pt* cn, float r) {
    struct circle* c = (struct circle*)malloc(sizeof(struct circle));
    c->cnter=copy_pt(cn);
    c->radius=r;
    c->tag=Circle;
    return c;
};


/* The following rectangle struct is our representation of a   */
/* rectangle. The first field is used to indicate that this    */
/* struct represents a rectangle. The next two fields store    */
/* the rectangle's topleft and bottom right corners.           */

struct rectangle {
    enum shape_tag tag;
    struct pt* topleft;
    struct pt* botright;
};


/* The function new_rectangle creates a rectangle in the location */
/* specified by parameters tl and br. It sets the rectangle's     */
/* type tag to "Rectangle".                                       */

struct rectangle* new_rectangle(struct pt* tl, struct pt* br) {
    struct rectangle* r = (struct rectangle*)malloc(sizeof(struct rectangle*));
    r->topleft=copy_pt(tl);
    r->botright=copy_pt(br);
    r->tag=Rectangle;
    return r;
};


/* The center function returns the center point of whatever shape */
/* it is passed. Because the code to compute the center of a      */
/* shape depends on whether the shape is a Circle or a Rectangle, */
/* the function consists of a switch statement that branches      */
/* according to the type tag of the shape s. Within the Circle    */
```

```
/* case, for example, we know the shape in question is actually a  */
/* circle, and hence that it has a "cnter" component storing     */
/* the circle's center. Note that we need to insert a typecast    */
/* to instruct the compiler that we have a circle and not just a   */
/* shape. Note also that this program organization depends on      */
/* the typetags, which are simply struct fields, being set     */
/* correctly. If some programmer incorrectly modifies a type tag   */
/* field, the program will no longer work and the problem can not */
/* be detected at compile time because of the typecasts.      */

struct pt* center (struct shape* s) {
   switch (s->tag) {
   case Circle: {
     struct circle* c = (struct circle*) s;
     return c->cnter;
   };

   case Rectangle: {
     struct rectangle* r = (struct rectangle*) s;
     struct pt* p = new_pt((r->botright->x - r->topleft->x)/2,
             (r->botright->x - r->topleft->x)/2);
     return p;
   };
  };
};

/* The move function moves the shape s dx units in the x-direction */
/* and dy units in the y-direction. Because the code to move a    */
/* shape depends on the kind of shape, this function is a switch */
/* statement that branches depending on the value of the "tag"    */
/* field. Within the individual cases, typecasts are used to     */
/* convert the generic shape s to a circle or rectangle as      */
/* appropriate.                           */

void move (struct shape* s,float dx, float dy) {
   switch (s->tag) {
      case Circle: {
        struct circle* c = (struct circle*) s;
        c->cnter->x += dx;
```

```
                c->cnter->y += dy;
                break;
            };


        case Rectangle: {
            struct rectangle* r = (struct rectangle*) s;
            r->topleft->x += dx;
            r->topleft->y += dy;
            r->botright->x += dx;
            r->botright->y += dy;
            };
        };
    };
```

```
/* The rotate function rotates the shape s ninety degrees. Since  */
/* the code depends on the kind of shape to be rotated, this    */
/* function is a switch statement that branches according to the */
/* type tag.                              */
void rotate (struct shape* s) {
    switch (s->tag) {
        case Circle:
            break;
        case Rectangle: {
            struct rectangle* r = (struct rectangle*)s;
            float d;
            d = ((r->botright->x - r->topleft->x) -
                (r->topleft->y - r->botright->y))/2.0;
            r->topleft->x += d;
            r->topleft->y += d;
            r->botright->x -= d;
            r->botright->y -= d;
            break;
        };
    };
};
```

```
/* The print function prints a descriptive statement about the  */
/* location and kind of shape s. This function is again a switch */
/* statement that branches according to the "tag" field.      */
```

```
void print (struct shape* s) {
    switch (s->tag) {
        case Circle: {
            struct circle* c = (struct circle*) s;
            printf("circle at %.1f %.1f radius %.1f \n",c->cnter->x,
                c->cnter->y, c->radius);
            break;
        };

        case Rectangle:{
            struct rectangle* r = (struct rectangle*) s;
            printf("rectangle at %.1f %.1f %.1f %.1f \n",
                r->topleft->x, r->topleft->y,
                r->botright->x, r->botright->y);
        };
    };
};

/* The body of this program just tests some of the above functions. */

main() {

pt* origin = new_pt(0,0);
pt* p1 = new_pt(0,2);
pt* p2 = new_pt(4,6);

shape* s1 = new_circle(origin,2);
shape* s2 = new_rectangle(p1,p2);

print(s1);
print(s2);

rotate(s1);
rotate(s2);

move(s1,1,1);
move(s2,1,1);

print(s1);
 print(s2);

};
```

A.1.2 Shape Program: Object-Oriented Version

```
#include <stdio.h>

/* The following class pt is used in the implementations of */
/* the shape objects below. Since pt is a class in this    */
/* version of the program, instead of simply a struct, we  */
/* may include the "new_pt" and "copy_pt" functions of   */
/* the typecase version within the pt class. For      */
/* convenience, both these functions are named "pt";      */
/* they are differentiated by the static types of their     */
/* arguments.                                    */

class pt {
public:
 float x;
 float y;
 pt(float xval, float yval) {x = xval; y=yval;};
 pt(pt* p) {x = p->x; y = p->y;};
};

/* Class shape is an example of a "pure abstract base class",   */
/* which means that it exists solely to provide an interface to  */
/* classes derived from it. Since it provides no implementations */
/* for the methods center, move, rotate, and print, no "shape"  */
/* objects can be created. Instead, we use this class as a base   */
/* class. Our circle and rectangle shapes will be derived from    */
/* it. This class is useful because it allows us to write      */
/* functions that expect "shape" objects as arguments. Since   */
/* our circles and rectangles are subtypes of shape, we may pass    */
/* them to such functions in a type-safe way.              */

class shape {
public:
 virtual pt* center()=0;
 virtual void move(float dx, float dy)=0;
 virtual void rotate()=0;
 virtual void print()=0;
};
```

```
/* Class circle, defined below, consolidates the code for circles */
/* from the center, move, rotate, and print functions in the     */
/* typecase version. It also contains the object constructor      */
/* "circle", corresponding to the function "new_circle" in        */
/* the typecase version. Note that in this version of the     */
/* program, the compiler guarantees that the circle move method, */
/* for example, is called on a circle. We do not have to rely on */
/* programmers keeping the tag field accurate for the program to  */
/* work correctly.                              */

class circle : public shape {
    pt* cnter;
    float radius;
  public:
    circle(pt* cn, float r)
        {cnter = new pt(cn); radius = r;};
    pt* center()
        {return cnter;};
    void move(float dx, float dy)
        {cnter->x += dx;
          cnter->y += dy;
        };
    void rotate() {};
    void print ()
        { printf("circle at %.1f %.1f radius %.1f \n",
                cnter->x, cnter->y, radius);
        };
};


/* Class rectangle, defined below, consolidates the code for */
/* rectangles from the center, move, rotate, and print functions */
/* in the typecase version. It also contains the object       */
/* constructor "rectangle", corresponding to the function   */
/* new_rectangle in the typecase version.                */

class rectangle : public shape {
  private:
    pt* topleft;
    pt* botright;
```

```
  public:
    rectangle(pt* tl, pt* br)
      {topleft=new pt(tl);botright=new pt(br);};
    pt* center()
      {pt* p = new
       pt((botright->x - topleft->x)/2, (botright->x - topleft->x)/2);
       return p;};
    void move(float dx,float dy)
      {topleft->x += dx;
       topleft->y += dy;
       botright->x += dx;
       botright->y += dy;
      };
    void rotate ()
      { float d;
       d = ((botright->x - topleft->x) -
           (topleft->y - botright->y))/2.0;
       topleft->x += d;
       topleft->y += d;
       botright->x -= d;
       botright->y -= d;
      };
    void print ()
      { printf("rectangle coordinates %.1f %.1f %.1f %.1f \n",topleft->x,
           topleft->y, botright->x, botright->y);
      };
};

main() {

pt* origin = new pt(0,0);
pt* p1 = new pt(0,2);
pt* p2 = new pt(4,6);

shape* s1 = new circle(origin, 2 );
shape* s2 = new rectangle(p1, p2);

s1->print();
s2->print();
```

```
    s1->rotate();
    s2->rotate();

    s1->move(1,1);
    s2->move(1,1);

    s1->print();
    s2->print();


    }
}
```

Glossary

activation record Data structure created for each procedure call. It contains parameters, return address, return result address, local variables, and temporary storage.

alias When two or more variables share the same location or two or more pointers point to the same memory cell, they are aliases of each other. Essentially, it is one variable (pointer) but it is known under different names.

alpha conversion Renaming of bound variables in a lambda term. For example, lambda $x.x + z$ can be alpha converted to lambda $y.y + z$.

beta conversion (lambda $x.M)N = [N/x]M$. Substitute N for every free occurrence of x in M, renaming bound variables of M as needed to avoid variable capture.

(beta) reduction Modeling of program execution as directed by beta conversion: (lambda $x.M)N \rightarrow [N/x]M$.

bound and free variables A bound variable is simply a place holder. The particular name of a bound variable is unimportant. For example, the functions lambda $x.x$ and lambda $y.y$ define exactly the same function (the identity function). In contrast, the name of a free variable is important. Free variables cannot be renamed without potentially changing the value of an expression. For example, in the following code fragment (in which x appears as a free variable), we cannot rename x to y without changing the value of the expression: $3 + x$ (assume x is bound to 2 and y to 3).

class A class defines the behavior of its instances. Usually the class contains definitions of all methods shared by its instances.

class interface The interface of an object in Smalltalk is the set of messages that can be sent to the object without receiving the error "message not understood." The interface of an object is determined by its class, as a class lists the messages that each object will answer.

class template In C++, templates are the mechanism for parameterizing a class with a type or a function. This allows the programmer to implement a class that operates on values of an arbitrary type (e.g., a general-purpose array class that may store elements of any type).

class variable Class variables are shared by all instances of a class.

confluence Property of lambda calculus guaranteeing that, if an expression has a normal form, the normal form is unique. This implies that the order in which reduction rules are applied is unimportant.

conformance A relation between two types that serves as the basis of subtyping. Conformance relies on messages understood (i.e., the object's interface), not the internal representation or inheritance hierarchy.

constructor (in object-oriented programming sense) A procedure that is used for creating and initializing objects. In C++, a constructor is called after the object has been created and is used mainly to initialize the object's internal state.

dangling pointer A pointer referring to an area of memory that has been deallocated. Dereferencing such a pointer usually produces garbage.

data type induction A process of formal reasoning about properties of abstract data types.

denotational semantics A technique of describing the "meaning" of programs as mathematical functions, allowing people to prove theorems and reason about programs as mathematical entities.

dynamic lookup When a message is sent to an object at run time, dynamic method lookup is performed to determine which method should be called.

dynamic scoping The variable that is not defined in the current scope is looked for in the most recent activation record.

dynamic type checking Checking for type errors when the program is executed.

encapsulation Language mechanism for restricting access to some of the object's components.

exception Exceptions are a control transfer mechanism, usually used to treat a special case or handle an error condition.

exception handler When an exception-raising condition occurs, control is transferred to a special procedure called the exception handler.

fixed point A fixed point of function f is a value x such that $x = f(x)$.

funarg problem The failure of traditional stack-based implementations of procedure calls in the presence of first-class functions (functions that can be passed as procedure parameters and returned as procedure results).

    upward funarg problem: The problem of returning a function as a procedure result; requires allocating activation records on the heap and returning a closure containing a pointer to code and a pointer to the enclosing activation record.

    downward funarg problem: The problem of passing a function as a procedure parameter; requires a tree structure for activation records.

garbage Memory allocated by a program that will not be accessed in any future execution of a given program.

garbage collection An automatic process that attempts to free memory that is storing garbage.

halting problem The problem of determining whether a given program halts when executed on a given input.

higher-order function Function that takes other functions as arguments or returns a function as its result.

implementation of an abstract type Hidden internal representation of an abstract type.

inheritance An object's definition may be given as an incremental modification to existing object definitions, in which case it is said that the object *inherits* from other objects.

instance variable Local variable defined in each instance of the class. Instance variables of different instances are independent.

interface of an abstract type Operations visible to the clients of an abstract type.

lambda calculus Mathematical system for defining functions, proving equations between expressions, and calculating values of expressions.

lazy function A lazy function evaluates its arguments only when it needs them. For example, a lazy implementation of or will not evaluate its second argument if the first argument is true, and thus the result can be determined without looking at the second argument. Compare with *strict* function.

L-value The L-value of variable x is the storage associated with x.

mark-and-sweep garbage collection A form of garbage collection that uses two phases: First, it marks all memory that can be possibly reached by the program from its current state; second, it frees (sweeps) all memory that has not been marked.

message A name and a list of parameter values. Objects in Smalltalk communicate by sending messages to each other.

method Code found in a class for responding to a message.

method dictionary Method dictionary of a class contains all methods defined in the class.

multimethods In a language that uses multiple dispatch, more than one argument to a message may be used to determine which method is called at run time.

normal form A lambda term that cannot be reduced.

objects Run-time entities that contain both data and operations.

overloading (ad hoc polymorphism) A function name is overloaded if it has two or more implementations associated with it. Different implementations are distinguished by type (e.g., function name "+" may have two implementations, one for adding integers, the other for adding real numbers).

parametric polymorphism A function is parametrically polymorphic if it has one implementation that can be applied to arguments of different types.

pass-by-reference Method of parameter passing: passes the L-value (address) of an actual parameter. Allows changing the actual parameter.

pass-by-value Method of parameter passing: passes the R-value (contents of address) of an actual parameter. Does not allow changing the actual parameter.

private data Private data can be accessed only by the methods of the class in which they are defined.

protected data Protected data can be accessed by the methods of the class in which they are defined as well as by the subclasses.

public data Public data can be accessed by the methods of the class in which they are defined, subclasses, and the clients.

raising an exception Raising an exception transfers control to an exception handler. Exception can be raised either implicitly if a certain condition occurs or explicitly by executing an appropriate command.

representation independence Property of a data type according to which different computer representations of values of the data type do not affect behavior of any program that uses them (i.e., different underlying representations are indistinguishable by the type's clients).

R-value The R-value of variable x is the contents of storage associated with x.

selector Name of a message (Smalltalk terminology).

static scoping The variable that is not defined in the current scope is looked for in the closest lexically enclosing scope.

strict function A function is strict if it always evaluates all of its arguments. Compare with lazy function.

subclass (derived class) If class A inherits from class B, A is the subclass of B.

subtyping Type A is a subtype of type B if any context expecting an expression of type B may take an expression of type A without introducing a type error.

superclass (base class) If class A inherits from class B, B is the superclass of A.

static type checking Checking for type errors at compile time.

tail recursion A function is tail recursive if it either returns a value without making a recursive call or if it returns directly the result of a recursive call. All possible branches of the function must satisfy one of these conditions.

template (in Smalltalk) Part of the object that stores pattern of instance variables.

type A basic notion (like set in set theory). A type can also be described as a set of values defined by a type expression. The precise meaning of a type is provided by the type system, which includes type expressions, value expressions, rules for assigning types to expressions, and equations or evaluation rules for value expressions.

type error A situation in which an execution of the program is not faithful to the intended semantics, i.e., in which the program interprets data in ways other than how they were intended to be used (e.g., machine representation of a floating-point number interpreted as an integer).

type inference Determining the type of an expression based on the known types of some of its subexpressions.

type tag A tag attached to each value and containing information about its type. Used for dynamic type checking.

variable capture This term is best explained by example. When an expression e is substituted for a variable x in another expression lambda $y.e'$, without any renaming of variables, then free occurrences of y within e are "captured" (i.e., bound) by the binding lambda y. For example, in

$$(\lambda x.(\lambda y.x))y = [y/x](\lambda y.x)! = \lambda y.y,$$

y should be free, but accidentally becomes bound. To avoid variable capture, all bound variables should be renamed so that their names are different from those of all free variables and all other bound variables.

von Neumann bottleneck Backus' term for the connection between CPU and main memory. Every computer program operating on the contents of main memory must send pieces of data back and forth through this connection, thus making it a bottleneck.

vtable In C++, vtable is the virtual method table. It contains pointers to all virtual member functions defined in the class.

the Y combinator When applied to a function, it returns its fixed point. $Y = \lambda f. (\lambda x. f(xx)) (\lambda x. f(xx))$.

Index